PRINCIPLES OF CONTRACT LAW

Third Edition

By

Steven J. Burton

John F. Murray Professor of Law
University of Iowa

AMERICAN CASEBOOK SERIES®

THOMSON
WEST

Mat #40293788

COPYRIGHT © 1995 WEST PUBLISHING CO.
© West, a Thomson business, 2001
© 2006 Thomson/West
     610 Opperman Drive
     P.O. Box 64526
     St. Paul, MN 55164–0526
     1–800–328–9352

Printed in the United States of America

ISBN–13: 978–0–314–15575–7
ISBN–10: 0–314–15575–9

 TEXT IS PRINTED ON 10% POST CONSUMER RECYCLED PAPER

For my Father

*

Foreword

American contract law constitutes a legal environment that encourages people to exchange goods and services by promising. It does so by enforcing promises as provided by legal rules and precedents, which are the grist for a practical lawyer's mill. Considered alone, rules and precedents are sure to seem a hopeless jumble of conflicting ideas. The rules and precedents, however, implement more general legal principles and policies—the purposes of the rules and precedents. Principles and policies guide the use of rules and precedents, bringing order to the law if anything does. In practice, principles and policies usually operate without being articulated, just as baseball players need not recite the principles of running, throwing, and batting while playing a game. Principles and policies are largely learned in advance, absorbed, and then taken for granted in ordinary legal discourse.

Unlike most casebooks, this one makes the principles and policies, hereafter called "principles" for convenience, explicit. There are three main reasons for this. First, the traditional goal of a comprehensive contracts casebook, one that at least mentions all of the law relevant to contractual relations, has become hopeless. When Christopher Columbus Langdell put together the first contracts casebook over a hundred years ago, comprehensiveness might have been a reasonable goal. There were many fewer cases then, to be sure. More important, few statutes affected contractual relations. Today, a survey of all of the laws governing contractual relations would take one far into legislation involving consumer protection, regulated industries, employment discrimination, labor law, and more. A comprehensive contracts casebook would be unwieldly at best and intimidating to the point of inducing despair at worst. The principles approach permits a class to survey the broad themes running through the law applying to contracts in the absence of special legislation. It seeks to equip students to work through the law governing specific problems when the problem arises. In truth, no contracts course, indeed, no law school, tries to provide students with a knowledge of all the law they will need in practice.

Second, contemporary thinking about contract law is notable for a multitude of contending theories and understandings, reflecting all of the disagreements in legal theory and politics more generally. A casebook can attempt to be neutral toward the contenders, giving each more or less equal time, without regard to practical considerations. Alternately, a casebook can offer a small cluster of ideas both as a rich example of one approach and as a foil for exploring competing approaches. This casebook takes the latter approach. It is doubtful that any "neutral" casebook could be composed. It, too, would be unwieldly and instructionally ineffective. Moreover, a major reason for law schools to have diverse faculties is to allow students to contend with a range of ways of thinking about law across the curriculum, though not necessarily within each class. The bias in this casebook is toward the law as it is applied by the courts in contemporary judicial practice.

The third reason stems from the fact that legal rules and cases can be understood in two fundamentally different ways. On one hand, rules might be regarded as social scientific descriptions and explanations of the regularities in the cases: We could suppose that the rules represent an observer's beliefs about these regularities. On this theoretical understanding, the good legal rules ground reliable predictions of what courts and other legal officials will do. The social scientific approach has been a popular one in recent years, but it has one major untoward consequence: Legal rules make for very bad social scientific theory. The consequence can be a deep skepticism about the law, sometimes disabling the student from doing his or her best at the practical tasks of lawyering. This skepticism is inapt to the extent that a second understanding of rules is appropriate.

Legal rules and cases can be understood as standards that guide the conduct of law-abiding people and justify coercing lawbreakers. They say something about what people ought to do. So the law that requires motorists to stop at a red light does not enable a motorist to predict that he or she will stop; rather, it guides conduct by providing a reason for the motorist to stop and by excluding many reasons for not stopping. On this practical understanding, the law licenses use of the state's coercive power, and this requires justification in political morality. The law as currently applied by the courts thus should be criticized when it is unjustified because it provides bad guidance. Principles are the medium for evaluating the laws in a way that has more to do with ethics than social science.

This casebook will treat the law of contracts in relevant part under five general principles.

The Autonomy Principle: The law empowers people to make and receive enforceable promises when they communicate decisions to act or refrain from acting in some definite way in the future, subject to other principles.

The Security Principle: The law requires each party to a contract formation or performance to do its part to respect the other party's reasonable expectations and reliance.

The Justification Principle: The law enforces promises when prima facie there are sufficient legal reasons for a court to enforce the promise.

The Justice Principle: The law refrains from enforcing promises when the prima facie justification for enforcing the promise is overridden by considerations of justice.

The Compensation Principle: The law enforces promises mainly by compensating nonbreaching parties for unavoidable, foreseeable, and reasonably certain harms caused by a breach.

These principles operate, of course, together with general rule-of-law values requiring the law to be applied to settle disputes consistently, predictably, administrably, with procedural regularity, and with appropriate finality.

To be clear, the law in my view does not determine a single set of correct results in all possible cases. Over time, the relative weights of principles change as the practices and dispositions of members of the legal community adapt to changing circumstances. The rules and precedents change accordingly. At times, principles play out in ways that leave the law unsettled and confusing. For the most part, however, the law moves with arguments of principle. The best lawyers tap principles in their arguments in difficult cases.

*

Summary of Contents

Table of Contents

_____

*

Table of Cases

The principal cases are in bold type. Cases cited or discussed in the text are roman type. References are to pages. Cases cited in principal cases and within other quoted materials are not included.

PRINCIPLES OF CONTRACT LAW

Third Edition

*

Chapter 1

THE AUTONOMY AND SECURITY PRINCIPLES

The law empowers people to make and receive enforceable promises when they communicate decisions to act or refrain from acting in some definite way in the future, subject to other principles.

The law requires each party to a contract formation or performance to do its part to respect the other party's reasonable expectations and reliance.

In moral theory, one of the least controversial principles is that promises ordinarily obligate promisors to perform as promised. The law enforces some promises in any society that allows individuals sometimes to pursue their own interests, in fairness to others, as they think best. Enforceable promises are conventionally called *contracts*. The law of contracts defines the conditions under which people have the legal power to make and receive enforceable promises, together with many of the consequences of having used that power.

We begin, accordingly, with the general idea of a promise and continue with agreements in which there is a promise on at least one side—promissory agreements. In the U.S. and similar societies, where economic and other activities take place largely at individual initiative, promises and agreements are important currencies. Some business activities occur without promises, as when two people trade specific used items, both sold "as is," both delivered on the spot. By far, however, most involve promises. Consider: A tenant promises not to bring pets onto the premises, an employer promises to provide child care to employees, a seller warrants a computer to operate without error for a time, a retailer agrees to buy from one product distributor exclusively, a borrower promises to repay a loan, corporate shareholders approve a merger in exchange for stock, a supplier of parts agrees to keep an adequate inventory, or an insurer agrees to repair a car should it be damaged in a collision. To generalize, the market is a domain of free contracting. Contract law governs transactions in the unregulated sector of the economy.

1

SECTION 1. PROMISES

To promise is to say something which creates an obligation for the promisor. In order that words should have this kind of effect, rules must exist providing that if words are used by appropriate persons on appropriate occasions (i.e. by sane persons understanding their position and free from various sorts of pressure) those who use these words shall be bound to do the things designated by them. So, when we promise, we make use of specified procedures to change our own moral situation by imposing obligations on ourselves and conferring rights on others; in lawyers' parlance we exercise "a power" conferred by rules to do this.

H.L.A. Hart, The Concept of Law 42–3 (1961).

A promise is an act by which a person imagines a possible world and signals a commitment to bring that world into being by future action. The imagined world may be like the extant world at the time of the promise in all respects save at least one. For example, a promisor can imagine a book in a promisee's hands rather than his or her own. A promise to give a book to someone else is a commitment to bring that world into existence by the act of handing over the book. It is not fundamentally different for an architect to imagine and describe a bridge and undertake to build it, for a business person to imagine a better way for a market to register its cash flow and to commit his or her company to make that happen, or for you to imagine torn clothing repaired and secure the promise of a tailor or seamstress to make it right.

A promise must be made to another person in a social context. Robinson Crusoe, shipwrecked and alone on a remote island, cannot make a promise because there is no promisee and no practice of promising which he can join. He can utter the sounds that we make when we promise, but, on the island, they do not have the significance of a promise. That significance depends on two things—the existence of another person to whom Crusoe can be bound, and a social practice in which the sounds fit and signal an obligation. Not all cultures have a practice of promising. Participants in those that have such a practice should recognize as a promise something like the preceding idea.

A practice of promising can emerge informally in a society and remain a matter of custom only. When that is so, however, the practice tends to be poorly defined, to resist change, and to produce interminable disputes. We can clarify and improve a practice by making it into formal law. We can institutionalize and systematize it; we can settle disputes with finality by adjudication or arbitration under the rule of law. We do this by articulating the principles, rules, and precedents that constitute the practice and by authorizing courts to settle disputes according to those standards of conduct.

RESTATEMENT (SECOND) OF CONTRACTS §§ 1–3

HAWKINS v. McGEE

Supreme Court of New Hampshire, 1929.
84 N.H. 114, 146 A. 641.

Assumpsit against a surgeon for breach of an alleged warranty of the success of an operation. Trial by jury. Verdict for the plaintiff. The writ also contained a count in negligence upon which a nonsuit was ordered, without exception.

Defendant's motions for a nonsuit and for a directed verdict on the count in assumpsit were denied, and the defendant excepted. During the argument of plaintiff's counsel to the jury, the defendant claimed certain exceptions, and also excepted to the denial of his requests for instructions and to the charge of the court upon the question of damages, as more fully appears in the opinion. The defendant seasonably moved to set aside the verdict upon the grounds that it was (1) contrary to the evidence; (2) against the weight of the evidence; (3) against the weight of the law and evidence; and (4) because the damages awarded by the jury were excessive. The court denied the motion upon the first three grounds, but found that the damages were excessive, and made an order that the verdict be set aside, unless the plaintiff elected to remit all in excess of $500. The plaintiff having refused to remit, the verdict was set aside "as excessive and against the weight of the evidence," and the plaintiff excepted.

The foregoing exceptions were transferred by Scammon, J. The facts are stated in the opinion....

BRANCH, JUDGE. 1. The operation in question consisted in the removal of a considerable quantity of scar tissue from the palm of the plaintiff's right hand and the grafting of skin taken from the plaintiff's chest in place thereof. The scar tissue was the result of a severe burn caused by contact with an electric wire, which the plaintiff received about nine years before the time of the transactions here involved. There was evidence to the effect that before the operation was performed the plaintiff and his father went to the defendant's office, and that the defendant, in answer to the question, "How long will the boy be in the hospital?" replied, "Three or four days, not over four; then the boy can go home and it will be just a few days when he will go back to work with a good hand." Clearly this and other testimony to the same effect would not justify a finding that the doctor contracted to complete the hospital treatment in three or four days or that the plaintiff would be able to go back to work within a few days thereafter. The above statements could only be construed as expressions of opinion or predictions as to the probable duration of the treatment and plaintiff's resulting disability, and the fact that these estimates were exceeded would impose no contractual liability upon the defendant. The only substantial basis for the plaintiff's claim is the testimony that the defendant also said before the operation was decided upon, "I will guarantee to make the hand a hundred per cent perfect hand or a hundred per cent good hand." The plaintiff was present when these words were alleged to have been spoken, and, if they are to be taken at their face value, it seems obvious that proof of their utterance would establish the giving of a warranty in accordance with his contention.

The defendant argues, however, that, even if these words were uttered by him, no reasonable man would understand that they were used with the intention of entering "into any contractual relation whatever," and that they could reasonably be understood only "as his expression in strong language that he believed and expected that as a result of the operation he would give the plaintiff a very good hand." It may be conceded, as the defendant contends, that, before the question of the making of a contract should be submitted to a jury, there is a preliminary question of law for the trial court to pass upon, i.e. "whether the words could possibly have the meaning imputed to them by the party who founds his case upon a certain interpretation," but it cannot be held that the trial court decided this question erroneously in the present case. It is unnecessary to determine at this time whether the argument of the defendant, based upon "common knowledge of the uncertainty which attends all surgical operations," and the improbability that a surgeon would ever contract to make a damaged part of the human body "one hundred per cent perfect," would, in the absence of countervailing considerations, be regarded as conclusive, for there were other factors in the present case which tended to support the contention of the plaintiff. There was evidence that the defendant repeatedly solicited from the plaintiff's father the opportunity to perform this operation, and the theory was advanced by plaintiff's counsel in cross-examination of the defendant that he sought an opportunity to "experiment on skin grafting," in which he had little previous experience. If the jury accepted this part of plaintiff's contention, there would be a reasonable basis for the further conclusion that, if defendant spoke the words attributed to him, he did so with the intention that they should be accepted at their face value, as an inducement for the granting of consent to the operation by the plaintiff and his father, and there was ample evidence that they were so accepted by them. The question of the making of the alleged contract was properly submitted to the jury.

2. The substance of the charge to the jury on the question of damages appears in the following quotation: "If you find the plaintiff entitled to anything, he is entitled to recover for what pain and suffering he has been made to endure and for what injury he has sustained over and above what injury he had before." To this instruction the defendant seasonably excepted. By it, the jury was permitted to consider two elements of damage: (1) Pain and suffering due to the operation; and (2) positive ill effects of the operation upon the plaintiff's hand. Authority for any specific rule of damages in cases of this kind seems to be lacking,

but, when tested by general principle and by analogy, it appears that the foregoing instruction was erroneous.

"By 'damages,' as that term is used in the law of contracts, is intended compensation for a breach, measured in the terms of the contract." Davis v. New England Cotton Yarn Co., 77 N.H. 403, 404, 92 A. 732, 733. The purpose of the law is "to put the plaintiff in as good a position as he would have been in had the defendant kept his contract." 3 Williston Cont. § 1338. The measure of recovery "is based upon what the defendant should have given the plaintiff, not what the plaintiff has given the defendant or otherwise expended." 3 Williston Cont. § 1341. "The only losses that can be said fairly to come within the terms of a contract are such as the parties must have had in mind when the contract was made, or such as they either knew or ought to have known would probably result from a failure to comply with its terms." Davis v. New England Cotton Yarn Co., 77 N.H. 403, 404, 92 A. 732, 733....

The present case is closely analogous to one in which a machine is built for a certain purpose and warranted to do certain work. In such cases, the usual rule of damages for breach of warranty in the sale of chattels is applied, and it is held that the measure of damages is the difference between the value of the machine, if it had corresponded with the warranty and its actual value, together with such incidental losses as the parties knew, or ought to have known, would probably result from a failure to comply with its terms....

The rule thus applied is well settled in this state. "As a general rule, the measure of the vendee's damages is the difference between the value of the goods as they would have been if the warranty as to quality had been true, and the actual value at the time of the sale, including gains prevented and losses sustained, and such other damages as could be reasonably anticipated by the parties as likely to be caused by the vendor's failure to keep his agreement, and could not by reasonable care on the part of the vendee have been avoided." Union Bank v. Blanchard, 65 N.H. 21, 23, 18 A. 90, 91.... We therefore conclude that the true measure of the plaintiff's damage in the present case is the difference between the value to him of a perfect hand or a good hand, such as the jury found the defendant promised him, and the value of his hand in its present condition, including any incidental consequences fairly within the contemplation of the parties when they made their contract. 1 Sutherland, Damages (4th Ed.) § 92. Damages not thus limited, although naturally resulting, are not to be given.

The extent of the plaintiff's suffering does not measure this difference in value. The pain necessarily incident to a serious surgical operation was a part of the contribution which the plaintiff was willing to make to his joint undertaking with the defendant to produce a good hand. It was a legal detriment suffered by him which constituted a part of the price which he was willing to pay for a good hand, but it furnished no test of the value of a good hand or the difference between the value of the hand which the defendant promised and the one which resulted from the operation.

It was also erroneous and misleading to submit to the jury as a separate element of damage any change for the worse in the condition of the plaintiff's hand resulting from the operation, although this error was probably more prejudicial to the plaintiff than to the defendant. Any such ill effect of the operation would be included under the true rule of damages set forth above, but damages might properly be assessed for the defendant's failure to improve the condition of the hand, even if there were no evidence that its condition was made worse as a result of the operation.

It must be assumed that the trial court, in setting aside the verdict, undertook to apply the same rule of damages which he had previously given to the jury, and, since this rule was erroneous, it is unnecessary for us to consider whether there was any evidence to justify his finding that all damages awarded by the jury above $500 were excessive. . . .

New trial.

Questions

1.   Who sued whom for what? What happened in the trial court? Who appealed to the Supreme Court of New Hampshire? On what grounds?

2.   Did Dr. McGee promise that Hawkins would have a perfect hand? If so, what reasons support that conclusion? How is the promise different from an opinion or prediction? How is it different from an expression of belief or expectation? Does it matter in the appellate court whether Dr. McGee promised or not?

3.   What does it mean for a court *to enforce* Dr. McGee's promise? What remedy does the court endorse as law? What alternative possibilities are considered by the court? What are the court's reasons for endorsing this remedy as against the alternatives? Are they sound reasons? Why should the court consider "the purpose of the law" of damages, in addition to the rules and precedents?

NOTE ON "INTERESTS," "RIGHTS," AND "DUTIES"

Among the most frequently used basic legal concepts are *interests*, *rights* and *duties* (also called *obligations*). There are, of course, many ways to explain these concepts, and not everyone would agree that they are basic. Some, for example, understand rights and duties solely as predictions of what courts will do. E.g., Oliver Wendell Holmes, Jr., *The Path of the Law*, 10 Harv. L. Rev. 61 (1897). On that approach, predictions are basic. Judges, however, are not predicting what they themselves will do. Advocates are not making predictive arguments. Rather, judges are duty-bound to reach decisions that are justified in law. Advocates try to persuade judges of what the law requires them to do. Another way to understand rights and duties follows. See if it provides part of a framework for making sense of the judicial opinions you read in this course and others.

A person has an interest when he or she has a stake in how another person acts. In *Hawkins v. McGee*, for example, young Hawkins had, among others, two distinct interests in relation to Dr. McGee: It mattered to Hawkins (1) whether Dr. McGee did the surgery competently, whether or not he had promised to do so; and (2) whether Dr. McGee kept his promise to produce a perfect hand, if such a promise was made. In each corresponding aspect of their relationship, Hawkins might be left worse off (than he should be) as a consequence of Dr. McGee's actions.

Distinguishing the various interests at play in a relationship is a key part of legal analysis. Only some interests, however, are protected by the law. For example, Hawkins might have an interest in being served gourmet food while in the hospital for surgery. He has no legal redress, however, against Dr. McGee or the hospital if the food is decent only by common hospital standards. Moreover, some interests are protected by one body of law but not another. Hawkins thus brought counts in "negligence" and "assumpsit" (an archaic label for a contract action). The negligence count sought to vindicate his interest that Dr. McGee perform the operation with due care, which might or might not produce a perfect hand. The assumpsit count sought to vindicate the different interest that Dr. McGee keep the alleged promise to produce a perfect hand.

The law of contracts generally protects three interests—the *expectation*, *reliance*, and *restitution* interests. The expectation interest stems from the psychological fact that, at formation, each party anticipates that the world of the contract will come into existence as promised. Hawkins, for example, might have had a reasonable expectation that Dr. McGee would produce a perfect hand as promised. He had an expectation interest from the moment of contracting. Such an expectation often leads a party to change position in advance of performance by action or inaction. Hawkins may have undergone the surgery and refrained from going to other surgeons in reliance on Dr. McGee's promise. Such a change of position gives rise to a reliance interest. The expectation and reliance interests may be harmed for a variety of familiar reasons, including mistakes, misunderstandings, changed circumstances, and misplaced trust. These two related interests define the harms that are the distinctive concerns of contract law.

The restitution interest is protected by contract law and also, more broadly, the law of restitution. This interest is concerned with benefits one party may receive at the expense of the other. Consider, for example, the fee paid by Hawkins to Dr. McGee. For Dr. McGee to keep the fee after failing to perform his promise might be unjust. If so, the law allows Hawkins to get his money back. This protects his restitution interest by restoring the benefit.

Even when one party has a legally protected interest, it does not follow that it will be vindicated in a lawsuit. Injured parties often cannot or will not sue due to the expense and aggravation involved. Procedural and evidentiary problems, as well as mistakes by the lawyers, can intrude and distort the process, leaving meritorious claims unrecognized. Further, both parties might have legally protected interests that clash. When they do not settle their differences by negotiation, a judge may be asked to decide which interest is the more worthy of legal protection under the circumstances. In civil cases, it need not be so that one party is a good guy while the other is a bad guy. Both can be good guys even if one must lose the lawsuit; both can be bad guys even though one of them should win!

On this understanding of interests, we can say that one person has a *right* when he or she has an interest strong enough (in its appeal in principle) to justify imposing a *duty* on another person to act with respect for that right. That is to say that the person under the duty *ought to act* as urged by the rightholder. Hawkins' interest that Dr. McGee perform the operation with due care thus can be a right because it is strong enough to justify imposing a duty on Dr. McGee to use due care in surgery. Surely Dr. McGee ought to do that, regardless of whether he promised due care. Moreover, this interest in the safety of another person's action is legally protected by the law of torts, which enforces duties whether or not they were undertaken autonomously. So Hawkins has a *legal right* while Dr. McGee has a *legal duty* to perform the surgery with due care.

In addition, Hawkins' expectation interest that Dr. McGee keep his promise to produce a perfect hand, if he indeed made such a promise, is protected by the law of contracts. So, Hawkins is claiming that he has a *contract right* and that Dr. McGee is under a *contract duty*. In principle, the validity of that claim depends on whether Hawkins' legally protected contractual interest is sufficient to justify imposing a duty on Dr. McGee to produce a perfect hand. If Hawkins' claim is well-grounded in the law, then Dr. McGee should pay compensation for failing to do it. A court should order Dr. McGee to pay compensation.

––––––

RESTATEMENT (SECOND) OF CONTRACTS § 344

––––––

NOTE ON THE RESTATEMENTS

The Restatement [First] of Contracts (1932) was the first in a series of "restatements of the law" published by the American Law Institute (ALI). The ALI is a private organization, formed under the leadership of Elihu Root in 1923, with the object of "improving the law." Its membership includes the justices of the U.S. Supreme Court, senior judges of the United States Circuit Courts of Appeals, the chief judges of the highest courts of the several states, the presidents of the American Bar Association and the state bar associations, the president of the National Conference of the Commissioners on Uniform State Laws, deans of the member schools of the Association of American Law Schools, and a large number of other judges, practitioners, and professors of law elected in recognition of their leadership and expertise.

The original idea of a "restatement" of the law was expressed as follows:

> The vast and ever increasing volume of the decisions of the courts establishing new rules or precedents, and the numerous instances in which the decisions are irreconcilable has resulted in ever increasing uncertainty in the law. The American Law Institute was formed in the belief that in order to clarify and simplify the law and to render it more certain, the first step must be the preparation of an orderly restatement of the common law, including in that term not only the law developed solely by judicial decisions but also the law which has grown from the application by the courts of generally and long adopted statutes. . . .
>
> The function of the courts is to decide the controversies brought before them. The function of the Institute is to state clearly and precisely in the light of the decisions the principles and rules of the common law.
>
> The sections of the Restatement express the result of a careful analysis of the subject and a thorough examination and discussion of pertinent cases—often very numerous and sometimes conflicting. The accuracy of the statements of law made rests on the authority of the Institute. They may be regarded both as the product of expert opinion and as the expression of the law by the legal profession.

Introduction, in Restatement [First] of Contracts viii-ix, xi-xii (1932).

The Restatement [First] of Contracts was written mainly by Professor Samuel Williston of the Harvard Law School, with the advice of Arthur L. Corbin of the Yale Law School and other respected lawyers and scholars. It was a remarkable success for a private effort to clarify the law. The first restatement swiftly became a standard citation in contracts cases decided by the courts of almost all American jurisdictions, as well as a standard resource for law students and practitioners. It was especially successful in jurisdictions with small populations and less diverse economies, whose own case law could be scant in many areas of the law. To some extent, moreover, the first restatement probably contributed to a more uniform law of contracts among the American jurisdictions.

The Restatement (Second) of Contracts was begun in 1962 and completed in 1979. A large part was written by Professor Robert Braucher of the Harvard Law School until he resigned upon appointment to the Supreme Judicial Court of Massachusetts; Professor E. Allan Farnsworth of Columbia Law School mainly completed the task. The relationship of the second to the first restatement was expressed by the Director of the American Law Institute as follows:

> The Reporters, their Advisers and the Institute approached the text of the first Restatement with the respect and tenderness that are appropriate in dealing with a classic. As the work proceeded, it uncovered relatively little need for major revision, in the sense of changing the positions taken on important issues, although the Uniform Commercial Code inspired a number of significant additions. . . . It does not denigrate the 1932 volumes to say that the revisions and additions here presented greatly augment their quality. This is, indeed, very close to a new work.

Foreword, in 1 RESTATEMENT (SECOND) OF CONTRACTS viii (1979).

The Restatement (Second) of Contracts has received considerable but not uniform recognition by the courts. A court, therefore, may follow the common law precedents in the relevant jurisdiction or the Restatement [First] of Contracts as endorsed by precedent, or it may follow provisions of the Restatement (Second). In practice, accordingly, a lawyer must consult the law of the jurisdiction on the particular legal issue. The restatements may be used when there is no clear law on the point or when there is reason to believe that the law might be changed by the courts. In the latter respect, the Restatement (Second) of Contracts serves as a conventional statement of "the modern view" of the law, even when it differs from the formal law on the books in a particular jurisdiction. It has considerable "persuasive authority," but it is not formally a part of the law that judges have a duty to uphold.

SECTION 2. PROMISSORY AGREEMENTS

Two persons can cooperate by jointly imagining a possible world and, by entering an agreement with a promise on at least one side, committing themselves to each other to bring that world into being by their actions. The imagined world may be like the actual world at the time of the promises in all respects save two changes. For example, when Crusoe discovers he is not alone on the island, he can imagine his coconut in Friday's hands while Friday's fish is in Crusoe's hands. He can communicate this imagined world to Friday, and they may exchange promises to trade the fish for the coconut. Crusoe's and Friday's promises then represent a joint commitment to bring the imagined world into existence by the coordinated actions of handing over the two objects. Again, two persons cannot contract unless they participate in a social practice of contracting. The people are bound by the principles, rules, and precedents used in the practice, much as the players are bound by the rules of a game, because they chose to participate and fairness so requires. Two aliens from radically different cultures, one of which has a practice of contracting, the other of which does not, can make any sounds and go through any motions they want. But they will understand those sounds and motions as a contract only if both know a social practice that gives them contractual significance.

a. *The Intention of the Parties*

The contracts cases you read will make frequent reference to the intention of the parties to an agreement. You should understand this intention with reference to the parties' promises and the world they represent. There are several ways to understand it. One equates intention with the world present in the mind of a promisor when promising. On this view, a misunderstanding occurs, for example, when a promisor has one world in mind when promising while the promisee has a different world in mind. It was Humpty Dumpty who scorned Alice by saying, " '[w]hen I use a word, ... it means just what I choose it to mean—neither more nor less.' " LEWIS CARROLL, THROUGH THE LOOKING-GLASS, reprinted in THE COMPLETE WORKS OF LEWIS CARROLL 213–14 (Mod. Lib. ed. 1947). To avoid such a strange understanding of language, we can distinguish between what the speaker intended his words to mean and what the words mean within a relevant practice. The latter view allows Humpty Dumpty to be mistaken about the meaning of his words, whether he likes it or not!

Consider whether the following cases succeed in avoiding a bizarre view of language while respecting the parties' autonomy.

RESTATEMENT (SECOND) OF CONTRACTS § 201

LUCY v. ZEHMER

Supreme Court of Appeals of Virginia, 1954.
196 Va. 493, 84 S.E.2d 516.

BUCHANAN, JUSTICE. This suit was instituted by W. O. Lucy and J. C. Lucy, complainants, against A. H. Zehmer and Ida S. Zehmer, his wife, defendants, to have specific performance of a contract by which it was alleged the Zehmers had sold to W. O. Lucy a tract of land owned by A. H. Zehmer in Dinwiddie county containing 471.6 acres, more or less, known as the Ferguson farm, for $50,000. J. C. Lucy, the other complainant, is a brother of W. O. Lucy, to whom W. O. Lucy transferred a half interest in his alleged purchase.

The instrument sought to be enforced was written by A. H. Zehmer on December 20, 1952, in these words: "We hereby agree to sell to W. O. Lucy the Ferguson Farm complete for $50,000.00, title satisfactory to buyer," and signed by the defendants, A. H. Zehmer and Ida S. Zehmer.

The answer of A. H. Zehmer admitted that at the time mentioned W. O. Lucy offered him $50,000 cash for the farm, but that he, Zehmer, considered that the offer was made in jest; that so thinking, and both he and Lucy having had several drinks, he wrote out "the memorandum" quoted above and induced his wife to sign it; that he did not deliver the memorandum to Lucy, but that Lucy picked it up, read it, put it in his pocket, attempted to offer Zehmer $5 to bind the bargain, which Zehmer refused to accept, and realizing for the first time that Lucy was serious, Zehmer assured him that he had no intention of selling the farm and that the whole matter was a joke. Lucy left the premises insisting that he had purchased the farm.

Depositions were taken and the decree appealed from was entered holding that the complainants had failed to establish their right to specific performance, and dismissing their bill. The assignment of error is to this action of the court.

W. O. Lucy, a lumberman and farmer, thus testified in substance. He had known Zehmer for fifteen or twenty years and had been familiar with the Ferguson farm for ten years. Seven or eight years ago he had offered Zehmer $20,000 for the farm which Zehmer had accepted, but the agreement was verbal and Zehmer backed out. On the night of December 20, 1952, around eight o'clock, he took an employee to McKenney, where Zehmer lived and operated a restaurant, filling station and motor court. While there he decided to see Zehmer and again try to buy the Ferguson farm. He entered the restaurant and talked to Mrs. Zehmer until Zehmer came in. He asked Zehmer if he had sold the Ferguson farm. Zehmer replied that he had not. Lucy said, "I bet you wouldn't take $50,000.00 for that place." Zehmer replied, "Yes, I would too; you wouldn't give fifty." Lucy said he would and told Zehmer to write up an agreement to that effect. Zehmer took a restaurant check and wrote on the back of it, "I do hereby agree to sell to W. O. Lucy the Ferguson Farm for $50,000 complete." Lucy told him he had better change it to "We" because Mrs. Zehmer would have to sign it too. Zehmer then tore up what he had written, wrote the agreement quoted above and asked Mrs. Zehmer, who was at the other end of the counter ten or twelve feet away, to sign it. Mrs. Zehmer said she would for $50,000 and signed it. Zehmer brought it back and gave it to Lucy, who offered him $5 which Zehmer refused, saying, "You don't need to give me any money, you got the agreement there signed by both of us."

The discussion leading to the signing of the agreement, said Lucy, lasted thirty or forty minutes, during which Zehmer seemed to doubt that Lucy could raise $50,000. Lucy suggested the provision for having the title examined and Zehmer made the suggestion that he would sell it "complete, everything there," and stated that all he had on the farm was three heifers.

Lucy took a partly filled bottle of whiskey into the restaurant with him for the purpose of giving Zehmer a drink if he wanted it. Zehmer did, and he and Lucy had had one or two drinks together. Lucy said that while he felt the drinks he took he was not intoxicated, and from the way Zehmer handled the transaction he did not think he was either.

December 20 was on Saturday. Next day Lucy telephoned to J. C. Lucy and arranged with the latter to take a half interest in the purchase and pay half of the consideration. On Monday he engaged an attorney to examine the title. The attorney reported favorably on December 31 and on January 2 Lucy wrote Zehmer stating that the title was satisfactory, that he was ready to pay the purchase price in cash and asking when Zehmer would be ready to close the deal. Zehmer replied by letter, mailed on January 13, asserting that he had never agreed or intended to sell.

Mr. and Mrs. Zehmer were called by the complainants as adverse witnesses. Zehmer testified in substance as follows:

He bought this farm more than ten years ago for $11,000. He had had twenty-five offers, more or less, to buy it, including several from Lucy, who had never offered any specific sum of money. He had given them all the same answer, that he was not interested in selling it. On this Saturday night before Christmas it looked like everybody and his brother came by there to have a drink. He took a good many drinks during the afternoon and had had a pint of his own. When he entered the restaurant around eight-thirty Lucy was there and he could see that he was "pretty high." He said to Lucy, "Boy, you got some good liquor, drinking, ain't you?" Lucy then offered him a drink. "I was already high as a Georgia pine, and didn't have any more better sense than to pour another great big slug out and gulp it down, and he took one too."

After they had talked a while Lucy asked whether he still had the Ferguson farm. He replied that he had not sold it and Lucy said, "I bet you wouldn't take $50,000.00 for it." Zehmer asked him if he would give $50,000 and Lucy said yes. Zehmer replied, "You haven't got $50,000 in cash." Lucy said he did and Zehmer replied that he did not believe it. They argued "pro and con for a long time," mainly about "whether he had $50,000 in cash that he could put up right then and buy that farm."

Finally, said Zehmer, Lucy told him if he didn't believe he had $50,000, "you sign that piece of paper here and say you will take $50,000.00 for the farm." He, Zehmer, "just grabbed the back off of a guest check there" and wrote on the back of it. At that point in his testimony Zehmer asked to see what he had written to "see if I recognize my own handwriting." He examined the paper and exclaimed, "Great balls of fire, I got 'Firgerson' for Ferguson. I have got satisfactory spelled wrong. I don't recognize that writing if I would see it, wouldn't know it was mine."

After Zehmer had, as he described it, "scribbled this thing off," Lucy said, "Get your wife to sign it." Zehmer walked over to where she was and she at first refused to sign but did so after he told her that he "was just needling him [Lucy], and didn't mean a thing in the world, that I was not selling the farm." Zehmer then "took it back over there ... and I was still looking at the dern thing. I had the drink right there by my hand, and I reached over to get a drink, and he said, 'Let me see it.' He reached and picked it up, and when I looked back again he had it in his pocket and he dropped a five dollar bill over there, and he said, 'Here is five dollars payment on it.' ... I said, 'Hell no, that is beer and liquor talking. I am not going to sell you the farm. I have told you that too many times before.' " . . .

The defendants insist that the evidence was ample to support their contention that the writing sought to be enforced was prepared as a bluff or dare to force Lucy to admit that he did not have $50,000; that the whole matter was a joke; that the writing was not delivered to Lucy and no binding contract was ever made between the parties.

It is an unusual, if not bizarre, defense. When made to the writing admittedly prepared by one of the defendants and signed by both, clear evidence is required to sustain it.

In his testimony Zehmer claimed that he "was high as a Georgia pine," and that the transaction "was just a bunch of two doggoned drunks bluffing to see who could talk the biggest and say the most." That claim is inconsistent with his attempt to testify in great detail as to what was said and what was done. It is contradicted by other evidence as to the condition of both parties, and rendered of no weight by the testimony of his wife that when Lucy left the restaurant she suggested that Zehmer drive him home. The record is convincing that Zehmer was not intoxicated to the extent of being unable to comprehend the nature and consequences of the instrument he executed, and hence that instrument is not to be invalidated on that ground. 17 C.J.S., Contracts, § 133, b., p. 483; Taliaferro v. Emery, 124 Va. 674, 98 S.E. 627. It was in fact conceded by defendants' counsel in oral argument that under the evidence Zehmer was not too drunk to make a valid contract. . . .

The appearance of the contract, the fact that it was under discussion for forty minutes or more before it was signed; Lucy's objection to the first draft because it was written in the singular, and he wanted Mrs. Zehmer to sign it also; the rewriting to meet that objection and the signing by Mrs. Zehmer; the discussion of what was to be included in the sale, the provision for the examination of the title, the completeness of the instrument that was executed, the taking possession of it by Lucy with no request or suggestion by either of the defendants that he give it back, are facts which furnish persuasive evidence that the execution of the contract was a serious business transaction rather than a casual, jesting matter as defendants now contend. . . .

If it be assumed, contrary to what we think the evidence shows, that Zehmer was jesting about selling his farm to Lucy and that the transaction was intended by him to be a joke, nevertheless the evidence shows that Lucy did not so understand it but considered it to be a serious business transaction and the contract to be binding on the Zehmers as well as on himself. . . .

Not only did Lucy actually believe, but the evidence shows he was warranted in believing, that the contract represented a serious business transaction and a good faith sale and purchase of the farm.

In the field of contracts, as generally elsewhere, "We must look to the outward expression of a person as manifesting his intention rather than to his secret and unexpressed intention. 'The law imputes to a person an intention corresponding to the reasonable meaning of his words and acts.'" First Nat. Bank of Roanoke v. Roanoke Oil Co., 169 Va. 99, 114, 192 S.E. 764, 770.

At no time prior to the execution of the contract had Zehmer indicated to Lucy by word or act that he was not in earnest about selling the farm. They had argued about it and discussed its terms, as Zehmer admitted, for a long time. Lucy testified that if there was any jesting it was about paying $50,000 that night. The contract and the evidence show that he was not expected to pay the money that night. Zehmer said that after the writing was signed he laid it down on the counter in front of Lucy. Lucy said Zehmer handed it to him. In any event there had been what appeared to be a good faith offer and a good faith acceptance, followed by the execution and apparent delivery of a written contract. Both said that Lucy put the writing in his pocket and then offered Zehmer $5 to seal the bargain. Not until then, even under the defendants' evidence, was anything said or done to indicate that the matter was a joke. Both of the Zehmers testified that when Zehmer asked his wife to sign he whispered that it was a joke so Lucy wouldn't hear and that it was not intended that he should hear.

The mental assent of the parties is not requisite for the formation of a contract. If the words or other acts of one of the parties have but one reasonable meaning, his undisclosed intention is immaterial except when an unreasonable meaning which he attaches to his manifestations is known to the other party....

So a person cannot set up that he was merely jesting when his conduct and words would warrant a reasonable person in believing that he intended a real agreement, 17 C.J.S., Contracts, § 47, p. 390; Clark on Contracts, 4 ed., § 27, at p. 54.

Whether the writing signed by the defendants and now sought to be enforced by the complainants was the result of a serious offer by Lucy and a serious acceptance by the defendants, or was a serious offer by Lucy and an acceptance in secret jest by the defendants, in either event it constituted a binding contract of sale between the parties....

The complainants are entitled to have specific performance of the contracts sued on. The decree appealed from is therefore reversed and the cause is remanded for the entry of a proper decree requiring the defendants to perform the contract in accordance with the prayer of the bill.

Reversed and remanded.

Questions

1. Who sued whom for what? What happened in the trial court that became the ground for appeal? What were the contentions of the parties on appeal? What exactly is the "holding" in *Lucy v. Zehmer*?

2. Why must Lucy establish that Zehmer promised? Should it matter if Zehmer was drunk? What facts in evidence suggest that Zehmer was serious? What facts suggest that Zehmer was jesting?

3. In justifying its holding, does the court employ an objective or subjective theory of contract interpretation? As indicated in the following Note, a subjective theory would require a "meeting of the minds" while an objective theory would give manifestations of intention the meaning they would have to a reasonable person under the circumstances. Which approach is more consistent with the autonomy principle? Consider, also, the security principle stated in the Foreword to this book.

NOTE ON SUBJECTIVE AND OBJECTIVE THEORIES

The standard way of understanding mutual assent takes its cue from Professor Samuel Williston, who wrote in 1919:

> It is a commonplace of the law that mutual assent is necessary for the formation of contracts....
>
> As is too often the case in the law, though the words in which the principle is stated have become indisputably commonplace, their fundamental meaning is unsettled. The point of dispute is whether actual mental assent of the parties is a legal requisite, or merely such an expression by them as would normally indicate assent, whatever may have been in the minds of the parties. Is the test objective or subjective?

Samuel Williston, *Mutual Assent in the Formation of Contracts*, 14 ILL. L. REV. 85 (1919). Williston thought that the courts of his time had generally turned away from the subjective theory of assent. He believed that an "expression of mutual assent, and not the assent itself, is the essential element of contractual liability." Id. The other great contracts scholar of the early twentieth century agreed. ARTHUR CORBIN, CORBIN ON CONTRACTS § 9 (1952). The objective theory has gained widespread acceptance in judicial practice. E. ALLEN FARNSWORTH, CONTRACTS § 3.6 (4th ed. 2004). However, a few recent scholars criticize the objective theory because it expands "the scope of 'consent' far beyond anything remotely close to what the parties ever had in mind." E.g., Ian R. MacNeil, *Contracts: Adjustment of Long-Term Economic Relations Under Classical, Neo-Classical and Relational Contract Law*, 72 NW. U. L. REV. 854, 884 (1978). If this consent-centered view were a sound view of contract formation, the objective theory would seem illicit indeed, leaving the enforcement of promises and agreements without adequate justification.

The distinction between subjective and objective theories of contract, however, employs an odd idea of the people who are contracting. It reminds me of an old Walt Disney cartoon in which Mickey Mouse personifies some ideas about vision. The camera's eye opens on a scene being viewed by Mickey Mouse, then cuts to a profile of Mickey's head as he views that scene, and then pans around to face his eyes; it zooms through his eyes to the inside of his head. Lo and behold! Inside Mickey's head is a Little Mickey Mouse, sitting on an easy chair and watching a movie screen against the inside back of Big Mickey's head. The inside of Big Mickey's eyes are portrayed as movie projectors casting images of the scene we had seen on the outside, and the Little Mickey is watching the very same scene with which we had opened. There was a time when such a Little Mickey Mouse would be called a "homunculus" and would personify the human mind. This metaphor of the person splits us into two parts—a body like the Big Mickey Mouse and a mind like the homuncular Mickey.

We can understand the subjective and objective theories of contract law within this metaphor. An objective agreement is reached when Big Mickey Mouse shakes hands with Donald Duck's body; a subjective agreement is reached when little Mickey Mouse, to speak figuratively, shakes hands with Donald's homunculus. There would be no problem of mutual assent when the bodies and homunculi shake hands simultaneously. The problems arise when bodies shake hands while homunculi do not, or the reverse.

The standard legal litany of mistake and misunderstanding is an ordered mix of subjective and objective theory that presupposes this mind/body dualism. See RESTATEMENT (SECOND) OF CONTRACTS §§ 20, 201. In terms of our metaphor, these provisions say that there is no manifestation of mutual assent to an exchange if the two homunculi attach materially different meanings to what their bodies do and neither homunculus knows or has reason to know what the other homunculus is thinking, or each homunculus knows or has reason to know what the other homunculus is thinking.

A problem arises if we imagine ourselves now inside Big Mickey's head from the camera-eye point of view and zoom through Little Mickey's eyes into his head where, not surprisingly, there is a Little Little Mickey Mouse watching a movie of Little Mickey Mouse watching a movie of Big Mickey Mouse watching the scene with which the story opened. We can of course repeat this move over and over. It is hard to imagine solving a problem once we start down this path to absurdity.

Is there another and better way to think of contract, consistent with the autonomy principle? Or is contract law's emphasis on the parties' voluntary obligations an illusion because consent is required and consent is always subjective? See Note on Consent and Fair Play, below at p. 66.

EMBRY v. HARGADINE, McKITTRICK DRY GOODS CO.

St. Louis Court of Appeals, Missouri, 1907.
127 Mo.App. 383, 105 S.W. 777.

GOODE, JUDGE. We dealt with this case on a former appeal (115 Mo.App. 130, 91 S.W. 170). It has been retried, and is again before us for the determination of questions not then reviewed. The appellant was an employé of the respondent company under a written contract to expire

December 15, 1903, at a salary of $2,000 per annum. His duties were to attend to the sample department of respondent, of which he was given complete charge. It was his business to select samples for the traveling salesmen of the company, which is a wholesale dry goods concern, to use in selling goods to retail merchants. Appellant contends that on December 23, 1903, he was re-engaged by respondent, through its president, Thos. H. McKittrick, for another year at the same compensation and for the same duties stipulated in his previous written contract. On March 1, 1904, he was discharged, having been notified in February that, on account of the necessity of retrenching expenses, his services and that of some other employés would no longer be required. The respondent company contends that its president never re-employed appellant after the termination of his written contract, and hence that it had a right to discharge him when it chose. The point with which we are concerned requires an epitome of the testimony of appellant and the counter testimony of McKittrick, the president of the company, in reference to the alleged re-employment. Appellant testified: That several times prior to the termination of his written contract on December 15, 1903, he had endeavored to get an understanding with McKittrick for another year, but had been put off from time to time. That on December 23d, eight days after the expiration of said contract, he called on McKittrick, in the latter's office, and said to him that as appellant's written employment had lapsed eight days before, and as there were only a few days between then and the 1st of January in which to seek employment with other firms, if respondent wished to retain his services longer he must have a contract for another year, or he would quit respondent's service then and there. That he had been put off twice before and wanted an understanding or contract at once so that he could go ahead without worry. That McKittrick asked him how he was getting along in his department, and appellant said he was very busy, as they were in the height of the season getting men out—had about 110 salesmen on the line and others in preparation. That McKittrick then said: "Go ahead, you're all right. Get your men out and don't let that worry you." That appellant took McKittrick at his word and worked until February 15th without any question in his mind. It was on February 15th that he was notified his services would be discontinued on March 1st. McKittrick denied this conversation as related by appellant, and said that, when accosted by the latter on December 23d, he (McKittrick) was working on his books in order to get out a report for a stockholders' meeting, and, when appellant said if he did not get a contract he would leave, that he (McKittrick) said: "Mr. Embry, I am just getting ready for the stockholders' meeting tomorrow. I have no time to take it up now. I have told you before I would not take it up until I had these matters out of the way. You will have to see me at a later time. I said: 'Go back upstairs and get your men out on the road.' I may have asked him one or two other questions relative to the department, I don't remember. The whole conversation did not take more than a minute."

Embry also swore that, when he was notified he would be discharged, he complained to McKittrick about it, as being a violation of their contract, and McKittrick said it was due to the action of the board of directors, and not to any personal action of his, and that others would suffer by what the board had done as well as Embry. Appellant requested an instruction to the jury setting out, in substance, the conversation between him and McKittrick according to his version, and declaring that those facts, if found to be true, constituted a contract between the parties that defendant would pay plaintiff the sum of $2,000 for another year, provided the jury believed from the evidence that plaintiff commenced said work believing he was to have $2,000 for the year's work. This instruction was refused, but the court gave another embodying in substance appellant's version of the conversation, and declaring it made a contract "if you (the jury) find both parties thereby intended and did contract with each other for plaintiff's employment for one year from and including December 23, 1903, at salary of $2,000 per annum." Embry swore that, on several occasions when he spoke to McKittrick about employment for the ensuing year, he asked for a renewal of his former contract, and that on December 23rd, the date of the alleged renewal, he went into Mr. McKittrick's office and told him his contract had expired, and he wanted to renew it for a year, having always worked under year contracts. Neither the refused instruction nor the one given by the court embodied facts quite as strong as appellant's testimony, because neither referred to appellant's alleged statement to McKittrick that unless he was re-employed he would stop work for respondent then and there.

It is assigned for error that the court required the jury, in order to return a verdict for appellant, not only to find the conversation occurred as appellant swore, but that both parties intended by such conversation to contract with each other for plaintiff's employment for the year from December, 1903, at a salary of $2,000. If it appeared from the record that there was a dispute between the parties as to the terms on which appellant wanted re-employment, there might have been sound reason for inserting this clause in the instruction; but no issue was made that they split on terms; the testimony of McKittrick tending to prove only that he refused to enter into a contract with appellant regarding another year's employment until the annual meeting of stockholders was out of the way. Indeed, as to the proposed terms McKittrick agrees with Embry, for the former swore as follows: "Mr. Embry said he wanted to know about the renewal of his contract. Said if he did not have the contract made he would leave." As the two witnesses coincided as to the terms of the proposed re-employment, there was no reason for inserting the above-mentioned clause in the instruction in order that it might be settled by the jury whether or not plaintiff, if employed for one year from December 23, 1903, was to be paid $2,000 a year. Therefore it remains to determine whether or not this part of the instruction was a correct statement of the law in regard to what was necessary to constitute a contract between the parties; that is to say, whether the formation of a contract by what, according to Embry, was said, depended on the intention of both Embry and McKittrick. Or, to put the question more precisely: Did what was said constitute a contract of re-employment on the previous terms irrespective of the intention or purpose of McKittrick?

Judicial opinion and elementary treatises abound in statements of the rule that to constitute a contract there must be a meeting of the minds of the parties, and both must agree to the same thing in the same sense. Generally speaking, this may be true; but it is not literally or universally true. That is to say, the inner intention of parties to a conversation subsequently alleged to create a contract cannot either make a contract of what transpired, or prevent one from arising, if the words used were sufficient to constitute a contract. In so far as their intention is an influential element, it is only such intention as the words or acts of the parties indicate; not one secretly cherished which is inconsistent with those words or acts. The rule is thus stated by a text-writer, and many decisions are cited in support of his text: "The primary object of construction in contract law is to discover the intention of the parties. This intention in express contracts is, in the first instance, embodied in the words which the parties have used and is to be deduced therefrom. This rule applies to oral contracts, as well as to contracts in writing, and is the rule recognized by courts of equity." 2 Paige, Contracts, § 1104. So it is said in another work: "Now this measure of the contents of the promise will be found to coincide in the usual dealings of men of good faith and ordinary competence, both with the actual intention of the promisor and with the actual expectation of the promisee. But this is not a constant or a necessary coincidence. In exceptional cases a promisor may be bound to perform something which he did not intend to promise, or a promisee may not be entitled to require that performance which he understood to be promised to him." Walds–Pollock, Contracts (3d Ed.) 309.... In view of those authorities, we hold that, though McKittrick may not have intended to employ Embry by what transpired between them according to the latter's testimony, yet if what McKittrick said would have been taken by a reasonable man to be an employment, and Embry so understood it, it constituted a valid contract of employment for the ensuing year.

The next question is whether or not the language used was of that character, namely, was such that Embry, as a reasonable man, might consider he was re-employed for the ensuing year on the previous terms, and act accordingly. We do not say that in every instance it would be for the court to pronounce on this question, because, peradventure, instances might arise in which there would be such an ambiguity in the language relied on to show an assent by the obligor to the proposal of the obligee that it would be for the jury to say whether a reasonable mind would take it to signify acceptance of the proposal. Belt v. Goode, 31 Mo. 128.... In Lancaster v. Elliott, 28 Mo.App. 86, 92, the opinion, as to the immediate point, reads: "The interpretation of a contract in writing is always a matter of law for determination by the court, and equally so, upon like principles, is the question what acts and words, in nearly every case, will suffice to constitute an acceptance by one party, of a proposal submitted by the other, so that a contract or agreement thereby becomes matured." The general rule is that it is for the court to construe the effect of writings relied on to make a contract, and also the effect of unambiguous oral words. Belt v. Goode, supra. . . . However, if the words are in dispute, the question of whether they were used or not is for the jury. Belt v. Goode, supra. With these rules of law in mind, let us recur to the conversation of December 23rd between Embry and McKittrick as related by the former. Embry was demanding a renewal of his contract, saying he had been put off from time to time, and that he had only a few days before the end of the year in which to seek employment from other houses, and that he would quit then and there unless he was re-employed. McKittrick inquired how he was getting along with the department, and Embry said they, i.e., the employés of the department were very busy getting out salesmen. Whereupon McKittrick said: "Go ahead, you are all right. Get your men out, and do not let that worry you." We think no reasonable man would construe that answer to Embry's demand that he be employed for another year, otherwise than as an assent to the demand, and that Embry had the right to rely on it as an assent. The natural inference is, though we do not find it testified to, that Embry was at work getting samples ready for the salesmen to use during the ensuing season. Now, when he was complaining of the worry and mental distress he was under because of his uncertainty about the future, and his urgent need, either of an immediate contract with respondent, or a refusal by it to make one, leaving him free to seek employment elsewhere, McKittrick must have answered as he did for the purpose of assuring appellant that any apprehension was needless, as appellant's services would be retained by the respondent. The answer was unambiguous, and we rule that if the conversation was according to appellant's version, and he understood he was employed, it constituted in law a valid contract of re-employment, and the court erred in making the formation of a contract depend on a finding that both parties intended to make one. It was only necessary that Embry, as a reasonable man, had a right to and did so understand.

Some other rulings are assigned for error by the appellant, but we will not discuss them because we think they are devoid of merit.

The judgment is reversed, and the cause remanded. All concur.

Questions

1. What words constitute the promise that is sued upon in *Embry*? What makes these words a promise? What is the agreement?

2. What is the procedural context in which the manifestation of intention is to be interpreted? What will happen on remand to the trial court? What is left to be done on remand? Why was that issue not resolved on this, the second, appeal in the case?

3. In justifying its holding, does the court employ the objective or subjective theory of contract interpretation? Did the defendant consent to

the obligation found by the court? Would it be fair for the defendant to leave Embry under the impression his employment had been renewed without undertaking such an obligation? How would you decide this case? Why?

OSWALD v. ALLEN

United States Court of Appeals, Second Circuit, 1969.
417 F.2d 43.

MOORE, CIRCUIT JUDGE. Dr. Oswald, a coin collector from Switzerland, was interested in Mrs. Allen's collection of Swiss coins. In April of 1964 Dr. Oswald was in the United States and arranged to see Mrs. Allen's coins. The parties drove to the Newburgh Savings Bank of Newburgh, New York, where two of her collections referred to as the Swiss Coin Collection and the Rarity Coin Collection were located in separate vault boxes. After examining and taking notes on the coins in the Swiss Coin Collection, Dr. Oswald was shown several valuable Swiss coins from the Rarity Coin Collection. He also took notes on these coins and later testified that he did not know that they were in a separate "collection." The evidence showed that each collection had a different key number and was housed in labeled cigar boxes.

On the return to New York City, Dr. Oswald sat in the front seat of the car while Mrs. Allen sat in the back with Dr. Oswald's brother, Mr. Victor Oswald, and Mr. Cantarella of the Chase Manhattan Bank's Money Museum, who had helped arrange the meeting and served as Dr. Oswald's agent. Dr. Oswald could speak practically no English and so depended on his brother to conduct the transaction. After some negotiation a price of $50,000 was agreed upon. Apparently the parties never realized that the references to "Swiss coins" and the "Swiss Coin Collection" were ambiguous. The trial judge found that Dr. Oswald thought the offer he had authorized his brother to make was for all of the Swiss coins, while Mrs. Allen thought she was selling only the Swiss Coin Collection and not the Swiss coins in the Rarity Coin Collection.

On April 8, 1964, Dr. Oswald wrote to Mrs. Allen to "confirm my purchase of all your Swiss coins (gold, silver and copper) at the price of $50,000.00." The letter mentioned delivery arrangements through Mr. Cantarella. In response Mrs. Allen wrote on April 15, 1964, that "Mr. Cantarella and I have arranged to go to Newburgh Friday April 24." This letter does not otherwise mention the alleged contract of sale or the quantity of coins sold. On April 20, realizing that her original estimation of the number of coins in the Swiss Coin Collection was erroneous, Mrs. Allen offered to permit a re-examination and to undertake not to sell to anyone else. Dr. Oswald cabled from Switzerland to Mr. Alfred Barth of the Chase Manhattan Bank, giving instruction to proceed with the transaction. Upon receiving the cable, Barth wrote a letter to Mrs. Allen stating Dr. Oswald's understanding of the agreement and requesting her signature on a copy of the letter as a "mere formality." Mrs. Allen did not sign and return this letter. On April 24, Mrs. Allen's husband told

Barth that his wife did not wish to proceed with the sale because her children did not wish her to do so.

Appellant attacks the conclusion of the Court below that a contract did not exist since the minds of the parties had not met. The opinion below states:

> "... plaintiff believed that he had offered to buy all Swiss coins owned by the defendant while defendant reasonably understood the offer which she accepted to relate to those of her Swiss coins as had been segregated in the particular collection denominated by her as the 'Swiss Coin Collection'...."

285 F. Supp. 488, 492 (S.D.N.Y.1968). The trial judge based his decision upon his evaluation of the credibility of the witnesses, the records of the defendant, the values of the coins involved, the circumstances of the transaction and the reasonable probabilities. Such findings of fact are not to be set aside unless "clearly erroneous." Fed.R.Civ.P. 52(a). There was ample evidence upon which the trial judge could rely in reaching this decision.

In such a factual situation the law is settled that no contract exists. The Restatement of Contracts in section 71(a) adopts the rule of Raffles v. Wichelhaus, 2 Hurl. & C. 906, 159 Eng.Rep. 375 (Ex. 1864). Professor Young states that rule as follows:

> "when any of the terms used to express an agreement is ambivalent, and the parties understand it in different ways, there cannot be a contract unless one of them should have been aware of the other's understanding."

Young, Equivocation in Agreements, 64 Colum. L. Rev. 619, 621 (1964). Even though the mental assent of the parties is not requisite for the formation of a contract (see Comment to Restatement of Contracts § 71 (1932)), the facts found by the trial judge clearly place this case within the small group of exceptional cases in which there is "no sensible basis for choosing between conflicting understandings." Young, at 647....

Questions

1. What was the language to be interpreted in *Oswald*? What does Oswald take to be its meaning? What does Allen claim? Does either know or have reason to know of the meaning attached by the other? Does the context provide a meaning to that language?

2. Who should decide who gets the Swiss coins in the Rarity Coin Collection? Should a court decide on the basis of fairness, rather than autonomy? What would justice require here? Or should the law leave things as they stand?

3. *Problem.*

    Assume that, at Oswald's home in Switzerland, the law required interpretation on the basis of documents alone. His letter of April 8 is the only written record of the agreement. At Allen's home in New York, however, the law required interpretation of documents in light of their context. Should a court find that each party's contract rights and duties are those established by his home law or culture?

NOTE ON APPLICABLE LAW

An international transaction, like *Oswald v. Allen*, raises a question about the law applicable to a contract. The laws of Switzerland and the U.S. differ on many points; so too do the laws of New York and Texas. Special problems arise when the law of one jurisdiction requires an outcome that is incompatible with the outcome required by the law of another jurisdiction. The law of Switzerland, for example, might give the Swiss Coins to Oswald while the law of New York gives them to Allen. Each party may argue that the applicable law is the law that favors the outcome he or she prefers. There is a separate body of law, called the law of conflicts or choice of law, containing rules and principles for deciding the applicable law.

When the parties live, and the making and performance of the contract occur, within a single jurisdiction, the law of that jurisdiction applies. In international transactions, however, it is common for the parties to come from different countries, to negotiate the deal in a third country, to conclude it in a fourth, to perform it in yet other countries, and so on. Similarly dispersed contracting can occur among the states of the U.S. The law of conflicts might provide that the applicable law is the law of the place where the contract is made or the law of the place where the transaction has its "center of gravity." On the latter view, all of the jurisdictions with which the transaction has contacts are considered in an effort to find one with which it is most closely associated. To avoid uncertainty, the parties generally can determine the applicable law by agreement if they wish.

Note that *Oswald* was decided by a federal court. U.S. law provides for federal court jurisdiction in large contract cases in which the parties are from different states or one is from a foreign state. This is called "diversity of citizenship jurisdiction;" you will study it in Civil Procedure. Otherwise, state courts hear contract cases. In principle, the applicable law should be the same in whatever court obtains jurisdiction over the parties and the subject matter of their dispute. In practice, it does not always turn out to be so neat.

b. *Offers*

Promissory agreements can be made when one party makes an "offer" and the other "accepts" it. This is familiar enough. For legal purposes, however, more distinctions are needed. To begin, not all agreements are contracts, and all offers are not offers to contract. Two people may agree that the President's economic policy is unwise, but this is surely not a contract. There is no commitment to action, only to a belief. A barter, as when two people trade goods on the spot on an "as is" basis, is an agreement to act but not a contract. There is no promise on either side because no action is to occur in the future. For the same reason, an offer to a barter is not an offer to contract.

Offers to contract are promises manifesting a commitment to some specified action in the future in return for some promise or performance by the offeree. An offer, in legal consequence, creates a "power of acceptance" in the offeree. An offeree can exercise this power by assenting to the offer, without changing its terms or equivocating on his or her commitment, thereby concluding an agreement. The following three subsections consider the offer, the power of acceptance, and the acceptance.

In contemporary contract law, a sequential offer and acceptance process is not the only way to reach agreement. Many contracts are made by negotiating a single document or using a standard form contract, which both parties sign at the same time. In these cases, the fact of agreement is patent from the writing, assuming it genuine. There is no need to analyze who was offeror and who was offeree (though, if necessary, the first to sign can be called the offeror). There are other circumstances, especially in some commercial contracts, when the fact of agreement is clearer than the details of how it came about (and sometimes what was agreed). The Uniform Commercial Code's provisions on contract formation, to be considered later in this chapter, make it unnecessary to parse the technicalities of the common law of offer and acceptance. The law of offer and acceptance, however, may be a helpful guide in difficult cases.

Having reached agreement, whether by offer and acceptance or otherwise, the parties do not necessarily have a contract. Their transaction must meet further conditions for the promises constituting the agreement to be enforceable. We will consider these conditions in Chapters 2 and 3.

RESTATEMENT (SECOND) OF CONTRACTS §§ 24, 26, 33, 35

MESAROS v. UNITED STATES

United States Court of Appeals, Federal Circuit, 1988.
845 F.2d 1576.

SKELTON, SENIOR CIRCUIT JUDGE. On May 23, 1986, plaintiffs Mary Mesaros and husband Anthony C. Mesaros filed a class action lawsuit for themselves and others similarly situated (thirty-three of whom were named) in the United States District Court for the Southern District of Georgia, Savannah Division, against the United States of America, the United States Department of the Treasury, the Bureau of the Mint, James Baker, Secretary of the Treasury, and Donna Pope, Director of the United States Mint (defendants) seeking damages for an alleged breach of contract by defendants in failing to deliver a quantity of Statue of Liberty commemorative coins they had ordered from defendants pursuant to an advertisement mailed to plaintiffs and published in newspapers and other news media by the United States Mint. In the alternative they sought mandamus relief for the delivery of the coins. Plaintiffs also filed a motion for certification of the class.

The defendants filed a motion to dismiss plaintiffs' suit, or in the alternative for summary judgment. On April 13, 1987, the court granted judgment for defendants on their motion in its entirety. No action was taken by the court on the class action motion because it was moot after the other action by the court. The plaintiffs filed an appeal (No. 87–8445) in the United States Court of Appeals for the Eleventh Circuit. On motion of defendants, the case was transferred to this court.

The facts in the case, as stated in an order of the district court dated April 13, 1987, (with a few omissions and additions), and as shown by the record are as follows.

In July 1985, Congress passed the Statue of Liberty–Ellis Island Commemorative Coin Act. Pub.L. No. 99–61, 99 Stat. 113 (July 9, 1985). The purpose of the Act was to provide funds, through the sale of a limited number of specially-minted commemorative coins, "to restore and renovate the Statue of Liberty and the facilities used for immigration at Ellis Island," and to establish an endowment to provide for the upkeep and maintenance of these national monuments. The Act, which by modern standards is a commendable example of brevity, instructed the Secretary of the Treasury: to mint a stated number of coins; to follow certain procedures with respect to the marketing of the coins; to disburse specified surcharges included in the price of each coin to the Statue of Liberty Foundation; and to take all actions necessary to ensure that the project would result in no net cost to the government.

. . .

The provision of the Act that is directly implicated in this action is § 105(c), which reads: "The Secretary [of the Treasury] shall accept prepaid orders for [commemorative] coins prior to the issuance of the coins. Sales under this subsection shall be at a reasonable discount to reflect the benefit of prepayment." A related provision, § 105(d), authorized bulk sales of commemorative coins at a discount. Pursuant to these provisions, in November and December 1985, the Mint mailed certain advertising materials to persons, including the plaintiffs, whose names were included on a list of previous customers/coin collectors. These materials described the various coins the issuance of which was authorized by the Act, and encouraged potential purchasers to forward early payment for commemorative coins. The materials represented, inter alia, that "[i]f [the Mint] receive[s] your reservation by December 31, 1985, you will enjoy a favorable Pre–Issue Discount saving you up to 16% on your coins." Payment could be made either by check, money order, or credit card. Apparently, the Mint had not previously dealt with credit card sales, and the processing of credit card orders, which in this case turned out to be an almost impossible ordeal, was contracted to the Mellon Bank in Pittsburgh, Pennsylvania.

The materials included an order form. Directly above the space provided on this form for the customer's signature was the following:

VERY IMPORTANT—PLEASE READ: YES, Please accept my order for the U.S. Liberty Coins I have indicated. I understand that all sales are final and not subject to refund. Verification of my order will be made by the Department of the Treasury, U.S. Mint. My coins may be delivered in multiple shipments. If my order is received by December 31, 1985, I will be entitled to purchase the coins at the Pre–Issue Discount price shown. I have read, understand and agree to the above.[2]

Demand for the coins far exceeded the Mint's expectations.... [T]here was an insufficient quantity of five-dollar gold coins, however, with which to fill the orders of many of those who responded to the Mint's promotional materials. According to the Mint's "knowledge and belief," the last order for gold coins that was filled was accepted "some time between December 31, 1985, and January 6, 1986. This exhausted the supply of 500,000 gold coins the issuance of which was authorized by the Act.

A great many would-be acquisitors of gold coins were disappointed by the news of the sell-out. These individuals, many of whom were coin dealers, developed a more serious case of disappointment when it became apparent that the gold coins had increased in value by approximately 200% within the first few months of 1986. Notwithstanding the foregoing facts, which understandably would be cause for tears on the part of those turned away, collectors and dealers alike, it is quite possible that no legal action against the Mint would have been contemplated had not certain matters concerning the treatment of credit card orders come to light. In this regard, the ordeal faced by plaintiffs Mary and Anthony Mesaros appears not to have been atypical.

Plaintiffs allege that on November 26, 1985, Mary Mesaros forwarded to the Mint an order for certain Statue of Liberty coins. Information concerning Anthony Mesaros' credit card was included on the order form, reflecting that the sum of $1,675 should be charged against Mr.

---

2. On the opposite side of the form the following language appeared:

As a special courtesy to collectors, you are receiving advance notice of the minting and issuing of three new U.S. coins authorized by Congress to commemorate the centennial of the Statue of Liberty. If you place your reservation prior to December 31, 1985, you will be eligible for a Congressionally authorized Pre–Issue Discount on all coins and sets of coins. Use this form to reserve your Liberty Coins direct from the U.S. Mint. All coins will be accompanied by a Liberty Coin presentation case and certificate.

. . .

Please allow 6 to 8 weeks for delivery after issue date of January 1, 1986. The U.S. Mint reserves the right to limit quantities shipped, subject to availability. Mint may discontinue accepting orders should bullion prices increase significantly. Credit card orders will be billed upon receipt by the U.S. Mint.

Mesaros' credit account. Subsequently, on December 30, 1985, Anthony Mesaros forwarded orders for an additional eighteen gold coins to the Mint. These orders were placed in the names of members of the Mesaros family, and were paid for with nine separate checks.

On February 18, 1986, the Mesaroses were informed by form letter that the Mint "had tried but was unable" to process the Mesaroses' November 26, 1985, credit card order. The letter directed the plaintiffs to contact their financial institution for details relating to the rejection of their order. A new order form was forwarded to the Mesaroses along with the form letter, with which the plaintiffs were informed that they could order "the options currently available." The options then available, of course, did not include five-dollar gold coins. Investigation by Mr. Mesaros revealed that his bank had not been responsible for the rejection of his credit card order. By letter of April 7, 1986, an officer of the Columbus (Georgia) Bank and Trust Company informed Mr. Mesaros that, in fact, on December 27, 1985, that bank had given authorization to the Mellon Bank (responsible for processing credit card orders for the Mint) with respect to the coin order charged to Mr. Mesaros' account. In or about May 1986, the Mesaroses received the eighteen coins that had been paid for by checks dated December 30, 1985.

.   .   .

On May 23, 1986, plaintiffs filed suit in the district court, seeking . . . damages on a breach of contract theory. . . .

The plaintiffs claim that the Mint breached an express contract with them and that they are entitled to recover money damages from defendants for this breach. They allege that the district court has jurisdiction over the claim under 28 U.S.C. § 1346 known as the Tucker Act.[4] We agree because the plaintiffs have alleged the existence of a contract with the government, the breach of that contract by the government, and a claim of damages for the breach not in excess of $10,000.

The plaintiffs contend that the materials sent to them by the Mint, including the order form, constituted an offer that upon acceptance by the plaintiffs created a binding contract between them and the government whereby the government was bound and obligated to deliver the coins ordered by them. The great weight of authority is against the plaintiffs. It is well established that materials such as those mailed to prospective customers by the Mint are no more than advertisements or invitations to deal. . . . Restatement (Second) Contracts, § 26.

It is stated in Williston, A Treatise on the Law of Contracts, § 27 (3rd ed. 1957):

Thus, if goods are advertised for sale at a certain price, it is not an offer, and no contract is formed by the statement of an intending

4. The Tucker Act grants to the federal district courts original jurisdiction, concurrent with that of the Claims Court, over, inter alia, contractual suits against the United States where the amount in controversy is not in excess of $10,000. 28 U.S.C. § 1346(a)(2).

purchaser that he will take a specified quantity of the goods at that price. The construction is rather favored that such an advertisement is a mere invitation to enter into a bargain rather than an offer. So a published price list is not an offer to sell the goods listed at the published prices.

See also Corbin, Contracts, §§ 25, 28 (1963 ed.). . . .

A basic rule of contracts holds that whether an offer has been made depends on the objective reasonableness of the alleged offeree's belief that the advertisement or solicitation was intended as an offer. Generally, it is considered unreasonable for a person to believe that advertisements and solicitations are offers that bind the advertiser. Otherwise, the advertiser could be bound by an excessive number of contracts requiring delivery of goods far in excess of amounts available. That is particularly true in the instant case where the gold coins were limited to 500,000 by the Act of Congress. We conclude that a thorough reading, construction, and interpretation of the materials sent to the plaintiffs by the Mint makes clear that the contention of the plaintiffs that they reasonably believed the materials were intended as an offer is unreasonable as a matter of law. This is especially true in view of the words "YES, Please accept my order . . ." that were printed on the credit card form, which showed that the credit card order was an offer from the plaintiffs to the Mint to buy the coins, which offer might or might not be accepted by the Mint. Accordingly, the Mint materials were intended solely as solicitations of offers from customers that were subject to acceptance by the Mint before the Mint would be bound by a contract. This is in accord with the following statement from I Corbin, Contracts, 375–76 § 88 (1963):

> Where one party solicits and receives an order or other expression of agreement from another, clearly specifying that there is to be no contract until ratification or assent by some officer or representative of the solicitor, the solicitation is not itself an offer; it is a request for an offer.

The plaintiffs rely on *Lefkowitz v. Great Minneapolis Surplus Store*, 251 Minn. 188, 86 N.W.2d 689 (1957). In that case a store advertised one fur stole worth $139.50 for sale for $1.00 on a first-come, first-served basis when the store opened at 9:00 a.m. The plaintiff arrived first, but the store refused to sell the stole to him. The plaintiff sued for breach of contract. The court held under these unusual facts that the advertisement constituted an offer. That case is clearly distinguishable from our case on the facts. Here the Mint had 35,500,000 coins for sale to the general public for which it received over 756,000 orders. The Mint advertisement did not state that the coins would be sold on a first-come, first-served basis, as in *Lefkowitz*, or on any other particular basis. Since the coins could be paid for with checks, money orders or credit cards, it would have been impossible for the Mint to have processed the sales on a first-come, first-served basis. The situation in *Lefkowitz* was so different that it is of no help to the plaintiffs.

We hold that the Mint advertisement materials were not an offer of sale of the coins that could be accepted by the plaintiffs to create a contract, and that no contract was made between the plaintiffs and the government with reference to the coins.

The plaintiffs failed to allege any genuine issue of material fact, and, therefore, the court was correct as a matter of law in granting summary judgment for the defendants.

. . .

The decision of the district court in his well-written order is affirmed.

Questions

1. In *Mesaros*, why is it significant that the Congress limited the quantity of coins to 500,000? Why is it significant that the order form began, "Yes, please accept my order...." Does the government win for sound legal reasons or, perhaps, because it is the government?

2. The court distinguishes the *Lefkowitz* case on the ground that the communication in that case said "First come, First Served." Why is that fact so important? *See Lefkowitz*, below.

LEFKOWITZ v. GREAT MINNEAPOLIS SURPLUS STORE

Supreme Court of Minnesota, 1957.
251 Minn. 188, 86 N.W.2d 689.

MURPHY, JUSTICE. This is an appeal from an order of the Municipal Court of Minneapolis denying the motion of the defendant for amended findings of fact, or, in the alternative, for a new trial. The order for judgment awarded the plaintiff the sum of $138.50 as damages for breach of contract.

This case grows out of the alleged refusal of the defendant to sell to the plaintiff a certain fur piece which it had offered for sale in a newspaper advertisement. It appears from the record that on April 6, 1956, the defendant published the following advertisement in a Minneapolis newspaper:

> "Saturday 9 A.M. Sharp
> 3 Brand New Fur Coats
> Worth to $100.00
> First Come First Served
> $1 Each"

On April 13, the defendant again published an advertisement in the same newspaper as follows:

> "Saturday 9 A.M.
> 2 Brand New Pastel Mink
> 3-Skin Scarfs

Selling for $89.50
Out they go
Saturday. Each.... $1.00
1 Black Lapin Stole
Beautiful, worth $139.50.... $1.00
First Come First Served"

The record supports the findings of the court that on each of the Saturdays following the publication of the above-described ads the plaintiff was the first to present himself at the appropriate counter in the defendant's store and on each occasion demanded the coat and the stole so advertised and indicated his readiness to pay the sale price of $1. On both occasions, the defendant refused to sell the merchandise to the plaintiff, stating on the first occasion that by a "house rule" the offer was intended for women only and sales would not be made to men, and on the second visit that plaintiff knew defendant's house rules.

The trial court properly disallowed plaintiff's claim for the value of the fur coats since the value of these articles was speculative and uncertain. The only evidence of value was the advertisement itself to the effect that the coats were "Worth to $100.00," how much less being speculative especially in view of the price for which they were offered for sale. With reference to the offer of the defendant on April 13, 1956, to sell the "1 Black Lapin Stole ... worth $139.50 ..." the trial court held that the value of this article was established and granted judgment in favor of the plaintiff for that amount less the $1 quoted purchase price.

1. The defendant contends that a newspaper advertisement offering items of merchandise for sale at a named price is a "unilateral offer" which may be withdrawn without notice. He relies upon authorities which hold that, where an advertiser publishes in a newspaper that he has a certain quantity or quality of goods which he wants to dispose of at certain prices and on certain terms, such advertisements are not offers which become contracts as soon as any person to whose notice they may come signifies his acceptance by notifying the other that he will take a certain quantity of them. Such advertisements have been construed as an invitation for an offer of sale on the terms stated, which offer, when received, may be accepted or rejected and which therefore does not become a contract of sale until accepted by the seller; and until a contract has been so made, the seller may modify or revoke such prices or terms....

. . .

There are numerous authorities which hold that a particular advertisement in a newspaper or circular letter relating to a sale of articles may be construed by the court as constituting an offer, acceptance of which would complete a contract....

The test of whether a binding obligation may originate in advertisements addressed to the general public is "whether the facts show that some performance was promised in positive terms in return for something requested." 1 Williston, Contracts (Rev. ed.) § 27.

The authorities above cited emphasize that, where the offer is clear, definite, and explicit, and leaves nothing open for negotiation, it constitutes an offer, acceptance of which will complete the contract. The most recent case on the subject is Johnson v. Capital City Ford Co., La.App., 85 So.2d 75, in which the court pointed out that a newspaper advertisement relating to the purchase and sale of automobiles may constitute an offer, acceptance of which will consummate a contract and create an obligation in the offeror to perform according to the terms of the published offer.

Whether in any individual instance a newspaper advertisement is an offer rather than an invitation to make an offer depends on the legal intention of the parties and the surrounding circumstances. Annotation, 157 A.L.R. 744, 751; 77 C.J.S., Sales, § 25b; 17 C.J.S., Contracts, § 389. We are of the view on the facts before us that the offer by the defendant of the sale of the Lapin fur was clear, definite, and explicit, and left nothing open for negotiation. The plaintiff having successfully managed to be the first one to appear at the seller's place of business to be served, as requested by the advertisement, and having offered the stated purchase price of the article, he was entitled to performance on the part of the defendant. We think the trial court was correct in holding that there was in the conduct of the parties a sufficient mutuality of obligation to constitute a contract of sale.

2.   The defendant contends that the offer was modified by a "house rule" to the effect that only women were qualified to receive the bargains advertised. The advertisement contained no such restriction. This objection may be disposed of briefly by stating that, while an advertiser has the right at any time before acceptance to modify his offer, he does not have the right, after acceptance, to impose new or arbitrary conditions not contained in the published offer. . . .

Questions

1.   Is the advertisement for three fur coats an offer? What about the advertisement for the black lapin stole? What are the plaintiff's probable contentions? The defendant's? Why does the defendant lose? Is the court's judgment justified? On what grounds? To what law does it appeal?

2.   The court states, "where the offer is clear, definite, and explicit, and leaves nothing open for negotiation, it constitutes an offer, acceptance of which will complete the contract." Is this statement true?

3.   *Problems.*

a.   Fred sent a telegram to Ginger asking, "Will you sell me Palace Theater? Telegraph lowest cash price." Ginger replied: "Lowest cash price for Palace Theater $897,000.00." Did Ginger make an offer? See Harvey v. Facey, [1893] A.C. 552 (P.C.) (Jamaica).

b. Douglas announced an auction of his 1937 Mercedes Benz, to be held at a specified time and place, "to be sold to the highest bidder." When Humphrey turned out to be the highest bidder, at what seemed too low a price, Douglas took the car off the auction block before the hammer fell. Who was the offeror? Was there a deal? See Uniform Commercial Code § 2–328.

c. *Powers of Acceptance*

In addition to rights and duties, the law creates and governs legal powers. A legal power is simply the ability to change legal relations—the parties' rights, duties, and other powers. For example, when a seller of a home is called out of town in an emergency and cannot be present to sign the deed at the closing, the seller can execute a power of attorney, appointing her broker to sign in her place. The broker then has the legal power to transfer ownership of the property, changing the legal rights and duties of the seller, the buyer, and others. The seller, for example, will no longer have a duty to pay further property taxes, and the county will have no right to further taxes from the seller. Instead, the buyer will have a duty to pay the property taxes.

People make offers by exercising a legal power—the power of contract. By exercising that power, an offeror changes his or her legal relations with the offeree. In particular, the offer creates a power of acceptance in the offeree. An agreement is made when the offeree exercises that legal power by accepting. If the agreement is enforceable, the parties then have contract rights and duties. Acceptance thus concludes the deal, assuming that the power of acceptance remains alive at the moment the offeree accepts.

———

RESTATEMENT (SECOND) OF CONTRACTS §§ 36, 41

———

AKERS v. J.B. SEDBERRY, INC.

Court of Appeals of Tennessee, 1955.
39 Tenn.App. 633, 286 S.W.2d 617.

FELTS, JUDGE. These two consolidated causes are before us upon a writ of error sued out by J.B. Sedberry, Inc., and Mrs. M.B. Sedberry, defendants below, to review a decree of the Chancery Court, awarding a recovery against them in favor of each of the complainants, Charles William Akers and William Gambill Whitsitt, for damages for breach of a contract of employment.

The principal question presented is whether complainants resigned their employment, or were wrongfully discharged by defendants; and if there was a breach of contract for which complainants are entitled to recover, there are some further questions as to the measure or extent of the recovery.

J.B. Sedberry, Inc., was a Tennessee corporation with its principal place of business at Franklin, Tennessee. Mrs. M.B. Sedberry owned practically all of its stock and was its president and in active charge of its affairs. It was engaged in the business of distributing "Jay Bee" hammer mills, which were manufactured for it under contract by Jay Bee Manufacturing Company, a Texas corporation, whose plant was in Tyler, Texas, and whose capital stock was owned principally by L.M. Glasgow and B.G. Byars.

On July 1, 1947, J.B. Sedberry, Inc., by written contract, employed complainant Akers as Chief Engineer for a term of five years at a salary of $12,000 per year, payable $1,000 per month, plus 1% of its net profits for the first year, 2% the second, 3% the third, 4% the fourth, and 5% the fifth year. His duties were to carry on research for his employer, and to see that the Jay Bee Manufacturing Company, Tyler, Texas, manufactured the mills and parts according to proper specifications. Mrs. M.B. Sedberry guaranteed the employer's performance of this contract.

On August 1, 1947, J.B. Sedberry, Inc., by written contract, employed complainant Whitsitt as Assistant Chief Engineer for a term of five years at a salary of $7,200 per year, payable $600 per month, plus 1% of the corporation's net profits for the first year, 2% for the second, 3% for the third, 4% for the fourth, and 5% for the fifth year. His duties were to assist in the work done by the Chief Engineer. Mrs. M.B. Sedberry guaranteed the employer's performance of this contract.

Under Mrs. Sedberry's instructions, Akers and Whitsitt moved to Tyler, Texas, began performing their contract duties in the plant of the Jay Bee Manufacturing Company, continued working there, and were paid under the contracts until October 1, 1950, when they ceased work, under circumstances hereafter stated. . . .

There soon developed considerable friction between [plant manager] Sorenson and complainants Akers and Whitsitt. The Jay Bee Manufacturing Company owed large sums to the Tyler State Bank & Trust Co.; and the bank's officers, fearing the company might fail under Sorenson's management, began talking to Akers and Whitsitt about the company's financial difficulties. . . .

While these matters were pending, Akers and Whitsitt flew to Nashville and went to Franklin to talk with Mrs. Sedberry about them. They had a conference with her at her office on Friday, September 29, 1950, lasting from 9:30 a.m. until 4:30 p.m. As they had come unannounced, and unknown to Sorenson, they felt Mrs. Sedberry might mistrust them; and at the outset, to show their good faith, they offered to resign, but she did not accept their offer. Instead, she proceeded with them in discussing the operation and refinancing of the business.

Testifying about this conference, Akers said that, at the very beginning, to show their good faith, he told Mrs. Sedberry that they would offer their resignations on a ninety-day notice, provided they were paid according to the contract for that period; that she pushed the offers aside—"would not accept them," but went into a full discussion of the business; that nothing was thereafter said about the offers to resign; and that they spent the whole day discussing the business, Akers making notes of things she instructed him to do when he got back to Texas.

Whitsitt testified that at the beginning of the meeting Akers stated the position for both of them, and told Mrs. Sedberry, as evidence of their good faith, "we would resign with ninety-days notice if she paid us the monies that she owed us to that date, and on the other hand, if she did not accept that resignation, we would carry forth the rest of our business." He said that she did not accept the offer, but proceeded with the business, and nothing further was said about resigning.

Mrs. Sedberry testified that Akers and Whitsitt came in and "offered their resignations;" that they said they could not work with Sorenson and did not believe the bank would go along with him; and that "they said if it would be of any help to the organization they would be glad to tender their resignation and pay them what was due them." She further said that she "did not accept the resignation," that she "felt it necessary to contact Mr. Sorenson and give consideration to the resignation offer." But she said nothing to complainants about taking the offer under consideration.

On cross-examination she said that in the offer to resign "no mention was made of any ninety-day notice." Asked what response she made to the offer she said, "I treated it rather casually because I had to give it some thought and had to contact Mr. Sorenson." She further said she excused herself from the conference with complainants, went to another room, tried to telephone Sorenson in Tyler, Texas, but was unable to locate him.

She then resumed the conference, nothing further was said about the offers to resign, nothing was said by her to indicate that she thought the offers were left open or held under consideration by her. But the discussion proceeded as if the offers had not been made. She discussed with complainants future plans for refinancing and operating the business, giving them instructions, and Akers making notes of them.

Following the conference, complainants, upon Mrs. Sedberry's request, flew back to Texas to proceed to carry out her instructions. . . . On Monday, October 2, 1950, Mrs. Sedberry sent to complainants similar telegrams, signed by "J.B. Sedberry, Inc., by M.B. Sedberry, President," stating that their resignations were accepted, effective immediately. We quote the telegram to Akers, omitting the formal parts:

> "Account present unsettled conditions which you so fully are aware we accept your kind offer of resignation effective immediately. Please discontinue as of today with everyone employed in Sedberry, Inc., Engineering Department, discontinuing all expenses in this department writing."

While this said she was "writing," she did not write. . . . Akers [wrote] that he was amazed to get her telegram, and called her attention to the fact that no offer to resign by him was open or outstanding when she sent the telegram; that while he had made a conditional offer to resign at their conference on September 29, she had immediately rejected the offer, and had discussed plans for the business and had instructed him and Whitsitt as to things she wanted them to do in the business on their return to Tyler.

This letter further stated that Akers was expecting to be paid according to the terms of his contract until he could find other employment that would pay him as much income as that provided in his contract, and that if he had to accept a position with less income, he would expect to be paid the difference, or whatever losses he suffered by her breach of the contract. Whitsitt's letter contained a similar statement of his position. . . .

As it takes two to make a contract, it takes two to unmake it. It cannot be changed or ended by one alone, but only by mutual assent of both parties. A contract of employment for a fixed period may be terminated by the employee's offer to resign, provided such offer is duly accepted by the employer. Gentry Co. v. Margolius, 110 Tenn. 669, 674, 75 S.W. 959. . . .

An employee's tender of his resignation, being a mere offer is, of course, not binding until it has been accepted by the employer. Such offer must be accepted according to its terms and within the time fixed. The matter is governed by the same rules as govern the formation of contracts. . . .

An offer may be terminated in a number of ways, as, for example, where it is rejected by the offeree, or where it is not accepted by him within the time fixed, or, if no time is fixed, within a reasonable time. An offer terminated in either of these ways ceases to exist and cannot thereafter be accepted. 1 Williston on Contracts (1936), secs. 50A, 51, 53, 54. . . .

The question what is a reasonable time, where no time is fixed, is a question of fact, depending on the nature of the contract proposed, the usages of business and other circumstances of the case. Ordinarily, an offer made by one to another in a face to face conversation is deemed to continue only to the close of their conversation, and cannot be accepted thereafter.

The rule is illustrated by Restatement of Contracts, section 40, Illustration 2, as follows:

> "2. While A and B are engaged in conversation, A makes B an offer to which B then makes no reply, but a few hours later meeting A again, B states that he accepts the offer. There is no contract unless the offer or the surrounding circumstances indicate that the offer is intended to continue beyond the immediate conversation."
> . . .

Professor Williston says:

> "A reasonable time for the acceptance of most offers made in conversation will not extend beyond the time of the conversation

unless special words or circumstances indicate an intention on the part of the offeror that it shall do so." Williston on Contracts (1938), section 54.

Professor Corbin says:

"When two negotiating parties are in each other's presence, and one makes an offer to the other without indicating any time for acceptance, the inference that will ordinarily be drawn by the other party is that an answer is expected at once.... If, when the first reply is not an acceptance, the offeror turns away in silence, the proper inference is that the offer is no longer open to acceptance." 1 Corbin on Contracts (1950), section 36, p. 111.

The only offer by Akers and Whitsitt to resign was the offer made by them in their conversation with Mrs. Sedberry. They made that offer at the outset, and on the evidence it seems clear that they expected an answer at once. Certainly, there is nothing in the evidence to show that they intended the offer to continue beyond that conversation; and on the above authorities, we think the offer did not continue beyond that meeting.

Indeed, it did not last that long, in our opinion, but was terminated by Mrs. Sedberry's rejection of it very early in that meeting. While she did not expressly reject it, and while she may have intended, as she says, to take the offer under consideration, she did not disclose such an intent to complainants; but, by her conduct, led them to believe she rejected the offer, brushed it aside, and proceeded with the discussion as if it had not been made.

"An offer is rejected when the offeror is justified in inferring from the words or conduct of the offeree that the offeree intends not to accept the offer or to take it under further advisement (Rest. Contracts sec. 36)." 1 Williston on Contracts, section 51.

So, we agree with the Trial Judge that when defendants sent the telegrams, undertaking to accept offers of complainants to resign, there was no such offer in existence; and that this attempt of defendants to terminate their contract was unlawful and constituted a breach for which they are liable to complainants....

Finally, defendants contend that if complainants are entitled to any recovery at all, such recovery should have been limited to the ninety-day period from and after October 2, 1950, because complainants themselves admitted that they had offered to resign upon ninety days notice with pay for that period.

The answer to this contention is that their offer to resign on ninety days notice was not accepted, but had terminated, and there was no offer in existence when Mrs. Sedberry undertook to accept their offers of resignation. Such attempt by defendants to terminate their contract was unlawful and was a breach for which they become liable for the measure of recovery as above stated....

Questions

1.   What is the legal issue in *Akers*? What is the court's holding? Are there alternative holdings?

2.   How many different justifications for the result can you find in the opinion in *Akers*?

3.   Why should offerors be allowed to revoke an offer at any time before it is accepted? What is the offeror's interest in revocation? What is the offeree's competing interest? Which is in the better position to protect their own interest? Which interest is more worthy of protection by the law?

4.   Why should an offer lapse at the end of a conversation? Why should it matter what is ordinarily expected? Can this rule be justified by the autonomy principle alone? Or must the autonomy principle be supplemented by the security principle or something similar?

5.   *Problem.*

Tex Rebel made a living for many years writing books and speaking against the federal income tax. On the live Sammy Sewer television show one night, Sammy ridiculed Tex's claim that "nothing in the Internal Revenue Code says anybody is legally required to pay the tax." Tex replied, "if anybody calls this station and cites any section of this code saying an individual is required to file a tax return, I'll pay them $100,000." Ann, a law student, phoned the television station twenty minutes later, citing eight sections of the code making the income tax mandatory. She claims $100,000 in an action against Tex. Does she get it? Does she get it if she called the next morning, ten minutes after seeing the offer on a taped rebroadcast? See Newman v. Schiff, 778 F.2d 460 (8th Cir.1985).

RESTATEMENT (SECOND) OF CONTRACTS §§ 38, 39, 59

ARDENTE v. HORAN

Supreme Court of Rhode Island, 1976.
117 R.I. 254, 366 A.2d 162.

Doris, Justice. Ernest P. Ardente, the plaintiff, brought this civil action in Superior Court to specifically enforce an agreement between himself and William A. and Katherine L. Horan, the defendants, to sell certain real property. The defendants filed an answer together with a motion for summary judgment pursuant to Super.R.Civ.P. 56. Following the submission of affidavits by both the plaintiff and the defendants and a hearing on the motion, judgment was entered by a Superior Court justice for the defendants. The plaintiff now appeals.

In August 1975, certain residential property in the city of Newport was offered for sale by defendants. The plaintiff made a bid of $250,000 for the property which was communicated to defendants by their attorney. After defendants' attorney advised plaintiff that the bid was acceptable to defendants, he prepared a purchase and sale agreement at the direction of defendants and forwarded it to plaintiff's attorney for plaintiff's signature. After investigating certain title conditions, plaintiff executed the agreement. Thereafter plaintiff's attorney returned the document to defendants along with a check in the amount of $20,000 and a letter dated September 8, 1975, which read in relevant part as follows:

> "My clients are concerned that the following items remain with the real estate. a) dining room set and tapestry wall covering in dining room; b) fireplace fixtures throughout; c) the sun parlor furniture. I would appreciate your confirming that these items are a part of the transaction, as they would be difficult to replace."

The defendants refused to agree to sell the enumerated items and did not sign the purchase and sale agreement. They directed their attorney to return the agreement and the deposit check to plaintiff and subsequently refused to sell the property to plaintiff. This action for specific performance followed.

In Superior Court, defendants moved for summary judgment on the ground that the facts were not in dispute and no contract had been formed as a matter of law.[1] The trial justice ruled that the letter quoted above constituted a conditional acceptance of defendants' offer to sell the property and consequently must be construed as a counteroffer. Since defendants never accepted the counteroffer, it followed that no contract was formed, and summary judgment was granted.

Summary judgment is a drastic remedy and should be cautiously applied; nevertheless, where there is no genuine issue as to any material fact and the moving party is entitled to judgment as a matter of law, summary judgment properly issues. . . .

The plaintiff assigns several grounds for appeal in his brief. He urges first that summary judgment was improper because there existed a genuine issue of fact. The factual question, according to plaintiff, was whether the oral agreement which preceded the drafting of the purchase and sale agreement was intended by the parties to take effect immediately to create a binding oral contract for the sale of the property.

We cannot agree with plaintiff's position. A review of the record shows that the issue was never raised before the trial justice. The plaintiff did not, in his affidavit in opposition to summary judgment or by any other means, bring to the attention of the trial court any facts which established the existence of a relevant factual dispute. Indeed, at the hearing on the motion plaintiff did not even mention the alleged factual dispute which he now claims the trial justice erred in overlooking. The only issue plaintiff addressed was the proper interpretation of

---

1. Although the contract would appear to be within the statute of frauds, defendants did not raise this defense in the trial court, nor do they raise it here. Where a party makes no claim to the benefit of the statute, the court sua sponte will not interpose it for him. Conti v. Fisher, 48 R.I. 33, 36, 134 A. 849, 850 (1926).

the language used in plaintiff's letter of acceptance. This was solely a question of law. . . .

It is well-settled that one who opposes a motion for summary judgment may not rest upon the mere allegations or denials of his pleading. He has an affirmative duty to set forth specific facts which show that there is a genuine issue of fact to be resolved at trial. If he does not do so, summary judgment, if appropriate, will be entered against him. . . . Accordingly, since no genuine issue of fact was presented to the trial justice, we hold that he did not err in ruling that summary judgment was appropriate.[2]

The plaintiff's second contention is that the trial justice incorrectly applied the principles of contract law in deciding that the facts did not disclose a valid acceptance of defendants' offer. Again we cannot agree.

The trial justice proceeded on the theory that the delivery of the purchase and sale agreement to plaintiff constituted an offer by defendants to sell the property. Because we must view the evidence in the light most favorable to the party against whom summary judgment was entered, in this case plaintiff, we assume as the trial justice did that the delivery of the agreement was in fact an offer.[3]

The question we must answer next is whether there was an acceptance of that offer. The general rule is that where, as here, there is an offer to form a bilateral contract, the offeree must communicate his acceptance to the offeror before any contractual obligation can come into being. A mere mental intent to accept the offer, no matter how carefully formed, is not sufficient. The acceptance must be transmitted to the offeror in some overt manner. *Bullock v. Harwick*, 158 Fla. 834, 30 So.2d 539 (1947). . . . A review of the record shows that the only expression of acceptance which was communicated to defendants was the delivery of the executed purchase and sale agreement accompanied by the letter of September 8. Therefore it is solely on the basis of the language used in these two documents that we must determine whether there was a valid acceptance. Whatever plaintiff's unexpressed intention may have been in sending the documents is irrelevant. We must be concerned only with

---

2. We note that not only did plaintiff fail to present the supposed factual issue to the trial justice, he also did not raise the issue at oral argument before us. Moreover, in his Memorandum in Opposition to Motion to Affirm Judgment Below, filed in this court after briefs were filed, plaintiff conceded that no factual dispute existed. The plaintiff stated:

"Your appellant readily acknowledges that there was no genuine issue of fact to be resolved and that the trial justice, in this regard, did not err in granting appellee's motion for Summary Judgment. However, having granted appellee's motion, the trial justice proceeded to render

decision for the wrong party. This, in substance, is the thrust of appellant's appeal." *Id.* at 1.

3. The conclusion that the delivery of the agreement was an offer is not unassailable in view of the fact that defendants did not sign the agreement before sending it to plaintiff, and the fact that plaintiff told defendants' attorney *after* the agreement was received that he would have to investigate certain conditions of title before signing the agreement. If it was not an offer, plaintiff's execution of the agreement could itself be no more than an offer, which defendants never accepted.

the language actually used, not the language plaintiff thought he was using or intended to use.

There is no doubt that the execution and delivery of the purchase and sale agreement by plaintiff, without more, would have operated as an acceptance. The terms of the accompanying letter, however, apparently conditioned the acceptance upon the inclusion of various items of personalty. In assessing the effect of the terms of that letter we must keep in mind certain generally accepted rules. To be effective, an acceptance must be definite and unequivocal. "An offeror is entitled to know in clear terms whether the offeree accepts his proposal. It is not enough that the words of a reply justify a probable inference of assent." 1 Restatement *Contracts* § 58, comment *a* (1932). The acceptance may not impose additional conditions on the offer, nor may it add limitations. "An acceptance which is equivocal or upon condition or with a limitation is a counteroffer and requires acceptance by the original offeror before a contractual relationship can exist." *John Hancock Mut. Life Ins. Co. v. Dietlin*, 97 R.I. 515, 518, 199 A.2d 311, 313 (1964)....

However, an acceptance may be valid despite conditional language if the acceptance is clearly independent of the condition. Many cases have so held. Williston states the rule as follows:

> "Frequently an offeree, while making a positive acceptance of the offer, also makes a request or suggestion that some addition or modification be made. So long as it is clear that the meaning of the acceptance is positively and unequivocally to accept the offer whether such request is granted or not, a contract is formed." 1 Williston, *Contracts* § 79 at 261–62 (3d ed. 1957).

Corbin is in agreement with the above view. 1 Corbin *[Corbin on Contracts]*, § 84 at 363–65. Thus our task is to decide whether plaintiff's letter is more reasonably interpreted as a qualified acceptance or as an absolute acceptance together with a mere inquiry concerning a collateral matter.

In making our decision we recognize that, as one text states, "The question whether a communication by an offeree is a conditional acceptance or counter-offer is not always easy to answer. It must be determined by the same common-sense process of interpretation that must be applied in so many other cases." 1 Corbin, *supra* § 82 at 353. In our opinion the language used in plaintiff's letter of September 8 is not consistent with an absolute acceptance accompanied by a request for a gratuitous benefit. We interpret the letter to impose a condition on plaintiff's acceptance of defendants' offer. The letter does not unequivocally state that even without the enumerated items plaintiff is willing to complete the contract. In fact, the letter seeks "confirmation" that the listed items "are a part of the transaction." Thus, far from being an independent, collateral request, the sale of the items in question is explicitly referred to as a part of the real estate transaction. Moreover, the letter goes on to stress the difficulty of finding replacements for these items. This is a further indication that plaintiff did not view the inclusion of the listed items as merely collateral or incidental to the real estate transaction. . . .

Accordingly, we hold that since the plaintiff's letter of acceptance dated September 8 was conditional, it operated as a rejection of the defendants' offer and no contractual obligation was created. . . .

Questions

1. In *Ardente*, was there an oral contract for the sale of the property when the buyer's attorney advised the seller that the bid was acceptable to the buyer? Was the delivery of the unsigned writing by the seller's attorney an offer for the sale of the property? Assuming that the delivery of the written agreement by the seller's attorney was an offer, was it accepted by the buyer? What are the specific legal reasons supporting the court's answer to the last of these questions?

2. Which of the parties' contractual interests are involved in the dispute in *Ardente*? Which party's contractual interests are more worthy of legal protection? Does legal doctrine—the rules of law—require an outcome that protects the more worthy interests?

3. How many mistakes did the attorneys make in litigating *Ardente*?

4. *Problems*.

    a. Assume that, in a residential housing deal like that in *Ardente*, the buyer offered to buy "on condition that Broker reduce its commission to 4%." The seller accepts. Before the Broker agrees to reduce its commission, however, the seller revokes its acceptance. Is the deal dead?

    b. Assume that, in a residential housing deal like that in *Ardente*, the buyer's offer was unconditional but the seller accepted "on condition that Broker reduce its commission to 4%." Before Broker agrees to reduce its commission, however, the buyer revokes its offer. Is the deal dead? Would the result differ if the buyer revokes its offer after Broker agrees to reduce the commission? See Corr v. Braasch, 97 N.M. 279, 639 P.2d 566 (1981).

NOTE ON DOCTRINAL MANIPULATION

Could the court have decided *Ardente* any way it liked? The rules of offer and acceptance allowed the court two possible conclusions. It could decide that the letter of September 8 was a conditional acceptance and therefore a counteroffer or that it was an unconditional acceptance with an offer to modify the contract. The court must make a judgment in order to classify the case in one of the legal categories thus designated. One way to think of the law that frames the alternatives is in terms of a "rule" and a "counterrule." Some argue that many, if not most or all, legal rules have their counter-rules. When this is so, "the authoritative tradition speaks with a forked tongue." Karl Llewelyn, *Some Realism About Realism*, 44 HARV. L. REV. 1222, 1252 (1931). Can the judges then manipulate the legal doctrines to reach any results they want?

A case like *Ardente* reaches the appellate courts and produces a thoughtful opinion only because, logically speaking, the rules allowed incompatible conclusions. It does not follow, however, that the judges could decide whatever they want to decide. Judges are, by all accounts, under a duty to uphold the law. If "the law" consists only of legal rules, the rule and counterrule would leave them legally unfettered in such a case. However, matters are more complicated if the law consists of rules together with other resources, such as precedents, principles, and policies. Courts might interpret and apply the rules to reach the results that are most like the authoritative precedents in light of the legal principles and policies. When incompatible outcomes are logically possible, then, judges would be bound to act as indicated by the more convincing argument of principle or policy. See STEVEN J. BURTON, AN INTRODUCTION TO LAW AND LEGAL REASONING (2d ed. 1995).

Doctrinal manipulation is an important lawyerly skill. In developing that skill, however, remember that lawyers often must predict what a court will do or persuade a court to act as wanted. To do either, you will need to assess whether your doctrinal argument will persuade an impartial decisionmaker. You can always *say* that the acceptance was conditional. The question, however, is whether a judge will or should *believe* it.

RESTATEMENT (SECOND) OF CONTRACTS
§§ 42, 43, 46, 50, 53

PETTERSON v. PATTBERG

Court of Appeals of New York, 1928.
248 N.Y. 86, 161 N.E. 428.

KELLOGG, JUDGE. The evidence given upon the trial sanctions the following statement of facts. John Petterson, of whose last will and testament the plaintiff is the executrix, was the owner of a parcel of real estate in Brooklyn, known as 5301 Sixth Avenue. The defendant was the owner of a bond executed by Petterson, which was secured by a third mortgage upon the parcel. On April 4, 1924, there remained unpaid upon the principal the sum of $5,450. This amount was payable in installments of $250 on April 25, 1924, and upon a like monthly date every three months thereafter. Thus the bond and mortgage had more than five years to run before the entire sum became due. Under date of the 4th of April, 1924, the defendant wrote Petterson as follows:

"I hereby agree to accept cash for the mortgage which I hold against premises 5301 6th Ave., Brooklyn, N.Y. It is understood and agreed as a consideration I will allow you $780 providing said mortgage is paid on or before May 31, 1924, and the regular quarterly payment due April 25, 1924, is paid when due."

On April 25, 1924, Petterson paid the defendant the installment of principal due on that date. Subsequently, on a day in the latter part of May, 1924, Petterson presented himself at the defendant's home, and knocked at the door. The defendant demanded the name of his caller. Petterson replied. "It is Mr. Petterson. I have come to pay off the mortgage." The defendant answered that he had sold the mortgage. Petterson stated that he would like to talk with the defendant, so the defendant partly opened the door. Thereupon Petterson exhibited the cash, and said he was ready to pay off the mortgage according to the agreement. The defendant refused to take the money. Prior to this conversation, Petterson had made a contract to sell the land to a third person free and clear of the mortgage to the defendant. Meanwhile, also, the defendant had sold the bond and mortgage to a third party. It therefore became necessary for Petterson to pay to such person the full amount of the bond and mortgage. It is claimed that he thereby sustained a loss of $780, the sum which the defendant agreed to allow upon the bond and mortgage, if payment in full of principal, less that sum, was made on or before May 31, 1924. The plaintiff has had a recovery for the sum thus claimed, with interest.

Clearly the defendant's letter proposed to Petterson the making of a unilateral contract, the gift of a promise in exchange for the performance of an act. The thing conditionally promised by the defendant was the reduction of the mortgage debt. The act requested to be done, in consideration of the offered promise, was payment in full of the reduced principal of the debt prior to the due date thereof. "If an act is requested, that very act, and no other, must be given." Williston on Contracts, § 73. "In case of offers for a consideration, the performance of the consideration is always deemed a condition." Langdell's Summary of the Law of Contracts, § 4. It is elementary that any offer to enter into a unilateral contract may be withdrawn before the act requested to be done has been performed. Williston on Contracts, § 60.... A bidder at a sheriff's sale may revoke his bid at any time before the property is struck down to him. Fisher v. Seltzer, 23 Pa. 308, 62 Am. Dec. 335. The offer of a reward in consideration of an act to be performed is revocable before the very act requested has been done. Shuey v. United States, 92 U.S. 73, 23 L.Ed. 697.... So, also, an offer to pay a broker commissions, upon a sale of land for the offeror, is revocable at any time before the land is sold, although prior to revocation the broker performs services in an effort to effectuate a sale. Stensgaard v. Smith, 43 Minn. 11, 44 N.W. 669, 19 Am. St. Rep. 205....

An interesting question arises when, as here, the offeree approaches the offeror with the intention of proffering performance and, before actual tender is made, the offer is withdrawn. Of such a case Williston says:

"The offeror may see the approach of the offeree and know that an acceptance is contemplated. If the offeror can say 'I revoke' before the offeree accepts, however brief the interval of time between the two acts, there is no escape from the conclusion that the offer is terminated." Williston on Contracts, § 60b.

In this instance Petterson, standing at the door of the defendant's house, stated to the defendant that he had come to pay off the mortgage. Before a tender of the necessary moneys had been made, the defendant informed Petterson that he had sold the mortgage. That was a definite notice to Petterson that the defendant could not perform his offered promise, and that a tender to the defendant, who was no longer the creditor, would be ineffective to satisfy the debt. "An offer to sell property may be withdrawn before acceptance without any formal notice to the person to whom the offer is made. It is sufficient if that person has actual knowledge that the person who made the offer has done some act inconsistent with the continuance of the offer, such as selling the property to a third person." Dickinson v. Dodds, 2 Ch. Div. 463. . . . Thus it clearly appears that the defendant's offer was withdrawn before its acceptance had been tendered. It is unnecessary to determine, therefore, what the legal situation might have been had tender been made before withdrawal. It is the individual view of the writer that the same result would follow. This would be so, for the act requested to be performed was the completed act of payment, a thing incapable of performance, unless assented to by the person to be paid. Williston on Contracts, § 60b. Clearly an offering party has the right to name the precise act performance of which would convert his offer into a binding promise. Whatever the act may be until it is performed, the offer must be revocable. However, the supposed case is not before us for decision. We think that in this particular instance the offer of the defendant was withdrawn before it became a binding promise, and therefore that no contract was ever made for the breach of which the plaintiff may claim damages.

The judgment of the Appellate Division and that of the Trial Term should be reversed, and the complaint dismissed, with costs in all courts.

LEHMAN, JUDGE (dissenting). The defendant's letter to Petterson constituted a promise on his part to accept payment at a discount of the mortgage he held, provided the mortgage is paid on or before May 31, 1924. Doubtless, by the terms of the promise itself, the defendant made payment of the mortgage by the plaintiff, before the stipulated time, a condition precedent to performance by the defendant of his promise to accept payment at a discount. If the condition precedent has not been performed, it is because the defendant made performance impossible by refusing to accept payment, when the plaintiff came with an offer of immediate performance. "It is a principle of fundamental justice that if a promisor is himself the cause of the failure of performance either of an obligation due him or of a condition upon which his own liability depends, he cannot take advantage of the failure." Williston on Contracts, § 677. The question in this case is not whether payment of the mortgage is a condition precedent to the performance of a promise made by the defendant, but, rather, whether, at the time the defendant refused the offer of payment, he had assumed any binding obligation, even though subject to condition.

The promise made by the defendant lacked consideration at the time it was made. Nevertheless, the promise was not made as a gift or mere gratuity to the plaintiff. It was made for the purpose of obtaining from the [plaintiff] something which the [defendant] desired. It constituted an offer which was to become binding whenever the plaintiff should give, in return for the defendant's promise, exactly the consideration which the defendant requested.

Here the defendant requested no counter promise from the plaintiff. The consideration requested by the defendant for his promise to accept payment was, I agree, some act to be performed by the plaintiff. Until the act requested was performed, the defendant might undoubtedly revoke his offer. Our problem is to determine from the words of the letter, read in the light of surrounding circumstances, what act the defendant requested as consideration for his promise.

The defendant undoubtedly made his offer as an inducement to the plaintiff to "pay" the mortgage before it was due. Therefore, it is said, that "the act requested to be performed was the completed act of payment, a thing incapable of performance, unless assented to by the person to be paid." In unmistakable terms the defendant agreed to accept payment, yet we are told that the defendant intended, and the plaintiff should have understood, that the act requested by the defendant, as consideration for his promise to accept payment, included performance by the defendant himself of the very promise for which the act was to be consideration. The defendant's promise was to become binding only when fully performed; and part of the consideration to be furnished by the plaintiff for the defendant's promise was to be the performance of that promise by the defendant. So construed, the defendant's promise or offer, though intended to induce action by the plaintiff, is but a snare and delusion. The plaintiff could not reasonably suppose that the defendant was asking him to procure the performance by the defendant of the very act which the defendant promised to do, yet we are told that, even after the plaintiff had done all else which the defendant requested, the defendant's promise was still not binding because the defendant chose not to perform.

I cannot believe that a result so extraordinary could have been intended when the defendant wrote the letter. "The thought behind the phrase proclaims itself misread when the outcome of the reading is injustice or absurdity." See opinion of Cardozo, C. J., in Surace v. Danna, 248 N.Y. 18, 161 N.E. 315. If the defendant intended to induce payment by the plaintiff and yet reserve the right to refuse payment when offered he should have used a phrase better calculated to express his meaning than the words. "I agree to accept." A promise to accept payment, by its very terms, must necessarily become binding, if at all, not later than when a present offer to pay is made.

I recognize that in this case only an offer of payment, and not a formal tender of payment, was made before the defendant withdrew his offer to accept payment. Even the plaintiff's part in the act of payment was then not technically complete. Even so, under a fair construction of the words of the letter, I think the plaintiff had done the act which the defendant requested as consideration for his promise. The plaintiff offered to pay, with present intention and ability to make that payment. A formal tender is seldom made in business transactions, except to lay the foundation for subsequent assertion in a court of justice of rights which spring from refusal of the tender. If the defendant acted in good faith in making his offer to accept payment, he could not well have intended to draw a distinction in the act requested of the plaintiff in return, between an offer which, unless refused, would ripen into completed payment, and a formal tender. Certainly the defendant could not have expected or intended that the plaintiff would make a formal tender of payment without first stating that he had come to make payment. We should not read into the language of the defendant's offer a meaning which would prevent enforcement of the defendant's promise after it had been accepted by the plaintiff in the very way which the defendant must have intended it should be accepted, if he acted in good faith.

The judgment should be affirmed.

Questions

1. Did Pattberg make an offer? If so, did Petterson accept Pattberg's offer? Should Pattberg's promise empower Petterson to accept by doing what Petterson did?

2. What is the best justification for holding Pattberg's offer to be unrevoked before acceptance? What interests might Petterson (and others in similar situations) have in holding Pattberg (and others in similar situations) to contracts? Are those interests deserving of legal protection under the circumstances? Would they be deserving of legal protection had Pattberg phoned Petterson and said, "I revoke" on May 15, before Petterson's visit?

RESTATEMENT (SECOND) OF CONTRACTS §§ 25, 37, 45, 54

MARCHIONDO v. SCHECK

Supreme Court of New Mexico, 1967.
78 N.M. 440, 432 P.2d 405.

WOOD, JUDGE, Court of Appeals. The issue is whether the offeror had a right to revoke his offer to enter a unilateral contract.

Defendant, in writing, offered to sell real estate to a specified prospective buyer and agreed to pay a percentage of the sales price as a commission to the broker. The offer fixed a six-day time limit for acceptance. Defendant, in writing, revoked the offer. The revocation was received by the broker on the morning of the sixth day. Later that day, the broker obtained the offeree's acceptance.

Plaintiff, the broker, claiming breach of contract, sued defendant for the commission stated in the offer. On the above facts, the trial court dismissed the complaint.

We are not concerned with the revocation of the offer as between the offeror and the prospective purchaser. With certain exceptions (see 12 C.J.S. Brokers § 95(2), pp. 223–224), the right of a broker to the agreed compensation, or damages measured thereby, is not defeated by the refusal of the principal to complete or consummate a transaction. Southwest Motel Brokers, Inc. v. Alamo Hotels, Inc., 72 N.M. 227, 382 P.2d 707 (1963).

Plaintiff's appeal concerns the revocation of his agency....

When defendant made his offer to pay a commission upon sale of the property, he offered to enter a unilateral contract; the offer was for an act to be performed, a sale. 1 Williston on Contracts, § 13 at 23 (3rd ed. 1957); Hutchinson v. Dobson–Bainbridge Realty Co., 31 Tenn.App. 490, 217 S.W.2d 6 (1946).

Many courts hold that the principal has the right to revoke the broker's agency at any time before the broker has actually procured a purchaser. See Hutchinson v. Dobson–Bainbridge Realty Co., supra, and cases therein cited. The reason given is that until there is performance, the offeror has not received that contemplated by his offer, and there is no contract. Further, the offeror may never receive the requested performance because the offeree is not obligated to perform. Until the offeror receives the requested performance, no consideration has passed from the offeree to the offeror. Thus, until the performance is received, the offeror may withdraw the offer. Williston, supra, § 60; Hutchinson v. Dobson-Bainbridge Realty Co., supra.

Defendant asserts that the trial court was correct in applying this rule. However, plaintiff contends that the rule is not applicable where there has been part performance of the offer.

Hutchinson v. Dobson-Bainbridge Realty Co., supra, states:

"A greater number of courts, however, hold that part performance of the consideration may make such an offer irrevocable and that where the offeree or broker manifests his assent to the offer by entering upon performance and spending time and money in his efforts to perform, then the offer becomes irrevocable during the time stated and binding upon the principal according to its terms...."

Defendant contends that the decisions giving effect to a part performance are distinguishable. He asserts that in these cases the offer was of an exclusive right to sell or of an exclusive agency. Because neither factor is present here, he asserts that the "part performance" decisions are not applicable.... Many of the decisions do seem to emphasize the exclusive aspects of the offer.... Defendant's offer did not specifically state that it was exclusive. Under § 70–1–43, N.M.S.A. 1953, it was not an exclusive agreement. It is not the exclusiveness of the offer that deprives the offeror of the right to revoke. It is the action taken by the offeree which deprives the offeror of that right. Until there is action by the offeree—a partial performance pursuant to the offer—the offeror may revoke even if his offer is of an exclusive agency or an exclusive right to sell. Levander v. Johnson, 181 Wis. 68, 193 N.W. 970 (1923).

Once partial performance is begun pursuant to the offer made, a contract results. This contract has been termed a contract with conditions or an option contract. This terminology is illustrated as follows:

> "If an offer for a unilateral contract is made, and part of the consideration requested in the offer is given or tendered by the offeree in response thereto, the offeror is bound by a contract, the duty of immediate performance of which is conditional on the full consideration being given or tendered within the time stated in the offer, or, if no time is stated therein, within a reasonable time." Restatement of Contracts, § 45 (1932).

Restatement (Second) of Contracts, § 45, Tent. Draft No. 1, (approved 1964, Tent. Draft No. 2, p. vii) states:

> "(1) Where an offer invites an offeree to accept by rendering a performance and does not invite a promissory acceptance, an option contract is created when the offeree begins the invited performance or tenders part of it.
>
> "(2) The offeror's duty of performance under any option contract so created is conditional on completion or tender of the invited performance in accordance with the terms of the offer."

Restatement (Second) of Contracts, § 45, Tent. Draft No. 1, comment (g), says:

> "This Section frequently applies to agency arrangements, particularly offers made to real estate brokers." ...

The reason for finding such a contract is stated in Hutchinson v. Dobson–Bainbridge Realty Co., supra, as follows:

> "This rule avoids hardship to the offeree, and yet does not hold the offeror beyond the terms of his promise. It is true by such terms he was to be bound only if the requested act was done; but this implies that he will let it be done, that he will keep his offer open till the offeree who has begun can finish doing it. At least this is so where the doing of it will necessarily require time and expense. In such a case it is but just to hold that the offeree's part performance furnishes the 'acceptance' and the 'consideration' for a binding subsidiary promise not to revoke the offer, or turns the offer into a

presently binding contract conditional upon the offeree's full performance."

We hold that part performance by the offeree of an offer of a unilateral contract results in a contract with a condition. The condition is full performance by the offeree. Here, if plaintiff-offeree partially performed prior to receipt of defendant's revocation, such a contract was formed. Thereafter, upon performance being completed by plaintiff, upon defendant's failure to recognize the contract, liability for breach of contract would arise. Thus, defendant's right to revoke his offer depends upon whether plaintiff had partially performed before he received defendant's revocation. In re Ward's Estate, 47 N.M. 55, 134 P.2d 539, 146 A.L.R. 826 (1943), does not conflict with this result. Ward is clearly distinguishable because there the prospective purchaser did not complete or tender performance in accordance with the terms of the offer.

What constitutes partial performance will vary from case to case since what can be done toward performance is limited by what is authorized to be done. Whether plaintiff partially performed is a question of fact to be determined by the trial court.

The trial court denied plaintiff's requested finding concerning his partial performance. It did so on the theory that partial performance was not material. In this the trial court erred. . . .

The cause is remanded for findings on the issue of plaintiff's partial performance of the offer prior to its revocation, and for further proceedings consistent with this opinion and the findings so made. . . .

Questions

1.   What was the offer to contract upon which plaintiff sues? Why is the plaintiff suing? What is an "option contract"?

2.   Under the law reflected in *Petterson v. Pattberg* and RESTATEMENT (SECOND) OF CONTRACTS § 36(1)(c), would the broker's power of acceptance be alive when the buyer's assent was secured?

3.   What is the justification for the law reflected in *Marchiondo* and RESTATEMENT (SECOND) OF CONTRACTS § 45? What are the relevant contractual interests of such offerors and offerees? Which is more worthy of legal protection in a situation like that in *Marchiondo*? See also Drennan v. Star Paving Co., below at p. 189.

4.   *Problems.*

   a.   On June 10, Leontyne sent a letter to Shirley, offering to sell her ranch for $1,325,000, "payment in cash or check before 5:00 p.m. Friday, June 21." During the evening of June 20, Shirley decided to accept the offer. She wrote "I accept" on Leontyne's letter and signed it. On the afternoon of June 21, Shirley went to Leontyne's home. When Leontyne answered the door, Shirley announced she had come to buy the ranch. Leontyne replied, "You snooze, you lose." It turns out that Leontyne had sold the ranch to Anna the previous week and had sent

Shirley a letter revoking the offer, but the letter never reached Shirley. Did Shirley accept the offer?

b. The facts are the same as in Problem a, except that, on the morning of June 21, Shirley heard from Beverly, her real estate broker, that Leontyne had sold the ranch to Anna. Shirley promptly went over to hand the acceptance to Leontyne. When Leontyne answered the door, Shirley announced she had come to buy the ranch. Leontyne replied, "You're slow. It's no-go." Did Shirley accept the offer? See Normile v. Miller, 313 N.C. 98, 326 S.E.2d 11 (1985).

c. The Great Minneapolis Department Store placed an ad in the local newspaper: "One Black Lapin Stole, Beautiful, Worth $2800.00, First Come, First Served on the First of Each Month, Only $1." The store had no intention of selling such a valuable stole for $1. Upon being advised by counsel that its ad was an offer to contract, the store seeks your advice on how to avoid selling to the first person to accept. What should you advise?

d. *Acceptance*

Recall that an offer changes the legal relations between offeror and offeree by creating a power of acceptance in the offeree. When the offeree exercises that legal power by accepting, an agreement is made. A valid acceptance normally concludes the deal, though whether it will be enforced by the law depends on additional requirements to be considered in Chapters 2 and 3. Acceptance signifies the offeree's assent, implying a promise to do what the promissory agreement requires of him or her.

Because "the offeror is master of the offer," as the saying goes, the offeror can specify exactly what will constitute acceptance. Often, however, offerors do not make the mode or manner of acceptance clear. In that situation, the law must resolve a dispute based on suppletory or "default" rules. In this context, default rules are the rules governing a dispute over contract formation unless the offer manifests a contrary intention. Here is a default rule we have already learned: An offeree's power of acceptance terminates at the time specified in the offer or, if no time is specified, at the end of a reasonable time. RESTATEMENT (SECOND) OF CONTRACTS § 41(1). Other contractual default rules, to be considered in Chapters 4–7, govern disputes in contract performance unless the parties agreed to different terms.

Default rules respect party autonomy because the offeror can override or the parties can contract around them. The prevalence of default rules in contract law indicates the importance of the autonomy principle. Contract law generally is loath to impose duties on the parties, preferring to enforce their voluntary undertakings.

The autonomy principle, however, does not give the offeror unbridled power to specify what will count as an acceptance. Offerors sometimes try to trap unwary offerees into acceptance, as by specifying in the offer that the offeree shall be deemed to accept unless the offeree expressly rejects the offer within a short time. In such a case, the offeror would be imposing on the offeree in a manner incompatible with the offeree's autonomy. The law then steps in with mandatory rules ensuring that acceptance is a voluntary and intentional commitment by the offeree or would reasonably be so understood by the offeror.

RESTATEMENT (SECOND) OF CONTRACTS
§§ 32, 50, 54, 56, 58, 63

DAVIS v. JACOBY

Supreme Court of California, 1934.
1 Cal.2d 370, 34 P.2d 1026.

PER CURIAM. Plaintiffs appeal from a judgment refusing to grant specific performance of an alleged contract to make a will. The facts are not in dispute and are as follows.

The plaintiff Caro M. Davis was the niece of Blanche Whitehead who was married to Rupert Whitehead. Prior to her marriage in 1913 to her coplaintiff Frank M. Davis, Caro lived for a considerable time at the home of the Whiteheads, in Piedmont, California. The Whiteheads were childless and extremely fond of Caro. The record is replete with uncontradicted testimony of the close and loving relationship that existed between Caro and her aunt and uncle. During the period that Caro lived with the Whiteheads she was treated as and often referred to by the Whiteheads as their daughter. In 1913, when Caro was married to Frank Davis the marriage was arranged at the Whitehead home and a reception held there. After the marriage Mr. and Mrs. Davis went to Mr. Davis' home in Canada, where they have resided ever since. During the period 1913 to 1931, Caro made many visits to the Whiteheads, several of them being of long duration. The Whiteheads visited Mr. and Mrs. Davis in Canada on several occasions. After the marriage and continuing down to 1931, the closest and most friendly relationship at all times existed between these two families. They corresponded frequently, the record being replete with letters showing the loving relationship.

By the year 1930, Mrs. Whitehead had become seriously ill. She had suffered several strokes and her mind was failing. Early in 1931, Mr. Whitehead had her removed to a private hospital. The doctors in attendance had informed him that she might die at any time or she might linger for many months. Mr. Whitehead had suffered severe financial reverses. He had had several sieges of sickness and was in poor health. The record shows that during the early part of 1931, he was desperately in need of assistance with his wife, and in his business affairs, and that he did not trust his friends in Piedmont. On March 18, 1931, he wrote to Mrs. Davis telling her of Mrs. Whitehead's condition and added that Mrs. Whitehead was very wistful. "Today I endeavored to find out what she wanted. I finally asked her if she wanted to see you.

She burst out crying and we had great difficulty in getting her to stop. Evidently, that is what is on her mind. It is a very difficult matter to decide. If you come it will mean that you will have to leave again, and then things may be serious. I am going to see the doctor, and get his candid opinion and will then write you again.... Since writing the above, I have seen the doctor, and he thinks it will help considerably if you come." Shortly thereafter, Mr. Whitehead wrote to Caro Davis further explaining the physical condition of Mrs. Whitehead and himself. On March 24, 1931, Mr. Davis, at the request of his wife, telegraphed to Mr. Whitehead as follows. "Your letter received. Sorry to hear Blanche not so well. Hope you are feeling better yourself. If you wish Caro to go to you can arrange for her to leave in about two weeks. Please wire me if you think it advisable for her to go." On March 30, 1931, Mr. Whitehead wrote a long letter to Mr. Davis, in which he explained in detail the condition of Mrs. Whitehead's health and also referred to his own health. He pointed out that he had lost a considerable portion of his cash assets but still owned considerable realty, that he needed someone to help him with his wife and some friend he could trust to help him with his business affairs and suggested that perhaps Mr. Davis might come to California. He then pointed out that all his property was community property; that under his will all the property was to go to Mrs. White-head; that he believed that under Mrs. Whitehead's will practically everything was to go to Caro. Mr. Whitehead again wrote to Mr. Davis under date of April 9, 1931, pointing out how badly he needed someone he could trust to assist him, and giving it as his belief that if properly handled he could still save about $150,000. He then stated: "Having you [Mr. Davis] here to depend on and to help me regain my mind and courage would be a big thing." Three days later, on April 12, 1931, Mr. Whitehead again wrote, addressing his letter to "Dear Frank and Caro," and in this letter made the definite offer, which offer it is claimed was accepted and is the basis of this action. In this letter he first pointed out that Blanche, his wife, was in a private hospital and that "she cannot last much longer ... my affairs are not as bad as I supposed at first. Cutting everything down I figure 150,000 can be saved from the wreck." He then enumerated the values placed upon his various properties and then continued.

> "My trouble was caused by my friends taking advantage of my illness and my position to skin me.

> "Now if Frank could come out here and be with me, and look after my affairs, we could easily save the balance I mentioned, provided I don't get into another panic and do some more foolish things.

> "The next attack will be my end, I am 65 and my health has been bad for years, so, the Drs. don't give me much longer to live. So if you can come, Caro will inherit everything and you will make our lives happier and see Blanche is provided for to the end.

"My eyesight has gone back on me, I cant (sic) read only for a few lines at a time. I am at the house alone with Stanley [the chauffeur] who does everything for me and is a fine fellow. Now, what I want is some one who will take charge of my affairs and see I don't lose any more. Frank can do it, if he will and cut out the booze.

"Will you let me hear from you as soon as possible, I know it will be a sacrifice but times are still bad and likely to be, so by settling down you can help me and Blanche and gain in the end. If I had you here my mind would get better and my courage return, and we could work things out."

This letter was received by Mr. Davis at his office in Windsor, Canada, about 9:30 a.m. April 14, 1931. After reading the letter to Mrs. Davis over the telephone, and after getting her belief that they must go to California, Mr. Davis immediately wrote Mr. Whitehead a letter, which, after reading it to his wife, he sent by air mail. This letter was lost, but there is no doubt that it was sent by Davis and received by Whitehead; in fact the trial court expressly so found. Mr. Davis testified in substance as to the contents of this letter. After acknowledging receipt of the letter of April 12, 1931, Mr. Davis unequivocally stated that he and Mrs. Davis accepted the proposition of Mr. Whitehead and both would leave Windsor to go to him on April 25th. This letter of acceptance also contained the information that the reason they could not leave prior to April 25th was that Mr. Davis had to appear in court on April 22nd as one of the executors of his mother's estate. The testimony is uncontradicted and ample to support the trial court's finding that this letter was sent by Davis and received by Whitehead. In fact under date of April 15, 1931, Mr. Whitehead again wrote to Mr. Davis and stated:

"Your letter by air mail received this a.m. Now, I am wondering if I have put you to unnecessary trouble and expense, if you are making any money dont leave it, as things are bad here.... You know your business and I dont and I am half crazy in the bargain but I don't want to hurt you or Caro.

"Then on the other hand if I could get some one to trust and keep me straight I can save a good deal, about what I told you in my former letter."

This letter was received by Mr. Davis on April 17, 1931, and the same day Mr. Davis telegraphed to Mr. Whitehead "Cheer up—we will soon be there, we will wire you from the train."

Between April 14, 1931, the date the letter of acceptance was sent by Mr. Davis, and April 22, Mr. Davis was engaged in closing out his business affairs, and Mrs. Davis in closing up their home and in making other arrangements to leave. On April 22, 1931, Mr. Whitehead committed suicide. Mr. and Mrs. Davis were immediately notified and they at once came to California. From almost the moment of her arrival Mrs. Davis devoted herself to the care and comfort of her aunt, and gave her aunt constant attention and care until Mrs. Whitehead's death on May

30, 1931. On this point the trial court found: "From the time of their arrival in Piedmont, Caro M. Davis administered in every way to the comforts of Blanche Whitehead and saw that she was cared for and provided for down to the time of the death of Blanche Whitehead on May 30, 1931; during said time Caro M. Davis nursed Blanche Whitehead, cared for her and administered to her wants as a natural daughter would have done toward and for her mother."

This finding is supported by uncontradicted evidence and in fact is conceded by respondents to be correct. In fact, the record shows that after their arrival in California Mr. and Mrs. Davis fully performed their side of the agreement.

After the death of Mrs. Whitehead, for the first time it was discovered that the information contained in Mr. Whitehead's letter of March 30, 1931, in reference to the contents of his and Mrs. Whitehead's wills was incorrect. By a duly witnessed will dated February 28, 1931, Mr. Whitehead, after making several specific bequests, had bequeathed all of the balance of his estate to his wife for life, and upon her death to respondents Geoff Doubble and Rupert Ross Whitehead, his nephews. Neither appellant was mentioned in his will. It was also discovered that Mrs. Whitehead by a will dated December 17, 1927, had devised all of her estate to her husband. The evidence is clear and uncontradicted that the relationship existing between Whitehead and his two nephews, respondents herein, was not nearly as close and confidential as that existing between Whitehead and appellants.

After the discovery of the manner in which the property had been devised was made, this action was commenced upon the theory that Rupert Whitehead had assumed a contractual obligation to make a will whereby "Caro Davis would inherit everything;" that he had failed to do so; that plaintiffs had fully performed their part of the contract; that damages being insufficient, quasi specific performance should be granted in order to remedy the alleged wrong, upon the equitable principle that equity regards that done which ought to have been done. The requested relief is that the beneficiaries under the will of Rupert Whitehead, respondents herein, be declared to be involuntary trustees for plaintiffs of Whitehead's estate.

It should also be added that the evidence shows that as a result of Frank Davis leaving his business in Canada he forfeited not only all insurance business he might have written if he had remained, but also forfeited all renewal commissions earned on past business. According to his testimony this loss was over $8,000.

The trial court found that the relationship between Mr. and Mrs. Davis and the Whiteheads was substantially as above recounted and that the other facts above stated were true.... The court then finds that the offer of April 12th was not accepted. As already stated, the court found that plaintiffs sent a letter to Rupert Whitehead on April 14th purporting to accept the offer of April 12th, and also found that this letter was received by the Whiteheads, but finds that in fact such letter was not a legal acceptance....

The court also found that plaintiffs did not know that the statements made by Whitehead in reference to the wills were not correct until after Mrs. Whitehead's death, that after plaintiffs arrived in Piedmont they cared for Mrs. Whitehead until her death and "Blanche Whitehead was greatly comforted by the presence, companionship and association of Caro M. Davis, and by her administering to her wants."

The theory of the trial court and of respondents on this appeal is that the letter of April 12th was an offer to contract, but that such offer could only be accepted by performance and could not be accepted by a promise to perform, and that said offer was revoked by the death of Mr. Whitehead before performance. In other words, it is contended that the offer was an offer to enter into a unilateral contract, and that the purported acceptance of April 14th was of no legal effect.

The distinction between unilateral and bilateral contracts is well settled in the law. It is well stated in section 12 of the American Institute's Restatement of the Law of Contracts as follows: "A unilateral contract is one in which no promisor receives a promise as consideration for his promise. A bilateral contract is one in which there are mutual promises between two parties to the contract; each party being both a promisor and a promisee." This definition is in accord with the law of California. Chrisman v. Southern Cal. Edison Co., 83 Cal.App. 249, 256 P. 618.

In the case of unilateral contracts no notice of acceptance by performance is required. Section 1584 of the Civil Code provides: "Performance of the conditions of a proposal ... is an acceptance of the proposal." See Cuthill v. Peabody, 19 Cal.App. 304, 125 P. 926....

Although the legal distinction between unilateral and bilateral contracts is thus well settled, the difficulty in any particular case is to determine whether the particular offer is one to enter into a bilateral or unilateral contract. Some cases are quite clear cut. Thus an offer to sell which is accepted is clearly a bilateral contract, while an offer of a reward is a clear-cut offer of a unilateral contract which cannot be accepted by a promise to perform, but only by performance. Berthiaume v. Doe, 22 Cal.App. 78, 133 P. 515. Between these two extremes is a vague field where the particular contract may be unilateral or bilateral depending upon the intent of the offerer and the facts and circumstances of each case. The offer to contract involved in this case falls within this category. By the provisions of the Restatement of the Law of Contracts it is expressly provided that there is a *presumption* that the offer is to enter into a bilateral contract. Section 31 provides: "In case of doubt it is presumed that an offer invites the formation of a bilateral contract by an acceptance amounting in effect to a promise by the offeree to perform what the offer requests, rather than the formation of one or more unilateral contracts by actual performance on the part of the offeree."

Professor Williston in his Treatise on Contracts, volume 1, § 60, also takes the position that a presumption in favor of bilateral contracts exists. In the comment following section 31 of the Restatement the reason for such presumption is stated as follows.

> "It is not always easy to determine whether an offerer requests an act or a promise to do the act. As a bilateral contract immediately and fully protects both parties, the interpretation is favored that a bilateral contract is proposed."

While the California cases have never expressly held that a presumption in favor of bilateral contracts exists, the cases clearly indicate a tendency to treat offers as offers of bilateral rather than of unilateral contracts. Roth v. Moeller, 185 Cal. 415, 197 P. 62. . . .

Keeping these principles in mind we are of the opinion that the offer of April 12th was an offer to enter into a bilateral as distinguished from a unilateral contract. Respondents argue that Mr. Whitehead had the right as offerer to designate his offer as either unilateral or bilateral. That is undoubtedly the law. It is then argued that from all the facts and circumstances it must be implied that what Whitehead wanted was performance and not a mere promise to perform. We think this is a non sequitur, in fact the surrounding circumstances lead to just the opposite conclusion. These parties were not dealing at arm's length. Not only were they related, but a very close and intimate friendship existed between them. The record indisputably demonstrates that Mr. Whitehead had confidence in Mr. and Mrs. Davis, in fact that he had lost all confidence in everyone else. The record amply shows that by an accumulation of occurrences Mr. Whitehead had become desperate, and that what he wanted was the promise of appellants that he could look to them for assistance. He knew from his past relationship with appellants that if they gave their promise to perform he could rely upon them. The correspondence between them indicates how desperately he desired this assurance. Under these circumstances he wrote his offer of April 12th, above quoted, in which he stated, after disclosing his desperate mental and physical condition, and after setting forth the terms of his offer: *"Will you let me hear from you as soon as possible*—I know it will be a sacrifice but times are still bad and likely to be, so by settling down you can help me and Blanche and gain in the end." By thus specifically requesting an immediate reply Whitehead expressly indicated the nature of the acceptance desired by him, namely, appellant's promise that they would come to California and do the things requested by him. This promise was immediately sent by appellants upon receipt of the offer, and was received by Whitehead. It is elementary that when an offer has indicated the mode and means of acceptance, an acceptance in accordance with that mode or means is binding on the offerer.

Another factor which indicates that Whitehead must have contemplated a bilateral rather than a unilateral contract, is that the contract required Mr. and Mrs. Davis to perform services until the death of both Mr. and Mrs. Whitehead. It is obvious that if Mr. Whitehead died first some of these services were to be performed after his death, so that he would have to rely on the promise of appellants to perform these services. It is also of some evidentiary force that Whitehead received the letter of acceptance and acquiesced in that means of acceptance....

For the foregoing reasons we are of the opinion that the offer of April 12, 1931, was an offer to enter into a bilateral contract which was accepted by the letter of April 14, 1931. Subsequently appellants fully performed their part of the contract. Under such circumstances it is well settled that damages are insufficient and specific performance will be granted. Wolf v. Donahue, 206 Cal. 213, 273 P. 547. Since the consideration has been fully rendered by appellants the question as to mutuality of remedy becomes of no importance. 6 Cal. Jur., § 140.

.   .   .

For the foregoing reasons the judgment appealed from is reversed.

Questions

1. What was the offer? Did it create a power of acceptance to be exercised by a performance or a return promise? Is there any interpretation of the "let me hear from you ASAP" that is wholly consistent with a power of acceptance to be exercised by a performance? How likely is it that Mr. Davis thought about whether he wanted an acceptance by performance or by promise?

2. Why did the court hold that the power of acceptance was to be exercised by a promise? Why should the mode of acceptance matter as long as the offeree's commitment is manifest?

3. *Problems.*

a. Field's Naturopathics, Inc. markets "mercuriam pills" through health food stores. The package contains the following notice: "Guaranteed to prevent hives. We will pay $1,000 to anyone contracting hives after using this product for 2 weeks." Annabelle took mercuriam pills for a month and then contracted hives. She immediately requested $1,000 from Field's, enclosing a letter from her doctor. Can Field's avoid payment because Annabelle did not promise or notify them of acceptance earlier?

b. Dreyfuss received a promotional letter in the mail offering him membership in the Tin Man CD Club, the fee for which is $20.00 per year. The letter concluded, "This offer to be accepted if we do not hear from you otherwise within two weeks." Dreyfuss did nothing. Must he pay the membership fee?

———

RESTATEMENT (SECOND) OF CONTRACTS §§ 19, 69

———

HOUSTON DAIRY, INC. v. JOHN HANCOCK MUTUAL LIFE INSURANCE CO.

United States Court of Appeals, Fifth Circuit, 1981.
643 F.2d 1185.

AINSWORTH, CIRCUIT JUDGE. This is an appeal from a Mississippi diversity action in which appellant Houston Dairy, Inc. attempted to recover $16,000 sent to appellee John Hancock Mutual Life Insurance Company as a "Good Faith Deposit" on a loan application which Houston Dairy claims never became binding. At the conclusion of the nonjury trial, the district court ruled that there was a binding contract between the parties and that the $16,000 deposit represented valid, liquidated damages forfeited by Houston Dairy when it breached the contract. We reverse.

I. FACTS

John Hancock mailed a commitment letter to Houston Dairy on December 30, 1977 in which it agreed to lend Houston Dairy $800,000 at 9¼% provided that within seven days Houston Dairy would return the commitment letter with a written acceptance and enclose either a letter of credit or a cashier's check in the amount of $16,000. The commitment letter stated the $16,000 was a "Good Faith Deposit" and was the appropriate measure of liquidated damages to be awarded John Hancock should Houston Dairy default. Dr. Dyer, president and principal shareholder of Houston Dairy, did not execute the letter until eighteen days later, on January 17, 1978. Along with the letter, Houston Dairy mailed a $16,000 cashier's check.

Upon receiving the returned commitment letter on January 23, an agent for John Hancock mailed the cashier's check to the John Hancock Depository and Service Center in Champaign, Illinois, for deposit and sent the loan-closing attorney, Harvey Henderson, the necessary information to close the loan. Meanwhile, Dr. Dyer delivered a copy of the commitment letter to Houston Dairy's attorney and asked him to call Henderson to ascertain his fee for closing the loan. On January 28, the two attorneys talked and agreed to the method they would use to close the loan and the manner in which the fee would be charged. However, on January 30, Houston Dairy was able to obtain a 9% loan from a state bank. Houston Dairy then requested a refund of its $16,000 deposit, which was refused by John Hancock.

In the district court, Houston Dairy contended that the return of the commitment letter constituted a counter offer since the seven-day time period for acceptance had expired, that John Hancock never communicated its acceptance of the counter offer, thus allowing Houston Dairy to revoke the counter offer, which it did on January 31. Therefore, the argument proceeds, no contract was ever formed and Houston Dairy was entitled to a refund of $16,000.

The district court disagreed, finding that John Hancock had both waived the seven-day limitation and validly accepted a counter offer. Accordingly, the court held that the parties had entered into a binding contract and awarded John Hancock the $16,000 deposit as valid, liquidated damages for breach of the loan agreement.

II. WAS THERE A CONTRACT?

It is . . . clear in the instant case that upon expiration of the seven-day time period, John Hancock's offer terminated. Thus the action taken by Houston Dairy in signing and returning the commitment letter subsequent to the termination of the offer constituted a counter offer which John Hancock could accept within a reasonable time.

In Mississippi, the courts have long recognized that for acceptance to have effect, it must be communicated to the proposer of the offer. *See Pioneer Box Co. v. Price Veneer & Lumber Co.*, 132 Miss. 189, 96 So. 103, 105 (1923). John Hancock contends it did accept Houston Dairy's counter offer and that the acceptance was communicated to Houston Dairy.

According to John Hancock, depositing Houston Dairy's check was itself sufficient to operate as communication of its acceptance of the counter offer. John Hancock argues that its silence plus retention of Houston Dairy's money constituted acceptance and notification. Indeed, Mississippi has specifically recognized the validity of acceptance by silence within the guidelines laid down in Restatement § 72. . . . However, the present facts do not fit within these guidelines. Houston Dairy neither had previous dealings nor had otherwise been led to understand that John Hancock's silence and temporary retention of its deposit would operate as acceptance. In addition, Houston Dairy had no knowledge that its check had been deposited in John Hancock's depository. Since Houston Dairy sent a cashier's check, it could not have known the check had even been deposited unless notified by John Hancock or its bank. No such notice arrived from John Hancock and none is required from the bank.

The Mississippi Supreme Court held in *L. A. Becker v. Clardy*, 96 Miss. 301, 51 So. 211 (1910) that the mere depositing of a check was insufficient to constitute acceptance of an offer. There, an offeror sent a $100 down payment along with its order for merchandise to the offeree. As was its policy, the offeree immediately deposited the check in its account, which was later paid in due course by the bank upon which the check was drawn. However, the offeree subsequently mailed a letter to the offeror rejecting the offer and enclosed a check for $100. The court held that upon receipt of the order and down payment, the offeree was "entitled to a reasonable time in which to examine and determine whether it would accept or reject [the order]. . . . Depositing the check for collection, therefore, did not constitute acceptance of the order." *Id.*, 51 So. at 213.[3]

3. John Hancock attempts to distinguish *L. A. Becker* by stating that the offer-   ee in *L. A. Becker* did not have a policy of immediately returning checks on offers it

John Hancock also contends that Houston Dairy was notified of its acceptance in the conversation between the attorneys for both parties on January 28. However, a review of the testimony concerning that conversation shows no communication of acceptance. Indeed, John Hancock's closing attorney testified that at the time of his conversation with Houston Dairy's attorney, he had not received the executed commitment letter and had no knowledge a counter offer had even been made. His conversation only concerned the method to be used to close the loan and the distribution of the fee to be charged, not acceptance of the counter offer. Houston Dairy cannot be deemed to have knowledge of John Hancock's acceptance simply by requesting and receiving information on the procedures for closing a loan should an agreement be reached.

III. CONCLUSION

In summary, Houston Dairy could not accept John Hancock's offer once the time period had lapsed. Thus, when Houston Dairy executed and returned the commitment letter several days late, it was proposing a counter offer which John Hancock could either accept or reject. Since the actions and policies of John Hancock were unknown to Houston Dairy, mere silence was not operative as an acceptance of the counter offer, no communication of acceptance having been received. Houston Dairy therefore was entitled to revoke its counter offer, which it did on January 31. Accordingly, we reverse the judgment of the district court and render judgment in favor of Houston Dairy for the amount of its deposit, $16,000.

COLE–McINTYRE–NORFLEET CO. v. HOLLOWAY

Supreme Court of Tennessee, 1919.
141 Tenn. 679, 214 S.W. 817, 7 A.L.R. 1683.

LANSDEN, CHIEF JUDGE. This case presents a question of law, which, so far as we are advised, has not been decided by this court in its exact phases. March 26, 1917, a traveling salesman of plaintiff in error[*], solicited and received from defendant in error, at his country store in Shelby County, Tenn., an order for certain goods, which he was authorized to sell. Among these goods were 50 barrels of meal. The meal was to be ordered out by defendant by the 31st day of July, and afterwards 5 cents per barrel per month was to be charged him for storage.

After the order was given the defendant in error heard nothing from it until the 26th of May, 1917, when he was in the place of business of

---

did not wish to accept, as was John Hancock's policy here. With this argument, John Hancock suggests that since the $16,000 deposit was not returned immediately in accord with its policy, then Houston Dairy had notice the counter offer had been accepted. This argument is valid only if Houston Dairy first had knowledge of John Hancock's policy. Upon a review of

the record, we have found no previous dealings or statements that would indicate knowledge by Houston Dairy of John Hancock's policy concerning offers it would not accept.

* [That is, the appellant, who was the defendant in the trial court and, in this case, the seller.—Ed.]

plaintiff in error, and told it to begin shipment of the meal on his contract. He was informed by plaintiff in error that it did not accept the order of March 26th, and for that reason the defendant had no contract for meal.

The defendant in error never received confirmation or rejection from plaintiff in error, or other refusal to fill the order. The same traveling salesman of plaintiff in error called on defendant as often as once each week, and this order was not mentioned to defendant, either by him or by his principals, in any way. Between the day of the order and the 26th of May, the day of its alleged rejection, prices on all of the articles in the contract greatly advanced. All of the goods advanced about 50 per cent in value.

Some jobbers at Memphis received orders from their drummers, and filled the orders or notified the purchaser that the orders were rejected; but this method was not followed by plaintiff in error.

The contract provided that it was not binding until accepted by the seller at its office in Memphis, and that the salesman had no authority to sign the contract for either the seller or buyer. It was further stipulated that the order should not be subject to countermand.

It will be observed that plaintiff in error was silent upon both the acceptance and rejection of the contract. It sent forth its salesman to solicit this and other orders. The defendant in error did not have the right to countermand orders and the contract was closed, if and when it was accepted by plaintiff in error. The proof that some jobbers in Memphis uniformly filled such orders unless the purchaser was notified to the contrary is of no value because it does not amount to a custom.

The case, therefore, must be decided upon its facts. The circuit court and the court of civil appeals were both of opinion that the contract was completed because of the lapse of time before plaintiff in error rejected it. The time intervening between the giving of the order by defendant and its alleged repudiation by plaintiff in error was about 60 days. Weekly opportunities were afforded the salesman of plaintiff in error to notify the defendant in error of the rejection of the contract, and, of course, daily occasions were afforded plaintiff in error to notify him by mail or wire. The defendant believed the contract was in force on the 26th of May, because he directed plaintiff in error to begin shipment of the meal on that day. Such shipments were to have been completed by July 31st, or defendant to pay storage charges. From this evidence the Circuit Court found as an inference of fact that plaintiff in error had not acted within a reasonable time, and therefore its silence would be construed as an acceptance of the contract. The question of whether the delay of plaintiff in error was reasonable or unreasonable was one of fact, and the circuit court was justified from the evidence in finding that the delay was unreasonable. Hence the case, as it comes to us, is whether delay upon the part of plaintiff in error for an unreasonable time in notifying the defendant in error of its action upon the contract is an acceptance of its terms.

We think such delay was unreasonable, and effected an acceptance of the contract. . . .

Plaintiff's agent in this case was authorized to do precisely that which he did do, both as to time and substance. The only thing which was left open by the contract was the acceptance or rejection of its terms by plaintiff in error. It will not do to say that a seller of goods like these could wait indefinitely to decide whether or not he will accept the offer of the proposed buyer. This was all done in the usual course of business, and the articles embraced within the contract were consumable in the use, and some of them would become unfitted for the market within a short time.

It is undoubtedly true that an offer to buy or sell is not binding until its acceptance is communicated to the other party. The acceptance, however, of such an offer, may be communicated by the other party either by a formal acceptance, or acts amounting to an acceptance. Delay in communicating action as to the acceptance may amount to an acceptance itself. When the subject of a contract, either in its nature or by virtue of conditions of the market, will become unmarketable by delay, delay in notifying the other party of his decision will amount to an acceptance by the [offeree]. Otherwise, the [offeree] could place his goods upon the market, and solicit orders, and yet hold the other party to the contract, while he reserves time to himself to see if the contract will be profitable.

Writ denied.

Questions

1. Can *Cole–McIntyre–Norfleet* be reconciled with *Houston Dairy*? Are both cases decided consistently? If the two cases were governed by the same law, would one be in error? If so, which one?

2. What would be the vice were the offeree in *Cole–McIntyre–Norfleet* to speculate on the contract, as described at the end of the court's opinion? Is there a similar vice when the offeror speculates similarly, perhaps as in *Houston Dairy*?

3. *Problems.*

    a. Assume the facts are as stated in *Cole–McIntyre–Norfleet*, except that the buyer sent a check with the order. The seller cashed the check and then rejected the offer while tendering a refund, all within a week of the order. Was there an agreement?

    b. Assume the facts are as stated in *Houston Dairy*, except that an officer of John Hancock signed a letter of acceptance and placed it in the company mailbox. It was picked up by the Postal Service, but it never arrived at Houston Dairy. Was there an agreement? See RESTATEMENT (SECOND) OF CONTRACTS § 63.

    c. Assume the facts are as stated in Problem b, except that the letter remained in the mail room in John Hancock's basement when Dr. Dyer phoned the officer and revoked the counteroffer. Was there an agreement? See First Dev. Corp. of Ky. v. Martin Marietta Corp., 959 F.2d 617 (6th Cir.1992).

d.   Assume that the Registrar of Internet Domain Names maintains a website that permits users to download its database of domain names. On the first screen, there was a paragraph titled "Contract" in which the user was to agree not to use the database for mass solicitation by mail, telephone or e-mail. Following this paragraph was a button labeled "I agree," but failure to click on this button did not prevent a user from downloading the database. Kidman downloaded the database and used it to send spam by e-mail. She had not clicked on the "I agree" button. Can the Registrar sue her successfully for breach of contract? See Register.Com, Inc. v. Verio, Inc., 356 F.3d 393 (2d Cir.2004).

SEAVIEW ASS'N OF FIRE ISLAND, N.Y., INC. v. WILLIAMS

Court of Appeals of New York, 1987.
69 N.Y.2d 987, 517 N.Y.S.2d 709, 510 N.E.2d 793.

MEMORANDUM OPINION

... Plaintiff is an association of homeowners formed more than 30 years ago in Seaview, an unincorporated Fire Island community of some 330 homes largely populated for summer recreation. Plaintiff owns and maintains the streets, walkways and beaches of Seaview. Additionally, it employs a community manager; it provides a rent-free home for a resident doctor in the summer; and it maintains shelters for lifeguards and for the Suffolk County police, as well as snowfences and antierosion devices, a nature area, and recreational facilities such as a ballfield and tennis courts. Seaview property owners are each assessed a share of plaintiff's annual costs. The assessment covers all services and facilities except the water company and the tennis courts. Defendants are a husband, wife and son who, by deeds, enjoy easements entitling them to the use of ocean beaches and walkways; two of the three defendants are in the real estate business, and are among the only five year-round residents of Seaview. Prior to purchasing their first house in Seaview in 1963, they lived in an adjoining community. They now own seven houses in Seaview, but refuse to pay any of the assessments, contending that as nonmembers of plaintiff association and nonusers of the recreational facilities maintained by plaintiff, they cannot be charged. Plaintiff brought the present action to recover assessments for the years 1976 through 1984. After a five-day bench trial, the court awarded judgment for plaintiff, concluding that there was an implied contract to pay the assessments arising out of defendants' purchase of property in Seaview with knowledge of the nature of the community and the conditions imposed upon ownership there. The Appellate Division affirmed for the reasons stated by the Trial Judge, one Justice dissenting, and granted leave to appeal to this court. We now affirm.

Where there is knowledge that a private community homeowners' association provides facilities and services for the benefit of community residents, the purchase of property there may manifest acceptance of conditions of ownership, among them payment for the facilities and services offered. The resulting implied-in-fact contract includes the obligation to pay a proportionate share of the full cost of maintaining those facilities and services, not merely the reasonable value of those actually used by any particular resident (*see, Sea Gate Assn. v. Fleischer*, 211 N.Y.S.2d 767, 778, 781). The issues of notice given by plaintiff and actual or constructive knowledge of defendants, gained from familiarity with the area, from signs or from other sources, are largely factual, and were the focus of the trial. There is ample evidence in the record to support the findings of the trial court, affirmed by the Appellate Division, that defendants knew the nature of the community and by their purchase—indeed, successive purchases—impliedly accepted the conditions accompanying ownership of property in Seaview. The issue is thus beyond our review (*see, Humphrey v. State of New York*, 60 N.Y.2d 742, 469 N.Y.S.2d 661, 457 N.E.2d 767).

Order affirmed, with costs, in a memorandum.

Questions

1. What words or acts constituted the offer in *Seaview Ass'n*? What were its terms? Did the defendant accept the offer? If so, what words or acts manifested the acceptance? Was the defendant under a duty to speak or be bound to a contract from silence? Or did the court impose a contract on the parties for reasons of Justice?

2. What were the homeowners' association's contractual interests in the payments by the defendant? Did the association have an expectation interest arising from a promise? Did the association have a restitution interest? Did the defendant have legally cognizable interests that would justify his position? Were other contractual interests implicated on these facts?

3. *Problems.*

    a. Assume the facts are otherwise as in *Seaview Ass'n*, but Li Po, a first-time buyer unfamiliar with the community, proves he did not know of the association's services. Same result?

    b. Assume the facts are otherwise as in Problem 3(a) above and that Li Po knew of the services but did not know who was providing them.

    c. Assume Li Po knew of the association's services and assessments but, before purchasing the home, sent a letter to the association refusing to enter into any contract with the association. Same result?

NOTE ON CONSENT AND FAIR PLAY

Would it be fair for the defendant in *Seaview Ass'n* to take the benefit of the association's services without paying a share of their cost? John Rawls has suggested that

> when a number of persons engage in a mutually advantageous cooperative venture according to rules, and thus restrict their liberty in ways necessary to yield advantages for all, those who have submitted to these restrictions have a right to a similar acquiescence on the part of those who have benefited from their submission.

JOHN RAWLS, A THEORY OF JUSTICE 12 (1971). The basis of such a right, with the corresponding duty on the benefitted party, is fair play: A person should do his or her part as defined by the rules of an institution when the institution is just and that person has voluntarily accepted the benefits of the arrangement or taken advantage of the opportunities it offers to further his or her interests.

Fair play is an alternative to consent as a basis of contractual obligation, implementing the autonomy principle. Like consent, fair play attaches obligations to voluntary acts of the parties. Consent theory, however, standardly bases the obligation on the parties' knowing, deliberate, and intentional undertakings. Fair play, by contrast, bases the obligation on the relationship between voluntary benefit-taking and the need for cooperation to keep the benefits coming. Would fair play or consent supply a better basis for the result in *Seaview Ass'n*? Would fair play better undergird the opinion in *Embry v. Hargadine, McKittrick Dry Goods Co.*, above at p. 17? Would fair play require different results in any of the cases considered heretofore? Does it avoid the problem with subjective and objective theories of mutual assent, considered in the Note on mutual assent, above at p. 16?

e. *Formation Under the U.C.C.*

In the abstract, the law of offer and acceptance has a neat formality that can be misleading. In real estate transactions, like many of the preceding cases, the parties are strangers who expect to deal once over a fairly short time period and not to deal again. It is prudent for parties to such transactions to make offers, counteroffers, and acceptances that can be separately identified, on terms that are set forth with relative completeness. The common law of offer and acceptance works best to implement the autonomy principle in such circumstances.

Consider, by contrast, contracts made by people in business when they deal with each other repeatedly over an extended time period. Often, such parties care to maintain a good reputation and to develop continuing relationships. In such circumstances, it may be reasonable to trust much to the other party's interest in maintaining the relationship and preserving its reputation as an honest and reliable contract partner. Consequently, contracting in commercial relationships often leaves much of the agreement implicit or open for ongoing cooperation.

Rigidly following the rules of offer and acceptance can do violence to the intentions and reasonable expectations of the parties to agreements in some commercial contexts. In part to better implement the autonomy principle, formation now may be governed by a statute—the Uniform Commercial Code (U.C.C.)—instead of the common law. As we will see, the relevant part of the U.C.C. takes a more flexible approach to contract formation, allowing the law to respond to reasonable commercial practices instead of withholding enforcement unless the transaction fits into the law's pre-set categories. To be sure, the U.C.C. does not govern the making of all commercial agreements. The formation of loan agreements and guarantees, for example, are governed by the common law. They are generally concluded with considerable formality. Contracts for the sale of goods, however, are governed by Article 2 of the U.C.C. As we will see, they are often concluded with striking informality.

NOTE ON THE UNIFORM COMMERCIAL CODE

Efforts to promote the uniformity of laws governing private transactions have a long history in the U.S. In the nineteenth century, David Dudley Field led these efforts by proposing "codes" to be adopted as law by the legislatures of the states. The general failure of his efforts led early in this century to the formation of the National Conference of Commissioners on Uniform State Laws. The Conference is an unofficial organization whose membership consists of commissioners appointed by the governor of each state. It has commissioned the drafting of a number of statutes for enactment by the states, many of which have achieved a high degree of acceptance.

Perhaps the most successful effort by the Commissioners, jointly with the American Law Institute, is the Uniform Commercial Code. Drafting began in 1942 under the leadership of Karl N. Llewellyn, then professor of law at Columbia Law School, and involving a large number of judges, practitioners, and professors with expertise in commercial law. The Commissioners and the ALI adopted a version of the U.C.C. in 1954, but this version failed to gain acceptance by the New York legislature. They adopted a revised version in 1956 to meet the objections of that crucial state in commercial matters. Forty-nine states now have adopted the U.C.C., with slight variations. It also has been adopted or used as a model in some foreign nations and was a major influence on the United Nations Convention on Contracts for the International Sale of Goods, U.N. Doc A/CONF.97/18 (1980); 19 I.L.M. 671 (1980), reproduced in CONTRACT LAW: BASIC SOURCE MATERIALS.

The U.C.C. is an unusual statute in that it begins with a statutory command concerning its interpretation: "This Act shall be liberally construed and applied to promote its underlying purposes and policies." U.C.C. § 1–102(1). The underlying purposes (i.e., principles) and policies of the act are to simplify, clarify, and modernize the law governing commercial transactions; to permit continued expansion of commercial practices through custom, usage, and agreement of the parties; and to make uniform the law among the various jurisdictions. U.C.C. § 1–102(2). The U.C.C. implements these goals through "articles" containing legal rules and standards.

In this casebook, we will consider Article 2 when its provisions displace the common law of contracts; parts of Article 9 will be relevant in Chapter 8, § 2. Article 2 "applies to transactions in goods." U.C.C.

§ 2–102. "Goods" is defined to include "all things (including specially manufactured goods) which are movable at the time of identification to the contract for sale other than the money in which the price is to be paid, investment securities ... and things in action." "Goods" also includes the "unborn young of animals and growing crops and other identified things attached to realty...." U.C.C. § 2–105(1). See also U.C.C. § 2–107. Since a statute supplants the common law within the scope of its application, it is important to consider in any contracts case whether the problem involves a "transaction in goods" within the meaning of the above provisions. If it does, the U.C.C. is the applicable law and governs the transaction as a matter of priority. An example of what happens when it is unclear whether Article 2 applies is *Gross Valentino Printing Co. v. Clarke,* below at pp. 157, 158–159.

Note that Article 2 has been amended and proposed for adoption by the states. Excerpts from the revision will be found in CONTRACT LAW: SELECTED SOURCE MATERIALS. The prospects for adoption of the amended Article 2 are scant.

U.C.C. §§ 2–204, 2–206

ProCD, INC. v. ZEIDENBERG

United States Court of Appeals, Seventh Circuit, 1996.
86 F.3d 1447.

EASTERBROOK, CIRCUIT JUDGE. Must buyers of computer software obey the terms of shrinkwrap licenses? The district court held not, for two reasons: first, they are not contracts because the licenses are inside the box rather than printed on the outside; .... 908 F.Supp. 640 (W.D.Wis. 1996). The parties and numerous amici curiae have briefed many other issues, but these are the only two that matter—and we disagree with the district judge's conclusion on each. Shrinkwrap licenses are enforceable unless their terms are objectionable on grounds applicable to contracts in general (for example, if they violate a rule of positive law, or if they are unconscionable). Because no one argues that the terms of the license at issue here are troublesome, we remand with instructions to enter judgment for the plaintiff.

I

ProCD, the plaintiff, has compiled information from more than 3,000 telephone directories into a computer database. We may assume that this database cannot be copyrighted, although it is more complex, contains more information (nine-digit zip codes and census industrial codes), is organized differently, and therefore is more original than the single alphabetical directory at issue in *Feist Publications, Inc. v. Rural*

Telephone Service Co., 499 U.S. 340, 111 S.Ct. 1282, 113 L.Ed.2d 358 (1991).... ProCD sells a version of the database, called SelectPhone (trademark), on CD–ROM discs. (CD–ROM means "compact disc—read only memory." The "shrinkwrap license" gets its name from the fact that retail software packages are covered in plastic or cellophane "shrinkwrap," and some vendors, though not ProCD, have written licenses that become effective as soon as the customer tears the wrapping from the package. Vendors prefer "end user license," but we use the more common term.) A proprietary method of compressing the data serves as effective encryption too. Customers decrypt and use the data with the aid of an application program that ProCD has written. This program, which is copyrighted, searches the database in response to users' criteria (such as "find all people named Tatum in Tennessee, plus all firms with 'Door Systems' in the corporate name"). The resulting lists (or, as ProCD prefers, "listings") can be read and manipulated by other software, such as word processing programs.

The database in SelectPhone (trademark) cost more than $10 million to compile and is expensive to keep current. It is much more valuable to some users than to others. The combination of names, addresses, and zip codes enables manufacturers to compile lists of potential customers. Manufacturers and retailers pay high prices to specialized information intermediaries for such mailing lists; ProCD offers a potentially cheaper alternative. People with nothing to sell could use the database as a substitute for calling long distance information, or as a way to look up old friends who have moved to unknown towns, or just as an electronic substitute for the local phone book. ProCD decided to engage in price discrimination, selling its database to the general public for personal use at a low price (approximately $150 for the set of five discs) while selling information to the trade for a higher price. It has adopted some intermediate strategies too: access to the SelectPhone (trademark) database is available via the America Online service for the price America Online charges to its clients (approximately $3 per hour), but this service has been tailored to be useful only to the general public.

If ProCD had to recover all of its costs and make a profit by charging a single price—that is, if it could not charge more to commercial users than to the general public—it would have to raise the price substantially over $150. The ensuing reduction in sales would harm consumers who value the information at, say, $200. They get consumer surplus of $50 under the current arrangement but would cease to buy if the price rose substantially. If because of high elasticity of demand in the consumer segment of the market the only way to make a profit turned out to be a price attractive to commercial users alone, then all consumers would lose out—and so would the commercial clients, who would have to pay more for the listings because ProCD could not obtain any contribution toward costs from the consumer market.

To make price discrimination work, however, the seller must be able to control arbitrage. An air carrier sells tickets for less to vacationers than to business travelers, using advance purchase and Saturday-night-stay requirements to distinguish the categories. A producer of movies segments the market by time, releasing first to theaters, then to pay-per-view services, next to the videotape and laserdisc market, and finally to cable and commercial tv. Vendors of computer software have a harder task. Anyone can walk into a retail store and buy a box. Customers do not wear tags saying "commercial user" or "consumer user." Anyway, even a commercial-user-detector at the door would not work, because a consumer could buy the software and resell to a commercial user. That arbitrage would break down the price discrimination and drive up the minimum price at which ProCD would sell to anyone.

Instead of tinkering with the product and letting users sort themselves—for example, furnishing current data at a high price that would be attractive only to commercial customers, and two-year-old data at a low price—ProCD turned to the institution of contract. Every box containing its consumer product declares that the software comes with restrictions stated in an enclosed license. This license, which is encoded on the CD–ROM disks as well as printed in the manual, and which appears on a user's screen every time the software runs, limits use of the application program and listings to non-commercial purposes.

Matthew Zeidenberg bought a consumer package of SelectPhone (trademark) in 1994 from a retail outlet in Madison, Wisconsin, but decided to ignore the license. He formed Silken Mountain Web Services, Inc., to resell the information in the SelectPhone (trademark) database. The corporation makes the database available on the Internet to anyone willing to pay its price—which, needless to say, is less than ProCD charges its commercial customers. Zeidenberg has purchased two additional SelectPhone (trademark) packages, each with an updated version of the database, and made the latest information available over the World Wide Web, for a price, through his corporation. ProCD filed this suit seeking an injunction against further dissemination that exceeds the rights specified in the licenses (identical in each of the three packages Zeidenberg purchased). The district court held the licenses ineffectual because their terms do not appear on the outside of the packages. The court added that the second and third licenses stand no different from the first, even though they are identical, because they might have been different, and a purchaser does not agree to—and cannot be bound by— terms that were secret at the time of purchase. 908 F.Supp. at 654.

II

Following the district court, we treat the licenses as ordinary contracts accompanying the sale of products, and therefore as governed by the common law of contracts and the Uniform Commercial Code. Whether there are legal differences between "contracts" and "licenses" . . . is a subject for another day. See *Microsoft Corp. v. Harmony Computers & Electronics, Inc.*, 846 F.Supp. 208 (E.D.N.Y.1994). Zeidenberg does not argue that Silken Mountain Web Services is free of any restrictions that apply to Zeidenberg himself, because any effort to treat the two parties as distinct would put Silken Mountain behind the eight ball on ProCD's argument that copying the application program onto its hard disk violates the copyright laws. Zeidenberg does argue, and the district court held, that placing the package of software on the shelf is an "offer," which the customer "accepts" by paying the asking price and leaving the store with the goods. *Peeters v. State*, 154 Wis. 111, 142 N.W. 181 (1913). In Wisconsin, as elsewhere, a contract includes only the terms on which the parties have agreed. One cannot agree to hidden terms, the judge concluded. So far, so good—but one of the terms to which Zeidenberg agreed by purchasing the software is that the transaction was subject to a license. Zeidenberg's position therefore must be that the printed terms on the outside of a box are the parties' contract—except for printed terms that refer to or incorporate other terms. But why would Wisconsin fetter the parties' choice in this way? Vendors can put the entire terms of a contract on the outside of a box only by using microscopic type, removing other information that buyers might find more useful (such as what the software does, and on which computers it works), or both. The "Read Me" file included with most software, describing system requirements and potential incompatibilities, may be equivalent to ten pages of type; warranties and license restrictions take still more space. Notice on the outside, terms on the inside, and a right to return the software for a refund if the terms are unacceptable (a right that the license expressly extends), may be a means of doing business valuable to buyers and sellers alike. See *E. Allan Farnsworth, 1 Farnsworth on Contracts* § 4.26 (1990); *Restatement (2d) of Contracts* § 211 comment a (1981) ("Standardization of agreements serves many of the same functions as standardization of goods and services; both are essential to a system of mass production and distribution. Scarce and costly time and skill can be devoted to a class of transactions rather than the details of individual transactions."). Doubtless a state could forbid the use of standard contracts in the software business, but we do not think that Wisconsin has done so.

Transactions in which the exchange of money precedes the communication of detailed terms are common. Consider the purchase of insurance. The buyer goes to an agent, who explains the essentials (amount of coverage, number of years) and remits the premium to the home office, which sends back a policy. On the district judge's understanding, the terms of the policy are irrelevant because the insured paid before receiving them. Yet the device of payment, often with a "binder" (so that the insurance takes effect immediately even though the home office reserves the right to withdraw coverage later), in advance of the policy, serves buyers' interests by accelerating effectiveness and reducing transactions costs. Or consider the purchase of an airline ticket. The traveler calls the carrier or an agent, is quoted a price, reserves a seat, pays, and gets a ticket, in that order. The ticket contains elaborate terms, which the traveler can reject by canceling the reservation. To use the ticket is to accept the terms, even terms that in retrospect are disadvantageous. See *Carnival Cruise Lines, Inc. v. Shute*, 499 U.S. 585, 111 S.Ct. 1522, 113 L.Ed.2d 622 (1991); see also *Vimar Seguros y Reaseguros, S.A. v.*

M/V Sky Reefer, 515 U.S. 528, 115 S.Ct. 2322, 132 L.Ed.2d 462 (1995) (bills of lading). Just so with a ticket to a concert. The back of the ticket states that the patron promises not to record the concert; to attend is to agree. A theater that detects a violation will confiscate the tape and escort the violator to the exit. One *could* arrange things so that every concertgoer signs this promise before forking over the money, but that cumbersome way of doing things not only would lengthen queues and raise prices but also would scotch the sale of tickets by phone or electronic data service.

Consumer goods work the same way. Someone who wants to buy a radio set visits a store, pays, and walks out with a box. Inside the box is a leaflet containing some terms, the most important of which usually is the warranty, read for the first time in the comfort of home. By Zeidenberg's lights, the warranty in the box is irrelevant; every consumer gets the standard warranty implied by the UCC in the event the contract is silent; yet so far as we are aware no state disregards warranties furnished with consumer products. Drugs come with a list of ingredients on the outside and an elaborate package insert on the inside. The package insert describes drug interactions, contraindications, and other vital information—but, if Zeidenberg is right, the purchaser need not read the package insert, because it is not part of the contract.

Next consider the software industry itself. Only a minority of sales take place over the counter, where there are boxes to peruse. A customer may place an order by phone in response to a line item in a catalog or a review in a magazine. Much software is ordered over the Internet by purchasers who have never seen a box. Increasingly software arrives by wire. There is no box; there is only a stream of electrons, a collection of information that includes data, an application program, instructions, many limitations ("MegaPixel 3.14159 cannot be used with BytePusher 2.718"), and the terms of sale. The user purchases a serial number, which activates the software's features. On Zeidenberg's arguments, these unboxed sales are unfettered by terms—so the seller has made a broad warranty and must pay consequential damages for any shortfalls in performance, two "promises" that if taken seriously would drive prices through the ceiling or return transactions to the horse-and-buggy age.

According to the district court, the UCC does not countenance the sequence of money now, terms later. (Wisconsin's version of the UCC does not differ from the Official Version in any material respect, so we use the regular numbering system. Wis. Stat. § 402.201 corresponds to UCC § 2–201, and other citations are easy to derive.) One of the court's reasons—that by proposing as part of the draft Article 2B a new UCC § 2–2203 that would explicitly validate standard-form user licenses, the American Law Institute and the National Conference of Commissioners on Uniform Laws have conceded the invalidity of shrinkwrap licenses under current law, see 908 F.Supp. at 655–56—depends on a faulty inference. To propose a change in a law's text is not necessarily to propose a change in the law's effect. New words may be designed to fortify the current rule with a more precise text that curtails uncertainty. To judge by the flux of law review articles discussing shrinkwrap licenses, uncertainty is much in need of reduction—although businesses seem to feel less uncertainty than do scholars, for only three cases (other than ours) touch on the subject, and none directly addresses it. See *Step–Saver Data Systems, Inc. v. Wyse Technology*, 939 F.2d 91 (3d Cir.1991); *Vault Corp. v. Quaid Software Ltd.*, 847 F.2d 255, 268–70 (5th Cir.1988); Arizona Retail Systems, Inc. v. Software Link, Inc., 831 F.Supp. 759 (D.Ariz.1993). As their titles suggest, these are not consumer transactions. Step–Saver is a battle-of-the-forms case, in which the parties exchange incompatible forms and a court must decide which prevails.... Our case has only one form; UCC § 2–207 is irrelevant. *Vault* holds that Louisiana's special shrinkwrap-license statute is preempted by federal law, a question to which we return. And Arizona Retail Systems did not reach the question, because the court found that the buyer knew the terms of the license before purchasing the software.

What then does the current version of the UCC have to say? We think that the place to start is § 2–204(1): "A contract for sale of goods may be made in any manner sufficient to show agreement, including conduct by both parties which recognizes the existence of such a contract." A vendor, as master of the offer, may invite acceptance by conduct, and may propose limitations on the kind of conduct that constitutes acceptance. A buyer may accept by performing the acts the vendor proposes to treat as acceptance. And that is what happened. ProCD proposed a contract that a buyer would accept by using the software after having an opportunity to read the license at leisure. This Zeidenberg did. He had no choice, because the software splashed the license on the screen and would not let him proceed without indicating acceptance. So although the district judge was right to say that a contract can be, and often is, formed simply by paying the price and walking out of the store, the UCC permits contracts to be formed in other ways. ProCD proposed such a different way, and without protest Zeidenberg agreed. Ours is not a case in which a consumer opens a package to find an insert saying "you owe us an extra $10,000" and the seller files suit to collect. Any buyer finding such a demand can prevent formation of the contract by returning the package, as can any consumer who concludes that the terms of the license make the software worth less than the purchase price. Nothing in the UCC requires a seller to maximize the buyer's net gains.

. . .

Some portions of the UCC impose additional requirements on the way parties agree on terms. A disclaimer of the implied warranty of merchantability must be "conspicuous." UCC § 2–316(2), incorporating UCC § 1–201(10). Promises to make firm offers, or to negate oral modifications, must be "separately signed." UCC §§ 2–205, 2–209(2). These special provisos reinforce the impression that, so far as the UCC is concerned, other terms may be as inconspicuous as the forum-selection clause on the back of the cruise ship ticket in *Carnival Lines*. Zeidenberg has not located any Wisconsin case—for that matter, any case in any state—holding that under the UCC the ordinary terms found in shrinkwrap licenses require any special prominence, or otherwise are to be undercut rather than enforced. In the end, the terms of the license are conceptually identical to the contents of the package. Just as no court would dream of saying that SelectPhone (trademark) must contain 3,100 phone books rather than 3,000, or must have data no more than 30 days old, or must sell for $100 rather than $150—although any of these changes would be welcomed by the customer, if all other things were held constant—so, we believe, Wisconsin would not let the buyer pick and choose among terms. Terms of use are no less a part of "the product" than are the size of the database and the speed with which the software compiles listings. Competition among vendors, not judicial revision of a package's contents, is how consumers are protected in a market economy. *Digital Equipment Corp. v. Uniq Digital Technologies, Inc.*, 73 F.3d 756 (7th Cir.1996). ProCD has rivals, which may elect to compete by offering superior software, monthly updates, improved terms of use, lower price, or a better compromise among these elements. As we stressed above, adjusting terms in buyers' favor might help Matthew Zeidenberg today (he already has the software) but would lead to a response, such as a higher price, that might make consumers as a whole worse off.

. . . .

Questions

1. Does U.C.C., Article 2 apply to the transaction in *ProCD*? Why or why not?

2. Under the common law of offer and acceptance, what was the offer and what was the acceptance? Would the result differ from that in *ProCD*? Under U.C.C. § 2–204, is there any need thus to analyze the transaction? See also U.C.C. §§ 1–201(3), 1–201(11).

3. Does the result in *ProCD* best serve the interests of consumers, as Judge Easterbrook claimed? Is this a proper goal of the law of contracts? Why shouldn't courts rewrite contracts to improve the lot of consumers?

4. *Problems.*

a. McQueen telephoned Gateway Computers, Inc., an assembler and marketer of personal computers. He and Gateway's representative identified the model and configuration that McQueen wanted. He placed an order and gave Gateway his credit card number. Three weeks later, a Gateway computer meeting his telephonic specifications arrived in a box. He opened it, set it up, and worked with it for six weeks. Then he found, among the hardware and software in the box, a pamphlet containing Gateway's legal terms for the transaction. They provided for a less consumer-friendly limited warranty than he had expected. They also provided that he could return the computer at his own expense and get a refund of the price at any time within 30 days of delivery. Is McQueen stuck with Gateway's limited warranty? See Hill v. Gateway 2000, Inc., 105 F.3d 1147 (7th Cir.1997).

b.   McQueen bought a "nonrefundable, nonreturnable" airline ticket on the phone from Global Airlines, Inc. He and the airline's representative identified the origin, destination, time of departure, time of arrival, meal service, and price of the ticket. He then paid with a credit card. One week later, the ticket arrived in the mail. It included lengthy terms concerning the airline's liabilities. McQueen decided the limits on liability made the ticket too one-sided. He wants to cancel. What should you advise him as a matter of common law? Why?

c.   Net Software offered free Internet browsing software, dowloadable from its website. The first screen on the website included a button labeled "download now." It also allowed the viewer to scroll down, but it did not notify the user that anything important was on the next screen. On the next screen, however, Net Software presented a license agreement and a notice to the user that downloading the software constituted the user's agreement to the terms of the license. Net Software later sued User for breach of the license agreement. Can User argue successfully that no contract was formed? See Specht v. Netscape Communications Corp., 306 F.3d 17 (2d Cir.2002).

EMPIRE MACHINERY CO. v. LITTON BUSINESS TELEPHONE SYSTEMS

Court of Appeals of Arizona, 1977.
115 Ariz. 568, 566 P.2d 1044.

JACOBSON, PRESIDING JUDGE. This is a contract action in which we are called upon to determine whether execution of a "home office acceptance" clause is the exclusive means by which a contract can be made binding.

This action was instituted by Empire Machinery Co. (Empire) against Litton Systems Co. and various divisions and subsidiary companies of Litton Systems Co. (collectively referred to as Litton) seeking damages for breach of a contract to install an "interconnect" telephone system for Empire's use. On cross-motions for summary judgment, the trial court granted judgment in favor of Litton, in essence finding, as a matter of law, that a binding contract was never consummated between the parties. Empire has appealed.

The facts are not in material dispute between the parties.

Empire is the dealer for Caterpillar Tractor Company in Arizona. In the summer of 1973, Empire became interested in acquiring an "interconnect" telephone system. An "interconnect" system is one in which the telephone customer owns the "in-house" switching equipment, telephones and wiring, as compared to this equipment being owned by the telephone company, in this case, Mountain Bell. Litton is a manufacturer and seller of interconnect systems and on April 2, 1973, Russell R. Murphy, National Accounts Manager for Litton wrote Empire a letter extolling the virtues of the Litton system and enclosing a card to be returned to Litton if Empire was interested in its system. Empire returned the card and on April 17, 1973 Murphy personally contacted Empire.

During this visit, Murphy explained that Litton was developing a "Superplex" switching system which would be available in approximately a year. Mr. Ronald E. Mathis, Jr., communications coordinator for Empire, expressed interest in Litton's system which embraced the "Superplex" switch.

On June 5, 1973, Litton, through Murphy, submitted a proposal to Empire which was rejected. Negotiations continued between Murphy and Mathis until July 30, 1973. On that date, Murphy submitted a letter to Empire which stated in pertinent part that:

> "To confirm our previous discussions, upon receipt of a signed order and deposit, Litton BTS will install a Common Control Crossbar Telephone System on your premises. This system will be replaced upon your request and in accordance with our normal delivery schedule with our computer-controlled electronic solid state TDM system ['Superplex'] at no further expense to your company."

Following receipt of this letter from Murphy, Mr. Jack W. Whitman, president of Empire, signed an "Equipment Sales Agreement" and delivered to Murphy a check in the sum of $8,546.00, as the down payment. Murphy, on the Equipment Sales Agreement, acknowledged receipt of this amount.

This Equipment Sales Agreement contained on its face a clause which read:

> "6. This agreement shall become effective and binding upon the Purchaser and BTS [Litton] only upon approval, acceptance, and execution hereof by BTS and its home office."

At the right hand bottom of the front page, the following appeared:

> "Approved and Accepted by Litton Business Telephone, Division of Litton Systems, Inc. (Seller)

> "By:

> _____

> (Signature)

> _____

> (Type Name and Title)

> _____

> (Date)"

It is acknowledged that Murphy did not sign this portion of the contract. It is also acknowledged that Empire's President, Mr. Whitman, read and understood paragraph 6 quoted above. The estimated date for installation of the Litton system was set at November 15, 1973.

On August 9, 1973, Mathis, on behalf of Empire, was requested by Murphy to send a form letter to Mountain Bell designating Litton as Empire's representative with authority to act in connection with the installation of the interconnect system. The form letter supplied by Litton contained the following lead paragraph:

"We have this date entered into a contractual agreement with LITTON BTS Division, Litton Systems, Inc. for the installation an 'interconnect telephone system'."

On August 30, 1973, John Parlett, National Systems Representative for Litton, wrote Mountain Bell advising that company of the details of the installation of the interconnect system. The letter contained the following lead paragraph:

"We have this date entered into a contractual agreement with Empire Machinery Company for the installation of an 'interconnect' telephone system."

Empire, at Litton's request, purchased approximately $12,000 worth of electrical equipment to facilitate Litton's equipment.

On December 3, 1973, W. P. Scott, service manager of Litton, requested that Mountain Bell supply a new telephone number for Empire to be put in service as of December 21, 1973. Nothing further was done by either party in furtherance of the contract. Litton never shipped nor prepared the interconnect system.

Apparently Litton encountered difficulties in perfecting its "Superplex" system and on January 10, 1974, Mr. E.E. Bolles, then Mountain Area Manager for Litton, met with Murphy and Mathis and advised Mathis that Litton would be unable to supply Empire with a "Superplex" interconnect telephone system. At that time Bolles tendered back Empire's down payment. This oral tender was verified by a letter the following day.

Subsequently, Empire purchased a Stromborg–Carlson interconnect telephone system in lieu of the Litton system. The electrical equipment purchased by Empire was substantially adaptable to the Stromborg–Carlson system. This litigation then ensued.

The parties have presented several issues for our determination, which may be summarized into two issues as follows:

1. Did Murphy's letter of July 30, 1973 constitute an offer to sell which was accepted by Empire executing the Equipment Sales Agreement so as to constitute a binding agreement?

2. If not, did the Equipment Sales Agreement constitute an offer by Empire to purchase which could only be accepted and made

binding by Litton at its home office in accordance with paragraph 6 of that agreement?

Empire first contends that the letter from Litton dated July 30, 1973, signed by Murphy which stated "upon receipt of a signed order and deposit, Litton BTS will install an ('interconnect system') on your premises," constituted an offer to sell. They further argue that having complied with that offer by signing the Equipment Sales Agreement and giving Murphy a check in the sum of $8,546.00, they accepted that offer and a binding contract was created. The problem with this reasoning is that it ignores the express language of the Equipment Sales Agreement, stating that the agreement would become effective and binding "only upon approval, acceptance, and execution hereof by BTS and its home office." Because of this language, we believe the correct rule is that stated in 1 Corbin, Contracts § 88 (1963):

> "When one party solicits and receives an order or other expression of agreement from another, clearly specifying that there is to be no contract until ratification or assent by some officer or representative of the solicitor, the solicitation is not itself an offer; it is a request for an offer. The order that is given upon such a request is an offer, not an acceptance."

We therefore hold that Murphy's letter of July 30, 1973 constituted a request for an offer from Empire, and that the Equipment Sales Agreement was in compliance with that request and therefore an offer which required Litton's acceptance.

This brings us to the second issue presented, that is, the offer having designated the manner in which it would be accepted, is this the exclusive means by which that acceptance can occur? Empire has argued in this matter that future discovery might disclose that in fact Litton did accept, approve and execute the Equipment Sales Agreement. The simple answer to this contention is that Litton moved for summary judgment on the basis that the agreement was not accepted, approved or executed by "BTS and its home office." Empire did not request a continuance of this motion in order to complete discovery on this point. *See* Rule 56(f), Rules of Civil Procedure, 16 A.R.S. We therefore assume, for the purposes of this appeal, that there was no formal execution of the Equipment Sales Agreement by "BTS and its home office."

The crux of the problem is thus presented. Litton argues that because of clause 6 in the contract, Empire's offer was never accepted in the manner designated and therefore a binding contractual relationship never existed between the parties. Empire argues that clause number 6 can be waived by it and assented to by Litton and the conduct of Litton subsequent to the submission of the Equipment Sales Agreement shows such an assent or at least a fact issue which would preclude summary judgment. Litton counters this argument by contending that in any event, the conduct relied upon by Empire to show assent was performed by agents who had no authority to bind Litton.

As the ground floor for both Litton's and Empire's positions, both cite A.R.S. § 44–2313 (§ 2–206, Uniform Commercial Code)....

Empire points to the language contained under paragraph 1 of this statute and contends the conduct of Litton constitutes, as a matter of law, an acceptance of its offer under the Equipment Sales Agreement. Litton, on the other hand, points to the lead paragraph of this statute and argues that paragraph 6 of the Equipment Sales Agreement, as a matter of law, "otherwise unambiguously indicated" that only home office acceptance shall constitute an acceptance of the contract. In our opinion, both arguments miss the mark.

As the official comment to § 2–206 of the Uniform Commercial Code (adopted as A.R.S. § 44–313) makes clear, this section was an attempt to simplify the common law rule that an acceptance of a contract could only be made in the manner and medium of the offer, that is, a written offer could only be accepted by an acceptance in writing. Litton is correct that this statute did not intend to change the common law rule that if an offer by its terms indicated that acceptance would only be made in a particular manner, one must comply with the particular manner. *See* Uniform Commercial Code, § 2–206, Comment 1 (1969). Nor is such an acceptance clause contrary to the Uniform Commercial Code. *West Penn Power Co. v. Bethlehem Steel Corp.*, 236 Pa.Super. 413, 348 A.2d 144 (1975) (holding that U.C.C. § 2–206(1)(a) envisions "home office" acceptance clauses).

However, even under the common law, a contract containing a clause that acceptance can only be made by approval of officers at the home office could be accepted in a manner other than by such written approval. *See Pratt–Gilbert Co. v. Renaud*, 25 Ariz. 79, 213 P. 400 (1923) (holding that complete performance of contract constituted acceptance)....

. . .

With these principles in mind, the resolution of this appeal requires a determination of (1) whether the conduct of Litton in this matter was directed toward the fulfilling of its obligations so as to sufficiently express its assent to the Equipment Sales Agreement and (2) if so, whether such conduct was performed by individuals who had authority to bind Litton.

The conduct of Litton contended by Empire to constitute assent is as follows:

(1) Murphy's request to Empire that Empire inform Mountain Bell that Litton was Empire's representative to install the "interconnect" system and the existence of a contractual relationship between Litton and Empire.

(2) Parlett's letter of August 30, 1973, on behalf of Litton to Mountain Bell advising Mountain Bell of the contractual relationship existing between Litton and Empire and advising of the details of the installation of the "interconnect" system.

(3) The purchase by Empire of $12,000 worth of equipment in reliance upon the installation of the Litton "interconnect" system.

(4) The cashing of Empire's down payment check and the retention of the proceeds of that check.

(5) The request by Scott, Litton's Service Manager, to Mountain Bell for a new telephone number for Empire's business.

We will analyze each of these to determine whether the conduct, (1) constituted beginning performance of the contractual obligation and, (2) whether the conduct was performed by individuals who could bind Litton by its conduct.

As to Murphy's request that Empire inform Mountain States that a contractual obligation existed between Litton and Empire, we would agree that such conduct could be considered by a trier of fact as constituting assent to the formation of a binding contractual relationship between the parties, if performed by an individual having authority to bind Litton. However, we also agree upon the record presented here that Murphy had no authority expressed or apparent to bind Litton. . . .

The same cannot be said of Parlett, National Systems Representative, and his letter of August 30, 1973, advising Mountain Bell of the contractual relationship existing between Litton and Empire. . . . [W]e are of the opinion that a question of fact exists as to whether Parlett's letter of August 30, 1973 constituted an assent by Litton to be bound by the Equipment Sales Agreement and whether Parlett had apparent authority to so bind Litton. The same can be said of Scott's letter to Mountain Bell concerning change of telephone numbers. In this regard, Empire's purchase of equipment in reliance on this authority, if this be the fact, can be considered by the trier of fact.

Likewise, in our opinion the cashing of Empire's down payment check raises an issue of fact as to whether Litton assented to the contract. We view this conduct . . . as evidence that Litton assented to the contractual relationship by converting the negotiable instrument. *See Restatement of Contracts*, § 72(2) (1932). We agree with Litton that the mere acceptance of the check in accordance with the terms of the offer does not constitute any evidence of binding conduct on Litton's part. It is the cashing of that check and the retention of the proceeds over a period of several months that gives rise to the factual inferences as to Litton's intent to enter into a binding contractual relationship with Empire. Since the record is silent as to who in the Litton organization negotiated the instrument, that individual's authority to do so must abide the trial of this matter.

Litton argues that in any event all of the conduct referred to by Litton does not amount to "substantial performance" of the Equipment Sales Agreement and therefore as a matter of law cannot constitute an assent of that contract. In this regard, Litton equates substantial performance to conduct dealing with the actual installing, assembling or shipping of the "interconnect" system conduct Litton did not embark upon. Admittedly, the cases relied upon by Empire have these elements. However, in our opinion, the rule should be that if the offeree takes steps in furtherance of its contractual obligations which would lead a reasonable businessman to believe that the contract had been accepted, such conduct may, under the circumstances, constitute acceptance of the contract.

rule

We therefore hold that factual issues were presented, both as to whether the conduct shown here was in furtherance of Litton's contractual obligations and whether the persons engaging in that conduct had authority, actual or apparent to do so. Such material, factual issues preclude the granting of summary judgment to either party.

Judgment reversed and the matter remanded for proceedings consistent with this opinion.

Questions

1. Would the U.C.C. apply to this transaction had the alleged contract involved a duty for Litton to design, supply, and install a telephone system? Is it entirely a transaction in goods, or is there a mix of goods, services, and know-how? How should a court decide the applicable law when the contract is for both goods and services, as when a gardener fertilizes a lawn or a going business is sold?

2. What result if *Empire Machinery Co.* were governed by the common law? Why? Is a different result required to protect the contractual interests of the parties?

3. Does the court apply the U.C.C. correctly in your view? Does the U.C.C. better implement the autonomy principle than would the common law?

NOTE ON THE "BATTLE OF THE FORMS"

Recall the common law "mirror image rule" (*Ardente v. Horan*, above at p. 39), indicating that a purported acceptance is a counteroffer unless its terms match those of the offer exactly. However appropriate it may be for transactions between strangers, like real estate sales, it can produce uncomfortable results in commercial transactions. In these transactions, the parties often attend to the key business points in an agreement—descriptions of the goods, price, delivery times, payment terms—and trust to considerations of relationship and reputation on other matters. They often do business on preprinted forms, called "purchase orders" and "acknowledgments," containing inconsistent provisions, often in fine print on the back, concerning points likely to become important only should a dispute arise and not be resolved amicably. The written record can suggest to a reasonable interpreter that there is no agreement when the parties' reasonable understanding in the commercial context is surely that there is.

Consider a seller of rubber who wrote a buyer enclosing a letter offering 12 tons of rubber following discussions that day, to be shipped in equal monthly shipments, January to June, at $2.42 per pound, payable in cash within 30 days from delivery. In reply, the buyer sent a "purchase order," filling in all of the key terms on its own preprinted order form, which also contained in fine print on the back: "This order given on condition that seller in any event promptly acknowledges." Both parties are likely to understand that there is an agreement. But, when the seller does not send an acknowledgement, the mirror image rule denies there is a contract. The buyer then is free to reject delivery if it regrets having made the deal. See Poel v. Brunswick–Balke–Collender Co. of New York, 216 N.Y. 310, 110 N.E. 619 (1915). If the seller sends an acknowledgement with fine print for additional material terms, the seller rejects the buyer's terms and makes a counteroffer. The buyer then accepts the seller's counteroffer by taking delivery of the goods. The seller gets its terms.

There are a number of reasons for discomfort with the common law result. In the situation described above, most sellers will check the buyer's purchase order, if at all, for conformity to the key terms, neglecting the fine print on the back. The seller will then expect that the buyer is bound, but the buyer can get out of the deal. The seller's expectation may be reasonable, however, because buyers too often have no awareness of the fine print on the back of their own forms when sent. If so, the seller's interest then would seem the more worthy of legal protection. More often in commercial practice, it is the seller who sends the last form, acknowledging the buyer's purchase order. The buyer checks it only for the key business points, trusting to relationship and reputation on the less salient legal points. In that situation, the common law treats the seller's acknowledgement as a counteroffer which is accepted when the buyer takes dominion over the goods. See Hobbs v. Massasoit Whip Co., 158 Mass. 194, 33 N.E. 495 (1893). The seller's preprinted form may contain provisions not expressly negotiated, such as limitations on warranties or an agreement to resolve disputes by arbitration. The buyer then is bound even though it had no reasonable expectation as to those terms, allowing the seller to impose on the buyer's autonomy.

In effect, the common law mirror image rule produces a "last shot" effect, favoring the party who sends the last form before delivery, usually the seller. U.C.C. § 2–207(1) abolishes the mirror image rule for contracts governed by Article 2. Consistent with its underlying goal of favoring commercial practices, U.C.C. § 1–102(2)(b), an agreement may be found even though the parties' writings do not manifest assent to identical terms. U.C.C. § 2–207, however, does a questionable job of simplifying, clarifying, and modernizing the law governing this commercial problem. In particular, there are conflicting interpretations of what that provision determines are the terms of the contract when the parties' order and acknowledgment forms differ on a point. The Convention on Contracts for the International Sale of Goods, art. 19(1), reinstates the last shot effect for many international sales transactions. We will consider the problem of terms, however, in Chapter 5, § 1.

U.C.C. § 2–207

Amended Article 2 §§ 2–206, 2–207

IONICS, INC. v. ELMWOOD SENSORS, INC.

United States Court of Appeals, First Circuit, 1997.
110 F.3d 184.

TORRUELLA, C.J. Ionics, Inc. ("Ionics") purchased thermostats from Elmwood Sensors, Inc. ("Elmwood") for installation in water dispensers manufactured by the former. Several of the dispensers subsequently caused fires which allegedly resulted from defects in the sensors. Ionics filed suit against Elmwood in order to recover costs incurred in the wake of the fires. Before trial, the district court denied Elmwood's motion for partial summary judgment. The District Court of Massachusetts subsequently certified to this court "the question whether, in the circumstances of this case, § 2–207 of M.G.L. c. 106 has been properly applied." Order of the district court, November 6, 1995.

. . .

II. BACKGROUND

The facts of the case are not in dispute. Elmwood manufactures and sells thermostats. Ionics makes hot and cold water dispensers, which it leases to its customers. On three separate occasions, Ionics purchased thermostats from Elmwood for use in its water dispensers.[1] Every time Ionics made a purchase of thermostats from Elmwood, it sent the latter a purchase order form which contained, in small type, various "conditions." Of the 20 conditions on the order form, two are of particular relevance:

18. REMEDIES—The remedies provided Buyer herein shall be cumulative, and in addition to any other remedies provided by law or equity. A waiver of a breach of any provision hereof shall not constitute a waiver of any other breach. The laws of the state shown in Buyer's address printed on the masthead of this order shall apply in the construction hereof.

---

1. Orders were placed in March, June, and September 1990.

19. ACCEPTANCE—Acceptance by the Seller of this order shall be upon the terms and conditions set forth in items 1 to 17 inclusive, and elsewhere in this order. Said order can be so accepted only on the exact terms herein and set forth. No terms which are in any manner additional to or different from those herein set forth shall become a part of, alter or in any way control the terms and conditions herein set forth.

Near the time when Ionics placed its first order, it sent Elmwood a letter that it sends to all of its new suppliers. The letter states, in part:

The information preprinted, written and/or typed on our purchase order is especially important to us. Should you take exception to this information, please clearly express any reservations to us in writing. If you do not, we will assume that you have agreed to the specified terms and that you will fulfill your obligations according to our purchase order. If necessary, we will change your invoice and pay your invoice according to our purchase order.

Following receipt of each order, Elmwood prepared and sent an "Acknowledgment" form containing the following language in small type:

THIS WILL ACKNOWLEDGE RECEIPT OF BUYER'S ORDER AND STATE SELLER'S WILLINGNESS TO SELL THE GOODS ORDERED BUT ONLY UPON THE TERMS AND CONDITIONS SET FORTH HEREIN AND ON THE REVERSE SIDE HEREOF AS A COUNTEROFFER. BUYER SHALL BE DEEMED TO HAVE ACCEPTED SUCH COUNTEROFFER UNLESS IT IS REJECTED IN WRITING WITHIN TEN (10) DAYS OF THE RECEIPT HERE-OF, AND ALL SUBSEQUENT ACTION SHALL BE PURSUANT TO THE TERMS AND CONDITIONS OF THIS COUNTEROFFER ONLY; ANY ADDITIONAL OR DIFFERENT TERMS ARE HERE-BY OBJECTED TO AND SHALL NOT BE BINDING UPON THE PARTIES UNLESS SPECIFICALLY AGREED TO IN WRITING BY SELLER.

Although this passage refers to a "counteroffer," we wish to emphasize that this language is not controlling. The form on which the language appears is labeled an "Acknowledgment" and the language comes under a heading that reads "Notice of Receipt of Order." The form, taken as a whole, appears to contemplate an order's confirmation rather than an order's rejection in the form of a counteroffer.

.   .   .

As we have noted, the Acknowledgment Form expressed Elmwood's willingness to sell thermostats on "terms and conditions" that the Form indicated were listed on the reverse side. Among the terms and conditions listed on the back was the following:

9. WARRANTY

All goods manufactured by Elmwood Sensors, Inc. are guaranteed to be free of defects in material and workmanship for a period of ninety (90) days after receipt of such goods by Buyer or eighteen months from the date of manufacturer [sic] (as evidenced by the manufacturer's date code), whichever shall be longer. THERE IS NO IMPLIED WARRANTY OF MERCHANTABILITY AND NO OTHER WARRANTY, EXPRESSED OR IMPLIED, EXCEPT SUCH AS IS EXPRESSLY SET FORTH HEREIN. SELLER WILL NOT BE LIABLE FOR ANY GENERAL, CONSEQUENTIAL OR INCIDENTAL DAMAGES, INCLUDING WITHOUT LIMITATION ANY DAMAGES FROM LOSS OF PROFITS, FROM ANY BREACH OF WARRANTY OR FOR NEGLIGENCE, SELLER'S LIABILITY AND BUYER'S EXCLUSIVE REMEDY BEING EXPRESSLY LIMITED TO THE REPAIR OF DEFECTIVE GOODS F.O.B. THE SHIPPING POINT INDICATED ON THE FACE HEREOF OR THE REPAYMENT OF THE PURCHASE PRICE UPON THE RETURN OF THE GOODS OR THE GRANTING OF A REASONABLE ALLOWANCE ON ACCOUNT OF ANY DEFECTS, AS SELLER MAY ELECT.

Neither party disputes that they entered into a valid contract and neither disputes the quantity of thermostats purchased, the price paid, or the manner and time of delivery. The only issue in dispute is the extent of Elmwood's liability.

In summary, Ionics' order included language stating that the contract would be governed exclusively by the terms included on the purchase order and that all remedies available under state law would be available to Ionics. In a subsequent letter, Ionics added that Elmwood must indicate any objections to these conditions in writing. Elmwood, in turn, sent Ionics an Acknowledgment stating that the contract was governed exclusively by the terms in the Acknowledgment, and Ionics was given ten days to reject this "counteroffer." Among the terms included in the Acknowledgment is a limitation on Elmwood's liability. As the district court stated, "the terms are diametrically opposed to each other on the issue of whether all warranties implied by law were reserved or waived." Order of the District Court, August 23, 1995.

We face, therefore, a battle of the forms. This is purely a question of law. The dispute turns on whether the contract is governed by the language after the comma in § 2–207(1) of the Uniform Commercial Code, according to the rule laid down by this court in *Roto–Lith, Ltd. v. F.P. Bartlett & Co.*, 297 F.2d 497 (1st Cir.1962), or whether it is governed by subsection (3) of the Code provision, as enacted by both Massachusetts, Mass. Gen. L. ch. 106, § 2–207 (1990 and 1996 Supp.), and Rhode Island, R.I. Gen. Laws § 6A–2–207 (1992).[2] We find the rule of *Roto–Lith* to be in conflict with the purposes of section 2–207 and,

2. There is some uncertainty on the question of whether Massachusetts or Rhode Island law governs. We need not address this issue, however, because the two states have adopted versions of section 2–207 of the Uniform Commercial Code that are virtually equivalent.

accordingly, we overrule *Roto–Lith* and find that subsection (3) governs the contract.[3] Analyzing the case under section 2–207, we conclude that Ionics defeats Elmwood's motion for partial summary judgment.

III. LEGAL ANALYSIS

Our analysis begins with the statute.... [The court quoted U.C.C. Section 2–207.]

In *Roto–Lith*, Roto–Lith sent a purchase order to Bartlett, who responded with an acknowledgment that included language purporting to limit Bartlett's liability. Roto–Lith did not object. *Roto–Lith*, 297 F.2d at 498–99. This court held that "a response which states a condition materially altering the obligation solely to the disadvantage of the offeror is an 'acceptance ... expressly ... conditional on assent to the additional ... terms.'" Id. at 500. This holding took the case outside of section 2–207 by applying the exception after the comma in subsection (1). The court then reverted to common law and concluded that Roto–Lith "accepted the goods with knowledge of the conditions specified in the acknowledgment [and thereby] became bound." Id. at 500. In other words, the Roto–Lith court concluded that the defendant's acceptance was conditional on assent, by the buyer, to the new terms and, therefore, constituted a counter offer rather than an acceptance. When Roto–Lith accepted the goods with knowledge of Bartlett's conditions, it accepted the counteroffer and Bartlett's terms governed the contract. Elmwood argues that *Roto–Lith* governs the instant appeal, implying that the terms of Elmwood's acknowledgment govern.

. . .

Our inquiry, however, is not complete. Having found that we cannot distinguish this case from *Roto–Lith*, we turn to the Uniform Commercial Code, quoted above. A plain language reading of section 2–207 suggests that subsection (3) governs the instant case. Ionics sent an initial offer to which Elmwood responded with its "Acknowledgment." Thereafter, the conduct of the parties established the existence of a contract as required by section 2–207(3).

Furthermore, the case before us is squarely addressed in comment 6, which states:

> 6. If no answer is received within a reasonable time after additional terms are proposed, it is both fair and commercially sound to

---

3. Although panel decisions of this court are ordinarily binding on newly constituted panels, that rule does not obtain in instances where, as here, a departure is compelled by controlling authority (such as the interpreted statute itself). In such relatively rare instances, we have sometimes chosen to circulate the proposed overruling opinion to all active members of the court prior to publication even though the need to overrule precedent is reasonably clear. See, e.g., Wright v. Park, 5 F.3d 586, 591 n. 7 (1st Cir.1993); Trailer Marine Transport Corp. v. Rivera Vazquez, 977 F.2d 1, 9 n. 5 (1st Cir.1992). This procedure is, of course, informal, and does not preclude a suggestion of rehearing en banc on any issue. We have followed that praxis here and can report that none of the active judges of this court has objected to the panel's analysis or to its conclusion that Roto-Lith has outlived its usefulness as circuit precedent.

assume that their inclusion has been assented to. Where clauses on confirming forms sent by both parties conflict[,] each party must be assumed to object to a clause of the other conflicting with one on the confirmation sent by himself. As a result [,] the requirement that there be notice of objection which is found in subsection (2) [of § 2–207] is satisfied and the conflicting terms do not become part of the contract. The contract then consists of the terms originally expressly agreed to, terms on which the confirmations agree, and terms supplied by this Act.

Mass. Gen. L. ch. 106, § 2–207, Uniform Commercial Code Comment 6. This Comment addresses precisely the facts of the instant case. Any attempt at distinguishing the case before us from section 2–207 strikes us as disingenuous.

We are faced, therefore, with a contradiction between a clear precedent of this court, *Roto–Lith*, which suggests that the language after the comma in subsection (1) governs, and the clear dictates of the Uniform Commercial Code, which indicate that subsection (3) governs. It is our view that the two cannot coexist and the case at bar offers a graphic illustration of the conflict. We have, therefore, no choice but to overrule our previous decision in *Roto–Lith, Ltd. v. F.P. Bartlett & Co.*, 297 F.2d 497 (1st Cir.1962). Our decision brings this circuit in line with the majority view on the subject and puts to rest a case that has provoked considerable criticism from courts and commentators and alike.[4]

We hold, consistent with section 2–207 and Official Comment 6, that where the terms in two forms are contradictory, each party is assumed to object to the other party's conflicting clause. As a result, mere acceptance of the goods by the buyer is insufficient to infer consent to the seller's terms under the language of subsection (1).[5] Nor do such terms become part of the contract under subsection (2) because notification of objection has been given by the conflicting forms. See § 2–207(2)(c).

The alternative result, advocated by Elmwood and consistent with *Roto-Lith*, would undermine the role of section 2–207. Elmwood suggests that "a seller's expressly conditional acknowledgment constitutes a counteroffer where it materially alters the terms proposed by the buyer, and the seller's terms govern the contract between the parties when the buyer accepts and pays for the goods." Appellant's Brief at 12. Under this view, section 2–207 would no longer apply to cases in which forms

---

4. See, e.g., Step–Saver Data Systems, Inc. v. Wyse Technology, 939 F.2d 91, 101 (3d Cir.1991); St. Charles Cable TV, Inc. v. Eagle Comtronics, Inc., 687 F.Supp. 820, 828 & n. 19 (S.D.N.Y.1988); Daitom v. Pennwalt Corp., 741 F.2d 1569, 1576–77 (10th Cir.1984); Luria Bros. v. Pielet Bros. Scrap Iron & Metal, 600 F.2d 103, 113 (7th Cir.1979); Dorton v. Collins & Aikman Corp., 453 F.2d 1161, 1168 & n. 5 (6th Cir.1972); James J. White & Robert S. Sum-mers, 1 Uniform Commercial Code, § 1–3, at 12, 16–17 (1995); Murray, Intention over Terms: An Exploration of UCC 2–207 & New Section 60, Restatement of Contracts, 37 Fordham L.Rev. 317, 329 (1969).

5. See also Official Comment 3 ("If [additional or different terms] are such as materially to alter the original bargain, they will not be included unless expressly agreed to by the other party.").

have been exchanged and subsequent disputes reveal that the forms are contradictory. That is, the last form would always govern.

The purpose of section 2–207, as stated in *Roto–Lith,* "was to modify the strict principle that a response not precisely in accordance with the offer was a rejection and a counteroffer." Roto–Lith, 297 F.2d at 500; see also Dorton v. Collins & Aikman Corp., 453 F.2d 1161, 1165–66 (6th Cir.1972) (stating that section 2–207 "was intended to alter the 'ribbon-matching' or 'mirror' rule of common law, under which the terms of an acceptance or confirmation were required to be identical to the terms of the offer"). Under the holding advocated by Elmwood, virtually any response that added to or altered the terms of the offer would be a rejection and a counteroffer. We do not think that such a result is consistent with the intent of section 2–207 and we believe it to be expressly contradicted by Comment 6.

Applied to this case, our holding leads to the conclusion that the contract is governed by section 2–207(3). Section 2–207(1) is inapplicable because Elmwood's acknowledgment is conditional on assent to the additional terms. The additional terms do not become a part of the contract under section 2–207(2) because notification of objection to conflicting terms was given on the order form and because the new terms materially alter those in the offer. Finally, the conduct of the parties demonstrates the existence of a contract, as required by section 2–207(3). Thus, section 2–207(3) applies and the terms of the contract are to be determined in accordance with that subsection.

We conclude, therefore, that section 2–207(3) prevails and "the terms of the particular contract consist of those terms on which the writings of the parties agree, together with any supplementary terms incorporated under any other provisions of this chapter." Mass. Gen. L. ch. 106, § 2–207(3).

The reality of modern commercial dealings, as this case demonstrates, is that not all participants read their forms. See James J. White & Robert S. Summers, Uniform Commercial Code § 1–3 at 6–7 (4th ed. 1995). To uphold Elmwood's view would not only fly in the face of Official Comment 6 to section 2–207 of the Uniform Commercial Code, and the overall purpose of that section, it would also fly in the face of good sense. The sender of the last form (in the instant case, the seller) could insert virtually any conditions it chooses into the contract, including conditions contrary to those in the initial form. The final form, therefore, would give its sender the power to re-write the contract. Under our holding today, we at least ensure that a party will not be held to terms that are directly contrary to the terms it has included in its own form. Rather than assuming that a failure to object to the offeree's conflicting terms indicates offeror's assent to those terms, we shall make the more reasonable inference that each party continues to object to the other's contradictory terms. We think it too much to grant the second form the power to contradict and override the terms in the first form.

IV. Conclusion

For the reasons stated herein, the district court's order denying Elmwood's motion for partial summary judgment is affirmed and the case is remanded to the district court for further proceedings.

Questions

1. How would *Ionics* be decided under the common law? In the typical battle of the forms, where the buyer declares war by sending a purchase order, does the buyer win (first shot effect) or does the seller, who delivers the goods after receiving the buyer's order (last shot effect)? Could you advise a seller to do anything to become the offeror in most cases?

2. How should U.C.C. § 2–207 be read as applied to the facts in *Ionics*? Is the court correct that, under Elmwood's proposed holding, virtually any response that added to or altered the terms of the offer would be a rejection and a counteroffer? Would this be the case when the seller's form makes its acceptance expressly conditional on assent to the additional or different terms? How do the amendments to Article 2 treat the case of an acceptance made expressly conditional in this way? How would *Ionics* be decided under that document?

3. Did the *Ionics* solution to the U.C.C. § 2–207 problem achieve a fair solution?

4. Problem.

The facts are as in the *Ionics* case except that the buyer's purchase order was silent on damages while the seller's acknowledgement had a damages limitations clause. Could the buyer successfully argue that, under U.C.C. § 2–207(2), its silence implied its preference for the U.C.C. gap-filler provisions such that the seller's damages limitations clause did not become part of the contract? *See* JOM, Inc. v. Adell Plastics, Inc., 193 F.3d 47 (1st Cir.1999).

f. *Incomplete Agreements*

SUN PRINTING & PUBLISHING ASS'N v. REMINGTON PAPER & POWER CO., INC.

Court of Appeals of New York, 1923.
235 N.Y. 338, 139 N.E. 470.

Cardozo, Judge. Plaintiff agreed to buy and defendant to sell 1,000 tons of paper per month during the months of September, 1919, to December, 1920, inclusive, 16,000 tons in all. Sizes and quality were adequately described. Payment was to be made on the 20th of each month for all paper shipped the previous month. The price for shipments in September, 1919, was to be $3.73 ¾ per 100 pounds, and for shipments in October, November, and December, 1919, $4 per 100 pounds. "For the balance of the period of this agreement the price of the paper and length of terms for which such price shall apply shall be agreed upon by and between the parties hereto fifteen days prior to the expiration of each period for which the price and length of term thereof have been previously agreed upon, said price in no event to be higher than the contract price for news print charged by the Canadian Export Paper Company to the large consumers, the seller to receive the benefit of any differentials in freight rates.''

Between September, 1919, and December of that year, inclusive, shipments were made and paid for as required by the contract. The time then arrived when there was to be an agreement upon a new price and upon the term of its duration. The defendant in advance of that time gave notice that the contract was imperfect, and disclaimed for the future an obligation to deliver. Upon this the plaintiff took the ground that the price was to be ascertained by resort to an established standard. It made demand that during each month of 1920 the defendant deliver 1,000 tons of paper at the contract price for news print charged by the Canadian Export Paper Company to the large consumers, the defendant to receive the benefit of any differentials in freight rates. The demand was renewed month by month till the expiration of the year. This action has been brought to recover the ensuing damage.

Seller and buyer left two subjects to be settled in the middle of December and at unstated intervals thereafter. One was the price to be paid. The other was the length of time during which such price was to govern. Agreement as to the one was insufficient without agreement as to the other. If price and nothing more had been left open for adjustment, there might be force in the contention that the buyer would be viewed, in the light of later provisions, as the holder of an option. Cohen & Sons v. Lurie Woolen Co., 232 N.Y. 112, 133 N.E. 370. This would mean that, in default of an agreement for a lower price, the plaintiff would have the privilege of calling for delivery in accordance with a price established as a maximum. The price to be agreed upon might be less, but could not be more, than "the contract price for news print charged by the Canadian Export Paper Company to the large consumers." The difficulty is, however, that ascertainment of this price does not dispense with the necessity for agreement in respect of the term during which the price is to apply. Agreement upon a maximum payable this month or to-day is not the same as an agreement that it shall continue to be payable next month or to-morrow. Seller and buyer understood that the price to be fixed in December for a term to be agreed upon would not be more than the price then charged by the Canadian Export Paper Company to the large consumers. They did not understand that, if during the term so established the price charged by the Canadian Export Paper Company was changed, the price payable to the seller would fluctuate accordingly. This was conceded by plaintiff's counsel on the argument before us. The seller was to receive no more during the running of the prescribed term, though the Canadian Maximum was raised. The buyer was to pay no less during that term, though the maximum was lowered. In the brief, the standard was to be applied at the beginning of the successive terms, but once applied was to be maintained until the term should have expired. While the term was unknown, the contract was inchoate.

The argument is made that there was no need of an agreement as to time unless the price to be paid was lower than the maximum. We find no evidence of this intention in the language of the contract. The result would then be that the defendant would never know where it stood. The plaintiff was under no duty to accept the Canadian standard. It does not assert that it was. What it asserts is that the contract amounted to the concession of an option. Without an agreement as to time, however, there would be not one option, but a dozen. The Canadian price to-day might be less than the Canadian price to-morrow. Election by the buyer to proceed with performance at the price prevailing in one month would not bind it to proceed at the price prevailing in another. Successive options to be exercised every month would thus be read into the contract. Nothing in the wording discloses the intention of the seller to place itself to that extent at the mercy of the buyer. Even if, however, we were to interpolate the restriction that the option, if exercised at all, must be exercised only once, and for the entire quantity permitted, the difficulty would not be ended. Market prices in 1920 happened to rise. The importance of the time element becomes apparent when we ask ourselves what the seller's position would be if they had happened to fall. Without an agreement as to time, the maximum would be lowered from one shipment to another with every reduction of the standard. With such an agreement, on the other hand, there would be stability and certainty. The parties attempted to guard against the contingency of failing to come together as to price. They did not guard against the contingency of failing to come together as to time. Very likely they thought the latter contingency so remote that it could safely be disregarded. In any event, whether through design or through inadvertence, they left the gap unfilled. The result was nothing more than "an agreement to agree." St. Regis Paper Co. v. Hubbs & Hastings Paper Co., 235 N.Y. 30, 36, 138 N.E. 495. Defendant "exercised its legal right" when it insisted that there was need of something more. St. Regis Paper Co. v. Hubbs & Hastings Paper Co., supra; 1 Williston Contracts, § 45. The right is not affected by our appraisal of the motive. Mayer v. McCreery, 119 N.Y. 434, 440, 23 N.E. 1045.

We are told that the defendant was under a duty, in default of an agreement, to accept a term that would be reasonable in view of the nature of the transaction and the practice of the business. To hold it to such a standard is to make the contract over. The defendant reserved the privilege of doing its business in its own way, and did not undertake to conform to the practice and beliefs of others. United Press v. New York Press Co., 164 N.Y. 406, 413, 58 N.E. 527, 53 L. R. A. 288. We are told again that there was a duty, in default of other agreement, to act as if the successive terms were to expire every month. The contract says they are to expire at such intervals as the agreement may prescribe. There is need, it is true, of no high degree of ingenuity to show how the parties, with little change of language, could have framed a form of contract to which obligation would attach. The difficulty is that they framed another. We are not at liberty to revise while professing to construe.

We do not ignore the allegation of the complaint that the contract price charged by the Canadian Export Paper Company to the large consumers "constituted a definite and well-defined standard of price that was readily ascertainable." The suggestion is made by members of the court that the price so charged may have been known to be one established for the year, so that fluctuation would be impossible. If that was its character, the complaint should so allege. The writing signed by the parties calls for an agreement as to time. The complaint concedes that no such agreement has been made. The result, prima facie, is the failure of the contract. In that situation the pleader has the burden of setting forth the extrinsic circumstances, if there are any, that make agreement unimportant. There is significance, moreover, in the attitude of counsel. No point is made in brief or in argument that the Canadian price, when once established, is constant through the year. On the contrary, there is at least a tacit assumption that it varies with the market. The buyer acted on the same assumption when it renewed the demand from month to month, making tender of performance at the prices then prevailing. If we misconceive the course of dealing, the plaintiff by amendment of its pleading can correct our misconception. The complaint as it comes before us leaves no escape from the conclusion that agreement in respect of time is as essential to a completed contract as agreement in respect of price. The agreement was not reached, and the defendant is not bound.

The question is not here whether the defendant would have failed in the fulfillment of its duty by an arbitrary refusal to reach any agreement as to time after notice from the plaintiff that it might make division of the terms in any way it pleased. No such notice was given, so far as the complaint discloses. The action is not based upon a refusal to treat with the defendant and attempt to arrive at an agreement. Whether any such theory of liability would be tenable we need not now inquire. Even if the plaintiff might have stood upon the defendant's denial of obligation as amounting to such a refusal, it did not elect to do so. Instead, it gave its own construction to the contract, fixed for itself the length of the successive terms, and thereby coupled its demand with a condition which there was no duty to accept. Rubber Trading Co. v. Manhattan Rubber Mfg. Co., 221 N.Y. 120, 116 N.E. 789; 3 Williston, Contracts, § 1334. We find no allegation of readiness, and offer to proceed on any other basis. The condition being untenable, the failure to comply with it cannot give a cause of action.

The order of the Appellate Division should be reversed, and that of the Special Term affirmed, with costs in the Appellate Division and in this court, and the question certified answered in the negative.

CRANE, JUDGE. (dissenting). I cannot take the view of this contract that has been adopted by the majority. The parties to this transaction beyond question thought they were making a contract for the purchase and sale of 16,000 tons rolls news print. The contract was upon a form used by the defendant in its business, and we must suppose that it was intended to be what it states to be, and not a trick or device to defraud merchants. It begins by saying that, in consideration of the mutual covenants and agreements herein set forth the Remington Paper & Power Company, Incorporated, of Watertown, state of New York, hereinafter called the seller, agrees to sell and hereby does sell and the Sun Printing & Publishing Association of New York City, state of New York, hereinafter called the purchaser, agrees to buy and pay for and hereby does buy the following paper, 16,000 tons rolls news print. The sizes are then given. Shipment is to be at the rate of 1,000 tons per month to December, 1920, inclusive. There are details under the headings consignee, specifications, price and delivery, terms, miscellaneous, cores, claims, contingencies, cancellations.

Under the head of miscellaneous comes the following:

"The price agreed upon between the parties hereto, for all papers shipped during the month of September, 1919, shall be $3.73 ¾ per hundred pounds gross weight of rolls on board cars at mills.

"The price agreed upon between the parties hereto for all shipments made during the months of October, November and December, 1919, shall be $4.00 per hundred pounds gross weight of rolls on board cars at mills.

"For the balance of the period of this agreement the price of the paper and length of terms for which such price shall apply shall be agreed upon by and between the parties hereto fifteen days prior to the expiration of each period for which the price and length of term thereof has been previously agreed upon, said price in no event to be higher than the contract price for news print charged by the Canadian Export Paper Company to the large consumers, the seller to receive the benefit of any differentials in freight rates.

"It is understood and agreed by the parties hereto that the tonnage specified herein is for use in the printing and publication of the various editions of the Daily and Sunday New York Sun, and any variation from this will be considered a breach of contract."

After the deliveries for September, October, November, and December, 1919, the defendant refused to fix any price for the deliveries during the subsequent months, and refused to deliver any more paper. It has taken the position that this document was no contract; that it meant nothing; that it was formally executed for the purpose of permitting the defendant to furnish paper or not, as it pleased.

Surely these parties must have had in mind that some binding agreement was made for the sale and delivery of 16,000 tons rolls of paper, and that the instrument contained all the elements necessary to make a binding contract. It is a strain upon reason to imagine the paper house, the Remington Paper & Power Company, Incorporated, and the Sun Printing & Publishing Association, formally executing a contract drawn up upon the defendant's prepared form which was useless and amounted to nothing. We must, at least, start the examination of this agreement by believing that these intelligent parties intended to make a binding contract. If this be so, the court should spell out a binding contract, if it be possible. . . .

But, while all agree that the price on the 15th day of December could be fixed, the further objection is made that the period during which that price should continue was not agreed upon. There are many answers to this.

We have reason to believe that the parties supposed they were making a binding contract; that they had fixed the terms by which one was required to take and the other to deliver; that the Canadian Export Paper Company price was to be the highest that could be charged in any event. These things being so, the court should be very reluctant to permit a defendant to avoid its contract. Wakeman v. Wheeler & Wilson Mfg. Co., 101 N.Y. 205, 4 N.E. 264, 54 Am. Rep. 676.

On the 15th of the fourth month, the time when the price was to be fixed for subsequent deliveries, there was a price charged by the Canadian Export Paper Company to large consumers. As the defendant failed to agree upon a price, made no attempt to agree upon a price, and deliberately broke its contract, it could readily be held to deliver the rest of the paper, 1,000 rolls a month, at this Canadian price. There is nothing in the complaint which indicates that this is a fluctuating price, or that the price of paper as it was on December 15th was not the same for the remaining 12 months. Or we can deal with this contract month by month. The deliveries were to be made 1,000 tons per month. On December 15th 1,000 tons could have been demanded. The price charged by the Canadian Export Paper Company on the 15th of each month on and after December 15, 1919, would be the price for the 1,000–ton delivery for that month. Or, again, the word as used in the miscellaneous provision quoted is not "price," but "contract price"—"in no event to be higher than the contract price." Contract implies a term or period, and, if the evidence should show that the Canadian contract price was for a certain period of weeks or months, then this period could be applied to the contract in question. Failing any other alternative, the law should do here what it has done in so many other cases—apply the rule of reason and compel parties to contract in the light of fair dealing. It could hold this defendant to deliver its paper as it agreed to do, and take for a price the Canadian Export Paper Company contract price for a period which is reasonable under all the circumstances and conditions as applied in the paper trade.

To let this defendant escape from its formal obligations when any one of these rulings as applied to this contract would give a practical and just result is to give the sanction of law to a deliberate breach. Wood v. Lucy, Lady Duff–Gordon, 222 N.Y. 88, 118 N.E. 214. . . .

For these reasons I am for the affirmance of the courts below.

Questions

1. Would Judge Cardozo have had to "make a contract for the parties" in order to find a contract here? Do the facts in the opinion provide sufficient basis for implying a promise to pay a specific price for a specific time?

2. Did the parties intend to be bound? If so, should the courts allow that intention to be frustrated in circumstances like these? Does the majority or dissenting opinion better implement the autonomy principle?

3. Would the result in *Sun Printing* differ if it were governed by the U.C.C.? Should it? See U.C.C. §§ 2–204(3), 2–305.

4. *Problem.*

Roger held the lease for a decorator showroom in The Mart. The initial term was for four years, "renewable at the tenant's option for an additional four years, rental to be agreed on the basis of comparable rental opportunities at the time." When Roger exercised the option, the parties failed to agree on an adjusted rental. The Mart gave Roger notice to vacate the premises. What should you advise him? See Walker v. Keith, 382 S.W.2d 198, 204 (Ky.1964).

ARNOLD PALMER GOLF CO. v. FUQUA INDUSTRIES, INC.

United States Court of Appeals, Sixth Circuit 1976.
541 F.2d 584.

McCree, Circuit Judge. This is an appeal from the district court's grant of summary judgment in favor of defendant Fuqua Industries, Inc. (Fuqua) in an action for breach of contract. The district court determined that a document captioned "Memorandum of Intent" and signed by both parties was not a contract because it evidenced the intent of the parties not to be contractually bound. We reverse and remand for trial.

Arnold Palmer Golf Company (Palmer) was incorporated under Ohio law in 1961, and has been primarily engaged in designing and marketing various lines of golf clubs, balls, bags, gloves, and other golf accessories. Palmer did none of its own manufacturing, but engaged other companies to produce its products. In the late 1960's, Palmer's management concluded that it was essential for future growth and profitability to acquire manufacturing facilities.

To that end, in January, 1969, Mark McCormack, Palmer's Executive Vice–President, and E. D. Kenna, Fuqua's President, met in New York City to consider a possible business relationship between the two corporations. The parties' interest in establishing a business relationship continued and they held several more meetings and discussions where the general outline of the proposed relationship was defined. In November 1969, Fuqua, with Palmer's assistance and approval, acquired Fernquest and Johnson, a Calfornia manufacturer of golf clubs. The minutes of the Fuqua Board of Directors meeting on November 3, 1969, reveal that Fuqua:

proposed that this Corporation participate in the golf equipment industry in association with Arnold Palmer Golf Co. and Arnold Palmer Enterprises, Inc. The business would be conducted in two parts. One part would be composed of a corporation engaged in the manufacture and sale of golf clubs and equipment directly related to the playing of the game of golf. This Corporation would be owned to the extent of 25% by Fuqua and 75% by the Arnold Palmer interests. Fuqua would transfer the Fernquest & Johnson business to the new corporation as Fuqua's contribution.

In November and December of 1969 further discussions and negotiations occurred and revised drafts of a memorandum of intent were distributed.

The culmination of the discussions was a six page document denominated as a Memorandum of Intent. It provided in the first paragraph that:

> This memorandum will serve to confirm the general understanding which has been reached regarding the acquisition of 25% of the stock of Arnold Palmer Golf Company ("Palmer") by Fuqua Industries, Inc. ("Fuqua") in exchange for all of the outstanding stock of Fernquest and Johnson Golf Company, Inc. ("F & J"), a wholly-owned California subsidiary of Fuqua, and money in the amount of $700,000; and for the rendition of management services by Fuqua.

The Memorandum of Intent contained detailed statements concerning, *inter alia*, the form of the combination, the manner in which the business would be conducted, the loans that Fuqua agreed to make to Palmer, and the warranties and covenants to be contained in the definitive agreement.

Paragraph 10 of the Memorandum of Intent stated:

> (10) *Preparation of Definitive Agreement*. Counsel for Palmer and counsel for Fuqua will proceed as promptly as possible to prepare an agreement acceptable to Palmer and Fuqua for the proposed combination of businesses. Such agreement will contain the representations, warranties, covenants and conditions, as generally outlined in the example submitted by Fuqua to Palmer....

In the last paragraph of the Memorandum of Intent, the parties indicated that:

> (11) *Conditions*. The obligations of Palmer and Fuqua shall be subject to fulfillment of the following conditions:
>
> > (i) preparation of the definitive agreement for the proposed combination in form and content satisfactory to both parties and their respective counsel;
> >
> > (ii) approval of such definitive agreement by the Board of Directors of Fuqua.; ...

The Memorandum of Intent was signed by Palmer and by the President of Fuqua. Fuqua had earlier released a statement to the press upon Palmer's signing that "Fuqua Industries, Inc., and The Arnold Palmer Golf Co. have agreed to cooperate in an enterprise that will serve the golfing industry, from the golfer to the greens keeper."

In February, 1970, the Chairman of Fuqua's Board of Directors, J. B. Fuqua, told Douglas Kenna, Fuqua's President, that he did not want to go through with the Palmer deal. Shortly thereafter Kenna informed one of Palmer's corporate officers that the transaction was terminated.

Palmer filed the complaint in this case on July 24, 1970. Nearly three and one-half years later, on January 14, 1974, the defendant filed a motion for summary judgment. More than one year after the briefs had been filed by the parties, on May 30, 1975, the district court granted defendant's motion.

The district court determined that:

> The parties were not to be subject to any obligations until a definitive agreement satisfactory to the parties and their counsel had been prepared. The fact that this agreement had to be "satisfactory" implies necessarily that such an agreement might be unsatisfactory. . . . The parties by the terms they used elected not to be bound by this memorandum and the Court finds that they were not bound.

The primary issue in this case is whether the parties intended to enter into a binding agreement when they signed the Memorandum of Intent, and the primary issue in this appeal is whether the district court erred in determining this question on a motion for summary judgment. . . .

We agree with the district court that both parties must have a clear understanding of the terms of an agreement and an intention to be bound by its terms before an enforceable contract is created. . . .

[W]e determine that our proper course is to remand this case to the district court for trial because we believe that the issue of the parties' intention to be bound is a proper one for resolution by the trier of fact. Upon first blush it may appear that the Memorandum of Intent is no more than preliminary negotiation between the parties. A cursory reading of the conditions contained in paragraph 11, by themselves, may suggest that the parties did not intend to be bound by the Memorandum of Intent.

Nevertheless, the memorandum recited that a "general understanding (had) been reached." And, . . . the entire document and relevant circumstances surrounding its adoption must be considered in making a determination of the parties' intention.[3] In this case we find an extensive document that appears to reflect all essential terms concerning the

---

3. Parties may orally or by informal memoranda, or by both, agree upon all essential terms of the contract and effectively bind themselves, if that is their intention, even though they contemplate the execution, at a later time, of a formal document to memorialize their undertaking. *Comerata v. Chaumont, Inc.*, 52 N.J.Super. 299, 145 A.2d 471 (1958).

transfer of Arnold Palmer stock to Fuqua in exchange for all outstanding stock in Fernquest and Johnson. The form of combination, the location of the principal office of Palmer, the license rights, employment contracts of Palmer personnel and the financial obligations of Fuqua are a few of the many areas covered in the Memorandum of Intent, and they are all described in unqualified terms. The Memorandum states, for instance, that "Fuqua *will* transfer all of the ... stock," that the "principal office of Palmer *will* be moved to Atlanta," that "Palmer ... *shall* possess an exclusive license," and that "Fuqua agrees to advance to Palmer up to an aggregate of $700,000." (Emphasis added.)

Paragraph 10 of the Memorandum states, also in unqualified language, that counsel for the parties "will proceed as promptly as possible to prepare an agreement acceptable to [the parties]...." We believe that this paragraph may be read merely to impose an obligation upon the parties to memorialize their agreement. We do not mean to suggest that this is the correct interpretation. The provision is also susceptible to an interpretation that the parties did not intend to be bound.

As we have indicated above, it is permissible to refer to extrinsic evidence to determine whether the parties intended to be bound by the Memorandum of Intent. In this regard, we observe that Fuqua circulated a press release in January 1970 that would tend to sustain Palmer's claim that the two parties intended to be bound by the Memorandum of Intent. Fuqua's statement said that the two companies "have agreed to cooperate in an enterprise that will serve the golfing industry."

Upon a review of the evidence submitted in connection with the motion for summary judgment, we believe that there is presented a factual issue whether the parties contractually obligated themselves to prepare a definitive agreement in accordance with the understanding of the parties contained in the Memorandum of Intent.... Because the facts and the inferences from the facts in this case indicate that the parties may have intended to be bound by the Memorandum of Intent, we hold that the district court erred in determining that no contract existed as a matter of law.

Questions

1. What was the issue on appeal in this case? What did the appellate court decide? According to the appellate court, did the Memorandum of Intent bind the parties?

2. In your view, should the Memorandum of Intent bind the parties? What facts would support the view that they should be bound? What facts cut against that conclusion? To what should they be bound, if they should be bound to anything?

3. What implications does this case have should you be asked to draft or review the draft of a memorandum or letter of intent or the equivalent?

4. *Problem.*

Otherwise on the facts of *Arnold Palmer Golf Co.*, assume that, for lack of an intention to be bound, the Memorandum of Intent did not bind the parties to go through with the deal combining the two businesses. The parties' lawyers prepared a final, formal and definitive agreement implementing the Memorandum. Fuqua, however, refused to sign that agreement. It objected to a "boilerplate" clause providing that the written contract was the parties' final and complete agreement, such that there were no oral understandings or agreements affecting their rights. It would not negotiate on the issue, which had not been addressed in the Memorandum of Intent. Fuqua did not object to any of the terms that had been in the Memorandum of Intent, and there were no other substantive terms. The deal fell through. Might Fuqua be in breach of any contract? See Teachers Ins. & Annuity Ass'n v. Tribune Co., 670 F.Supp. 491 (S.D.N.Y. 1987).

NOTE ON AGREEMENTS IN NEGOTIATIONS

Contracts, of course, are often the product of negotiations. Negotiations may take place by making legal offers and counteroffers, as in several cases in the preceding section. To be sure, an offeror may make an offer that is accepted without further ado; in that case, there may be a contract without negotiation. As soon as the offeree makes a counteroffer, however, negotiations have commenced. Negotiations also may take place before anyone makes a legal offer. In that case, the parties make proposals and counterproposals, reaching agreement point-by-point until agreement is reached on the final whole. The whole agreement then may be concluded orally or recorded in a document that is either signed by both parties simultaneously or sent by one to the other for signature in duplicate.

When negotiations proceed point-by-point before anyone makes a legal offer, an agreement on a point is normally not intended or understood to have legal consequences unless and until agreement is reached on the final whole. Courts, of course, should not enforce such agreements in the course of negotiations. Since the parties have not reached a final agreement, they have not made the commitments required for contract formation. Indefiniteness is likely to be a problem; enforcement would involve the courts in judgments of what a party should have found acceptable. Such judgments plainly violate the autonomy principle and, unless a special statute authorizes compulsion, they invade the unregulated sector of the economy.

In some cases, however, agreements in the course of negotiations are intended to have legal consequences before the parties reach or formalize the final agreement. In principle, there is no reason why an agreement made during negotiations cannot have legal effect if it is not too indefinite and the parties intend to be bound.

NOTE ON GOOD FAITH IN NEGOTIATIONS

Unlike some European legal systems, the U.S. legal system contains no general duty to negotiate in "good faith." Such a duty would require parties to act fairly and reasonably in all contract negotiations, subject to legal liability for failing to do so. Despite the urgings of some scholars, U.S. courts generally refrain from second-guessing the parties' decisions to hang tough even to the point of terminating negotiations after considerable investments of effort by both sides. Compelling people to deal or to deal on terms they have not accepted voluntarily runs afoul of the autonomy principle. See, e.g., Friedrich Kessler and Edith Fine, Culpa in Contrahendo, *Bargaining in Good Faith, and Freedom of Contract: A Comparative Study,* 77 Harv. L. Rev. 401 (1964).

However, the fact that parties are engaged in contract negotiations does not immunize them from liability for misconduct, and the misconduct can affect the formation of their contract. A negotiating party would be guilty of assault for using a gun to make an offer the other party cannot refuse; moreover, the duress would invalidate any agreement reached under the threat. Restatement (Second) of Contracts §§ 175–76. A car salesman who turns back the speedometer on a used car would be liable in tort for fraud when the other party relies on the misrepresentation to its detriment, and the contract could be voided. Id. §§ 162–64. Restitution may be available to restore benefits conferred during negotiations, as when an architect provides plans for a project that falls through, and the recipient uses the plans on another project. Hill v. Waxberg, 237 F.2d 936 (9th Cir.1956). In a way, these liabilities are special good faith duties in negotiations. Such duties do not require fair and reasonable conduct in general. Rather, they constrain the use of force and lies, and avoid windfalls, to support the negotiation of genuine agreements reached by the parties on a voluntary basis. See generally E. Allan Farnsworth, *Precontractual Liability and Preliminary Agreements: Fair Dealing and Failed Negotiations,* 87 Colum. L. Rev. 217 (1987).

In addition, the parties are free to make agreements in the course of negotiations, which agreements can be enforceable contracts. For example, the negotiating parties may need a survey of a tract of land while negotiating a joint venture to build a shopping mall. They may agree to share the expenses of a surveyor while they continue their negotiations on the joint venture. The preliminary agreement may be a contract whether or not the main agreement on the joint venture is ever concluded. The following cases involve obligations of good faith resulting from similar agreements by the parties.

A/S APOTHEKERNES LABORATORIUM FOR SPECIALPRAEPARATER v. I.M.C. CHEMICAL GROUP, INC.

United States Court of Appeals, Seventh Circuit, 1989.
873 F.2d 155.

Coffey, Circuit Judge. This is a diversity case arising from Apothekernes' unsuccessful attempt to purchase the Biochemical Division of IMC. The parties negotiated for some months in an attempt to reach an agreement on the terms of the sale. In February of 1978, the two companies' negotiators were finally able to agree on all terms. However, IMC's board of directors refused to approve the deal. Apothekernes filed this action asserting state law claims of breach of contract, fraud and estoppel. Following a bench trial, the district court, 678 F.Supp. 193 (N.D.Ill.1988) entered judgment in favor of IMC on all counts. We affirm.

I.

Apothekernes brought this suit against IMC on the theories of breach of contract, fraud and estoppel, seeking damages and specific performance of what it perceived as a consummated deal for the sale of IMC's Biochemical Division....

The case ... proceeded to a bench trial and the district court made the following findings of fact and conclusions of law. In March of 1977, Apothekernes, through its president, E.W. Sissener, began negotiating with IMC and its president and chief executive officer, Dr. M.B. Gillis, for the purchase of various of IMC's assets. During the month of December in 1977, the scope of the deal had narrowed to the point that the parties were talking about the purchase of certain, though not all, of IMC's Terre Haute plant facilities. On the 9th of December 1977, the parties signed a letter "intended to set forth the terms upon which we and/or our nominee intend to negotiate and consummate an Agreement of Sale relative to the purchase of certain assets of the Biochemical Division of IMC...." The letter set forth and delineated those matters upon which Sissener and Gillis had previously reached substantial agreement, as well as those issues that required further negotiation. The letter then concluded that "[a]ll of the above is subject to our concluding an Agreement of Sale which shall be acceptable to the Boards of Directors of our respective corporations, whose discretion shall in no way be limited by this letter.... In the interim, [IMC] agree[s] not to initiate negotiations or discussions intended to lead to negotiations with others for the sale of these same assets." Finally, the letter provided for an Agreement of Sale to be executed within 60 days of December 9, 1977.

Initially, the court found that the December 9, 1977 letter of intent did not constitute a binding contract for the sale of IMC's assets, but that it did serve to obligate both parties to bargain in good faith with the goal of eventually reaching agreement. According to the district court, although negotiations proceeded in good faith, by February 23, 1978 the parties still had not resolved their differences on three matters that the court considered "deal breakers." The court concluded that because the sixty day period in which the parties had agreed to execute a final agreement had expired, Gillis was no longer obligated to continue negotiations and could have broken them off at any time. Nonetheless, Sissener capitulated on the three points of contention on February 24, and the court found that at that time, the parties had reached a "meeting of the minds on all substantial terms." The court specifically found that up to this point, Gillis had negotiated in good faith and had reached agreement with Sissener.

According to the district court, the February 24 meeting of the minds did not, however, constitute a binding contract of sale. Though it determined that the lack of a final executed written draft did not preclude finding an intent to contract on February 24, it did find that the board approval provision in the December 9 letter of intent prevented the formalization of a binding contract absent the approval of IMC's board of directors. The court also found that though Gillis "had perhaps indicated to Sissener his confidence that board approval would be forthcoming, there was no certainty that it would be granted." Instead, the district court found that the board approval provision was explicit in the letter of intent; Gillis had neither the authority nor the apparent authority to bind IMC to the sale of substantial corporate assets, especially when the deal would have involved joint use of a production facility. Nor was the board bound by the letter of intent to accept the terms of the February 24 deal, even though it was reasonably in accord with the terms in the letter of intent; the letter of intent explicitly reserved to the board unlimited discretion to either accept or reject the deal.

Before taking the agreement to the IMC board of directors for approval, Gillis initially went to discuss the matter with Lenon, the president of IMC's parent, as he told Sissener he would do. The court found that at the Gillis–Lenon meeting, Gillis did not take it upon himself to advocate the agreement, but rather focused on the protracted nature of the negotiations leading up to the agreement. Lenon in turn summarily rejected the deal. Lenon's decision was, according to the district court, binding on Gillis and IMC's board of directors. Accordingly, Gillis convened a telephone meeting of the board and induced them to reject the sale. The court concluded that the fact that the board's decision was not an independent one, but instead was a rubber-stamp for Lenon's decision, was in no way improper. It found that Lenon could reject the sale to the same extent that the IMC board could reject the sale. Having determined that the letter of intent reserved to the board of directors the right to reject the deal, the court concluded that, "[b]efore there was a contract the IMC board had to approve what its negotiator had approved, and the IMC board would not approve unless Lenon approved, and Lenon said no. There was no contract." Accordingly, the district court entered judgment in favor of IMC on all counts, which judgment Apothekernes now appeals.

II.

Apothekernes presents two arguments on appeal. First, it argues that the February 24 meeting of the minds constituted a binding contract which IMC breached by refusing to go through with the proposed sale. Alternatively, Apothekernes argues that the December 9 letter of intent imposed a duty upon IMC to negotiate in good faith, which IMC breached when its board of directors rejected the proposal. We address each of these arguments.

A. The February 24 Meeting of the Minds

The district court found that on February 24, following Sissener's capitulation on the three deal-breaking points, Sissener and Gillis had reached a meeting of the minds on all substantial points. All that remained to be accomplished was to formalize the agreement in writing and obtain the approval of the boards of directors of both parties. The question is whether either of these remaining steps were prerequisites to the formation of a binding contract, or whether the meeting of the minds in and of itself served to bind both parties to the sale.

Under Illinois law, courts focus on the parties' intentions to determine whether an enforceable contract comes into being during the course of negotiations, or whether some type of formalization of the agreement is required before it becomes binding. *Itek Corporation v. Chicago Aerial Industries, Inc.*, 248 A.2d 625, 629 (Del.1968) (applying Illinois law). The fact that some matters may have been left for future agreement does not necessarily preclude a finding of intent to contract during preliminary negotiations. *Borg–Warner Corp. v. Anchor Coupling Co.*, 16 Ill.2d 234, 243–44, 156 N.E.2d 513, 517–18 (1958). Courts look to all of the circumstances surrounding the negotiations, including the actions of the principals both during and after, to determine what the parties intended. *Itek,* 248 A.2d at 629. The intent of the parties in circumstances such as these is a question of fact, and we will not set aside the fact finder's determination on this issue unless it is clearly erroneous. *Lambert Corp. v. Evans*, 575 F.2d 132, 136 (7th Cir. 1978)....

In this case, the district court made two factual findings regarding what IMC and Apothekernes intended. First, it found that the parties did not intend the lack of a formally drawn and executed agreement to prevent formation of a binding obligation. Nevertheless, the court concluded that the absence of approval by IMC's board of directors prevented a finding that the parties intended to be bound by their February 24 meeting of the minds. In making this determination, the district court relied on the specific terms recited in the December 9 letter of intent as well as the circumstances surrounding the transaction itself. The letter explicitly stated that its terms were, "subject to our concluding an Agreement of Sale which shall be acceptable to the Board of Directors of our respective corporations, whose discretion shall in no way be limited by this letter...."

. . .

B. Breach of Duty to Negotiate in Good Faith

Apothekernes ... argued unsuccessfully in the district court that the December 9 letter of intent constituted a binding contract for the sale of IMC's assets. The district court correctly rejected this argument; as we recently stated in *Runnemede Owners, Inc. v. Crest Mortgage Corp.*, 861 F.2d 1053 (7th Cir.1988), the purpose and function of a preliminary letter of intent is not to bind the parties to their ultimate contractual objective. Instead, it is only "to provide the initial framework from which the parties might later negotiate a final ... agreement, if the deal works out." *Id.* at 1056; *Teachers Insurance and Annuity Ass'n v. Tribune Co.*, 670 F.Supp. 491, 498 (S.D.N.Y.1987). The district court nonetheless concluded that the December 9 letter of intent did impose upon the parties an obligation to negotiate in good faith. We agree that that conclusion was proper; a number of courts, including this court, have held that the terms of a letter of intent may impose such a duty. *Channel Home Centers v. Grossman*, 795 F.2d 291, 299 (3d Cir.1986).... Apothekernes argues that even if IMC did not breach a contract of sale, it did breach this duty to negotiate in good faith.

The obligation to negotiate in good faith has been generally described as preventing one party from, "renouncing the deal, abandoning the negotiations, or insisting on conditions that do not conform to the preliminary agreement." *Teachers Insurance*, 670 F.Supp. at 498. For instance, a party might breach its obligation to bargain in good faith by unreasonably insisting on a condition outside the scope of the parties' preliminary agreement, especially where such insistence is a thinly disguised pretext for scotching the deal because of an unfavorable change in market conditions. *Id.* at 506. The full extent of a party's duty to negotiate in good faith can only be determined, however, from the terms of the letter of intent itself. For example, our recent decision in *Feldman v. Allegheny International, Inc.*, 850 F.2d 1217 (7th Cir.1988), demonstrates how the terms of the letter of intent control the scope of the obligation to bargain in good faith. In that case, the letter provided only that the potential seller would not "hold discussions or negotiate with any person other than [the potential buyer] ... while the proposed acquisition [was] being pursued." 850 F.2d at 1219. With the exception of setting a minimum cash component for the proposed sale, the letter did not set forth any previously agreed upon terms much less provide a general framework within which the parties intended to conduct their negotiations. As it turned out, such a commitment was not much of a commitment at all. It simply bound the seller to negotiate exclusively with the buyer in good faith until they disagreed; this was the full extent of the parties' obligation. In the absence of any agreed upon terms or even a general framework within which to conduct the negotiations, the parties were free to insist on or reject any proposed terms to the contract that they wished. As we explained in *Feldman*,

> in a business transaction both sides presumably try to get the best of the deal. That is the essence of bargaining and the free market. And in the context of this case, no legal rule bounds the run of business interest. So one cannot characterize self-interest as bad faith. No particular demand in negotiations could be termed dishonest, even if it seemed outrageous to the other party. The proper recourse is to walk away from the bargaining table, not to sue for "bad faith" in negotiations.

Id. at 1223. Thus, the scope of any obligation to negotiate in good faith can only be determined from the framework the parties have established for themselves in their letter of intent.

Here, the district court found that Gillis did negotiate in good faith at all times and that he did reach agreement with Sissener on all substantial terms on February 24. In claiming that this duty was breached, Apothekernes does not argue that any of Gillis' actions leading up to the February 24 meeting of the minds evidenced bad faith in negotiation; it does not argue that Gillis insisted unreasonably on terms not contained in the letter of intent or attempted to alter terms already agreed upon. Instead, it argues that Gillis' obligations continued even after he and Sissener had reached agreement on the disputed terms. In short, Apothekernes argues that once the issues had been hammered out, IMC was further obligated by the letter of intent and its corresponding duty to negotiate in good faith to go ahead and approve the deal. The letter of intent, however, "was merely an agreement to *negotiate*, not a promise that those negotiations would be fruitful." *Feldman*, 850 F.2d at 1223 (emphasis added). A duty to *negotiate* in good faith does not encompass an automatic duty to approve the final deal. A letter of intent is no guarantee that the final contract will be concluded, even if the parties fulfill their good faith obligations. *Teachers Insurance*, 670 F.Supp. at 498.

Nor does the obligation to negotiate in good faith encompass any duty on the negotiator's part to advocate the deal to the ultimate decision maker. Apothekernes argues that Gillis breached his good faith duty by failing to more vigorously advocate the deal when he took it to Lenon for approval. In advancing this argument, Apothekernes erroneously relies upon broad principles dealing with the common law duty to perform contracts in good faith. Here, Gillis' duty to engage in good faith negotiations arose from the preliminary letter of intent, which established the framework for the negotiation process. It did not arise from principles of common law. Because nothing in the letter of intent provided that Gillis must act as an advocate for the proposed sale, he had no duty to do so....

III.

In conclusion, we hold that there was no contract for the sale of IMC's Biochemical Division to Apothekernes; therefore, there was no breach. Although IMC did agree to negotiate in good faith, it did not breach that duty. Accordingly, judgment in favor of IMC is AFFIRMED.

Questions

1. Why was there no contract for the sale of IMC's assets to Apothekernes?

2. Why was there a contract to negotiate in good faith? What would be bad faith? Should the agreement reached on February 24 obligate Gillis to

advocate approval to his board? Should it obligate the board to approve the agreement?

3. Should an agreement to negotiate in good faith be unenforceable because it is too indefinite for enforcement by a court?

ITEK CORP. v. CHICAGO AERIAL INDUS., INC.

Supreme Court of Delaware, 1968.
248 A.2d 625.

WOLCOTT, CHIEF JUSTICE. This is an appeal by Itek Corporation (Itek) from the grant of summary judgment for the defendants in a breach of contract action brought by Itek against Chicago Aerial Industries, Inc. (CAI) and individuals who collectively represented in the contract negotiations CAI and its controlling stockholders.

Both Itek and CAI are producers of photographic equipment. At the time of the events which ultimately led to this litigation, approximately 50% of the CAI stock was owned by its president and by the estates of two of its founders. The beneficiaries of the estates, particularly, desired to obtain cash for their CAI stock in order to diversify investments. Accordingly, in early 1964 the individual defendants, who made up a committee for the purpose, began to look for a way to realize cash for their CAI stock.

In the spring of 1964, Itek became interested in the acquisition of CAI's assets, either by merger or otherwise. CAI was interested in a combination of some sort with Itek which would produce cash for its stockholders.

Negotiations reached a climax in the fall of 1964 with the conditional acceptance by CAI of an offer by Itek to purchase all of CAI's assets at a total price based upon $12.00 per share of CAI stock plus one-twentieth of a share of Itek. This offer was intended to permit the passing on to CAI stockholders of approximately $13.00 per share in cash.

Ultimately, the agreement of the principal CAI stockholders to the Itek offer was obtained and the CAI Board agreed to recommend acceptance of the offer to the other CAI stockholders. The CAI acceptance was transmitted by telephone to Itek on January 4, 1965, subject to the following conditions:

(1) That Itek obtain the necessary financing;

(2) That an informal letter of intent be executed;

(3) That the details be worked out, and

(4) That formal documents be prepared to the satisfaction of the parties.

Itek arranged for the necessary financing and, on January 15, 1965, a letter of intent was drafted and signed by the parties. Since the letter is of prime importance in this lawsuit, it is set out in full:

"ITEK CORPORATION" January 15, 1965, "Chicago Aerial Industries, Inc. §§ 550 West Northwest Highway "Barrington, Illinois "Gentlemen:

"This is to confirm the terms on which Itek Corporation (Itek) and Chicago Aerial Industries, Inc. (CAI) have agreed, with the approval of their respective Board of Directors, to work towards a combination of the two companies through the purchase of the assets and assumption of specified liabilities of CAI by Itek, all subject to adoption of a plan of liquidation and approval of such sale by CAI stockholders:

"1. The purchase price to be paid by Itek for all of the assets of CAI (including name and goodwill), subject to the liabilities to be assumed by Itek, is $6,759,600 in cash plus 28,165 shares of Itek common stock, par value $1.00 per share, subject to proportionate increase for outstanding CAI stock options exercised after December 31, 1964. The liabilities of CAI to be assumed by Itek are only those which shall be shown in CAI's balance sheet as of December 31, 1964, together with any liabilities incurred in the ordinary course of business after that date and such other liabilities of CAI as the parties may agree upon.

"2. Itek and CAI shall make every reasonable effort to agree upon and have prepared as quickly as possible a contract providing for the foregoing purchase by Itek and sale by CAI, subject to the approval of CAI stockholders, embodying the above terms and such other terms and conditions as the parties shall agree upon. If the parties fail to agree upon and execute such a contract they shall be under no further obligation to one another.

"3. Pending the completion of the contract CAI will permit Itek and its representatives to examine CAI's finances, contracts and business and interview its officers and customers, all as designated by CAI, it being understood that CAI shall not be obligated to divulge trade secrets or confidential matters.

"4. Itek represents to CAI that Itek has received assurance from Time, Incorporated that Time, Incorporated, subject to the approval of its Board of Directors, is prepared to invest $4,350,000 in Itek convertible debentures and stock, and has received assurance from a director of an investment company that it is prepared to invest $1,200,000 for such debentures and stock. Both such investments would be contingent upon and for the purpose of financing the purchase by Itek of CAI assets.

"5. A joint announcement to the press in the form attached shall be made by both companies on the afternoon of January 19, 1965, for publication in the morning papers January 20.

"If you agree to the foregoing please so indicate by signing and returning the enclosed copy of this letter.

"Yours very truly,

"ITEK CORPORATION

"By Edwin D. Campbell

"Executive Vice President

"AGREED:

"CHICAGO AERIAL INDUSTRIES, INC.

"By Fred T. Sonne—President"

Thereafter, the parties commenced the preparation of a formal agreement. On February 23, 1965, CAI claimed that its potential tax liability would prohibit assuring the uncommitted CAI stockholders of an immediate distribution of $13.00 per share. Accordingly, CAI requested that Itek place a $3.00 floor on the value of the one-twentieth of a share of its stock, establish an escrow fund of $2.00 per share of CAI stock for the payment of all CAI liabilities, and guarantee payment of all CAI liabilities in excess of the escrow fund. Itek immediately agreed and so advised CAI on February 26, 1965.

Meanwhile, early in February, 1965, one of the committee representing CAI and its largest stockholders succeeded in reviving an earlier interest in purchasing CAI stock by Bourns, Inc. This culminated in a luncheon meeting between him and a Bourns representative on February 15, 1965. At this meeting, an offer was outlined under which Bourns would purchase the largest stockholders' CAI stock at $16.00 per share.

On February 23, 1965, as noted above, Itek and CAI representatives met and Itek agreed to the three new conditions insisted upon by CAI. Upon the departure of the Itek representatives, the CAI committee met with the representative of Bourns who was told that the CAI–Itek negotiations had reached an impasse and that they were free to go ahead with Bourns. On February 25, 1965, the formal Bourns offer was mailed, and on February 26, 1965, the principal stockholders accepted $1,000,000.00 in earnest money to cover the eventual sale of their CAI stock to Bourns at $16.00 per share.

On March 2, 1965, CAI by telegram notified Itek that it was terminating the transaction as a result of unforeseen circumstances and the failure on the part of the parties to reach agreement. This lawsuit followed.

Itek argues that the letter of January 15, 1965 is a binding contract and that CAI breached it by willfully refusing to negotiate in good faith toward the completion of the deal.

CAI argues that the letter of January 15, 1965 was, at most, a statement of intent, and was in no sense a binding contract. In particular, it points to the last sentence of paragraph 2 of the letter. That sentence is, "If the parties fail to agree upon and execute such a contract they shall be under no further obligation to one another." The argument is that since the parties in fact failed to agree upon a formal contract, the quoted sentence absolves CAI from liability.

The negotiations in this matter and all pertinent actions took place in Chicago which makes the law of Illinois applicable in the determination of whether or not Itek and CAI entered into an enforceable contract. Wilmington Trust Co. v. Pennsylvania Company, 40 Del.Ch. 1, 172 A.2d 63. We accordingly look to the law of Illinois to determine initially whether or not under any provable facts there is in existence an enforceable contract between Itek and CAI.

Under Illinois law, the question of whether an enforceable contract comes into being during the preliminary stages of negotiations, or whether its binding effect must await a formal agreement, depends on the intention of the parties. El Reno Wholesale Grocery Co. v. Stocking, 293 Ill. 494, 127 N.E. 642. In making that determination, the fact that some matters are left for future agreement among the parties does not necessarily preclude the finding that a binding agreement was entered into during the preliminary stages. Borg–Warner Corporation v. Anchor Coupling Co., 16 Ill.2d 234, 156 N.E.2d 513, 930.

In making that determination, the trier of fact, of necessity, must look at the circumstances surrounding the negotiations and the actions of the principals at the time and subsequently. Borg–Warner Corporation v. Anchor Coupling Co., supra. From all of these, the intention of the parties to be bound or not to be bound must be ascertained.

The trial judge, however, reached his decision solely because of the last sentence of paragraph 2 of the January 15, 1965 letter to the effect that the failure to execute a formal contract absolved the parties from "further obligation." We think, however, that it was error to separate the last sentence from the rest of paragraph 2. All its provisions must be read and considered together. If this is done, then it is apparent that the parties obligated themselves to "make every reasonable effort" to agree upon a formal contract, and only if such effort failed were they absolved from "further obligation" for having "failed" to agree upon and execute a formal contract. We think these provisions of the January 15 letter obligated each side to attempt in good faith to reach final and formal agreement.

We think the first issue to be resolved in this case is the existence or non-existence on January 15, 1965 of an enforceable agreement. If there was none, then obviously Itek's case falls. Under Illinois law, this decision is to be reached after consideration of the surrounding circumstances and what the parties intended and believed to have been the result. . . .

We have examined the record before us and are of the opinion that there is evidence which, if accepted by the trier of fact, would support the conclusion that on January 15, 1965 both Itek and CAI intended to be bound, the former to purchase and the latter to sell all the assets of CAI. There is also evidence which, if accepted by the trier of fact, would support the conclusion that subsequently, in order to permit its stockholders to accept a higher offer, CAI willfully failed to negotiate in good faith and to make "every reasonable effort" to agree upon a formal contract, as it was required to do. We do not say that the evidence requires these conclusions, particularly since they are contested by CAI, but we think the evidence would permit these conclusions.

There were, then, issues of material fact unresolved which make the disposition of the case against CAI on summary judgment inappropriate. CAI has failed to demonstrate to a reasonable certitude that there is no issue of fact which, if resolved in favor of Itek, would have held CAI liable. Therefore, summary judgment for CAI was improvidently granted. Allied Auto Sales, Inc. v. President, Directors and Company of Farmers Bank, Del., 216 A.2d 666.

With respect to the individual stockholders of CAI, a different situation exists. The contract, if there is a contract, was to purchase the assets of CAI at a price determined by a per share price of CAI stock. There was no contract between Itek and the CAI stockholders. This being the fact, it was proper to enter summary judgment in their favor.

The judgment below in favor of CAI will be reversed, and the judgment below in favor of the individual defendants will be affirmed.

Questions

1. What is the legal basis for finding an obligation to negotiate in good faith in *Itek Corp.*?

2. Should the obligation to negotiate in good faith be held too indefinite for enforcement here? What does it require?

3. Had the agreements in *A/S Apothekernes* and in *Itek Corp.* not contained promises pertaining to the contract formation process, should such promises have been implied? Should a general duty of good faith be required in all contract negotiations? If so, what should it require?

SECTION 3.   THE REQUIREMENT OF A WRITING

In 1677, the English Parliament passed "An Act for Prevention of Frauds and Perjuries," known as the "Statute of Frauds." All but three states in the U.S. now have general statutes of frauds in their law of contracts. These general statutes provide that agreements within certain categories of contracts are not enforceable unless memorialized in a signed writing. In addition, requirements that additional kinds of contracts be in writing can be found in various specialized statutes. For example, the United States Arbitration Act requires agreements to arbitrate to be in writing. 9 U.S.C. § 2.

Variations in the texts of statutes in different states make it hazardous to generalize on this topic. When a problem arises, you must consult the specific statute applicable to a concrete dispute and the case law construing it. In most cases, you will need to consider three main issues in light of the policies implemented by the statutory text.

The first main issue is whether the contract in question falls within the statute, and consequently must be in writing (unless exceptions apply). RESTATEMENT (SECOND) OF CONTRACTS § 110 sets forth five general categories that fairly reflect the common part in most state statutes. The more important categories are contracts in which one person promises to answer for the debt of another (the suretyship provision), contracts for the sale of an interest in land (the land contract provision), and contracts that cannot be performed within one year from their making (the one year provision). In addition, U.C.C. § 2–201 requires contracts for the sale of goods worth more than $500 to be in writing, subject to several exceptions. See Amended Article 2, § 2–201.

The second main issue concerns the conditions under which the statute of frauds is satisfied. In general, a writing must identify the contract parties and show that they made a contract, identify the subject matter, state the essential terms, and be signed. RESTATEMENT (SECOND) OF CONTRACTS § 131. U.C.C. § 2–201 requires only that the writing evidence a sale of goods, specify the quantity, and be signed or authenticated by the party to be charged. The writing need not be complete or formal. A price list on a scrap of paper, indicating the quantity and carrying the seller's initials, may satisfy § 2–201. See Southwest Engineering Co., Inc. v. Martin Tractor Co., Inc., 205 Kan. 684, 473 P.2d 18 (1970). In some cases, part performance of the alleged contract will satisfy the statute, as the performance itself may be reliable evidence of a real agreement. E.g., U.C.C. § 2–201(3).

The third main issue concerns the legal consequences of failing to satisfy the statute of frauds. No claim, counterclaim, set-off, or defense requiring enforcement of an oral contract will succeed when the contract is within the statute. However, the oral agreement is not void or voidable for all legal purposes. If a party who has not signed brings an action against one who has, defenses arising from the contract can be asserted against the one who has not signed. As in *Ardente v. Horan*, above at p. 39, a court will not raise the statute of frauds if a party does not. An oral agreement within the statute can be admitted into evidence for purposes other than its enforcement, and it can be the basis for an action in tort. The fact that an agreement is oral, moreover, should never preclude an action for restitution of a benefit conferred in performance of the contract, such as one seeking the return of a deposit or payment. RESTATEMENT (SECOND) OF CONTRACTS §§ 138–44.

The statute of frauds is not popular. If applied according to the plain meaning of its terms, a statute intended to prevent fraud will become an instrument of fraud in some cases. A lawyer is faced with an ethical question whether to comply with a client's wishes to plead the statute of frauds as a defense when the client admits that the contract was made. See Robert S. Stevens, *Ethics and the Statute of Frauds*, 37 CORNELL L.Q. 355 (1952). The statute has been almost eliminated in the country of its birth for several reasons: The categories of contracts within the statute bear no commonality distinguishing them from contracts outside it; business practice often dispenses with writings; and procedural changes in English law since 1677 have made the evidentiary value of a writing less critical. Law Reform (Enforcement of Contracts) Act, 1954, 2 & 3 Eliz. 2, c.34; Report of the Law Revision Committee on the Statute of Frauds and the Doctrine of Consideration 6–7 (Sixth Interim Report, Cmd. 5449, 1937). The United Nations Convention on Contracts for the International Sale of Goods, art. 11, does not require contracts within that convention to be in writing.

In the U.S., however, the problems have been left to the courts, producing a bewildering array of cases. Courts often manipulate the formal legal authorities and create exceptions to implement the statute's purposes. As the cases below will suggest, the courts sometimes take striking liberties with principles of legislative supremacy and statutory interpretation.

RESTATEMENT (SECOND) OF CONTRACTS § 110(1), 129, 131

VERMONT STATUTE OF FRAUDS
12 V.S.A. § 181.

§ 181. Agreements required to be written.

An action at law shall not be brought in the following cases unless the promise, contract or agreement upon which such action is brought or some memorandum or note thereof is in writing, signed by the party to be charged therewith or by some person thereunto by him lawfully authorized.

> (5) A contract for the sale of lands, tenements or hereditaments, or of an interest in or concerning them. Authorization to execute such a contract on behalf of another shall be in writing. . . .

CHOMICKY v. BUTTOLPH
Supreme Court of Vermont, 1986.
147 Vt. 128, 513 A.2d 1174.

HILL, JUSTICE. Defendants, Edward and Barbara Buttolph, appeal from the lower court's order granting specific performance of an alleged oral agreement for the sale of property. . . . We reverse the court's decree of specific performance on the basis that this dispute is properly resolved under the Statute of Frauds. . . .

Defendants are landowners of lakeside property on Lake Dunmore. Their property is divided by a road. Intending to retain title to the undeveloped back lot together with a 50–foot strip leading to the lake, defendants offered the front lakeside lot and summer cottage for sale.

Plaintiffs inspected the property, and entered into negotiations with defendants. The parties eventually reached an understanding, and plaintiffs' attorney drew up a purchase and sale contract that reflected the terms of their agreement. Both parties signed the contract in August, 1985; the closing was to occur in mid-October. The contract, however, was made contingent on the defendants obtaining a subdivision permit from the Leicester Planning Commission.

While defendants' subdivision petition was pending, plaintiff Eugene Chomicky telephoned defendants to discuss an alternative that would allow them to proceed with the sale in the event that the permit was denied. Plaintiff proposed that defendants retain an easement granting them a 50–foot right-of-way in lieu of outright ownership. Mr. Buttolph told Mr. Chomicky that they had considered that option, but that his wife was opposed to it. He agreed to discuss it with her again.

On October 1, Mr. Buttolph called the plaintiffs, and indicated that the right-of-way arrangement previously discussed was acceptable in the event that the Leicester Planning Commission did not approve their subdivision permit.

The Commission met on October 12, 1985, and denied defendants' permit application. On October 13, defendants called plaintiffs and advised them that "the deal was off." They now wanted to sell the whole parcel or nothing. Plaintiffs sued for specific performance on the oral contract allegedly concluded over the phone.

A contract involving the sale of land or interests therein is controlled by the Statute of Frauds. See 12 V.S.A. § 181(5). As a general rule, such contracts must be in writing to be enforceable. See *Couture v. Lowery*, 122 Vt. 239, 243, 168 A.2d 295, 298 (1961). Moreover, any proposed changes or modifications "are subjected to the same requirements of form as the original provisions." *Evarts v. Forte*, 135 Vt. 306, 311, 376 A.2d 766, 769 (1977).

According to plaintiffs, defendants have admitted to the existence of the oral contract in question, and are thus precluded from setting up the Statute of Frauds as a defense to this action. Plaintiffs cite a footnote in *Bryant v. Strong*, 141 Vt. 244, 245 n. 1, 448 A.2d 142, 143 n. 1 (1982), as controlling precedent on this issue. Even if we accept plaintiffs' characterization of the facts, a characterization which is very much contested by the defendants, we do not believe that such an admission takes the contract outside the Statute of Frauds.

First, ...

Second, while the writing requirement is imposed primarily as a shield against possible fraud, see *Couture, supra,* 122 Vt. at 243, 168 A.2d at 298, it also "promotes deliberation, seriousness, certainty, and shows that the act was a genuine act of volition." Rabel, *The Statute of Frauds and Comparative Legal History,* 63 L.Q. Rev. 174, 178 (1947). In short, it helps to ensure that contracts for the sale of land or interests therein are not entered into improvidently. Thus, in *Couture, supra,* 122

Vt. at 243, 168 A.2d at 298, we expressly stated that "[o]ne may admit the sale of land by a verbal contract, and yet defend an action for specific performance by pleading the statute." See also *Radke v. Brenon*, 271 Minn. 35, 37–38, 134 N.W.2d 887, 889–90 (1965) (fact that defendant admits parol contract sued upon does not preclude him from setting up and insisting upon the Statute of Frauds as a defense to the action)....

"The validation of an oral contract to convey real estate in spite of the prohibition against enforcement of the Statute of Frauds depends on the doctrine of part performance." *Jasmin v. Alberico*, 135 Vt. 287, 289, 376 A.2d 32, 33 (1977). The doctrine of part performance, as we have repeatedly stated, is invoked to give relief to those who substantially and irretrievably change their position in reliance on the oral agreement. *Id.* at 290, 376 A.2d at 34 (citing *Towsley v. Champlain Oil Co.*, 127 Vt. 541, 543, 254 A.2d 440, 442 (1969)).... Plaintiffs contend that the doctrine of part performance was properly invoked as they made financing arrangements, and conducted a title search in preparation for closing. "[A]ctivities in preparation for [a] proposed transfer of title ..., though perhaps troublesome, belong to that class of responsibilities that fall into the lot of any prospective seller [or purchaser] of real estate, and are not ... the kind of imposition supporting the equitable relief sought." *Towsley, supra*, 127 Vt. at 543–44, 254 A.2d at 442.

Plaintiffs also claim that their $5,000 downpayment constitutes sufficient reliance to warrant the granting of specific performance. This claim merits little or no comment as we have repeatedly emphasized that "money payments on the purchase are not enough to give the oral agreement enforceable status, even coupled with possession, in the face of the Statute of Frauds." *Jasmin, supra*, 135 Vt. at 290, 376 A.2d at 34....

Plaintiffs claim that they gave up other opportunities to acquire lakeside property in reliance on their oral agreement with defendants. This claim, however, cannot support an award of specific performance, as plaintiffs produced no evidence showing (1) that other properties were available, or (2) how they were precluded from pursuing such opportunities....

Judgment reversed as to court's decree of specific performance; judgment affirmed as to court's denial of plaintiffs' claim for damages.

Questions

1. Did the defendants in *Chomicky* deny that an agreement accepting the right-of-way arrangement was made? What is their defense? How does the plaintiff seek to overcome that defense?

2. Does the plaintiff have any contractual interests that the law should protect? Assuming the defendant admitted that an oral contract was made, are there any offsetting contractual interests that justify leaving the plaintiff's interests unprotected?

3. Why does the court reject the plaintiffs' argument? Is the holding required by the language of 12 V.S.A. § 181 or the policies implemented by

that statute? What are those policies in this court's view? Are they better implemented by rejecting or accepting the plaintiffs' argument?

RADKE v. BRENON

Supreme Court of Minnesota, 1965.
271 Minn. 35, 134 N.W.2d 887.

ROGOSHESKE, JUSTICE. Defendants appeal from a judgment of the district court decreeing specific performance of a contract for the sale of real estate.

The judgment was entered upon findings made after trial that "subsequent to the Defendant acquiring" the property in question they "did offer to sell the property to the Plaintiff for the sum of Two Hundred Sixty-two ($262.00) Dollars, which offer the Plaintiff did accept;" and that "at all times relevant, the Plaintiff has been ready, willing and able to complete the agreement for the sale of Defendants' property but the Defendants have refused to do so." The court concluded that defendants "have wrongfully and improperly failed and refused" to deliver a deed of the property to plaintiff.

Resolving the conflicts in the evidence in plaintiff's favor, as we must, these appear to be the facts. Plaintiff and defendants are neighbors owning adjoining lots in Wakefield Park addition in Ramsey County. At the times each acquired ownership, their lots and eight neighboring lots did not extend to the west shoreline of Wakefield Lake, located nearby. The strip of land between the shoreline of the lake and the east boundary of the platted lots was owned by Dr. Gulden, the developer of the addition, and his brother. They had been hopeful of selling the entire strip to the county for use of a park, but when the county finally declined the offer in 1956, Dr. Gulden attempted to sell to the several owners separated from the lake. These attempts were unsuccessful until December 1, 1959, when defendants acquired ownership of the entire strip. Preston Brenon, hereinafter referred to as defendant, was a licensed real estate agent. Following his purchase, he had the property surveyed, and on June 28, 1960, he sent an identical letter to plaintiff and the eight other neighbors offering to sell them the irregular parcels that separated their lots from the lake. In the letter he explained that since he was interested only in that part of the strip adjoining his property, he had no desire to retain the remainder. He stated he had "no desire to make any profit on this transaction if everyone owning adjoining property is willing to buy their portion" and divide the cost "equally among all 10 including [him]self." He itemized the total cost at $2,120 and offered to sell each lot for $212 on any terms agreeable. This letter was not signed by defendant but his name was typewritten thereon, he having authorized this and considered such to be tantamount to his signature. Previous to the receipt of this letter, plaintiff and defendant had discussed the latter's intent of acquiring the property for the neighborhood on at least two occasions. About 2 weeks after plaintiff received this offer, he orally accepted it. Sometime later, plaintiff learned from a neighbor that two neighbors declined to purchase, and thus the divided cost of each lot was increased to $262. Although he was agreeable to pay the increase, he did not immediately so inform defendant. Despite defendant's progress in completing sales to other interested neighbors, plaintiff, for reasons not explained except that he believed he was waiting for defendant to furnish him a copy of the survey and an abstract, delayed making a request for the abstract until May 7, 1961. On cross-examination, he admitted that the survey was received by him with the June 28 letter. In any event, it is clear that plaintiff accepted defendant's offer on May 7, at which time plaintiff knew of the price increase. Defendant testified:

"Q. . . . And did he agree to buy that time?

"A. At that time he did."

Later in May, defendant delivered to plaintiff a stub abstract covering entries from July 2, 1947, to May 9, 1961. At that time plaintiff offered "some money" but was told by defendant to "wait till it's all settled." There was a further delay before a title opinion could be given, made necessary when plaintiff's attorney insisted on procuring a complete abstract. On August 14, plaintiff delivered to his attorney a check for $262 payable to defendants for the purpose of completing the sale. On August 16, plaintiff's attorney wrote defendant informing him that he held the check for payment of the sale price to be delivered on receipt of a deed. Sometime after August 16, plaintiff received a letter from defendant dated August 16 informing him that the offer to sell was revoked.

From the time plaintiff bought his home in 1953, he occupied the parcel of land in dispute with consent of the owners. During the period it was owned by the Guldens, he cleaned, filled, graded, and planted grass upon it. However, after defendant purchased it, he did no more than continue to maintain the grass, fill in some "low spots that kind of wash away," and plant "a few trees."

The question is whether these facts establish a valid and enforceable contract for the sale of land. Defendants contend they do not.

As admitted by defendant, an oral contract to sell the land was made, and the trial court was clearly justified in so finding. There being no formal, integrated, written contract, however, the problem is whether the oral contract is unenforceable because it comes within Minn.St. 513.05[1] of the statute of frauds. Briefly, that provision decrees void any contract for the sale of lands unless the contract or some memorandum of the contract is in writing. The precise issue in this case is whether,

---

1. Minn.St. 513.05 provides: "Every contract for the leasing for a longer period than one year or for the sale of any lands, or any interest in lands, shall be void unless the contract, or some note or memorandum thereof, expressing the consideration, is in writing and subscribed by the party by whom the lease or sale is to be made, or by his lawful agent thereunto authorized in writing; and no such contract, when made by an agent, shall be entitled to record unless the authority of such agent be also recorded."

under the circumstances, the letter written by defendant offering the land to plaintiff is a memorandum sufficient to satisfy the requirements of the statute.

The statute expresses a public policy of preventing the enforcement by means of fraud and perjury of contracts that were never in fact made. To inhibit perversion of this policy by those who would deny an oral contract actually made, the statute itself permits enforcement of an oral contract if there exists a note or memorandum as evidence of the contract. To the courts, then, is left promotion of the policy of the statute, either by denying enforcement urged by defrauders or by granting enforcement against wrongful repudiators. As an aid in this objective, the statute itself lists some requisites of a memorandum and this court has added others, so that we have some indication of what content a memorandum normally must have in order to be sufficient evidence of the contract.

The statute requires that the writing express the consideration and that it be subscribed by the party by whom the sale is to be made or by his lawful agent authorized in writing. This court has stated that the memorandum is sufficient when, in addition to the above requirements, it states expressly or by necessary implication the parties to the contract, the lands involved, and the general terms and conditions upon which the sale will be made.[2]

These latter elements are clearly present in the letter written by defendant. Plaintiff's name is included in the inside address heading the letter, and Brenon's name is typewritten at the bottom. The land to be sold is positively delineated. The letter offers "their portion" to "everyone owning adjoining property," and the survey map accompanying the letter depicts each tract. Considering the conversation both before and after the letter was sent, it is inconceivable that the parties could be uncertain concerning the land to be sold. As to other terms of the contract, such as manner of payment, Brenon merely held himself ready "to work out any kind of terms" with the purchasers.

The elements expressly required by statute are not so obvious. First, the consideration of $212 stated in the letter is not the same as the $262 tendered in accord with the oral understanding. Despite this discrepancy, we think that the letter sufficiently expresses the consideration because the $212 represented an equal share of the cost divided by all ten interested parties. As Brenon said in the letter, "I feel the only fair way to share the cost is to divide equally among all 10 including myself." There is no dispute that the price was changed from that stated in the letter when two property owners declined to buy. The consideration then was simply a mathematical computation according to the formula specified in the letter.[3] We do not believe this variation in the dollar amount

2. Doyle v. Wohlrabe, 243 Minn. 107, 66 N.W.2d 757. . . .

3. This case thus differs from a case where no consideration at all is mentioned, such as William Weisman Realty Co. v. Cohen, 157 Minn. 161, 195 N.W. 898, or where the consideration expressed cannot be identified with reasonable certainty, as in

renders the letter's expression of the consideration insufficient, especially since plaintiff paid more under the admitted agreement than he would have paid according to the letter.

The necessity of a subscription presents the final problem. A "subscription" is the same as a "signing,"[4] and it is clear that Brenon's typewritten name, which according to his testimony was typed with the intent that it be tantamount to a written signature, is a sufficient subscription.[5] A problem here is that his wife, who owned the property with him in joint tenancy, apparently neither signed the letter nor authorized him in writing to sell her share. But this deficiency was at no time claimed or asserted before the trial court or in defendants' brief to this court. It was suggested for the first time upon oral argument. If it is a fact, it was not a part of the theory upon which the case was tried and submitted. We must therefore adhere to our well-settled rule that an unlitigated issue may not be asserted for the first time on appeal.[6]

We by no means intend to hold that Brenon's letter would be a sufficient memorandum in every case. We will overlook technical requirements only if proof of the oral contract is clear and uncontradicted as in this case where defendant admitted that a contract had been made. But those technical requirements are only aids to discern where the truth lies in a given case, and we will not blindly apply those technicalities if they lead to a conclusion repugnant to commonsense. As Professor Williston has said:

> "In brief, the Statute 'was intended to guard against the perils of perjury and error in the spoken word.' Therefore, if after a consideration of the surrounding circumstances, the pertinent facts and all the evidence in a particular case, the court concludes that enforcement of the agreement will not subject the defendant to fraudulent claims, the purpose of the Statute will best be served by holding the note or memorandum sufficient even though it be ambiguous or incomplete."[7]

Most persuasive is defendant's admission during trial that a contract was in fact made between plaintiff and himself. Although we have followed the majority rule that admission of the contract does not preclude assertion of the statute of frauds,[8] an admission that a contract was made certainly cannot be ignored when all other evidence submitted supports the same conclusion. Even though it may be argued that the

---

George v. Conhaim, 38 Minn. 338, 37 N.W. 791. See, also, D. M. Osborne & Co. v. Baker, 34 Minn. 307, 25 N.W. 606, where we held that "for value received" was a sufficient expression.

4. 2 Corbin, Contracts, § 521; 4 Williston, Contracts (3 ed.) § 585.

5. Conlan v. Grace, 36 Minn. 276, 30 N.W. 880; Restatement, Contracts, § 210.

6. E.g., American Surety Co. of New York v. Greenwald, 223 Minn. 37, 25 N.W.2d 681....

7. 4 Williston, Contracts (3 ed.) § 567A; 2 Corbin, Contracts, § 498.

8. Doyle v. Wohlrabe, supra; Holste v. Baker, 223 Minn. 321, 26 N.W.2d 473.... The rule is based on the belief that it is more important that a seller not be tempted to perjure himself by falsely denying a contract than it is to give effect to his judicial declarations....

formal requirements contemplated by the statute are lacking, when all the evidence is taken into account we are of the opinion that the letter should be held a sufficient memorandum in this case.[9] The policy of the statute of frauds would be perverted if the admitted contract were not enforced. The judgment of the trial court is therefore affirmed.

Questions

1. Did the letter offering the land to the plaintiff satisfy the requirements of Minn. St. § 513.05? Would it satisfy those stated in RESTATEMENT (SECOND) OF CONTRACTS § 131? Should it matter that the letter was merely an offer, not a completed contract? See RESTATEMENT (SECOND) OF CONTRACTS § 131, Ill. 2.

2. If the letter satisfies the statutory requirements, why would the court state: "We by no means intend to hold that Brenon's letter would be a sufficient memorandum in every case." If the letter is sufficient in this case, why should the same letter not be sufficient in any other case with the same facts? Is the court indicating that it will not treat like cases alike? What makes cases alike in the important respects, according to this court? Does the court pay appropriate respect to the principle of legislative supremacy?

3. Should the court in *Radke* have decided that the contract was unenforceable? Does the Minnesota statute make an exception for cases in which a party admits the oral contract was made? If not, of what relevance is the admission?

4. How does the Minnesota Supreme Court's view of the policies underlying the statute of frauds compare with the Vermont Supreme Court's view? Does *Chomicky v. Buttolph* cite *Radke v. Brenon* accurately? Were *Chomicky* governed by Minnesota law, would *Radke* require a different result?

———

U.C.C. §§ 2–201, 2–209

———

Amended U.C.C., § 2–201

———

CLOUD CORP. v. HASBRO, INC.

United States Court of Appeals, Seventh Circuit, 2002.
314 F.3d 289.

POSNER, CIRCUIT JUDGE. "Wonder World Aquarium" is a toy that Hasbro, Inc., the well-known designer and marketer of toys, sold for a

---

9. See Jones v. Jones, 333 Mo. 478, 63 S.W.2d 146, in which the Missouri court, although upholding the majority rule, thought that defendant's admission removed ambiguity from the evidence.

brief period in the mid–1990s. The toy comes as a package that contains (we simplify slightly) the aquarium itself, some plastic fish, and, depending on the size of the aquarium (for this varies), large or small packets of a powder that when dissolved in distilled water forms a transparent gelatinous filling for the aquarium. The gel simulates water, and the plastic fish can be inserted into it with tweezers to create the illusion of a real fish tank with living, though curiously inert, fish. "Pretend blood," included in some of the packages, can be added for even greater verisimilitude. The consumer can choose among versions of Wonder World Aquarium that range from "My Pretty Mermaid" to "Piranha Attack"—the latter a scenario in which the pretend blood is doubtless a mandatory rather than optional ingredient.

Hasbro contracted out the manufacture of this remarkable product. Southern Clay Products Company was to sell and ship Laponite HB, a patented synthetic clay, to Cloud Corporation, which was to mix the Laponite with a preservative according to a formula supplied by Hasbro, pack the mixture in the packets that we mentioned, and ship them to affiliates of Hasbro in East Asia. The affiliates would prepare and package the final product—that is the aquarium, the packet of gel, and the plastic fish (and "pretend blood")—and ship it back to Hasbro in the United States for distribution to retailers.

Beginning in mid–1995, Hasbro would from time to time issue purchase orders for a specified number of large and small packets to Cloud, which would in turn order the quantity of Laponite from Southern Clay Products that it needed in order to manufacture the specified number of packets. The required quantity of Laponite depended not only on the number of large and small packets ordered by Hasbro but also on the formula that Hasbro supplied to Cloud specifying the proportion of Laponite in each packet. The formula was changed frequently. The less Laponite per packet specified in the formula, the more packets could be manufactured for a given quantity of the ingredient.

Early in 1997 Hasbro discovered that its East Asian affiliates, the assemblers of the final package, had more than enough powder on hand to supply Hasbro's needs, which were diminishing, no doubt because Wonder World Aquarium was losing market appeal. Mistakenly believing that Hasbro's market was expanding rather than contracting, Cloud had manufactured a great many packets of powder in advance of receiving formal purchase orders for them from Hasbro. Hasbro refused to accept delivery of these packets or to pay for them. Contending that this refusal was a breach of contract, Cloud sued Hasbro in federal district court in Chicago, basing jurisdiction on diversity of citizenship and seeking more than $600,000 in damages based mainly on the price of the packets that it had manufactured and not delivered to Hasbro and now was stuck with—for the packets, being usable only in Wonder World Aquaria, had no resale value. After a bench trial, the district judge ruled in favor of Hasbro.

Cloud does not quarrel with the district judge's findings of fact, but only with her legal conclusions. The governing law is the Uniform Commercial Code as interpreted in Illinois.

The original understanding between Hasbro and Cloud regarding Cloud's role in the Wonder World Aquarium project either was not a contract or was not broken–probably the former, as the parties had not agreed on the price, quantity, delivery dates, or composition of the packets. These essential terms were set forth in the purchase orders that Hasbro sent Cloud, confirming discussions between employees of Cloud and Kathy Esposito, Hasbro's employee in charge of purchasing inputs for the company's foreign affiliates. Upon receipt of a purchase order, Cloud would send Hasbro an order acknowledgment and would order from Southern Clay Products the quantity of Laponite required to fill the purchase order.

In October 1995, which is to say a few months after the launch of Wonder World Aquarium, Hasbro sent a letter to all its suppliers, including Cloud, that contained a "terms and conditions" form to govern future purchase orders. One of the terms was that a supplier could not deviate from a purchase order without Hasbro's written consent. As requested, Cloud signed the form and returned it to Hasbro. Nevertheless, to make assurance doubly sure, every time Hasbro sent a purchase order to Cloud it would include an acknowledgment form for Cloud to sign that contained the same terms and conditions that were in the October letter. Cloud did not sign any of these acknowledgment forms. The order acknowledgments that it sent Hasbro in response to Hasbro's purchase orders contained on the back of each acknowledgment Cloud's own set of terms and conditions–and the provision in Hasbro's letter and forms requiring Hasbro's written consent to any modification of the purchase order was not among them. There was a space for Hasbro to sign Cloud's acknowledgment form but it never did so. Neither party complained about the other's failure to sign the tendered forms.

Hasbro placed its last purchase orders with Cloud in February and April 1996. The orders for February specified 2.3 million small packets and 3.2 million large ones. For April the numbers were 1.5 and 1.4 million. Hasbro notified Cloud of the formula that it was to use in making the packets and Cloud ordered Laponite from Southern Clay Products accordingly.

Now as it happened Southern Clay Products was having trouble delivering the Laponite in time to enable Cloud to meet its own delivery schedule. In June 1996, amidst complaints from Hasbro's East Asian affiliates that they were running out of powder, and concerned about the lag in Laponite deliveries, Hasbro notified Cloud that it was to use a new formula in manufacturing the powder, a formula that required so much less Laponite that the same quantity would enable Cloud to produce a third again as many packets. Cloud determined that by using the new formula it could produce from the quantity of Laponite that it had on hand 4.5 million small and 5 million large packets, compared to the 3.8

and 3.9 million called for by the February and April orders but not yet delivered. Cloud had delivered 700,000 of the large packets ordered in February and April; that is why it had 7.7 million packets still to deliver under those orders rather than 8.4 million, the total number of packets ordered $(2.3 + 3.2 + 1.5 + 1.4 = 8.4)$.

Although it had received no additional purchase orders, Cloud sent Hasbro an order acknowledgment for 4.5 million small and 5 million large packets with a delivery date similar to that for the April order, but at a lower price per packet, reflecting the smaller quantity of Laponite, the expensive ingredient in the powder, in each packet.

Cloud's acknowledgment was sent in June. Hasbro did not respond to it–at least not explicitly. It did receive it, however. And Kathy Esposito continued having e-mail exchanges and phone conversations with Cloud. These focused on delivery dates and, importantly, on the quantities to be delivered on those dates. Importantly because some very large numbers–much larger than the February and April numbers, numbers consistent however with Cloud's order acknowledgment sent to Hasbro in June–appear in these and other e-mails written by her. In two of the e-mails the quantity Cloud is to ship is described as "more or less depending on the formula," consistent with Cloud's understanding that if the formula reduced the amount of Laponite per packet Cloud should increase the number of packets it made rather than return unused Laponite to Southern Clay Products. A notation made in August by another member of Hasbro's purchasing department, Maryann Ricci– "Cloud O/S; 4,000,000 sm; 3.5 million lg."–indicates her belief that Cloud had outstanding ("O/S") purchase orders for 4 million small and 3.5 million large packets. These numbers were far in excess of the undelivered portions of the February and April orders; and since all the earlier orders had, so far as we can determine, already been filled and so were no longer outstanding, she must have been referring to the numbers in Cloud's June order acknowledgment.

The district judge, despite ruling for Hasbro, found that indeed "Hasbro intended to exceed the quantities of . . . packages it had ordered from Cloud in February and April of 1996," that "Hasbro was more concerned with prompt product than with the specific terms of its order[s]," and, most important, that "given Hasbro's repeated message that it could not get enough Laponite HB to fill its needs in a timely fashion, Cloud's decision to produce as many packets as possible appeared to be a safe course of action. Cloud was trying to keep pace with Hasbro's Laponite HB needs, a task made virtually impossible by the length of time it took Southern Clay to fill Cloud's Laponite HB orders." The judge even suggested that given Hasbro's desperation, Cloud could have persuaded Hasbro to execute additional purchase orders at prices equal to those in the February and April orders. Instead, rather than trying to take advantage of Hasbro's fix, Cloud reduced its price to reflect its lower cost. . . .

Was Cloud commercially unreasonable in producing the additional quantity without a purchase order? If not, should the Uniform Commercial Code, which was intended to conform sales law to the customs and usages of business people, UCC §§ 1–102(2)(b), 1–105 comment 3; *In re Merritt Dredging Co.*, 839 F.2d 203, 206 (4th Cir.1988); Kerry Lynn Macintosh, "Liberty, Trade, and the Uniform Commercial Code: When Should Default Rules Be Based on Business Practices?" 38 *Wm. & Mary L.Rev.* 1465, 1488–91 (1997), nevertheless condemn Cloud, as the district judge believed, for failing to request written purchase orders for the additional quantity that the change in formula enabled it to manufacture? Or was Hasbro contractually obligated to pay for that additional quantity?

The answers to these questions depend on whether there was a valid modification of the quantity specifications in the February and April purchase orders (obviously Hasbro cannot complain about the price modification!). The October letter provided that purchase orders could not be modified without Hasbro's written consent. Cloud signed the letter and so became bound by it, consideration being furnished by Hasbro's continuing to do business with Cloud. Hasbro's order acknowledgments accompanying its February and April purchase orders also provided that the orders could not be modified without Hasbro's written consent.

 . . .

For unexpressed reasons the district judge did not focus on the contractual provisions requiring that any modification of a purchase order be in writing. She considered only whether the UCC's statute of frauds required this, and ruled that it did. The quantity term in a contract for the sale of goods for more than $500 must be memorialized in a writing signed by the party sought to be held to that term, UCC § 2–201(1), and so, therefore, must a modification of that term. UCC § 2–209(3). However–and here we part company with the district judge–Kathy Esposito's e-mails, plus the notation that we quoted earlier signed by Maryann Ricci, another member of Hasbro's purchasing department, satisfy the statutory requirement. The UCC does not require that the contract itself be in writing, only that there be adequate documentary evidence of its existence and essential terms, which there was here. *Architectural Metal Systems, Inc. v. Consolidated Systems, Inc.*, 58 F.3d 1227, 1229–31 (7th Cir.1995). . . .

But what shall we make of the fact that Kathy Esposito's e-mails contained no signature? The Electronic Signatures in Global and National Commerce Act, 15 U.S.C. § 7001, provides that in all transactions in or affecting interstate or foreign commerce (the transactions between Cloud and Hasbro were in interstate commerce and affected both interstate and foreign commerce), a contract or other record relating to the transaction shall not be denied legal effect merely because it is in electronic form. That would be conclusive in this case–had the e-mails been sent after the Act took effect in 2000. But they were sent in 1996.

The Act does not purport to be applicable to transactions that occurred before its effective date, and, not being procedural, compare *Landgraf v. USI Film Products*, 511 U.S. 244, 275, 114 S.Ct. 1483, 128 L.Ed.2d 229 (1994), it is presumed not to apply retroactively. *Johnson v. Ventra Group, Inc.*, 191 F.3d 732, 745 (6th Cir.1999). But like the court in *Shattuck v. Klotzbach*, No. 011109A, 2001 WL 1839720, at *2–3 (Mass.Super.Dec. 11, 2001), we conclude without having to rely on the federal Act that the sender's name on an e-mail satisfies the signature requirement of the statute of frauds. . . .

. . .

The purpose of the statute of frauds is to prevent a contracting party from creating a triable issue concerning the terms of the contract–or for that matter concerning whether a contract even exists–on the basis of his say-so alone. That purpose does not require a handwritten signature, especially in a case such as this in which there is other evidence, and not merely say-so evidence, of the existence of the contract (more precisely, the contract modification) besides the writings. The fact that Cloud produced the additional quantity is pretty powerful evidence of a contract, *Consolidation Services, Inc. v. KeyBank National Ass'n*, 185 F.3d 817, 821 (7th Cir.1999) . . ., as it would have been taking a terrible risk in doing so had it thought it would have no right to be paid if Hasbro refused to accept delivery but would instead be stuck with a huge quantity of a product that had no salvage value. Actually, in the case of a contract for goods specially manufactured by the buyer, partial performance by the seller takes the contract outside the statute of frauds, without more. UCC § 2–201(3)(a). This may well be such a case; but we need not decide.

The background to the modification—the fact that the parties had dealt informally with each other (as shown by their disregard of the form contracts), and above all that Hasbro plainly wanted more product and wanted it fast–is further evidence that had Cloud asked for a written purchase order in June 1996 for the additional quantity, Hasbro would have given it, especially since Cloud was offering a lower price.

There is more: "between merchants [a term that embraces 'any transaction with respect to which both parties are chargeable with the knowledge or skill of merchants,' UCC § 2–104(3)] if within a reasonable time a writing in confirmation of the contract and sufficient against the sender is received and the party receiving it has reason to know its contents, it satisfies the requirements of subsection 1 [the statute of frauds] . . . unless written notice of objection to its contents is given within 10 days after it is received." UCC § 2–201(2). Cloud sent an order acknowledgment, reciting the increased quantity, shortly after the oral modification, and Hasbro did not object within ten days. *Campbell v. Yokel*, 20 Ill.App.3d 702, 313 N.E.2d628, 628–31 (1974). . . .

So Hasbro's statute of frauds defense fails on a number of independent grounds. . . .

That leaves intact, however, Cloud's argument, which we have accepted, that there was adequate evidence of written consent to the modification. And it leaves intact still another alternative argument by Cloud: "an attempt at modification" that does not satisfy the statute of frauds nevertheless "can operate as a waiver." § 2–209(4). The word "can" is key. To prevent the "attempt" provision from eviscerating the statute of frauds, the courts require that the attempting modifier, Cloud in this case, must show either that it reasonably relied on the other party's having waived the requirement of a writing, *Wisconsin Knife Works v. National Metal Crafters, supra*, 781 F.2d at 1286–87 (7th Cir.1986) . . ., or that the waiver was clear and unequivocal. *In re Nitz*, 317 Ill.App.3d 119, 250 Ill.Dec. 632, 739 N.E.2d 93 (2000). . . . This exception to the statute of frauds applies equally to the "buyer's written consent" provision of the parties' contracts, UCC § 2–209(4); *Wisconsin Knife Works v. National Metal Crafters*, supra, 781 F.2d at 1284–87, because waiver is a general doctrine of contract law rather than an appendage to the statute of frauds.

The district judge erred by requiring that Cloud show both reasonable reliance and that the waiver was clear and unequivocal. There was no clear and unequivocal waiver, but there was reliance. The judge found reliance. She found that Cloud had been acting in good faith in producing the additional quantity of packets because it reasonably believed that Hasbro wanted the additional quantity. But she concluded that Cloud had been unreasonable in relying on its reasonable belief because it could so easily have insisted on a written purchase order modifying the quantity terms in the February and April orders. Reasonableness, however, is relative to commercial practices and understandings rather than to the desire of judges and lawyers, reflecting their training and professional culture, to see a deal memorialized in a form that leaves no room for misunderstanding the legal consequences. The employees of Hasbro and Cloud who were responsible for the administration of the parties' contractual undertaking were not lawyers. Doubtless because of this, the parties had, as we have noted, been casual about documentation. Cloud had treated the purchase orders as sources of information on how much Hasbro wanted when and according to what formula, but had paid no attention to them as contracts containing terms and conditions that might bind it. Hasbro had treated Cloud's purchase-order acknowledgments with similar insouciance. The parties had a smooth working relationship the details of which were worked out in informal communications. With time of the essence and the parties on good terms and therefore careless or impatient with formalities, Cloud was reasonable in believing that if Hasbro didn't want to be committed to buying the additional quantity that it plainly wanted in the summer and autumn of 1996, it would so advise Cloud rather than leading Cloud down the primrose path. . . .

Cloud could have been more careful. But a failure to insist that every i be dotted and t crossed is not the same thing as being unreasonable. In any event, to repeat an earlier point, Hasbro did give its written consent to the modification.

We conclude that the June modification was enforceable and we therefore reverse the judgment and remand the case for a determination of Cloud's damages. . . .

Questions

1. What is a contract modification? What was the modification in *Cloud Corp.*? Why should one be in writing, if it should?

2. What does the court see as the purpose of the statute of frauds provisions of Article 2? Does it differ from the purposes identified in the preceding two cases? Does the court believe that, to further that purpose, the modification must be in writing to be enforceable? What significance does the court attach to the fact that Cloud Corp. went ahead and made the additional packets without securing a writing signed by Hasbro? What significance does it attach to the fact that the parties dealt with each other informally? Should these two facts be relevant to the statute of frauds question?

3. How many arguments does the court make for deeming the Article 2 statute of frauds satisfied? Which is the strongest argument in your view? Was there a writing, signed by Hasbro that satisfied the statute? Would the Amendments to Article 2 support the result in this case? If the Amendments are not enacted in the relevant jurisdiction, should a court give them weight?

4. What is a "waiver?" Does the attempted modification in *Cloud Corp.* constitute a waiver of the statute of frauds?

5. *Problems.*

a. Maurice and Leslie communicate by electronic mail. Maurice sent a message offering 400 cords of hickory firewood at $50 per cord, delivery on November 1. Leslie copied that message to her hard drive and replied, "I accept. Please deliver in the morning November 1." Maurice copied that message to his hard drive. When Leslie repudiates, can Maurice enforce the contract?

b. Assume that, after the electronic mail message from Maurice, Leslie sent Maurice a purchase order on a printed form listing the quantity, price and delivery time. It was not signed by Leslie, but carried Leslie's rubber stamp name and address at the center top. When Leslie repudiates, can Maurice enforce the contract? See First Valley Leasing, Inc. v. Goushy, 795 F.Supp. 693 (D.N.J.1992).

c. Maurice and Leslie met in person and agreed orally on the purchase and sale of 400 cords on the terms set forth above. Maurice suggested that they put the agreement in writing. Leslie balked, expressing her offense that Maurice would so distrust her and assuring Maurice that there was no need. Maurice agreed to leave things unwritten. When Leslie later repudiates, should Maurice be able to enforce the contract? See Loeb v. Gendel, 23 Ill.2d 502, 179 N.E.2d 7 (1961).

d. The facts are the same as in Problem b above, except that Leslie indicated she was late for a crucial appointment and promised to put the deal in writing later that day. She never did. When Leslie later repudiates, should Maurice be able to enforce the contract?

———

Chapter 2

THE JUSTIFICATION PRINCIPLE

The law enforces promises when prima facie there are sufficient legal reasons for a court to enforce the promise.

The fact that a person promises to act in some definite way in the future gives that person a reason to act as promised when the time comes. It also gives the promisee a reason to demand performance as promised. Assume that Clark promises to play tennis at noon with Vivian, and Veronica later asks him to play tennis at the same time with her. We usually think that Clark should decline Veronica's invitation because he made a promise to Vivian. We would not criticize Vivian for insisting that he play with her; we would criticize Clark for going with Veronica. Therefore, conventionally speaking, Clark would have a *moral obligation* to Vivian.

The law, however, will not enforce Clark's promise just because it is a promise and morally binding. Vivian must establish three main conditions before the law will intervene on her behalf. The existence of a promise is only one.

The second condition is that a court have sufficient legal reason to enforce the promise. Our tradition strongly condemns the use of official coercion without proper justification. A court, of course, invokes the state's coercive powers, at least as an unspoken threat, whenever it issues an order. Suppose that a court did order Clark to pay damages to Vivian for breaking his promise to play tennis. If Clark did not pay, the sheriff would take some of Clark's property, sell it, and give the proceeds to Vivian to satisfy the court's judgment. Courts should not use such intrusive powers without a good reason. Moreover, the fact of Clark's promise is not enough of a reason. That promise is a private affair between Clark and Vivian. Perhaps courts should enforce promises only when there is a reason for enforcement that reflects a public interest. After all, the public pays the freight for the legal system.

In this chapter, we explore the distinction between enforceable and unenforceable promises by considering reasons recognized by the law as justifications for enforcing promises. We do so on a "prima facie" basis. That is, we consider the legal reasons for enforcing promises on a temporary assumption—that there are no offsetting reasons. Consequently, a court may be prima facie justified in enforcing a promise and yet not enforce it because there turn out to be offsetting reasons. In Chapter 3, we will explore the third main condition for enforcement— that there be no reasons of justice that should defeat enforcement. Together, Chapters 2 and 3 make clear that the law may restrict the parties' autonomy for reasons of principle and public policy.

SECTION 1.   THE BARGAINED–FOR EXCHANGE

CONGREGATION KADIMAH TORAS– MOSHE v. DeLEO

Supreme Judicial Court of Massachusetts, 1989.
405 Mass. 365, 540 N.E.2d 691.

LIACOS, CHIEF JUSTICE. Congregation Kadimah Toras–Moshe (Congregation), an Orthodox Jewish synagogue, commenced this action in the Superior Court to compel the administrator of an estate (estate) to fulfill the oral promise of the decedent to give the Congregation $25,000. The Superior Court transferred the case to the Boston Municipal Court, which rendered summary judgment for the estate. The case was then transferred back to the Superior Court, which also rendered summary judgment for the estate and dismissed the Congregation's complaint. We granted the Congregation's application for direct appellate review. We now affirm.

The facts are not contested. The decedent suffered a prolonged illness, throughout which he was visited by the Congregation's spiritual leader, Rabbi Abraham Halbfinger. During four or five of these visits, and in the presence of witnesses, the decedent made an oral promise to give the Congregation $25,000. The Congregation planned to use the $25,000 to transform a storage room in the synagogue into a library named after the decedent. The oral promise was never reduced to writing. The decedent died intestate in September, 1985. He had no children, but was survived by his wife.

The Congregation asserts that the decedent's oral promise is an enforceable contract under our case law, because the promise is allegedly supported either by consideration and bargain, or by reliance. See *Loranger Constr. Corp. v. E.F. Hauserman Co.*, 376 Mass. 757, 761, 763, 384 N.E.2d 176 (1978) (distinguishing consideration and bargain from reliance in the absence of consideration). We disagree.

The Superior Court judge determined that "[t]his was an oral gratuitous pledge, with no indication as to how the money should be used, or what [the Congregation] was required to do if anything in return for this promise." There was no legal benefit to the promisor nor detriment to the promisee, and thus no consideration. See *Marine Contractors Co. v. Hurley*, 365 Mass. 280, 286, 310 N.E.2d 915 (1974);

Gishen v. Dura Corp., *362 Mass. 177, 186, 285 N.E.2d 117 (1972) (moral obligation is not legal obligation). Furthermore, there is no evidence in the record that the Congregation's plans to name a library after the decedent induced him to make or to renew his promise. Contrast* Allegheny College v. National Chautauqua County Bank, *246 N.Y. 369, 377–379, 159 N.E. 173 (1927) (subscriber's promise became binding when charity implicitly promised to commemorate subscriber).*

As to the lack of reliance, the judge stated that the Congregation's "allocation of $25,000 in its budget[,] for the purpose of renovating a storage room, is insufficient to find reliance or an enforceable obligation." We agree. The inclusion of the promised $25,000 in the budget, by itself, merely reduced to writing the Congregation's expectation that it would have additional funds. A hope or expectation, even though well founded, is not equivalent to either legal detriment or reliance. *Hall v. Horizon House Microwave, Inc.,* 24 Mass.App.Ct. 84, 94, 506 N.E.2d 178 (1987).

The Congregation cites several of our cases in which charitable subscriptions were enforced. These cases are distinguishable because they involved written, as distinguished from oral, promises and also involved substantial consideration or reliance. See, e.g., *Trustees of Amherst Academy v. Cowls,* 6 Pick. 427, 434 (1828) (subscribers to written agreement could not withdraw "after the execution or during the progress of the work which they themselves set in motion"); *Trustees of Farmington Academy v. Allen,* 14 Mass. 172, 176 (1817) (trustees justifiably "proceed[ed] to incur expense, on the faith of the defendant's subscription"). Conversely, in the case of *Cottage St. Methodist Episcopal Church v. Kendall,* 121 Mass. 528 (1877), we refused to enforce a promise in favor of a charity where there was no showing of any consideration or reliance.

The Congregation asks us to abandon the requirement of consideration or reliance in the case of charitable subscriptions.... [W]e are of the opinion that in this case there is no injustice in declining to enforce the decedent's promise.... The promise to the Congregation is entirely unsupported by consideration or reliance. Furthermore, it is an oral promise sought to be enforced against an estate. To enforce such a promise would be against public policy.

Judgment affirmed.

Questions

1. Should the court have enforced the promise against the estate in *Congregation Kadimah Toras–Moshe?* What are the arguments for and against enforcing informal promises to make gifts generally? Should the law enforce this promise because it is charitable? See Restatement (Second) of Contracts § 90(2).

2. Should the law enforce all promises? Why might it be significant that the promise in *Congregation Kadimah Toras–Moshe* was not in writing? Should the law enforce all formal promises? All written promises to make gifts?

RESTATEMENT (SECOND) OF CONTRACTS
§§ 17, 71, 72, 75, 79

SCHNELL v. NELL

Supreme Court of Indiana, 1861.
17 Ind. 29, 79 Am.Dec. 453.

PERKINS, JUDGE. Action by *J.B. Nell* against *Zacharias Schnell*, upon the following instrument:

"This agreement, entered into this 13th day of *February*, 1856, between *Zach. Schnell*, of *Indianapolis, Marion* county, State of *Indiana*, as party of the first part, and J.B. Nell, of the same place, *Wendelin Lorenz*, of *Stilesville, Hendricks* county, State of *Indiana*, and *Donata Lorenz*, of *Frickinger, Grand Duchy of Baden, Germany*, as parties of the second part, witnesseth: The said *Zacharias Schnell* agrees as follows: whereas his wife, *Theresa Schnell*, now deceased, has made a last will and testament, in which, among other provisions, it was ordained that every one of the above named second parties, should receive the sum of $200; and whereas the said provisions of the will must remain a nullity, for the reason that no property, real or personal, was in the possession of the said *Theresa Schnell*, deceased, in her own name, at the time of her death, and all property held by *Zacharias* and *Theresa Schnell* jointly, therefore reverts to her husband; and whereas the said *Theresa Schnell* has also been a dutiful and loving wife to the said *Zach. Schnell*, and has materially aided him in the acquisition of all property, real and personal, now possessed by him; for, and in consideration of all this, and the love and respect he bears to his wife; and, furthermore, in consideration of one cent, received by him of the second parties, he, the said *Zach. Schnell*, agrees to pay the above named sums of money to the parties of the second part, to wit: $200 to the said *J.B. Nell*; $200 to the said *Wendelin Lorenz*; and $200 to the said *Donata Lorenz*, in the following installments, viz., $200 in one year from the date of these presents; $200 in two years, and $200 in three years; to be divided between the parties in equal portions of $66⅔ each year, or as they may agree, till each one has received his full sum of $200.

"And the said parties of the second part, for, and in consideration of this, agree to pay the above named sum of money [one cent], and to deliver up to said *Schnell*, and abstain from collecting any real or supposed claims upon him or his estate, arising from the said last will and testament of the said *Theresa Schnell*, deceased.

"In witness whereof, the said parties have, on this 13th day of *February*, 1856, set hereunto their hands and seals.

"ZACHARIAS SCHNELL, [SEAL.]

"J.B. NELL, [SEAL.]

"WEN. LORENZ," [SEAL.]

The complaint contained no averment of a consideration for the instrument, outside of those expressed in it; and did not aver that the one cent agreed to be paid, had been paid or tendered.

A demurrer to the complaint was overruled.

The defendant answered, that the instrument sued on was given for no consideration whatever.

He further answered, that it was given for no consideration, because his said wife, *Theresa*, at the time she made the will mentioned, and at the time of her death, owned, neither separately, nor jointly with her husband, or any one else (except so far as the law gave her an interest in her husband's property), any property, real or personal, & c. . . .

The Court sustained a demurrer to these answers, evidently on the ground that they were regarded as contradicting the instrument sued on, which particularly set out the considerations upon which it was executed. But the instrument is latently ambiguous on this point. . . .

The case turned below, and must turn here, upon the question whether the instrument sued on does express a consideration sufficient to give it legal obligation, as against *Zacharias Schnell*. It specifies three distinct considerations for his promise to pay $600:

    1.   A promise, on the part of the plaintiffs, to pay him one cent.

    2.   The love and affection he bore his deceased wife, and the fact that she had done her part, as his wife, in the acquisition of property.

    3.   The fact that she had expressed her desire, in the form of an inoperative will, that the persons named therein should have the sums of money specified.

The consideration of one cent will not support the promise of *Schnell*. It is true, that as a general proposition, inadequacy of consideration will not vitiate an agreement. *Baker v. Roberts*, 14 Ind. 552. But this doctrine does not apply to a mere exchange of sums of money, of coin, whose value is exactly fixed, but to the exchange of something of, in itself, indeterminate value, for money, or, perhaps, for some other thing of indeterminate value. In this case, had the one cent mentioned, been some particular one cent, a family piece, or ancient, remarkable coin, possessing an indeterminate value, extrinsic from its simple money value, a different view might be taken. As it is, the mere promise to pay six hundred dollars for one cent, even had the portion of that cent due from the plaintiff been tendered, is an unconscionable contract, void, at first blush, upon its face, if it be regarded as an earnest one. *Hardesty v. Smith*, 3 Ind. 39. The consideration of one cent is, plainly, in this case, merely nominal, and intended to be so. As the will and testament of *Schnell's* wife imposed no legal obligation upon him to discharge her bequests out of his property, and as she had none of her own, his promise to discharge them was not legally binding upon him, on that ground. A moral consideration, only, will not support a promise.... And for the same reason, a valid consideration for his promise can not be found in the fact of a compromise of a disputed claim; for where such claim is legally groundless, a promise upon a compromise of it, or of a suit upon it, is not legally binding. *Spahr v. Hollingshead*, 8 Blackf. 415. There was no mistake of law or fact in this case, as the agreement admits the will inoperative and void. The promise was simply one to make a gift. The past services of his wife, and the love and affection he had borne her, are objectionable as legal considerations for *Schnell's* promise, on two grounds: 1. They are past considerations.... 2. The fact that *Schnell* loved his wife, and that she had been industrious, constituted no consideration for his promise to pay *J.B. Nell*, and the *Lorenzes*, a sum of money. Whether, if his wife, in her lifetime, had made a bargain with *Schnell*, that, in consideration of his promising to pay, after her death, to the persons named, a sum of money, she would be industrious, and worthy of his affection, such a promise would have been valid and consistent with public policy, we need not decide. Nor is the fact that *Schnell* now venerates the memory of his deceased wife, a legal consideration for a promise to pay any third person money.

The instrument sued on, interpreted in the light of the facts alleged in the second paragraph of the answer, will not support an action. The demurrer to the answer should have been overruled....

Per Curiam. The judgment is reversed, with costs.

Questions

1.   How many reasons could counsel for Nell and the Lorenzes advance in an effort to persuade a court to enforce Schnell's promise? With respect to each one, would a court be justified in enforcing Schnell's promise for that reason? Should the court enforce Schnell's promise just because it is a promise?

2.   Should people be able to make enforceable promises whenever they want, as long as they make it clear that this is what they want? Why or why not? Which of the following hypothetical cases is the more sound?

a.   "A wishes to make a binding promise to his son B to convey to B Blackacre, which is worth $5000. Being advised that a gratuitous promise is not binding, A writes to B an offer to sell Blackacre for $1. B accepts. B's promise to pay $1 is sufficient consideration." RESTATEMENT [FIRST] OF CONTRACTS § 84, Ill. 1 (1932).

b.   "A desires to make a binding promise to give $1000 to his son B. Being advised that a gratuitous promise is not binding, A offers to buy from B for $1000 a book worth less than $1. B accepts the offer knowing that the purchase of the book is a mere pretense. There is no consideration for A's promise to pay $1000." RESTATEMENT (SECOND) OF CONTRACTS § 71, Ill. 5 (1979).

NOTE ON "CONSIDERATION"

Promises are enforceable when supported by "consideration." In RESTATEMENT (SECOND) OF CONTRACTS terminology, consideration consists of a performance or a return promise that is *bargained-for in exchange* for the promise sought to be enforced. The word "consideration" is used in several other ways, both in the English language and by the courts in contracts cases. Thus, for example, the promise in *Schnell v. Nell* was made in consideration of the love and respect Schnell felt for his wife, thus referring to a sentiment or motive. But this is not the relevant meaning of consideration in law.

To determine whether courts are justified in enforcing a promise, we do not inquire into states of mind, seeking to determine the *motive* for making the promise. See *Hamer v. Sidway*, below at p. 135. Rather, as in ascertaining the existence of an agreement, courts usually look to external indices of intention and interpret them in light of the general practice. There is consideration (as a bargained-for exchange) when the promise and the return promise or performance stand in a relation of reciprocal conventional inducement. That is, a reasonable person would understand each to induce the giving of the other in ordinary circumstances. See OLIVER WENDELL HOLMES, JR., THE COMMON LAW 293–4 (1881).

There are two main rationales for courts to enforce promises made as part of a bargained-for exchange of values. The first, endorsed by the RESTATEMENT (SECOND) OF CONTRACTS, reflects the economics of exchange. From an economic perspective, exchange is efficient because it moves scarce resources to higher valued uses, increasing the total wealth in an economy. For example, assume Glenda sells a book to Lynn in exchange for $25. Both parties act freely and rationally upon full information under competitive conditions. It would seem that Glenda values $25 more than the book while Lynn values the book more than $25. The trade makes each better off by her own reckoning. If the transaction does not affect anyone else, the society is better off because two of its citizens are better off and no one was made worse off by the transaction. On utilitarian grounds, then, society has an interest in fostering exchange, as it does by promoting domestic and international trade. Similarly, enforcing promises made as part of exchanges may serve the greater good. See generally R. POSNER, ECONOMIC ANALYSIS OF THE LAW 89–95 (4th Ed. 1992).

The second rationale, endorsed by the RESTATEMENT [FIRST] OF CONTRACTS, is less interested in the gains of trade than the effect of the *form* of a bargain on the parties' choices. Historically under English law, promises were enforced when under seal without any further requirements. The justification was that the process of sealing a promise cautioned promisors that they were doing something with legal consequences, making it more likely that sealed promises were made deliberately. It also signalled to courts that the parties intended legal consequences, since the significance of the seal was widely appreciated. Enforcing formal promises supposes that people should have the freedom to bind themselves in law as long as they do so deliberately and make their intention clear to others. It may be thought that, similarly, the form of an exchange is not employed lightly or without intending legal consequences. In *Schnell v. Nell*, for example, the promise to pay one cent was probably part of an elaborate effort to enhance the prospects of court enforcement. When the law considers the form of a bargain sufficient to justify enforcement, it bases enforcement on the will of the parties, clearly and deliberately manifested. See generally Lon L. Fuller, *Consideration and Form*, 41 Colum. L. Rev. 799 (1941).

Neither view any longer purports to treat exchange as the exclusive basis for enforcing promises. Reliance and unjust enrichment, to be considered in §§ 2 and 3 below, are additional and alternative bases for enforcing promises in some circumstances. Terminologically, many courts will say that reliance is "consideration" or even that unjust enrichment is "consideration." These uses of the term have nothing to do with exchange. "Consideration" so used refers to *a reason to enforce a contract*, including among the reasons bargained for exchange, reliance, and unjust enrichment. The Restatement (Second) of Contracts, by contrast, uses "consideration" to refer only to a bargained for exchange of values, treating promises enforceable for reasons of reliance or unjust enrichment as "contracts without consideration." The terminological problem is unfortunate; nothing practical turns on it so long as the ideas are kept clear. However put, the prevailing law considers the bargain contract the central paradigm of an enforceable promises.

HAMER v. SIDWAY

Court of Appeals of New York, 1891.
124 N.Y. 538, 27 N.E. 256.

Appeal from an order of the general term of the supreme court in the fourth judicial department, reversing a judgment entered on the decision of the court at special term in the county clerk's office of Chemung county on the 1st day of October, 1889. The plaintiff presented a claim to the executor of William E. Story, Sr., for $5,000 and interest from the 6th day of February, 1875. She acquired it through several mesne assignments from William E. Story, 2d. The claim being rejected by the executor, this action was brought. It appears that William E. Story, Sr., was the uncle of William E. Story, 2d., that at the celebration of the golden wedding of Samuel Story and wife, father and mother of William E. Story, Sr., on the 20th day of March, 1869, in the presence of the family and invited guests, he promised his nephew that if he would refrain from drinking, using tobacco, swearing, and playing cards or billiards for money until he became 21 years of age, he would pay him the sum of $5,000. The nephew assented thereto, and fully performed the conditions inducing the promise. When the nephew arrived at the age of 21 years, and on the 31st day of January, 1875, he wrote to his uncle, informing him that he had performed his part of the agreement, and had thereby become entitled to the sum of $5,000. The uncle received the letter, and a few days later, and on the 6th day of February, he wrote and mailed to his nephew the following letter: "Buffalo, Feb. 6, 1875. W. E. Story, Jr.–Dear Nephew: Your letter of the 31st ult. came to hand all right, saying that you had lived up to the promise made to me several years ago. I have no doubt but you have, for which you shall have five thousand dollars, as I promised you. I had the money in the bank the day you was twenty-one years old that I intend for you, and you shall have the money certain. Now, Willie, I do not intend to interfere with this money in any way till I think you are capable of taking care of it, and the sooner that time comes the better it will please me. I would hate very much to have you start out in some adventure that you thought all right and lose this money in one year. The first five thousand dollars that I got together cost me a heap of hard work.... This money you have earned much easier than I did, besides acquiring good habits at the same time, and you are quite welcome to the money. Hope you will make good use of it. I was ten long years getting this together after I was your age.... Truly yours, W. E. Story. P. S. You can consider this money on interest." The nephew received the letter, and thereafter consented that the money should remain with his uncle in accordance with the terms and conditions of the letter. The uncle died on the 29th day of January, 1887, without having paid over to his nephew any portion of the said $5,000 and interest.

PARKER, J. The question which provoked the most discussion by counsel on this appeal, and which lies at the foundation of plaintiff's asserted right of recovery, is whether by virtue of a contract defendant's testator, William E. Story, became indebted to his nephew, William E. Story, 2d, on his twenty-first birthday in the sum of $5,000.... The defendant contends that the contract was without consideration to support it, and therefore invalid. He asserts that the promisee, by refraining from the use of liquor and tobacco, was not harmed, but benefited; that that which he did was best for him to do, independently of his uncle's promise, and insists that it follows that, unless the promisor was benefited, the contract was without consideration, a contention which, if well founded, would seem to leave open for controversy in many cases whether that which the promisee did or omitted to do was in fact of such benefit to him as to leave no consideration to support the enforcement of the promisor's agreement. Such a rule could not be tolerated, and is without foundation in the law. The exchequer chamber in 1875 defined "consideration" as follows: "A valuable consideration, in the sense of the law, may consist either in some right, interest, profit, or benefit accruing to the one party, or some forbearance, detriment, loss, or responsibility given, suffered, or undertaken by the other." Courts "will not ask whether the thing which forms the consideration does in fact benefit the promisee or a third party, or is of any substantial value to any one. It is enough that something is promised, done, forborne, or suffered by the party to whom the promise is made as consideration for the promise made to him." Anson, Cont. 63. "In general a waiver of any legal right at the request of another party is a sufficient consideration for a promise." Pars. Cont. *444. "Any damage, or suspension, or forbearance of a right will be sufficient to sustain a promise." 2 Kent, Comm. (12th Ed.) *465. Pollock in his work on Contracts, (page 166,) after citing the definition given by the exchequer chamber, already quoted, says: "The second branch of this judicial description is really the most important one. 'Consideration' means not so much that one party is profiting as that the other abandons some legal right in the present, or limits his legal freedom of action in the future, as an inducement for the promise of the first." Now, applying this rule to the facts before us, the promisee used tobacco, occasionally drank liquor, and he had a legal right to do so. That right he abandoned for a period of years upon the strength of the promise of the testator that for such forbearance he would give him $5,000. We need not speculate on the effort which may have been required to give up the use of those stimulants. It is sufficient that he restricted his lawful freedom of action within certain prescribed limits upon the faith of his uncle's agreement, and now, having fully performed the conditions imposed, it is of no moment whether such performance actually proved a benefit to the promisor, and the court will not inquire into it; but, were it a proper subject of inquiry, we see nothing in this record that would permit a determination that the uncle was not benefited in a legal sense. . . .

Questions

1. In *Hamer v. Sidway*, what were the benefits and detriments to Uncle William from performing his promise? What were the benefits and detriments to Nephew William from performing his? Which benefits and detriments are relevant to a question of consideration? Why, for example, does the court hold that it is not relevant if Nephew William benefitted on balance from performing his promise? Should it matter if Uncle William would suffer a detriment from performing his promise?

2. In your view, should the court have found the promise enforceable because it was supported by consideration, understood as a bargained-for exchange? Or was this a donative promise made on condition that Nephew William refrain from bad habits? Was this a genuine bargained-for exchange, or did it only have the form of a bargain?

3. *Problems*:

a. Charlie, a tramp, knocked on Mack's front door, pleaded hunger, and asked for a meal. Mack promised to give him a bowl of stew if Charlie would go to the back door. Charlie nodded. Charlie then waddled to the back door and knocked, but Mack never answered. Should Charlie be able to enforce Mack's promise because he gave up his right to go elsewhere at that time?

b. Charlie, a tramp, knocked on Mack's front door, pleaded hunger, and asked for a meal. Mack promised to give him a bowl of stew if Charlie would rake the fallen leaves. Charlie raked the leaves. Charlie then went to the back door and knocked, but Mack never answered. Is Mack's promise enforceable because supported by consideration?

c. Charlie, a tramp, knocked on Mack's front door, pleaded hunger, and asked for a meal. Mack promised to give him a bowl of stew if Charlie would promise to rake the fallen leaves. Charlie nodded and went to Mack's garage to get a rake. Mack met him at the garage door, thumbed his nose, made some hideous sounds, and told him to leave the premises. Is Mack's promise enforceable because supported by consideration?

BATSAKIS v. DEMOTSIS

Court of Civil Appeals of Texas, 1949.
226 S.W.2d 673.

McGILL, JUSTICE. This is an appeal from a judgment of the 57th Judicial District Court of Bexar County. Appellant was plaintiff and appellee was defendant in the trial court. The parties will be so designated.

Plaintiff sued defendant to recover $2,000 with interest at the rate of 8% per annum from April 2, 1942, alleged to be due on the following instrument, being a translation from the original, which is written in the Greek language:

"Mr. George Batsakis Peiraeus
"Konstantinou Diadohou #7 April 2, 1942
"Peiraeus
"Mr. Batsakis:

"I state by my present (letter) that I received today from you the amount of two thousand dollars ($2,000.00) of United States of America money, which I borrowed from you for the support of my family during these difficult days and because it is impossible for me to transfer dollars of my own from America.

"The above amount I accept with the expressed promise that I will return to you again in American dollars either at the end of the present war or even before in the event that you might be able to find a way to collect them (dollars) from my representative in America to whom I shall write and give him an order relative to this. You understand until the final execution (payment) to the above amount an eight per cent interest will be added and paid together with the principal.

"I thank you and I remain yours with respects.

"The recipient,

"(Signed) Eugenia The. Demotsis."

Trial to the court without the intervention of a jury resulted in a judgment in favor of plaintiff for $750.00 principal, and interest at the rate of 8% per annum from April 2, 1942 to the date of judgment, totaling $1163.83, with interest thereon at the rate of 8% per annum until paid. Plaintiff has perfected his appeal.

The court sustained certain special exceptions of plaintiff to defendant's first amended original answer on which the case was tried, and struck therefrom paragraphs II, III and V. Defendant excepted to such action of the court, but has not cross-assigned error here. The answer, stripped of such paragraphs, consisted of a general denial contained in paragraph I thereof, and of paragraph IV, which is as follows:

"IV. That under the circumstances alleged in Paragraph II of this answer, the consideration upon which said written instrument sued upon by plaintiff herein is founded, is wanting and has failed to the extent of $1975.00, and defendant pleads specially under the verification hereinafter made the want and failure of consideration stated, and now tenders, as defendant has heretofore tendered to plaintiff, $25.00 as the value of the loan of money received by defendant from plaintiff, together with interest thereon.

"Further, in connection with this plea of want and failure of consideration defendant alleges that she at no time received from plaintiff himself or from anyone for plaintiff any money or thing of value other than, as hereinbefore alleged, the original loan of 500,-000 drachmae. That at the time of the loan by plaintiff to defendant of said 500,000 drachmae the value of 500,000 drachmae in the Kingdom of Greece in dollars of money of the United States of America, was $25.00, and also at said time the value of 500,000 drachmae of Greek money in the United States of America in dollars was $25.00 of money of the United States of America. The plea of want and failure of consideration is verified by defendant as follows."

The allegations in paragraph II which were stricken, referred to in paragraph IV, were that the instrument sued on was signed and delivered in the Kingdom of Greece on or about April 2, 1942, at which time both plaintiff and defendant were residents of and residing in the Kingdom of Greece, and

"*Plaintiff* (emphasis ours) avers that on or about April 2, 1942 she owned money and property and had credit in the United States of America, but was then and there in the Kingdom of Greece in straitened financial circumstances due to the conditions produced by World War II and could not make use of her money and property and credit existing in the United States of America. That in the circumstances the plaintiff agreed to and did lend to defendant the sum of 500,000 drachmae, which at that time, on or about April 2, 1942, had the value of $25.00 in money of the United States of America. That the said plaintiff, knowing defendant's financial distress and desire to return to the United States of America, exacted of her the written instrument plaintiff sues upon, which was a promise by her to pay to him the sum of $2,000.00 of United States of America money.''

Plaintiff specially excepted to paragraph IV because the allegations thereof were insufficient to allege either want of consideration or failure of consideration, in that it affirmatively appears therefrom that defendant received what was agreed to be delivered to her, and that plaintiff breached no agreement. The court overruled this exception, and such action is assigned as error. Error is also assigned because of the court's failure to enter judgment for the whole unpaid balance of the principal of the instrument with interest as therein provided.

Defendant testified that she did receive 500,000 drachmas from plaintiff. It is not clear whether she received all the 500,000 drachmas or only a portion of them before she signed the instrument in question. Her testimony clearly shows that the understanding of the parties was that plaintiff would give her the 500,000 drachmas if she would sign the instrument. She testified:

> "Q.   . . . who suggested the figure of $2,000.00?

> "A.   That was how he asked me from the beginning. He said he will give me five hundred thousand drachmas provided I signed that I would pay him $2,000.00 American money.''

The transaction amounted to a sale by plaintiff of the 500,000 drachmas in consideration of the execution of the instrument sued on, by defendant. It is not contended that the drachmas had no value. Indeed, the judgment indicates that the trial court placed a value of $750.00 on them or on the other consideration which plaintiff gave defendant for the instrument if he believed plaintiff's testimony. Therefore the plea of want of consideration was unavailing. . . .

Mere inadequacy of consideration will not void a contract. 10 Tex. Jur., Contracts, § 89, p. 150; Chastain v. Texas Christian Missionary Society, Tex.Civ.App., 78 S.W.2d 728, loc. cit. 731(3), Wr. Ref.

. . .

Questions

1.   What was the deal? What was the promise sued upon? What was the court's legal reason for enforcing it? Why is it a legal reason? What were the contractual interests of the parties? Was the result unjustified? Can you make a better legal argument for Ms. Demotsis?

2.   Should it matter to the question of consideration that the values exchanged seem so unbalanced? Why did Ms. Demotsis agree to such an exchange? Why did Mr. Batsakis? What were their circumstances? Were she and Mr. Batsakis, in the words of RESTATEMENT (SECOND) OF CONTRACTS § 79, Comment c, "free to fix their own valuations"? Were they "better able than others to evaluate the circumstances" of this particular action? Were they better able than the judges of the Texas Court of Civil Appeals seven years after the events in question? Were they better able than us, decades later?

3.　Should it matter in deciding the question of consideration that Mr. Batsakis was probably a loan shark and war profiteer? Should it matter if the loan were illegal under the laws of the Nazi Occupation? Would it be in the interests of people in dire circumstances to withhold legal enforcement of agreements that would be enforceable in normal situations?

NOTE ON AUTONOMY IN CONTEXT

Contractual obligations are undertaken by free beings who are capable of rational deliberation about the commitments they undertake. It makes no sense to think of a turtle's obligations. So far as we know, turtle behavior is determined by genetic make-up and environmental stimuli without pause for the turtle to deliberate on what it shall do. Humans are like turtles to some extent; it makes no sense to think of the law of gravity as an obligation-imposing law. If it makes sense to think of obligations at all, it is because humans are free beings who can make choices.

Individuals need not be free of *all* constraints on conduct in order for us to be unlike turtles in an important way. The freedom presupposed by the law is not absolute; it consists only of a capacity for deliberate action. Humans are always situated within a physical body in a physical and social environment that offers a finite range of opportunities for action. The law is a powerful, partial determinant of this environment insofar as it defines many of the opportunities people can conceive of making for themselves (e.g., being a married person) or cannot so conceive (e.g., being a righteous cannibal). Individual freedom is surely constrained by a person's environment. The range of opportunities in a social environment can be limited, yet broad enough to allow people to make genuine choices. See JOSEPH RAZ, THE MORALITY OF FREEDOM (1986).

Perhaps, then, the mere fact that Ms. Demotsis's choices were constrained by her rather hostile environment is not a sufficient reason for refusing to enforce the contract she made. Everyone's choices are to some extent constrained. To justify refusing to enforce her contract, but not all contracts, we need some workable standard to distinguish her circumstances from everyone else's.

Social justice concerns the distribution of opportunities available to individuals in the social environment. When the distribution is uneven, the range of opportunities can be more or less rich for different people or groups in the same community. Like Ms. Demotsis, some people in our society have very limited options due to social conditions not of their making. A topical question involves the extent to which contract law should take into account socially unjust circumstances that limit a person's opportunities. The doctrine of consideration might be manipulated to take account of unjust circumstances (which it was not in *Batsakis v. Demotsis*). An alternative is to confine the function of this doctrine to ascertaining the presence of a reason for enforcing promises *generally*, regardless of social conditions. Other contract doctrines might be better suited to accounting for unjust circumstances with the kind of public accountability judges should allow in a democracy. See Chapter 3.

NEWMAN & SNELL'S STATE BANK v. HUNTER

Supreme Court of Michigan, 1928.
243 Mich. 331, 220 N.W. 665, 59 A.L.R. 311.

Action by Newman & Snell's State Bank against Zennetta H. Hunter, also known as Z. H. Hunter. Judgment for plaintiff. Case made; and defendant brings error. Reversed without new trial.

FELLOWS, JUDGE. Defendant is the widow of Lee C. Hunter, who died intestate January 25, 1926. His estate was insufficient to pay his funeral expenses and the widow's allowance. At the time of his death, plaintiff bank held his note for $3,700, with 50 shares of the capital stock of the Hunter Company as collateral. This company was insolvent, but was still doing business when the note was given; afterwards it was placed in the hands of a receiver, and its assets were insufficient to pay its debts. The facts were agreed upon on the trial in the court below. We quote from the agreed statement of facts:

> "On March 1, 1926, the defendant gave the plaintiff the note described in the plaintiff's declaration in this cause, and the plaintiff surrendered to her therefor, and, in consideration thereof, the note of said Lee C. Hunter. The defendant also paid the plaintiff the earned interest due on the deceased's note."

Defendant pleaded want of consideration. We shall presently consider the effect of what was done about the stock of the Hunter Company, and for the present will consider whether the surrender of the note of her deceased husband who left no estate was a sufficient consideration for the note sued upon. Counsel for both parties have furnished able briefs, and their arguments have been helpful. They have doubtless brought to our attention all the cases which would be of assistance to us in reaching a conclusion. While all the authorities cited have been examined, we shall not take up each one of them and discuss them, nor shall we cite them all, nor shall we attempt a reconciliation of the decisions of those states whose own decisions are claimed to be out of accord with each other. There is a definite conflict in the decisions from other states, and it is possible there is a conflict between cases from the same court. . . .

Doubtless plaintiff's strongest case is Judy v. Louderman, 48 Ohio St. 562, 29 N.E. 181. The father of an insolvent decedent took up decedent's note with his own. Although the note taken up was worthless, it was held that the consideration was adequate. The opinion largely rests on the desire of the father to acquire his son's note, and in part on the question of moral obligation. . . .

We now take up some of the cases relied upon by defendant. . . . In Home State Bank v. De Witt, 121 Kan. 29, 245 P. 1036, that court pointed out that, while the note of a living person who was presently without means would furnish a consideration, one of a deceased insolvent would not. . . .

This court in one case (Taylor v. Weeks, 129 Mich. 233, 88 N.W. 466) has held that the widow's note, given for the discharge of an unenforceable claim against the estate of her deceased husband, one outlawed under the statute of limitations, was one that was unenforceable as without sufficient consideration, and in two cases (Cawthorpe v. Clark, 173 Mich. 267, 138 N.W. 1075, and Steep v. Harpham, 241 Mich. 652, 217 N.W. 787) this court has held that the widow's note, given for the discharge of obligations of her husband, was enforceable, in the absence of any testimony showing that the estate was insolvent. In the more recent of these cases it was stressed that there was no evidence of insolvency of the estate, and that, while the duty of showing consideration rested on the plaintiff through the case, the recitals in the note made a prima facie case, and the duty of going forward with the testimony rested on the defendant. Here we have the widow's note given to take up the note of her insolvent husband, a worthless piece of paper. When plaintiff surrendered this worthless piece of paper to the defendant, it parted with nothing of value, and defendant received nothing of value, the plaintiff suffered no loss or inconvenience, and defendant received no benefit. The weight of authority sustains defendant's contention, but, going back to fundamentals, it seems clear to me that the transaction was without consideration. . . .

We have now reached the question of whether the manner of handling the stock of the Hunter Company furnished a consideration. So far as the record discloses, this stock was retained by the bank, and was treated as collateral to defendant's note, and it was so stated in that instrument. The bank, so far as the record discloses, never surrendered it to the defendant, but kept it, and has it to-day. But plaintiff's counsel insists that, as matter of law, it was transferred to defendant. They insist that whatever interest the bank had in the stock passed to defendant when her husband's note was surrendered to her, even though it was not as a matter of fact given to her. But, if we accept this theory, and thus create a legal fiction, we must have in mind that she at once and in the same transaction rehypothecated the stock to the bank. Stripped of all legal fiction, the cold facts are that, when the negotiations opened, plaintiff had this stock and the worthless note of defendant's husband. When they ended, the bank still had the stock and defendant's note. Defendant had her husband's worthless note, and she had nothing more. But this discussion is largely academic. The agreed statement of facts shows that the company was insolvent. The stock then had no book value. There is no statement that it had a market value, and, in the absence of anything showing, or tending to show, a market value, we cannot assume it had such value or what it was. It was suggested in the argument that, even though the company was insolvent, it might have been revived by the infusion of new money in the enterprise. But no one has come along with any infusion of such new blood, and value based on such a possibility is altogether too problematical to form a fixed basis of property rights. The record shows the affairs of the company have been wound up, and that creditors were not paid in full. Upon this record the stock was worthless. . . .

The judgment will be reversed without a new trial.

Questions

1. What was the deal? What is the promise sued upon? Why does the court not enforce that promise?

2. Was the decision justified? On what grounds? Did the bank have a contractual interest that was worthy of legal protection? Did Ms. Hunter have a countervailing interest?

3. Should the fact that the defendant was a widow have any legal significance in this case? Did the court manipulate consideration doctrine to see to it that the widow won? Does the decision do justice to the parties? If so, why should judges have to manipulate a legal doctrine to that end?

RESTATEMENT (SECOND) OF CONTRACTS § 74

DYER v. NATIONAL BY–PRODUCTS, INC.

Supreme Court of Iowa, 1986.
380 N.W.2d 732.

SCHULTZ, JUSTICE. The determinative issue in this appeal is whether good faith forbearance to litigate a claim, which proves to be invalid and unfounded, is sufficient consideration to uphold a contract of settlement. The district court determined, as a matter of law, that consideration for the alleged settlement was lacking because the forborne claim was not a viable cause of action. We reverse and remand.

On October 29, 1981, Dale Dyer, an employee of National By-Products, lost his right foot in a job-related accident. Thereafter, the employer placed Dyer on a leave of absence at full pay from the date of his injury until August 16, 1982. At that time he returned to work as a foreman, the job he held prior to his injury. On March 11, 1983, the employer indefinitely laid off Dyer.

Dyer then filed the present lawsuit against his employer claiming that his discharge was a breach of an oral contract. He alleged that he in good faith believed that he had a valid claim against his employer for his personal injury. Further, Dyer claimed that his forbearance from litigating his claim was made in exchange for a promise from his employer that he would have lifetime employment. The employer specifically denied that it had offered a lifetime job to Dyer after his injury.

Following extensive discovery procedures, the employer filed a motion for summary judgment claiming there was no genuine factual issue and that it was entitled to judgment as a matter of law. The motion was resisted by Dyer. The district court sustained the employer's motion on the basis that: (1) no reciprocal promise to work for the employer for life was present, and (2) there was no forbearance of any viable cause of action, apparently on the ground that workers' compensation provided Dyer's sole remedy.

On appeal, Dyer claims that consideration for the alleged contract of lifetime employment was his forbearance from pursuing an action against his employer. Accordingly, he restricts his claim of error to the second reason advanced by the district court for granting summary judgment. Summary judgment is only proper when there is no genuine issue of any material fact. Iowa R.Civ.P. 237(c). Dyer generally contends that an unresolved issue of material fact remains as to whether he reasonably and in good faith forbore from asserting a claim against his employer and his coemployees in exchange for the employer's alleged promise to employ him for life. Specifically, he asserts that the trial court erred because: (1) the court did not consider the reasonableness and good faith of his belief in the validity of the claim he forbore from asserting, and (2) the court considered the legal merits of the claim itself which Dyer forbore from asserting.

The employer, on the other hand, maintains that workers' compensation[1] benefits are Dyer's sole remedy for his injury and that his claim for damages is unfounded. It then urges that forbearance from asserting an unfounded claim cannot serve as consideration for a contract. For the purpose of this discussion, we shall assume that Dyer's tort action is clearly invalid and he had no basis for a tort suit against either his employer or his fellow employees. We recognize that the fact issue, as to whether Dyer in good faith believed that he had a cause of action based in tort against the employer, remains unresolved. The determinative issue before the district court and now on appeal is whether the lack of consideration for the alleged promise of lifetime employment has been established as a matter of law.

Preliminarily, we observe that the law favors the adjustment and settlement of controversies without resorting to court action. *Olson v. Wilson & Co.*, 244 Iowa 895, 899, 58 N.W.2d 381, 384 (1953). Compromise is favored by law. *White v. Flood*, 258 Iowa 402, 409, 138 N.W.2d 863, 867 (1965). Compromise of a doubtful right asserted in good faith is sufficient consideration for a promise. *Id.*

---

1. It is undisputed that the employee was covered under workers' compensation. The Iowa workers' compensation act states in pertinent part that:

The rights and remedies provided in this chapter ... for an employee on account of injury ... for which benefits under this chapter ... are recoverable, *shall be the exclusive and only rights and remedies of such employee ... at common law or otherwise, on account of such injury ... against:* (1) his or her employer....

Iowa Code § 85.20 (1983) (emphasis added).

The more difficult problem is whether the settlement of an unfounded claim asserted in good faith is consideration for a contract of settlement. Professor Corbin presents a view favorable to Dyer's argument when he states:

> [F]orbearance to press a claim, or a promise of such forbearance, may be a sufficient consideration even though the claim is wholly ill-founded. It may be ill-founded because the facts are not what he supposes them to be, or because the existing facts do not have the legal operation that he supposes them to have. In either case, his forbearance may be a sufficient consideration, although under certain circumstances it is not. The fact that the claim is ill-founded is not in itself enough to prevent forbearance from being a sufficient consideration for a promise.

1 *Corbin on Contracts* § 140, at 595 (1963). Further, in the same section, it is noted that:

> The most generally prevailing, and probably the most satisfactory view is that *forbearance is sufficient if there is any reasonable ground for the claimant's belief that it is just to try to enforce his claim. He must be asserting his claim "in good faith;"* but this does not mean he must believe that his suit can be won. It means that he must not be making his claim or threatening suit for purposes of vexation, or in order to realize on its "nuisance value."

Id. § 40, at 602 (emphasis added). Indeed, we find support for the Corbin view in language contained in our cases. *See White v. Flood*, 258 Iowa at 409, 138 N.W.2d at 867 ("[C]ompromise of a doubtful right asserted in good faith is sufficient consideration for a promise."). . . .

However, not all jurisdictions adhere to this view. Some courts require that the claim forborne must have some merit in fact or at law before it can provide consideration and these jurisdictions reject those claims that are obviously invalid. *See Bullard v. Curry–Cloonan*, 367 A.2d 127, 131 (D.C.App.1976) ("[A]s a general principle, the forbearance of a cause of action advanced in good faith, which is neither absurd in fact nor obviously unfounded in law, constitutes good and valuable consideration."). . . .

In fact, we find language in our own case law that supports the view which is favorable to the employer in this case. *See Vande Stouwe v. Bankers' Life Co.*, 218 Iowa 1182, 1190, 254 N.W. 790, 794 (1934) ("A claim that is entirely baseless and without foundation in law or equity will not support a compromise."). . . . Additionally, Professor Williston notes that:

> While there is a great divergence of opinion respecting the kind of forbearance which will constitute consideration, the *weight of authority holds that although forbearance from suit on a clearly invalid claim is insufficient consideration for a promise,* forbearance from suit on a claim of doubtful validity is sufficient consideration for a promise if there is a sincere belief in the validity of the claim.

1 *Williston on Contracts* § 135, at 581 (3rd ed. 1957) (emphasis added).

We believe, however, that the better reasoned approach is that expressed in the Restatement (Second) of Contracts section 74.... As noted before, as a matter of policy the law favors compromise and such policy would be defeated if a party could second guess his settlement and litigate the validity of the compromise. The requirement that the forbearing party assert the claim in good faith sufficiently protects the policy of law that favors the settlement of controversies. Our holdings which are to the contrary to this view are overruled.

In the present case, the invalidity of Dyer's claim against the employer does not foreclose him, as a matter of law, from asserting that his forbearance was consideration for the alleged contract of settlement. However, the issue of Dyer's good faith must still be examined. In so doing, the issue of the validity of Dyer's claim should not be entirely overlooked.... We conclude that the evidence of the invalidity of the claim is relevant to show a lack of honest belief in the validity of the claim asserted or forborne.

Under the present state of the record, there remains a material fact as to whether Dyer's forbearance to assert his claim was in good faith. Summary judgment should not have been rendered against him. Accordingly, the case is reversed and remanded for further proceedings consistent with this opinion.

Questions

1. What was the deal? What is the promise sued upon? Why was it not enforced by the trial court?

2. Should the law encourage settlements like the one in *Dyer*? If so, should the requirement of consideration, understood as a bargained-for exchange of objective values, stand in the way of enforcing a settlement of an invalid claim regardless of the good faith with which it is asserted? Assume that the law was indifferent to settlements. Same result?

3. Is there any reason of justice why Dyer's employer should have made the promise for lifetime employment? The technicalities of the law aside, is there any reason why a court should enforce that promise? If so, should the courts allow juries to impose the just result regardless of the promise? Would juries care about the promise in a case like this? Or should the doctrine of consideration bar a jury's discretion to do justice on the particulars of the situation? See Webb v. McGowin, below at p. 193.

4. *Problem.*

    Assume that Dyer's claim was legally invalid. Dyer did not know this because he did not have a lawyer. Reyd, however, lost his left foot while working for the same employer under otherwise identical circumstances. Reyd had a lawyer, who advised him that the claim was invalid. When Reyd wants to sue his employer to enforce a promise of lifetime employment, should you take the case?

LAKE LAND EMPLOYMENT GROUP
OF AKRON v. COLUMBER

Supreme Court of Ohio, 2004.
101 Ohio St.3d 242, 804 N.E.2d 27.

MOYER, C.J. Lake Land Employment Group of Akron, LLC ("Lake Land"), appellant, initiated this action by filing a complaint asserting that its ex-employee, appellee Lee Columber, had breached a noncompetition agreement the parties had executed. The agreement provided that for a period of three years after his termination of employment Columber would not engage in any business within a 50–mile radius of Akron, Ohio, that competed with the business of Lake Land. Lake Land further claimed that Columber's employment with Lake Land terminated in 2001 and that he thereafter violated the terms of the noncompetition agreement. Lake Land sought money damages and an order prohibiting Columber from engaging in any activities that violated the noncompetition agreement. Columber answered and admitted that he had been employed by Lake Land from 1988 until 2001. He further admitted that he had signed the noncompetition agreement and that following his discharge from Lake Land he had formed a corporation that is engaged in a business similar to that of Lake Land. Columber pled lack of consideration in his answer.

Columber moved for summary judgment, claiming that the noncompetition agreement was unenforceable. He asserted that the agreement was not supported by consideration and that the restrictions in the agreement were overly restrictive and imposed an undue hardship on him.

Columber could remember very little about the presentation or execution of the noncompetition agreement. He could not remember whether he had been told that his continued employment was dependent upon execution of the agreement or whether he had posed questions about the restrictions it contained. He testified that he vaguely remembered signing the agreement after his employer presented it to him and told him to read and sign it. He acknowledged that he had read the agreement, but had not talked to an attorney or anybody else about it. The at-will relationship of the parties continued for ten years thereafter.

The trial court granted summary judgment in Columber's favor. It found no dispute that Columber had been employed by Lake Land beginning in1988 and that Columber signed the agreement in September 1991. It further found no dispute that there "was no increase of salary, benefits, or other remunerations given as consideration for Columber signing the noncompetition agreement" and "no change in his employment status in connection with the signing of the noncompetition agreement." The trial court concluded that the noncompetition agreement lacked consideration, and was unenforceable. The trial court therefore found it unnecessary to determine the reasonableness of the temporal and geographical restrictions in the noncompetition agreement.

The court of appeals affirmed. It certified a conflict, however, between its decision and the judgments of the Eighth District Court of Appeals.... The certified issue is "Is subsequent employment alone sufficient consideration to support a covenant-not-to-compete agreement with an at-will employee entered into after employment has already begun?"

Generally, courts look upon noncompetition agreements with some skepticism and have cautiously considered and carefully scrutinized them. Ingram, Covenants Not to Compete (2002), 36 Akron L.Rev. 49, 50. Under English common law, agreements in restraint of trade, including noncompetition agreements, were disfavored as being against public policy, although partial restraints supported by fair consideration were upheld. *Lange v. Werk* (1853), 2 Ohio St. 519, 527–528, 1853 WL 117, citing *Mitchel v. Reynolds* (1711), 1 P.Wms. 181, 24 Eng.Rep. 347. In a society in which working men entered skilled trades only by serving apprenticeships, and mobility was minimal, restrictive covenants precluding an ex–employee from competing with his ex-employer "either destroyed a man's means of livelihood, or bound him to his master for life." *Raimonde v. Van Vlerah* (1975), 42 Ohio St.2d 21, 71 O.O.2d 12, 325 N.E.2d 544.

Modern economic realities, however, do not justify a strict prohibition of noncompetition agreements between employer and employee in an at-will relationship. "The law upholds these agreements because they allow the parties to work together to expand output and competition. If one party can trust the other with confidential information and secrets, then both parties are better positioned to compete with the rest of the world.... By protecting ancillary covenants not to compete, even after an employee has launched his own firm, the law 'makes it easier for people to cooperate productively in the first place.' " *KW Plastics v. United States Can Co.* (Feb. 2, 2001....

Accordingly, this court has long recognized the validity of agreements that restrict competition by an ex-employee if they contain reasonable geographical and temporal restrictions. *Briggs v. Butler* (1942), 140 Ohio St. 499, 507, 24 O.O. 523, 45 N.E.2d 757. Such an agreement does not violate public policy, "being reasonably necessary for the protection of the employer's business, and not unreasonably restrictive upon the rights of the employee." Id. at 508, 24 O.O. 523, 45 N.E.2d 757....

Jurisdictions throughout the country are split on the issue presented by the certified question.... As summarized by the Supreme Court of Minnesota, "cases which have held that continued employment is not a sufficient consideration stress the fact that an employee frequently has no bargaining power once he is employed and can easily be coerced. By signing a noncompetition agreement, the employee gets no more from his employer than he already has, and in such cases there is a danger that an employer does not need protection for his investment in the employee but instead seeks to impose barriers to prevent an employee from securing a better job elsewhere. Decisions in which continued employment has been deemed a sufficient consideration for a noncompetition agreement have focused on a variety of factors, including the possibility that the employee would otherwise have been discharged, the employee was actually employed for a substantial time after executing the contract, or the employee received additional compensation or training or was given confidential information after he signed the agreement." (Citations omitted.) *Davies & Davies Agency, Inc. v. Davies* (Minn. 1980) 298 N.W.2d 127, 130.

More recently, some courts have found sufficient consideration in an at-will employment situation where a *substantial* period of employment ensues after a noncompetition covenant is executed, especially when the continued employment is accompanied by raises, promotion, or similar tangible benefits. 6 Lord, Williston on Contracts (4th Ed.1995), Section 13:13. These courts thereby implicitly find that the execution of a noncompetition agreement changes the prior employment relationship from one purely at will. Id. at 577–584. In effect, these courts infer a promise on the part of the employer to continue the employment of his previously at-will employee for an indefinite yet substantial term. Under this approach, however, neither party knows whether the agreement is enforceable until events occur after its execution. The certified question puts in issue only the element of consideration. It asks, "Is subsequent employment alone sufficient consideration to support a covenant-not-to-compete agreement with an at-will employee entered into after employment has already begun?" We conclude that forbearance on the part of an at-will employer from discharging an at-will employee serves as consideration to support a noncompetition agreement.

This court has long recognized the rule that a contract is not binding unless supported by consideration. *Judy v. Louderman* (1891), 48 Ohio St. 562, 29 N.E. 181, paragraph two of the syllabus. Consideration may consist of either a detriment to the promisee or a benefit to the promisor. *Irwin v. Lombard Univ.* (1897), 56 Ohio St. 9, 19, 46 N.E. 63. A benefit may consist of some right, interest, or profit accruing to the promisor, while a detriment may consist of some forbearance, loss, or responsibility given, suffered, or undertaken by the promisee. Id. at 20, 46 N.E. 63.

. . .

At-will employment is contractual in nature. *Floyd v. DuBois Soap Co.* (1942), 139 Ohio St. 520, 530–531, 23 O.O. 20, 41 N.E.2d 393. In such a relationship, the employee agrees to perform work under the direction and control of the employer, and the employer agrees to pay the employee at an agreed rate. Moreover, either an employer or an employee in a pure at-will employment relationship may legally terminate the employment relationship at any time and for any reason. *Mers v. Dispatch Printing Co.* (1985), 19 Ohio St.3d 100, 103, 19 OBR 261, 483 N.E.2d 150. In the event that an at-will employee quits or is fired, he or she provides no further services for the employer and is generally entitled only to wages and benefits already earned.

It follows that either an employer or an employee in an at-will relationship may propose to change the terms of their employment relationship at any time. If, for instance, an employer notifies an employee that the employee's compensation will be reduced, the employee's remedy, if dissatisfied, is to quit. Similarly, if the employee proposes to the employer that he deserves a raise and will no longer work at his current rate, the employer may either negotiate an increase or accept the loss of his employee. In either event the employee is entitled to be paid only for services already rendered pursuant to terms to which they both have agreed. Thus, mutual promises to employ and to be employed on an ongoing at-will basis, according to agreed terms, are supported by consideration: the promise of one serves as consideration for the promise of the other.

The presentation of a noncompetition agreement by an employer to an at-will employee is, in effect, a proposal to renegotiate the terms of the parties' at-will employment. Where an employer makes such a proposal by presenting his employee with a noncompetition agreement and the employee assents to it, thereby accepting continued employment on new terms, consideration supporting the noncompetition agreement exists. The employee's assent to the agreement is given in exchange for forbearance on the part of the employer from terminating the employee.

We therefore hold that consideration exists to support a noncompetition agreement when, in exchange for the assent of an at-will employee to a proffered noncompetition agreement, the employer continues an at-will employment relationship that could legally be terminated without cause. Judgment reversed and cause remanded.

ALICE ROBIE RESNICK, J., dissenting. Courts everywhere are sharply divided on the present certified issue. However, I adhere to the principle that continued employment in an at-will situation does not by itself constitute consideration. I respectfully dissent.

As the majority confirms, "a contract is not binding unless supported by consideration," which is generally defined as "a detriment to the promisee or a benefit to the promisor." Thus, in order for the September 1991 noncompetition agreement executed between appellant, Lake Land Employment Group of Akron, LLC, and appellee, Lee Columber, to be binding, either Lake Land must have given something for it or Columber must have received something in return. Yet, when all is said and done, the only difference in the parties' employment relationship before and after September 1991 is the noncompetition agreement.

The majority's holding that "[c]onsideration exists to support a noncompetition agreement when ... the employer continues an at-will employment relationship ..." belies itself. If the same at-will employment relationship continues, where is the consideration? The employer has relinquished nothing, since it retains exactly the same preexisting right it always had to discharge the employee at any time, for any reason, for no reason, with or without cause. The employee has gained nothing, for he has not been given or promised anything other than that which he already had, which is "employment which need not last longer than the ink is dry upon [his] signature." *Kadis v. Britt* (1944), 224 N.C. 154, 163, 29 S.E.2d 543. It is precisely because the same at-will employment relationship continues that there is no consideration.

In fact, the majority endeavors to transform this mutual exchange of nothing into consideration by formulating such artful euphemisms as "forbearance on the part of an at-will employer from discharging an at-will employee," "mutual promises to employ and to be employed on an ongoing at-will basis," and "a proposal to renegotiate the terms of the parties' at-will employment." But in the end, the employer simply winds up with both the noncompetition agreement and the continued right to discharge the employee at will, while the employee is left with the same preexisting "nonright" to be employed for so long as the employer decides not to fire him. The only actual "forbearance," "proposal," or "promise" made by the employer in this situation is declining to fire the employee until he executes the noncompetition agreement. . . .

Questions

1. What is the deal regarding the covenant not to compete? What does the employee give the employer? What does the employer give the employee? Was the exchange identified by the court "bargained for."

2. Was there consideration for the employee's promise not to compete, in your view? What should be the role of policy, such as the "modern economic realities" identified by the court, in a decision on the consideration question? Are there any other relevant policies? Would you concur with the majority or the dissent?

3. *Problems.*

   a. Assume that a buyer of goods agrees to buy all that it may want from the seller at a fixed price. The seller agrees to sell all that the buyer may order at the same price. The price of the goods rises, and the seller refuses to fill a large order. Can the buyer successfully sue the seller? See Wickham & Burton Coal Co. v. Farmers' Lumber Co., 189 Iowa 1183, 179 N.W. 417 (1920).

   b. The facts are the same as in problem a above, except that the buyer ordered two carloads of the goods. The seller filled the order. The buyer then ordered two more carloads. The seller refused to fill this order. Does the buyer have any recourse on the second order?

   c. The facts are the same as in problem a above, except that the buyer and the seller agreed that the buyer would order its requirements of the goods from the seller at a fixed price. The buyer ordered some goods. The seller refused to fill the order. Was there consideration for the seller's promise? See U.C.C. § 2–306(1).

WOOD v. LUCY, LADY DUFF–GORDON

Court of Appeals of New York, 1917.
222 N.Y. 88, 118 N.E. 214.

CARDOZO, J. The defendant styles herself "a creator of fashions." Her favor helps a sale. Manufacturers of dresses, millinery, and like articles are glad to pay for a certificate of her approval. The things which she designs, fabrics, parasols, and what not, have a new value in the public mind when issued in her name. She employed the plaintiff to help her to turn this vogue into money. He was to have the exclusive right, subject always to her approval, to place her indorsements on the designs of others. He was also to have the exclusive right to place her own designs on sale, or to license others to market them. In return she was to have one-half of "all profits and revenues" derived from any contracts he might make. The exclusive right was to last at least one year from April 1, 1915, and thereafter from year to year unless terminated by notice of 90 days. The plaintiff says that he kept the contract on his part, and that the defendant broke it. She placed her indorsement on fabrics, dresses, and millinery without his knowledge, and withheld the profits. He sues her for the damages, and the case comes here on demurrer.

The agreement of employment is signed by both parties. It has a wealth of recitals. The defendant insists, however, that it lacks the elements of a contract. She says that the plaintiff does not bind himself to anything. It is true that he does not promise in so many words that he will use reasonable efforts to place the defendant's indorsements and market her designs. We think, however, that such a promise is fairly to be implied. The law has outgrown its primitive stage of formalism when the precise word was the sovereign talisman, and every slip was fatal. It takes a broader view today. A promise may be lacking, and yet the whole writing may be "instinct with an obligation," imperfectly expressed (Scott, J., in McCall Co. v. Wright, 133 App.Div. 62, 117 N.Y. Supp. 775 . . .). If that is so, there is a contract.

The implication of a promise here finds support in many circumstances. The defendant gave an exclusive privilege. She was to have no right for at least a year to place her own indorsements or market her own designs except through the agency of the plaintiff. The acceptance of the exclusive agency was an assumption of its duties. Phoenix Hermetic Co. v. Filtrine Mfg. Co., 164 App.Div. 424, 150 N.Y. Supp. 193. . . . Many other terms of the agreement point the same way. We are told at the outset by way of recital that:

> "The said Otis F. Wood possesses a business organization adapted to the placing of such indorsements as the said Lucy, Lady Duff–Gordon, has approved."

The implication is that the plaintiff's business organization will be used for the purpose for which it is adapted. But the terms of the defendant's compensation are even more significant. Her sole compensation for the grant of an exclusive agency is to be one-half of all the profits resulting from the plaintiff's efforts. Unless he gave his efforts, she could never get anything. Without an implied promise, the transaction cannot have such business "efficacy, as both parties must have intended that at all events it should have." Bowen, L. J., in the Moorcock, 14 P. D. 64, 68. But the contract does not stop there. The plaintiff goes on to promise that he will account monthly for all moneys received by him, and that he will take out all such patents and copyrights and trade-marks as may in his judgment be necessary to protect the rights and articles affected by the agreement. It is true, of course, as the Appellate Division has said, that if he was under no duty to try to market designs or to place certificates of indorsement, his promise to account for profits or take out copyrights would be valueless. But in determining the intention of the parties the promise has a value. It helps to enforce the conclusion that the plaintiff had some duties. His promise to pay the defendant one-half of the profits and revenues resulting from the exclusive agency and to render accounts monthly was a promise to use reasonable efforts to bring profits and revenues into existence. For this conclusion the authorities are ample. . . .

The judgment of the Appellate Division should be reversed, and the order of the Special Term affirmed, with costs in the Appellate Division and in this court.

Questions

1.   What was the deal? What is the promise sued upon? What is the defense?

2.   Why does Cardozo imply a promise? Does the implication of a promise here impose upon Mr. Wood's autonomy? Does it impose upon Lady Duff–Gordon's? Is the decision to enforce her promise justified? Did she have a contractual interest that was more important than Wood's?

3.   *Problems.*

a.   Newman promised Woodward that, in exchange for a sizable payment, he would deliver a described automobile to her in December. It was unclear, however, whether such an automobile would be available in December. Newman promised that, if he could not obtain the described automobile, he would deliver a described substitute. Woodward agreed to accept the substitute if delivered. Did Newman supply consideration for Woodward's promise to pay? See RESTATEMENT (SECOND) OF CONTRACTS § 77 (1981).

b.   Holden promised to work as a bus boy for a fast food restaurant. His employment was "at will"; that is, he could be discharged at any time for any reason. Is Holden's promise enforceable?

c.   The facts are the same as is Problem b above, except that Holden could be discharged for any reason with seven day's notice. Is his promise enforceable?

———

RESTATEMENT (SECOND) OF CONTRACTS § 73

———

LEVINE v. BLUMENTHAL
Supreme Court of New Jersey, 1936.
117 N.J.L. 23, 186 A. 457.

HEHER, JUSTICE. By an indenture dated April 16, 1931, plaintiff leased to defendants, for the retail merchandising of women's wearing apparel, store premises situate in the principal business district of the city of Paterson. The term was two years, to commence on May 1 next ensuing, with an option of renewal for the further period of three years; and the rent reserved was $2,100 for the first year, and $2,400 for the second year, payable in equal monthly installments in advance.

The state of the case settled by the district court judge sets forth that defendants adduced evidence tending to show that, in the month of April, 1932, before the expiration of the first year of the term, they advised plaintiff that "it was absolutely impossible for them to pay any increase in rent; that their business had so fallen down that they had great difficulty in meeting the present rent of $175 per month; that if the plaintiff insisted upon the increase called for in the lease, they would be forced to remove from the premises or perhaps go out of business altogether;" and that plaintiff "agreed to allow them to remain under the same rental 'until business improved.' " While conceding that defendants informed him that "they could not pay the increase called for in the lease because of adverse business conditions," plaintiff, on the other hand, testified that he "agreed to accept the payment of $175 each month, on account." For eleven months of the second year of the term rent was paid by defendants, and accepted by plaintiff, at the rate of $175 per month. The option of renewal was not exercised; and defendants surrendered the premises at the expiration of the term, leaving the last month's rent unpaid. This action was brought to recover the unpaid balance of the rent reserved by the lease for the second year—$25 per month for eleven months, and $200 for the last month.

The district court judge found, as a fact, that "a subsequent oral agreement had been made to change and alter the terms of the written lease, with respect to the rent paid," but that it was not supported by "a lawful consideration," and therefore was wholly ineffective.

The insistence is that the current trade depression had disabled the lessees in respect of the payment of the full rent reserved, and a consideration sufficient to support the secondary agreement arose out of these special circumstances; and that, in any event, the execution of the substituted performance therein provided is a defense at law, notwithstanding the want of consideration.... It is said also that, "insofar as the oral agreement has become executed as to the payments which had fallen due and had been paid and accepted in full as per the oral agreement," the remission of the balance of the rent is sustainable on the theory of gift, if not of accord and satisfaction. . . .

It is elementary that the subsequent agreement, to impose the obligation of a contract, must rest upon a new and independent consideration. The rule was laid down in very early times that even though a part of a matured liquidated debt or demand has been given and received in full satisfaction thereof, the creditor may yet recover the remainder. The payment of a part was not regarded in law as a satisfaction of the whole, unless it was in virtue of an agreement supported by a consideration. Pinnel's Case, 5 Coke 117, a, 77 Eng.Reprint 237; Fitch v. Sutton, 5 East. 230; Foakes v. Beer, 9 App.Cas. 605; Cumber v. Wane, 1 Strange 426. . . . The principle is firmly imbedded in our jurisprudence that a promise to do what the promisor is already legally bound to do is an unreal consideration. . . .

So tested, the secondary agreement at issue is not supported by a valid consideration; and it therefore created no legal obligation. General economic adversity, however disastrous it may be in its individual consequences, is never a warrant for judicial abrogation of this primary principle of the law of contracts.

It remains to consider the second contention that, in so far as the agreement has been executed by the payment and acceptance of rent at the reduced rate, the substituted performance stands, regardless of the want of consideration. This is likewise untenable. Ordinarily, the actual performance of that which one is legally bound to do stands on the same footing as his promise to do that which he is legally compellable to do. Anson on Contracts (Turck Ed.) p. 234; Williston on Contracts (Rev. Ed.) §§ 130, 130a. This is a corollary of the basic principle. Of course, a different rule prevails where bona fide disputes have arisen respecting the relative rights and duties of the parties to a contract, or the debt or demand is unliquidated, or the contract is wholly executory on both sides. Anson on Contracts (Turck Ed.) pp. 240, 241.

It is settled in this jurisdiction that, as in the case of other contracts, a consideration is essential to the validity of an accord and satisfaction. . . . It results that the issue was correctly determined.

Judgment affirmed, with costs.

Questions

1. What is the deal? What happens that leads to litigation? What is the lessee's defense? Would the court be justified in holding for the tenant? If so, what would be the justification in law?

2. In *Levine,* why was the then-current depression not a consideration sufficient to support the lessor's promise to reduce the rent?

3. *Problems.*

    a. Mason was a police detective assigned to investigate burglaries. He was snowed with work because there had been a rash of burglaries over the preceding month. Della was burglarized but was dissatisfied with the speed with which Mason was investigating her case. She promised to pay Mason a $1,000 bonus if he would move her case to the top of his "To-Do" list. Mason did so and solved her case. Is he entitled to the $1,000 she promised him? See Gray v. Martino, 91 N.J.L. 462, 103 A. 24 (1918).

b. Assume the facts are as in Problem a, except that Mason was a private investigator employed by Della's insurance company. Same result for the same reasons?

c. Assume the facts are as in Problem b, except that Mason let Della know he would move her case to the bottom of his "To-Do" list unless she promised to pay him $1,000 for investigating the case promptly. Same result for the same reasons?

d. Cousy contracted to build a stadium for the University of Basketball according to architectural plans he had drawn. When the stadium's steel frame was up, Cousy informed the University that he would walk off the job, taking all copies of the plans, unless his price was increased by 50%. Preferring to submit than to incur the expenses of salvaging the operation, the University agreed. Cousy completed the stadium, but the University then paid him only the original contract price. In an action by Cousy for the additional 50%, what result? Why? See Lingenfelder v. Wainwright Brewery Co., 103 Mo. 578, 15 S.W. 844 (1891); Austin Instrument, Inc. v. Loral Corp., 29 N.Y.2d 124, 324 N.Y.S.2d 22, 272 N.E.2d 533 (1971).

U.C.C. § 2–209(1)

Restatement (Second) of Contracts §§ 175–76.

GROSS VALENTINO PRINTING CO. v. CLARKE

Appellate Court of Illinois, First District, First Division, 1983.
120 Ill.App.3d 907, 76 Ill.Dec. 373, 458 N.E.2d 1027.

GOLDBERG, JUSTICE: Gross Valentino Printing Company (plaintiff) brought this action against Frederick S. Clarke, doing business as Cinefantastique (defendant) based on an alleged breach of contract. Defendant asserted three affirmative defenses: lack of consideration, fraudulent or innocent misrepresentation, and business compulsion.

Plaintiff moved for summary judgment. Both plaintiff and defendant filed depositions in support of their theories. The trial court granted plaintiff's motion with regard to the first and third defenses and allowed defendant to amend its pleadings with regard to the affirmative defense of fraud. Plaintiff then renewed its motion for summary judgment. After a hearing, the trial court granted plaintiff's motion and entered judgment of $5,116.20 for plaintiff. Defendant appeals.

Defendant publishes a magazine. After discussion, in July of 1979, plaintiff sent defendant a letter for printing the magazine including a price quotation of $6,695. Defendant accepted the terms. On August 8, 1979, the parties met to discuss the layout. The parties' depositions diverge as to the substance of that meeting. Because plaintiff was the movant for summary judgment, "this court will construe the pleadings, depositions and affidavits strictly against the movant and liberally in favor of the opponent" to determine if the summary judgment was proper. *Kolakowski v. Voris* (1980), 83 Ill.2d 388, 398, 47 Ill.Dec. 392, 415 N.E.2d 397.

According to defendant's deposition, he brought materials for printing the magazine to plaintiff's office on August 8, 1979. Defendant discussed problems concerning the layout with an agent of plaintiff corporation. The agent told defendant the job could still be done "in house" despite the problems. He also told defendant the price would remain the same over the next six issues of the magazine.

Defendant also stated the parties had a telephone conversation on August 14, 1979. Defendant was informed the job "was going to cost more than we thought." Plaintiff's agent told defendant the higher cost was incurred because plaintiff had to "send the stripping out." Defendant did not inform plaintiff's agent he wanted to get another printer because defendant did not believe he could meet his deadline if he changed printers. Defendant was also afraid plaintiff would not return defendant's materials if defendant argued about the price. Those materials were necessary for continued printing of defendant's magazine.

Defendant also deposed that sometime thereafter plaintiff sent defendant a letter dated August 15, 1979. The letter specified the same work as represented in the parties' earlier contract. However the price was increased to $9,300. Defendant made no objection to this increase until a later date.

On August 30, 1979, plaintiff delivered the first 5,000 magazines to defendant. Defendant signed the purchase order reflecting the new price and paid plaintiff $4,650 on account of the purchase. Defendant subsequently received the complete shipment of 15,000 magazines. However, on October 28, 1979, defendant informed plaintiff he would not accept the price increase.

I.

LACK OF CONSIDERATION.

The parties agree that the sufficiency of defendant's first affirmative defense of lack of consideration depends on the determination of whether the transactions at issue are subject to the Uniform Commercial Code

(UCC). (Ill. Rev. Stat. 1981, ch. 26, par. 1–101 *et seq.*) Under the UCC a modification of an existing contract "within this Article needs no consideration to be binding." (Ill. Rev. Stat. 1981, ch. 26, par. 2–209(1).) The parties also agree that the applicability of the UCC depends on the determination of whether they contracted for "goods" or "services."

The UCC defines "goods" as (Ill. Rev. Stat. 1981, ch. 26, par. 2–105(1)):

> " 'Goods' means all things, including specially manufactured goods, which are movable at the time of identification to the contract for sale other than the money in which the price is to be paid, investment securities (Article 8) and things in action. 'Goods' also includes the unborn young of animals and growing crops and other identified things attached to realty as described in the section on goods to be severed from realty (Section 2–107)."

The parties have not cited, and our research has not disclosed any case in Illinois in which the court specifically applied the above definition to printed magazines. . . . [In] *Lake Wales Publishing Co., Inc. v. Florida Visitor, Inc.* (Fla.App.1976), 335 So.2d 335[,] . . . the court specifically addressed the issue of whether a contract to compile, edit, and publish printed material constituted a sale of goods. The court concluded that it did (335 So.2d 335, 336):

> "We focus then on whether the printed materials which appellant allegedly furnished to appellee were 'goods' under the U.C.C., Fla. Stat. § 672.2–105(1), which defines 'goods' as:
>
>> " '. . . all things (including specially manufactured goods) which are movable at the time of identification to the contract for sale other than the money in which the price is to be paid, investment securities (chapter 678) and things in action.'
>
> "The specific point has not been passed on by the Florida courts; however, the Official Comment to U.C.C. § 2–105 states that the definition of goods is based upon the concept of their movability. The items allegedly furnished by the appellant were specially produced or manufactured and were movable. Moreover, any services rendered were of necessity directed to production of the items."

See also *Cardozo v. True* (Fla.App.1977), 342 So.2d 1053, 1055, where the court stated "[t]he definition of 'goods' under the U.C.C. is sufficiently broad to include books." . . .

In the case at bar, we conclude that the primary subject of the contract was the tangible printed magazines and not "printing services." Defendant's deposition indicates he worked with plaintiff in arriving at the "layout" of the magazine. Furthermore, defendant's deposition indicates he "shopped" for printers based solely on which printer submitted the lowest price estimate. Such an admission suggests that to defendant the "printing services" were largely fungible or interchangeable and were merely incidental to delivery of the final product. It is clear that defendant was simply interested in determining who could get him the magazines, the ultimate product, at the lowest possible price.

Defendant relies on three cases. We find them inapposite to the case at bar.... In all of these cases the responsibility of the publisher went beyond the simple printing of the material. Each of the contracts in the cited cases required more independent judgment, skill, and service than the contract in the case at bar. Therefore we hold that the agreement between these parties for printing the magazines was subject to the provisions of the UCC. It follows that proof of consideration was unnecessary. The trial court properly struck the first affirmative defense.

.   .   .

III.

BUSINESS COMPULSION.

[D]efendant has failed to allege sufficient facts to sustain the affirmative defense of business compulsion. "Economic duress is present where one is induced by a wrongful act of another to make a contract under circumstances which deprive him of the exercise of free will...." (*Alexander v. Standard Oil Co.* (1981), 97 Ill.App.3d 809, 814, 53 Ill.Dec. 194, 423 N.E.2d 578.) "The bare allegation of 'legal duress' is not sufficient even as an allegation of ultimate fact." *Scoa Industries, Inc. v. Howlett* (1975), 33 Ill.App.3d 90, 96, 337 N.E.2d 305.

"[T]he defense of duress cannot be predicated upon a demand which is lawful or upon doing or threatening to do that which a party has the legal right to do.... Rather, the conduct of the party obtaining the advantage must be shown to be tainted with some degree of fraud or wrongdoing in order to have an agreement invalidated on the basis of duress." (*Alexander*, 97 Ill.App.3d 809, 815, 53 Ill.Dec. 194, 423 N.E.2d 578.) To show compulsion, one must indicate how legal redress would be inadequate. *Kaplan v. Keith* (1978), 60 Ill.App.3d 804, 807, 18 Ill.Dec. 126, 377 N.E.2d 279, *appeal denied*, 71 Ill.2d 609.

In the case at bar, defendant has failed to indicate how his "free will" was overcome by any wrongdoing of plaintiff. As shown above, defendant has failed to show plaintiff was guilty of any fraud or wrongdoing. Defendant does not show how he would have been so damaged by possibly missing a deadline as to overcome his free will. Finally, defendant does not show how legal redress for possible breach of the original contract would have been inadequate.

For these reasons the summary judgment in favor of plaintiff is affirmed....

Questions

1.   What is the deal? What happens that leads to litigation? What is the buyer's chief defense? Why does it fail? Should the court have found economic duress?

2. Should the promises in *Levine* and *Gross Valentino Printing Co.* both be unenforceable unless supported by consideration? Should neither be enforceable unless supported by consideration? Or does the law get it right by requiring consideration at common law but not under U.C.C. Article 2?

3. *Problems*.

a. Nimoy purchased a new computer program from Software-Shops. The program came in a box which contained a warranty on the outside that the program would run on a computer of the kind he owned. When he got home, Nimoy opened the box and found the disks inside a plastic bag, which he opened. Upon installing the program, he found that the program would not work on his computer. When he contacted SoftwareShop, the manager pointed out that the plastic bag contained on it a printed disclaimer of all warranties, "this modification of any prior contract to be accepted by opening this bag." Did Nimoy lose his warranty? See Gold Kist, Inc. v. Citizens and Southern Nat'l Bank of South Carolina, 286 S.C. 272, 333 S.E.2d 67 (1985).

b. Shirley found herself in a contract dispute with her gardener, Gordon, over the amount due to Gordon for landscaping work on Shirley's property. Gordon claims that she agreed to pay $420 while she claims to have agreed to pay only $275. Shirley mailed a personal check to Gordon for $275, noting on the check "payment in full for landscaping services rendered." Gordon cashed the check. He wants to sue Shirley for the balance he claims is due. What should you advise him? Are there further facts that you should ascertain before advising him? If so, what questions would you ask? See U.C.C. § 3–311.

RESTATEMENT (SECOND) OF CONTRACTS § 89

ANGEL v. MURRAY

Supreme Court of Rhode Island, 1974.
113 R.I. 482, 322 A.2d 630.

ROBERTS, CHIEF JUSTICE. This is a civil action brought by Alfred L. Angel and others against John E. Murray, Jr., Director of Finance of the City of Newport, the city of Newport, and James L. Maher, alleging that Maher had illegally been paid the sum of $20,000 by the Director of Finance and praying that the defendant Maher be ordered to repay the city such sum. The case was heard by a justice of the Superior Court, sitting without a jury, who entered a judgment ordering Maher to repay the sum of $20,000 to the city of Newport. Maher is now before this court prosecuting an appeal.

The record discloses that Maher has provided the city of Newport with a refuse-collection service under a series of five-year contracts beginning in 1946. On March 12, 1964, Maher and the city entered into another such contract for a period of five years commencing on July 1, 1964, and terminating on June 30, 1969. The contract provided, among other things, that Maher would receive $137,000 per year in return for collecting and removing all combustible and noncombustible waste materials generated within the city.

In June of 1967, Maher requested an additional $10,000 per year from the city council because there had been a substantial increase in the cost of collection due to an unexpected and unanticipated increase of 400 new dwelling units. Maher's testimony, which is uncontradicted, indicates the 1964 contract had been predicated on the fact that since 1946 there had been an average increase of 20 to 25 new dwelling units per year. After a public meeting of the city council where Maher explained in detail the reasons for his request and was questioned by members of the city council, the city council agreed to pay him an additional $10,000 for the year ending on June 30, 1968. Maher made a similar request again in June of 1968 for the same reasons, and the city council again agreed to pay an additional $10,000 for the year ending on June 30, 1969.

The trial justice found that each such $10,000 payment was made in violation of law. His decision, as we understand it, is premised on two independent grounds. First, he found that the additional payments were unlawful because they had not been recommended in writing to the city council by the city manager. Second, he found that Maher was not entitled to extra compensation because the original contract already required him to collect all refuse generated within the city and, therefore, included the 400 additional units. The trial justice further found that these 400 additional units were within the contemplation of the parties when they entered into the contract. It appears that he based this portion of the decision upon the rule that Maher had a preexisting duty to collect the refuse generated by the 400 additional units, and thus there was no consideration for the two additional payments. . . .

II.

Having found that the city council had the power to modify the 1964 contract without the written recommendation of the city manager, we are still confronted with the question of whether the additional payments were illegal because they were not supported by consideration.

A.

As previously stated, the city council made two $10,000 payments. The first was made in June of 1967 for the year beginning on July 1, 1967, and ending on June 30, 1968. Thus, by the time this action was commenced in October of 1968, the [first] modification was completely executed. That is, the money had been paid by the city council, and Maher had collected all of the refuse. Since consideration is only a test of the enforceability of executory promises, the presence or absence of consideration for the first payment is unimportant because the city council's agreement to make the first payment was fully executed at the time of the commencement of this action.... However, since both payments were made under similar circumstances, our decision regarding the second payment (Part B, infra) is fully applicable to the first payment.

B.

It is generally held that a modification of a contract is itself a contract, which is unenforceable unless supported by consideration.... In Rose v. Daniels, 8 R.I. 381 (1866), this court held that an agreement by a debtor with a creditor to discharge a debt for a sum of money less than the amount due is unenforceable because it was not supported by consideration.

Rose is a perfect example of the preexisting duty rule. Under this rule an agreement modifying a contract is not supported by consideration if one of the parties to the agreement does or promises to do something that he is legally obligated to do or refrains or promises to refrain from doing something he is not legally privileged to do. See Calamari & Perillo, Contracts § 60 (1970); 1A Corbin, Contracts §§ 171–72 (1963); 1 Williston, *supra*, § 130; Annot., 12 A.L.R.2d 78 (1950). In *Rose* there was no consideration for the new agreement because the debtor was already legally obligated to repay the full amount of the debt.

Although the preexisting duty rule is followed by most jurisdictions, a small minority of jurisdictions, Massachusetts, for example, find that there is consideration for a promise to perform what one is already legally obligated to do because the new promise is given in place of an action for damages to secure performance. *See* Swartz v. Lieberman, 323 Mass. 109, 80 N.E.2d 5 (1948).... *Swartz* is premised on the theory that a promisor's forbearance of the power to breach his original agreement and be sued in an action for damages is consideration for a subsequent agreement by the promisee to pay extra compensation. This rule, however, has been widely criticized as an anomaly. *See* Calamari & Perillo, *supra*, § 61; Annot., 12 A.L.R.2d 78, 85–90 (1950).

The primary purpose of the preexisting duty rule is to prevent what has been referred to as the "hold-up game." *See* 1A Corbin, *supra*, § 171. A classic example of the "hold-up game" is found in Alaska Packers' Ass'n v. Domenico, 117 F. 99 (9th Cir.1902). There 21 seamen entered into a written contract with Domenico to sail from San Francisco to Pyramid Harbor, Alaska. They were to work as sailors and fishermen out of Pyramid Harbor during the fishing season of 1900. The contract specified that each man would be paid $50 plus two cents for each red salmon he caught. Subsequent to their arrival at Pyramid Harbor, the men stopped work and demanded an additional $50. They threatened to return to San Francisco if Domenico did not agree to their demand. Since it was impossible for Domenico to find other men, he agreed to pay the men an additional $50. After they returned to San Francisco, Domenico refused to pay the men an additional $50. The court found that the subsequent agreement to pay the men an additional

$50 was not supported by consideration because the men had a preexisting duty to work on the ship under the original contract, and thus the subsequent agreement was unenforceable.

Another example of the "hold-up game" is found in the area of construction contracts. Frequently, a contractor will refuse to complete work under an unprofitable contract unless he is awarded additional compensation. The courts have generally held that a subsequent agreement to award additional compensation is unenforceable if the contractor is only performing work which would have been required of him under the original contract. *See, e.g.,* Lingenfelder v. Wainwright Brewing Co., 103 Mo. 578, 15 S.W. 844 (1891), which is a leading case in this area. . . .

These examples clearly illustrate that the courts will not enforce an agreement that has been procured by coercion or duress and will hold the parties to their original contract regardless of whether it is profitable or unprofitable. However, the courts have been reluctant to apply the preexisting duty rule when a party to a contract encounters unanticipated difficulties and the other party, not influenced by coercion or duress, voluntarily agrees to pay additional compensation for work already required to be performed under the contract. For example, the courts have found that the original contract was rescinded, Linz v. Schuck, 106 Md. 220, 67 A. 286 (1907); abandoned, Connelly v. Devoe, 37 Conn. 570 (1871), or waived, Michaud v. McGregor, 61 Minn. 198, 63 N.W. 479 (1895).

Although the preexisting duty rule has served a useful purpose insofar as it deters parties from using coercion and duress to obtain additional compensation, it has been widely criticized as a general rule of law. With regard to the preexisting duty rule, one legal scholar has stated: "There has been a growing doubt as to the soundness of this doctrine as a matter of social policy. . . . In certain classes of cases, this doubt has influenced courts to refuse to apply the rule, or to ignore it, in their actual decisions. Like other legal rules, this rule is in process of growth and change, the process being more active here than in most instances. The result of this is that a court should no longer accept this rule as fully established. It should never use it as the major premise of a decision, at least without giving careful thought to the circumstances of the particular case, to the moral deserts of the parties, and to the social feelings and interests that are involved. It is certain that the rule, stated in general and all-inclusive terms, is no longer so well-settled that a court must apply it though the heavens fall." 1A Corbin, *supra*, § 171; *see also* Calamari & Perillo, *supra*, § 61.

The modern trend appears to recognize the necessity that courts should enforce agreements modifying contracts when unexpected or unanticipated difficulties arise during the course of the performance of a contract, even though there is no consideration for the modification, as long as the parties agree voluntarily.

Under the Uniform Commercial Code, § 2–209(1), which has been adopted by 49 states, "[a]n agreement modifying a contract [for the sale of goods] needs no consideration to be binding." *See* G.L.1956 (1969 Reenactment) § 6A–2–209(1). Although at first blush this section appears to validate modifications obtained by coercion and duress, the comments to this section indicate that a modification under this section must meet the test of good faith imposed by the Code, and a modification obtained by extortion without a legitimate commercial reason is unenforceable.

The modern trend away from a rigid application of the preexisting duty rule is reflected by § [89](a) of the American Law Institute's Restatement Second of the Law of Contracts, which provides: "A promise modifying a duty under a contract not fully performed on either side is binding (a) if the modification is fair and equitable in view of circumstances not anticipated by the parties when the contract was made...."

We believe that § [89](a) is the proper rule of law and find it applicable to the facts of this case.[2] It not only prohibits modifications obtained by coercion, duress, or extortion but also fulfills society's expectation that agreements entered into voluntarily will be enforced by the courts. *See generally* Horwitz, The Historical Foundations of Modern Contract Law, 87 Harv. L. Rev. 917 (1974). Section [89](a), of course, does not compel a modification of an unprofitable or unfair contract; it only enforces a modification if the parties voluntarily agree and if (1) the promise modifying the original contract was made before the contract was fully performed on either side, (2) the underlying circumstances which prompted the modification were unanticipated by the parties, and (3) the modification is fair and equitable.

The evidence, which is uncontradicted, reveals that in June of 1968 Maher requested the city council to pay him an additional $10,000 for the year beginning on July 1, 1968, and ending on June 30, 1969. This request was made at a public meeting of the city council, where Maher explained in detail his reasons for making the request. Thereafter, the city council voted to authorize the Mayor to sign an amendment to the 1964 contract which provided that Maher would receive an additional $10,000 per year for the duration of the contract. Under such circumstances we have no doubt that the city voluntarily agreed to modify the 1964 contract.

Having determined the voluntariness of this agreement, we turn our attention to the three criteria delineated above. First, the modification was made in June of 1968 at a time when the five-year contract which was made in 1964 had not been fully performed by either party. Second, although the 1964 contract provided that Maher collect all refuse generated within the city, it appears this contract was premised on Maher's

---

2. The fact that these additional payments were made by a municipal corporation rather than a private individual does not, in our opinion, affect the outcome of this case....

past experience that the number of refuse-generating units would increase at a rate of 20 to 25 per year. Furthermore, the evidence is uncontradicted that the 1967–1968 increase of 400 units "went beyond any previous expectation." Clearly, the circumstances which prompted the city council to modify the 1964 contract were unanticipated.[4] Third, although the evidence does not indicate what proportion of the total this increase comprised, the evidence does indicate that it was a "substantial" increase. In light of this, we cannot say that the council's agreement to pay Maher the $10,000 increase was not fair and equitable in the circumstances.

The judgment appealed from is reversed, and the cause is remanded to the Superior Court for entry of judgment for the defendants.

Questions

1. What was the original deal? What was the deal as modified? Why did Maher request the modification? Was it made as a bargained-for exchange? If not, why was the contract enforced as modified?

2. What is the proper function of the pre-existing duty rule? If it is to police cases of economic duress, should it be abolished and replaced with a doctrine that identifies that issue? Or does the pre-existing duty rule better protect against enforcing promises extracted by duress than would an inquiry directly into that subject? See Robert Hillman, *Policing Contract Modifications under the UCC: Good Faith and the Doctrine of Economic Duress,* 64 IOWA L. REV. 849 (1979).

3. Consider the three ways in which the law treats contract modifications doctrinally—RESTATEMENT (SECOND) OF CONTRACTS § 73, U.C.C. § 2–209(1), and RESTATEMENT (SECOND) OF CONTRACTS § 89. Does each operate within a clearly delineated domain so that the law of contract modifications is coherent? Or are these three rules available as rule and counterrule (recall

4. The trial justice found that sec. 2(a) of the 1964 contract precluded Maher from recovering extra compensation for the 400 additional units. Section 2(a) provided: *"The Contractor, having made his proposal after his own examinations and estimates, shall take all responsibility for, and bear, any losses resulting to him in carrying out the contract;* and shall assume the defence of, and hold the City, its agents and employees harmless from all suits and claims arising from the use of any invention, patent, or patent rights, material, labor or implement, by or from any act, omission or neglect of, the Contractor, his agents or employees, in carrying out the contract." (Emphasis added). The trial justice, quoting the italicized portion of sec. 2(a), found that this section required that any losses incurred in the performance of the contract were Maher's responsibility. In our opinion, however, the trial justice overlooked the thrust of sec. 2(a) when read in its entirety.

It is clearly a contractual provision requiring the contractor to hold the city harmless and to defend it in any litigation arising out of the performance of his obligations under the contract, whether a result of affirmative action or some omission or neglect on the part of Maher or his agents or employees. We are persuaded that the portion of sec. 2(a) specifically referred to by the court refers to losses resulting to Maher from some action or omission on the part of his own agents or employees. It cannot be disputed, however, that any losses that resulted from an increase in the cost of collecting from the increased number of units generating refuse in no way resulted from any action on the part of either Maher or his employees. Rather, whatever losses he did entail by reason of the requirement of such extra collection resulted from actions completely beyond his control and thus unanticipated.

the Note on Doctrinal Manipulation, above at p. 43) for manipulation on nondoctrinal grounds (*i.e.,* grounds of principle)? Does each operate within an appropriate sphere? Should one of the three doctrines govern all contract modifications?

SECTION 2. RELIANCE ON A PROMISE

Two problems would be apt to arise were the law to hold promises enforceable if and only if supported by consideration, understood to require a bargained-for exchange. First, the law would enforce some promises that should not be enforced. A carjacker who points a gun at a driver's head and says, "Your car or your life" is making an offer to a bargained-for exchange. The doctrine of consideration has no capacity to refuse enforcement of a comparable deal involving a promise. The bargain principle consequently is limited by doctrines such as those considered in Chapter 3. Second, when consideration is a necessary condition for enforcing a promise, the law would not enforce some promises that probably should be enforced. That is, the law would be both over- and underinclusive. A number of examples follow in the remainder of this chapter.

DEVECMON v. SHAW

Court of Appeals of Maryland, 1888.
69 Md. 199, 14 A. 464.

BRYAN, JUDGE. John Semmes Devecmon brought suit against the executors of John S. Combs, deceased. He declared on the common counts, and also filed a bill of particulars. After judgment by default, a jury was sworn to assess the damages sustained by the plaintiff. The evidence consisted of certain accounts taken from the books of the deceased, and testimony that the plaintiff was a nephew of the deceased, and lived for several years in his family, and was in his service as clerk for several years. The plaintiff then made an offer of testimony which is thus stated in the bill of exceptions: "That the plaintiff took a trip to Europe in 1878, and that said trip was taken by said plaintiff, and the money spent on said trip was spent by the said plaintiff, at the instance and request of said Combs, and upon a promise from him that he would reimburse and repay to the plaintiff all money expended by him in said trip; and that the trip was so taken, and the money so expended, by the said plaintiff, but that the said trip had no connection with the business of said Combs; and that said Combs spoke to the witness of his conduct, in being thus willing to pay his nephew's expenses, as liberal and generous on his part." On objection the court refused to permit the evidence to be given, and the plaintiff excepted.

It might very well be, and probably was the case, that the plaintiff would not have taken a trip to Europe at his own expense. But, whether this be so or not, the testimony would have tended to show that the plaintiff incurred expense at the instance and request of the deceased, and upon an express promise by him that he would repay the money spent. It was a burden incurred at the request of the other party, and was certainly a sufficient consideration for a promise to pay. Great injury might be done by inducing persons to make expenditures beyond their means, on express promise of repayment, if the law were otherwise. It is an entirely different case from a promise to make another a present, or render him a gratuitous service. It is nothing to the purpose that the plaintiff was benefited by the expenditure of his own money. He was induced by this promise to spend it in this way, instead of some other mode. If it is not fulfilled, the expenditure will have been procured by a false pretense. As the plaintiff, on the theory of this evidence, had fulfilled his part of the contract, and nothing remained to be done but the payment of the money by the defendant, there could be a recovery in *indebitatus assumpsit*, and it was not necessary to declare on the special contract. The fifth count in the declaration is for "money paid by the plaintiff for the defendant's testator in his life-time, at his request." In the bill of particulars we find this item: "To cash contributed by me, J. Semmes Devecmon, out of my own money, to defray my expenses to Europe and return, the said John S. Combs, now deceased, having promised me in 1878 that, if I would contribute part of my own money towards the trip, he would give me a part of his, and would make up to me my part, and the amount below named is my contribution, as follows," etc. It seems to us that this statement is a sufficient description of a cause of action covered by the general terms of the fifth count. The evidence ought to have been admitted.... Judgment reversed, and new trial ordered.

Questions

1. What is the nephew's contractual interest in his uncle's performance of his promise? Does the court treat reliance on a promise as "consideration"? Does it treat consideration as a bargained-for exchange? How does reliance differ from a bargained-for exchange as a ground that justifies enforcing a promise? Does reliance justify enforcing this uncle's promise?

2. Does reliance justify enforcing *any* promise, such as Mack's promise in problem 3(a) above at p. 137? Would *Hamer v. Sidway,* above at p. 135, better rest on the nephew's reliance on his uncle's promise?

3. *Problem.*

Assume that, after making the promise but before his nephew went to Europe, Uncle John discovered that Nephew John used cocaine. Uncle John repudiated his promise. Would the promise be enforceable by the nephew? What if Nephew John had purchased a nonrefundable, nontransferable airline ticket to Rome before Uncle John's repudiation of the promise? Would you advise him to go to Europe and then sue Uncle John for all of the expenses? Would you advise him not to go but to sue Uncle John for the cost of the ticket?

RESTATEMENT (SECOND) OF CONTRACTS § 90

FEINBERG v. PFEIFFER CO.

St. Louis Court of Appeals, Missouri, 1959.
322 S.W.2d 163.

DOERNER, COMMISSIONER. This is a suit brought in the Circuit Court of the City of St. Louis by plaintiff, a former employee of the defendant corporation, on an alleged contract whereby defendant agreed to pay plaintiff the sum of $200 per month for life upon her retirement. A jury being waived, the case was tried by the court alone. Judgment below was for plaintiff for $5,100, the amount of the pension claimed to be due as of the date of the trial, together with interest thereon, and defendant duly appealed.

The parties are in substantial agreement on the essential facts. Plaintiff began working for the defendant, a manufacturer of pharmaceuticals, in 1910, when she was but 17 years of age. By 1947, she had attained the position of bookkeeper, office manager, and assistant treasurer of the defendant, and owned 70 shares of its stock out of a total of 6,503 shares issued and outstanding. Twenty shares had been given to her by the defendant or its then president, she had purchased 20, and the remaining 30 she had acquired by a stock split or stock dividend. Over the years she received substantial dividends on the stock she owned, as did all of the other stockholders. Also, in addition to her salary, plaintiff from 1937 to 1949, inclusive, received each year a bonus varying in amount from $300 in the beginning to $2,000 in the later years.

On December 27, 1947, the annual meeting of the defendant's Board of Directors was held at the Company's offices in St. Louis, presided over by Max Lippman, its then president and largest individual stockholder. The other directors present were George L. Marcus, Sidney Harris, Sol Flammer, and Walter Weinstock, who, with Max Lippman, owned 5,007 of the 6,503 shares then issued and outstanding. At that meeting the Board of Directors adopted the following resolution, which, because it is the crux of the case, we quote in full:

"The Chairman thereupon pointed out that the Assistant Treasurer, Mrs. Anna Sacks Feinberg, has given the corporation many years of long and faithful service. Not only has she served the corporation devotedly, but with exceptional ability and skill. The President pointed out that although all of the officers and directors sincerely hoped and desired that Mrs. Feinberg would continue in her present position for as long as she felt able, nevertheless, in view of the length of service which she has contributed provision should be made to afford her retirement privileges and benefits which should become a firm obligation of the corporation to be available to her whenever she should see fit to retire from active duty, however many years in the future such retirement may become effective. It was, accordingly, proposed that Mrs. Feinberg's salary which is presently $350.00 per month, be increased to $400.00 per month, and that Mrs. Feinberg would be given the privilege of retiring from active duty at any time she may elect to see fit so to do upon a retirement pay of $200.00 per month for life, with the distinct understanding that the retirement plan is merely being adopted at the present time in order to afford Mrs. Feinberg security for the future and in the hope that her active services will continue with the corporation for many years to come. After due discussion and consideration, and upon motion duly made and seconded, it was

"Resolved, that the salary of Anna Sacks Feinberg be increased from $350.00 to $400.00 per month and that she be afforded the privilege of retiring from active duty in the corporation at any time she may elect to see fit so to do upon retirement pay of $200.00 per month, for the remainder of her life."

At the request of Mr. Lippman his sons-in-law, Messrs. Harris and Flammer, called upon the plaintiff at her apartment on the same day to advise her of the passage of the resolution. Plaintiff testified on cross-examination that she had no prior information that such a pension plan was contemplated, that it came as a surprise to her, and that she would have continued in her employment whether or not such a resolution had been adopted. It is clear from the evidence that there was no contract, oral or written, as to plaintiff's length of employment, and that she was free to quit, and the defendant to discharge her, at any time.

Plaintiff did continue to work for the defendant through June 30, 1949, on which date she retired. In accordance with the foregoing resolution, the defendant began paying her the sum of $200 on the first of each month. Mr. Lippman died on November 18, 1949, and was succeeded as president of the company by his widow. Because of an illness, she retired from that office and was succeeded in October, 1953, by her son-in-law, Sidney M. Harris. Mr. Harris testified that while Mrs. Lippman had been president she signed the monthly pension check paid plaintiff, but fussed about doing so, and considered the payments as gifts. After his election, he stated, a new accounting firm employed by the defendant questioned the validity of the payments to plaintiff on several occasions, and in the Spring of 1956, upon its recommendation, he consulted the Company's then attorney, Mr. Ralph Kalish. Harris testified that both Ernst and Ernst, the accounting firm, and Kalish told him there was no need of giving plaintiff the money. He also stated that he had concurred in the view that the payments to plaintiff were mere gratuities rather than amounts due under a contractual obligation, and that following his discussion with the Company's attorney plaintiff was sent a check for $100 on April 1, 1956. Plaintiff declined to accept the reduced amount, and this action followed. Additional facts will be referred to later in this opinion.

Appellant's first assignment of error relates to the admission in evidence of plaintiff's testimony over its objection, that at the time of trial she was sixty-five and a half years old, and that she was no longer able to engage in gainful employment because of the removal of a cancer and the performance of a colocholecystostomy operation on November 25, 1957. Its complaint is not so much that such evidence was irrelevant and immaterial, as it is that the trial court erroneously made it one basis for its decision in favor of plaintiff. As defendant concedes, the error (if it was error) in the admission of such evidence would not be a ground for reversal, since, this being a jury-waived case, we are constrained by the statutes to review it upon both the law and the evidence, Sec. 510.310 RSMo 1949, V.A.M.S., and to render such judgment as the court below ought to have given. Section 512.160, Minor v. Lillard, Mo., 289 S.W.2d 1; Thumm v. Lohr, Mo.App., 306 S.W.2d 604. We consider only such evidence as is admissible, and need not pass upon questions of error in the admission and exclusion of evidence. Hussey v. Robison, Mo., 285 S.W.2d 603. However, in fairness to the trial court it should be stated that while he briefly referred to the state of plaintiff's health as of the time of the trial in his amended findings of fact, it is obvious from his amended grounds for decision and judgment that it was not, as will be seen, the basis for his decision.

Appellant's next complaint is that there was insufficient evidence to support the court's findings that plaintiff would not have quit defendant's employ had she not known and relied upon the promise of defendant to pay her $200 a month for life, and the finding that, from her voluntary retirement until April 1, 1956, plaintiff relied upon the continued receipt of the pension installments. The trial court so found, and, in our opinion, justifiably so. Plaintiff testified, and was corroborated by Harris, defendant's witness, that knowledge of the passage of the resolution was communicated to her on December 27, 1947, the very day it was adopted. She was told at that time by Harris and Flammer, she stated, that she could take the pension as of that day, if she wished. She testified further that she continued to work for another year and a half, through June 30, 1949; that at that time her health was good and she could have continued to work, but that after working for almost forty years she thought she would take a rest. Her testimony continued:

"Q. Now, what was the reason? I'm sorry. Did you then quit the employment of the company after you—after this year and a half? A. Yes.

"Q. What was the reason that you left? A. Well, I thought almost forty years, it was a long time and I thought I would take a little rest.

"Q. Yes. A. And with the pension and what earnings my husband had, we figured we could get along.

"Q. Did you rely upon this pension? A. We certainly did.

"Q. Being paid? A. Very much so. We relied upon it because I was positive that I was going to get it as long as I lived.

"Q. Would you have left the employment of the company at that time had it not been for this pension? A. No.

"Mr. Allen: Just a minute, I object to that as calling for a conclusion and conjecture on the part of this witness.

"The Court: It will be overruled.

"Q. (Mr. Agatstein continuing): Go ahead, now. The question is whether you would have quit the employment of the company at that time had you not relied upon this pension plan? A. No, I wouldn't.

"Q. You would not have. Did you ever seek employment while this pension was being paid to you-A. (interrupting): No.

"Q. Wait a minute, at any time prior at any other place? A. No, sir.

"Q. Were you able to hold any other employment during that time? A. Yes, I think so.

"Q. Was your health good? A. My health was good."

It is obvious from the foregoing that there was ample evidence to support the findings of fact made by the court below.

We come, then, to the basic issue in the case. While otherwise defined in defendant's third and fourth assignments of error, it is thus succinctly stated in the argument in its brief: "... whether plaintiff has proved that she has a right to recover from defendant based upon a legally binding contractual obligation to pay her $200 per month for life."

It is defendant's contention, in essence, that the resolution adopted by its Board of Directors was a mere promise to make a gift, and that no contract resulted either thereby, or when plaintiff retired, because there was no consideration given or paid by the plaintiff. It urges that a promise to make a gift is not binding unless supported by a legal consideration; that the only apparent consideration for the adoption of the foregoing resolution was the "many years of long and faithful service" expressed therein; and that past services are not a valid consideration for a promise. Defendant argues further that there is nothing in the resolution which made its effectiveness conditional upon plaintiff's continued employment, that she was not under contract to work for any length of time but was free to quit whenever she wished, and that she had no contractual right to her position and could have been discharged at any time.

Plaintiff concedes that a promise based upon past services would be without consideration, but contends that there were two other elements which supplied the required element: First, the continuation by plaintiff in the employ of the defendant for the period from December 27, 1947, the date when the resolution was adopted, until the date of her retirement on June 30, 1949. And, second, her change of position, i.e., her retirement, and the abandonment by her of her opportunity to continue in gainful employment, made in reliance on defendant's promise to pay her $200 per month for life.

We must agree with the defendant that the evidence does not support the first of these contentions. There is no language in the resolution predicating plaintiff's right to a pension upon her continued employment. She was not required to work for the defendant for any period of time as a condition to gaining such retirement benefits. She was told that she could quit the day upon which the resolution was adopted, as she herself testified, and it is clear from her own testimony that she made no promise or agreement to continue in the employ of the defendant in return for its promise to pay her a pension. Hence there was lacking that mutuality of obligation which is essential to the validity of a contract. . . .

But as to the second of these contentions we must agree with plaintiff. By the terms of the resolution defendant promised to pay plaintiff the sum of $200 a month upon her retirement. . . .

Section 90 of the Restatement of the Law of Contracts states that: "A promise which the promisor should reasonably expect to induce action or forbearance of a definite and substantial character on the part of the promisee and which does induce such action or forbearance is binding if injustice can be avoided only by enforcement of the promise." This doctrine has been described as that of "promissory estoppel. . . ."

Was there such an act on the part of plaintiff, in reliance upon the promise contained in the resolution, as will estop the defendant, and therefore create an enforceable contract under the doctrine of promissory estoppel? We think there was. One of the illustrations cited under Section 90 of the Restatement is: "2. A promises B to pay him an annuity during B's life. B thereupon resigns a profitable employment, as A expected that he might. B receives the annuity for some years, in the meantime becoming disqualified from again obtaining good employment. A's promise is binding." This illustration is objected to by defendant as not being applicable to the case at hand. The reason advanced by it is that in the illustration B became "disqualified" from obtaining other employment *before* A discontinued the payments, whereas in this case the plaintiff did not discover that she had cancer and thereby became unemployable until *after* the defendant had discontinued the payments of $200 per month. We think the distinction is immaterial. The only reason for the reference in the illustration to the disqualification of A is in connection with that part of Section 90 regarding the prevention of injustice. The injustice would occur regardless of when the disability occurred. Would defendant contend that the contract would be enforceable if the plaintiff's illness had been discovered on March 31, 1956, the day before it discontinued the payment of the $200 a month, but not if it occurred on April 2nd, the day after? Furthermore, there are more ways to become disqualified for work, or unemployable, than as the result of illness. At the time she retired plaintiff was 57 years of age. At the time the payments were discontinued she was over 63 years of age. It is a matter of common knowledge that it is virtually impossible for a woman of that age to find satisfactory employment, much less a position comparable to that which plaintiff enjoyed at the time of her retirement.

The fact of the matter is that plaintiff's subsequent illness was not the "action or forbearance" which was induced by the promise contained in the resolution. As the trial court correctly decided, such action on plaintiff's part was her retirement from a lucrative position in reliance upon defendant's promise to pay her an annuity or pension. In a very similar case, Ricketts v. Scothorn, 57 Neb. 51, 77 N.W. 365, 367, 42 L.R.A. 794, the Supreme Court of Nebraska said:

> "... According to the undisputed proof, as shown by the record before us, the plaintiff was a working girl, holding a position in which she earned a salary of $10 per week. Her grandfather, desiring to put her in a position of independence, gave her the note accompanying it with the remark that his other grandchildren did not work, and that she would not be obliged to work any longer. In effect, he suggested that she might abandon her employment, and rely in the future upon the bounty which he promised. He doubtless desired that she should give up her occupation, but, whether he did or not, it is entirely certain that he contemplated such action on her part as a reasonable and probable consequence of his gift. Having intentionally influenced the plaintiff to alter her position for the worse on the faith of the note being paid when due, it would be grossly inequitable to permit the maker, or his executor, to resist payment on the ground that the promise was given without consideration."

The Commissioner therefore recommends, for the reasons stated, that the judgment be affirmed....

HAYES v. PLANTATIONS STEEL CO.

Supreme Court of Rhode Island, 1982.
438 A.2d 1091.

SHEA, JUSTICE. The defendant employer, Plantations Steel Company (Plantations), appeals from a Superior Court judgment for the plaintiff employee, Edward J. Hayes (Hayes). The trial justice, sitting without a jury, found that Plantations was obligated to Hayes on the basis of an implied-in-fact contract to pay him a yearly pension of $5,000. The award covered three years in which payment had not been made. The trial justice ruled, also, that Hayes had made a sufficient showing of detrimental reliance upon Plantations's promise to pay to give rise to its obligation based on the theory of promissory estoppel. The trial justice, however, found in part for Plantations in ruling that the payments to Hayes were not governed by the Employee Retirement Income Security Act, 29 U.S.C.A. §§ 1001–1461 (West 1975), and consequently he was not entitled to attorney's fees under § 1132(g) of that act. Both parties have appealed.

We reverse the findings of the trial justice regarding Plantations's contractual obligation to pay Hayes a pension. Consequently we need not deal with the cross-appeal concerning the award of attorney's fees under the federal statute.

Plantations is a closely held Rhode Island corporation engaged in the manufacture of steel reinforcing rods for use in concrete construction. The company was founded by Hugo R. Mainelli, Sr., and Alexander A. DiMartino. A dispute between their two families in 1976 and 1977 left the DiMartinos in full control of the corporation. Hayes was an employee of the corporation from 1947 until his retirement in 1972 at the age of sixty-five. He began with Plantations as an "estimator and draftsman" and ended his career as general manager, a position of considerable responsibility. Starting in January 1973 and continuing until January 1976, Hayes received the annual sum of $5,000 from Plantations. Hayes instituted this action in December 1977, after the then company management refused to make any further payments.

Hayes testified that in January 1972 he announced his intention to retire the following July, after twenty-five years of continuous service. He decided to retire because he had worked continuously for fifty-one years. He stated, however, that he would not have retired had he not expected to receive a pension. After he stopped working for Plantations, he sought no other employment.

Approximately one week before his actual retirement Hayes spoke with Hugo R. Mainelli, Jr., who was then an officer and a stockholder of Plantations. This conversation was the first and only one concerning payments of a pension to Hayes during retirement. Mainelli said that the company "would take care" of him. There was no mention of a sum of money or a percentage of salary that Hayes would receive. There was no formal authorization for payments by Plantations's shareholders and/or board of directors. Indeed, there was never any formal provision for a pension plan for any employee other than for unionized employees, who benefit from an arrangement through their union. The plaintiff was not a union member.

Mr. Mainelli, Jr., testified that his father, Hugo R. Mainelli, Sr., had authorized the first payment "as a token of appreciation for the many years of [Hayes's] service." Furthermore, "it was implied that that check would continue on an annual basis." Mainelli also testified that it was his "personal intention" that the payments would continue for "as long as I was around."

Mainelli testified that after Hayes's retirement, he would visit the premises each year to say hello and renew old acquaintances. During the course of his visits, Hayes would thank Mainelli for the previous check and ask how long it would continue so that he could plan an orderly retirement.

The payments were discontinued after 1976. At that time a succession of several poor business years plus the stockholders' dispute, resulting in the takeover by the DiMartino family, contributed to the decision to stop the payments.

The trial justice ruled that Plantations owed Hayes his annual sum of $5,000 for the years 1977 through 1979. The ruling implied that barring bankruptcy or the cessation of business for any other reason, Hayes had a right to expect continued annual payments.

The trial justice found that Hugo Mainelli, Jr.'s statement that Hayes would be taken care of after his retirement was a promise. Although no sum of money was mentioned in 1972, the four annual payments of $5,000 established that otherwise unspecified term of the contract. The trial justice also found that Hayes supplied consideration for the promise by voluntarily retiring, because he was under no obligation to do so. From the words and conduct of the parties and from the surrounding circumstances, the trial justice concluded that there existed an implied contract obligating the company to pay a pension to Hayes for life. The trial justice made a further finding that even if Hayes had not truly bargained for a pension by voluntarily retiring, he had nevertheless incurred the detriment of foregoing other employment in reliance upon the company's promise. He specifically held that Hayes's retirement was in response to the promise and held also that Hayes refrained from seeking other employment in further reliance thereon.

The findings of fact of a trial justice sitting without a jury are entitled to great weight when reviewed by this court. His findings will not be disturbed unless it can be shown that they are clearly wrong or that the trial justice misconceived or overlooked material evidence. *Lisi v. Marra*, 424 A.2d 1052 (1981).... After careful review of the record, however, we conclude that the trial justice's findings and conclusions must be reversed.

Assuming for the purpose of this discussion that Plantations in legal effect made a promise to Hayes, we must ask whether Hayes did supply the required consideration that would make the promise binding? And, if Hayes did not supply consideration, was his alleged reliance sufficiently induced by the promise to estop defendant from denying its obligation to him? We answer both questions in the negative.

We turn first to the problem of consideration. The facts at bar do not present the case of an express contract. As the trial justice stated, the existence of a contract in this case must be determined from all the circumstances of the parties' conduct and words. Although words were expressed initially in the remark that Hayes "would be taken care of," any contract in this case would be more in the nature of an implied contract. Certainly the statement of Hugo Mainelli, Jr., standing alone is not an expression of a direct and definite promise to pay Hayes a pension. Though we are analyzing an implied contract, nevertheless we must address the question of consideration.

Contracts implied in fact require the element of consideration to support them as is required in express contracts. The only difference between the two is the manner in which the parties manifest their assent. *J. Koury Steel Erectors, Inc. v. San-Vel Concrete Corp.*, R.I., 387 A.2d 694 (1978).... In this jurisdiction, consideration consists either in some right, interest, or benefit accruing to one party or some forbearance, detriment, or responsibility given, suffered, or undertaken by the

other. *See Dockery v. Greenfield*, 86 R.I. 464, 136 A.2d 682 (1957)....
Valid consideration furthermore must be bargained for. It must induce
the return act or promise. To be valid, therefore, the purported consideration must not have been delivered before a promise is executed, that is,
given without reference to the promise. *Plowman v. Indian Refining Co.*,
20 F.Supp. 1 (E.D.Ill.1937). Consideration is therefore a test of the
enforceability of executory promises, *Angel v. Murray*, 113 R.I. 482, 322
A.2d 630 (1974), and has no legal effect when rendered in the past and
apart from an alleged exchange in the present. *Zanturjian v. Boornazian*,
25 R.I. 151, 55 A. 199 (1903).

In the case before us, Plantations's promise to pay Hayes a pension
is quite clearly not supported by any consideration supplied by Hayes.
Hayes had announced his intent to retire well in advance of any promise,
and therefore the intention to retire was arrived at without regard to
any promise by Plantations. Although Hayes may have had in mind the
receipt of a pension when he first informed Plantations, his expectation
was not based on any statement made to him or on any conduct of the
company officer relative to him in January 1972. In deciding to retire,
Hayes acted on his own initiative. Hayes's long years of dedicated service
also is legally insufficient because his service too was rendered without
being induced by Plantation's promise. *See Plowman v. Indian Refining
Co.*, *supra*.

Clearly then this is not a case in which Plantations's promise was
meant to induce Hayes to refrain from retiring when he could have
chosen to do so in return for further service. 1 *Williston on Contracts*,
§ 130B (3d ed., Jaeger 1957). Nor was the promise made to encourage
long service from the start of his employment. *Weesner v. Electric Power
Board of Chattanooga*, 344 S.W.2d 766 (Tenn.App.1961). Instead, the
testimony establishes that Plantations's promise was intended "as a
token of appreciation for [Hayes's] many years of service." As such it
was in the nature of a gratuity paid to Hayes for as long as the company
chose. In *Spickelmier Industries, Inc. v. Passander*, 359 N.E.2d 563
(Ind.App.1977), an employer's promise to an employee to pay him a year-
end bonus was unenforceable because it was made after the employee
had performed his contractual responsibilities for that year.

. . .

Hayes argues in the alternative that even if Plantations's promise
was not the product of an exchange, its duty is grounded properly in the
theory of promissory estoppel. This court adopted the theory of promissory estoppel in *East Providence Credit Union v. Geremia*, 103 R.I. 597,
601, 239 A.2d 725, 727 (1968) (quoting 1 Restatement *Contracts* § 90 at
110 (1932)) stating:

> "A promise which the promisor should reasonably expect to induce
> action or forbearance of a definite and substantial character on the
> part of the promisee and which does induce such action or forbear-
> ance is binding if injustice can be avoided only by enforcement of its
> promise."

In *East Providence Credit Union* this court said that the doctrine of promissory estoppel is invoked "as a substitute for a consideration, rendering a gratuitous promise enforceable as a contract." *Id*. To restate the matter differently, "the acts of reliance by the promisee to his detriment [provide] a substitute for consideration." *Id*.

Hayes urges that in the absence of a bargained-for promise the facts require application of the doctrine of promissory estoppel. He stresses that he retired voluntarily while expecting to receive a pension. He would not have otherwise retired. Nor did he seek other employment.

We disagree with this contention largely for the reasons already stated. One of the essential elements of the doctrine of promissory estoppel is that the promise must *induce* the promisee's action or forbearance. The particular act in this regard is plaintiff's decision whether or not to retire. As we stated earlier, the record indicates that he made the decision on his own initiative. In other words, the conversation between Hayes and Mainelli which occurred a week before Hayes left his employment cannot be said to have induced his decision to leave. He had reached that decision long before.

An example taken from the restatement provides a meaningful contrast:

> "2. A promises B to pay him an annuity during B's life. B *thereupon* resigns profitable employment *as A expected* that he might. B receives the annuity for some years, in the meantime becoming disqualified from again obtaining good employment. A's promise is binding." (Emphasis added.) 1 Restatement *Contracts* § 90 at 111 (1932).

In *Feinberg v. Pfeiffer Co.*, 322 S.W.2d 163 (Mo.App.1959), the plaintiff-employee had worked for her employer for nearly forty years. The defendant corporation's board of directors resolved, in view of her long years of service, to obligate itself to pay "retirement privileges" to her. The resolution did not require the plaintiff to retire. Instead, the decision whether and when to retire remained entirely her own. The board then informed her of its resolution. The plaintiff worked for eighteen months more before retiring. She sued the corporation when it reduced her monthly checks seven years later. The court held that a pension contract existed between the parties. Although continued employment was not a consideration to her receipt of retirement benefits, the court found sufficient reliance on the part of the plaintiff to support her claim. The court based its decision upon the above restatement example, that is, the defendant informed the plaintiff of its plan, and the plaintiff in reliance thereon, retired. *Feinberg* presents factors that also appear in the case at bar. There, the plaintiff had worked many years and desired to retire; she would not have left had she not been able to rely on a pension; and once retired, she sought no other employment.

However, the important distinction between *Feinberg* and the case before us is that in *Feinberg* the employer's decision definitely shaped the thinking of the plaintiff. In this case the promise did not. It is not reasonable to infer from the facts that Hugo R. Mainelli, Jr., expected retirement to result from his conversation with Hayes. Hayes had given notice of his intention seven months previously. Here there was thus no inducement to retire which would satisfy the demands of § 90 of the Restatement. Nor can it be said that Hayes's refraining from other employment was "action or forbearance of a definite and substantial character." The underlying assumption of Hayes's initial decision to retire was that upon leaving the defendant's employ, he would no longer work. It is impossible to say that he changed his position any more so because of what Mainelli had told him in light of his own initial decision. These circumstances do not lead to a conclusion that injustice can be avoided only by enforcement of Plantations's promise. Hayes received $20,000 over the course of four years. He inquired each year about whether he could expect a check for the following year. Obviously, there was no absolute certainty on his part that the pension would continue. Furthermore, in the face of his uncertainty, the mere fact that payment for several years did occur is insufficient by itself to meet the requirements of reliance under the doctrine of promissory estoppel.

For the foregoing reasons, the defendant's appeal is sustained and the judgment of the Superior Court is reversed. The papers of the case are remanded to the Superior Court.

Questions

1. What exactly was Ms. Feinberg's action in reliance on the promise of a pension? Were all of the elements of § 90 satisfied? What is the "injustice" that could be avoided only by enforcement of the promise? How is it related to the interests that are protected by the law of contracts?

2. In *Hayes*, on which element of RESTATEMENT [FIRST] OF CONTRACTS § 90 did his claim founder? Should it have? Would the result differ under RESTATEMENT (SECOND) OF CONTRACTS § 90? Does the *Hayes* court succeed in distinguishing *Feinberg*? If so, what is the key distinction? If not, which is the better justified decision?

3. *Problems.*

a. Chamberlain was working as a pharmacist's assistant at Massey Stores when he received an offer to be the pharmacist at Young Drugs. His employment at Massey Stores was for a year, renewable for additional years by mutual agreement. The employment offered at Young Drugs was to be terminable at the will of either party. Chamberlain resigned his employment at Massey Stores and worked for two days at Young Drugs, at which time he was terminated when a customer complained that he was rude. It took him three months to find employment again as a pharmacist's assistant. Should Chamberlain have an action against Young Drugs? Compare Grouse v. Group Health Plan, Inc., 306 N.W.2d 114 (Minn.1981) with Rosatone v. GTE Sprint Communications, 761 S.W.2d 670 (Mo.App.1988).

b. Assume the facts as in Problem a above, except that Chamberlain's employment at Massey Stores was terminable at the will of either party. Same result?

RESTATEMENT (SECOND) OF CONTRACTS § 87

U.C.C. § 2–205

DRENNAN v. STAR PAVING CO.

Supreme Court of California, 1958.
51 Cal.2d 409, 333 P.2d 757.

TRAYNOR, JUSTICE. Defendant appeals from a judgment for plaintiff in an action to recover damages caused by defendant's refusal to perform certain paving work according to a bid it submitted to plaintiff.

On July 28, 1955, plaintiff, a licensed general contractor, was preparing a bid on the "Monte Vista School Job" in the Lancaster school district. Bids had to be submitted before 8:00 p.m. Plaintiff testified that it was customary in that area for general contractors to receive the bids of subcontractors by telephone on the day set for bidding and to rely on them in computing their own bids. Thus on that day plaintiff's secretary, Mrs. Johnson, received by telephone between fifty and seventy-five subcontractors' bids for various parts of the school job. As each bid came in, she wrote it on a special form, which she brought into plaintiff's office. He then posted it on a master cost sheet setting forth the names and bids of all subcontractors. His own bid had to include the names of subcontractors who were to perform one-half of one per cent or more of the construction work, and he had also to provide a bidder's bond of ten per cent of his total bid of $317,385 as a guarantee that he would enter the contract if awarded the work.

Late in the afternoon, Mrs. Johnson had a telephone conversation with Kenneth R. Hoon, an estimator for defendant. He gave his name and telephone number and stated that he was bidding for defendant for the paving work at the Monte Vista School according to plans and specifications and that his bid was $7,131.60. At Mrs. Johnson's request he repeated his bid. Plaintiff listened to the bid over an extension telephone in his office and posted it on the master sheet after receiving the bid form from Mrs. Johnson. Defendant's was the lowest bid for the paving. Plaintiff computed his own bid accordingly and submitted it with the name of defendant as the subcontractor for the paving. When the bids were opened on July 28th, plaintiff's proved to be the lowest, and he was awarded the contract.

On his way to Los Angeles the next morning plaintiff stopped at defendant's office. The first person he met was defendant's construction engineer, Mr. Oppenheimer. Plaintiff testified: "I introduced myself and he immediately told me that they had made a mistake in their bid to me the night before, they couldn't do it for the price they had bid, and I told him I would expect him to carry through with their original bid because I had used it in compiling my bid and the job was being awarded them. And I would have to go and do the job according to my bid and I would expect them to do the same."

Defendant refused to do the paving work for less than $15,000. Plaintiff testified that he "got figures from other people" and after trying for several months to get as low a bid as possible engaged L & H Paving Company, a firm in Lancaster, to do the work for $10,948.60.

The trial court found on substantial evidence that defendant made a definite offer to do the paving on the Monte Vista job according to the plans and specifications for $7,131.60, and that plaintiff relied on defendant's bid in computing his own bid for the school job and naming defendant therein as the subcontractor for the paving work. Accordingly, it entered judgment for plaintiff in the amount of $3,817.00 (the difference between defendant's bid and the cost of the paving to plaintiff) plus costs.

Defendant contends that there was no enforceable contract between the parties on the ground that it made a revocable offer and revoked it before plaintiff communicated his acceptance to defendant.

There is no evidence that defendant offered to make its bid irrevocable in exchange for plaintiff's use of its figures in computing his bid. Nor is there evidence that would warrant interpreting plaintiff's use of defendant's bid as the acceptance thereof, binding plaintiff, on condition he received the main contract, to award the subcontract to defendant. In sum, there was neither an option supported by consideration nor a bilateral contract binding on both parties.

Plaintiff contends, however, that he relied to his detriment on defendant's offer and that defendant must therefore answer in damages for its refusal to perform. Thus the question is squarely presented: Did plaintiff's reliance make defendant's offer irrevocable?

Section 90 of the Restatement of Contracts states: "A promise which the promisor should reasonably expect to induce action or forbearance of a definite and substantial character on the part of the promisee and which does induce such action or forbearance is binding if injustice can be avoided only by enforcement of the promise." This rule applies in this state. . . .

Defendant's offer constituted a promise to perform on such conditions as were stated expressly or by implication therein or annexed thereto by operation of law. (See 1 Williston, Contracts [3rd. ed.], § 24A, p. 56, § 61, p. 196.) Defendant had reason to expect that if its bid proved the lowest it would be used by plaintiff. It induced "action ... of a definite and substantial character on the part of the promisee."

Had defendant's bid expressly stated or clearly implied that it was revocable at any time before acceptance we would treat it accordingly. It was silent on revocation, however, and we must therefore determine whether there are conditions to the right of revocation imposed by law or reasonably inferable in fact. In the analogous problem of an offer for a unilateral contract, the theory is now obsolete that the offer is revocable at any time before complete performance. Thus section 45 of the Restatement of Contracts provides: "If an offer for a unilateral contract is made, and part of the consideration requested in the offer is given or tendered by the offeree in response thereto, the offeror is bound by a contract, the duty of immediate performance of which is conditional on the full consideration being given or tendered within the time stated in the offer, or, if no time is stated therein, within a reasonable time." In explanation, comment *b* states that the "main offer includes as a subsidiary promise, necessarily implied, that if part of the requested performance is given, the offeror will not revoke his offer, and that if tender is made it will be accepted. Part performance or tender may thus furnish consideration for the subsidiary promise. Moreover, merely acting in justifiable reliance on an offer may in some cases serve as sufficient reason for making a promise binding (see § 90)."

Whether implied in fact or law, the subsidiary promise serves to preclude the injustice that would result if the offer could be revoked after the offeree had acted in detrimental reliance thereon. Reasonable reliance resulting in a foreseeable prejudicial change in position affords a compelling basis also for implying a subsidiary promise not to revoke an offer for a bilateral contract.

The absence of consideration is not fatal to the enforcement of such a promise. It is true that in the case of unilateral contracts the Restatement finds consideration for the implied subsidiary promise in the part performance of the bargained-for exchange, but its reference to section 90 makes clear that consideration for such a promise is not always necessary. The very purpose of section 90 is to make a promise binding even though there was no consideration "in the sense of something that is bargained for and given in exchange." (See 1 Corbin, Contracts 634 et seq.) Reasonable reliance serves to hold the offeror in lieu of the consideration ordinarily required to make the offer binding. In a case involving similar facts the Supreme Court of South Dakota stated that "we believe that reason and justice demand that the doctrine [of section 90] be applied to the present facts. We cannot believe that by accepting this doctrine as controlling in the state of facts before us we will abolish the requirement of a consideration in contract cases, in any different sense than an ordinary estoppel abolishes some legal requirement in its application. We are of the opinion, therefore, that the defendants in executing the agreement [which was not supported by consideration] made a promise which they should have reasonably expected would induce the plaintiff to submit a bid based thereon to the Government, that such promise did induce this action, and that injustice can be avoided only by enforcement of the promise." Northwestern Engineering Co. v. Ellerman, 69 S.D. 397, 408, 10 N.W.2d 879, 884. . . .

When plaintiff used defendant's offer in computing his own bid, he bound himself to perform in reliance on defendant's terms. Though defendant did not bargain for this use of its bid neither did defendant make it idly, indifferent to whether it would be used or not. On the contrary it is reasonable to suppose that defendant submitted its bid to obtain the subcontract. It was bound to realize the substantial possibility that its bid would be the lowest, and that it would be included by plaintiff in his bid. It was to its own interest that the contractor be awarded the general contract; the lower the subcontract bid, the lower the general contractor's bid was likely to be and the greater its chance of acceptance and hence the greater defendant's chance of getting the paving subcontract. Defendant had reason not only to expect plaintiff to rely on its bid but to want him to. Clearly defendant had a stake in plaintiff's reliance on its bid. Given this interest and the fact that plaintiff is bound by his own bid, it is only fair that plaintiff should have at least an opportunity to accept defendant's bid after the general contract has been awarded to him.

It bears noting that a general contractor is not free to delay acceptance after he has been awarded the general contract in the hope of getting a better price. Nor can he reopen bargaining with the subcontractor and at the same time claim a continuing right to accept the original offer. See, R. J. Daum Const. Co. v. Child, Utah, 247 P.2d 817, 823. In the present case plaintiff promptly informed defendant that plaintiff was being awarded the job and that the subcontract was being awarded to defendant. . . .

The judgment is affirmed.

SOUTHERN CALIFORNIA ACOUSTICS CO., INC. v. C.V. HOLDER, INC.

Supreme Court of California, 1969.
71 Cal.2d 719, 79 Cal.Rptr. 319, 456 P.2d 975.

Traynor, Chief Justice. Plaintiff appeals from a judgment of dismissal entered after a demurrer to its second amended complaint was sustained without leave to amend.

Plaintiff alleged that it is a licensed specialty subcontractor. On November 24, 1965, it submitted by telephone to defendant C.V. Holder, Inc., a general contractor, a subcontract bid in the amount of $83,400 for the furnishing and installation of acoustical tile on a public construction job. Later that day Holder submitted a bid for the prime contract to codefendant Los Angeles Unified School District. As required by law, Holder listed the subcontractors who would perform work on the project of a value in excess of one-half of one percent of the total bid.[1] Holder

---

1. Government Code section 4104 provides:

"Any officer, department, board or commission taking bids for the construction

listed plaintiff as the acoustical tile subcontractor. Holder was subsequently awarded the prime contract for construction of the facility and executed a written contract with the school district on December 9, 1965. A local trade newspaper widely circulated among subcontractors reported that Holder had been awarded the contract and included in its report the names of the subcontractors listed in Holder's bid. Plaintiff read the report and, acting on the assumption that its bid had been accepted, refrained from bidding on other construction jobs in order to remain within its bonding limits.

Sometime between December 27, 1965, and January 10, 1966, Holder requested permission from the school district to substitute another subcontractor for plaintiff, apparently on the ground that plaintiff had been inadvertently listed in the bid in place of the intended subcontractor. The school district consented, and the substitution was made. Plaintiff then sought a writ of mandamus to compel the school district to rescind its consent to the change in subcontractors. The trial court sustained the district's demurrer and thereafter dismissed the proceeding. Plaintiff did not appeal. Plaintiff then brought this action for damages against Holder and the school district.

Plaintiff contends that the trial court erred in sustaining the demurrer on the ground that the facts alleged in its complaint would support recovery of damages for breach of contract, breach of a statutory duty, and for negligence. We conclude that plaintiff has stated a cause of action for breach of a statutory duty.

There was no contract between plaintiff and Holder, for Holder did not accept plaintiff's offer. Silence in the face of an offer is not an acceptance, unless there is a relationship between the parties or a previous course of dealing pursuant to which silence would be understood as acceptance. (See Wold v. League of the Cross (1931) 114 Cal.App. 474, 479–481, 300 P. 57 . . . .) No such relationship or course of dealing is alleged. Nor did Holder accept the bid by using it in presenting its own bid. In the absence of an agreement to the contrary, listing of the subcontractor in the prime bid is not an implied acceptance of the subcontractor's bid by the general contractor. (Klose v. Sequoia Union High School Dist. (1953) 118 Cal.App.2d 636, 641, 258 P.2d 515 . . . .) The listing by the general contractor of the subcontractors he intends to retain is in response to statutory command (Gov. Code, § 4104) and

of any public work or improvement shall provide in the specifications prepared for the work or improvement or in the general conditions under which bids will be received for the doing of the work incident to the public work or improvement that any person making a bid or offer to perform the work, shall, in his bid or offer, set forth:

"(a) The name and the location of the place of business of each subcontractor who will perform work or labor or render service to the prime contractor in or about the construction of the work or improvement in an amount in excess of one-half of 1 percent of the prime contractor's total bid.

"(b) The portion of the work which will be done by each such subcontractor under this act. The prime contractor shall list only one subcontractor for each such portion as is defined by the prime contractor in his bid."

cannot reasonably be construed as an expression of acceptance. (Cf. Western Concrete Structures Co. v. James I. Barnes Constr. Co. (1962) 206 Cal.App.2d 1, 13, 23 Cal.Rptr. 506. . . .)

Plaintiff contends, however, that its reliance on Holder's use of its bid and Holder's failure to reject its offer promptly after Holder's bid was accepted constitute acceptance of plaintiffs bid by operation of law under the doctrine of promissory estoppel. Section 90 of the Restatement of Contracts states: 'A promise which the promisor should reasonably expect to induce action or forbearance of a definite and substantial character on the part of the promisee and which does induce such action or forbearance is binding if injustice can be avoided only by enforcement of the promise.' This rule applies in this state. Drennan v. Star Paving Co. (1958) 51 Cal.2d 409, 333 P.2d 757.) Before it can be invoked, however, there must be a promise that was relied upon. . . . .

In *Drennan*, we held that implicit in the subcontractor's bid was a subsidiary promise to keep his bid open for a reasonable time after award of the prime contract to give the general contractor an opportunity to accept the offer on which he relied in computing the prime bid. The subsidiary promise was implied 'to preclude the injustice that would result if the offer could be revoked after the offeree had acted in detrimental reliance thereon.' (51 Cal.2d at p. 414, 333 P.2d at p. 760).

Plaintiff urges us to find an analogous subsidiary promise not to reject its bid in this case, but it fails to allege facts showing the existence of any promise by Holder to it upon which it detrimentally relied. Plaintiff did not rely on any promise by Holder, but only on the listing of subcontractors required by section 4104 of the Government Code and on the statutory restriction on Holder's right to change its listed subcontractors without the consent of the school district. Gov. Code. § 4107. Holder neither accepted plaintiff's offer, nor made any promise or offer to plaintiff intended to 'induce action or forbearance of a definite and substantial character. . . .'

[The court's opinion on the statutory question is omitted.]

Questions

1. In *Drennan*, what was the offer that was relevant to the legal action? Was that offer accepted before the power of acceptance died? Why does the general contractor win the lawsuit? Is *Drennan* like *Devecmon* and *Feinberg* in the important respects? What are these similarities? What are the differences? Should the differences make a difference in result?

2. In *Southern California Acoustics Co.*, how does the problem differ from the problem in *Drennan*? Is the nonreciprocal relationship between subcontractors and general contractors in California, which results from the two cases, justified? See Home Elec. Co. of Lenoir, Inc. v. Hall and Underdown Heating and Air Cond. Co., 86 N.C.App. 540, 358 S.E.2d 539 (1987).

3. After these cases, what might you advise a subcontractor who seeks to bind a general contractor in order to prevent bid-shopping? What might

you advise a general who seeks to bind a sub? Would your advice be different if the common practice in contractor bidding almost never involves legally binding contracts but, rather, depends on good will and reputational considerations? See Frank Schultz, *The Firm Offer Puzzle: A Study of Business Practice in the Construction Industry*, 19 U. CHI. L. REV. 237 (1952).

SECTION 3. UNJUST ENRICHMENT

Assume that Harvey mistakenly wrote a check for $1,000 in payment of a bill for $100 in charges incurred on his credit card with Stewart Savings. When Harvey discovers the error and requests repayment of $900 from Stewart Savings, must Stewart Savings return his money? Since ancient times, it has seemed clear that justice requires Stewart Savings to return the overpayment. Indeed, the justice of Stewart Savings' obligation seems so obvious as to need no explication. Yet Stewart Savings made no promise to do so. It did nothing wrong that would count as a tort.

Redress is available to Harvey on a noncontractual, nontortious basis known as quasi-contract, implied-in-law contract, restitution, or unjust enrichment. Do not be misled by the seemingly unbounded reach of the labels. The injustice and the enrichment needed to qualify for restitutionary relief must satisfy specific conditions. To recover, Harvey must show that he conferred a measurable benefit on Stewart Savings nonofficiously and nongratuitously, which benefit was unjustly retained. "Injustice" in this context has little to do with its more common use to characterize a maldistribution of wealth or power in a group. Rather, the required injustice involves a disruption in the equality of two persons when one gains at the expense of the other for no good reason. See Chapter 3, introductory remarks. A thief thus should make restitution to the victim in addition to undergoing some form of punishment. So, too, Stewart Savings should make restitution to Harvey, though no punishment seems appropriate here.

The law of restitution is a large subject sometimes taught as a course in its own right. To be clear, restitution may be available whether or not a promise was made. Claims for restitution, however, commonly supplement or accompany contract claims. See Note on "Interests," "Rights," and "Duties," above at p. 7. Accordingly, a brief overview is provided below. See generally I–IV GEORGE E. PALMER, LAW OF RESTITUTION (1978).

SPARKS v. GUSTAFSON

Supreme Court of Alaska, 1988.
750 P.2d 338.

MATTHEWS, JUSTICE. Robert J. Sparks, Jr., executor of his father's estate (Estate), appeals from a superior court decision ordering the Estate to pay $65,706.07 to the plaintiff, Ernie Gustafson, in compensation for management services that Gustafson rendered to the Estate and for maintaining and improving Estate property. The central issue presented here is whether it is unjust to allow the Estate to retain these benefits without paying for them. In particular, Sparks argues that Gustafson gave his services to the Estate gratuitously, without the Estate's knowledge or consent....

The decedent, Robert Sparks, Sr., and the plaintiff, Ernie Gustafson, were personal friends and business associates for many years. In 1980 Sparks purchased a one-half interest in the Nome Center Building. Gustafson managed the building for Sparks without charge until Sparks died on March 1, 1981. Thereafter Gustafson continued to manage the building and collect rents on behalf of Sparks, Sr.'s estate, with the knowledge and approval of the executor, Robert Sparks, Jr. Gustafson did not request any compensation for his services.

Under Gustafson's management, Nome Center operated at a loss. The Estate deposited $10,000 in a Nome Center account to cover operating expenses, but the amount was not sufficient to meet the necessary costs of insurance, mortgage payments, utility bills, and repairs. Gustafson often paid Nome Center expenses out of his own pocket. Maintenance and remodeling work were performed by Gustafson, using in part his own funds. Although he mailed monthly reports of the Nome Center's income and expenses, these reports did not include all of his own expenditures.

In February, 1982, the Estate signed a document entitled "purchase agreement" which indicated that Gustafson had purchased the building from the Estate, and would assume the deed of trust as soon as the purchase details could be worked out. However, no purchase details were ever agreed upon. The Estate sold the building to a third party in February, 1983, and Gustafson ceased to manage the property at that time.

On July 14, 1983, Gustafson and his business corporation, Nome Business Venture, Inc., filed suit against the Estate and the executor in Nome, claiming that the defendants breached an oral agreement to sell the Nome Center Building to Gustafson. Plaintiffs subsequently filed an amended complaint which further alleged that Gustafson was entitled to recover for funds and services that he expended on the building under a statutory or equitable lien theory. Defendants filed an answer and counterclaimed for an accounting of all monies collected and expended on the building.

At trial the superior court found that Gustafson had no enforceable lien. The court also concluded that it would be inequitable to allow the Estate to retain the benefits that Gustafson had conferred upon Nome Center at his own expense. The court ordered the Estate to pay Gustafson $65,706.07 in compensation for the services and improvements that he conferred upon the Estate during his two years of managing the Nome Center Building. This appeal followed....

Unjust enrichment exists where the defendant has received a benefit from the plaintiff and it would be inequitable for defendant to retain the benefit without compensating plaintiff for its value. *E.g., Bevins v.*

Peoples Bank & Trust Co., 671 P.2d 875, 881 (Alaska 1983).... Sparks claims that plaintiffs failed to prove either element of unjust enrichment: first, that the Estate received any benefit from plaintiffs, and second, that if a benefit was received then its retention would be unjust.

A person confers a benefit upon another if he gives the other some interest in money, land or possessions; performs services beneficial to or at the request of the other; satisfies a debt of the other; or in any way adds to the other's advantage. *Restatement of the Law of Restitution* § 1, comment b (1937). In this case Gustafson made substantial repairs and improvements to the Nome Center, provided management services that kept Nome Center operating, and paid debts incurred by Nome Center, all arguably on the Estate's behalf. There is no question that Gustafson conferred a benefit upon the Estate.

Even where a person has conferred a benefit upon another, however, he is entitled to compensation only if it would be just and equitable to require compensation under the circumstances. *Restatement of the Law of Restitution* § 1, comment c (1937). Courts will allow the defendant to retain a benefit without compensating plaintiff in several situations, one of which is relevant to the case at hand: where the benefit was given gratuitously without expectation of payment. *Murdock–Bryant Construction v. Pearson*, 146 Ariz. 48, 703 P.2d 1197, 1203 (1985). *See also* Dawson, *The Self–Serving Intermeddler*, 87 Harv.L.Rev. 1409 (1974).... Appellants argue that this situation is present in the case before us.

This court has not yet addressed the circumstances which give rise to a finding of gratuitous intent. A good discussion of this issue in the context of a decedent's estate can be found in *Kershaw v. Tracy Collins Bank & Trust Co.*, 561 P.2d 683 (Utah 1977). In that case the decedent's best friend provided a variety of services to the decedent's widow, including chauffeuring, buying groceries, running errands, and performing minor repair work. *Id.* at 684. The court looked at the extent of the services provided to the widow, the closeness of the relationship between the parties, and the fact that the plaintiff never sought compensation until after the widow died. The court found that the widow had not been unjustly enriched, since plaintiff's services were not necessary for the widow's existence and were of the sort which could reasonably be expected from a long time friend. *Id.* at 687.

In this case there was a similarly close relationship between the plaintiff and the decedent. It appears that Gustafson managed the Nome Center Building for the decedent without requesting compensation, in recognition of many long years of friendship and business association together. At trial, the executor testified that he thought Gustafson would continue to manage the building for two years after Sparks' death out of the goodness of his heart, without expectation of payment. Gustafson never requested compensation for his services during his tenure as the Nome Center manager for the Estate. The closeness of the parties' relationship and Gustafson's failure to request compensation in a timely manner suggest that Gustafson offered his services to the Estate gratuitously.

However, the services that Gustafson performed for the Estate were not the sort which one would ordinarily expect to receive from a friend as a mere gratuity. Gustafson spent approximately five hours a day for two years collecting rents for Nome Center, soliciting new tenants, making repairs and improvements, paying utility, insurance and mortgage bills out of his own pocket when rental income fell short of expenses, and performing other general maintenance and management services for the Estate. These are the types of extensive business services for which one would ordinarily expect to be paid. We therefore agree with the trial court that Gustafson's services were not offered gratuitously.[4] . . .

Questions

1. Does the court in your view succeed in distinguishing *Sparks* from *Kershaw*? What is the injustice in *Sparks*?

2. Should Sparks, Jr. have protected the estate's interest by monitoring the situation and clarifying matters with Gustafson? Should Gustafson have indicated his expectation of payment to Sparks, Jr. before doing the work? Should either party's omission bear on the claim for restitution?

3. *Problems.*

a. Assume that, the facts otherwise being as in *Sparks*, Gustafson had performed the same services for his friend before his friend's death and billed the estate for the value of all services rendered before and after the death. Same result?

b. Assume that, the facts otherwise being as in *Sparks*, Gustafson had painted the exterior of the building while Sparks, Jr. was out of town because, he testified, he had expected Sparks, Jr. to object. But, he said, Sparks, Sr. surely would have wanted the job done. Is the estate liable for the increased value of the building? For the value of goods and services employed in the work?

c. Assume that, the facts otherwise being as in *Sparks*, Sparks, Jr. told Gustafson soon after Sparks, Sr.'s death that he was making no promises of remuneration for Gustafson's good works, which were nonetheless appreciated. Same result?

4. The trial court's finding stated:

8. That this court, after examining all the evidence presented by the parties and personally observing the demeanor of the witnesses herein, finds that plaintiffs, Gustafson and NBV, expended time and money on behalf of the Estate of Sparks, Sr. and to the benefit of the estate, at the implied request of the executor of the Estate, Sparks, Jr., with the implied promise of the Estate to pay plaintiffs therefore, and the services and money that plaintiffs Gustafson and NBV rendered were value to the Estate and to the executor and did preserve the assets of the Estate in the amount of $62,506.07, the reasonable value thereof and the reasonable value plaintiffs deserve therefore, and the defendant Estate of Sparks, Sr. would be unjustly enriched by these activities of plaintiffs in this said amount, if not awarded the said $62,506.07.

(Footnote omitted).

MILLS v. WYMAN

Supreme Judicial Court of Massachusetts, 1825.
3 Pick. (20 Mass.) 207.

This was an action of *assumpsit* brought to recover a compensation for the board, nursing, & c., of Levi Wyman, son of the defendant, from the 5th to the 20th of February, 1821. The plaintiff then lived at Hartford, in Connecticut; the defendant, at Shrewsbury, in this county. Levi Wyman, at the time when the services were rendered, was about 25 years of age, and had long ceased to be a member of his father's family. He was on his return from a voyage at sea, and being suddenly taken sick at Hartford, and being poor and in distress, was relieved by the plaintiff in the manner and to the extent above stated. On the 24th of February, after all the expenses had been incurred, the defendant wrote a letter to the plaintiff promising to pay him such expenses. There was no consideration for this promise, except what grew out of the relation which subsisted between Levi Wyman and the defendant, and *Howe* J., before whom the cause was tried in the Court of Common Pleas, thinking this not sufficient to support the action, directed a nonsuit. To this direction the plaintiff filed exceptions.

PARKER, CHIEF JUSTICE. General rules of law established for the protection and security of honest and fair-minded men, who may inconsiderately make promises without any equivalent, will sometimes screen men of a different character from engagements which they are bound in *foro conscientiae* to perform. This is a defect inherent in all human systems of legislation. The rule that a mere verbal promise, without any consideration, cannot be enforced by action, is universal in its application, and cannot be departed from to suit particular cases in which a refusal to perform such a promise may be disgraceful.

The promise declared on in this case appears to have been made without any legal consideration. The kindness and services towards the sick son of the defendant were not bestowed at his request. The son was in no respect under the care of the defendant. He was twenty-five years old, and had long left his father's family. On his return from a foreign country, he fell sick among strangers, and the plaintiff acted the part of the good Samaritan, giving him shelter and comfort until he died. The defendant, his father, on being informed of this event, influenced by a transient feeling of gratitude, promises in writing to pay the plaintiff for the expenses he had incurred. But he has determined to break this promise, and is willing to have his case appear on record as a strong example of particular injustice sometimes necessarily resulting from the operation of general rules.

It is said a moral obligation is a sufficient consideration to support an express promise; and some authorities lay down the rule thus broadly; but upon examination of the cases we are satisfied that the universality of the rule cannot be supported, and that there must have been some preexisting obligation, which has become inoperative by positive law, to form a basis for an effective promise. The cases of debts barred by the statute of limitations, of debts incurred by infants, of debts of bankrupts, are generally put for illustration of the rule. Express promises founded on such preexisting equitable obligations may be enforced; there is a good consideration for them; they merely remove an impediment created by law to the recovery of debts honestly due, but which public policy protects the debtors from being compelled to pay. In all these cases there was originally a *quid pro quo*; and according to the principles of natural justice the party receiving ought to pay; but the legislature has said he shall not be coerced; then comes the promise to pay the debt that is barred, the promise of the man to pay the debt of the infant, of the discharged bankrupt to restore to his creditor what by the law he had lost. In all these cases there is a moral obligation founded upon an antecedent valuable consideration. These promises therefore have a sound legal basis. They are not promises to pay something for nothing; not naked pacts; but the voluntary revival or creation of obligation which before existed in natural law, but which had been dispensed with, not for the benefit of the party obliged solely, but principally for the public convenience. If moral obligation, in its fullest sense, is a good substratum for an express promise, it is not easy to perceive why it is not equally good to support an implied promise. What a man ought to do, generally he ought to be made to do, whether he promise or refuse. But the law of society has left most of such obligations to the *interior* forum, as the tribunal of conscience has been aptly called. Is there not a moral obligation upon every son who has become affluent by means of the education and advantages bestowed upon him by his father, to relieve that father from pecuniary embarrassment, to promote his comfort and happiness, and even to share with him his riches, if thereby he will be made happy? And yet such a son may, with impunity, leave such a father in any degree of penury above that which will expose the community in which he dwells, to the danger of being obliged to preserve him from absolute want. Is not a wealthy father under strong moral obligation to advance the interest of an obedient, well disposed son, to furnish him with the means of acquiring and maintaining a becoming rank in life, to rescue him from the horrors of debt incurred by misfortune? Yet the law will uphold him in any degree of parsimony, short of that which would reduce his son to the necessity of seeking public charity.

Without doubt there are great interests of society which justify withholding the coercive arm of the law from these duties of imperfect obligation, as they are called; imperfect, not because they are less binding upon the conscience than those which are called perfect, but because the wisdom of the social law does not impose sanctions upon them.

A deliberate promise, in writing, made freely and without any mistake, one which may lead the party to whom it is made into contracts and expenses, cannot be broken without a violation of moral duty. But if there was nothing paid or promised for it, the law, perhaps wisely, leaves the execution of it to the conscience of him who makes it. It is only when the party making the promise gains something, or he to whom it is made loses something, that the law gives the promise validity. And in the case of the promise of the adult to pay the debt of the infant, of the debtor discharged by the statute of limitations or bankruptcy, the principle is preserved by looking back to the origin of the transaction, where an equivalent is to be found. An exact equivalent is not required by the law; for there being a consideration, the parties are left to estimate its value: though here the courts of equity will step in to relieve from gross inadequacy between the consideration and the promise.

These principles are deduced from the general current of decided cases upon the subject, as well as from the known maxims of the common law. The general position, that moral obligation is a sufficient consideration for an express promise, is to be limited in its application, to cases where at some time or other a good or valuable consideration has existed.

A legal obligation is always a sufficient consideration to support either an express or an implied promise; such as an infant's debt for necessaries, or a father's promise to pay for the support and education of his minor children. But when the child shall have attained to manhood, and shall have become his own agent in the world's business, the debts he incurs, whatever may be their nature, create no obligation upon the father; and it seems to follow, that his promise founded upon such a debt has no legally binding force.

The cases of instruments under seal and certain mercantile contracts, in which considerations need not be proved, do not contradict the principles above suggested. They first import a consideration in themselves, and the second belong to a branch of the mercantile law, which has found it necessary to disregard the point of consideration in respect to instruments negotiable in their nature and essential to the interests of commerce. . . .

For the foregoing reasons we are all of opinion that the nonsuit directed by the Court of Common Pleas was right, and that judgment be entered thereon for costs for the defendant.

Questions

1. What is the promise sued upon in *Mills*? Is the court's argument for not enforcing it sound? If not, are there grounds that justify enforcing the promise? What is the contractual interest that is worthy of legal protection?

2. What is the court's distinction between legal and moral obligation? Is it sound? Does it depend on the view that promises are enforceable *only* when part of a bargained-for exchange of values? If so, in light of the foregoing cases on consideration, is that a sound reason for refusing to enforce the promise in *Mills*?

3. *Problems.*

    a. Sturges owed Capra $1,000 under a contract that became unenforceable when the statute of limitations ran on the claim. Being an upright person, Sturges then promised Capra that he would keep the promise nonetheless. Should Capra be able to recover from Sturges's estate when Sturges suddenly dies? See RESTATEMENT (SECOND) OF CONTRACTS § 82.

b. Sturges owed Capra $1,000 under a contract that was discharged when Sturges went bankrupt. Being an upright person, Sturges later promised Capra that he would keep the promise nonetheless. Should Capra be able to recover from Sturges's estate when Sturges suddenly dies? See *Id.,* § 83; 11 U.S.C. § 524(c), (d) (Bankruptcy Code).

c. Bette was seriously injured and unconscious from an automobile accident when Kathrine, a physician, stopped at the scene, gave emergency treatment, and stayed with Bette until the ambulance arrived at the hospital. When Kathrine sends Bette a bill for services rendered, must Bette pay at the usual and customary rate, assuming no statutes are applicable? See In re Crisan's Estate, 362 Mich. 569, 107 N.W.2d 907 (1961).

d. Assume the facts are as in Problem c, except that Bette is a Christian Scientist who deeply resents having been treated medically at all. Same result? See RESTATEMENT OF RESTITUTION § 116.

e. Assume the facts are as in Problem c, except that Kathrine is not a physician. Same result?

––––––––

RESTATEMENT (SECOND) OF CONTRACTS § 86

––––––––

WEBB v. McGOWIN

Court of Appeals of Alabama, 1935.
27 Ala.App. 82, 168 So. 196.

BRICKEN, PRESIDING JUDGE. This action is in assumpsit. The complaint as originally filed was amended. The demurrers to the complaint as amended were sustained, and because of this adverse ruling by the court the plaintiff took a nonsuit, and the assignment of errors on this appeal are predicated upon said action or ruling of the court.

A fair statement of the case presenting the questions for decision is set out in appellant's brief, which we adopt.

"On the 3d day of August, 1925, appellant while in the employ of the W.T. Smith Lumber Company, a corporation, and acting within the scope of his employment, was engaged in clearing the upper floor of mill No. 2 of the company. While so engaged he was in the act of dropping a pine block from the upper floor of the mill to the ground below; this being the usual and ordinary way of clearing the floor, and it being the duty of the plaintiff in the course of his employment to so drop it. The block weighed about 75 pounds.

"As appellant was in the act of dropping the block to the ground below, he was on the edge of the upper floor of the mill. As he started to turn the block loose so that it would drop to the ground, he saw J. Greeley McGowin, testator of the defendants, on the ground below and directly under where the block would have fallen had appellant turned it loose. Had he turned it loose it would have struck McGowin with such force as to have caused him serious bodily harm or death. Appellant could have remained safely on the upper floor of the mill by turning the block loose and allowing it to drop, but had he done this the block would have fallen on McGowin and caused him serious injuries or death. The only safe and reasonable way to prevent this was for appellant to hold to the block and divert its direction in falling from the place where McGowin was standing and the only safe way to divert it so as to prevent its coming into contact with McGowin was for appellant to fall with it to the ground below. Appellant did this, and by holding to the block and falling with it to the ground below, he diverted the course of its fall in such way that McGowin was not injured. In thus preventing the injuries to McGowin appellant himself received serious bodily injuries, resulting in his right leg being broken, the heel of his right foot torn off and his right arm broken. He was badly crippled for life and rendered unable to do physical or mental labor.

"On September 1, 1925, in consideration of appellant having prevented him from sustaining death or serious bodily harm and in consideration of the injuries appellant had received, McGowin agreed with him to care for and maintain him for the remainder of appellant's life at the rate of $15 every two weeks from the time he sustained his injuries to and during the remainder of appellant's life; it being agreed that McGowin would pay this sum to appellant for his maintenance. Under the agreement McGowin paid or caused to be paid to appellant the sum so agreed on up until McGowin's death on January 1, 1934. After his death the payments were continued to and including January 27, 1934, at which time they were discontinued. Thereupon plaintiff brought suit to recover the unpaid installments accruing up to the time of the bringing of the suit. . . ."

The action was for the unpaid installments accruing after January 27, 1934, to the time of the suit.

The principal grounds of demurrer to the original and amended complaint are: (1) It states no cause of action; (2) its averments show the contract was without consideration; (3) it fails to allege that McGowin had, at or before the services were rendered, agreed to pay appellant for them; (4) the contract declared on is void under the statute of frauds.

1. The averments of the complaint show that appellant saved McGowin from death or grievous bodily harm. This was a material benefit to him of infinitely more value than any financial aid he could have received. Receiving this benefit, McGowin became morally bound to compensate appellant for the services rendered. Recognizing his moral obligation, he expressly agreed to pay appellant as alleged in the com-

plaint and complied with this agreement up to the time of his death; a period of more than 8 years.

Had McGowin been accidentally poisoned and a physician, without his knowledge or request, had administered an antidote, thus saving his life, a subsequent promise by McGowin to pay the physician would have been valid. Likewise, McGowin's agreement as disclosed by the complaint to compensate appellant for saving him from death or grievous bodily injury is valid and enforceable.

Where the promisee cares for, improves, and preserves the property of the promisor, though done without his request, it is sufficient consideration for the promisor's subsequent agreement to pay for the service, because of the material benefit received. . . .

In Boothe v. Fitzpatrick, 36 Vt. 681, the court held that a promise by defendant to pay for the past keeping of a bull which had escaped from defendant's premises and been cared for by plaintiff was valid, although there was no previous request, because the subsequent promise obviated that objection; it being equivalent to a previous request. On the same principle, had the promisee saved the promisor's life or his body from grievous harm, his subsequent promise to pay for the services rendered would have been valid. Such service would have been far more material than caring for his bull. Any holding that saving a man from death or grievous bodily harm is not a material benefit sufficient to uphold a subsequent promise to pay for the service, necessarily rests on the assumption that saving life and preservation of the body from harm have only a sentimental value. The converse of this is true. Life and preservation of the body have material pecuniary values, measurable in dollars and cents. Because of this, physicians practice their profession charging for services rendered in saving life and curing the body of its ills, and surgeons perform operations. The same is true as to the law of negligence, authorizing the assessment of damages in personal injury cases based upon the extent of the injuries, earnings, and life expectancies of those injured.

In the business of life insurance, the value of a man's life is measured in dollars and cents according to his expectancy, the soundness of his body, and his ability to pay premiums. The same is true as to health and accident insurance.

It follows that if, as alleged in the complaint, appellant saved J. Greeley McGowin from death or grievous bodily harm, and McGowin subsequently agreed to pay him for the service rendered, it became a valid and enforceable contract.

2. It is well settled that moral obligation is a sufficient consideration to support a subsequent promise to pay where the promisor has received a material benefit, although there was no original duty or liability resting on the promisor. . . .

The case at bar is clearly distinguishable from the class of cases where the consideration is a mere moral obligation or conscientious duty unconnected with receipt by promisor of benefits of a material or pecuniary nature.... Here the promisor received a material benefit constituting a valid consideration for his promise.

3. Some authorities hold that, for a moral obligation to support a subsequent promise to pay, there must have existed a prior legal or equitable obligation, which for some reason had become unenforceable, but for which the promisor was still morally bound. This rule, however, is subject to qualification in those cases where the promisor, having received a material benefit from the promisee, is morally bound to compensate him for the services rendered and in consideration of this obligation promises to pay. In such cases the subsequent promise to pay is an affirmance or ratification of the services rendered carrying with it the presumption that a previous request for the service was made....

McGowin's express promise to pay appellant for the services rendered was an affirmance or ratification of what appellant had done raising the presumption that the services had been rendered at McGowin's request.

4. The averments of the complaint show that in saving McGowin from death or grievous bodily harm, appellant was crippled for life. This was part of the consideration of the contract declared on. McGowin was benefited. Appellant was injured. Benefit to the promisor or injury to the promisee is a sufficient legal consideration for the promisor's agreement to pay....

5. Under the averments of the complaint the services rendered by appellant were not gratuitous. The agreement of McGowin to pay and the acceptance of payment by appellant conclusively shows the contrary.

6. The contract declared on was not void under the statute of frauds (Code 1923, § 8034). The demurrer on this ground was not well taken....

From what has been said, we are of the opinion that the court below erred in the ruling complained of; that is to say, in sustaining the demurrer, and for this error the case is reversed and remanded.

Reversed and remanded.

SAMFORD, JUDGE (concurring).

The questions involved in this case are not free from doubt, and perhaps the strict letter of the rule, as stated by judges, though not always in accord, would bar a recovery by plaintiff, but following the principle announced by Chief Justice Marshall in Hoffman v. Porter, Fed.Cas. No. 6,577, 2 Brock. 156, 159, where he says, "I do not think that law ought to be separated from justice, where it is at most doubtful," I concur in the conclusions reached by the court.

Questions

1. What is the promise sued upon in *Webb*? Was it supported by consideration? Did Mr. Webb have a contractual interest that deserved

protection? Should it be legally relevant, in this action, that he was a "good Samaritan"?

2.   Would *Mills* be decided differently after *Webb*?

3.   Should *Dyer*, above at p. 154, have been litigated on the same basis as *Webb*? Should the holding in *Dyer* be understood as a manipulation of consideration doctrine to protect the interests protected in *Webb*?

4.   *Problem.*

Nick and Nora were married just before Nick started law school. They agreed that Nora would stop school and work to put Nick through law school, and that Nick would then work to put Nora through graduate school in art history. Shortly after the law school graduation, however, Nick and Nora decided to get divorced. Special family law issues aside, does Nora have a claim for breach of contract against Nick? For restitution? If either claim is sound, how should her recovery be measured? See Pyeatte v. Pyeatte, 135 Ariz. 346, 661 P.2d 196 (App. 1982).

Chapter 3

THE JUSTICE PRINCIPLE

The law refrains from enforcing promises when the prima facie justification for enforcing the promise is overridden by considerations of justice.

"Justice" is a word with many meanings. Perfect justice would treat all people as they should be treated ideally—as God, who is infinitely just, would treat them. God has no need for rules or principles, as He, if anyone, would know what is just in the particular circumstances of each situation.

The laws in force in all societies fall short of perfect justice. Not infrequently, we humans make mistakes, even when lawmakers and judges aim at justice. Moreover, particularized justice would not be humanly administrable or predictable. In principle, for example, young children should not have the power to make contracts because they are too easily separated from their property by the unscrupulous. Children do not all mature at the same age. To allow children to contract "when mature" would leave it highly unclear whether a contract is enforceable in many cases, producing much litigation with uncertain results and making it risky for people to contract with the young. Setting an age makes things administrable and predictable, but at some cost to perfect justice. No matter what age is set, there will be individuals who, in justice, should be allowed to make contracts before that age and others who should not be allowed to make contracts even later. Thus, the law does not always do justice in the particular.

If perfect justice is unattainable by us, we can nonetheless evaluate our laws by three more practical conceptions of justice. One is formal justice, which requires that like cases be treated alike, a rule be applied consistently, or that persons be treated equally under law. Presumably all law should conform to formal justice. Laws that do not do so are arbitrary and unjustifiable. However, achieving formal justice would be a minimal achievement because this conception of justice says nothing about the content of just laws. Odious laws, such as the laws of apartheid, can be applied consistently.

A second conception of justice is "corrective justice." This is the conception underlying the law of unjust enrichment, considered in Chapter 2, § 3, and many civil laws requiring compensation for injuries inflicted on another person. Here, an injustice involves two people, one of whom takes the other's property without consent. The injustice lies in the disturbance of the equality of their personhoods that is implicit in an uninvited taking. Compensation aims at corrective justice by reconstituting that equality.

A third conception of justice is "distributive justice." This is the conception that underlies theories of social justice requiring wealth and power to be distributed fairly in a society. Injustice in this sense is a state of affairs in the aggregate affecting groups of people, not a relation between two individuals. An unjust distribution might be perpetuated by laws allowing the rich and powerful to exploit their disproportionate assets to maintain their dominant position. A related idea is paternalism—the view that courts should protect the weak by prohibiting them from contracting against their own interests.

In this chapter, we explore various legal doctrines that might be understood to implement principles of corrective or distributive justice. We saw in Chapter 2 that promises are not enforceable unless there are sufficient legal reasons for a court to wield its powers. Sufficient legal reasons are bargained-for exchange, reliance, unjust enrichment and, in some cases, formality. Even when a court is prima facie justified in enforcing a promise, however, the promise may be unenforceable because justice overrides the autonomy principle and the prima facie justification for judicial action. Section 1 explores the boundaries of autonomy's domain by considering limits placed on free contracting by public policy. Section 2 considers the boundaries of autonomy and corrective justice, focusing on mistakes. Section 3 explores the role of distributive justice by considering consumer sales in low-income markets. Section 4 considers unfair surprise and contracts of adhesion using recent cases involving agreements to arbitrate.

SECTION 1.   THE DOMAIN OF FREEDOM OF CONTRACT

"Freedom of Contract" once was used as a political slogan favoring strong individualism in a laissez faire economy. In Lochner v. New York, 198 U.S. 45, 25 S.Ct. 539, 49 L.Ed. 937 (1905), for example, the U.S. Supreme Court held unconstitutional a state statute setting maximum hours and minimum wages for workers in bakeries. It reasoned that liberty of contract meant that "one has as much right to purchase as the other to sell labor." Id., 198 U.S. at 56, 25 S.Ct. at 543. Moreover, the court wrote:

> There is no reasonable ground for interfering with the liberty of person or the right of free contract, by determining the hours of labor, in the occupation of a baker. There is no contention that bakers as a class are not ... able to assert their rights and care for

themselves without the protecting arm of the State, interfering with their independence of judgment and of action.

Id., 198 U.S. at 57, 25 S.Ct. at 543. On this view, it would seem, the domain of freedom of contract must be large indeed. In this domain, people are neither disabled from contracting on terms they choose (freedom of contract) nor, as a corollary, forced to contract on terms imposed by the other party or the state (freedom from contract). The state's role is limited to protecting baseline property rights, setting rules for fair competition, and enforcing promises that meet the conditions considered above in Chapters 1 and 2, § 1.

Lochner was overruled during the Great Depression. Almost everyone today acknowledges that the government has constitutional authority to regulate contracts in a great many ways. The debate, rather, is over when it may be wise policy to limit free contracting. On one hand, few today would replace freedom of contract with central planning, by which the state regulates all terms of exchange for the entire economy. The sad experiences of Soviet-style communism and developing country socialism have all but extinguished this view for the time being. On the other hand, few now advocate complete liberty of contract. No one, for example, insists that children have the power to contract. On the most popular conservative view, moreover, market failures do occur, requiring state intervention to make the free market more efficient.

Much legislation and public debate involves a constant struggle over the shape and location of the boundaries of the free market. Statutes and administrative regulations, such as the minimum wage and maximum hours laws, commonly override autonomy. In this course, however, we will examine restrictions imposed by the common law to indicate that there is a boundary. We will here consider issues involving exclusions of certain kinds of people and certain kinds of contracts from the domain of free contracting.

CIVIL RIGHTS ACT OF 1866

Act of Apr. 9, 1866, ch. 31, § 1, 14 Stat. 27.

[C]itizens, of every race and color, without regard to any previous condition of slavery or involuntary servitude, . . . shall have the same right, in every State and Territory in the United States, to make and enforce contracts . . . as is enjoyed by white citizens. . . .

———

RESTATEMENT (SECOND) OF CONTRACTS §§ 7, 12, 15

———

ORTELERE v. TEACHERS' RETIREMENT BOARD

Court of Appeals of New York, 1969.
25 N.Y.2d 196, 250 N.E.2d 460, 303 N.Y.S.2d 362.

BREITEL, J. This appeal involves the revocability of an election of benefits under a public employees' retirement system and suggests the need for a renewed examination of the kinds of mental incompetency which may render voidable the exercise of contractual rights. The particular issue arises on the evidently unwise and foolhardy selection of benefits by a 60-year-old teacher, on leave for mental illness and suffering from cerebral arteriosclerosis, after service as a public schoolteacher and participation in a public retirement system for over 40 years. The teacher died a little less than two months after making her election of maximum benefits, payable to her during her life, thus causing the entire reserve to fall in. She left surviving her husband of 38 years of marriage and two grown children.

There is no doubt that any retirement system depends for its soundness on an actuarial experience based on the purely prospective selections of benefits and mortality rates among the covered group, and that retrospective or adverse selection after the fact would be destructive of a sound system. It is also true that members of retirement systems are free to make choices which to others may seem unwise or foolhardy. The issue here is narrower than any suggested by these basic principles. It is whether an otherwise irrevocable election may be avoided for incapacity because of known mental illness which resulted in the election when, except in the barest actuarial sense, the system would sustain no unfavorable consequences.

The husband and executor of Grace W. Ortelere, the deceased New York City schoolteacher, sues to set aside her application for retirement without option, in the event of her death. It is alleged that Mrs. Ortelere, on February 11, 1965, two months before her death from natural causes, was not mentally competent to execute a retirement application. By this application, effective the next day, she elected the maximum retirement allowance (Administrative Code of City of New York, § B20–46.0). She thus revoked her earlier election of benefits under which she named her husband a beneficiary of the unexhausted reserve upon her death. Selection of the maximum allowance extinguished all interests upon her death.

Following a nonjury trial in Supreme Court, it was held that Grace Ortelere had been mentally incompetent at the time of her February 11 application, thus rendering it 'null and void and of no legal effect'. The Appellate Division, by a divided court, reversed the judgment of the Supreme Court and held that, as a matter of law, there was insufficient proof of mental incompetency as to this transaction (31 A.D.2d 139, 295 N.Y.S.2d 506).

Mrs. Ortelere's mental illness, indeed, psychosis, is undisputed. It is not seriously disputable, however, that she had complete cognitive judgment or awareness when she made her selection. A modern understanding of mental illness, however, suggests that incapacity to contract or exercise contractual rights may exist, because of volitional and affective impediments or disruptions in the personality, despite the intellectual or cognitive ability to understand. It will be recognized as the civil law parallel to the question of criminal responsibility which has been the recent concern of so many and has resulted in statutory and decisional changes in the criminal law (e.g., A.L.I. Model Penal Code, § 4.01; Penal Law, § 30.05; Durham v. United States, 214 F.2d 862).

Mrs. Ortelere, an elementary school teacher since 1924, suffered a 'nervous breakdown' in March, 1964 and went on a leave of absence expiring February 5, 1965. She was then 60 years old and had been happily married for 38 years. On July 1, 1964, she came under the care of Dr. D'Angelo, a psychiatrist, who diagnosed her breakdown as involutional psychosis, melancholia type. Dr. D'Angelo prescribed, and for about six weeks decedent underwent, tranquilizer and shock therapy. Although moderately successful, the therapy was not continued since it was suspected that she also suffered from cerebral arteriosclerosis, an ailment later confirmed. However, the psychiatrist continued to see her at monthly intervals until March, 1965. On March 28, 1965, she was hospitalized after collapsing at home from an aneurysm. She died to days later; the cause of death was 'Cerebral thrombosis due to H(ypertensive) H(eart) D(isease).'

. . .

Some years before, on June 28, 1958, she had executed a 'Selection of Benefits under Option One' naming her husband as beneficiary of the unexhausted reserve. Under this option upon retirement her allowance would be less by way of periodic retirement allowances, but if she died before receipt of her full reserve the balance of the reserve would be payable to her husband. On June 16, 1960, two years later, she had designated her husband as beneficiary of her service death benefits in the event of her death prior to retirement.

Then on February 11, 1965, when her leave of absence had just expired and she was still under treatment, she executed a retirement application, the one here involved, selecting the maximum retirement allowance payable during her lifetime with nothing payable on or after death. She also, at this time, borrowed from the system the maximum cash withdrawal permitted, namely, $8,760. Three days earlier she had written the board, stating that she intended to retire on February 12 or 15 or as soon as she received 'the information I need in order to decide whether to take an option or maximum allowance.' She then listed eight specific questions, reflecting great understanding of the retirement system, concerning the various alternatives available. An extremely detailed reply was sent, by letter of February 15, 1965, although by that date it was technically impossible for her to change her selection. However, the board's chief clerk, before whom Mrs. Ortelere executed the application, testified that the questions were 'answered verbally by me on February

11th.' Her retirement reserve totaled $62,165 (after deducting the $8,760 withdrawal), and the difference between electing the maximum retirement allowance (no option) and the allowance under 'option one' was $901 per year or $75 per month. That is, had the teacher selected 'option one' she would have received an annual allowance of $4,494 or $375 per month, while if no option had been selected she would have received an annual allowance of $5,395 or $450 per month. Had she not withdrawn the cash the annual figures would be $5,247 and $6,148 respectively.

Following her taking a leave of absence for her condition, Mrs. Ortelere had become very depressed and was unable to care for herself. As a result her husband gave up his electrician's job, in which he earned $222 per week, to stay home and take care of her on a full-time basis. She left their home only when he accompanied her. Although he took her to the Retirement Board on February 11, 1965, he did not know why she went, and did not question her for fear 'she'd start crying hysterically that I was scolding her. That's the way she was. And I wouldn't upset her.'

The Orteleres were in quite modest circumstances. They owned their own home, valued at $20,000, and had $8,000 in a savings account. They also owned some farm land worth about $5,000. Under these circumstances, as revealed in this record, retirement for both of the Orteleres or the survivor of them had to be provided, as a practical matter, largely out of Mrs. Ortelere's retirement benefits.

According to Dr. D'Angelo, the psychiatrist who treated her, Mrs. Ortelere never improved enough to 'warrant my sending her back (to teaching).' A physician for the Board of Education examined her on February 2, 1965 to determine her fitness to return to teaching. Although not a psychiatrist but rather a specialist in internal medicine, this physician 'judged that she had apparently recovered from the depression' and that she appeared rational. However, before allowing her to return to teaching, a report was requested from Dr. D'Angelo concerning her condition. It is notable that the Medical Division of the Board of Education on February 24, 1965 requested that Mrs. Ortelere report to the board's 'panel psychiatrist' on March 11, 1965.

Dr. D'Angelo stated '[a]t no time since she was under my care was she ever mentally competent'; that '[m]entally she couldn't make a decision of any kind, actually, of any kind, small or large.' He also described how involutional melancholia affects the judgment process: 'They can't think rationally, no matter what the situation is. They will even tell you, 'I used to be able to think of anything and make any decision. Now,' they say, 'even getting up, I don't know whether I should get up or whether I should stay in bed.' Or, 'I don't even know how to make a slice of toast any more.' Everything is impossible to decide, and everything is too great an effort to even think of doing. They just don't have the effort, actually, because their nervous breakdown drains them of all their physical energies.'

While the psychiatrist used terms referring to 'rationality', it is quite evident that Mrs. Ortelere's psychopathology did not lend itself to a classification under the legal test of irrationality. It is undoubtedly, for this reason, that the Appellate Division was unable to accept his testimony and the trial court's finding of irrationality in the light of the prevailing rules as they have been formulated.

The well-established rule is that contracts of a mentally incompetent person who has not been adjudicated insane are voidable. Even where the contract has been partly or fully performed it will still be avoided upon restoration of the status quo. (Verstandig v. Schlaffer, 296 N.Y. 62, 64, 70 N.E.2d 15, 16. . . .)

Traditionally, in this State and elsewhere, contractual mental capacity has been measured by what is largely a cognitive test (Aldrich v. Bailey, 132 N.Y. 85, 30 N.E. 264; 2 Williston, Contracts (3d ed.) . . .). Under this standard the 'inquiry' is whether the mind was 'so affected as to render him wholly and absolutely incompetent to comprehend and understand the nature of the transaction' (Aldrich v. Bailey, *supra*, at p. 89, 30 N.E. at p. 265). A requirement that the party also be able to make a rational judgment concerning the particular transaction qualified the cognitive test (Paine v. Aldrich, 133 N.Y. 544, 546, 30 N.E. 725, 726 . . .). Conversely, it is also well recognized that contractual ability would be affected by insane delusions intimately related to the particular transaction (Moritz v. Moritz, 153 App.Div. 147, 138 N.Y.S. 124, aff'd. 211 N.Y. 580, 105 N.E. 1090 . . .).

These traditional standards governing competency to contract were formulated when psychiatric knowledge was quite primitive. They fail to account for one who by reason of mental illness is unable to control his conduct even though his cognitive ability seems unimpaired. When these standards were evolving it was thought that all the mental faculties were simultaneously affected by mental illness. . . . This is no longer the prevailing view (Note, Mental Illness and the Law of Contracts, 57 Mich.L.Rev. 1020, 1033–1036).

Of course, the greatest movement in revamping legal notions of mental responsibility has occurred in the criminal law. The nineteenth century cognitive test embraced in the M'Naghten rules has long been criticized and changed by statute and decision in many jurisdictions (see M'Naghten's Case, 10 Clark & Fin. 200; 8 Eng.Rep. 718 (House of Lords, 1843); Weihofen, Mental Disorder as a Criminal Defense (1954), pp. 65–68; British Royal Comm. on Capital Punishment (1953), ch. 4; A.L.I. Model Penal Code, § 4.01, *supra*; cf. Penal Law, § 30.05).

While the policy considerations for the criminal law and the civil law are different, both share in common the premise that policy considerations must be based on a sound understanding of the human mind and, therefore, its illnesses. Hence, because the cognitive rules are, for the most part, too restrictive and rest on a false factual basis they must be re-examined. Once it is understood that, accepting plaintiff's proof, Mrs. Ortelere was psychotic and because of that psychosis could have been incapable of making a voluntary selection of her retirement system benefits, there is an issue that a modern jurisprudence should not exclude, merely because her mind could pass a 'cognition' test based on nineteenth century psychology.

. . .

It is quite significant that Restatement, 2d, Contracts, states the modern rule on competency to contract. This is in evident recognition, and the Reporter's Notes support this inference, that, regardless of how the cases formulated their reasoning, the old cognitive test no longer explains the results. Thus, the new Restatement section reads: '(1) A person incurs only voidable contractual duties by entering into a transaction if by reason of mental illness or defect . . . (b) he is unable to act in a reasonable manner in relation to the transaction and the other party has reason to know of his condition.' (Restatement, 2d, Contracts [§ 15(1)(b)]). . . .

The avoidance of duties under an agreement entered into by those who have done so by reason of mental illness, but who have understanding, depends on balancing competing policy considerations. There must be stability in contractual relations and protection of the expectations of parties who bargain in good faith. On the other hand, it is also desirable to protect persons who may understand the nature of the transaction but who, due to mental illness, cannot control their conduct. Hence, there should be relief only if the other party knew or was put on notice as to the contractor's mental illness. Thus, the Restatement provision for avoidance contemplates that 'the other party has reason to know' of the mental illness (Id.).

. . .

The system was, or should have been, fully aware of Mrs. Ortelere's condition. They, or the Board of Education, *knew* of her leave of absence for medical reasons and the resort to staff psychiatrists by the Board of Education. Hence, the other of the conditions for avoidance is satisfied.

Lastly, there are no significant changes of position by the system other than those that flow from the barest actuarial consequences of benefit selection.

Nor should one ignore that in the relationship between retirement system and member, and especially in a public system, there is not involved a commercial, let alone an ordinary commercial, transaction. Instead the nature of the system and its announced goal is the protection of its members and those in whom its members have an interest. It is not a sound scheme which would permit 40 years of contribution and participation in the system to be nullified by a one-instant act committed by one known to be mentally ill. This is especially true if there would be no substantial harm to the system if the act were avoided. On the record none may gainsay that her selection of a 'no option' retirement while under psychiatric care, ill with cerebral arteriosclerosis, aged 60, and with a family in which she had always manifested concern, was so unwise and foolhardy that a factfinder might conclude that it was explainable only as a product of psychosis.

On this analysis it is not difficult to see that plaintiff's evidence was sufficient to sustain a finding that, when she acted as she did on February 11, 1965, she did so solely as a result of serious mental illness, namely, psychosis. Of course, nothing less serious than medically classified psychosis should suffice or else few contracts would be invulnerable to some kind of psychological attack. Mrs. Ortelere's psychiatrist testified quite flatly that as an involutional melancholiac in depression she was incapable of making a voluntary 'rational' decision. Of course, as noted earlier, the trial court's finding and perhaps some of the testimony attempted to fit into the rubrics of the traditional rules. For that reason rather than reinstatement of the judgment at Trial Term there should be a new trial under the proper standards frankly considered and applied.

Accordingly, the order of the Appellate Division should be reversed, without costs, and the action remanded to Special Term for a new trial.

JASEN, JUDGE (dissenting). Where there has been no previous adjudication of incompetency, the burden of proving mental incompetence is upon the party alleging it. I agree with the majority at the Appellate Division that the plaintiff, the husband of the decedent, failed to sustain the burden incumbent upon him of proving deceased's incompetence.

The evidence conclusively establishes that the decedent, at the time she made her application to retire, understood not only that she was retiring, but also that she had selected the maximum payment during her lifetime.

Indeed, the letter written by the deceased to the Teachers' Retirement System prior to her retirement demonstrates her full mental capacity to understand and to decide whether to take an option or the maximum allowance. The full text of the letter reads as follows:

February 8, 1965

Gentlemen:

I would like to retire on Feb. 12 or Feb. 15. In other words, just as soon as possible after I receive the information I need in order to decide whether to take an option or maximum allowance. Following are the questions I would like to have answered:

1. What is my 'average' five-year salary?

2. What is my maximum allowance?

3. I am 60 years old. If I select option four-a with a beneficiary (female) 27 years younger, what is my allowance?

4. If I select four-a on the pension part only, and take the maximum annuity, what is my allowance?

5. If I take a loan of 89% of my year's salary before retirement, what would my maximum allowance be?

6. If I take a loan of $5,000 before retiring, and select option four-a on both the pension and annuity, what would my allowance be?

7. What is my total service credit? I have been on a leave without pay since Oct. 26, 1964.

8. What is the 'factor' used for calculating option four-a with the above beneficiary?

Thank you for your promptness in making the necessary calculations. I will come to your office on Thursday afternoon of this week.

It seems clear that this detailed, explicit and extremely pertinent list of queries reveals a mind fully in command of the salient features of the Teachers' Retirement System. Certainly, it cannot be said that the decedent could possess sufficient capacity to compose a letter indicating such a comprehensive understanding of the retirement system, and yet lack the capacity to understand the answers.

As I read the record, the evidence establishes that the decedent's election to receive maximum payments was predicated on the need for a higher income to support two retired persons—her husband and herself. Since the only source of income available to decedent and her husband was decedent's retirement pay, the additional payment of $75 per month which she would receive by electing the maximal payment was a necessity. Indeed, the additional payments represented an increase of 20% *over* the benefits payable under option 1. Under these circumstances, an election of maximal income during decedent's lifetime was not only a rational, but a necessary decision.

Further indication of decedent's knowledge of the financial needs of her family is evidenced by the fact that she took a loan for the maximum amount ($8,760) permitted by the retirement system at the time she made application for retirement.

Moreover, there is nothing in the record to indicate that the decedent had any warning, premonition, knowledge or indication at the time of retirement that her life expectancy was, in any way, reduced by her condition.

Decedent's election of the maximum retirement benefits, therefore, was not so contrary to her best interests so as to create an inference of her mental incompetence.

Indeed, concerning election of options under a retirement system, it has been held: 'Even where no previous election has been made, the court must make the election for an incompetent which would be in accordance with what would have been his manifest and reasonable choice if he were sane, and, in the absence of convincing evidence that the incompetent would have made a different selection, it is *presumed* that he would have chosen the option yielding the largest returns in his lifetime.' (Schwartzberg v. Teachers' Retirement Bd., 273 App.Div. 240, 242–243, 76 N.Y.S.2d 488, aff'd. 298 N.Y. 741, 83 N.E.2d 146; emphasis supplied.)

Nor can I agree with the majority's view that the traditional rules governing competency to contract 'are, for the most part, too restrictive and rest on a false factual basis'.

The issue confronting the courts concerning mental capacity to contract is under what circumstances and conditions should a party be relieved of contractual obligations freely entered. This is peculiarly a legal decision, although, of course, available medical knowledge forms a datum which influences the legal choice. It is common knowledge that the present state of psychiatric knowledge is inadequate to provide a fixed rule for each and every type of mental disorder. Thus, the generally accepted rules which have evolved to determine mental responsibility are general enough in application to encompass all types of mental disorders, and phrased in a manner which can be understood and practically applied by juries composed of laymen.

The generally accepted test of mental competency to contract which has thus evolved is whether the party attempting to avoid the contract was capable of understanding and appreciating the nature and consequences of the particular act or transaction which he challenges. . . . This rule represents a balance struck between policies to protect the security of transactions between individuals and freedom of contract on the one hand, and protection of those mentally handicapped on the other hand. In my opinion, this rule has proven workable in practice and fair in result. . . . In the final analysis, the lay jury will infer the state of the party's mind from his observed behavior as indicated by the evidence presented at trial. Each juror instinctively judges what is normal and what is abnormal conduct from his own experience, and the generally accepted test harmonizes the competing policy considerations with human experience to achieve the fairest result in the greatest number of cases.

. . .

The Appellate Division correctly found that the deceased was capable of understanding the nature and effect of her retirement benefits, and exercised rational judgment in electing to receive the maximum allowance during her lifetime. I fear that the majority's refinement of the generally accepted rules will prove unworkable in practice, and make many contracts vulnerable to psychological attack. Any benefit to those who understand what they are doing, but are unable to exercise self-discipline, will be outweighed by frivolous claims which will burden our courts and undermine the security of contracts. The reasonable expectations of those who innocently deal with persons who appear rational and who understand what they are doing should be protected.

Questions

1. What is the traditional test for mental incapacity? How would this court alter the test? Does it render a contract void or voidable? What difference does this make? Was it necessary to alter the test in order to invalidate Ms. Ortelere's election of a retirement option?

2.   Should Ms. Ortelere's election have been invalidated? Why? Should it be invalidated because her plight invokes our sympathy or empathy? Because, could she speak from the dead, she would regret her decision? Because giving effect to her election would be correctively or distributively unjust? Because Mr. Ortelere would otherwise be treated unjustly? Would invalidating her election be consistent with requirements of justice?

3.   *Problems.*

a.   Kevin purchased a used motor vehicle from Gwyneth Motors when he was seventeen years old, married, a father, and working. After he turned eighteen, the vehicle developed serious mechanical problems. Can he return it and recover the price? See RESTATEMENT (SECOND) OF CONTRACTS § 14.

b.   Assume that the facts are otherwise as in Problem a, except that Kevin was 16 years old when he concluded the contract. The dealer allowed him to pay one-half the purchase price on delivery and the balance in six months. The mechanical problems arose after four months. Kevin solicits your advice on whether he has a right to keep the car and use the balance owing to make the needed repairs. What should you advise him?

c.   Assume that the facts are otherwise as in Problem b, except that Kevin was two months shy of 18 when he concluded the contract and is now two months past his eighteenth birthday. Moreover, the dealer had allowed him to pay one-half the purchase price on delivery and the balance in three months. One month past his eighteenth birthday, he paid the balance due. The mechanical problems arose after four months. Can Kevin now disaffirm the contract?

––––––––

RESTATEMENT (SECOND) OF CONTRACTS §§ 178–179

––––––––

IN THE MATTER OF BABY M

Supreme Court of New Jersey, 1988.
109 N.J. 396, 537 A.2d 1227.

WILENTZ, CHIEF JUSTICE. In this matter the Court is asked to determine the validity of a contract that purports to provide a new way of bringing children into a family. For a fee of $10,000, a woman agrees to be artificially inseminated with the semen of another woman's husband; she is to conceive a child, carry it to term, and after its birth surrender it to the natural father and his wife. The intent of the contract is that the child's natural mother will thereafter be forever separated from her child. The wife is to adopt the child, and she and the natural father are to be regarded as its parents for all purposes. The contract providing for this is called a "surrogacy contract," the natural mother inappropriately called the "surrogate mother."

We invalidate the surrogacy contract because it conflicts with the law and public policy of this State. While we recognize the depth of the yearning of infertile couples to have their own children, we find the payment of money to a "surrogate" mother illegal, perhaps criminal, and potentially degrading to women. Although in this case we grant custody to the natural father, the evidence having clearly proved such custody to be in the best interests of the infant, we void both the termination of the surrogate mother's parental rights and the adoption of the child by the wife/stepparent. We thus restore the "surrogate" as the mother of the child. We remand the issue of the natural mother's visitation rights to the trial court, since that issue was not reached below and the record before us is not sufficient to permit us to decide it *de novo*.

We find no offense to our present laws where a woman voluntarily and without payment agrees to act as a "surrogate" mother, provided that she is not subject to a binding agreement to surrender her child. Moreover, our holding today does not preclude the Legislature from altering the current statutory scheme, within constitutional limits, so as to permit surrogacy contracts. Under current law, however, the surrogacy agreement before us is illegal and invalid.

I. FACTS

In February 1985, William Stern and Mary Beth Whitehead entered into a surrogacy contract. It recited that Stern's wife, Elizabeth, was infertile, that they wanted a child, and that Mrs. Whitehead was willing to provide that child as the mother with Mr. Stern as the father.

The contract provided that through artificial insemination using Mr. Stern's sperm, Mrs. Whitehead would become pregnant, carry the child to term, bear it, deliver it to the Sterns, and thereafter do whatever was necessary to terminate her maternal rights so that Mrs. Stern could thereafter adopt the child. Mrs. Whitehead's husband, Richard, was also a party to the contract; Mrs. Stern was not. Mr. Whitehead promised to do all acts necessary to rebut the presumption of paternity under the Parentage Act. *N.J.S.A.* 9:17–43a(1), –44a. Although Mrs. Stern was not a party to the surrogacy agreement, the contract gave her sole custody of the child in the event of Mr. Stern's death. Mrs. Stern's status as a nonparty to the surrogate parenting agreement presumably was to avoid the application of the baby-selling statute to this arrangement. *N.J.S.A.* 9:3–54.

Mr. Stern, on his part, agreed to attempt the artificial insemination and to pay Mrs. Whitehead $10,000 after the child's birth, on its delivery to him. In a separate contract, Mr. Stern agreed to pay $7,500 to the Infertility Center of New York ("ICNY"). The Center's advertising campaigns solicit surrogate mothers and encourage infertile couples to consider surrogacy. ICNY arranged for the surrogacy contract by bringing the parties together, explaining the process to them, furnishing the contractual form, and providing legal counsel.

The history of the parties' involvement in this arrangement suggests their good faith. William and Elizabeth Stern were married in July 1974, having met at the University of Michigan, where both were Ph.D. candidates. Due to financial considerations and Mrs. Stern's pursuit of a medical degree and residency, they decided to defer starting a family until 1981. Before then, however, Mrs. Stern learned that she might have multiple sclerosis and that the disease in some cases renders pregnancy a serious health risk. Her anxiety appears to have exceeded the actual risk, which current medical authorities assess as minimal. Nonetheless that anxiety was evidently quite real, Mrs. Stern fearing that pregnancy might precipitate blindness, paraplegia, or other forms of debilitation. Based on the perceived risk, the Sterns decided to forgo having their own children. The decision had special significance for Mr. Stern. Most of his family had been destroyed in the Holocaust. As the family's only survivor, he very much wanted to continue his bloodline.

Initially the Sterns considered adoption, but were discouraged by the substantial delay apparently involved and by the potential problem they saw arising from their age and their differing religious backgrounds. They were most eager for some other means to start a family.

The paths of Mrs. Whitehead and the Sterns to surrogacy were similar. Both responded to advertising by ICNY. The Sterns' response, following their inquiries into adoption, was the result of their long-standing decision to have a child. Mrs. Whitehead's response apparently resulted from her sympathy with family members and others who could have no children (she stated that she wanted to give another couple the "gift of life"); she also wanted the $10,000 to help her family.

Both parties, undoubtedly because of their own self-interest, were less sensitive to the implications of the transaction than they might otherwise have been. Mrs. Whitehead, for instance, appears not to have been concerned about whether the Sterns would make good parents for her child; the Sterns, on their part, while conscious of the obvious possibility that surrendering the child might cause grief to Mrs. Whitehead, overcame their qualms because of their desire for a child. At any rate, both the Sterns and Mrs. Whitehead were committed to the arrangement; both thought it right and constructive. . . .

Mrs. Whitehead realized, almost from the moment of birth, that she could not part with this child. She had felt a bond with it even during pregnancy. Some indication of the attachment was conveyed to the Sterns at the hospital when they told Mrs. Whitehead what they were going to name the baby. She apparently broke into tears and indicated that she did not know if she could give up the child. She talked about how the baby looked like her other daughter, and made it clear that she was experiencing great difficulty with the decision.

Nonetheless, Mrs. Whitehead was, for the moment, true to her word. Despite powerful inclinations to the contrary, she turned her child over to the Sterns on March 30 at the Whiteheads' home.

The Sterns were thrilled with their new child. They had planned extensively for its arrival, far beyond the practical furnishing of a room for her. It was a time of joyful celebration—not just for them but for their friends as well. The Sterns looked forward to raising their daughter, whom they named Melissa. While aware by then that Mrs. Whitehead was undergoing an emotional crisis, they were as yet not cognizant of the depth of that crisis and its implications for their newly-enlarged family.

Later in the evening of March 30, Mrs. Whitehead became deeply disturbed, disconsolate, stricken with unbearable sadness. She had to have her child. She could not eat, sleep, or concentrate on anything other than her need for her baby. The next day she went to the Sterns' home and told them how much she was suffering.

The depth of Mrs. Whitehead's despair surprised and frightened the Sterns. She told them that she could not live without her baby, that she must have her, even if only for one week, that thereafter she would surrender her child. The Sterns, concerned that Mrs. Whitehead might indeed commit suicide, not wanting under any circumstances to risk that, and in any event believing that Mrs. Whitehead would keep her word, turned the child over to her. It was not until four months later, after a series of attempts to regain possession of the child, that Melissa was returned to the Sterns, having been forcibly removed from the home where she was then living with Mr. and Mrs. Whitehead, the home in Florida owned by Mary Beth Whitehead's parents.

The struggle over Baby M began when it became apparent that Mrs. Whitehead could not return the child to Mr. Stern. Due to Mrs. Whitehead's refusal to relinquish the baby, Mr. Stern filed a complaint seeking enforcement of the surrogacy contract. He alleged, accurately, that Mrs. Whitehead had not only refused to comply with the surrogacy contract but had threatened to flee from New Jersey with the child in order to avoid even the possibility of his obtaining custody. The court papers asserted that if Mrs. Whitehead were to be given notice of the application for an order requiring her to relinquish custody, she would, prior to the hearing, leave the state with the baby. And that is precisely what she did. After the order was entered, *ex parte*, the process server, aided by the police, in the presence of the Sterns, entered Mrs. Whitehead's home to execute the order. Mr. Whitehead fled with the child, who had been handed to him through a window while those who came to enforce the order were thrown off balance by a dispute over the child's current name.

The Whiteheads immediately fled to Florida with Baby M. . . . Eventually the Sterns discovered where the Whiteheads were staying, commenced supplementary proceedings in Florida, and obtained an order requiring the Whiteheads to turn over the child. Police in Florida enforced the order, forcibly removing the child from her grandparents' home. She was soon thereafter brought to New Jersey and turned over to the Sterns. The prior order of the court, issued *ex parte*, awarding custody of the child to the Sterns *pendente lite*, was reaffirmed by the trial court after consideration of the certified representations of the parties (both represented by counsel) concerning the unusual sequence of events that had unfolded. Pending final judgment, Mrs. Whitehead was awarded limited visitation with Baby M.

The Sterns' complaint, in addition to seeking possession and ultimately custody of the child, sought enforcement of the surrogacy contract. Pursuant to the contract, it asked that the child be permanently placed in their custody, that Mrs. Whitehead's parental rights be terminated, and that Mrs. Stern be allowed to adopt the child, *i.e.*, that, for all purposes, Melissa become the Sterns' child.

The trial took thirty-two days over a period of more than two months.... [The trial court] held that the surrogacy contract was valid; ordered that Mrs. Whitehead's parental rights be terminated and that sole custody of the child be granted to Mr. Stern; and, after hearing brief testimony from Mrs. Stern, immediately entered an order allowing the adoption of Melissa by Mrs. Stern, all in accordance with the surrogacy contract. Pending the outcome of the appeal, we granted a continuation of visitation to Mrs. Whitehead, although slightly more limited than the visitation allowed during the trial....

Mrs. Whitehead appealed. This Court granted direct certification. 107 *N.J.* 140, 526 *A.2d* 203 (1987). The briefs of the parties on appeal were joined by numerous briefs filed by *amici* expressing various interests and views on surrogacy and on this case. We have found many of them helpful in resolving the issues before us.

Mrs. Whitehead contends that the surrogacy contract, for a variety of reasons, is invalid.... The Sterns claim that the surrogacy contract is valid and should be enforced, largely for the reasons given by the trial court.... Of considerable interest in this clash of views is the position of the child's guardian *ad litem*, wisely appointed by the court at the outset of the litigation. As the child's representative, her role in the litigation, as she viewed it, was solely to protect the child's best interests. She therefore took no position on the validity of the surrogacy contract, and instead devoted her energies to obtaining expert testimony uninfluenced by any interest other than the child's. We agree with the guardian's perception of her role in this litigation. She appropriately refrained from taking any position that might have appeared to compromise her role as the child's advocate. She first took the position, based on her experts' testimony, that the Sterns should have primary custody, and that while Mrs. Whitehead's parental rights should not be terminated, no visitation should be allowed for five years. As a result of subsequent developments, mentioned *infra*, her view has changed. She now recommends that no visitation be allowed at least until Baby M reaches maturity....

II.   INVALIDITY AND UNENFORCEABILITY OF SURROGACY CONTRACT

We have concluded that this surrogacy contract is invalid. Our conclusion has two bases: direct conflict with existing statutes and conflict with the public policies of this State, as expressed in its statutory and decisional law.

One of the surrogacy contract's basic purposes, to achieve the adoption of a child through private placement, though permitted in New Jersey "is very much disfavored." *Sees v. Baber*, 74 *N.J.* 201, 217, 377 *A.2d* 628 (1977). Its use of money for this purpose—and we have no doubt whatsoever that the money is being paid to obtain an adoption and not, as the Sterns argue, for the personal services of Mary Beth Whitehead—is illegal and perhaps criminal. *N.J.S.A.* 9:3–54. In addition to the inducement of money, there is the coercion of contract: the natural mother's irrevocable agreement, prior to birth, even prior to conception, to surrender the child to the adoptive couple. Such an agreement is totally unenforceable in private placement adoption. *See*, 74 *N.J.* at 212–14, 377 *A.2d* 628. Even where the adoption is through an approved agency, the formal agreement to surrender occurs only *after* birth (as we read *N.J.S.A.* 9:2–16 and –17, and similar statutes), and then, by regulation, only after the birth mother has been offered counseling. *N.J.A.C.* 10:121A–5.4(c). Integral to these invalid provisions of the surrogacy contract is the related agreement, equally invalid, on the part of the natural mother to cooperate with, and not to contest, proceedings to terminate her parental rights, as well as her contractual concession, in aid of the adoption, that the child's best interests would be served by awarding custody to the natural father and his wife—all of this before she has even conceived, and, in some cases, before she has the slightest idea of what the natural father and adoptive mother are like.

The foregoing provisions not only directly conflict with New Jersey statutes, but also offend long-established State policies. These critical terms, which are at the heart of the contract, are invalid and unenforceable; the conclusion therefore follows, without more, that the entire contract is unenforceable....

The surrogacy contract's invalidity, resulting from its direct conflict with the above statutory provisions, is further underlined when its goals and means are measured against New Jersey's public policy. The contract's basic premise, that the natural parents can decide in advance of birth which one is to have custody of the child, bears no relationship to the settled law that the child's best interests shall determine custody. *See Fantony v. Fantony*, 21 *N.J.* 525, 536–37, 122 *A.2d* 593 (1956).... The fact that the trial court remedied that aspect of the contract through the "best interests" phase does not make the contractual provision any less offensive to the public policy of this State.

The surrogacy contract guarantees permanent separation of the child from one of its natural parents. Our policy, however, has long been that to the extent possible, children should remain with and be brought up by both of their natural parents. That was the first stated purpose of the previous adoption act, *L.* 1953, *c.* 264, § 1, codified at *N.J.S.A.* 9:3–17 (repealed).... While not so stated in the present adoption law, this purpose remains part of the public policy of this State. *See, e.g., Wilke v.*

Culp, 196 *N.J.Super.* 487, 496, 483 A.2d 420 (App.Div.1984), certif. den., 99 *N.J.* 243, 491 A.2d 728 (1985).... This is not simply some theoretical ideal that in practice has no meaning. The impact of failure to follow that policy is nowhere better shown than in the results of this surrogacy contract. A child, instead of starting off its life with as much peace and security as possible, finds itself immediately in a tug-of-war between contending mother and father.

The surrogacy contract violates the policy of this State that the rights of natural parents are equal concerning their child, the father's right no greater than the mother's. "The parent and child relationship extends equally to every child and to every parent, regardless of the marital status of the parents." *N.J.S.A.* 9:17–40....

The policies expressed in our comprehensive laws governing consent to the surrender of a child ... stand in stark contrast to the surrogacy contract and what it implies. Here there is no counseling, independent or otherwise, of the natural mother, no evaluation, no warning.

The only legal advice Mary Beth Whitehead received regarding the surrogacy contract was provided in connection with the contract that she previously entered into with another couple. Mrs. Whitehead's lawyer was referred to her by the Infertility Center, with which he had an agreement to act as counsel for surrogate candidates. His services consisted of spending one hour going through the contract with the Whiteheads, section by section, and answering their questions. Mrs. Whitehead received no further legal advice prior to signing the contract with the Sterns.

Mrs. Whitehead was examined and psychologically evaluated, but if it was for her benefit, the record does not disclose that fact. The Sterns regarded the evaluation as important, particularly in connection with the question of whether she would change her mind. Yet they never asked to see it, and were content with the assumption that the Infertility Center had made an evaluation and had concluded that there was no danger that the surrogate mother would change her mind. From Mrs. Whitehead's point of view, all that she learned from the evaluation was that "she had passed." It is apparent that the profit motive got the better of the Infertility Center. Although the evaluation was made, it was not put to any use, and understandably so, for the psychologist warned that Mrs. Whitehead demonstrated certain traits that might make surrender of the child difficult and that there should be further inquiry into this issue in connection with her surrogacy. To inquire further, however, might have jeopardized the Infertility Center's fee. The record indicates that neither Mrs. Whitehead nor the Sterns were ever told of this fact, a fact that might have ended their surrogacy arrangement.

Under the contract, the natural mother is irrevocably committed before she knows the strength of her bond with her child. She never makes a totally voluntary, informed decision, for quite clearly any decision prior to the baby's birth is, in the most important sense, uninformed, and any decision after that, compelled by a pre-existing contractual commitment, the threat of a lawsuit, and the inducement of a $10,000 payment, is less than totally voluntary. Her interests are of little concern to those who controlled this transaction....

Worst of all, however, is the contract's total disregard of the best interests of the child. There is not the slightest suggestion that any inquiry will be made at any time to determine the fitness of the Sterns as custodial parents, of Mrs. Stern as an adoptive parent, their superiority to Mrs. Whitehead, or the effect on the child of not living with her natural mother.

This is the sale of a child, or, at the very least, the sale of a mother's right to her child, the only mitigating factor being that one of the purchasers is the father. Almost every evil that prompted the prohibition on the payment of money in connection with adoptions exists here.

The differences between an adoption and a surrogacy contract should be noted, since it is asserted that the use of money in connection with surrogacy does not pose the risks found where money buys an adoption. Katz, "Surrogate Motherhood and the Baby-Selling Laws," 20 *Colum. J. L. & Soc. Probs.* 1 (1986).... The main difference, that the unwanted pregnancy is unintended while the situation of the surrogate mother is voluntary and intended, is really not significant. Initially, it produces stronger reactions of sympathy for the mother whose pregnancy was unwanted than for the surrogate mother, who "went into this with her eyes wide open." On reflection, however, it appears that the essential evil is the same, taking advantage of a woman's circumstances (the unwanted pregnancy or the need for money) in order to take away her child, the difference being one of degree.

In the scheme contemplated by the surrogacy contract in this case, a middle man, propelled by profit, promotes the sale. Whatever idealism may have motivated any of the participants, the profit motive predominates, permeates, and ultimately governs the transaction. The demand for children is great and the supply small. The availability of contraception, abortion, and the greater willingness of single mothers to bring up their children has led to a shortage of babies offered for adoption. *See* N. Baker, *Baby Selling: The Scandal of Black Market Adoption, supra; Adoption and Foster Care, 1975: Hearings on Baby Selling Before the Subcomm. On Children and Youth of the Senate Comm. on Labor and Public Welfare*, 94th Cong. 1st Sess. 6 (1975) (Statement of Joseph H. Reid, Executive Director, Child Welfare League of America, Inc.). The situation is ripe for the entry of the middleman who will bring some equilibrium into the market by increasing the supply through the use of money.

Intimated, but disputed, is the assertion that surrogacy will be used for the benefit of the rich at the expense of the poor. *See, e.g.*, Radin, "Market Inalienability," 100 *Harv. L. Rev.* 1849, 1930 (1987). In response it is noted that the Sterns are not rich and the Whiteheads not poor. Nevertheless, it is clear to us that it is unlikely that surrogate mothers will be as proportionately numerous among those women in the top twenty percent income bracket as among those in the bottom twenty percent. *Ibid.* Put differently, we doubt that infertile couples in the low-income bracket will find upper income surrogates.

In any event, even in this case one should not pretend that disparate wealth does not play a part simply because the contrast is not the dramatic "rich versus poor." At the time of trial, the Whiteheads' net assets were probably negative—Mrs. Whitehead's own sister was fore-closing on a second mortgage. Their income derived from Mr. White-head's labors. Mrs. Whitehead is a homemaker, having previously held part-time jobs. The Sterns are both professionals, she a medical doctor, he a biochemist. Their combined income when both were working was about $89,500 a year and their assets sufficient to pay for the surrogacy contract arrangements.

The point is made that Mrs. Whitehead *agreed* to the surrogacy arrangement, supposedly fully understanding the consequences. Putting aside the issue of how compelling her need for money may have been, and how significant her understanding of the consequences, we suggest that her consent is irrelevant. There are, in a civilized society, some things that money cannot buy. In America, we decided long ago that merely because conduct purchased by money was "voluntary" did not mean that it was good or beyond regulation and prohibition. *West Coast Hotel Co. v. Parrish*, 300 U.S. 379, 57 S.Ct. 578, 81 L.Ed. 703 (1937). Employers can no longer buy labor at the lowest price they can bargain for, even though that labor is "voluntary," 29 U.S.C. § 206 (1982), or buy women's labor for less money than paid to men for the same job, 29 U.S.C. § 206(d), or purchase the agreement of children to perform oppressive labor, 29 U.S.C. § 212, or purchase the agreement of workers to subject themselves to unsafe or unhealthful working conditions, 29 U.S.C. §§ 651 to 678. (Occupational Safety and Health Act of 1970). There are, in short, values that society deems more important than granting to wealth whatever it can buy, be it labor, love, or life. Whether this principle recommends prohibition of surrogacy, which presumably sometimes results in great satisfaction to all of the parties, is not for us to say. We note here only that, under existing law, the fact that Mrs. Whitehead "agreed" to the arrangement is not dispositive.

The long-term effects of surrogacy contracts are not known, but feared—the impact on the child who learns her life was bought, that she is the offspring of someone who gave birth to her only to obtain money; the impact on the natural mother as the full weight of her isolation is felt along with the full reality of the sale of her body and her child; the impact on the natural father and adoptive mother once they realize the consequences of their conduct. Literature in related areas suggests these are substantial considerations, although, given the newness of surrogacy, there is little information. . . .

The surrogacy contract is based on principles that are directly contrary to the objectives of our laws. It guarantees the separation of a child from its mother; it looks to adoption regardless of suitability; it totally ignores the child; it takes the child from the mother regardless of her wishes and her maternal fitness; and it does all of this, it accomplishes all of its goals, through the use of money.

Beyond that is the potential degradation of some women that may result from this arrangement. In many cases, of course, surrogacy may bring satisfaction, not only to the infertile couple, but to the surrogate mother herself. The fact, however, that many women may not perceive surrogacy negatively but rather see it as an opportunity does not diminish its potential for devastation to other women.

In sum, the harmful consequences of this surrogacy arrangement appear to us all too palpable. In New Jersey the surrogate mother's agreement to sell her child is void. Its irrevocability infects the entire contract, as does the money that purports to buy it. . . .

V. Custody

Having decided that the surrogacy contract is illegal and unenforceable, we now must decide the custody question without regard to the provisions of the surrogacy contract that would give Mr. Stern sole and permanent custody. (That does not mean that the existence of the contract and the circumstances under which it was entered may not be considered to the extent deemed relevant to the child's best interests.) With the surrogacy contract disposed of, the legal framework becomes a dispute between two couples over the custody of a child produced by the artificial insemination of one couple's wife by the other's husband. Under the Parentage Act the claims of the natural father and the natural mother are entitled to equal weight, *i.e.*, one is not preferred over the other solely because he or she is the father or the mother. *N.J.S.A.* 9:17–40. The applicable rule given these circumstances is clear: the child's best interests determine custody. . . .

[W]e have concluded, independent of the trial court's identical conclusion, that Melissa's best interests call for custody in the Sterns. . . .

VI. Visitation

The trial court's decision to terminate Mrs. Whitehead's parental rights precluded it from making any determination on visitation. 217 *N.J.Super.* at 399, 408, 525 A.2d 1128. Our reversal of the trial court's order, however, requires delineation of Mrs. Whitehead's rights to visitation. It is apparent to us that this factually sensitive issue, which was never addressed below, should not be determined *de novo* by this Court. We therefore remand the visitation issue to the trial court for an abbreviated hearing and determination as set forth below. . . .

The judgment is affirmed in part, reversed in part, and remanded for further proceedings consistent with this opinion.

Questions

1. How many different reasons (arguments) does the court give in the above excerpt for finding the surrogacy contract unenforceable in *Baby M?*

2. Consider the court's argument that the contract required termination of parental rights and adoption in violation of the state's statutes. Why should the statutes take precedence over freedom of contract? If all of the parties agree to the arrangement, why should they not be able to make enforceable promises as they see fit? Should such statutes be default rules, applying only when the parties have not otherwise agreed? Or should the state act paternalistically here? See Anthony T. Kronman, *Paternalism and the Law of Contracts*, 92 YALE L.J. 673 (1983).

3. Consider the court's argument that the contract should not be enforced because Ms. Whitehead never made a "totally voluntary, informed decision" prior to making an irrevocable commitment. Should contracts generally be unenforceable unless the party against whom enforcement is sought made a totally voluntary, informed decision? Does anyone ever make a *totally* voluntary, informed decision? If not, why should surrogacy contracts be singled out? See Note on Autonomy in Context, above at p. 151.

4. Consider the court's arguments that surrogacy contracts for pay are degrading to women and will benefit the rich at the expense of the poor. Is that so? If it is, should surrogacy contracts be unenforceable for reasons of distributive justice? Should all contracts that degrade women be unenforceable? Should all contracts that benefit the rich at the expense of the poor be unenforceable? If not all such contracts should be unenforceable, why should surrogacy contracts be singled out? See Anthony T. Kronman, *Contract Law and Distributive Justice*, 89 YALE L.J. 472 (1980).

5. Should the law of contracts concern itself with the virtues of surrogacy? Or is it sufficient for contract law to provide that illegal contracts and contracts against public policy are void or voidable under conditions like those in RESTATEMENT (SECOND) OF CONTRACTS §§ 178, 179?

SECTION 2. MISTAKES

Contract law aims to protect reasonable expectations arising from promises and justified reliance thereon. Doing so is thought to enhance the security of contractual transactions, thereby encouraging trade and planning within the domain of free contracting. It is important, to these ends, that the enforceability of promises be well-defined and that the obligation be created with considerable finality. Consequently, courts hesitate to review an agreement and invalidate or change it when one or both parties made a mistake.

It will help to distinguish a mistake from regret. A party regrets having made a contract when, for example, it promised to pay $12 per barrel of oil next Tuesday and the market price of the same oil drops to $11 on Monday. In ordinary English, that buyer might say she made a mistake. Courts do not relieve parties from their bargains on the basis of hindsight. On the conventional view, a key purpose of a contract is to allocate risks of future events between the parties. Thus, agreement on a $50 price for oil implies that the seller takes the risk of a rising market while the buyer takes the risk that the price will fall. Courts are averse to reallocating such risks even when the burden of a losing contract is great.

By contrast, the parties make a mistake when they act on beliefs that are not in accord with the facts existing at the time of contracting. There are times when a mistake seems to undermine the authority of a contract as a joint commitment stemming from the parties' autonomous undertakings and enforceable because of their will or because socially beneficial. The world of the contract then will not reflect the intentions or reasonable expectations of the parties, and performance may impose an unjust hardship on one of them. The disadvantaged party, under conditions to be explored in this section, may then have a power to avoid the contract ("rescind" it). In unusual circumstances, moreover, one party may act in ignorance of a fact known to the other when the knowledgeable party should disclose it. The ignorant party makes a mistake, while the knowledgeable party may commit a fraud for which rescission is allowed. In some cases, the mistake concerns the expression of the parties' agreement in a way that can be easily corrected without undue prejudice to either party. In that case, the disadvantaged party can ask a court to reform the contract.

RESTATEMENT (SECOND) OF CONTRACTS
§§ 151, 153–54, 159, 161–64

STAMBOVSKY v. ACKLEY

Supreme Court of New York, Appellate Division, First Department, 1991.
169 A.D.2d 254, 572 N.Y.S.2d 672.

RUBIN, J. Plaintiff, to his horror, discovered that the house he had recently contracted to purchase was widely reputed to be possessed by poltergeists, reportedly seen by defendant seller and members of her family on numerous occasions over the last nine years. Plaintiff promptly commenced this action seeking rescission of the contract of sale. Supreme Court reluctantly dismissed the complaint, holding that plaintiff has no remedy at law in this jurisdiction.

The unusual facts of this case, as disclosed by the record, clearly warrant a grant of equitable relief to the buyer who, as a resident of New York City, cannot be expected to have any familiarity with the folklore of the Village of Nyack. Not being a "local," plaintiff could not readily learn that the home he had contracted to purchase is haunted.

Whether the source of the spectral apparitions seen by defendant seller are parapsychic or psychogenic, having reported their presence in both a national publication ("Readers' Digest") and the local press (in 1977 and 1982, respectively), defendant is estopped to deny their existence and, as a matter of law, the house is haunted. More to the point, however, no divination is required to conclude that it is defendant's promotional efforts in publicizing her close encounters with these spirits which fostered the home's reputation in the community. In 1989, the house was included in a five-home walking tour of Nyack and described in a November 27th newspaper article as "a riverfront Victorian (with ghost)." The impact of the reputation thus created goes to the very essence of the bargain between the parties, greatly impairing both the value of the property and its potential for resale. The extent of this impairment may be presumed for the purpose of reviewing the disposition of this motion to dismiss the cause of action for rescission (*Harris v. City of New York*, 147 A.D.2d 186, 188–189, 542 N.Y.S.2d 550) and represents merely an issue of fact for resolution at trial.

While I agree with the Supreme Court [*i.e.*, the trial court in New York] that the real estate broker, as agent for the seller, is under no duty to disclose to a potential buyer the phantasmal reputation of the premises and that, in his pursuit of a legal remedy for fraudulent misrepresentation against the seller, plaintiff hasn't a ghost of a chance, I am nevertheless moved by the spirit of equity to allow the buyer to seek rescission of the contract of sale and recovery of his down payment. New York law fails to recognize any remedy for damages incurred as a result of the seller's mere silence, applying instead the strict rule of caveat emptor. Therefore, the theoretical basis for granting relief, even under the extraordinary facts of this case, is elusive if not ephemeral.

> "Pity me not but
>
> lend thy serious hearing to what I shall unfold"
>
> (William Shakespeare, Hamlet, Act I, Scene V. [Ghost]).

From the perspective of a person in the position of plaintiff herein, a very practical problem arises with respect to the discovery of a paranormal phenomenon: "Who you gonna' call?" as the title song to the movie "Ghostbusters" asks. Applying the strict rule of caveat emptor to a contract involving a house possessed by poltergeists conjures up visions of a psychic or medium routinely accompanying the structural engineer and Terminix man on an inspection of every home subject to a contract of sale. It portends that the prudent attorney will establish an escrow account lest the subject of the transaction come back to haunt him and his client—or pray that his malpractice insurance coverage extends to supernatural disasters. In the interest of avoiding such untenable consequences, the notion that a haunting is a condition which can and should be ascertained upon reasonable inspection of the premises is a hobgoblin which should be exorcised from the body of legal precedent and laid quietly to rest.

It has been suggested by a leading authority that the ancient rule which holds that mere non-disclosure does not constitute actionable misrepresentation "finds proper application in cases where the fact undisclosed is patent, or the plaintiff has equal opportunities for obtaining information which he may be expected to utilize, or the defendant has no reason to think that he is acting under any misapprehension" (Prosser, Law of Torts § 106, at 696 [4th ed., 1971]). However, with respect to transactions in real estate, New York adheres to the doctrine of caveat emptor and imposes no duty upon the vendor to disclose any information concerning the premises (*London v. Courduff*, 141 A.D.2d 803, 529 N.Y.S.2d 874) unless there is a confidential or fiduciary relationship between the parties (*Moser v. Spizzirro*, 31 A.D.2d 537, 295 N.Y.S.2d 188, *aff'd*, 25 N.Y.2d 941, 305 N.Y.S.2d 153, 252 N.E.2d 632 ...) or some conduct on the part of the seller which constitutes "active concealment" (*see, 17 East 80th Realty Corp. v. 68th Associates*, 173 A.D.2d 245, 569 N.Y.S.2d 647 [dummy ventilation system constructed by seller]; *Haberman v. Greenspan*, 82 Misc.2d 263, 368 N.Y.S.2d 717 [foundation cracks covered by seller]). Normally, some affirmative misrepresentation (*e.g., Tahini Invs., Ltd. v. Bobrowsky*, 99 A.D.2d 489, 470 N.Y.S.2d 431 [industrial waste on land allegedly used only as farm]; *Jansen v. Kelly*, 11 A.D.2d 587, 200 N.Y.S.2d 561 [land containing valuable minerals allegedly acquired for use as campsite]) or partial disclosure (*Junius Constr. Corp. v. Cohen*, 257 N.Y. 393, 178 N.E. 672 [existence of third unopened street concealed]; *Noved Realty Corp. v. A.A.P. Co.*, 250 A.D. 1, 293 N.Y.S. 336 [escrow agreements securing lien concealed]) is required to impose upon the seller a duty to communicate undisclosed conditions affecting the premises (*contra, Young v. Keith*, 112 A.D.2d 625, 492 N.Y.S.2d 489 [defective water and sewer systems concealed]).

Caveat emptor is not so all-encompassing a doctrine of common law as to render every act of non-disclosure immune from redress, whether legal or equitable. "In regard to the necessity of giving information which has not been asked, the rule differs somewhat at law and in equity, and while the law courts would permit no recovery of *damages* against a vendor, because of mere concealment of facts *under certain circumstances*, yet if the vendee refused to complete the contract because of the concealment of a material fact on the part of the other, equity would refuse to compel him so to do, because equity only compels the specific performance of a contract which is fair and open, and in regard to which all material matters known to each have been communicated to the other" (*Rothmiller v. Stein*, 143 N.Y. 581, 591–592 [emphasis added]). Even as a principle of law, long before exceptions were embodied in statute law (see, e.g., UCC §§ 2–312, 2–313, 2–314, 2–315; 3–417[2][e]), the doctrine was held inapplicable to contagion among animals, adulteration of food, and insolvency of a maker of a promissory note and of a tenant substituted for another under a lease (*see, Rothmiller v. Stein, supra*, at 592–593 and cases cited therein). Common law is not moribund. *Ex facto jus oritur* (law arises out of facts). Where fairness and common sense dictate that an exception should be created, the evolution of the law should not be stifled by rigid application of a legal maxim.

The doctrine of caveat emptor requires that a buyer act prudently to assess the fitness and value of his purchase and operates to bar the purchaser who fails to exercise due care from seeking the equitable remedy of rescission (*see, e.g., Rodas v. Manitaras*, 159 A.D.2d 341, 552 N.Y.S.2d 618). For the purposes of the instant motion to dismiss the action pursuant to CPLR 3211(a)(7), plaintiff is entitled to every favorable inference which may reasonably be drawn from the pleadings (*Arrington v. New York Times Co.*, 55 N.Y.2d 433, 442, 449 N.Y.S.2d 941, 434 N.E.2d 1319....), specifically, in this instance, that he met his obligation to conduct an inspection of the premises and a search of available public records with respect to title. It should be apparent, however, that the most meticulous inspection and the search would not reveal the presence of poltergeists at the premises or unearth the property's ghoulish reputation in the community. Therefore, there is no sound policy reason to deny plaintiff relief for failing to discover a state of affairs which the most prudent purchaser would not be expected to even contemplate (*see, Da Silva v. Musso*, 53 N.Y.2d 543, 551, 444 N.Y.S.2d 50, 428 N.E.2d 382).

The case law in this jurisdiction dealing with the duty of a vendor of real property to disclose information to the buyer is distinguishable from the matter under review. The most salient distinction is that existing cases invariably deal with the physical condition of the premises (*e.g., London v. Courduff*, supra [use as a landfill]; *Perin v. Mardine Realty Co.*, 5 A.D.2d 685, 168 N.Y.S.2d 647, affd. 6 N.Y.2d 920, 190 N.Y.S.2d 995, 161 N.E.2d 210 [sewer line crossing adjoining property without owner's consent]), defects in title (*e.g., Sands v. Kissane*, 282 App.Div. 140, 121 N.Y.S.2d 634 [remainderman]), liens against the property (*e.g., Noved Realty Corp. v. A.A.P. Co.*, supra), expenses or income (*e.g., Rodas v. Manitaras*, supra [gross receipts]) and other factors affecting its operation. No case has been brought to this court's attention in which the property value was impaired as the result of the reputation created by information disseminated to the public by the seller (or, for that matter, as a result of possession by poltergeists).

Where a condition which has been created by the seller materially impairs the value of the contract and is peculiarly within the knowledge of the seller or unlikely to be discovered by a prudent purchaser exercising due care with respect to the subject transaction, nondisclosure constitutes a basis for rescission as a matter of equity. Any other outcome places upon the buyer not merely the obligation to exercise care in his purchase but rather to be omniscient with respect to any fact which may affect the bargain. No practical purpose is served by imposing such a burden upon a purchaser. To the contrary, it encourages predatory business practice and offends the principle that equity will suffer no wrong to be without a remedy. . . .

To the extent New York law may be said to require something more than "mere concealment" to apply even the equitable remedy of rescission, the case of *Junius Construction Corporation v. Cohen*, 257 N.Y. 393, 178 N.E. 672, *supra*, while not precisely on point, provides some guidance. In that case, the seller disclosed that an official map indicated two as yet unopened streets which were planned for construction at the edges of the parcel. What was not disclosed was that the same map indicated a third street which, if opened, would divide the plot in half. The court held that, while the seller was under no duty to mention the planned streets at all, having undertaken to disclose two of them, he was obliged to reveal the third. . . .

In the case at bar, defendant seller deliberately fostered the public belief that her home was possessed. Having undertaken to inform the public at large, to whom she has no legal relationship, about the supernatural occurrences on her property, she may be said to owe no less a duty to her contract vendee. It has been remarked that the occasional modern cases which permit a seller to take unfair advantage of a buyer's ignorance so long as he is not actively misled are "singularly unappetizing" (Prosser, Law of Torts § 106, at 696 [4th ed. 1971]). Where, as here, the seller not only takes unfair advantage of the buyer's ignorance but has created and perpetuated a condition about which he is unlikely to even inquire, enforcement of the contract (in whole or in part) is offensive to the court's sense of equity. Application of the remedy of rescission, within the bounds of the narrow exception to the doctrine of caveat emptor set forth herein, is entirely appropriate to relieve the unwitting purchaser from the consequences of a most unnatural bargain.

Accordingly, the judgment of the Supreme Court, New York County (Edward H. Lehner, J.), entered April 9, 1990, which dismissed the complaint pursuant to CPLR 3211(a)(7), should be modified, on the law and the facts and in the exercise of discretion, and the first cause of action seeking rescission of the contract reinstated, without costs.

SMITH, JUSTICE (dissenting). I would affirm the dismissal of the complaint by the motion court.

Plaintiff seeks to rescind his contract to purchase defendant Ackley's residential property and recover his down payment. Plaintiff alleges that Ackley and her real estate broker, defendant Ellis Realty, made material misrepresentations of the property in that they failed to disclose that Ackley believed that the house was haunted by poltergeists. Moreover, Ackley shared this belief with her community and the general public through articles published in *Reader's Digest* (1977) and the local newspaper (1982). In November 1989, approximately two months after the parties entered into the contract of sale but subsequent to the scheduled October 2, 1989 closing, the house was included in a five-house walking tour and again described in the local newspaper as being haunted.

Prior to closing, plaintiff learned of this reputation and unsuccessfully sought to rescind the $650,000 contract of sale and obtain return of his $32,500 down payment without resort to litigation. The plaintiff then commenced this action for that relief and alleged that he would not have entered into the contract had he been so advised and that as a result of the alleged poltergeist activity, the market value and resaleability of the property was greatly diminished. Defendant Ackley has counterclaimed for specific performance.

"It is settled law in New York that the seller of real property is under no duty to speak when the parties deal at arm's length. The mere silence of the seller, without some act or conduct which deceived the purchaser, does not amount to a concealment that is actionable as a fraud (*see Perin v. Mardine Realty Co., Inc.*, 5 A.D.2d 685, 168 N.Y.S.2d 647, *aff'd.*, 6 N.Y.2d 920, 190 N.Y.S.2d 995, 161 N.E.2d 210; *Moser v. Spizzirro*, 31 A.D.2d 537, 295 N.Y.S.2d 188, *aff'd.*, 25 N.Y.2d 941, 305 N.Y.S.2d 153, 252 N.E.2d 632). The buyer has the duty to satisfy himself as to the quality of his bargain pursuant to the doctrine of caveat emptor, which in New York State still applies to real estate transactions." *London v. Courduff*, 141 A.D.2d 803, 804, 529 N.Y.S.2d 874 (1988), *app. dism'd.*, 73 N.Y.2d 809, 537 N.Y.S.2d 494, 534 N.E.2d 332 (1988).

The parties herein were represented by counsel and dealt at arm's length. This is evidenced by the contract of sale which, *inter alia*, contained various riders and a specific provision that all prior understandings and agreements between the parties were merged into the contract, that the contract completely expressed their full agreement and that neither had relied upon any statement by anyone else not set forth in the contract. There is no allegation that defendants, by some specific act, other than the failure to speak, deceived the plaintiff. Nevertheless, a cause of action may be sufficiently stated where there is a confidential or fiduciary relationship creating a duty to disclose and there was a failure to disclose a material fact, calculated to induce a false belief. *County of Westchester v. Welton Becket Assoc.*, 102 A.D.2d 34, 50–51, 478 N.Y.S.2d 305, *aff'd.*, 66 N.Y.2d 642, 495 N.Y.S.2d 364, 485 N.E.2d 1029 (1985). However, plaintiff herein has not alleged and there is no basis for concluding that a confidential or fiduciary relationship existed between these parties to an arm's length transaction such as to give rise to a duty to disclose. In addition, there is no allegation that defendants thwarted plaintiff's efforts to fulfill his responsibilities fixed by the doctrine of caveat emptor. *See London v. Courduff, supra*, 141 A.D.2d at 804, 529 N.Y.S.2d 874.

Finally, if the doctrine of caveat emptor is to be discarded, it should be for a reason more substantive than a poltergeist. The existence of a poltergeist is no more binding upon the defendants than it is upon this court. . . .

Questions

1. What is the plaintiff's claim in *Stambovsky*? What is the defense? Why does the defense fail? Should it?

2. If rescission should be allowed when there is a unilateral nondisclosure like the one in *Stambovsky*, what would be the reason? Does such a unilateral nondisclosure undermine the autonomy principle or the justification principle? Or would enforcing a contract based on nondisclosure be unjust? If the latter, would it be a matter of corrective or distributive justice?

3. *Problems*.

    a. Marilyn, who knows little about cars, owned a white 1965 Ford Mustang. One day, in need of money, she took it to Tony's Used Car Lot and asked Tony if he would like to buy it. Tony looked at it carefully and gave it a run around the block. He offered her $450.00. Marilyn accepted the money and signed over the pink slip. Marilyn later found out that the car was a collector's item worth $5,000. Can Marilyn rescind?

    b. Tony is a genetic engineer who reads the scientific journals regularly. Upon reading two reports in two journals, he concluded that a breakthrough was imminent in the effort of ADN, Inc. to make biodegradable plastic bags out of corn. He bought a large quantity of ADN stock from Marilyn. Two months later, ADN announced a patented breakthrough and the value of its stock quintupled. Can Marilyn rescind?

    c. Tony is a merchant who buys tobacco from farmers and sells it to cigarette companies. On Saturday, he received a phone call from a friend in the Department of Agriculture in Washington advising him that the Surgeon General would, on the following Monday, issue a surprise report finding that cigarette smoking does not cause cancer after all. Tony thereupon visited Marilyn and several other tobacco farmers, concluding contracts for a large quantity of tobacco. On Monday, the report was issued and the price of tobacco in the relevant market quintupled. Can Marilyn rescind? See Anthony T. Kronman, *Mistake, Disclosure, Information, and the Law of Contracts*, 7 J. Leg. Stud. 1 (1978).

RESTATEMENT (SECOND) OF CONTRACTS § 152

WOOD v. BOYNTON

Supreme Court of Wisconsin, 1885.
64 Wis. 265, 25 N.W. 42.

Taylor, Justice. This action was brought in the circuit court for Milwaukee county to recover the possession of an uncut diamond of the alleged value of $1,000. The case was tried in the circuit court, and after hearing all the evidence in the case, the learned circuit judge directed the jury to find a verdict for the defendants. The plaintiff excepted to such instruction, and, after a verdict was rendered for the defendants, moved for a new trial upon the minutes of the judge. The motion was denied, and the plaintiff duly excepted, and after judgment was entered in favor of the defendants, appealed to this court. The defendants are partners in the jewelry business. On the trial it appeared that on and before the twenty-eighth of December, 1883, the plaintiff was the owner of and in the possession of a small stone of the nature and value of which she was ignorant; that on that day she sold it to one of the defendants for the sum of one dollar. Afterwards it was ascertained that the stone was a rough diamond, and of the value of about $700. After hearing this fact the plaintiff tendered the defendants the one dollar, and ten cents as interest, and demanded a return of the stone to her. The defendants refused to deliver it, and therefore she commenced this action.

The plaintiff testified to the circumstances attending the sale of the stone to Mr. Samuel B. Boynton, as follows: "The first time Boynton saw that stone he was talking about buying the topaz, or whatever it is, in September or October. I went into the store to get a little pin mended, and I had it in a small box,—the pin,—a small earring; ... this stone, and a broken sleeve-button were in the box. Mr. Boynton turned to give me a check for my pin. I thought I would ask him what the stone was, and I took it out of the box and asked him to please tell me what that was. He took it in his hand and seemed some time looking at it. I told him I had been told it was a topaz, and he said it might be. He says, 'I would buy this; would you sell it?' I told him I did not know but what I would. What would it be worth? And he said he did not know; he would give me a dollar and keep it as a specimen, and I told him I would not sell it; and it was certainly pretty to look at. He asked me where I found it, and I told him in Eagle. He asked about how far out, and I said right in the village, and I went out. Afterwards, and about the twenty-eighth of December, I needed money pretty badly, and thought every dollar would help, and I took it back to Mr. Boynton and told him I had brought back the topaz, and he says, 'Well yes; what did I offer you for it?' and I says, 'One dollar'; and he stepped to the change drawer and gave me the dollar, and I went out." In another part of her testimony she says: "Before I sold the stone I had no knowledge whatever that it was a diamond. I told him that I had been advised that it was probably a topaz, and he said probably it was. The stone was about the size of a canary bird's egg, nearly the shape of an egg,—worn pointed at one end; it was nearly straw color,—a little darker." She also testified that before this action was commenced she tendered the defendants $1.10, and demanded the return of the stone, which they refused. This is substantially all the evidence of what took place at and before the sale to the defendants, as testified to by the plaintiff herself. She produced no other witness on that point.

The evidence on the part of the defendant is not very different from the version given by the plaintiff, and certainly is not more favorable to the plaintiff. Mr. Samuel B. Boynton, the defendant to whom the stone was sold, testified that at the time he bought this stone, he had never seen an uncut diamond; had seen cut diamonds, but they are quite different from the uncut ones; "he had no idea this was a diamond, and it never entered his brain at the time." Considerable evidence was given as to what took place after the sale and purchase, but that evidence has very little if any bearing, upon the main point in the case.

This evidence clearly shows that the plaintiff sold the stone in question to the defendants, and delivered it to them in December 1883, for a consideration of one dollar. By such sale the title to the stone passed by the sale and delivery to the defendants. How has that title been divested and again vested in the plaintiff? The contention of the learned counsel for the appellant is that the title became vested in the plaintiff by the tender to the Boyntons of the purchase money with interest, and a demand of a return of the stone to her. Unless such tender and demand revested the title in the appellant, she cannot maintain her action. The only question in the case is whether there was anything in the sale which entitled the vendor (the appellant) to rescind the sale and so revest the title in her. The only reasons we know of for rescinding a sale and revesting the title in the vendor so that he may maintain an action at law for the recovery of the possession against his vendee are (1) that the vendee was guilty of some fraud in procuring a sale to be made to him; (2) that there was a mistake made by the vendor in delivering an article which was not the article sold,—a mistake in fact as to the identity of the thing sold with the thing delivered upon the sale. This last is not in reality a rescission of the sale made, as the thing delivered was not the thing sold, and no title ever passed to the vendee by such delivery.

 In this case, upon the plaintiff's own evidence, there can be no just ground for alleging that she was induced to make the sale she did by any fraud or unfair dealings on the part of Mr. Boynton. Both were entirely ignorant at the time of the character of the stone and of its intrinsic value. Mr. Boynton was not an expert in uncut diamonds, and had made no examination of the stone, except to take it in his hand and look at it before he made the offer of one dollar, which was refused at the time, and afterwards accepted without any comment or further examination made by Mr. Boynton. The appellant had the stone in her possession for a long time, and it appears from her own statement that she had made some inquiry as to its nature and qualities. If she chose to sell it without further investigation as to its intrinsic value to a person who was guilty of no fraud or unfairness which induced her to sell it for a small sum, she cannot repudiate the sale because it is afterwards ascertained that she made a bad bargain. *Kennedy v. Panama, etc., Mail Co. L.R.*, 2 Q.B. 580. There is no pretense of any mistake as to the identity of the thing sold. It was produced by the plaintiff and exhibited to the vendee before the sale was made, and the thing sold was delivered to the vendee when the purchase price was paid. . . . Suppose the appellant had produced the stone, and said she had been told that it was a diamond, and she believed it was, but had no knowledge herself as to its character or value, and Mr. Boynton had given her $500 for it, could he have rescinded the sale if it had turned out to be a topaz or any other stone of very small value? Could Mr. Boynton have rescinded the sale on the ground of mistake?

Clearly not, nor could he rescind it on the ground that there had been a breach of warranty, because there was no warranty, nor could he rescind it on the ground of fraud, unless he could show that she falsely declared that she had been told it was a diamond, or, if she had been so told, still she knew it was not a diamond. . . .

It is urged, with a good deal of earnestness, on the part of the counsel for the appellant that, because it has turned out that the stone was immensely more valuable than the parties at the time of the sale supposed it was, such fact alone is a ground for the rescission of the sale, and that fact was evidence of fraud on the part of the vendee. Whether inadequacy of price is to be received as evidence of fraud, even in a suit in equity to avoid a sale, depends upon the facts known to the parties at the time the sale is made. When this sale was made the value of the thing sold was open to the investigation of both parties, neither knowing its intrinsic value, and, so far as the evidence in this case shows, both supposed that the price paid was adequate. How can fraud be predicated upon such a sale, even though after investigation showed that the intrinsic value of the thing sold was hundreds of times greater than the price paid? It certainly shows no such fraud as would authorize the vendor to rescind the contract and bring an action at law to recover the possession of the thing sold. Whether that fact would have any influence in an action in equity to avoid the sale we need not consider. . . . We can find nothing in the evidence from which it could be justly inferred that Mr. Boynton, at the time he offered the plaintiff one dollar for the stone, had any knowledge of the real value of the stone, or that he entertained even a belief that the stone was a diamond. It cannot, therefore, be said that there was a suppression of knowledge on the part of the defendant as to the value of the stone which a court of equity might seize upon to avoid the sale. . . .

However unfortunate the plaintiff may have been in selling this valuable stone for a mere nominal sum, she has failed entirely to make out a case either of fraud or mistake in the sale such as will entitle her to a rescission of such sale so as to recover the property sold in an action at law. . . .

LENAWEE COUNTY BOARD OF HEALTH v. MESSERLY

Supreme Court of Michigan, 1982.
417 Mich. 17, 331 N.W.2d 203.

RYAN, JUSTICE. In March of 1977, Carl and Nancy Pickles, appellees, purchased from appellants, William and Martha Messerly, a 600–square-foot tract of land upon which is located a three-unit apartment building. Shortly after the transaction was closed, the Lenawee County Board of Health condemned the property and obtained a permanent injunction which prohibits human habitation on the premises until the defective sewage system is brought into conformance with the Lenawee County sanitation code.

We are required to determine whether appellees should prevail in their attempt to avoid this land contract on the basis of mutual mistake.... We conclude that the parties did entertain a mutual misapprehension of fact, but that the circumstances of this case do not warrant rescission.

I

The facts of the case are not seriously in dispute. In 1971, the Messerlys acquired approximately one acre plus 600 square feet of land. A three-unit apartment building was situated upon the 600–square-foot portion. The trial court found that, prior to this transfer, the Messerlys' predecessor in title, Mr. Bloom, had installed a septic tank on the property without a permit and in violation of the applicable health code. The Messerlys used the building as an income investment property until 1973 when they sold it, upon land contract, to James Barnes who likewise used it primarily as an income-producing investment.

Mr. and Mrs. Barnes, with the permission of the Messerlys, sold approximately one acre of the property in 1976, and the remaining 600 square feet and building were offered for sale soon thereafter when Mr. and Mrs. Barnes defaulted on their land contract. Mr. and Mrs. Pickles evidenced an interest in the property, but were dissatisfied with the terms of the Barnes–Messerly land contract. Consequently, to accommodate the Pickleses' preference to enter into a land contract directly with the Messerlys, Mr. and Mrs. Barnes executed a quit-claim deed which conveyed their interest in the property back to the Messerlys. After inspecting the property, Mr. and Mrs. Pickles executed a new land contract with the Messerlys on March 21, 1977. It provided for a purchase price of $25,500. A clause was added to the end of the land contract form which provides:

> "17. Purchaser has examined this property and agrees to accept same in its present condition. There are no other or additional written or oral understandings."

Five or six days later, when the Pickleses went to introduce themselves to the tenants, they discovered raw sewage seeping out of the ground. Tests conducted by a sanitation expert indicated the inadequacy of the sewage system. The Lenawee County Board of Health subsequently condemned the property and initiated this lawsuit in the Lenawee Circuit Court against the Messerlys as land contract vendors, and the Pickleses, as vendees, to obtain a permanent injunction proscribing human habitation of the premises until the property was brought into conformance with the Lenawee County sanitation code. The injunction was granted, and the Lenawee County Board of Health was permitted to withdraw from the lawsuit by stipulation of the parties.

When no payments were made on the land contract, the Messerlys filed a cross-complaint against the Pickleses seeking foreclosure, sale of the property, and a deficiency judgment. Mr. and Mrs. Pickles then counterclaimed for rescission against the Messerlys, and filed a third-party complaint against the Barneses, which incorporated, by reference, the allegations of the counterclaim against the Messerlys. In count one, Mr. and Mrs. Pickles alleged failure of consideration. Count two charged Mr. and Mrs. Barnes with willful concealment and misrepresentation as a result of their failure to disclose the condition of the sanitation system. Additionally, Mr. and Mrs. Pickles sought to hold the Messerlys liable in equity for the Barneses' alleged misrepresentation. The Pickleses prayed that the land contract be rescinded.

After a bench trial, the court concluded that the Pickleses had no cause of action against either the Messerlys or the Barneses as there was no fraud or misrepresentation. This ruling was predicated on the trial judge's conclusion that none of the parties knew of Mr. Bloom's earlier transgression or of the resultant problem with the septic system until it was discovered by the Pickleses, and that the sanitation problem was not caused by any of the parties. The trial court held that the property was purchased "as is", after inspection and, accordingly, its "negative ... value cannot be blamed upon an innocent seller". Foreclosure was ordered against the Pickleses, together with a judgment against them in the amount of $25,943.09.

Mr. and Mrs. Pickles appealed from the adverse judgment. The Court of Appeals unanimously affirmed the trial court's ruling with respect to Mr. and Mrs. Barnes but, in a two-to-one decision, reversed the finding of no cause of action on the Pickleses' claims against the Messerlys. Lenawee County Board of Health v. Messerly, 98 Mich. App. 478, 295 N.W.2d 903 (1980). It concluded that the mutual mistake between the Messerlys and the Pickleses went to a basic, as opposed to a collateral, element of the contract, and that the parties intended to transfer income-producing rental property but, in actuality, the vendees paid $25,500 for an asset without value.[7]

We granted the Messerlys' application for leave to appeal. 411 Mich. 900 (1981).[8]

II

We must decide initially whether there was a mistaken belief entertained by one or both parties to the contract in dispute and, if so, the resultant legal significance.[9]

7. The trial court found that the only way that the property could be put to residential use would be to pump and haul the sewage, a method which is economically unfeasible, as the cost of such a disposal system amounts to double the income generated by the property. There was speculation by the trial court that the adjoining land might be utilized to make the property suitable for residential use, but, in the absence of testimony directed at that point, the court refused to draw any conclusions. The trial court and the Court of Appeals both found that the property was valueless, or had a negative value.

8. The Court of Appeals decision to affirm the trial court's finding of no cause of action against Mr. and Mrs. Barnes has not been appealed to this Court and, accordingly, the propriety of that ruling is not before us today.

9. We emphasize that this is a bifurcated inquiry. Legal or equitable remedial measures are not mandated in every case in which a mutual mistake has been established.

A contractual mistake "is a belief that is not in accord with the facts". 1 Restatement Contracts, 2d, § 151, p. 383. The erroneous belief of one or both of the parties must relate to a fact in existence at the time the contract is executed. *Richardson Lumber Co. v. Hoey*, 219 Mich. 643, 189 N.W. 923 (1922); *Sherwood v. Walker*, 66 Mich. 568, 580, 33 N.W. 919 (1887) (Sherwood, J., dissenting). That is to say, the belief which is found to be in error may not be, in substance, a prediction as to a future occurrence or non-occurrence. *Henry v. Thomas*, 241 Ga. 360, 245 S.E.2d 646 (1978).... But see *Denton v. Utley*, 350 Mich. 332, 86 N.W.2d 537 (1957).

The Court of Appeals concluded, after a de novo review of the record, that the parties were mistaken as to the income-producing capacity of the property in question. 98 Mich. App. at 487–488, 295 N.W.2d 903. We agree. The vendors and the vendees each believed that the property transferred could be utilized as income-generating rental property. All of the parties subsequently learned that, in fact, the property was unsuitable for any residential use.

Appellants assert that there was no mistake in the contractual sense because the defect in the sewage system did not arise until after the contract was executed. The appellees respond that the Messerlys are confusing the date of the inception of the defect with the date upon which the defect was discovered.

This is essentially a factual dispute which the trial court failed to resolve directly. Nevertheless, we are empowered to draw factual inferences from the facts found by the trial court. GCR 1963, 865.1(6).

An examination of the record reveals that the septic system was defective prior to the date on which the land contract was executed. The Messerlys' grantor installed a nonconforming septic system without a permit prior to the transfer of the property to the Messerlys in 1971. Moreover, virtually undisputed testimony indicates that, assuming ideal soil conditions, 2,500 square feet of property is necessary to support a sewage system adequate to serve a three-family dwelling. Likewise, 750 square feet is mandated for a one-family home. Thus, the division of the parcel and sale of one acre of the property by Mr. and Mrs. Barnes in 1976 made it impossible to remedy the already illegal septic system within the confines of the 600–square-foot parcel.

Appellants do not dispute these underlying facts which give rise to an inference contrary to their contentions.

Having determined that when these parties entered into the land contract they were laboring under a mutual mistake of fact, we now direct our attention to a determination of the legal significance of that finding.

A contract may be rescinded because of a mutual misapprehension of the parties, but this remedy is granted only in the sound discretion of the court. *Harris v. Axline*, 323 Mich. 585, 36 N.W.2d 154 (1949). Appellants argue that the parties' mistake relates only to the quality or value of the real estate transferred, and that such mistakes are collateral to the agreement and do not justify rescission, citing *A & M Land Development Co. v. Miller*, 354 Mich. 681, 94 N.W.2d 197 (1959).

In that case, the plaintiff was the purchaser of 91 lots of real property. It sought partial rescission of the land contract when it was frustrated in its attempts to develop 42 of the lots because it could not obtain permits from the county health department to install septic tanks on these lots. This Court refused to allow rescission because the mistake, whether mutual or unilateral, related only to the value of the property.

. . .

Appellees contend ... that in this case the parties were mistaken as to the very nature of the character of the consideration and claim that the pervasive and essential quality of this mistake renders rescission appropriate. They cite in support of that view *Sherwood v. Walker*, 66 Mich. 568, 33 N.W. 919 (1887), the famous "barren cow" case. In that case, the parties agreed to the sale and purchase of a cow which was thought to be barren, but which was, in reality, with calf. When the seller discovered the fertile condition of his cow, he refused to deliver her. [The court permitted rescission.]

As the parties suggest, the foregoing precedent arguably distinguishes mistakes affecting the essence of the consideration from those which go to its quality or value, affording relief on a per se basis for the former but not the latter. See, e.g., *Lenawee County Board of Health v. Messerly*, 98 Mich.App. 478, 492, 295 N.W.2d 903 (1980) (Mackenzie, J., concurring in part).

However, the distinctions which may be drawn from *Sherwood and A & M Land Development Co.* do not provide a satisfactory analysis of the nature of a mistake sufficient to invalidate a contract. Often, a mistake relates to an underlying factual assumption which, when discovered, directly affects value, but simultaneously and materially affects the essence of the contractual consideration. It is disingenuous to label such a mistake collateral. . . .

Appellant and appellee both mistakenly believed that the property which was the subject of their land contract would generate income as rental property. The fact that it could not be used for human habitation deprived the property of its income-earning potential and rendered it less valuable. However, this mistake, while directly and dramatically affecting the property's value, cannot accurately be characterized as collateral because it also affects the very essence of the consideration. "The thing sold and bought [income generating rental property] had in fact no existence". *Sherwood v. Walker*, 66 Mich. 568, 33 N.W. 919.

We find that the inexact and confusing distinction between contractual mistakes running to value and those touching the substance of the consideration serves only as an impediment to a clear and helpful analysis for the equitable resolution of cases in which mistake is alleged and proven. Accordingly, the holdings of *A & M Land Development Co.*

and *Sherwood* with respect to the material or collateral nature of a mistake are limited to the facts of those cases.

Instead, we think the better-reasoned approach is a case-by-case analysis whereby rescission is indicated when the mistaken belief relates to a basic assumption of the parties upon which the contract is made, and which materially affects the agreed performances of the parties. *Denton v. Utley*, 350 Mich. 332, 86 N.W.2d 537 (1957); ... 1 Restatement Contracts, 2d, § 152, p. 385–386. Rescission is not available, however, to relieve a party who has assumed the risk of loss in connection with the mistake. *Denton v. Utley*, 350 Mich. at 344–345, 86 N.W.2d 537; ... 1 Restatement Contracts, 2d, §§ 152, 154, pp. 385–386, 402–406.

All of the parties to this contract erroneously assumed that the property transferred by the vendors to the vendees was suitable for human habitation and could be utilized to generate rental income. The fundamental nature of these assumptions is indicated by the fact that their invalidity changed the character of the property transferred, thereby frustrating, indeed precluding, Mr. and Mrs. Pickles' intended use of the real estate. Although the Pickleses are disadvantaged by enforcement of the contract, performance is advantageous to the Messerlys, as the property at issue is less valuable absent its income-earning potential. Nothing short of rescission can remedy the mistake. Thus, the parties' mistake as to a basic assumption materially affects the agreed performances of the parties.

Despite the significance of the mistake made by the parties, we reverse the Court of Appeals because we conclude that equity does not justify the remedy sought by Mr. and Mrs. Pickles.

Rescission is an equitable remedy which is granted only in the sound discretion of the court. *Harris v. Axline*, 323 Mich. 585, 36 N.W.2d 154 (1949).... A court need not grant rescission in every case in which the mutual mistake relates to a basic assumption and materially affects the agreed performance of the parties.

In cases of mistake by two equally innocent parties, we are required, in the exercise of our equitable powers, to determine which blameless party should assume the loss resulting from the misapprehension they shared.[13] Normally that can only be done by drawing upon our "own notions of what is reasonable and just under all the surrounding circumstances".

Equity suggests that, in this case, the risk should be allocated to the purchasers. We are guided to that conclusion, in part, by the standards

---

13. This risk-of-loss analysis is absent in both A & M Land Development Co. and Sherwood, and this omission helps to explain, in part, the disparate treatment in the two cases. Had such an inquiry been undertaken in Sherwood, we believe that the result might have been different. Moreover, a determination as to which party assumed the risk in A & M Land Development Co. would have alleviated the need to characterize the mistake as collateral so as to justify the result denying rescission. Despite the absence of any inquiry as to the assumption of risk in those two leading cases, we find that there exists sufficient precedent to warrant such an analysis in future cases of mistake.

announced in § 154 of the Restatement of Contracts 2d, for determining when a party bears the risk of mistake. Section 154(a) suggests that the court should look first to whether the parties have agreed to the allocation of the risk between themselves. While there is no express assumption in the contract by either party of the risk of the property becoming uninhabitable, there was indeed some agreed allocation of the risk to the vendees by the incorporation of an "as is" clause into the contract which, we repeat, provided:

> "Purchaser has examined this property and agrees to accept same in its present condition. There are no other or additional written or oral understandings."

That is a persuasive indication that the parties considered that, as between them, such risk as related to the "present condition" of the property should lie with the purchaser. If the "as is" clause is to have any meaning at all, it must be interpreted to refer to those defects which were unknown at the time that the contract was executed.[15] Thus, the parties themselves assigned the risk of loss to Mr. and Mrs. Pickles.

We conclude that Mr. and Mrs. Pickles are not entitled to the equitable remedy of rescission and, accordingly, reverse the decision of the Court of Appeals.

Questions

1. Was there a mutual mistake of fact in *Wood*? What was the deal? What if it could be fairly inferred that, at the time he offered the plaintiff one dollar for the stone, the buyer did know its true value? Should the buyer then have disclosed that to the seller? Why or why not? Would there have been a mutual mistake of fact?

2. In *Lenawee County Board of Health*, how does the holding differ from the holding in *Sherwood v. Walker,* as the court reports it? Assume that the contract had not included an "as is" clause. What result? Why?

3. If rescission should be allowed when there is a mutual mistake of fact as to a basic assumption, and there is no assumption of the risk, what is the reason? Does a mutual mistake undermine the autonomy principle or the justification principle? Or would enforcing a contract based on such a mistake be unjust?

4. *Problems*.

    a. Assume the facts are otherwise as in *Lenawee County Board of Health*, except that the buyer had discovered the sewage problem one year after taking title to the property? What would you advise the buyer?

---

15. An "as is" clause waives those implied warranties which accompany the sale of a new home, Tibbitts v. Openshaw, 18 Utah 2d 442, 425 P.2d 160 (1967), or the sale of goods. M.C.L. § 440.2316(3)(a); M.S.A. § 19.2316(3)(a). Since implied war- ranties protect against latent defects, an "as is" clause will impose upon the purchaser the assumption of the risk of latent defects, such as an inadequate sanitation system, even when there are no implied warranties.

b. Assume the facts are as in Problem a, except that the buyer discovered the problem five years later. Same advice?

_____

RESTATEMENT (SECOND) OF CONTRACTS § 155

_____

ELSINORE UNION ELEMENTARY SCH. DIST. v. KASTORFF

Supreme Court of California, 1960.
54 Cal.2d 380, 6 Cal.Rptr. 1, 353 P.2d 713.

SCHAUER, JUSTICE. Defendants, who are a building contractor and his surety, appeal from an adverse judgment in this action by plaintiff school district to recover damages allegedly resulting when defendant Kastorff, the contractor, refused to execute a building contract pursuant to his previously submitted bid to make certain additions to plaintiff's school buildings. We have concluded that because of an honest clerical error in the bid and defendant's subsequent prompt rescission he was not obliged to execute the contract, and that the judgment should therefore be reversed.

Pursuant to plaintiff's call for bids, defendant Kastorff secured a copy of the plans and specifications of the proposed additions to plaintiff's school buildings and proceeded to prepare a bid to be submitted by the deadline hour of 8 p.m., August 12, 1952, at Elsinore, California. Kastorff testified that in preparing his bid he employed worksheets upon which he entered bids of various subcontractors for such portions of the work as they were to do, and that to reach the final total of his own bid for the work he carried into the right-hand column of the work sheets the amounts of the respective sub bids which he intended to accept and then added those amounts to the cost of the work which he would do himself rather than through a subcontractor; that there is "a custom among subcontractors, in bidding on jobs such as this, to delay giving . . . their bids until the very last moment;" that the first sub bid for plumbing was in the amount of $9,285 and he had received it "the afternoon of the bid-opening," but later afternoon when "the time was drawing close for me to get [my] bids together and get over to Elsinore" (from his home in San Juan Capistrano) he received a $6,500 bid for the plumbing. Erroneously thinking he had entered the $9,285 plumbing bid in his total column and had included that sum in his total bid and realizing that the second plumbing bid was nearly $3,000 less than the first, Kastorff then deducted $3,000 from the total amount of his bid and entered the resulting total of $89,994 on the bid form as his bid for the school construction. Thus the total included no allowance whatsoever for the plumbing work.

Kastorff then proceeded to Elsinore and deposited his bid with plaintiff. When the bids were opened shortly after 8 p.m. that evening, it was discovered that of the five bids submitted that of Kastorff was some $11,306 less than the next lowest bid. The school superintendent and the four school board members present thereupon asked Kastorff whether he was sure his figures were correct, Kastorff stepped out into the hall to check with the person who had assisted in doing the clerical work on the bid, and a few minutes later returned and stated that the figures were correct. He testified that he did not have his worksheets or other papers with him to check against at the time. The board thereupon, on August 12, 1952, voted to award Kastorff the contract.

The next morning Kastorff checked his worksheets and promptly discovered his error. He immediately drove to the Los Angeles office of the firm of architects which had prepared the plans and specifications for plaintiff, and there saw Mr. Rendon. Mr. Rendon testified that Kastorff "had his maps and estimate work-sheets of the project, and indicated to me that he had failed to carry across the amount of dollars for the plumbing work. It was on the sheet, but not in the total sheet. We examined that evidence, and in our opinion we felt that he had made a clerical error in compiling his bill. . . . In other words, he had put down a figure, but didn't carry it out to the 'total' column when he totaled his column to make up his bid. . . . He exhibited . . . at that time . . . his work-sheets from which he had made up his bid." That same morning (August 13) Rendon telephoned the school superintendent and informed him of the error and of its nature and that Kastorff asked to be released from his bid. On August 14, Kastorff wrote a letter to the school board explaining his error and again requesting that he be permitted to withdraw his bid. On August 15, after receiving Kastorff's letter, the board held a special meeting and voted not to grant his request. Thereafter, on August 28, *written notification* was given to Kastorff of award of the contract to him.[1] Subsequently plaintiff submitted to Kastorff a contract to be signed in accordance with his bid, and on September 8, 1952, Kastorff returned the contract to plaintiff with a letter again explaining his error and asking the board to reconsider his request for withdrawal of his bid.

Plaintiff thereafter received additional bids to do the subject construction; let the contract to the lowest bidder, in the amount of $102,900; and brought this action seeking to recover from Kastorff the $12,906 difference between that amount and the amount Kastorff had bid.[2] Recovery of $4,499.60 is also sought against Kastorff's surety under the terms of the bond posted with his bid.

1. On the bid form, provided by plaintiff, the bidder agreed "that if he is notified of the acceptance of the proposal within forty-five (45) days from the time set for the opening of bids, he will execute and deliver to you within five (5) days after having received *written notification* a contract as called for in the 'Notice to Contractors.'" (Italics added.)

2. Plaintiff's original published call for bids contained the following statement: "No Bidder may withdraw his bid for a period of forty-five (45) days after the date set for the opening thereof." Whether upon

Defendants in their answer to the complaint pleaded, among other things, that Kastorff had made an honest error in compiling his bid; that "he thought he was bidding, and intended to bid, $9,500.00 more, making a total of $99,494,00 as his bid;" that upon discovering his error he had promptly notified plaintiff and rescinded the $89,994 bid. The trial court found that it was true that Kastorff made up a bid sheet, which was introduced in evidence; that the subcontractor's bids thereupon indicated were those received by Kastorff; that he "had 16 subcontracting bids to ascertain from 31 which were submitted;" and that Kastorff had neglected to carry over from the left-hand column on the bid sheet to the right-hand column on the sheet a portion of the plumbing (and heating) subcontractor's bid. Despite the uncontradicted evidence related hereinabove, including that of plaintiff's architect and of its school superintendent, both of whom testified as plaintiff's witnesses, the court further found, however, that "it is not true that the right hand column of figures was totaled for the purpose of arriving at the total bid to be submitted by E. J. Kastorff.... It cannot be ascertained from the evidence for what purpose the total of the right hand column of figures on the bid sheet was used nor can it be ascertained from the evidence for what purpose the three bid sheets were used in arriving at the total bid." And although finding that "on or about August 15, 1952," plaintiff received Kastorff's letter of August 14 explaining that he "made an error of omitting from my bid the item of Plumbing," the court also found that "It is not true that plaintiff knew at any time that defendant Kastorff's bid was intended to be other than $89,994.00.... It is not true that the plaintiff knew at the time it requested the execution of the contract by defendant Kastorff that he had withdrawn his bid because of an honest error in the compilation thereof. It is not true that plaintiff had notice of an error in the compilation of the bid by defendant Kastorff and tried nevertheless to take advantage of defendant Kastorff by forcing him to enter a contract on the basis of a bid he had withdrawn.... It is not true that it would be either inequitable or unjust to require defendant Kastorff to perform the contract awarded to him for the sum of $89,994.00, and it is not true that he actually intended to bid for said work the sum of $99,494.00."[3] Judgment was given for plaintiff in the amounts sought, and this appeal by defendants followed.

In reliance upon M. F. Kemper Const. Co. v. City of Los Angeles (1951), 37 Cal.2d 696, 235 P.2d 7, and Lemoge Electric v. County of San Mateo (1956), 46 Cal.2d 659, 662, 664 [1a, 1b, 2, 3], 297 P.2d 638, defendants urged that where, as defendants claim is the situation here, a

Kastorff's rescission for good cause prior to expiration of the 45 day period plaintiff could have accepted the next lowest bid is not an issue before us.

3. Other findings are that Kastorff "in the company of his wife and another couple left San Juan Capistrano for Elsinore ... at 6:00 P.M. on August 12, 1952, a distance of 34 miles by way of California State High-

way ... Kastorff had ample time and opportunity after receiving his last subcontractor's bid to extend the figures on his bid sheet from one column to the other, to check and recheck his bid sheet figures and to take his papers to Elsinore and to check them there prior to close of receipt to bids at 8:00 P.M."

contractor makes a clerical error in computing a bid on a public work he is entitled to rescind.

In the Kemper case one item on a worksheet in the amount of $301,769 was inadvertently omitted by the contractor from the final tabulation sheet and was overlooked in computing the total amount of a bid to do certain construction work for the defendant city. The error was caused by the fact that the men preparing the bid were exhausted after working long hours under pressure. When the bids were opened it was found that plaintiff's bid was $780,305, and the next lowest bid was $1,049,592. Plaintiff discovered its error several hours later and immediately notified a member of defendant's board of public works of its mistake in omitting one item while preparing the final accumulation of figures for its bid. Two days later it explained its mistake to the board and withdrew its bid. A few days later it submitted to the board evidence which showed the unintentional omission of the $301,769 item. The board nevertheless passed a resolution accepting plaintiff's erroneous bid of $780,305, and plaintiff refused to enter into a written contract at that figure. The board then awarded the contract to the next lowest bidder, the city demanded forfeiture of plaintiff's bid bond, and plaintiff brought action to cancel its bid and obtain discharge of the bond. The trial court found that the bid had been submitted as the result of an excusable and honest mistake of a material and fundamental character, that plaintiff company had not been negligent in preparing the proposal, that it had acted promptly to notify the board of the mistake and to rescind the bid, and that the board had accepted the bid with knowledge of the error. The court further found and concluded that it would be unconscionable to require the company to perform for the amount of the bid, that no intervening rights had accrued, and that the city had suffered no damage or prejudice.

On appeal by the city this court affirmed, stating the following applicable rules (at pages 700–703 of 37 Cal.2d, at pages 10, 11 of 235 P.2d):

"(1) Once opened and declared, the company's bid was in the nature of an irrevocable option, a contract right of which the city could not be deprived without its consent unless the requirements for rescission were satisfied. [Citations.] ... (2) ... the city had actual notice of the error in the estimates before it attempted to accept the bid, and knowledge by one party that the other is acting under mistake is treated as equivalent to mutual mistake for purposes of rescission. [Citations.] (3) Relief from mistaken bids is consistently allowed where one party knows or has reason to know of the other's error and the requirements for rescission are fulfilled. [Citations.]

"(4) Rescission may be had for mistake of fact if the mistake is material to the contract and was not the result of neglect of a legal duty, if enforcement of the contract as made would be unconscionable, and if the other party can be placed in statu quo. [Citations.] In addition, the party seeking relief must give prompt notice of his election to rescind and must restore or offer to restore to the other party everything of value which he has received under the contract. [Citations.]

"(5) Omission of the $301,769 item from the company's bid was, of course, a material mistake.... [E]ven if we assume that the error was due to some carelessness, it does not follow that the company is without remedy. Civil Code section 1577, which defines mistake of facts for which relief may be allowed, describes it as one not caused by 'the neglect of a legal duty' on the part of the person making the mistake. (6) It has been recognized numerous times that not all carelessness constitutes a 'neglect of legal duty' within the meaning of the section. [Citations.] On facts very similar to those in the present case, courts of other jurisdictions have stated that there was no culpable negligence and have granted relief from erroneous bids. [Citations.] (7) The type of error here involved is one which will sometimes occur in the conduct of reasonable and cautious business-men, and, under all the circumstances, we cannot say as a matter of law that it constituted a neglect of legal duty such as would bar the right to equitable relief.

"(8) The evidence clearly supports the conclusion that it would be unconscionable to hold the company to its bid at the mistaken figure. The city had knowledge before the bid was accepted that the company had made a clerical error which resulted in the omission of an item amounting to nearly one third of the amount intended to be bid, and, under all the circumstances, it appears that it would be unjust and unfair to permit the city to take advantage of the company's mistake. (9, 10) There is no reason for denying relief on the ground that the city cannot be restored to status quo. It had ample time in which to award the contract without readvertising, the contract was actually awarded to the next lowest bidder, and the city will not be heard to complain that it cannot be placed in statu quo because it will not have the benefit of an inequitable bargain. [Citations.] (11) Finally, the company gave notice promptly upon discovering the facts entitling it to rescind, and no offer of restoration was necessary because it had received nothing of value which it could restore. [Citation.] We are satisfied that all the requirements for rescission have been met."

In the Lemoge case (Lemoge Electric v. County of San Mateo (1956), supra, 46 Cal.2d 659, 662, 664 [1a, 1b, 2, 3]), 297 P.2d 638, the facts were similar to those in Kemper, except that plaintiff Lemoge did not attempt to rescind but instead, after discovering and informing defendant of inadvertent clerical error in the bid, entered into a formal contract with defendant on the terms specified in the erroneous bid, performed the required work, and then sued for reformation. Although this court affirmed the trial court's determination that plaintiff was not, under the circumstances, entitled to have the contract reformed, we also reaffirmed the rule that "Once opened and declared, plaintiff's bid was in the nature of an irrevocable option, a contract right of which defendant could not be deprived without its consent unless the requirements for rescission were satisfied. [Citation.] Plaintiff then had the right to rescind, and it could have done so without incurring any liability on its bond." (See also Brunzell Const. Co. v. G. J. Weisbrod, Inc. (1955), 134 Cal.App.2d 278, 286–287 [1, 2], 285 P.2d 989; Klose v. Sequoia Union High School Dist. (1953), 118 Cal.App.2d 636, 641–642 [5], 258 P.2d 515.)

The rules stated in the Kemper and Lemoge cases would appear to entitle defendant to relief here, were it not for the findings of the trial court adverse to defendant. However, certain of such findings are clearly not supported by the evidence and others are immaterial to the point at issue. The finding that it is not true that the right hand column of figures on the bid sheet was totaled for the purpose of arriving at the total bid, and that it cannot be ascertained from the evidence for what purpose either the bid sheets or the right hand column total thereon were used in arriving at the total bid, is without evidentiary support in the face of the worksheets which were introduced in evidence and of the uncontradicted testimony not alone of defendant Kastorff, but also of plaintiff's own architect and witness Rendon, explaining the purpose of the worksheets and the nature of the error which had been made. We have examined such sheets, and they plainly show the entry of the sums of $9,285 and of $6,500 in the left hand columns as the two plumbing sub bids which were received by defendant, and the omission from the right hand totals column of any sum whatever for plumbing.

The same is true of the finding that although "on or about August 15" plaintiff received Kastorff's letter of August 14 explaining the error in his bid, it was not true that plaintiff knew at any time that the bid was intended to be other than as submitted. Again, it was shown by the testimony of plaintiff's architect, its school superintendent, and one of its school board members, all produced as plaintiff's witnesses, that the board was informed of the error and despite such information voted at its special meeting of August 15 not to grant defendant's request to withdraw his bid.

Further, we are persuaded that the trial court's view, as expressed in the finding set forth in the margin, that "Kastorff had ample time and opportunity after receiving his last subcontractor's bid" to complete and check his final bid, does not convict Kastorff of that "neglect of legal duty" which would preclude his being relieved from the inadvertent clerical error of omitting from his bid the cost of the plumbing. (See Civ.Code, § 1577; M. F. Kemper Const. Co. v. City of Los Angeles (1951), supra, 37 Cal.2d 696, 702 [6], 235 P.2d 7.) Neither should he be denied relief from an unfair, inequitable, and unintended bargain simply because, in response to inquiry from the board when his bid was discovered to be much the lowest submitted, he informed the board, after checking with his clerical assistant, that the bid was correct. He did not have his worksheets present to inspect at that time, he did thereafter inspect them at what would appear to have been the earliest practicable moment, and thereupon promptly notified plaintiff and rescinded his bid. Further, as shown in the margin, Kastorff's bid agreement, as provided by plaintiff's own bid form, was to execute a formal written contract only after receiving written notification of acceptance of his bid, and such notice was not given to him until some two weeks following his rescission.

If the situations of the parties were reversed and plaintiff and Kastorff had even executed a formal written contract (by contrast with the preliminary bid offer and acceptance) calling for a fixed sum payment to Kastorff large enough to include a reasonable charge for plumbing but inadvertently through the *district's* clerical error omitting a mutually intended provision requiring Kastorff to furnish and install plumbing, we have no doubt but that the district would demand and expect reformation or recession. In the case before us the district expected Kastorff to furnish and install plumbing; surely it must also have understood that he intended to, and that his bid did, include a charge for such plumbing. The omission of any such charge was as unexpected by the board as it was unintended by Kastorff. Under the circumstances the "bargain" for which the board presses (which action we, of course, assume to be impelled by advice of counsel and a strict concept of official duty) appears too sharp for law and equity to sustain.

Plaintiff suggests that in any event the amount of the plumbing bid omitted from the total was immaterial. The bid as submitted was in the sum of $89,994, and whether the sum for the omitted plumbing was $6,500 or $9,285 (the two sub bids), the omission of such a sum is plainly material to the total. In Lemoge (Lemoge Electric v. County of San Mateo (1956), supra, 46 Cal.2d 659, 661–662, 297 P.2d 638) the error which it was declared would have entitled plaintiff to rescind was the listing of the cost of certain materials as $104.52, rather than $10,452, in a total bid of $172,421. Thus the percentage of error here was larger than in Lemoge, and was plainly material.

The judgment is reversed.

Questions

1. What is the District's complaint? Was there a contract supported by a bargained-for exchange? Why was Kastorff's promise not enforced?

2. Should Kastorff's promise have been enforced? Is *Kastorff* more like *Sherwood*, *Wood* or *Stambovsky*? What are the relevant contractual interests and principles in each case? Which are stronger in *Kastorff*?

3. Would enforcement against Kastorff be justified by the autonomy principle? Would it be unjust? If it would be unjust, is it for reasons of corrective or distributive justice? Are the holdings in *Sherwood*, *Wood* and *Stambovsky* justified by respect for the parties' autonomy? Or is justice the relevant principle at play in these cases?

SECTION 3. UNCONSCIONABILITY

In principle, a regime of free contracting treats all persons equally. In law, every capable adult has the same rights to contract or not as they see fit. Promises are enforceable or not under the same circumstances. The rules of offer, acceptance, and consideration, however, do not include within the relevant circumstances the relative wealth or power of the parties. Realistically, a homeless person whose sole income comes from begging cannot exercise the power of contract as does a wealthy tycoon. True, both have the same legal power to contract for delivery of a yacht. But it is idle or misleading to insist on that point as though the differences in their situations did not far outweigh the legal similarity.

Professor Friedrich Kessler sounded a theme that has resonated through the law of contracts in recent decades:

> [T]he law, by protecting the unequal distribution of property, does nothing to prevent freedom of contract from becoming a one-sided privilege. Society, by proclaiming freedom of contract, guarantees that it will not interfere with the exercise of power by contract. Freedom of contract enables enterprisers to legislate by contract and, what is even more important, to legislate in a substantially authoritarian manner without using the appearance of authoritarian forms. Standard contracts in particular could thus become effective instruments in the hands of powerful industrial and commercial overlords enabling them to impose a new feudal order of their own making upon a vast host of vassals.

Friedrich Kessler, *Contracts of Adhesion—Some Thoughts about Freedom of Contract*, 43 COLUM. L. REV. 629, 640 (1943). The concern here is not with the state's coercive powers as such, as is the concern underlying the justification principle. Rather, it is with granting enforcement of contracts in which one party enjoys disproportionate private power. Enforcement of such contracts, some fear, might have the consequence of maintaining or aggravating an unjust distribution of wealth and power generally.

Traditionally, contract law did little to prevent powerful entities from using the power of contract to maintain and extend their privileged positions. The law of consideration, for example, forecloses inquiry into the equivalence of values exchanged, allowing exploitative or unfair contracts the same enforceability as productive and fair ones. To be sure, the law of offer, acceptance, and consideration is manipulable to some extent. Rules and counterrules can be selected as needed to achieve results desired on grounds of justice (or other grounds), as in some of the cases in Chapter 2, § 1. However, many thoughtful people are convinced that the law in action, hidden beneath doctrinal manipulations of the law on the books, should be made explicit through law reform. The unconscionability doctrine, considered in the next two sections, has been partly an attempt to bring justice out of the closet.

As you read the following cases, consider whether contract law should be reshaped to protect the socially disadvantaged in our society. If it should, under what conditions should courts refuse to enforce agreed terms? Or would other means, such as tax strategies, economic growth, or government programs, better improve distributive justice?

In this section, we consider consumer transactions involving the sale of goods. A consumer is a buyer and end-user of a good. Consumers may not be sophisticated about contracting practices. Consumers should not, however, be equated in this respect with buyers. Consumers buy from retailers who buy from wholesalers who buy from manufacturers who buy component parts, labor, and services from suppliers. If we consider all buys made in a day, probably most are made by the U.S. Government. General Motors probably places second. So it would be a mistake to assume that buyers as such have less bargaining power than sellers. Even consumers may have considerable bargaining power, as in highly competitive markets, especially with the recent decline in brand name loyalties. Some, however, are not able to use that power effectively.

The consumer in each case in this section claimed that a contract was not binding, in whole or in part, because it was not a product of meaningful choice on the consumer's part, because it was one-sided, or for both reasons. Some courts that are unwilling to help a businessman are willing to help disadvantaged consumers avoid unconscionable contracts. As you read the following cases, consider whether the specific arguments for judicial relief from apparently oppressive contracts are stronger than the arguments for enforcing these agreements as made.

U.C.C. §§ 1–103, 2–302

RESTATEMENT (SECOND) OF CONTRACTS § 208

WILLIAMS v. WALKER–THOMAS FURNITURE CO.

United States Court of Appeals, District of Columbia Circuit, 1965.
121 U.S.App.D.C. 315, 350 F.2d 445.

J. SKELLY WRIGHT, CIRCUIT JUDGE. Appellee, Walker–Thomas Furniture Company, operates a retail furniture store in the District of Columbia. During the period from 1957 to 1962 each appellant in these cases purchased a number of household items from Walker–Thomas, for which payment was to be made in installments. The terms of each purchase were contained in a printed form contract which set forth the value of the purchased item and purported to lease the item to appellant for a stipulated monthly rent payment. The contract then provided, in substance, that title would remain in Walker–Thomas until the total of all the monthly payments made equaled the stated value of the item, at which time appellants could take title. In the event of a default in the payment of any monthly installment, Walker–Thomas could repossess the item.

The contract further provided that "the amount of each periodical installment payment to be made by [purchaser] to the Company under this present lease shall be inclusive of and not in addition to the amount of each installment payment to be made by [purchaser] under such prior leases, bills or accounts; *and all payments now and hereafter made by [purchaser] shall be credited pro rata on all outstanding leases, bills and accounts* due the Company by [purchaser] at the time each such payment is made." (Emphasis added.) The effect of this rather obscure provision was to keep a balance due on every item purchased until the balance due on all items, whenever purchased, was liquidated. As a result, the debt incurred at the time of purchase of each item was secured by the right to repossess all the items previously purchased by the same purchaser, and each new item purchased automatically became subject to a security interest arising out of the previous dealings.

On May 12, 1962, appellant Thorne purchased an item described as a Daveno, three tables, and two lamps, having total stated value of \$391.10. Shortly thereafter, he defaulted on his monthly payments and appellee sought to replevy all the items purchased since the first transaction in 1958. Similarly, on April 17, 1962, appellant Williams bought a stereo set of stated value of \$514.95.[1] She too defaulted shortly thereafter, and appellee sought to replevy all the items purchased since December, 1957. The Court of General Sessions granted judgment for appellee. The District of Columbia Court of Appeals affirmed, and we granted appellants' motion for leave to appeal to this court.

Appellants' principal contention, rejected by both the trial and the appellate courts below, is that these contracts, or at least some of them, are unconscionable and, hence, not enforceable. In its opinion in Williams v. Walker-Thomas Furniture Company, 198 A.2d 914, 916 (1964), the District of Columbia Court of Appeals explained its rejection of this contention as follows:

"Appellant's second argument presents a more serious question. The record reveals that prior to the last purchase appellant had reduced the balance in her account to \$164. The last purchase, a stereo set, raised the balance due to \$678. Significantly, at the time of this and the preceding purchases, appellee was aware of appellant's financial position. The reverse side of the stereo contract listed the name of appellant's social worker and her \$218 monthly stipend from the government. Nevertheless, with full knowledge that appellant had to feed, clothe and support both herself and seven children on this amount, appellee sold her a \$514 stereo set.

"We cannot condemn too strongly appellee's conduct. It raises serious questions of sharp practice and irresponsible business dealings. A review of the legislation in the District of Columbia affecting retail sales and the pertinent decisions of the highest court in this

---

1. At the time of this purchase her account showed a balance of \$164 still owing from her prior purchases. The total of all the purchases made over the years in question came to \$1,800. The total payments amounted to \$1,400.

jurisdiction disclose, however, no ground upon which this court can declare the contracts in question contrary to public policy. We note that were the Maryland Retail Installment Sales Act, Art. 83 §§ 128–153, or its equivalent, in force in the District of Columbia, we could grant appellant appropriate relief. We think Congress should consider corrective legislation to protect the public from such exploitive contracts as were utilized in the case at bar."

We do not agree that the court lacked the power to refuse enforcement to contracts found to be unconscionable. In other jurisdictions, it has been held as a matter of common law that unconscionable contracts are not enforceable.[2] While no decision of this court so holding has been found, the notion that an unconscionable bargain should not be given full enforcement is by no means novel. In Scott v. United States, 79 U.S. (12 Wall.) 443, 445, 20 L.Ed. 438 (1870), the Supreme Court stated:

> ". . . If a contract be unreasonable and unconscionable, but not void for fraud, a court of law will give to the party who sues for its breach damages, not according to its letter, but only such as he is equitably entitled to. . . ."

Since we have never adopted or rejected such a rule, the question here presented is actually one of first impression.

Congress has recently enacted the Uniform Commercial Code, which specifically provides that the court may refuse to enforce a contract which it finds to be unconscionable at the time it was made. 28 D.C.CODE § 2–302 (Supp. IV 1965). The enactment of this section, which occurred subsequent to the contracts here in suit, does not mean that the common law of the District of Columbia was otherwise at the time of enactment, nor does it preclude the court from adopting a similar rule in the exercise of its powers to develop the common law for the District of Columbia. In fact, in view of the absence of prior authority on the point, we consider the congressional adoption of § 2–302 persuasive authority for following the rationale of the cases from which the section is explicitly derived. Accordingly, we hold that where the element of unconscionability is present at the time a contract is made, the contract should not be enforced.

Unconscionability has generally been recognized to include an absence of meaningful choice on the part of one of the parties together with contract terms which are unreasonably favorable to the other party.[6] Whether a meaningful choice is present in a particular case can only be determined by consideration of all the circumstances surrounding the transaction. In many cases the meaningfulness of the choice is negated by a gross inequality of bargaining power.[7] The manner in which the

2. Campbell Soup Co. v. Wentz, 3 Cir., 172 F.2d 80 (1948); Indianapolis Morris Plan Corporation v. Sparks, 132 Ind.App. 145, 172 N.E.2d 899 (1961); Henningsen v. Bloomfield Motors, Inc., 32 N.J. 358, 161 A.2d 69, 84–96, 75 A.L.R.2d 1 (1960). Cf. 1 CORBIN, CONTRACTS 128 (1963).

6. See Henningsen v. Bloomfield Motors, Inc., *supra* Note 2; Campbell Soup Co. v. Wentz, *supra* Note 2.

7. See Henningsen v. Bloomfield Motors, Inc., *supra* Note 2, 161 A.2d at 86, and authorities there cited. Inquiry into the rel-

contract was entered is also relevant to this consideration. Did each party to the contract, considering his obvious education or lack of it, have a reasonable opportunity to understand the terms of the contract, or were the important terms hidden in a maze of fine print and minimized by deceptive sales practices? Ordinarily, one who signs an agreement without full knowledge of its terms might be held to assume the risk that he has entered a one-sided bargain. But when a party of little bargaining power, and hence little real choice, signs a commercially unreasonable contract with little or no knowledge of its terms, it is hardly likely that his consent, or even an objective manifestation of his consent, was ever given to all the terms. In such a case the usual rule that the terms of the agreement are not to be questioned should be abandoned and the court should consider whether the terms of the contract are so unfair that enforcement should be withheld.

In determining reasonableness or fairness, the primary concern must be with the terms of the contract considered in light of the circumstances existing when the contract was made. The test is not simple, nor can it be mechanically applied. The terms are to be considered "in the light of the general commercial background and the commercial needs of the particular trade or case."[11] Corbin suggests the test as being whether the terms are "so extreme as to appear unconscionable according to the mores and business practices of the time and place." 1 CORBIN, *op. cit.* supra Note 2. We think this formulation correctly states the test to be applied in those cases where no meaningful choice was exercised upon entering the contract.

Because the trial court and the appellate court did not feel that enforcement could be refused, no findings were made on the possible unconscionability of the contracts in these cases. Since the record is not sufficient for our deciding the issue as a matter of law, the cases must be remanded to the trial court for further proceedings.

So ordered.

DANAHER, CIRCUIT JUDGE (dissenting). The District of Columbia Court of Appeals obviously was as unhappy about the situation here presented as any of us can possibly be. Its opinion in the *Williams* case, quoted in the majority text, concludes: "We think Congress should consider corrective legislation to protect the public from such exploitive contracts as were utilized in the case at bar."

ative bargaining power of the two parties is not an inquiry wholly divorced from the general question of unconscionability, since a one-sided bargain is itself evidence of the inequality of the bargaining parties. This fact was vaguely recognized in the common law doctrine of intrinsic fraud, that is, fraud which can be presumed from the grossly unfair nature of the terms of the contract. See the oft-quoted statement of Lord Hardwicke in Earl of Chesterfield v. Janssen, 28 Eng.Rep. 82, 100 (1751):

> ". . . [Fraud] may be apparent from the intrinsic nature and subject of the bargain itself; such as no man in his senses and not under delusion would make. . . ."

. . .

11. Comment, Uniform Commercial Code § 2–307.

My view is thus summed up by an able court which made no finding that there had actually been sharp practice. Rather the appellant seems to have known precisely where she stood.

There are many aspects of public policy here involved. What is a luxury to some may seem an outright necessity to others. Is public oversight to be required of the expenditures of relief funds? A washing machine, e.g., in the hands of a relief client might become a fruitful source of income. Many relief clients may well need credit, and certain business establishments will take long chances on the sale of items, expecting their pricing policies will afford a degree of protection commensurate with the risk. Perhaps a remedy when necessary will be found within the provisions of the "Loan Shark" law, D.C.CODE §§ 26–601 *et seq.* (1961).

I mention such matters only to emphasize the desirability of a cautious approach to any such problem, particularly since the law for so long has allowed parties such great latitude in making their own contracts. I dare say there must annually be thousands upon thousands of installment credit transactions in this jurisdiction, and one can only speculate as to the effect the decision in these cases will have.

I join the District of Columbia Court of Appeals in its disposition of the issues.

Questions

1. What was the deal in *Williams*? What was the promise sued upon? Why was Ms. Williams unhappy with her agreement? Was there a legal reason to enforce it? Why was Ms. Williams unhappy enough to sue?

2. What overriding reasons might justify nullifying the parties' agreement? What evidence would you want to present to the trial court on remand on behalf of Ms. Williams? On behalf of the Walker-Thomas Furniture Co.? Should it matter whether Ms. Williams read the add-on clause? Should it matter whether the salesman called it to her attention and explained it to her?

3. *Problem.*

Assume that a statute makes it mandatory, in any consumer credit sale where the seller secures credit by taking a security interest in goods sold previously and currently, for the seller to apply each entire payment first to pay off the debts arising from the sales made first. The manager of the Walker-Thomas Furniture Co. is upset because, his experience suggests, the company's loans will not be sufficiently secure without offsetting changes in the contract. How would you advise the Walker-Thomas Furniture Co. to redo its contracts for transactions like the one in *Williams*?

NOTE ON "EASY CREDIT" CONSUMER TRANSACTIONS

Popular images sometimes cast merchants like the Walker-Thomas Furniture Co. as unscrupulous capitalists getting rich by exploiting low-income buyers. See D. CAPLOVITZ, THE POOR PAY MORE (1967). A study of credit practices by the Federal Trade Commission (FTC), following the decision in *Williams*, confirmed that merchants like the Walker-Thomas Furniture Co. charge much higher prices than those charged by general-market retailers, including appliance, furniture, and department stores that sell for cash or on credit cards. But merchants with poor customers do not make great profits.

"Profit" can be measured as a percentage of sales revenue or as a rate of return on investment. In 1966, low-income market retailers in the District of Columbia made a net profit after taxes, as a percentage of sales, of 4.7%. By comparison, department stores by the same measure made 4.6%, furniture stores 3.9%, and appliance stores 2.1%. Low-income market retailers made a 10.1% rate of return on investment after taxes. By comparison, department stores made 13%, furniture stores 17.6%, and appliance stores 20.3%. From an investor's point of view, it clearly would have been most profitable to have opened a general market appliance store in that year in the District of Columbia. FEDERAL TRADE COMM'N, ECONOMIC REPORT ON INSTALLMENT CREDIT AND RETAIL SALES PRACTICES OF DISTRICT OF COLUMBIA RETAILERS 20–21 (1968).

The reason why higher prices do not yield higher returns for low-income retailers seems to be that these retailers have very high costs. The contracts in *Williams v. Walker-Thomas Furniture Co.* were consumer transactions with a merchant who catered to low-income customers in need of "easy credit." Buyers in situations like these are often unemployed and on government assistance. They are unable to purchase goods for cash. They do not have credit cards, which are issued only after a check to exclude those who are not "creditworthy." The risk of default is too great for creditors to extend credit to poor people on the same terms offered to people with jobs and histories of timely repayments.

The FTC study indicated, in particular, that low-income market retailers had far higher costs due to the high risks of extending credit to their customers. Based on samples of 10 low-income and 10 general market retailers, 28.2% of low-income market sales revenues was spent on salaries and commissions. The FTC explained, "A major reason for low-income market retailers' higher personnel expense is believed to be their use of outside salesmen who canvass house-to-house or followup requests for home demonstrations and often make collections of installment payments at the home of the customer." *Id.* at 19. These salesmen often received commissions on both sales and collections. Low-income market retailers also tend to finance their own installment contracts, requiring more administrative personnel than do general market retailers. Most significant, however, low-income market retailers have far higher collection expenses. Bad-debt losses accounted for 6.7% of sales revenues, compared to .3% for general market retailers. Other expenses, mainly lawyer's fees and court costs for enforcing credit agreements, amounted to 21.3% of sales revenues for low-income market retailers, compared to 11.2% for general market retailers. *Id.*

TOKER v. WESTERMAN

District Court, Union County, New Jersey, 1970.
113 N.J.Super. 452, 274 A.2d 78.

McKENZIE, J.D.C. On November 7, 1966 plaintiff's assignor, People's Foods of New Jersey, sold a refrigerator-freezer to defendant under a retail installment contract. The cash price for the unit was $899.98. With sales tax, group life insurance and time-price-differential the total amount was $1,229.76, to be paid in 36 monthly installments of $34.16 each.

Defendants made payments over a period of time, but resist payment of the balance in the sum of $573.89, claiming that the unit was so greatly over-priced as to make the contract unenforceable under N.J.S. 12A:2–302. "Unconscionable Contract or Clause...."

At the trial defendant presented an appliance dealer who had inspected the refrigerator-freezer in question. He stated that the same had a capacity of approximately 18 cubic feet, was not frost-free, and, with no special features, was known in the trade as a stripped unit. He estimated the reasonable retail price at the time of sale as between $350 and $400. He testified that the most expensive refrigerator-freezer of comparable size, with such additional features as butter temperature control and frost-free operation, at that time sold for $500.

The questions presented are simply whether or not the contract price for the unit is unconscionable, and, if so, whether the provisions of the cited section of the Uniform Commercial Code apply.

The Code does not define the term "unconscionable." Elsewhere an unconscionable contract has been defined as:

> ... one such as no man in his senses and not under a delusion would make on the one hand, and as no honest and fair man would accept on the other. To what extent inadequacy of consideration must go to make a contract unconscionable is difficult to state, except in abstract terms, which gives but little practical help. It has been said that there must be an inequality so strong, gross, and manifest that it must be impossible to state it to a man of common sense without producing an exclamation at the inequality of it. 43 Words and Phrases p. 143.

It is apparent that the court should not allow the statutory provision in question to be used as a manipulative tool to allow a purchaser to avoid the consequences of a bargain which he later finds to be unfavorable. Suffice it to say that in the instant case the court finds as shocking, and therefore unconscionable, the sale of goods for approximately 2½ times their reasonable retail value. This is particularly so where, as here, the sale was made by a door-to-door salesman for a dealer who therefore would have less overhead expense than a dealer maintaining a store or showroom. In addition, it appeared that defendants during the course of the payments they made to plaintiff were obliged to seek welfare assistance.

A flagrantly excessive purchase price was held to be within the intendment of N.J.S. 12A:2–302 in the case of Toker v. Perl, 103 N.J.Super. 500, 247 A.2d 701 (Law Div.1968). There the same dealer as in the present case sold a refrigerator-freezer to defendant for a purchase price of $799.95. The court found that the maximum value of the unit was $300 and held the excessive price to be unconscionable. The claim for the balance of the purchase price was therefore held to be unenforceable under the statute. On appeal, the Appellate Division affirmed. Toker v. Perl, 108 N.J.Super. 129, 260 A.2d 244 (1970). However, defendants there charged, and the trial court found, that the dealer had fraudulently procured defendants' signatures to the contract. The affirmance of the Appellate Division was on this ground alone, the court specifically expressing no opinion on the finding of the trial court that the excessive price of the unit also rendered the contract unenforceable.

There appear to be no other cases in New Jersey on this precise point and the reported cases in other states are sparse. However, it would also appear that those states which have considered this question have uniformly held that the purchase price alone may be found to be unconscionable, therefore bringing the statutory provision into play. See Frostifresh Corp. v. Reynoso, 52 Misc.2d 26, 274 N.Y.S.2d 757 (Dist.Ct. 1966), rev'd on other grounds, 54 Misc.2d 119, 281 N.Y.S.2d 964 (Sup. App.1967); Central Budget Corp. v. Sanchez, 53 Misc.2d 620, 279 N.Y.S.2d 391, 392 (Civ..Ct. 1967); American Home Improvement, Inc. v. MacIver, 105 N.H. 435, 201 A.2d 886 (Sup.Ct. 1964)....

In Frostifresh Corp. v. Reynoso, *supra*, the Appellate Court upheld the finding of unconscionability where a home freezer costing the plaintiff $348 was sold to a welfare recipient for a total price, including time-price-differential, of $1,145.88. However, it also reversed the lower court in permitting the seller to recover only the cost of the item, holding that the seller was entitled to the reasonable profit. These decisions are clearly in the mainstream of current judicial concepts in the area of consumer goods, as set forth by our Supreme Court:

> ... Although courts continue to recognize that persons should not be unnecessarily restricted in their freedom to contract, there is an increasing willingness to invalidate unconscionable contractual provisions which clearly tend to injure the public in some way. [Ellsworth Dobbs, Inc. v. Johnson, 50 N.J. 528, 236 A.2d 843 (1967)]

In the instant case the court finds that in receiving a total of $655.85 plaintiff and his assignor have received a reasonable sum. The payment of the balance of the purchase price will therefore not be enforced. Judgment for defendants.

Questions

1. What was the deal in *Toker*? What was the promise sued upon? Was there a legal reason to enforce it? Was that reason overridden by other sound reasons? What were they?

2. If contracts like the one in *Toker* are held to be unconscionable, what consequences would you expect for people whose creditworthiness is weak? If you were representing People's Foods, what would you advise it to do to protect its interests after *Toker*?

FROSTIFRESH CORP. v. REYNOSO

District Court, Nassau County, Second District, 1966.
52 Misc.2d 26, 274 N.Y.S.2d 757.

FRANCIS J. DONOVAN, JUDGE.

DECISION AFTER TRIAL

Plaintiff brings this action for $1,364.10, alleging that the latter amount is owed by the defendants to the plaintiff on account of the purchase of a combination-refrigerator-freezer for which they agreed to pay the sum of $1,145.88. The balance of the amount consists of a claim for attorney fees in the amount of $227.35 and a late charge of $22.87. The only payment made on account of the original indebtedness is the sum of $32.00.

The contract for the refrigerator-freezer was negotiated orally in Spanish between the defendants and a Spanish speaking salesman representing the plaintiff. In that conversation the defendant husband told the salesman that he had but one week left on his job and he could not afford to buy the appliance. The salesman distracted and deluded the defendants by advising them that the appliance would cost them nothing because they would be paid bonuses or commissions of $25.00 each on the numerous sales that would be made to their neighbors and friends. Thereafter there was submitted to and signed by the defendants a retail installment contract entirely in English. The retail contract was neither translated nor explained to the defendants. In that contract there was a cash sales price set forth of $900.00. To this was added a credit charge of $245.88, making a total of $1,145.88 to be paid for the appliance.

The plaintiff admitted that cost to the plaintiff corporation for the appliance was $348.00.

No defense of fraud was set forth in the pleadings and accordingly such defense is not available.

However, in the course of the trial, it did appear to the court that the contract might be unconscionable. The court therefore continued the trial at an adjourned date to afford a reasonable opportunity to the parties to present evidence as to the commercial setting, purpose and effect of the contract.

The court finds that the sale of the appliance at the price and terms indicated in this contract is shocking to the conscience. The service charge, which almost equals the price of the appliance is in and of itself indicative of the oppression which was practiced on these defendants. Defendants were handicapped by a lack of knowledge, both as to the commercial situation and the nature and terms of the contract which was submitted in a language foreign to them.

The question presented in this case is simply this: Does the court have the power under section 2–302 of the Uniform Commercial Code to refuse to enforce the price and credit provisions of the contract in order to prevent an unconscionable result.

It is normally stated that the parties are free to make whatever contracts they please so long as there is no fraud or illegality (Allegheny College v. National Chautauqua County Bank, 246 N.Y. 369, 159 N.E. 173, 57 A.L.R. 980).

However, it is the apparent intent of the Uniform Commercial Code to modify this general rule by giving the courts power "to police explicitly against the contracts or clauses which they find to be unconscionable. . . . The principle is one of the prevention of oppression and unfair surprise." (See the official comment appended to the statute in the note on page 193, McKinney's Uniform Commercial Code, volume 62½ Part I.)

The comment cites Campbell Soup Company v. Wentz, 3 Cir., 172 F.2d 80, to illustrate the principle. It is interesting to note that the *Wentz* case involved oppression with respect to the price Campbell Company agreed to pay for carrots, the price specified in the contract being $23.00 to $33.00 a ton. In the particular case Wentz, the farmer, refused to deliver carrots at the contract price, since the market price at such time had increased to $90.00 a ton. The Court of Appeals said "We think it too hard a bargain and too one-sided an agreement to entitle the plaintiff to relief in a court of conscience" (p. 83).

In the instant case the court finds that here, too, it was "too hard a bargain" and the conscience of the court will not permit the enforcement of the contract as written. Therefore the plaintiff will not be permitted to recover on the basis of the price set forth in the retail installment contract, namely $900.00 plus $245.85 as a service charge.

However, since the defendants have not returned the refrigerator-freezer, they will be required to reimburse the plaintiff for the cost to the plaintiff, namely $348.00. No allowance is made on account of any commissions the plaintiff may have paid to salesmen or for legal fees, service charges or any other matters of overhead.

Accordingly the plaintiff may have judgment against both defendants in the amount of $348.00 with interest, less the $32.00 paid on account, leaving a net balance of $316.00 with interest from December 26, 1964.

FROSTIFRESH CORP. v. REYNOSO

Supreme Court, Appellate Term, Second Department, New York, 1967.
54 Misc.2d 119, 281 N.Y.S.2d 964.

PER CURIAM. Judgment unanimously reversed, without costs, and a new trial ordered limited to an assessment of plaintiff's damages and entry of judgment thereon.

While the evidence clearly warrants a finding that the contract was unconscionable (Uniform Commercial Code, § 2–302), we are of the opinion that plaintiff should recover its net cost for the refrigerator-freezer, plus a reasonable profit, in addition to trucking and service charges necessarily incurred and reasonable finance charges.

Questions

1. What was the deal in *Frostifresh*? Was there a legal reason for the court to enforce the buyer's promise? Was it overridden by other reasons? What were they?

2. Were the overriding reasons internal to the law of contracts (e.g., autonomy-based reasons), or external (e.g., reasons of distributive justice or paternalism)?

3. Did the court in *Toker* cite *Frostifresh* accurately?

4. *Problems.*

a. Assume the facts are as in *Frostifresh*, except that the contract was written in Spanish. Same result?

b. Assume the facts are as in *Frostifresh*, except that there was no evidence of high pressure sales tactics and the salesman translated the contract into Spanish. Same result?

c. Assume the facts are as in *Frostifresh*, except that the total sales price was $696.00, including all charges and fees. Same result?

SECTION 4. STANDARD FORM CONTRACTS

NOTE ON STANDARD FORM CONTRACTS

Most contracting is done today on standard form contracts. Such contracts are drafted in advance of any particular transaction. They are pre-printed with blanks for the parties to fill in the identity of one party, the goods or services to be provided, price, time for performance, and little else, with all other terms standard for all transactions of the type. Among the terms that are standardized will be exculpatory clauses, disclaimers or limitations of warranty, arbitration clauses, notice requirements, and other terms that become important only after a dispute has arisen. Few people bother to read the "fine print." Not infrequently, the forms are designed to discourage careful reading. Even those who read the fine print may underestimate their significance because they deal with remote and unwelcome contingencies.

Forms are sometimes drafted by trade associations representing both sides to a standard transaction. In that case, the terms are likely to be fairly balanced. Often, however, they are drafted by the lawyers for one of the parties. Thus, automobile manufacturers have standard form sales agreements used by their respective dealers, parking lot and theater tickets contain contract terms that are accepted by taking the ticket, credit card agreements contain standard terms; insurance companies often do not even send the insureds copies of the full policies unless requested. When one party drafts the standard form, the undickered-for terms are apt to be one-sided. In some markets, such as automobile warranties, competition may constrain this tendency. In other situations, such as exculpatory clauses in residential leases, tenants probably do not shop for attractive contract clauses.

Standard form contracts serve some highly useful functions. Within an enterprise, they are an efficient means of organizing sales on terms acceptable to the firm, constraining sales personnel from going off in many directions without incurring high costs of supervision. A firm can use copies of the form to communicate among its parts, as when sales sends an order to production with a copy to billing, and production sends a copy with the product to shipping. Customer service does not need a file with copies of all the firm's contracts; when a customer calls with a complaint, service personnel can read the firm's obligations from the relevant standard contract. Moreover, customer service personnel need not be trained to worry about legal relationships that vary from sale to sale. Should litigation occur, the result in one case will be readily transferable to many other disputes involving the same form. Consequently, the costs of doing business are less with standardized contracts, allowing parties greater flexibility on matters such as price. The law often respects these functions. See RESTATEMENT (SECOND) OF CONTRACTS § 211(2).

On the other hand, standardized form contracts expose how great can be the gap between objective and subjective theories of contract formation. A buyer's signature on a lengthy form provided by the seller traditionally binds buyer to all of the terms on the form, whether they were read, understood and appreciated, or not. Yet, since it is common even for sophisticated people not to read the fine print, the contract may not represent a knowing agreement on all of its terms. To be sure, it would wreak havoc with modern efficient business practices to hold that the parties are bound only by the terms they filled in on the form. But it may inflict injustice to allow form providers to effectively dictate terms. The courts have as yet found it difficult to accommodate both concerns in a principled doctrine. See generally Rakoff, *Contracts of Adhesion: An Essay in Reconstruction*, 96 Harv.L.Rev.1173 (1983).

NOTE ON ARBITRATION

With dramatically increasing frequency in the United States, contract parties are including arbitration clauses in their contracts. The main thrust of such clauses is that all disputes arising out of or in connection with the contract shall be settled by arbitration. When the parties so agree and a dispute arises, they must proceed to arbitration in a private forum in lieu of litigation in a court of law. *See* Federal Arbitration Act ("F.A.A.") §§ 3, 4.

Though roughly similar, arbitration differs significantly from litigation. For example, the case is heard and decided by a disinterested, nongovernmental decision-maker called the "arbitrator" (or "arbitral tribunal" where there are several arbitrators) instead of a judge or judge and jury. The parties can determine their own procedure as appropriate for their case instead of following a fixed procedure designed for a wide variety of cases. The arbitrator need not be a lawyer and may be an expert in the subject matter of the dispute. In part because there are no juries in arbitration, the adjudicative rules of evidence need not apply. The arbitrator still hears the parties' evidence and arguments. After doing so, the arbitrator issues an "award", which purports to settle the dispute. Arbitrations are often more private, flexible, faster and cheaper than litigation. Yet, a winning party can easily enforce an award as though it were the judgment of a court. *See* F.A.A. § 13.

Historically, courts were hostile to arbitration; thus, they often refused to enforce agreements to arbitrate future disputes. Recently, the U.S. Supreme Court and many state courts have expanded the enforceability of such agreements. There is, in the Court's words, an "emphatic federal policy in favor of arbitral dispute resolution." Mitsubishi Motors Corp. v. Soler Chrysler–Plymouth, Inc., 473 U.S. 614, 631, 105 S.Ct. 3346, 87 L.Ed.2d 444 (1985). In such a favorable environment, it is perhaps not surprising that some parties have sought to take unjust advantage of others by manipulating them into one-sided agreements to arbitrate. Arbitration law is ill-suited to protect against questionable practices when making arbitral agreements. *See* F.A.A. § 2. Agreements to arbitrate, however, are contracts. The following cases and materials explore contract law's capacity to police unjust arbitral agreements notwithstanding the strong policy in favor of arbitration.

FEDERAL ARBITRATION ACT, §§ 2, 3, 4

WASHINGTON MUTUAL FINANCE GROUP v. BAILEY

United States Court of Appeals, Fifth Circuit, 2004.
364 F.3d 260.

JOLLY, C.J: This case requires us to determine the effect of an individual's illiteracy on the enforcement of an arbitration agreement, which the individual admits he signed, but because of his illiteracy, denies he understood. The district court held that the individual's illiteracy, coupled with a lack of oral disclosure, rendered the agreement procedurally unconscionable. We conclude the district court erred and REVERSE.

Washington Mutual Finance Group ("WM Finance") is a financial institution providing, among other things, consumer credit services. John Phinizee, Willie Curry ("Curry"), Beulah Tate ("Tate"), Violet Smith ("Smith"), John Bailey ("Bailey") and Helen Spellman ("Spellman") (collectively "the Illiterate Appellees") obtained loans from WM Finance or its predecessors. As part of the same transaction, the Illiterate Appellees also purchased credit, life, disability, and property insurance from American Bankers Life Assurance Company of Florida, American Security Insurance Company, Union Security Life Insurance Company and American Bankers Insurance Company of Florida (collectively "the Insurer Appellants"). Each of the Illiterate Appellees signed an agreement to arbitrate any disputes they might have with WM Finance.

Sometime thereafter, a dispute did arise. The Illiterate Appellees and Miriah Phinizee, wife of Illiterate Appellee John Phinizee, sued WM Finance and the Insurer Appellants in Mississippi state court, alleging primarily that they were sold and charged for insurance that they did not need or want. In response, WM Finance brought separate federal actions under the Federal Arbitration Act (FAA). [9 U.S.C. § 4] against the Illiterate Appellees and Miriah Phinizee, seeking an order staying the state actions and compelling the appellees to arbitrate their disputes. The Insurer Appellants, who were also defendants in the state court suit, intervened. The district court consolidated the cases into the instant one. The district court was persuaded by the Illiterate Appellees' arguments. It found that they were illiterate and that WM Finance never specifically informed them that they were signing arbitration agreements. The district court went on to conclude that these circumstances rendered the arbitration agreements procedurally unconscionable and therefore unenforceable. The district court also found that Miriah Phinizee did not sign an arbitration agreement and therefore could not be compelled to arbitrate. Accordingly, the district court denied WM Finance's motion to compel arbitration, denied the Insurer Appellants' motion for summary judgment, and granted the Illiterate Appellees' motion to dismiss.

.　.　.

We review a grant or denial of a petition to compel arbitration pursuant to § 4 of the FAA de novo. *Will-Drill Resources, Inc. v. Samson Resources Co.*, 352 F.3d 211, 214 (5th Cir. 2003). "The FAA expresses a strong national policy favoring arbitration of disputes, and all doubts concerning the arbitrability of claims should be resolved in favor of arbitration." *Primerica Life Ins. Co. v. Brown*, 304 F.3d 469, 471 (5th Cir. 2002). Courts conduct a bifurcated inquiry to determine whether parties should be compelled to arbitrate a dispute. *Id.* First, the court must determine whether the parties agreed to arbitrate the dispute. Once the court finds that the parties agreed to arbitrate, it must consider whether any federal statute or policy renders the claims nonarbitrable. *Id.* In this case, the district court based its refusal to compel arbitration on a finding that there was no valid or enforceable arbitration agreement between the parties. It did not find, nor do the Illiterate Appellees now argue, that the arbitration clause here is rendered unenforceable by any contrary federal statute or policy. Accordingly, the sole question presented by this appeal is whether the arbitration agreement admittedly signed by the Illiterate Appellees is valid.

The purpose of the FAA is to give arbitration agreements the same force and effect as other contracts–no more and no less. 9 U.S.C. § 2. *See Pennzoil Exploration and Production Co. v. Ramco Energy Ltd.*, 139 F.3d 1061, 1064 (5th Cir. 1998) ("Arbitration is a matter of contract between the parties"). Accordingly, in determining whether the parties agreed to arbitrate a certain matter, courts apply the contract law of the particular state that governs the agreement. *First Options of Chicago, Inc. v. Kaplan*, 514 U.S. 938, 944, 115 S.Ct. 1920, 131 L.Ed.2d 985 (1995). Both parties acknowledge that this means Mississippi state law applies here.

Under Mississippi law, a contract can be unconscionable in one of two ways: procedurally and/or substantively. *Russell v. Performance Toyota, Inc.*, 826 So.2d 719, 725 (Miss. 2002)....

Procedural unconscionability is proved by showing "a lack of knowledge, lack of voluntariness, inconspicuous print, the use of complex legalistic language, disparity in sophistication or bargaining power of the parties and/or a lack of opportunity to study the contract and inquire about the contract terms." *Id.* (citations omitted). There are no allegations here that the Illiterate Appellees were coerced into signing the arbitration agreements in question, nor is the complexity of the legal language, conspicuousness of the print or the relative bargaining power of the two parties in dispute here today. Evidently recognizing the absence of these more customary grounds, the district court based its finding of procedural unconscionability on its conclusion that the Illiterate Appellees' professed illiteracy rendered them unable to comprehend the arbitration agreement and that they therefore lacked any form of knowledge about the agreement when they signed it. The district court also appeared to rest its finding of unconscionability on the fact that WM Finance failed specifically to inform the Illiterate Appellees that they were signing an arbitration agreement after the Illiterate Appellees had informed WM Finance of their inability to read.

We find both bases of the district court's unconscionability conclusion unsupported by Mississippi law. First, the district court erred in concluding that the Illiterate Appellees' inability to read rendered them incapable of possessing adequate knowledge of the arbitration agreement they signed. The Mississippi Supreme Court has held that, as a matter of law, an individual's inability to understand a contract because of his or her illiteracy is not a sufficient basis for concluding that a contract is unenforceable. *See Mixon v. Sovereign Camp, W.O.W.*, 155 Miss. 841, 125 So. 413, 415 (1930) (noting that "the suggestion of illiteracy cannot prevail, for the manifest reason that there cannot be two separate departments in the law of contracts, one for the educated and another for those who are not"). This case is an old one, but its holding has never been contested and accords with subsequent Mississippi Supreme Court cases presenting similar issues. For example, Mississippi courts have consistently held that parties to an insurance contract have an affirmative duty to read that contract and thus, knowledge of the contract's terms is imputed to those parties irrespective of whether they read the contract. In *Russell*, the Mississippi Supreme Court found that "[i]n Mississippi, a person is charged with knowing the contents of any document that he executes." 826 So.2d at 726. Therefore, "[a] person cannot avoid a written contract which he has entered into on the ground that he did not read it or have it read to him." *J.R. Watkins Co. v. Runnels*, 252 Miss. 87, 172 So.2d 567, 571 (1965) (emphasis added). *See Tel–Com Management, Inc. v. Waveland Resort Inns, Inc.*, 782 So.2d 149, 153 (Miss. 2001) (holding that "[t]o permit a party when sued on a written contract, to admit that he signed it ... but did not read it or know its stipulations would absolutely destroy the value of all contracts. . . .

Accordingly, we hold that under Mississippi law, the inability to read and understand the arbitration agreement does not render the agreement unconscionable or otherwise unenforceable.

We similarly reject the district court's holding that the agreement is unconscionable and unenforceable because WM Finance failed specifically to inform the Illiterate Appellees that they were signing an arbitration agreement after having been made aware of the Illiterate Appellees' inability to read. As we previously have noted, Mississippi law charges parties to a contract with the obligation to read that contract or "have it read to [them]," *Russell*, 826 So.2d at 726, and does not permit such a party "to admit that he signed it.... but did not read it or know its stipulations." *Tel–Com Management Inc.*, 782 So.2d at 153. We find no authority supporting the district court's assertion that illiteracy removes this affirmative obligation from a signatory.

Questions

1. Was there "mutual assent" between the illiterate appellants and the lender with respect to the arbitration clause? Would the court's reasoning apply to someone who read the contract but did not understand the arbitration clause? How many people who sign a contract containing an arbitration clause understand what arbitration is?

2. Would it make a difference whether the relevant jurisdiction follows the objective or subjective theory of contract formation? Which theory should be favored in a case like *Washington Mutual*? If the subjective theory should be favored, should it be applied to all form contracts, which are rarely read completely by those who sign them? (Over 90% of all contracts probably are form contracts.) Or should it only be favored in the cases of consumers, employees and similarly "unsophisticated" parties? If a jurisdiction follows the subjective theory in cases involving all or some form contracts, should the law of offer and acceptance follow the same theory? Or should there be a different contract law for unsophisticated parties?

3.   Contracts are sometimes "assigned" to parties who were not involved in their formation ("third parties"). That is, a third party may by assignment acquire rights under a contract it did not make. A creditor, for example, may assign its right to repayment of a loan to a collection agency. If the law were as the district court would have it in *Washington Mutual*, what effect would it have on the assignment of contracts? Would that effect be a good thing?

RESTATEMENT 2D OF CONTRACTS § 211

BROEMMER v. ABORTION SERVICES OF PHOENIX, LTD.

Supreme Court of Arizona, In Banc, 1992.
173 Ariz. 148, 840 P.2d 1013.

MOELLER, VICE CHIEF JUSTICE.... Melinda Kay Broemmer (plaintiff) asks this court to review a court of appeals opinion that held that an "Agreement to Arbitrate" which she signed prior to undergoing a clinical abortion is an enforceable, albeit an adhesive, contract. Broemmer v. Otto, 169 Ariz. 543, 821 P.2d 204 (1991). The opinion affirmed the trial court's grant of summary judgment in favor of Abortion Services of Phoenix and Dr. Otto (defendants). Because we hold the agreement to arbitrate is unenforceable as against plaintiff, we reverse the trial court and vacate in part the court of appeals opinion....

FACTS AND PROCEDURAL HISTORY

In December 1986, plaintiff, an Iowa resident, was 21 years old, unmarried, and 16 or 17 weeks pregnant. She was a high school graduate earning less than $100.00 a week and had no medical benefits. The father-to-be insisted that plaintiff have an abortion, but her parents advised against it. Plaintiff's uncontested affidavit describes the time as one of considerable confusion and emotional and physical turmoil for her.

Plaintiff's mother contacted Abortion Services of Phoenix and made an appointment for her daughter for December 29, 1986. During their visit to the clinic that day, plaintiff and her mother expected, but did not receive, information and counselling on alternatives to abortion and the nature of the operation. When plaintiff and her mother arrived at the clinic, plaintiff was escorted into an adjoining room and asked to complete three forms, one of which is the agreement to arbitrate at issue in this case. The agreement to arbitrate included language that "any dispute aris[ing] between the Parties as a result of the fees and/or services" would be settled by binding arbitration and that "any arbitrators appointed by the AAA [American Arbitration Association] shall be licensed medical doctors who specialize in obstetrics/gynecology." The two other documents plaintiff completed at the same time were a 2–page consent-to-operate form and a questionnaire asking for a detailed medical history. Plaintiff completed all three forms in less than 5 minutes and returned them to the front desk. Clinic staff made no attempt to explain the agreement to plaintiff before or after she signed, and did not provide plaintiff with copies of the forms.

After plaintiff returned the forms to the front desk, she was taken into an examination room where pre-operation procedures were performed. She was then instructed to return at 7:00 a.m. the next morning for the termination procedure. Plaintiff returned the following day and Doctor Otto performed the abortion. As a result of the procedure, plaintiff suffered a punctured uterus that required medical treatment.

Plaintiff filed a malpractice complaint in June 1988, approximately 1 1/2 years after the medical procedure. By the time litigation commenced, plaintiff could recall completing and signing the medical history and consent-to-operate forms, but could not recall signing the agreement to arbitrate. Defendants moved to dismiss, contending that the trial court lacked subject matter jurisdiction because arbitration was required. In opposition, plaintiff submitted affidavits that remain uncontroverted. The trial court considered the affidavits, apparently treated the motion to dismiss as one for summary judgment, and granted summary judgment to the defendants. Plaintiff's motion to vacate, quash or set aside the order, or to stay the claim pending arbitration, was denied.

On appeal, the court of appeals held that although the contract was one of adhesion, it was nevertheless enforceable because it did not fall outside plaintiff's reasonable expectations and was not unconscionable. Following the court of appeals opinion, the parties stipulated to dismiss the Ottos from the lawsuit and from this appeal. We granted plaintiff's petition for review.

ISSUE

Plaintiff presents 5 potential issues in her petition for review. Some of the parties and amici have urged us to announce a "bright-line" rule of broad applicability concerning the enforceability of arbitration agreements. Arbitration proceedings are statutorily authorized in Arizona, A.R.S. §§ 12–1501 to–1518, and arbitration plays an important role in dispute resolution, as do other salutary methods of alternative dispute resolution. Important principles of contract law and of freedom of contract are intertwined with questions relating to agreements to utilize alternative methods of dispute resolution. We conclude it would be unwise to accept the invitation to attempt to establish some "bright-line" rule of broad applicability in this case. We will instead resolve the one issue which is dispositive: Under the undisputed facts in this case, is the agreement to arbitrate enforceable against plaintiff? We hold that it is not.

Discussion

I. The Contract is One of Adhesion

When the facts are undisputed, this court is not bound by the trial court's conclusions and may make its own analysis of the facts or legal instruments on which the case turns. *Tovrea Land & Cattle Co. v. Linsenmeyer*, 100 Ariz. 107, 114, 412 P.2d 47, 51 (1966). A.R.S. § 12–1501 authorizes written agreements to arbitrate and provides that they are "valid, enforceable and irrevocable, save upon such grounds as exist at law or in equity for the revocation of any contract." Thus, the enforceability of the agreement to arbitrate is determined by principles of general contract law. The court of appeals concluded, and we agree, that, under those principles, the contract in this case was one of adhesion.

An adhesion contract is typically a standardized form "offered to consumers of goods and services on essentially a 'take it or leave it' basis without affording the consumer a realistic opportunity to bargain and under such conditions that the consumer cannot obtain the desired product or services except by acquiescing in the form contract." *Wheeler v. St. Joseph Hosp.*, 63 Cal.App.3d 345, 356, 133 Cal.Rptr. 775, 783 (1976) (citations omitted).... Likewise, in *Contractual Problems in the Enforcement of Agreements to Arbitrate Medical Malpractice*, 58 Va. L.Rev. 947, 988 (1972), Professor Stanley Henderson recognized "the essence of an adhesion contract is that bargaining position and leverage enable one party 'to select and control risks assumed under the contract.'" (quoting Friedrich Kessler, *Contracts of Adhesion—Some Thoughts About Freedom of Contract*, 43 Colum.L.Rev. 629 (1943)).

The printed form agreement signed by plaintiff in this case possesses all the characteristics of a contract of adhesion. The form is a standardized contract offered to plaintiff on a "take it or leave it" basis. In addition to removing from the courts any potential dispute concerning fees or services, the drafter inserted additional terms potentially advantageous to itself requiring that any arbitrator appointed by the American Arbitration Association be a licensed medical doctor specializing in obstetrics/gynecology. The contract was not negotiated but was, instead, prepared by defendant and presented to plaintiff as a condition of treatment. Staff at the clinic neither explained its terms to plaintiff nor indicated that she was free to refuse to sign the form; they merely represented to plaintiff that she had to complete the three forms. The conditions under which the clinic offered plaintiff the services were on a "take it or leave it" basis, and the terms of service were not negotiable. Applying general contract law to the undisputed facts, the court of appeals correctly held that the contract was one of adhesion.

II. Reasonable Expectations

Our conclusion that the contract was one of adhesion is not, of itself, determinative of its enforceability. "[A] contract of adhesion is fully enforceable according to its terms [citations omitted] unless certain other factors are present which, under established legal rules—legislative or judicial—operate to render it otherwise." *Graham v. Scissor–Tail, Inc.*, 28 Cal.3d 807, 171 Cal.Rptr. 604, 611, 623 P.2d 165, 172 (1981) (footnotes omitted). To determine whether this contract of adhesion is enforceable, we look to two factors: the reasonable expectations of the adhering party and whether the contract is unconscionable. As the court stated in *Graham*:

> Generally speaking, there are two judicially imposed limitations on the enforcement of adhesion contracts or provisions thereof. The first is that such a contract or provision which does not fall within the reasonable expectations of the weaker or "adhering" party will not be enforced against him. [citations omitted] The second—a principle of equity applicable to all contracts generally—is that a contract or provision, even if consistent with the reasonable expectations of the parties, will be denied enforcement if, considered in its context, it is unduly oppressive or "unconscionable."

171 Cal.Rptr. at 612, 623 P.2d at 172–73 (citations omitted)....

Plaintiff argues that the trial court should have adopted, and we should now adopt, the analysis provided in *Obstetrics & Gynecologists v. Pepper*, 101 Nev. 105, 693 P.2d 1259 (1985), because it is virtually indistinguishable from the present case. In *Pepper*, the patient was required to sign an agreement before receiving treatment which waived her right to jury trial and submitted all disputes to arbitration. The clinic did not explain the contents of the agreement to the patient. The clinic's practice was to have staff instruct patients to complete two medical history forms and the agreement to arbitrate and to inform patients that any questions would be answered. If the patient refused to sign the agreement, the clinic refused treatment.

The plaintiff in *Pepper* signed the agreement, but did not recall doing so, nor did she recall having the agreement explained to her. The plaintiff later brought suit for injuries suffered due to improperly prescribed oral contraceptives. The trial court made no findings of fact or conclusions of law, but the Nevada Supreme Court, upon review of the record before it, held the agreement unenforceable because plaintiff did not give a knowing consent to the agreement to arbitrate.

The facts in the instant case present an even stronger argument in favor of holding the agreement unenforceable than do the facts in *Pepper*. In both cases, plaintiffs stated that they did not recall signing the agreement to arbitrate or having it explained to them. Unlike the clinic in *Pepper*, the clinic in this case did not show that it was the procedure of clinic staff to offer to explain the agreement to patients. The clinic did not explain the purpose of the form to plaintiff and did not show whether plaintiff was required to sign the form or forfeit treatment. In *Pepper*, the fact that both parties were waiving their right to a jury trial was explicit, which is not so in the present case.

Clearly, the issues of knowing consent and reasonable expectations are closely related and intertwined. In *Darner Motor Sales, Inc. v.*

Universal Underwriters Ins. Co., 140 Ariz. 383, 682 P.2d 388 (1984), this court used the Restatement (Second) of Contracts § 211 (Standardized Agreements), as a guide to analyzing, among other things, contracts that contain non-negotiated terms. The comment to subsection (3), quoted with approval in *Darner*, states in part:

> Although customers typically adhere to standardized agreements and are bound by them without even appearing to know the standard terms in detail, they are not bound to unknown terms which are beyond the range of reasonable expectation.

See 140 Ariz. at 391, 682 P.2d at 396.

The Restatement focuses our attention on whether it was beyond plaintiff's reasonable expectations to expect to arbitrate her medical malpractice claims, which includes waiving her right to a jury trial, as part of the filling out of the three forms under the facts and circumstances of this case. Clearly, there was no conspicuous or explicit waiver of the fundamental right to a jury trial or any evidence that such rights were knowingly, voluntarily and intelligently waived. The only evidence presented compels a finding that waiver of such fundamental rights was beyond the reasonable expectations of plaintiff. Moreover, as Professor Henderson writes, "[i]n attempting to effectuate reasonable expectations consistent with a standardized medical contract, a court will find less reason to regard the bargaining process as suspect if there are no terms unreasonably favorable to the stronger party." Henderson, supra, at 995. In this case failure to explain to plaintiff that the agreement required all potential disputes, including malpractice disputes, to be heard only by an arbitrator who was a licensed obstetrician/gynecologist requires us to view the "bargaining" process with suspicion. It would be unreasonable to enforce such a critical term against plaintiff when it is not a negotiated term and defendant failed to explain it to her or call her attention to it.

Plaintiff was under a great deal of emotional stress, had only a high school education, was not experienced in commercial matters, and is still not sure "what arbitration is." Given the circumstances under which the agreement was signed and the nature of the terms included therein, our reading of *Pepper, Darner*, the Restatement and the affidavits in this case compel us to conclude that the contract fell outside plaintiff's reasonable expectations and is, therefore, unenforceable. Because of this holding, it is unnecessary for us to determine whether the contract is also unconscionable.

III.   *A Comment on The Dissent*

In view of the concern expressed by the dissent, we restate our firm conviction that arbitration and other methods of alternative dispute resolution play important and desirable roles in our system of dispute resolution. We encourage their use. When agreements to arbitrate are freely and fairly entered, they will be welcomed and enforced. They will not, however, be exempted from the usual rules of contract law, as A.R.S. § 12–1501 itself makes clear.

. . .

MARTONE, JUSTICE, dissenting. The court's conclusion that the agreement to arbitrate was outside the plaintiff's reasonable expectations is without basis in law or fact. I fear today's decision reflects a preference for litigation over alternative dispute resolution that I had thought was behind us. I would affirm the court of appeals.

We begin with the undisputed facts that the court ignores. Appendix "A" to this dissent is the agreement to arbitrate. At the top it states in bold capital letters "PLEASE READ THIS CONTRACT CAREFULLY AS IT EFFECTS [sic] YOUR LEGAL RIGHTS." Directly under that in all capital letters are the words "AGREEMENT TO ARBITRATE." The recitals indicate that "the Parties deem it to be in their respective best interest to settle any such dispute as expeditiously and economically as possible." The parties agreed that disputes over services provided would be settled by arbitration in accordance with the rules of the American Arbitration Association. They further agreed that the arbitrators appointed by the American Arbitration Association would be licensed medical doctors who specialize in obstetrics/gynecology. Plaintiff, an adult, signed the document.

Under A.R.S. § 12–1501, a written contract to submit to arbitration any controversy that might arise between the parties is "valid, enforceable and irrevocable, save upon such grounds as exist at law or in equity for the revocation of any contract." The statute applies to any controversy. Under A.R.S. § 12–1503, if the arbitration agreement provides a method of appointment of arbitrators, "this method shall be followed." Under A.R.S. § 12–1518, the American Arbitration Association is expressly acknowledged as an entity that the state itself may use in connection with arbitration. There is judicial review of any award. A.R.S. § 12–1512. Thus, on the face of it, the contract to arbitrate is plainly reasonable and enforceable unless there are grounds to revoke it. A.R.S. § 12–1501.

The court seizes upon the doctrine of reasonable expectations to revoke this contract. But there is nothing in this record that would warrant a finding that an agreement to arbitrate a malpractice claim was not within the reasonable expectations of the parties. On this record, the exact opposite is likely to be true. For all we know, both sides in this case might wish to avoid litigation like the plague and seek the more harmonious waters of alternative dispute resolution. Nor is there anything in this record that would suggest that arbitration is bad. Where is the harm? In the end, today's decision reflects a preference in favor of litigation that is not shared by the courts of other states and the courts of the United States.

In *Doyle v. Giuliucci*, 62 Cal.2d 606, 43 Cal.Rptr. 697, 699, 401 P.2d 1, 3 (1965), Chief Justice Roger J. Traynor of the California Supreme

Court said, in connection with a medical malpractice claim, that "[t]he arbitration provision in such contracts is a reasonable restriction, for it does no more than specify a forum for the settlement of disputes." And, in *Madden v. Kaiser Foundation Hospitals*, 17 Cal.3d 699, 131 Cal.Rptr. 882, 890, 552 P.2d 1178, 1186 (1976), the California Supreme Court outlined "the benefits of the arbitral forum":

> [t]he speed and economy of arbitration, in contrast to the expense and delay of jury trial, could prove helpful to all parties; the simplified procedures and relaxed rules of evidence in arbitration may aid an injured plaintiff in presenting his case. Plaintiffs with less serious injuries, who cannot afford the high litigation expenses of court or jury trial, disproportionate to the amount of their claim, will benefit especially from the simplicity and economy of arbitration; that procedure could facilitate the adjudication of minor malpractice claims which cannot economically be resolved in a judicial forum.

The Federal Arbitration Act, 9 U.S.C. § 2, is just like Arizona's, A.R.S. § 12–1501. There was a time when judicial antipathy towards arbitration prevailed. Poor Justice Frankfurter had to say in dissent in *Wilko v. Swan*, 346 U.S. 427, 439, 74 S.Ct. 182, 189, 98 L.Ed. 168 (1953) that "[t]here is nothing in the record before us, nor in the facts of which we can take judicial notice, to indicate that the arbitral system ... would not afford the plaintiff the rights to which he is entitled."

Justice Frankfurter's views have now been vindicated. The Supreme Court of the United States has upheld arbitration agreements under the Federal Arbitration Act in a variety of contexts, from the commercial setting in *Shearson/American Express Inc. v. McMahon*, 482 U.S. 220, 107 S.Ct. 2332, 96 L.Ed.2d 185 (1987) (Securities Exchange Act of 1934 and RICO claims) and *Rodriguez de Quijas v. Shearson/American Express, Inc.*, 490 U.S. 477, 109 S.Ct. 1917, 104 L.Ed.2d 526 (1989) (Securities Act of 1933) to employment discrimination claims. *Gilmer v. Interstate/Johnson Lane Corp.*, 500 U.S. 20, 111 S.Ct. 1647, 114 L.Ed.2d 26 (1991) (Age Discrimination in Employment Act claim).

Indeed, in *Gilmer*, the Supreme Court expressly rejected the arguments that regrettably this court has accepted. 500 U.S. at 30–33, 111 S.Ct. at 1654–55. The Supreme Court has expressly rejected the "outmoded presumption" and "suspicion of arbitration as a method of weakening the protections afforded in the substantive law." *Rodriguez de Quijas*, 490 U.S. at 481, 109 S.Ct. at 1920.

Against this background, how does this court reach its conclusion that arbitration is beyond the reasonable expectations of the parties? Its reliance on *Obstetrics and Gynecologists v. Pepper*, 101 Nev. 105, 693 P.2d 1259 (1985), *Darner Motor Sales, Inc. v. Universal Underwriters Insurance Co.*, 140 Ariz. 383, 682 P.2d 388 (1984), and the *Restatement (Second) of Contracts* § 211 (1979), is misplaced.

Pepper is a brief per curiam opinion of the Nevada Supreme Court which merely affirmed the finding of a trial court. The trial court held a hearing to determine whether there was an enforceable arbitration contract. However, the trial court did not make findings of facts and conclusions of law. That court simply denied a motion to stay pending arbitration. The Nevada Supreme Court said "[t]he district court could certainly have found that the arbitration agreement was an adhesion contract." 693 P.2d at 1260. It then said "[s]ince appellant's counsel failed to pursue the entry of findings of facts and conclusions of law, we are bound to presume that the district court found that respondent did not give a knowing consent to the arbitration agreement prepared by appellant clinic." *Id.*, 693 P.2d at 1261. If *Pepper* stands for anything, it stands for the proposition that "knowing consent" is a factual question, and that an appellate court will affirm a factual finding if there is any evidence to support it. The basis for the court's decision was "knowing consent" under Nevada law, not reasonable expectations under ours.

Nor are *Darner* and the *Restatement* support for this court's conclusion. *Darner* held that an adhesive contract term that is "contrary to the negotiated agreement made by the parties," 140 Ariz. at 387, 682 P.2d at 392, will not be enforced because it collides with expectations that "have been induced by the making of a promise." 140 Ariz. at 390, 682 P.2d at 395 (quoting 1 Corbin, *Contracts* § 1 at 2 (1963)). The defendant here did not promise the plaintiff that malpractice claims could be litigated. Thus, the agreement to arbitrate is not contrary to any negotiated deal.

Gordinier v. Aetna Casualty & Surety Co., 154 Ariz. 266, 742 P.2d 277 (1987), of course, extended *Darner* to the entire scope of the *Restatement (Second) of Contracts* § 211 (1979). But even that section does not support today's decision. Under *Restatement (Second) of Contracts* § 211(3), standardized agreements are enforceable except where a party has reason to believe that the other party would not manifest assent if he knew that the writing contained a particular term. *Comment f* to § 211 tells us:

> Such a belief or assumption may be shown by the prior negotiations or inferred from the circumstances. Reason to believe may be inferred from the fact that the term is bizarre or oppressive, from the fact that it eviscerates the non-standard terms explicitly agreed to, or from the fact that it eliminates the dominant purpose of the transaction. The inference is reinforced if the adhering party never had an opportunity to read the term, or if it is illegible or otherwise hidden from view.

Plainly, there are no facts in this case to support any of these factors. There were no prior negotiations that were contrary to arbitration. An agreement to arbitrate is hardly bizarre or oppressive. It is a preferred method of alternative dispute resolution that our legislature has expressly acknowledged in A.R.S. § 12–1501. Arbitration does not eviscerate any agreed terms. Nor does it eliminate the dominant purpose of the transaction. The plaintiff here had an opportunity to read the document, the document was legible and was hardly hidden from plaintiff's view. This arbitration agreement was in bold capital letters. Thus, the reasonable expectations standard of the *Restatement (Second) of Contracts* § 211 does not support this court's conclusion.

There is another reason why § 211(3) fails to support the court's conclusion. The Restatement (Second) of Contracts chapter 8 describes the whole range of unenforceable contracts. Its introductory note states:

> A particularly important change has been effected by statutes relating to arbitration, which have now been enacted in so many jurisdictions that it seems likely that even in the remaining states, there has been a change in the former judicial attitude of hostility toward agreements to arbitrate future disputes.... Such agreements are now widely used and serve the public interest by saving court time. The rules stated in this Chapter do not preclude their enforcement even in the absence of legislation.

Restatement (Second) of Contracts ch. 8, intro. note at 4 (emphasis added). It is difficult to reconcile the court's reliance on the Restatement in light of this.

The court tells us that there is no explicit waiver of the fundamental right to a jury trial in the arbitration agreement. But under Rule 38(d), Ariz.R.Civ.P., the failure of a party to serve a demand for a jury trial and file it constitutes a waiver by that party of a trial by jury. In contrast to the criminal process, no complicated proceeding is required to waive a trial by jury in a civil case. It is ironic that the majority prefers litigation, in which the plaintiff would lose her right to trial by jury by failing to know about it and demand it under Rule 38, but then somehow assumes that a document which in bold capital letters informs the plaintiff that it affects her legal rights and is denominated in bold capital letters as "agreement to arbitrate" is insufficient warning.

At bottom, all that could explain the court's decision is a preference for litigation over arbitration. The court expresses sympathy for the plaintiff as though arbitration were harmful to her interests. But Arizona public policy has long supported arbitration as good, not evil. Court annexed arbitration of civil actions under A.R.S. § 12–133 is now an entrenched part of our culture. About 90% of these cases end at arbitration and are not appealed. Arizona Supreme Court Commission on the Courts, Report of the Commission on the Courts 36 (1989). Indeed, the Commission on the Courts specifically recommended that medical malpractice cases be subject to alternative dispute resolution procedures. Id. at 38. It noted that many lawyers will not take a malpractice case unless the damages exceed $100,000. "A large number of potential plaintiffs, therefore, may never receive the representation and opportunity for compensation they deserve. Both plaintiff and defense attorneys indicate that they would prefer a different form of dispute resolution." Id. at 39.

... For all these reasons, I dissent.

APPENDIX A

**F. / ⁀. READ THIS CONTRACT C..⸗.f 'LLY
A⸗ IT EFFECTS YOUR LEGAL RIGHTS**

AGREEMENT TO ARBITRATE   DEC 2 9 1986

THIS AGREEMENT is made and entered into at Phoenix, Arizona this _____ day of _____ , 19___ , by and between Robert H. Tamis, M.D., Abortion Services of Phoenix, referred to hereinafter as Doctor, its agents, servants and employees and _____ referred to hereinafter as Patient. (Doctor and Patient hereinafter sometimes collectively referred to as Parties).

WITNESSETH:

WHEREAS, Doctor will be performing certain services on behalf of Patient; and

WHEREAS, the Parties hereto recognize that a dispute could develop regarding the fees and or services rendered by Doctor; and

WHEREAS, the Parties deem it to be in their respective best interest to settle any such dispute as expeditiously and economically as possible.

NOW, THEREFORE, in accordance with the provisions herein set forth, and other good and valuable consideration the sufficiency of which is hereby acknowledged, the Parties agree as follows.

1. In the event any dispute arises between the Parties as a result of the fees and/or services provided by Doctor the Parties hereto mutually agree that any such dispute shall be settled by binding arbitration in the City of Phoenix in accordance with the rules then prevailing of the American Arbitration Association (AAA). The Parties further agree that any arbitrators appointed by the AAA shall be licensed medical doctors who specialize in obstetrics/gynecology.

2. This Agreement shall be binding not only upon the parties hereto, but also as appropriate their respective heirs, devisees, personal representatives, guardians or any person deriving any claim through or on behalf of them.

It is understood by the Patient that he or she is not required to use the aforesaid Doctor and that there are numerous other physicians in Phoenix, Arizona who are qualified to provide the same services as aforesaid Doctor.

IN WITNESS WHEREOF, the Parties hereto have executed this Agreement the Day and year first above written.

Doctor   Patient

By _____   By _____
           Authorized Agent   Patient

                                             _____
                                             Patient's Spouse (if present)

The above parties appeared and signed this document before me on _____ day of _____ 198___ , in witness thereof I set my seal. _____

Questions

1. In *Broemmer,* what legal points does the majority make in support of its refusal to enforce the parties' agreement to arbitrate? What legal points does the dissent make? Assuming the court must follow the legal authorities (*i.e.,* putting justice aside for the moment), who gets the better of the argument?

2. Now consider the justice of the case. Does the majority or the dissent come to the more just conclusion? Why? Do the legal authorities highlight the facts which are crucial to the justice of the case?

3. Does it add anything to the court's analysis to find that the agreement to arbitrate was a contract of adhesion? Is the unconscionability doctrine limited to or dependent upon a contract of adhesion? Is the doctrine of reasonable expectations thus limited?

WE CARE HAIR DEVELOPMENT, INC. v. ENGEN

United States Court of Appeals, Seventh Circuit, 1999.
180 F.3d 838.

HARLINGTON WOOD, JR., CIRCUIT JUDGE. Defendants-appellants, franchisees of We Care Hair Development, Inc. ("We Care Hair"), appeal from a judgment of the district court ordering them to arbitrate their various state law claims against plaintiff-appellee We Care Hair and enjoining them from proceeding in a pending state court lawsuit.

BACKGROUND

. . .

... Doctor's Associates, Inc., is a Florida corporation owned by Frederick DeLuca and Peter Buck. Doctor's Associates, Inc., is the franchisor of the Subway sandwich shops and the fried chicken franchise chain Cajun Joe's. Doctor's Associates, Inc., together with John Amico, also owns We Care Hair, Inc., the franchisor of the We Care Hair salons.

All of the appellant-franchisees entered into franchise agreements with We Care Hair, Inc. Each of these franchise agreements contains a clause requiring arbitration as a condition precedent to the commencement of legal action for all disputes arising out of or relating to the franchise agreement. The franchise agreements all provide that they shall be governed by and construed in accordance with the laws of the State of Illinois. All of the franchisees were required to sublease their premises from a leasing company, We Care Hair Realty, which is an alter ego of We Care Hair, Inc. The rent under the subleases is the same as the rent under the master leases between the landlords and We Care Hair Realty, and the franchisees are directed to pay their rent directly to the landlords.

Under the subleases, arbitration is not required; the leasing company may file an eviction lawsuit against a franchisee for any breach of the sublease. The subleases contain cross-default provisions which make every breach of the franchise agreement a breach of the sublease. The uniform offering circular for We Care Hair salons clearly states that "the provisions in the franchise agreement concerning ... arbitration ... do not apply to [the] sublease." The offering circular also advises prospective franchisees that the leasing company, We Care Hair Realty, could terminate a franchisee's sublease without We Care Hair also terminating the franchise agreement, a situation which could render the franchise agreement valueless. Appellants concede that the offering circulars disclosed that, notwithstanding the arbitration clause in the franchise agreement, the leasing company could terminate the sublease and evict the franchisee for any breach of the sublease, including a breach of the franchise agreement.

ANALYSIS

. . .

Under the FAA, arbitration clauses "shall be valid, irrevocable, and enforceable, save upon such grounds as exist at law or in equity for the revocation of any contract." 9 U.S.C. § 2. In the present case, the district court found the arbitration clauses to be valid and enforceable and entered an order compelling arbitration. Appellants' contend that this ruling was in error because the arbitration clauses and the cross-default provisions in the subleases are both unconscionable and against public policy. We review a district court's decision to compel arbitration de novo. Kiefer Specialty Flooring, Inc. v. Tarkett, Inc., 174 F.3d 907, 909 (7th Cir.1999).

State contract defenses may be applied to invalidate arbitration clauses if those defenses apply to contracts generally. Doctor's Associates, Inc. v. Casarotto, 517 U.S. 681, 687, 116 S.Ct. 1652, 1656, 134 L.Ed.2d 902 (1996). In the present case, Illinois law applies. Appellants claim that the arbitration clause, when coupled with the cross-default provision of the sublease, is unconscionable because it requires the franchisees to arbitrate their claims while permitting the franchisor to litigate its claims through eviction actions filed in the name of the alter ego leasing company. As we have noted, "[i]n assessing whether a contractual provision should be disregarded as unconscionable, Illinois courts look to the circumstances existing at the time of the contract's formation, including the relative bargaining positions of the parties and whether the provision's operation would result in unfair surprise." Cognitest Corp. v. Riverside Pub. Co., 107 F.3d 493, 499 (7th Cir. 1997).... A contract is unconscionable when, viewed as a whole, "it is improvident, oppressive, or totally one-sided." Streams Sports Club, Ltd. v. Richmond, 99 Ill.2d 182, 75 Ill.Dec. 667, 457 N.E.2d 1226, 1232 (1983). "The presence of a commercially unreasonable term, in the sense of a term that no one in his right mind would have agreed to, can be relevant to drawing an inference of unconscionability but cannot be equated to it." The Original Great Am. Chocolate Chip Cookie Co., Inc. v. River Valley Cookies, Ltd., 970 F.2d 273, 281 (7th Cir.1992)....

The arbitration clauses in the present case cannot be viewed as creating unfair surprise. Before signing the franchise agreement and the sublease, each franchisee was provided with a copy of the uniform offering circular which clearly disclosed that the leasing company could bring eviction proceedings for any breach of the sublease, including a breach of the franchise agreement. Furthermore, the franchisees were "not vulnerable consumers or helpless workers," but rather "business people who bought a franchise." The Original Great Am. Chocolate Chip Cookie Co., Inc., 970 F.2d at 281. We cannot conclude that, in acquiring their franchises, the franchisees were "forced to swallow unpalatable terms." Id. The arbitration clauses, even when coupled with the cross-default provisions of the subleases, are not unconscionable.

Questions

1. What was the relevant contract in *We Care Hair Development*? Was it a standard form contract? A "contract of adhesion"? If it is standard and/or a contract of adhesion, what legal consequence should follow, if any?

2. Did the parties have relatively equal bargaining power? What is "bargaining power"? If the parties were unequal in this respect, what legal consequence should follow? By contrast, why might it matter that the franchisees "were 'not vulnerable consumers or helpless workers,' but rather 'business people who bought a franchise.' "?

3. Were the terms one-sided? In what respect? What legal consequence, if any, should follow from such one-sidedness? From one-sidedness and unequal bargaining power?

4. Did the franchisees give a knowing consent to the arbitration clause? Should a knowing consent be required when a party agrees to give up its right to a trial by jury? Did the franchisor explain the arbitration clause and the relation between the franchise and sublease agreements? Should this be required to avoid unfair surprise?

5. Did the franchisees have a meaningful choice when signing the franchise agreement? Should the franchisor have given them several contracts with differing terms among which the franchisees could choose? Do the franchisees have no meaningful choice when presented with one standard franchise agreement and one sublease like the one in *We Care Hair Development*?

Chapter 4

THE COMPENSATION PRINCIPLE

The law enforces promises mainly by compensating nonbreaching parties for unavoidable, foreseeable, and reasonably certain harms caused by a breach.

"The traditional goal of the law of contract remedies has not been compulsion of the promisor to perform his promise but compensation of the promisee for the loss resulting from breach." RESTATEMENT (SECOND) OF CONTRACTS, Introductory Note to Ch. 16. In general, the losses resulting from breach are understood as harms to the interests protected by the law of contracts generally. See Note on "Interests," "Rights," and "Duties," above at p. 7. These are the expectation, reliance, and restitution interests. RESTATEMENT (SECOND) OF CONTRACTS § 344. With exceptions, the laws of contract formation and enforcement aim at congruence. That is, in principle, the law holds that a contract is formed when one party has an expectation, reliance, or restitution interest arising from a promise and deserving of legal protection. That party then has a contract right, and the other has a duty to respect that right. Upon breach, the remedy generally aims at compensating the injured party for harm to the contractual interest that sustains the right, insofar as possible. Of course, such tidy symmetry is sometimes unattainable for reasons to be explored below. See Lon L. Fuller and William Perdue, *The Reliance Interest in Contract Damages*, 46 YALE L.J. 52, 373 (1936).

The compensation principle is easily understood at an abstract level. Its justification and practical implications are not so easy to grasp. In recent years, the advent of economic analysis of the law has made the way somewhat easier. Though controversial when applied to many legal problems, its value in explaining and evaluating the law of contract remedies is widely respected. As we shall see, the law prefers to put a party injured by a breach into the position he or she would have been in had the contract been performed, insofar as money can do so. That is, the law gives the injured party the benefit of the bargain by compensating for harm to the expectation interest. Identifying the expected position requires imagining how events would have unfolded when they did

273

not go that way in fact. Economics, as a discipline that traces the implications of rational behavior, helps to identify the expected position, at least in business contracts where both parties generally try to maximize profits. Consequently, economics helps us to assess whether existing legal rules are over- or undercompensatory.

Notice that this chapter is placed in a way that does not reflect the logical flow of contract analysis. Before awarding a remedy for breach, a court must determine whether there was a breach. In many cases, litigation centers on identifying and interpreting the terms of the contract and ascertaining whether obligations thereby created were or were not fulfilled. We will consider these topics in Chapters 5 and 6. We consider remedies first because the consequence of finding a breach will affect a court's propensity to find one. (Some instructors may take up this chapter before contract formation for an analogous reason.) Thus, to dramatize, if the consequence of finding a breach were life imprisonment, we would expect courts to be reluctant to find contracts and breaches at all. In fact, under the prevailing law, contract remedies are mild.

SECTION 1. COMPENSATION OR PUNISHMENT?

In the lion's share of cases, a breach of contract consists simply of a party's failure to do what he or she expressly or impliedly promised to do, without excuse or justification. Morally, promise-breaking is wrong. In law, however, it is not a tort. Many say that torts involve wrongs to the public, while promise-breaking is a private wrong because it affects only the parties. E.g., Parke–Hayden, Inc. v. Loews Theatre Management Corp., 789 F.Supp. 1257, 1267 (S.D.N.Y.1992). Consequently,

> Punitive damages are not recoverable for a breach of contract unless the conduct constituting the breach is also a tort for which punitive damages are recoverable.

RESTATEMENT (SECOND) OF CONTRACTS § 355. Why is this so? Often, the standard response is a doctrinaire assertion that "the purposes [sic] of awarding contract damages is to compensate the injured party.... For this reason, courts in contract cases do not award damages to punish the party in breach or to serve as an example to others unless the breach is also a tort...." Id., Comment a.

The distinction between public and private wrongs is hard to maintain. When Randolph hits Joel in a fight in Randolph's backyard, it seems as private a matter as when Randolph fails to deliver goods as promised. The immediate harms are confined to the parties. The fight yields a tort because the public has a general interest in containing violence. Joel can get punitive damages if Randolph started the fight maliciously. But the public also has a general interest in the security of contractual transactions. If Randolph withholds the goods maliciously, why should Joel not get punitive damages?

WHITE v. BENKOWSKI

Supreme Court of Wisconsin, 1967.
37 Wis.2d 285, 155 N.W.2d 74.

This case involves a neighborhood squabble between two adjacent property owners.

Prior to November 28, 1962, Virgil and Gwynneth White, the plaintiffs, were desirous of purchasing a home in Oak Creek. Unfortunately, the particular home that the Whites were interested in was without a water supply. Despite this fact, the Whites purchased the home.

The adjacent home was owned and occupied by Paul and Ruth Benkowski, the defendants. The Benkowskis had a well in their yard which had piping that connected with the Whites' home.

On November 28, 1962, the Whites and Benkowskis entered into a written agreement wherein the Benkowskis promised to supply water to the White home for ten years or until an earlier date when either water was supplied by the municipality, the well became inadequate, or the Whites drilled their own well. The Whites promised to pay $3 a month for the water and one-half the cost of any future repairs or maintenance that the Benkowski well might require. As part of the transaction, but not included in the written agreement, the Whites gave the Benkowskis $400 which was used to purchase and install a new pump and an additional tank that would increase the capacity of the well.

Initially, the relationship between the new neighbors was friendly. With the passing of time, however, their relationship deteriorated and the neighbors actually became hostile. In 1964, the water supply, which was controlled by the Benkowskis, was intermittently shut off. Mrs. White kept a record of the dates and durations that her water supply was not operative. Her record showed that the water was shut off on the following occasions:

    (1) March 5, 1964, from 7:10 p.m. to 7:25 p.m.

    (2) March 9, 1964, from 3:40 p.m. to 4:00 p.m.

    (3) March 11, 1964, from 6:00 p.m. to 6:15 p.m.

    (4) June 10, 1964, from 6:20 p.m. to 7:03 p.m.

The record also discloses that the water was shut off completely or partially for varying lengths of time on July 1, 6, 7, and 17, 1964, and on November 25, 1964.

Mr. Benkowski claimed that the water was shut off either to allow accumulated sand in the pipes to settle or to remind the Whites that their use of the water was excessive. Mr. White claimed that the Benkowskis breached their contract by shutting off the water.

Following the date when the water was last shut off (November 25, 1964), the Whites commenced an action to recover compensatory and punitive damages for an alleged violation of the agreement to supply water. A jury trial was held. Apparently it was agreed by counsel that for purposes of the trial "plaintiffs' case was based upon an alleged deliberate violation of the contract consisting of turning off the water at the times specified in the plaintiffs' complaint." [Trial court's decision-motions after verdict.] Accordingly, in the special verdict the jury was asked:

"QUESTION 1: Did the defendants maliciously, vindictively or wantonly shut off the water supply of the plaintiffs for the purpose of harassing the plaintiffs?"

The jury was also asked:

"QUESTION 2: If you answered Question 1 'Yes', then answer this question:

"(a) What compensatory damages did the plaintiffs suffer?

"(b) What punitive damages should be assessed?"

Before the case was submitted to the jury, the defendants moved to strike the verdict's punitive-damage question. The court reserved its ruling on the motion. The jury returned a verdict which found that the Benkowskis maliciously shut off the Whites' water supply for harassment purposes. Compensatory damages were set at $10 and punitive damages at $2,000. On motions after verdict, the court reduced the compensatory award to $1 and granted defendants' motion to strike the punitive damage question and answer.

Judgment for plaintiffs of $1 was entered and they appeal.

WILKIE, JUSTICE. Two issues are raised on this appeal.

1. Was the trial court correct in reducing the award of compensatory damages from $10 to $1?

2. Are punitive damages available in actions for breach of contract?

REDUCTION OF JURY AWARD.

The evidence of damage adduced during the trial here was that the water supply had been shut off during several short periods. Three incidents of inconvenience resulting from these shut-offs were detailed by the plaintiffs. Mrs. White testified that the lack of water in the bathroom on one occasion caused an odor and that on two other occasions she was forced to take her children to a neighbor's home to bathe them. Based on this evidence, the court instructed the jury that:

". . . in an action for a breach of contract the plaintiff is entitled to such damages as shall have been sustained by him which resulted naturally and directly from the breach if you find that the defendants did in fact breach the contract. Such damages include pecuniary loss and inconvenience suffered as a natural result of the breach and are called compensatory damages. In this case the plaintiffs have proved no pecuniary damages which you or the Court could compute. In a situation where there has been a breach of contract which you find to have damaged the plaintiff but for which the plaintiffs have proven no actual damages, the plaintiffs may recover nominal damages.

"By nominal damages is meant trivial—a trivial sum of money."

Plaintiffs did not object to this instruction. In the trial court's decision on motions after verdict it states that the court so instructed the jury because, based on the fact that the plaintiffs paid for services they did not receive, their loss in proportion to the contract rate was approximately 25 cents. This rationale indicates that the court disregarded or overlooked Mrs. White's testimony of inconvenience. In viewing the evidence most favorable to the plaintiffs, there was some injury. The plaintiffs are not required to ascertain their damages with mathematical precision, but rather the trier of fact must set damages at a reasonable amount. Notwithstanding this instruction, the jury set the plaintiffs' damages at $10. The court was in error in reducing that amount to $1.

The jury finding of $10 in actual damages, though small, takes it out of the mere nominal status. The award is predicated on an actual injury. This was not the situation present in Sunderman v. Warnken [(1947), 251 Wis. 471, 29 N.W.2d 496]. *Sunderman* was a wrongful-entry action by a tenant against his landlord. No actual injury could be shown by the mere fact that the landlord entered the tenant's apartment, therefore damages were nominal and no punitory award could be made. Here there was credible evidence which showed inconvenience and thus actual injury, and the jury's finding as to compensatory damages should be reinstated.

PUNITIVE DAMAGES.

"If a man shall steal an ox, or a sheep, and kill it, or sell it; he shall restore five oxen for an ox, and four sheep for a sheep." [Exodus 22:1.]

Over one hundred years ago this court held that, under proper circumstances, a plaintiff was entitled to recover exemplary or punitive damages. [McWilliams v. Bragg (1854), 3 Wis. 377 (*424).]

Kink v. Combs [(1965), 28 Wis.2d 65, 135 N.W.2d 789] is the most recent case in this state which deals with the practice of permitting punitive damages. In *Kink* the court relied on Fuchs v. Kupper [(1963), 22 Wis.2d 107, 125 N.W.2d 360] and reaffirmed its adherence to the rule of punitive damages.

In Wisconsin compensatory damages are given to make whole the damage or injury suffered by the injured party. [Malco, Inc. v. Midwest Aluminum Sales (1961), 14 Wis.2d 57, 66, 109 N.W.2d 516, 521.] On the other hand, punitive damages are given

"... on the basis of punishment to the injured party not because he has been injured, which injury has been compensated with compensatory damages, but to punish the wrongdoer for his malice and to deter others from like conduct." [Id.]

Thus we reach the question of whether the plaintiffs are entitled to punitive damages for a breach of the water agreement.

The overwhelming weight of authority supports the proposition that punitive damages are not recoverable in actions for breach of contract. [Annot. (1933), 84 A.L.R. 1345, 1346.] In Chitty on Contracts, the author states that the right to receive punitive damages for breach of contract is now confined to the single case of damages for breach of a promise to marry. [1 Chitty, Contracts, (22d ed. 1961), p. 1339.]

Simpson states:

"Although damages in excess of compensation for loss are in some instances permitted in tort actions by way of punishment ... in contract actions the damages recoverable are limited to compensation for pecuniary loss sustained by the breach." [Simpson, Contracts, (2d ed. hornbook series), p. 394, sec. 195.]

Corbin states that as a general rule punitive damages are not recoverable for breach of contract. [5 Corbin, Contracts, p. 438, sec. 1077.]

In Wisconsin, the early case of Gordon v. Brewster [(1858), 7 Wis. 309 (*355)] involved the breach of an employment contract. The trial court instructed the jury that if the nonperformance of the contract was attributable to the defendant's wrongful act of discharging the plaintiff, then that would go to increase the damages sustained. On appeal, this court said that the instruction was unfortunate and might have led the jurors to suppose that they could give something more than actual compensation in a breach of contract case. We find no Wisconsin case in which breach of contract (other than breach of promise to marry [Simpson v. Black (1870), 27 Wis. 206]) has led to the award of punitive damages.

Persuasive authority from other jurisdictions supports the proposition (without exception) that punitive damages are not available in breach of contract actions. [White, Inc. v. Metropolitan Merchandise Mart (1954), 48 Del. 526, 9 Terry 526, 107 A.2d 892....] This is true even if the breach, as in the instant case, is willful. [McDonough v. Zamora (Tex.Civ.App.1960), 338 S.W.2d 507....]

Although it is well recognized that breach of a contractual duty may be a tort, [Colton v. Foulkes (1951), 259 Wis. 142, 47 N.W.2d 901 ...,] in such situations the contract creates the relation out of which grows the duty to use care in the performance of a responsibility prescribed by the contract. [38 Am.Jur., Negligence, p. 661, sec. 20.] Not so here. No tort was pleaded or proved.

Reversed in part by reinstating the jury verdict relating to compensatory damages and otherwise affirmed. Costs to appellant.

Questions

1. Why should people generally not be punished for breaching a contract? If people should generally not be punished for breaching a contract, should they be punished when the breach is willful or malicious? Is the damage award in *White* enough to do justice? What would you award if you were judge and factfinder?

2. *Problems.*

a. Lex is a hacker who sold Clark a computer program. When Clark ran the program, his hard drive crashed due to a virus implanted by Lex. A $390 component and 200 hours of Clark's not-backed-up work were destroyed. The work was intended to entertain Clark and his friends, not to produce income, though Clark is employed as a computer programmer at $35 per hour. In an action for breach of contract against Lex, what should Clark recover? See Werner, Zaroff, Slotnick, Stern & Askenazy v. Lewis, 155 Misc.2d 558, 588 N.Y.S.2d 960 (Civ.Ct.1992).

b. Joker Auto Leasing contracted to purchase eight automobiles from Batman Autosales, payment to be made within 30 days of delivery. Joker took delivery and immediately sold the vehicles to third parties on the black market. Three checks tendered to Batman were returned marked "payment stopped." Three more checks were returned marked "insufficient funds." When Batman called to inquire, Joker denied making a contract. Further efforts to communicate failed. Should Joker be liable for punitive damages? See Seaman's Direct Buying Service, Inc. v. Standard Oil Co., 36 Cal.3d 752, 206 Cal.Rptr. 354, 686 P.2d 1158 (1984) (overruled).

c. The facts are as in Problem b, except that, in addition, Joker denied in a legal proceeding by Batman that any contract had been made, thereby committing perjury. Should Joker now be liable for punitive damages? Or should contempt of court be the sole sanction for the perjury? See Hudson Motors Partnership v. Crest Leasing Enterprises, Inc., 845 F.Supp. 969 (E.D.N.Y.1994).

———

RESTATEMENT (SECOND) OF CONTRACTS § 356

———

CITY OF RYE v. PUBLIC SERV. MUT. INS. CO.

Court of Appeals of New York, 1974.
34 N.Y.2d 470, 358 N.Y.S.2d 391, 315 N.E.2d 458.

BREITEL, CHIEF JUDGE. In this action to recover on a surety bond given to secure timely completion of some six buildings, the City of Rye, as obligee under the bond, seeks to recover the face amount of $100,000. The surety and the developers are defendants. Special Term denied the city's motion for summary judgment, and a divided Appellate Division affirmed the denial. In his concurring opinion at the Appellate Division, Mr. Justice Shapiro reasoned that the bond was penal in nature and therefore not enforceable. The dissenters, in an opinion by Mr. Justice Hopkins, would have sustained the city's contention that, as a governmental entity pursuing its governmental responsibilities, it had the power, without violating any public policy, to exact a substantial bond to secure performance of obligations imposed on a developer by the zoning ordinance and action taken under it.

The order of the Appellate Division denying plaintiff city's motion for summary judgment should be affirmed. The bond of $100,000 posted by the developers with the city to ensure completion of the remaining six "peripheral" buildings by a date certain did not reflect a reasonable estimate of probable monetary harm or damages to the city, but a penalty, and, in the absence of statutory authority for the penal bond may not be recovered upon.

The developers, under a plan approved by the City Planning Commission, had constructed six luxury co-operative apartment buildings and were to construct six more. In order to obtain certificates of occupancy for the six completed buildings the developers were required to post a bond with the city to ensure completion of the remaining six buildings. By letter agreement with the city in the fall of 1967, they agreed to post a $100,000 bond and to pay $200 per day for each day after April 1, 1971 that the six remaining buildings were not completed, up to the aggregate amount of the bond. More than 500 days have passed without the additional buildings having been completed within the time limit. The city seeks to recover the entire $100,000 amount of the bond.

Concededly, no statute authorizes the city to exact a penalty or forfeiture from the developers. If there were such a statute, the statutory penalty would undoubtedly be upheld. . . . Hence, general principles of contract law governing the enforceability of liquidated damage clauses should apply (cf. Priebe & Sons v. United States, 332 U.S. 407, 411, 68 S.Ct. 123, 92 L.Ed. 32, see 5 Williston, Contracts [3d ed.], § 775B, at p. 664). The sole issue, then, becomes whether the agreement exacted from the developers and the conditional bond supplied provide for a penalty or for liquidated damages. If the agreement provides for a penalty or forfeiture without statutory authority, it is unenforceable. Where, however, damages flowing from a breach are difficult to ascertain, a provision fixing the damages in advance will be upheld if the amount is a reasonable measure of the anticipated probable harm (Ward v. Hudson Riv. Bldg. Co., 125 N.Y. 230, 235, 26 N.E. 256, 257 . . .). If, on the other hand, the amount fixed is grossly disproportionate to the anticipated probable harm or if there were no anticipatable harm, the provision will not be enforced.

The harm which the city contends it would suffer by delay in construction is minimal, speculative, or simply not cognizable. The city urges that its inspectors and employees will be required to devote more time to the project than anticipated because it has taken extra years to complete. It also urges that it will lose tax revenues for the years the buildings are not completed. It contends, too, that it is harmed by a continuing violation of the height restrictions of its zoning ordinance. This is entailed because the 12 buildings in the entire complex vary in height between two and four stories; the ordinance sets a maximum average height of 30 feet for the complex; and the taller buildings, those higher than the allowable average, were built first. Only after all of the structures in the complex are built will the project comply with the average height requirement of the ordinance.

The most serious disappointments in expectation suffered by the city are not pecuniary in nature and therefore not measurable in monetary damages. The effect on increased inspectorial services or on tax revenue are not likely to be substantial and, in any event, are not developed in the record on summary judgment. There is nothing to show that either the sum of $200 per day or the aggregate amount of the bond bear any reasonable relationship to the pecuniary harm likely to be suffered or in fact suffered.

There is, as noted, no statutory authority for the city to exact harsh penal bonds from developers who are perforce dependent on approvals by local officials at the various stages of construction, and after construction for certificates of occupancy. For municipalities, without statutory authorization or restriction, to condition perhaps arbitrarily the grant of building permits or certificates of occupancy on large penalty bonds raises potential for grave abuse. A developer, especially an outside developer, is rarely in a position to bargain on an equal basis with local officials, after completion of buildings rendered useless and an economic drain without a certificate of occupancy. Whether, and under what circumstances, the drastic remedy of penal bonds may be exacted is a matter best left to legislated authority, standards, and limitations.

There is no suggestion in this case that the developers' delay was purposeful. Apparently, the mortgage market "dried up" and the developers could not obtain additional financing for the remaining six buildings in the time planned. (The court is informed by the developers in their brief that, while this litigation has been pending, the remaining six buildings have almost been completed.)

Developers ask not only that the denial of summary judgment to the city be affirmed, but that summary judgment be granted to defendants dismissing the city's complaint. Since the city by this action sought, not actual damages, but only to recover the face amount of the bond, for the reasons discussed above, defendants perhaps might have been entitled to judgment dismissing the complaint. In denying the city's motion for summary judgment, the motion court and perhaps the Appellate Division, could have, but did not, grant summary judgment for defendants (see CPLR 3212, subd. [b], Consol. Laws, c. 8). Defendants, however, took no appeal from that determination. This court has no power to grant defendants, respondents on this appeal, affirmative relief (People

v. Consolidated Edison Co. of N.Y., 34 N.Y.2d 646, 648, 355 N.Y.S.2d 379, 380, 311 N.E.2d 511, 512).

Accordingly, the order of the Appellate Division should be affirmed, without costs, and the question certified by that court answered in the affirmative.

Questions

1.   What is meant by "liquidated damages"? What is meant by a "penalty"? What is the distinction?

2.   In *Rye*, did the court not enforce the agreed damages clause because the expectable harm from breach was "minimal, speculative, or simply not cognizable"? Or was it because the harm turned out to be "minimal, speculative, or simply not cognizable"? Did it so turn out? Or, instead, does the case turn on the unequal bargaining power of the parties and related unconscionability concerns? Or, instead again, does it turn on the low salience to the parties at formation time of the contract clause and the events that would invoke it, undermining the authority of their assent to that clause?

3.   Should the parties be free to increase the security of the contract by agreement? In *Rye*, was there a legal reason to enforce the promise to pay $200 per day after April 1, 1971 until completion? If so, were there other legal reasons, such as unconscionability, to offset that reason? Does the result in *Rye* defeat the autonomy principle? On what basis is it justified, if it is? See Charles Goetz & Robert Scott, *Liquidated Damages, Penalties and the Just Compensation Principle: Some Notes on an Enforcement Model and a Theory of Efficient Breach*, 77 COLUM. L. REV. 558 (1977).

NOTE ON THE EFFICIENT BREACH HYPOTHESIS

Why should the law compensate, not punish, even when the parties agree to a penalty in the event of a breach? Many contracts scholars have sought the answer in the economic analysis of law. Economics studies the efficiency properties of markets and rational behavior within markets. As it happens, the law of contract remedies has long looked to markets for measures of harm to a nonbreaching party. It seems natural, then, to employ economics to ask whether contract remedies promote or retard efficiency. The compensation principle might be justified by the contribution of compensatory legal rules to enhanced market efficiency.

Efficiency is generally understood as the state of affairs in which no one can be made better off without someone else being made worse off. A legal rule or act is efficient when it induces people to behave in ways that make at least one person better off while no one else is made worse off, moving the state of affairs in a superior direction. Several assumptions are needed to make this intelligible. The most important is that people act rationally to maximize their own wealth or welfare. Economists may also assume, for analytical purposes, that contracting parties operate within competitive markets, where there are many buyers and sellers of the relevant goods or services; that they act without compulsion on full information regarding their preferences and available opportunities; and that the costs of transacting are otherwise insignificant. Of course these assumptions do not describe real markets. For some economists, the more important question is whether predictions of human behavior made on these assumptions turn out to be reliable. For others, after initial analytical baselines have been established on a tentative basis, the unrealistic assumptions are relaxed in further, more complicated studies.

As a first approximation, consider why efficiency values might commend the compensation principle. If a party breaches and is acting rationally, that party must consider itself better off by breaching than by performing. The nonbreaching party, however, may be left worse off by the breach than it would be from the performance to which it is entitled. Upon receiving full compensation for all losses caused by a breach, however, the nonbreaching party will be indifferent as between performance and breach. (If this is not so, compensation must not have been "full.") If the other party considers itself better off after breaching and paying full compensation, and no third parties are affected, then the efficiency condition will be satisfied: One party will be better off while no one is made worse off. Consequently, it seems, compensatory remedies for breach of contract enhance economic efficiency.

Here is an example. Assume that Buyer A contracts with Seller A for delivery of a new widget in exchange for $110. At the time for delivery, Seller A prefers to sell the widget to Buyer B, who is willing to pay $130 because the market has risen, and Buyer B needs it urgently. Assume further that Seller B is willing to sell a similar widget to Buyer A for $125, the new market price. If Seller A breaches, sells the widget to Buyer B, and pays Buyer A $15 compensation, the conditions for an efficiency gain seem to have been met. Assuming $15 is full compensation, Buyer A will be indifferent as between performance and breach; she gets a widget at a net cost to her of $110, as contracted. Buyer B is better off because he valued the widget more highly than Buyer A. Seller A is better off because he has a net profit from the breach and resale of $5. Thus, two parties are better off while no one is made worse off.

Of course, this is just too neat. It turns out, for example, that the compensation principle will affect several behaviors in addition to Seller A's decision to breach. It may also affect the parties' searches for contract partners, the number of contracts made, the terms of the contracts made, and the promisee's propensity to rely. The compensation principle might induce less efficient behavior at any of these points with inefficient consequences on balance. Lewis A. Kornhauser, *An Introduction to the Economic Analysis of Contract Remedies*, 57 U. COLO. L. REV. 683 (1986). Moreover, identifying the dollar figure that amounts to full compensation is far more complicated than the example suggests, as we shall see in the next section. Most economic analysts would fix compensation at the amount the parties would have agreed to had they negotiated a right to breach in a transaction-costless market. Such hypothetical questions, however, often do not yield clear and realistic answers. Finally, some question whether efficiency should be the goal of contract remedies, by contrast with upholding the morality of promise-keeping in any of several ways.

Nonetheless, the prevailing law of contract remedies assumes a model of contract breach behavior highly similar to the one sketched above. The insights of economic analysis consequently make it easier to grasp the prevailing law as a practical matter. The jury is still out on the question whether the law of contract remedies is or should be efficient. This is a largely theoretical question that might become of practical value should the courts become more receptive to economic arguments. See generally, R. POSNER, ECONOMIC ANALYSIS OF THE LAW 117–31 (4th ed. 1992); A. MITCHELL POLINSKY, AN INTRODUCTION TO LAW AND ECONOMICS 25–31 (1983). For criticism, see, e.g., Daniel Friedmann, *The Efficient Breach Fallacy*, 18 J. LEGAL STUD. 1 (1989).

SECTION 2.   EXPECTATION REMEDIES

Expectation remedies seek to put the nonbreaching party in the position it would have been in had the contract been performed. That is, they aim to give the nonbreaching party the benefit of the bargain in order to protect its contractual expectation interest. This goal can be accomplished in two ways—by ordering the party in breach to perform as promised or by ordering that party to pay enough money to fully compensate the nonbreaching party for its contractual losses.

The expectation interest has two calculable components. One is the value of out-of-pocket losses sustained in reliance on the promise. A carpenter, for example, may buy lumber for $15 and cut it for a custom job, only to have the customer cancel the project. Since the lumber cannot be reused, it represents a loss of $15. Since it would not have been bought and cut had the customer not promised to pay, the lumber and the carpenter's time represent losses in reliance on the customer's promise. The second component is the value of opportunities forgone in reliance on the promise. Thus, the carpenter might have taken another job that would have yielded a profit, while he could not have done both jobs at once; therefore, he let the alternative opportunity go when contracting with the party who later breached. The gain prevented by the breach is the distinctive harm to the expectation interest. In the example above at p. 283, Buyer A relied on Seller A's promise at the moment of contracting with Seller A by giving up the opportunity to contract with Seller B at the prevailing market price of $110. When Seller A later breaches and the market price has risen to $125, the value of the lost opportunity is $15.

A "mere expectation" seems to pale next to an out-of-pocket loss in reliance on a promise. Compensating it gives the nonbreaching party something it never had. Economically, however, a lost opportunity worth $15 is as real as the carpenter's loss of $15 spent on lumber he cut for a cancelled custom job. Together, lost opportunities and reliance losses represent the primary calculable harms that may be caused by a breach.

a. *Specific Performance*

Remedies awarded for breach of contract are of two kinds—specific relief and damages. Specific relief gives the nonbreaching party the promised performance, as when a defaulting seller of goods is ordered to deliver the goods or a defaulting buyer is ordered to pay the price. Damages substitute money for the promised performance, as when Seller A above is ordered to pay $15 to Buyer A. For largely historical reasons, the prevailing law prefers to award money damages, except in land sale contracts. Thus, courts regularly say, specific relief is unavailable unless money damages would be inadequate; when available, specific relief is awarded in the court's discretion. In general, specific relief is available when goods are unique, regularly in land sale contracts, and rarely in personal services contracts. See generally, E. Allan Farnsworth, *Legal Remedies for Breach of Contract*, 70 COLUM. L. REV. 1145 (1970).

The relevant history runs roughly as follows. Early in its legal history, England developed two court systems—law and equity. The law courts were governed by the common law and came to award only monetary remedies. The equity courts represented the King's conscience and awarded nonmonetary remedies, including specific relief. The function of the equity courts was to do justice when the law court was unable to do so because of the rigidities of the common law or the limitations on its remedial powers. Accordingly, since the sixteenth century, the law court's prerogatives were primary. Equity would not act when legal remedies were available and adequate; even then, equitable relief was discretionary.

We no longer have two systems of courts in the English tradition. Law and equity were "merged" in the late nineteenth century. The history remains apparent, however, in the distinction still made in legal pleadings between "actions at law" and "suits in equity" and the different bodies of law that accompany them. Both proceedings are now brought in the same court (except in Delaware). Actions at law remain subject to the common law and applicable statutes; they produce money judgments when plaintiffs are victorious. Equity suits are judged in the court's discretion and produce specific relief. As the merger recedes into history, however, the sharp distinction is slowly breaking down. An impressive recent study suggests, for example, that plaintiffs can generally get specific relief if they ask for it. DOUGLAS LAYCOCK, THE DEATH OF THE IRREPARABLE INJURY RULE (1991). See also Alan Schwartz, *The Case for Specific Performance*, 89 YALE L.J. 271 (1979).

———

RESTATEMENT (SECOND) OF CONTRACTS
§§ 344, 347, 359(1)

———

U.C.C. § 2-716

McCALLISTER v. PATTON

Supreme Court of Arkansas, 1948.
214 Ark. 293, 215 S.W.2d 701.

MILLWEE, JUSTICE. A. J. McCallister was plaintiff in the chancery court in a suit for specific performance of an alleged contract for the sale and purchase of a new Ford automobile from the defendant, R. H. Patton. The complaint alleges:

"That on or about the 15th day of September, 1945, the Plaintiff entered into a contract with the Defendant, whereby the Plaintiff contracted to purchase and the Defendant to sell, one Ford super deluxe tudor sedan and radio.

"That the Defendant is an automobile dealer and sells Ford automobiles and trucks within the city of Jonesboro, Craighead County, Arkansas and that at the time this Plaintiff entered into this contract the Defendant had no new Ford automobiles in stock of any kind and was engaged in taking orders by contract, numbering the contracts in the order that they were executed and delivered to him. As the cars were received the Defendant would fill the orders as he had previously received the contracts. The Plaintiff's number was number 37.

"As consideration and as part of the purchase price the Plaintiff paid to this Defendant the sum of $25.00 and at all times stood ready, able and willing to pay the balance upon the purchase price in accordance with the terms of the contract. That a copy of this contract is hereto attached marked Exhibit 'A' and made a part of this Complaint, the original being held subject to the orders of this Court and the inspection of the interested parties.

"The Plaintiff is informed and verily believes and the Defendant has admitted to this Plaintiff that he has received more than 37 cars since the execution of this contract. The Defendant refuses to sell an automobile of the above make and description to this Plaintiff.

"Since the execution of this contract and to the present date, new Ford automobiles have been hard to obtain and this Plaintiff is unable to purchase an automobile at any other place or upon the open market of the description named in this contract and there is not an adequate remedy at law and the Court should direct specific performance of this contract."

The prayer of the complaint was that the defendant be ordered to sell the automobile to plaintiff in compliance with the contract, and for all other proper relief. Under the terms of the "New Car Order" attached to the complaint as Exhibit "A," delivery of the car was to be made "as soon as possible out of current or future production" at defendant's regularly established price. Plaintiff was not required to trade in a used car but might do so, if the price of such car could be agreed upon and, if not, plaintiff was entitled to cancel the order and to the return of his deposit. The deposit of $25 was to be held in trust for the plaintiff and returned to him at his option on surrender of his rights under the agreement. There was no provision for forfeiture of the deposit in the event plaintiff refused to accept delivery of the car.

Defendant demurred to the complaint on the grounds that it did not state facts sufficient to entitle plaintiff to the relief of specific performance, and that the alleged contract was lacking in mutuality of obligation and certainty of subject matter. There were further allegations in the demurrer constituting an answer to the effect that plaintiff was engaged in the sale of used cars and had contracted to resell whatever vehicle he obtained from the defendant; and that upon being so informed, defendant tendered and plaintiff refused to accept return of the $25 deposit. Plaintiff filed a motion to strike this part of the pleading.

The chancellor sustained the demurrer to the complaint and overruled the motion to strike. The plaintiff refused to plead further and his complaint was dismissed. This appeal follows.

In testing the correctness of the trial court's ruling in sustaining the demurrer we first determine whether the allegations of the complaint are sufficient to bring plaintiff within the rule that equity will not grant specific performance of a contract for the sale of personal property if damages in an action at law afford a complete and adequate remedy. . . .

Among the various exceptions to the general rule are those cases involving contracts relating to personal property which has a peculiar, unique or sentimental value to the buyer not measurable in money damages. In Chamber of Commerce v. Barton, 195 Ark. 274, 112 S.W.2d 619, 625, this court held that the purchaser, Barton, was entitled to specific performance of a contract for the sale of Radio Station KTHS as an organized business. Justice Baker, speaking for the court, said:

> "A judgment for a bit of lumber from which a picture frame might be made and also for a small lot of tube paint and a yard of canvas would not compensate one who had purchased a great painting.

> "By the same token Barton would not be adequately compensated by a judgment for a bit of wire, a steel tower or two, more or less, as the mere instrumentalities of KTHS when he has purchased an organized business including these instrumentalities, worth perhaps not more than one-third of the purchase price. Moreover, he has also contracted for the good will of KTHS, which is so intangible as to be incapable of delivery or estimation of value. So the property is unique in character and, so far as the contract is capable of enforcement, the vendee is entitled to relief."

Exhaustive annotations involving many cases of specific performance of contracts for the sale of various types of personal property are found in L.R.A. 1918E, 597 and 152 A.L.R. 4. Comparatively few cases involving suits for specific performance of contracts for the sale of new automobiles have reached the appellate courts. Plaintiff relies on the case of De Moss v. Conart Motor Sales, Inc., 72 N.E.2d 158, where an Ohio Common Pleas Court directed specific performance of a contract similar to the one under consideration on the ground that the purchaser was without an adequate remedy at law due to the fact that new automobiles were difficult to obtain.

A different result was reached in Kirsch v. Zubalsky, 139 N.J.Eq. 22, 49 A.2d 773, 775, where the court sustained defendant's motion to strike the bill of complaint for specific performance in which plaintiff alleged that he was unable to purchase an identical automobile elsewhere at regular O.P.A. price limitations because of the extreme scarcity of such cars and would be forced to pay an illegal bonus above O.P.A. regulations for any similar automobile available on the market. The court said: "The complainant mentions no characteristic which adds a special value to the automobile so as to put it in the category of an unique chattel; and he presents no facts which can be considered by this court as elements of value adding to the intrinsic worth of the automobile itself, so as to permit it to be classed as special or unique. While automobiles may be difficult to procure under the economic or industrial conditions of the present day, they are not in the category of unique chattels."

In Welch v. Chippewa Sales Co., 252 Wis. 166, 31 N.W.2d 170, 171, the plaintiff contended that the vehicle contracted for was invested with the quality of uniqueness due to a current shortage of automobiles and that a judgment for damages did not furnish an adequate remedy. In holding that the complaint did not state a cause of action for specific performance, the court cited Kirsch v. Zubalsky, supra, and said: "In spite of the failure of production fully to meet the demands of customers, automobiles, and indeed, the very make and type of automobile ordered by plaintiff in this case, are being produced by the thousands. There is no sentimental consideration worth while protecting that has to do with the particular make, color or style of automobile. Hence, the mere contention that plaintiff needs cars in his business is not impressive. . . ."

In the still more recent case of Poltorak v. Jackson Chevrolet Co., 322 Mass. 699, 79 N.E.2d 285, the plaintiff contracted for the purchase of a new passenger automobile and delivered to the dealer his automobile for which he was to be allowed a credit on the purchase price of a new car. It was held that plaintiff was not entitled to specific performance of the contract upon showing a scarcity of automobiles and in the absence of a showing of substantial harm of a character which could not be adequately compensated in an action at law for damages. . . .

Plaintiff says we will take judicial knowledge of the scarcity of new automobiles as a result of the recent world war. If so, we would also take judicial notice of the fact that large numbers of cars of the type mentioned in the alleged contract have been produced since 1945, and sold through both new and used car dealers in the open market. Although the complaint alleges inadequacy of the remedy at law, it does not set forth facts sufficient to demonstrate such conclusion. It is neither alleged nor contended that the car ordered has any special or peculiar qualities not commonly possessed by others of the same make so as to make it practically impossible to replace it in the market. While it is alleged that new Ford automobiles have been hard to obtain, no harm or inconvenience of a kind which could not be fully compensated by an award of damages in a law action is set forth in the complaint.

We conclude that the allegations of the complaint are insufficient to entitle plaintiff to equitable relief and that his remedy at law is adequate. The demurrer was, therefore, properly sustained. In view of this conclusion we do not find it necessary to examine the contention that lack of consideration and mutuality renders the contract specifically unenforceable.

The decree is affirmed.

Questions

1. What is specific performance? Why does the plaintiff think it is entitled to specific performance here? Why does the court reject plaintiff's prayer for relief? Would damages be an adequate remedy? How so?

2. Is there any reason to prefer damages over specific performance as a means of protecting the injured party's expectation interest? Under what economic circumstances does an award of damages compensate the injured party? Under what circumstances does it not? Consider, in this regard, the sale of a painting and the sale of a radio station. Was specific performance properly awarded in *Chamber of Commerce v. Barton*, summarized in *McCallister* at p. 287?

LONDON BUCKET CO. v. STEWART

Court of Appeals of Kentucky, 1951.
314 Ky. 832, 237 S.W.2d 509.

STANLEY, COMMISSIONER. This is an appeal from a judgment decreeing specific performance of a contract to properly furnish and install a heating system for a large motel. The basic contention of the appellant, London Bucket Company, is that the remedy of specific performance will not lie for breach of this type of contract.

The chancellor overruled a demurrer to the petition and this is the first assignment of error. Stewart's petition set out the contract, the pertinent parts of which are as follows: "The parties of the first part agree and bind themselves to furnish and install (subletting installation) in said building the following equipment. . . ." The only standard as to the quality of work to be performed was that the defendant was to "guarantee to heat this said court to 75 degrees in winter, and to supervise all work," etc. The plaintiff alleged that the defendant "soon thereafter and within one year installed a plant in an incompleted, unskilled, unworkmanlike manner, never finishing same, and of such size, type and inferior quality of materials that same does not to a reasonable degree perform the purpose contemplated." The petition further states: "Plaintiff here now demands of the court of equity that defendant be compelled to specifically perform the terms of said contract and complete said installation and furnish the type of furnace provided in said contract and all the things necessary to properly heat said building and rooms and same to be done forthwith, before the fall of cold weather."

The plaintiff prayed that "immediate specific performance be adjudged" and also asked $8,250 damages for faulty and negligent construction and resulting expense, loss of business, etc. On being required to elect his remedy, he chose specific performance and dismissed without prejudice his action for damages.

The defendant, among other defenses, pleaded there had been a mutual cancellation of the contract insofar as it covered the completion of the job. Upon sharply conflicting evidence, but with some documents strongly supporting the plaintiff's contention, the court found as a fact that there had been no such cancellation. This was an issue necessary to be decided before deciding there could be a decree of specific performance.

The court decreed: "The defendant is hereby mandatorily ordered and directed to comply with the terms of said contract, in its entirety. He shall proceed diligently so to do and continue its obligation, assumed by it under the said contract, therein specifically set out."

No matter what the evidence may have been, the plaintiff's legal right could be no greater than that which the basic facts pleaded authorized. So if the demurrer should have been sustained to his pleading which undertook to state his whole case, that is all the court need consider. In other words, if the plaintiff did not state a cause of action for specific performance, the demurrer should have been sustained instead of overruled. That is the way the trial court treated the case except to find that the work done was defective, the heating system was not properly functioning, and the job was incomplete. In his opinion, the court recognized the difficulty of the question whether the contract and the conditions were such as required specific performance. He considered the familiar principle that such an equitable decree will not be adjudged unless the ordinary common law remedy of damages for a breach of contract is an inadequate and incomplete remedy for injuries arising from the failure to carry out its terms. Edelen v. Samuels & Co., 126 Ky. 295, 103 S.W. 360. The court concluded, nevertheless, that this case was within Schmidt v. Louisville & N.R. Co., 101 Ky. 441, 41 S.W. 1015, 19 Ky. Law Rep. 666, 38 L.R.A. 809, and Pennsylvania Railroad Co. v. City of Louisville, 277 Ky. 402, 126 S.W.2d 840.

It seems to us the two cases are not altogether apt. In the *Schmidt* case it was held a decree of specific performance to operate the railroad under the terms of the lease for the benefit of both holders was proper since there was no adequate remedy at law. The Pennsylvania Railroad Case was a suit to declare the rights of the parties and to require several railroad companies to proceed with the elimination of grade crossings as they had contracted to do. Both cases involve matters of great magnitude and were of public interest and welfare. In each case the court in effect said, "Proceed to do what you contracted to do." There was no question of partial or incomplete or faulty performance of a building contract. The Schmidt case is distinguished in the leading case of Edelen v. Samuels & Co., supra. In the present case the decree was in effect to direct a building contractor to go back, correct defective work and complete its job. It is the general rule that contracts for building construction will not be specifically enforced because ordinarily damages are an adequate remedy and, in part, because of the incapacity of the court to superintend the performance. 9 Am.Jur., Building and Construction Contracts, § 124; 58 C.J. 1046. The case at bar is not within the exceptions to the rule or of the class where specific performance should be decreed. 49 Am.Jur., Specific performance, § 12. That there may be difficulty in proving the damages as appellee suggests, is not enough to put the case within the exceptions.

Under our conclusion that specific performance should not have been decreed, the decision on the issue of cancellation of the contract must follow it. This will leave the question open in the common-law action for damages should it be filed.

Wherefore, the judgment is reversed.

Questions

1. Why does the court not award specific performance here? Should it? How might you calculate the motel's damages? Could they be adequate to compensate the motel for all harm to its contractual interests?

2. Does the court give persuasive reasons for distinguishing the *Schmidt* and *Pennsylvania Railroad* cases? Can you think of better distinctions? Or was *London Bucket Co.* wrongly decided?

3. *Problems.*

a. Assume that the facts are otherwise as in *McCallister v. Patton*, except that the parties had agreed in their contract that, upon breach, the buyer should be able to obtain specific performance from a court. Same result?

b. Assume that the facts are otherwise as in *London Bucket Co. v. Stewart*, except that the parties had agreed in their contract that, upon breach, the motel owner should be able to obtain specific performance from a court. Same result?

c. Bob and Bing concluded a contract for Bob to sell Bing his 120 acre estate in Palm Springs, California for $12 million. Should Bob breach, can Bing get specific performance? Should Bing breach instead, can Bob get specific performance?

d.   Bob and Bing concluded a contract for Bob to sell Bing his tract home in Levittown, Pa. for $72,000. Should Bob breach, can Bing get specific performance? Should Bing breach, can Bob get specific performance?

b.   General Damages

The losses suffered by nonbreaching parties are often highly patterned. For example, when a seller fails to deliver in a rising market, any buyer will suffer a loss equal to the difference between the contract price and the market price at the time for delivery. Any carpenter may have unrecoverable losses from cut lumber that cannot be reused. These kinds of losses are known as "general damages" because they are suffered generically by general categories of nonbreaching parties. To be sure, a nonbreaching party must prove the extent of its general damages to put a number on the loss. It may turn out to be zero. But the fact of the loss is presupposed due to the pattern, and the breaching party's duty to pay the damages is set by the law in advance.

Other damages are not suffered so regularly. They are known as "special damages" because they depend on the nonbreaching party's special circumstances. Special damages are considered in the next subsection.

To compensate for harm to the nonbreaching party's expectation interest, general damages must be measured differently depending on the type of contract and which party is in breach. It may make sense to award the seller the contract price when the buyer takes delivery and fails to pay; it makes no sense, however, to award the buyer the price when the seller breaches and the buyer has not prepaid. The cases that follow indicate how we vary the measure in pursuit of one goal in different types of contracts and breaches—breach by a buyer of goods, breach by a seller of goods, breach by a recipient of services, and breach by a provider of services. The goal, of course, is compensation for harm to the contractual expectation interest, when possible.

U.C.C. §§ 1–106, 2–703, 2–704, 2–706, 2–708, 2–709, 2–718

Problems

Solve the following hypothetical problems using U.C.C. § 2–703 *et seq.*:

1.   Ingrid sold Grace a new gold watch for $750, delivery on Oct. 1. On Oct. 1, the market price is $600. Grace repudiates on Sept. 28. How much may Ingrid recover?

2.   The facts are as stated in Problem #1, except that Ingrid sells the watch to Lauren on Oct. 3 for $575.

3. The facts are as stated in Problem #1, except that Ingrid gives notice of her intent to resell the watch at her store on Oct. 3. Ingrid then sells to her cousin on Oct. 3 for $500. The market price on Oct. 3 is $600.

4. Grace takes delivery of the watch on Oct. 1, but it is stolen from her home on Oct. 2. Grace refuses to pay Ingrid. What may Ingrid recover?

NERI v. RETAIL MARINE CORP.

Court of Appeals of New York, 1972.
30 N.Y.2d 393, 334 N.Y.S.2d 165, 285 N.E.2d 311.

GIBSON, JUDGE. The appeal concerns the right of a retail dealer to recover loss of profits and incidental damages upon the buyer's repudiation of a contract governed by the Uniform Commercial Code. This is, indeed, the correct measure of damage in an appropriate case and to this extent the code (§ 2–708, subsection [2]) effected a substantial change from prior law, whereby damages were ordinarily limited to "the difference between the contract price and the market or current price."[1] Upon the record before us, the courts below erred in declining to give effect to the new statute and so the order appealed from must be reversed.

The plaintiffs contracted to purchase from defendant a new boat of a specified model for the price of $12,587.40, against which they made a deposit of $40. They shortly increased the deposit to $4,250 in consideration of the defendant dealer's agreement to arrange with the manufacturer for immediate delivery on the basis of "a firm sale," instead of the delivery within approximately four to six weeks originally specified. Some six days after the date of the contract plaintiffs' lawyer sent to defendant a letter rescinding the sales contract for the reason that plaintiff Neri was about to undergo hospitalization and surgery, in consequence of which, according to the letter, it would be "impossible for Mr. Neri to make any payments." The boat had already been ordered from the manufacturer and was delivered to defendant at or before the time the attorney's letter was received. Defendant declined to refund plaintiffs' deposit and this action to recover it was commenced. Defendant counterclaimed, alleging plaintiffs' breach of the contract and defendant's resultant damage in the amount of $4,250, for which sum defendant demanded judgment. Upon motion, defendant had summary judgment on the issue of liability tendered by its counterclaim; and Special Term directed an assessment of damages, upon which it would be determined whether plaintiffs were entitled to the return of any portion of their down payment.

Upon the trial so directed, it was shown that the boat ordered and received by defendant in accordance with plaintiffs' contract of purchase was sold some four months later to another buyer for the same price as that negotiated with plaintiffs. From this proof the plaintiffs argue that

---

1. Personal Property Law, Consol. Laws, c. 41, § 145, repealed by Uniform Commercial Code, § 10–102 (L. 1962, ch. 553, eff. Sept. 27, 1964)....

defendant's loss on its contract was recouped, while defendant argues that but for plaintiffs' default, it would have sold two boats and have earned two profits instead of one. Defendant proved, without contradiction, that its profit on the sale under the contract in suit would have been $2,579 and that during the period the boat remained unsold incidental expenses aggregating $674 for storage, upkeep, finance charges and insurance were incurred. Additionally, defendant proved and sought to recover attorneys' fees of $1,250.

The trial court found "untenable" defendant's claim for loss of profit, inasmuch as the boat was later sold for the same price that plaintiffs had contracted to pay; found, too, that defendant had failed to prove any incidental damages; further found "that the terms of section 2–718, subsection 2(b), of the Uniform Commercial Code are applicable and same make adequate and fair provision to place the sellers in as good a position as performance would have done" and, in accordance with paragraph (b) of subsection (2) thus relied upon, awarded defendant $500 upon its counterclaim and directed that plaintiffs recover the balance of their deposit, amounting to $3,750. The ensuing judgment was affirmed, without opinion, at the Appellate Division, 37 A.D.2d 917, 326 N.Y.S.2d 984, and defendant's appeal to this court was taken by our leave.

The issue is governed in the first instance by section 2–718 of the Uniform Commercial Code which provides, among other things, that the buyer, despite his breach, may have restitution of the amount by which his payment exceeds: (a) reasonable liquidated damages stipulated by the contract or (b) absent such stipulation, 20% of the value of the buyer's total performance or $500, whichever is smaller (§ 2–718, subsection [2], pars. [a], [b]). As above noted, the trial court awarded defendant an offset in the amount of $500 under paragraph (b) and directed restitution to plaintiffs of the balance. Section 2–718, however, establishes, in paragraph (a) of subsection (3), an alternative right of offset in favor of the seller, as follows: "(3) The buyer's right to restitution under subsection (2) is subject to offset to the extent that the seller establishes (a) a right to recover damages under the provisions of this Article other than subsection (1)."

Among "the provisions of this Article other than subsection (1)" are those to be found in section 2–708, which the courts below did not apply. Subsection (1) of that section provides that "the measure of damages for non-acceptance or repudiation by the buyer is the difference between the market price at the time and place for tender and the unpaid contract price together with any incidental damages provided in this Article (Section 2–710), but less expenses saved in consequence of the buyer's breach." However, this provision is made expressly subject to subsection (2), providing: "(2) If the measure of damages provided in subsection (1) is inadequate to put the seller in as good a position as performance would have done then the measure of damages is the profit (including reasonable overhead) which the seller would have made from full performance by the buyer, together with any incidental damages provided in this Article (Section 2–710), due allowance for costs reasonably incurred and due credit for payments or proceeds of resale."

The provision of the code upon which the decision at Trial Term rested (§ 2–718, subsection [2], par. [b]) does not differ greatly from the corresponding provisions of the prior statute (Personal Property Law, § 145–a, subd. 1, par. [b]), except as the new act includes the alternative remedy of a lump sum award of $500. Neither does the present reference (in § 2–718, subsection [3], par. [a]) to the recovery of damages pursuant to other provisions of the article differ from a like reference in the prior statute (Personal Property Law, § 145–a, subd. 2, par. [a]) to an alternative measure of damages under section 145 of that act; but section 145 made no provision for recovery of lost profits as does section 2–708 (subsection [2]) of the code. The new statute is thus innovative and significant and its analysis is necessary to the determination of the issues here presented.

Prior to the code, the New York cases "applied the 'profit' test, contract price less cost of manufacture, only in cases where the seller [was] a manufacturer or an agent for a manufacturer" (1955 Report of N.Y. Law Rev. Comm., vol. 1, p. 693). Its extension to retail sales was "designed to eliminate the unfair and economically wasteful results arising under the older law when fixed price articles were involved. This section permits the recovery of lost profits in all appropriate cases, which would include all standard priced goods." (Official Comment 2, McKinney's Cons.Laws of N.Y., Book 62½, Part 1, p. 605, under Uniform Commercial Code, § 2–708.) Additionally, and "[i]n all cases the seller may recover incidental damages" (*id.*, Comment 3). The buyer's right to restitution was established at Special Term upon the motion for summary judgment, as was the seller's right to proper offsets, in each case pursuant to section 2–718; and, as the parties concede, the only question before us, following the assessment of damages at Special Term, is that as to the proper measure of damage to be applied. The conclusion is clear from the record—indeed with mathematical certainty—that "the measure of damages provided in subsection (1) is inadequate to put the seller in as good a position as performance would have done" (Uniform Commercial Code, § 2–708, subsection [2]) and hence—again under subsection (2)—that the seller is entitled to its "profit (including reasonable overhead) ... together with any incidental damages ..., due allowance for costs reasonably incurred and due credit for payments or proceeds of resale."

It is evident, first, that this retail seller is entitled to its profit and, second, that the last sentence of subsection (2), as hereinbefore quoted, referring to "due credit for payments or proceeds of resale" is inapplicable to this retail sales contract.[2] Closely parallel to the factual situation

---

2. The concluding clause, "due credit for payments or proceeds of resale," is intended to refer to "the privilege of the seller to realize junk value when it is manifestly useless to complete the operation of manufacture" (Supp. No. 1 to the 1952 Official Draft of Text and Comments of the Uniform Commercial Code, as Amended by

now before us is that hypothesized by Dean Hawkland as illustrative of the operation of the rules: "Thus, if a private party agrees to sell his automobile to a buyer for $2,000, a breach by the buyer would cause the seller no loss (except incidental damages, i.e., expense of a new sale) if the seller was able to sell the automobile to another buyer for $2,000. But the situation is different with dealers having an unlimited supply of standard-priced goods. Thus, if an automobile dealer agrees to sell a car to a buyer at the standard price of $2,000, a breach by the buyer injures the dealer, even though he is able to sell the automobile to another for $2,000. If the dealer has an inexhaustible supply of cars, the resale to replace the breaching buyer costs the dealer a sale, because, had the breaching buyer performed, the dealer would have made two sales instead of one. The buyer's breach, in such a case, depletes the dealer's sales to the extent of one, and the measure of damages should be the dealer's profit on one sale. Section 2–708 recognizes this, and it rejects the rules developed under the Uniform Sales Act by many courts that the profit cannot be recovered in this case." (Hawkland, Sales and Bulk Sales [1958 ed.], pp. 153–154; and see Comment, 31 Fordham L.Rev. 749, 755–756.)

The record which in this case establishes defendant's entitlement to damages in the amount of its prospective profit, at the same time confirms defendant's cognate right to "any incidental damages provided in this Article (Section 2–710)" (Uniform Commercial Code, § 2–708, subsection [2]). From the language employed it is too clear to require discussion that the seller's right to recover loss of profits is not exclusive and that he may recoup his "incidental" expenses as well (Procter & Gamble Distr. Co. v. Lawrence Amer. Field Warehousing Corp., 16 N.Y.2d 344, 354, 266 N.Y.S.2d 785, 792, 213 N.E.2d 873, 878). Although the trial court's denial of incidental damages in the uncontroverted amount of $674 was made in the context of its erroneous conclusion that paragraph (b) of subsection (2) of section 2–718 was applicable and was "adequate ... to place the sellers in as good a position as performance would have done," the denial seems not to have rested entirely on the court's mistaken application of the law, as there was an explicit finding "that defendant completely failed to show that it suffered any incidental damages." We find no basis for the court's conclusion with respect to a deficiency of proof inasmuch as the proper items of the $674 expenses (being for storage, upkeep, finance charges and insurance for the period between the date performance was due and the time of the resale) were proven without objection and were in no way controverted, impeached or otherwise challenged, at the trial or on appeal. Thus the court's finding

the Action of the American Law Institute of the National Conference of Commissioners on Uniform Laws [1954], p. 14). The commentators who have considered the language have uniformly concluded that "the reference is to a resale as scrap under ... Section 2–704" (1956 Report of N.Y. Law Rev. Comm., p. 397; 1955 Report of N.Y. Law Rev. Comm., vol. 1, p. 761....) Another writer, reaching the same conclusion, after detailing the history of the clause, says that "'proceeds of resale' previously meant the resale value of the goods in finished form; now it means the resale value of the components on hand at the time plaintiff learns of breach" (Harris, Seller's Damages, 18 Stanf. L. Rev. 66, 104).

of a failure of proof cannot be supported upon the record and, therefore, and contrary to plaintiffs' contention, the affirmance at the Appellate Division was ineffective to save it.

The trial court correctly denied defendant's claim for recovery of attorney's fees incurred by it in this action. Attorney's fees incurred in an action such as this are not in the nature of the protective expenses contemplated by the statute (Uniform Commercial Code, § 1–106, subd. [1]; § 2–710; § 2–708, subsection [2]) and by our reference to "legal expense" in Procter & Gamble Distr. Co. v. Lawrence Amer. Field Warehousing Corp. (16 N.Y.2d 344, 354–355, 266 N.Y.S.2d 785, 792–793, 213 N.E.2d 873, 878–879, *supra*), upon which defendant's reliance is in this respect misplaced.

It follows that plaintiffs are entitled to restitution of the sum of $4,250 paid by them on account of the contract price less an offset to defendant in the amount of $3,253 on account of its lost profit of $2,579 and its incidental damages of $674.

The order of the Appellate Division should be modified, with costs in all courts, in accordance with this opinion, and, as so modified, affirmed.

Questions

1. Why should Neri, a buyer in breach, be entitled to get his deposit back under U.C.C. § 2–718(2), subject to the relevant offsets? What are the relevant offsets? Do they leave the seller over- or undercompensated?

2. Why would the drafters of the U.C.C. have made the innovation represented by § 2–708(2)? Under what conditions would the remedy provided in § 2–708(1) be "inadequate to put the seller in as good a position as performance would have done"? Was the court correct to endorse Dean Hawkland's statement that the conditions include dealers with an unlimited supply of standard priced goods?

3. Should the profit Retail Marine received from the resale be deducted from the amount due from Neri?

4. *Problems*.

    a. The facts are otherwise as in *Neri*, except that Neri proved in addition that, had he kept the contract, he would have resold the boat to the same person who bought it from Retail Marine. Same result?

    b. Frank, a middleman, and Dean, a supplier, concluded a fixed-price supply contract for Frank to acquire goods to fulfill a pending contract with Sammy. Frank would have made a $95,000 profit. However, the market price for the contract goods fell $300,000 at the time for performance. Sammy breached before Frank had acquired the goods from Dean, and Dean released Frank of all liability under the supply contract. In an action by Frank against Sammy, what should be Frank's damages? See Nobs Chemical, U.S.A., Inc. v. Koppers Co., Inc., 616 F.2d 212 (5th Cir.1980).

U.C.C. §§ 2–711, 2–712, 2–713, 2–714, 2–715(1)

Problems

Solve the following hypothetical problems using U.C.C. §§ 2–711 *et seq.*:

1. Ingrid sold Grace her new gold watch, which has a market price of $1,000, for $750. Grace resold it to Lauren for $1,050. Ingrid fails to deliver. What may Grace recover?

2. Ingrid sold Grace her new gold watch for $750, delivery on Oct. 1. The market price for the watch on Oct. 1 is $1,000, and Ingrid fails to deliver. Grace buys another similar watch on Oct. 5 for $1,200, after the price of gold has risen dramatically. What may Grace recover?

3. The facts are as stated in Problem #2, except that Grace bought the other watch on Oct. 20.

4. The facts are as stated in Problem #2, except that Grace bought the other watch from her cousin on Oct. 2.

5. Ingrid sold and delivered a watch worth $1,000 to Grace for $750. Grace unpacked it and put it on. After working for 24 hours, the watch failed. In fact, the watch has a defective part and requires an $85 repair, which will take 2 weeks. Assuming the defect is a breach of warranty, what can Grace recover from Ingrid?

FERTICO BELGIUM S.A. v. PHOSPHATE CHEMICALS EXPORT ASS'N

Court of Appeals of New York, 1987.
70 N.Y.2d 76, 517 N.Y.S.2d 465, 510 N.E.2d 334.

BELLACOSA, JUDGE. A seller (Phoschem) breached its contract to timely deliver goods to a buyer-trader (Fertico) who properly sought cover (under the Uniform Commercial Code that means acquiring substitute goods) from another source (Unifert) in order to avoid breaching that buyer-trader's obligation to a third-party buyer (Altawreed). The sole issue involves the applicable principles and computation of damages for breach of the Phoschem-to-Fertico contract.

We hold that under the exceptional circumstances of this case plaintiff Fertico, as a buyer-trader, is entitled to damages from seller Phoschem equal to the increased cost of cover plus consequential and incidental damages minus expenses saved (UCC 2–712[2]). In this case, expenses saved as a result of the breach are limited to costs or expenditures which would have arisen had there been no breach. Thus, the seller Phoschem is not entitled to a credit from the profits of a subsequent sale by the first buyer-trader Fertico to a fourth party (Janssens) of nonconforming goods from Phoschem. Fertico's letter of credit had been presented by Phoschem and honored so, under the specific facts of this case, Fertico had no commercially reasonable alternative but to retain and resell the fertilizer. This is so despite Fertico's exercise of cover in connection with the first set of transactions, i.e., Phoschem to

Fertico to Altawreed. The covering buyer-trader may not, however, as in this case, recover other consequential damages when the third party to which it made its sale provides increased compensation to offset additional costs arising as a consequence of the breach.

In October 1978, appellant Fertico Belgium S.A. (Fertico), an international trader of fertilizer, contracted with Phosphate Chemicals Export Association, Inc. (Phoschem), a corporation engaged in exporting phosphate fertilizer, to purchase two separate shipments of fertilizer for delivery to Antwerp, Belgium. The first shipment was to be 15,000 tons delivered no later than November 20, 1978, and the second was to be 20,000 tons delivered by November 30, 1978. Phoschem knew that Fertico required delivery on the specified dates so that the fertilizer could be bagged and shipped in satisfaction of a secondary contract Fertico had with Altawreed, Iraq's agricultural ministry. Fertico secured a letter of credit in a timely manner with respect to the first shipment. After Phoschem projected a first shipment delivery date of December 4, 1978, Fertico advised Phoschem, on November 13, 1978, that the breach as to the first shipment presented "huge problems" and canceled the second shipment which had not as of that date been loaded, thus ensuring its late delivery. The first shipment did not actually arrive in Antwerp until December 17 and was not off-loaded until December 21, 1978. Despite the breach as to the first shipment, Fertico retained custody and indeed acquired title over that first shipment because, as its president testified "[w]e had no other choice" (Rec on app, at 597–598) as defendant seller Phoschem had presented Fertico's $1.7 million letter of credit as of November 17, 1978, and the same had been honored by the issuer (*see*, UCC 5–114).

Fertico's predicament from the breach by delay of even the first shipment, a breach which Phoschem does not deny, was that it, in turn, would breach its contract to sell to Altawreed unless it acquired substitute goods. In an effort to avoid that secondary breach, Fertico took steps in mid-November to cover (UCC 2–712) the goods by purchasing 35,000 tons of the same type fertilizer from Unifert, a Lebanese concern. The cost of the fertilizer itself under the Phoschem-to-Fertico contract was $4,025,000, and under the Unifert-to-Fertico contract $4,725,000, a differential of $700,000. On the same day Fertico acquired cover, November 15, 1978, Fertico's president traveled to Baghdad, Iraq, to renegotiate its contract with Altawreed. In return for a postponed delivery date and an additional payment of $20.50 per ton, Fertico agreed to make direct inland delivery rather than delivery to the seaport of Basra. Fertico fulfilled its renegotiated Altawreed contract with the substitute fertilizer purchased as cover from Unifert.

In addition to the problems related to its Altawreed contract, Fertico was left with 15,000 tons of late-delivered fertilizer which it did not require but which it had been compelled to take because Phoschem had received payment on Fertico's letter of credit. This aggrieved international buyer-seller was required to store the product and seek out a new purchaser. Fertico sold the 15,000 tons of the belatedly delivered Phoschem fertilizer to another buyer, Janssens, on March 19, 1979, some three months after the nonconforming delivery, and earned a profit of $454,000 based on the cost to it from Phoschem and its sale price to Janssens.

In 1981 Fertico commenced this action against Phoschem seeking $1.25 million in damages for Phoschem's breach of the October 1978 agreement. A jury returned a verdict of $1.07 million which the trial court refused to overturn on a motion for judgment notwithstanding the verdict. The Appellate Division vacated the damage award, ordered a new trial on the damages issue only and ruled, as a matter of law, (1) that the increased transportation costs on the Altawreed contract were not consequential damages; (2) that the higher purchase price paid by Altawreed to Fertico was an expense saved as a consequence of the Phoschem breach; and (3) that the Fertico damages had to be reduced by the profits from the Janssens' sale (*Fertico Belgium v. Phosphate Chems. Export Assn.*, 120 A.D.2d 401, 501 N.Y.S.2d 867). Fertico appealed to this court on a stipulation for judgment absolute. We disagree with propositions (2) and (3) in the Appellate Division ruling, and conclude that the Uniform Commercial Code and our analysis support a modification and reinstatement of $700,000 of the damage award in a final judgment resolving this litigation between the parties. . . .

[The court held that the increased price paid by Altawreed was erroneously treated as an expense saved in consequence of the breach. It was, rather, compensation for the additional shipment responsibilities incurred by Fertico.]

The third prong of the damages analysis relates to the profit made from the independent sale of the Phoschem fertilizer to Janssens. The Appellate Division erred in offsetting this profit against the damages otherwise suffered since that court mistakenly concluded that the sale stemmed from and was dependent upon Phoschem's breach. This offset, on these peculiar facts, would severely disadvantage Fertico, a trader in fertilizer who both buys and sells, and who would have pursued such commercial transactions had there been no breach by Phoschem. It would be anomalous to conclude that had it not been for Phoschem's breach Fertico would not have continued its trade and upon such reasoning to counterpoise the profits from the Janssens' sale against the damages arising from Phoschem's breach. Inasmuch as the facts here are exceptional because Fertico met its subsale obligations with the cover fertilizer and yet acquired title and control over the late-delivered fertilizer from Phoschem, our decision does not fit squarely within the available Uniform Commercial Code remedies urged by the dissent. Thus, strict reliance on *Neri v. Retail Mar. Corp.*, 30 N.Y.2d 393, 334 N.Y.S.2d 165, 285 N.E.2d 311 (*supra*) and on Hawkland's commentary (3 Hawkland, Uniform Commercial Code Series § 2–714:05, at 384), as undertaken by the dissent, does not provide an adequate resolution to the particular problem presented in this case.

Fertico learned of Phoschem's breach after Phoschem had negotiated Fertico's $1.7 million letter of credit, which constituted complete payment for the first shipment. With no commercially reasonable alternative, Fertico took custody of the first shipment but canceled the second (UCC 2–601[c]), having previously notified Phoschem of its breach (UCC 2–607). The loss resulting to Fertico by having to acquire cover, even in the face of its acceptance of a late-delivered portion of the fertilizer, is properly recoverable under section 2–714(1) (3 Hawkland, Uniform Commercial Code Series § 2–714:05, at 384–385). At the same time, Uniform Commercial Code § 1–106 directs that the remedies provided by the Uniform Commercial Code should be liberally administered so as to put the aggrieved party in as good a position as if the other party had fully performed. Had Phoschem fully performed, Fertico would have had the benefit of the Altawreed transaction and, as a trader of fertilizer, the profits from the Janssens' sale as well. "Gains made by the injured party on other transactions after the breach are never to be deducted from the damages that are otherwise recoverable, unless such gains could not have been made, had there been no breach" (5 Corbin, Contracts § 1041, at 256 ...). Fertico's profit made on the sale of a nonspecific article such as fertilizer, of which the supply in the market is not limited, should not therefore be deducted from the damages recoverable from Phoschem (5 Corbin, Contracts § 1041, at 258–260; *see also, Neri v. Retail Mar. Corp.*, 30 N.Y.2d 393, 401, 334 N.Y.S.2d 165, 285 N.E.2d 311, *supra*).

Fertico was concededly wronged by Phoschem's breach and Fertico resorted to Uniform Commercial Code remedies which are rooted in what we perceive to be the realities of the marketplace. Fertico did what reasonable traders would do and would like to do in mitigating risks inflicted in this case by Phoschem and in exerting its commercial resourcefulness. That is, it took steps to save its business, its customers, its good will and its deals and ultimately to also recover appropriate damages from a wrongdoer. That did not produce a "windfall" or a "double benefit" to the aggrieved party as the dissenting opinion asserts. The result we reach today countenances no such thing. On the contrary, to deprive the buyer-trader Fertico of its rightful differential damages of $700,000 and to credit this transactionally independent profit to Phoschem would perversely enrich the wrongdoer at the expense of the wronged party, a result those in the marketplace would find perplexing and a result which the generous remedial purpose of the Uniform Commercial Code does not compel or authorize. The dissent's characterization of the recovery by an injured party of damages for a breach of contract as a "benefit" is wrong, since that functionally attributes a kind of lien against the independently pursued benefit derived out of that separate transaction.

Accordingly, the order of the Appellate Division affirming liability but vacating, on the law, the damage award and remanding the matter for a new trial on the issue of damages, as appealed to this court on a stipulation for judgment absolute, should be modified and damages awarded to Fertico in the amount of $700,000 in accordance with this opinion.

TITONE, JUDGE (dissenting). At issue in this appeal is the relationship among the various remedies that Article 2 of the Uniform Commercial Code provides for buyers aggrieved by sellers' defaults. Central to the analysis is the principle that the Code's remedies "shall be liberally administered to the end that the aggrieved party may be put in *as good a position* as if the other party had fully performed" (UCC 1–106[1] [emphasis supplied]). Here, the majority has concluded that the aggrieved buyer may retain both cover damages and the profit from the resale of the late-delivered goods, in effect, securing the benefit of its bargain twice. Since that result is not required by, and indeed is not even consistent with, the purpose of Code's generous remedial provisions, I must respectfully dissent.

I begin with the premise that an aggrieved buyer who has purchased substitute goods and sued for "cover" damages under UCC 2–712 has impliedly rejected the seller's nonconforming performance and, consequently, holds the seller's goods only as security for any prepayments made to the seller (*see,* UCC 2–706[6]; 2–711[3]). I find the contrary position—that an aggrieved buyer may compatibly resort to cover and also retain and resell the nonconforming goods for its own account—to be legally insupportable and economically unsound. The "cover" remedy represents a recognition by the Code's drafters that a buyer aggrieved by a breach or repudiation "may not be made whole by the mere recovery of damages, because he is left, thereby, in a position in which he does not have the goods he wants" (3 Hawkland, Uniform Commercial Code Series § 2–712:01, at 360). The Code's "cover" provision, which authorizes the buyer to purchase equivalent goods in the open market and then sue the breaching seller for any price differential (*see,* UCC 2–712), was intended as a practical method of furnishing the buyer with a fair substitute for the goods it bargained for but did not receive. Thus, from an economic standpoint, the buyer receives the full benefit of his bargain when he obtains cover damages under UCC 2–712. Allowing the buyer to retain and resell the goods in addition obviously leads to a windfall, since the buyer is receiving more than the benefit of the transaction it bargained for.

Moreover, the language of the Code makes clear that the buyer cannot both sue for cover and accept the goods. UCC 2–712(1) defines "cover" as a purchase of goods "*in substitution for* those due from the seller" (emphasis supplied) and authorizes an aggrieved buyer to resort to cover only "[a]fter a breach within [UCC 2–711(1)]," which specifically states that cover "under [UCC 2–712(1)]" is available when "the seller fails to make delivery ... or the buyer rightfully rejects or justifiably revokes acceptance" (UCC 2–711[1]). Finally, any doubt about the applicability of the cover remedy referred to in UCC 2–711 is dispelled by comment 1: "The remedies listed here are those available to a buyer *who has not accepted the goods or who has justifiably revoked his acceptance*" (emphasis supplied).

In short, consistent with its purpose, the cover remedy is, by its terms, available only in situations where the buyer either does not have the needed goods because of nondelivery or cannot use the goods that were delivered because of a defect in the seller's performance. In all other situations, the aggrieved buyer must resort to the remedies provided in UCC 2–714, which concerns nonconforming goods that have been accepted (*see*, UCC 2–711, comment 1). While there are instances in which an accepting buyer may also seek cover damages under UCC 2–714(1), even the commentary the majority cites makes clear that the cover remedy is not intended to be used with respect to those nonconforming goods that the buyer has received *and accepted*; rather, the remedy is properly used only to replace the portion of needed goods the buyer either does not have or does not take (3 Hawkland, *op. cit.* § 2–714:05, at 384–385).

Viewed within the framework of these basic principles, cases such as this one involving late delivery are not difficult to resolve. As in cases where there has been a total failure to deliver, the buyer in late-delivery cases may reject the untimely performance and cover with substitute goods. Additionally, unlike the buyer aggrieved by a total failure to deliver, the buyer aggrieved by a late delivery has the alternative option of accepting the belatedly delivered goods and retaining for itself any profit realized on resale. However, contrary to Fertico's claims, the aggrieved buyer may not pursue both courses simultaneously, since it would then benefit twice from what was a single bargain–a result that is unacceptable under UCC 1–106 (*see*, *Melby v. Hawkins Pontiac*, 13 Wash.App. 745, 537 P.2d 807 [alternative remedies may be pursued under UCC, but not where double recovery would result]).

The majority has attempted to rationalize that result here by relying on a damages rule that has previously been applied only to aggrieved sellers. The rule permits a seller who regularly deals in goods of a particular type to sue the breaching buyer for lost profit even though the wrongfully rejected goods have been sold to another buyer without loss. The rule applies only where the seller has an *unlimited* supply of *standard-price* goods (*see*, *Neri v. Retail Mar. Corp.*, 30 N.Y.2d 393, 399–400, 334 N.Y.S.2d 165, 285 N.E.2d 311; 3 Hawkland, op. cit. § 2–708:04, at 331–332). In those situations, "it may safely be assumed that" the seller would have made two sales instead of one if the buyer had not breached, and, consequently, it can fairly be said that the buyer's breach deprived the seller of an opportunity for additional profit (3 Hawkland, *op. cit.*, at 332). Thus, traditional remedies such as resale or market price differential are "inadequate to put the seller in as good a position as performance would have done," and the seller may sue for the lost profit (UCC 2–708[2]).

The Code, however, does not contain an analogous provision allowing aggrieved buyers to recover profits from lost sales, and there is good reason for that omission, since neither of the conditions necessary for application of the sellers' lost-profit remedy may be satisfied in the case of an aggrieved buyer. First, a party in the position of a buyer cannot, by definition, be said to have an unlimited supply of the goods at his disposal for resale; even where the goods are fungible, the buyer who intends to resell must go into the marketplace to acquire the goods in the first instance. Second, a buyer who must go into the market to obtain goods will ordinarily not be able to rely on the availability of a "standard price;" rather, unlike the seller who has an unlimited supply of standard-price goods in its inventory, the reselling buyer remains at the mercy of the wholesale market's price fluctuations. Because of these differences, it *cannot* "be safely assumed" that the aggrieved buyer-dealer would have made a second sale at a particular profit were it not for the seller's breach. . . .

Finally, I cannot agree with the majority's reliance on the supposedly "exceptional" circumstance that Fertico both "met its subsale obligations with the cover fertilizer and . . . acquired title and control over the late-delivered fertilizer" (majority opn., at 83, at 467 of 517 N.Y.S.2d, at 336 of 510 N.E.2d). . . .

[U]nder the terms of the majority's holding the outcome in a given case would turn, in large measure, on the fortuity of which party had possession of the goods after the breach. In the case of a simple late delivery the buyer will ordinarily have possession after the breach. Under the majority's holding, that buyer may *both* obtain cover damages *and* resell the seller's goods, retaining any profit for itself. In the case of a complete failure to deliver, however, the seller will ordinarily have possession of the goods after the breach. Under the Code, the buyer in such a case may obtain *either* cover damages *or* the goods (if they have been specifically identified to the contract), but not both (UCC 2–716[3]). Thus, the buyer aggrieved by a late delivery is placed in a substantially better position than a buyer aggrieved by a complete failure to deliver, although there is no apparent legal or commercial justification for the distinction. Even more seriously, a seller who completely repudiates is placed in a more advantageous position than one who merely delivers late. While both must pay cover damages, the repudiating seller may resell the undelivered goods in its possession for its own account–an option unavailable to the seller who has delivered, albeit late. Since I cannot agree with a rule of law that ultimately imposes a greater penalty on the less serious of two similar breaches, I dissent and vote to affirm.

Questions

1. What is the contract sued upon by Fertico? Why did Fertico contract with Unifert? Why did Fertico contract with the Janssens? What is its preferred measure of damages in the action against Phoschem?

2. Would Fertico have made the sale to the Janssens had Phoschem not breached? Was the profit on that sale made possible by the breach? Why does it not belong to Phoschem, in the majority's view? Should it be relevant that the buyer paid the price? Should it be relevant that the buyer held the goods in a warehouse for three months?

3. Is the dissenting opinion correct that U.C.C. § 2–712 is unavailable to a buyer who accepts the goods and that the cover remedy is unavailable

under § 2–714? Is the dissenting opinion correct that the majority relied significantly on *Neri v. Retail Marine Corp.* in justifying its result? Is the dissenting opinion correct that the majority would put the buyer aggrieved by a late delivery in a substantially better position than a buyer aggrieved by a complete failure to deliver? In your view, does the dissenting judge treat U.C.C. § 1–106 as centrally as he represents?

VITEX MFG. CORP. v. CARIBTEX CORP.

United States Court of Appeals, Third Circuit, 1967.
377 F.2d 795.

STALEY, CHIEF JUDGE. This is an appeal by Caribtex Corporation from a judgment of the District Court of the Virgin Islands finding Caribtex in breach of a contract entered into with Vitex Manufacturing Company, Ltd., and awarding $21,114 plus interest to Vitex for loss of profits. The only substantial question raised by Caribtex is whether it was error for the district court, sitting without a jury, not to consider overhead as part of Vitex's costs in determining the amount of profits lost. We conclude that under the facts presented, the district court was not compelled to consider Vitex's overhead costs, and we will affirm the judgment.

Before discussing the details of the controversy between the parties, it will be helpful to briefly describe the peculiar legal setting in which this suit arose. At the time of the events in question, there were high tariff barriers to the importation of foreign wool products. However, under § 301 of the Tariff Act of 1930, 19 U.S.C.A. § 1301a, repealed but the provision continued under Revised Tariff Schedules, 19 U.S.C.A. § 1202, note 3(a)(i)(ii) (1965), if such goods were imported into the Virgin Islands and were processed in some manner so that their finished value exceeded their importation value by at least 50%, then the high tariffs to importation into the continental United States would be avoided. Even after the processing, the foreign wool enjoyed a price advantage over domestic products so that the business flourished. However, to keep the volume of this business at such levels that Congress would not be stirred to change the law, the Virgin Islands Legislature imposed "quotas" on persons engaging in processing, limiting their output. 33 V.I.C. § 504 (Supp.1966).

Vitex was engaged in the business of chemically shower-proofing imported cloth so that it could be imported duty-free into the United States. For this purpose, Vitex maintained a plant in the Virgin Islands and was entitled to process a specific quantity of material under the Virgin Islands quota system. Caribtex was in the business of importing cloth into the islands, securing its processing, and exporting it to the United States.

In the fall of 1963, Vitex found itself with an unused portion of its quota but no customers, and Vitex closed its plant. Caribtex acquired some Italian wool and subsequently negotiations for a processing contract were conducted between the principals of the respective companies in New York City. Though the record below is clouded with differing versions of the negotiations and the alleged final terms, the trial court found upon substantial evidence in the record that the parties did enter into a contract in which Vitex agreed to process 125,000 yards of Caribtex's woolen material at a price of 26 cents per yard.

Vitex proceeded to re-open its Virgin Islands plant, ordered the necessary chemicals, recalled its work force and made all the necessary preparations to perform its end of the bargain. However, no goods were forthcoming from Caribtex, despite repeated demands by Vitex, apparently because Caribtex was unsure that the processed wool would be entitled to duty-free treatment by the customs officials. Vitex subsequently brought this suit to recover the profits lost through Caribtex's breach.

Vitex alleged, and the trial court found, that its gross profits for processing said material under the contract would have been $31,250 and that its costs would have been $10,136, leaving Vitex's damages for loss of profits at $21,114. On appeal, Caribtex asserted numerous objections to the detailed computation of lost profits.[1] While the record below is sometimes confusing, we conclude that the trial court had substantial evidence to support its findings on damages. It must be remembered that the difficulty in exactly ascertaining Vitex's costs is due to Caribtex's wrongful conduct in repudiating the contract before performance by Vitex. Caribtex will not be permitted to benefit by the uncertainty it has caused. Thus, since there was a sufficient basis in the record to support the trial court's determination of substantial damages, we will not set aside its judgment. Stentor Elec. Mfg. Co. v. Klaxon Co., 115 F.2d 268 (C.A.3, 1940), rev'd other grounds 313 U.S. 487, 61 S.Ct. 1020, 85 L.Ed. 1477 (1941); 5 Williston, Contracts § 1345 (rev. ed. 1937).

Caribtex first raised the issue at the oral argument of this appeal that the trial court erred by disregarding Vitex's overhead expenses in determining lost profits. In general, overhead "... may be said to include broadly the continuous expenses of the business, irrespective of the outlay on a particular contract." Grand Trunk W.R.R. Co. v. H. W. Nelson Co., 116 F.2d 823, 839 (C.A.6, 1941). Such expenses would include executive and clerical salaries, property taxes, general administration expenses, etc.[2] Although Vitex did not expressly seek recovery for

---

1. As originally transcribed, Vitex's costs appeared to have been understated by $4,500 because the transcript read "Q. But, at 5 cents a gallon for oil what is necessary to run the plant for one week ...? A. We estimated that we would need 37,000 gallons and at 5 cents a gallon, that came to $350 and the balance of the $37, we estimated for the trucking of the oil to our plant. Court: What is that total? A. (Witness) $387."

However, 37,000 x $0.05 = $1,850 per week, not $350 and since the plant required fuel oil for three weeks, Vitex appeared to be understating its costs by $4,500. Subse-

quently, the official reporter reviewed his notes and certified to this court that the witness replied "We estimated we would need *7,000* gallons ..." rather than 37,000. As such, no error appears in the cost of fuel oil.

2. Caribtex could not be referring to overhead expenses as including labor costs and the like, because the trial judge did charge as costs all the expenses directly associated with the reactivation of Vitex's plant, and the actual processing of Caribtex's goods according to the terms of the contract.

overhead, if a portion of these fixed expenses should be allocated as costs to the Caribtex contract, then under the judgment of the district court Vitex tacitly recovered these expenses as part of its damages for lost profits, and the damages should be reduced accordingly. Presumably, the portion to be allocated to costs would be a pro rata share of Vitex's annual overhead according to the volume of business Vitex would have done over the year if Caribtex had not breached the contract.

Although there is authority to the contrary, we feel that the better view is that normally, in a claim for lost profits, overhead should be treated as a part of gross profits and recoverable as damages, and should not be considered as part of the seller's costs. A number of cases hold that since overhead expenses are not affected by the performance of the particular contract, there should be no need to deduct them in computing lost profits. E.g., Oakland California Towel Co. v. Sivils, 52 Cal. App.2d 517, 520, 126 P.2d 651, 652 (1942). . . . The theory of these cases is that the seller is entitled to recover losses incurred and gains prevented in excess of savings made possible, Restatement, Contracts § 329 (made part of the law of the Virgin Islands, 1 V.I.C. § 4); since overhead is fixed and nonperformance of the contract produced no overhead cost savings, no deduction from profits should result.

The soundness of the rule is exemplified by this case. Before negotiations began between Vitex and Caribtex, Vitex had reached a lull in business activity and had closed its plant. If Vitex had entered into no other contracts for the rest of the year, the profitability of its operations would have been determined by deducting its production costs and overhead from gross receipts yielded in previous transactions. When this opportunity arose to process Caribtex's wool, the only additional expenses Vitex would incur would be those of re-opening its plant and the direct costs of processing, such as labor, chemicals and fuel oil. Overhead would have remained the same whether or not Vitex and Caribtex entered their contract and whether or not Vitex actually processed Caribtex's goods. Since this overhead remained constant, in no way attributable-to or affected-by the Caribtex contract, it would be improper to consider it as a cost of Vitex's performance to be deducted from the gross proceeds of the Caribtex contract.

However, Caribtex may argue that this view ignores modern accounting principles, and that overhead is as much a cost of production as other expenses. It is true that successful businessmen must set their prices at sufficient levels to recoup all their expenses, including overhead, and to gain profits. Thus, the price the businessman should charge on each transaction could be thought of as that price necessary to yield a pro rata portion of the company's fixed overhead, the direct costs associated with production, and a "clear" profit. Doubtless this type of calculation is used by businessmen and their accountants. Pacific Portland Cement Co. v. Food Mach. & Chem. Corp., 178 F.2d 541 (C.A.9, 1949). However, because it is useful for planning purposes to allocate a portion of overhead to each transaction, it does not follow that this allocated share of fixed overhead should be considered a cost factor in the computation of lost profits on individual transactions.

First, it must be recognized that the pro rata allocation of overhead costs is only an analytical construct. In a similar manner one could allocate a pro rata share of the company's advertising cost, taxes and/or charitable gifts. The point is that while these items all are paid from the proceeds of the business, they do not normally bear such a direct relationship to any individual transaction to be considered a cost in ascertaining lost profits.

Secondly, even were we to recognize the allocation of overhead as proper in this case, we should uphold the tacit award of overhead expense to Vitex as a "loss incurred." Conditioned Air Corp. v. Rock Island Motor Transit Co., 253 Iowa 961, 114 N.W.2d 304, 3 A.L.R.3d 679, cert. denied, 371 U.S. 825, 83 S.Ct. 46, 9 L.Ed.2d 64 (1962). By the very nature of this allocation process, as the number of transaction[s] over which overhead can be spread becomes smaller, each transaction must bear a greater portion or allocate share of the fixed overhead cost. Suppose a company has fixed overhead of $10,000 and engages in five similar transactions; then the receipts of each transaction would bear $2000 of overhead expense. If the company is now forced to spread this $10,000 over only four transactions, then the overhead expense per transaction will rise to $2500, significantly reducing the profitability of the four remaining transactions. Thus, where the contract is between businessmen familiar with commercial practices, as here, the breaching party should reasonably foresee that his breach will not only cause a loss of "clear" profit, but also a loss in that the profitability of other transactions will be reduced. Resolute Ins. Co. v. Percy Jones, Inc., 198 F.2d 309 (C.A.10, 1952). . . . Therefore, this loss is within the contemplation of "losses caused and gains prevented," and overhead should be considered to be a compensable item of damage.

Significantly, the Uniform Commercial Code, adopted in the Virgin Islands, 11A V.I.C. §§ 1–101 et seq., and in virtually every state today, provides for the recovery of overhead in circumstances similar to those presented here. Under 11A V.I.C. § 2–708, the seller's measure of damage for non-acceptance or repudiation is the difference between the contract price and the market price, but if this relief is inadequate to put the seller in as good position as if the contract had been fully performed, ". . . then the measure of damages is the *profit (including reasonable overhead)* which the seller would have made from full performance by the buyer. . . ." 11A V.I.C. § 2–708(2) (emphasis added). While this contract is not controlled by the Code, the Code is persuasive here because it embodies the foremost modern legal thought concerning commercial transactions. Indeed, it may overrule some of the cases denying recovery for overhead. E.g., Wilhelm Lubrication Co. v. Brattrud, 197 Minn. 626, 632, 268 N.W. 634, 636, 106 A.L.R. 1279 (1936). . . .

The judgment of the district court will be affirmed.

Questions

1. Why does the defendant in *Vitex* think that overhead should be deducted from the plaintiff's damages? Is overhead a "cost" or a "profit"? Would an accountant agree with the court's opinion?

2. Why does the court think overhead should not be deducted from the plaintiff's damages? Does the court's opinion better protect the nonbreaching party's expectation interest?

———

RESTATEMENT (SECOND) OF CONTRACTS § 350

———

PARKER v. TWENTIETH CENTURY–FOX FILM CORP.

Supreme Court of California, In Bank, 1970.
3 Cal.3d 176, 89 Cal.Rptr. 737, 474 P.2d 689.

BURKE, JUSTICE. Defendant Twentieth Century–Fox Film Corporation appeals from a summary judgment granting to plaintiff the recovery of agreed compensation under a written contract for her services as an actress in a motion picture. As will appear, we have concluded that the trial court correctly ruled in plaintiff's favor and that the judgment should be affirmed.

Plaintiff is well known as an actress, and in the contract between plaintiff and defendant is sometimes referred to as the "Artist." Under the contract, dated August 6, 1965, plaintiff was to play the female lead in defendant's contemplated production of a motion picture entitled "Bloomer Girl." The contract provided that defendant would pay plaintiff a minimum "guaranteed compensation" of $53,571.42 per week for 14 weeks commencing May 23, 1966, for a total of $750,000. Prior to May 1966, defendant decided not to produce the picture and by a letter dated April 4, 1966, it notified plaintiff of that decision and that it would not "comply with our obligations to you under" the written contract.

By the same letter and with the professed purpose "to avoid any damage to you," defendant instead offered to employ plaintiff as the leading actress in another film tentatively entitled "Big Country, Big Man" (hereinafter, "Big Country"). The compensation offered was identical, as were 31 of the 34 numbered provisions or articles of the original contract.[1] Unlike "Bloomer Girl," however, which was to have been a musical production, "Big Country" was a dramatic "western type"

———

1. Among the identical provisions was the following found in the last paragraph of Article 2 of the original contract: "We [defendant] shall not be obligated to utilize   your [plaintiff's] services in or in connection with the Photoplay hereunder, our sole obligation, subject to the terms and conditions of this Agreement, being to pay you

movie. "Bloomer Girl" was to have been filmed in California; "Big Country" was to be produced in Australia. Also, certain terms in the proffered contract varied from those of the original.[2] Plaintiff was given one week within which to accept; she did not and the offer lapsed. Plaintiff then commenced this action seeking recovery of the agreed guaranteed compensation.

The complaint sets forth two causes of action. The first is for money due under the contract; the second, based upon the same allegations as the first, is for damages resulting from defendant's breach of contract. Defendant in its answer admits the existence and validity of the contract, that plaintiff complied with all the conditions, covenants and promises and stood ready to complete the performance, and that defendant breached and "anticipatorily repudiated" the contract. It denies, however, that any money is due to plaintiff either under the contract or as a result of its breach, and pleads as an affirmative defense to both causes of action plaintiff's allegedly deliberate failure to mitigate damages, asserting that she unreasonably refused to accept its offer of the leading role in "Big Country."

Plaintiff moved for summary judgment under Code of Civil Procedure section 437c, the motion was granted, and summary judgment for $750,000 plus interest was entered in plaintiff's favor. This appeal by defendant followed.

The familiar rules are that the matter to be determined by the trial court on a motion for summary judgment is whether facts have been presented which give rise to a triable factual issue. The court may not pass upon the issue itself. Summary judgment is proper only if the

---

the guaranteed compensation herein provided for."

2. Article 29 of the original contract specified that plaintiff approved the director already chosen for "Bloomer Girl" and that in case he failed to act as director plaintiff was to have approval rights of any substitute director. Article 31 provided that plaintiff was to have the right of approval of the "Bloomer Girl" dance director, and Article 32 gave her the right of approval of the screenplay.

Defendant's letter of April 4 to plaintiff, which contained both defendant's notice of breach of the "Bloomer Girl" contract and offer of the lead in "Big Country," eliminated or impaired each of those rights. It read in part as follows: "The terms and conditions of our offer of employment are identical to those set forth in the 'BLOOMER GIRL'" Agreement, Articles 1 through 34 and Exhibit A to the Agreement, except as follows:

"1. Article 31 of said Agreement will not be included in any contract of employment regarding 'BIG COUNTRY,

BIG MAN' as it is not a musical and it thus will not need a dance director.

"2. In the 'BLOOMER GIRL' agreement, in Articles 29 and 32, you were given certain director and screenplay approvals and you had preapproved certain matters. Since there simply is insufficient time to negotiate with you regarding your choice of director and regarding the screenplay and since you already expressed an interest in performing the role in 'BIG COUNTRY, BIG MAN,' we must exclude from our offer of employment in 'BIG COUNTRY, BIG MAN' any approval rights as are contained in said Articles 29 and 32; however, we shall consult with you respecting the director to be selected to direct the photoplay and will further consult with you with respect to the screenplay and any revisions or changes therein, provided, however, that if we fail to agree ... the decision of ... [defendant] with respect to the selection of a director and to revisions and changes in the said screenplay shall be binding upon the parties to said agreement."

affidavits or declarations in support of the moving party would be sufficient to sustain a judgment in his favor and his opponent does not by affidavit show facts sufficient to present a triable issue of fact. . . .

However, before projected earnings from other employment opportunities not sought or accepted by the discharged employee can be applied in mitigation, the employer must show that the other employment was comparable, or substantially similar, to that of which the employee has been deprived; the employee's rejection of or failure to seek other available employment of a different or inferior kind may not be resorted to in order to mitigate damages. (Gonzales v. Internat. Assn. of Machinists (1963) 213 Cal.App.2d 817, 822–824, 29 Cal.Rptr. 190. . . .)

In the present case defendant has raised no issue of *reasonableness of efforts* by plaintiff to obtain other employment; the sole issue is whether plaintiff's refusal of defendant's substitute offer of "Big Country" may be used in mitigation. Nor, if the "Big Country" offer was of employment different or inferior when compared with the original "Bloomer Girl" employment, is there an issue as to whether or not plaintiff acted reasonably in refusing the substitute offer. Despite defendant's arguments to the contrary, no case cited or which our research has discovered holds or suggests that reasonableness is an element of a wrongfully discharged employee's option to reject, or fail to seek, different or inferior employment lest the possible earnings therefrom be charged against him in mitigation of damages.[5]

Applying the foregoing rules to the record in the present case, with all intendments in favor of the party opposing the summary judgment motion—here, defendant—it is clear that the trial court correctly ruled that plaintiff's failure to accept defendant's tendered substitute employment could not be applied in mitigation of damages because the offer of the "Big Country" lead was of employment both different and inferior, and that no factual dispute was presented on that issue. The mere circumstance that "Bloomer Girl" was to be a musical review calling upon plaintiff's talents as a dancer as well as an actress, and was to be

---

5. Instead, in each case the reasonableness referred to was that of the *efforts* of the employee to obtain other employment that was not different or inferior; his right to reject the latter was declared as an unqualified rule of law. Thus, Gonzales v. Internat. Assn. of Machinists, *supra*, 213 Cal.App.2d 817, 823?824, 29 Cal.Rptr. 190, 194, holds that the trial court correctly instructed the jury that plaintiff union member, a machinist, was required to make "such *efforts* as the average [member of his union] desiring employment would make at that particular time and place" (italics added); but, further, that the court *properly rejected* defendant's *offer of proof of the availability of other kinds of employment* at the same or higher pay than plaintiff usually received and all outside the jurisdiction of his union, as plaintiff could not be required to accept different employment or a nonunion job.

In Harris v. Nat. Union, etc., Cooks and Stewards, *supra*, 116 Cal.App.2d 759, 761, 254 P.2d 673, 676, the issues were stated to be, inter alia, whether comparable employment was open to each plaintiff employee, and if so whether each plaintiff made a *reasonable effort* to secure such employment. It was held that the trial court *properly sustained an objection to an offer to prove a custom of accepting a job in a lower rank* when work in the higher rank was not available, as "The duty of mitigation of damages . . . does not require the plaintiff 'to seek or to accept other employment of a different or inferior kind.'" (p. 764 [5], 254 P.2d p. 676.). . . .

produced in the City of Los Angeles, whereas "Big Country" was a straight dramatic role in a "Western Type" story taking place in an opal mine in Australia, demonstrates the difference in kind between the two employments; the female lead as a dramatic actress in a western style motion picture can by no stretch of imagination be considered the equivalent of or substantially similar to the lead in a song-and-dance production.

Additionally, the substitute "Big Country" offer proposed to eliminate or impair the director and screenplay approvals accorded to plaintiff under the original "Bloomer Girl" contract (see fn. 2, *ante*), and thus constituted an offer of inferior employment. No expertise or judicial notice is required in order to hold that the deprivation or infringement of an employee's rights held under an original employment contract converts the available "other employment" relied upon by the employer to mitigate damages, into inferior employment which the employee need not seek or accept. (See Gonzales v. Internat. Assn. of Machinists, *supra*, 213 Cal.App.2d 817, 823–824, 29 Cal.Rptr. 190; and fn. 5 . . . .)

Statements found in affidavits submitted by defendant in opposition to plaintiff's summary judgment motion, to the effect that the "Big Country" offer was not of employment different from or inferior to that under the "Bloomer Girl" contract, merely repeat the allegations of defendant's answer to the complaint in this action, constitute only conclusionary assertions with respect to undisputed facts, and do not give rise to a triable factual issue so as to defeat the motion for summary judgment. . . .

In view of the determination that defendant failed to present any facts showing the existence of a factual issue with respect to its sole defense—plaintiff's rejection of its substitute employment offer in mitigation of damages—we need not consider plaintiff's further contention that for various reasons, including the provisions of the original contract set forth in footnote 1, *ante*, plaintiff was excused from attempting to mitigate damages.

The judgment is affirmed.

SULLIVAN, ACTING CHIEF JUSTICE (dissenting). The basic question in this case is whether or not plaintiff acted reasonably in rejecting defendant's offer of alternate employment. The answer depends upon whether that offer (starring in "Big Country, Big Man") was an offer of work that was substantially similar to her former employment (starring in "Bloomer Girl") or of work that was of a different or inferior kind. To my mind this is a factual issue which the trial court should not have determined on a motion for summary judgment. The majority have not only repeated this error but have compounded it by applying the rules governing mitigation of damages in the employer-employee context in a misleading fashion. Accordingly, I respectfully dissent.

The familiar rule requiring a plaintiff in a tort or contract action to mitigate damages embodies notions of fairness and socially responsible behavior which are fundamental to our jurisprudence. Most broadly stated, it precludes the recovery of damages which, through the exercise of due diligence, could have been avoided. Thus, in essence, it is a rule requiring reasonable conduct in commercial affairs. This general principle governs the obligations of an employee after his employer has wrongfully repudiated or terminated the employment contract. Rather than permitting the employee simply to remain idle during the balance of the contract period, the law requires him to make a reasonable effort to secure other employment.[1] He is not obliged, however, to seek or accept any and all types of work which may be available. Only work which is in the same field and which is of the same quality need be accepted.[2]

Over the years the courts have employed various phrases to define the type of employment which the employee, upon his wrongful discharge, is under an obligation to accept. Thus in California alone it has been held that he must accept employment which is "substantially similar" ...; "comparable employment" ...; employment "in the same general line of the first employment" ...; "equivalent to his prior position" ...; "employment in a similar capacity" ...; employment which is "not ... of a different or inferior kind...." (Gonzales v. Internat. Assn. of Machinists (1963) 213 Cal.App.2d 817, 822, 29 Cal. Rptr. 190, 193.)

For reasons which are unexplained, the majority cite several of these cases yet select from among the various judicial formulations which contain one particular phrase, "Not of a different or inferior kind," with which to analyze this case. I have discovered no historical or theoretical reason to adopt this phrase, which is simply a negative restatement of the affirmative standards set out in the above cases, as the exclusive standard. Indeed, its emergence is an example of the dubious phenomenon of the law responding not to rational judicial choice or changing social conditions, but to unrecognized changes in the language of opinions or legal treatises. However, the phrase is a serviceable one and my concern is not with its use as the standard but rather with what I consider its distortion.

The relevant language excuses acceptance only of employment which is of a *different kind*. (Gonzales v. Internat. Assn. of Machinists, *supra*,

---

1. The issue is generally discussed in terms of a duty on the part of the employee to minimize loss. The practice is long-established and there is little reason to change despite Judge Cardozo's observation of its subtle inaccuracy. "The servant is free to accept employment or reject it according to his uncensored pleasure. What is meant by the supposed duty is merely this: That if he unreasonably reject, he will not be heard to say that the loss of wages from then on shall be deemed the jural consequence of the earlier discharge. He has broken the chain of causation, and loss resulting to him thereafter is suffered through his own act."

(McClelland v. Climax Hosiery Mills (1930) 252 N.Y. 347, 359, 169 N.E. 605, 609, concurring opinion.)

2. This qualification of the rule seems to reflect the simple and humane attitude that it is too severe to demand of a person that he attempt to find and perform work for which he has no training or experience. Many of the older cases hold that one need not accept work in an inferior rank or position nor work which is more menial or arduous. This suggests that the rule may have had its origin in the bourgeois fear of resubmergence in lower economic classes.

213 Cal.App.2d 817, 822, 29 Cal.Rptr. 190....) It has never been the law that the mere existence of *differences between two jobs in the same field* is sufficient, as a matter of law, to excuse an employee wrongfully discharged from one from accepting the other in order to mitigate damages. Such an approach would effectively eliminate any obligation of an employee to attempt to minimize damage arising from a wrongful discharge. The only alternative job offer an employee would be required to accept would be an offer of his former job by his former employer.

Although the majority appear to hold that there was a difference "in kind" between the employment offered plaintiff in "Bloomer Girl" and that offered in "Big Country" ..., an examination of the opinion makes crystal clear that the majority merely point out differences between the two *films* (an obvious circumstance) and then apodictically assert that these constitute a difference in the *kind of employment*. The entire rationale of the majority boils down to this: that the *"mere circumstances"* that "Bloomer Girl" was to be a musical review while "Big Country" was a straight drama "demonstrates the difference in kind" since a female lead in a western is not "the equivalent of or substantially similar to" a lead in a musical. This is merely attempting to prove the proposition by repeating it. It shows that the vehicles for the display of the star's talents are different but it does not prove that her employment as a star in such vehicles is of necessity different *in kind* and either inferior or superior.

I believe that the approach taken by the majority (a superficial listing of differences with no attempt to assess their significance) may subvert a valuable legal doctrine.[5] The inquiry in cases such as this should not be whether differences between the two jobs exist (there will always be differences) but whether the differences which are present are substantial enough to constitute differences in the *kind* of employment or, alternatively, whether they render the substitute work employment of an *inferior kind*.

It seems to me that *this* inquiry involves, in the instant case at least, factual determinations which are improper on a motion for summary judgment....

Questions

1. Why should a provider of services, like Ms. Parker (Shirley MacLaine), not recover the contract price? Should a seller of goods recover the contract price when the buyer breaches? Why is there an explicit mitigation doctrine in services contracts but not in the main remedies for breach of a contract for the sale of goods? Is the same interest of the party in breach nonetheless being protected in sales of goods?

5. The values of the doctrine of mitigation of damages in this context are that it minimizes the unnecessary personal and social (e.g., nonproductive use of labor, litigation) costs of contractual failure. If a wrongfully discharged employee can, through his own action and without suffering financial or psychological loss in the process, reduce the damages accruing from the breach of contract, the most sensible policy is to require him to do so. I fear the majority opinion will encourage precisely opposite conduct.

2. What is the key difference between the majority and the dissent? Is it about the film business? The law of summary judgment? Or the place of an artist's subjective preferences in the law of contract damages? Consider, in connection with the last question, the first sentence of the dissenting opinion.

3. *Problem.*

On January 20, Rock, a general building contractor, entered into a contract with Doris to build a house on Doris's land. Rock then contracted with Cary Plumbing Co. for Cary to do the plumbing, in accordance with specifications attached to the contract, for a price of $32,000. In March, before building had progressed to the point that plumbing could be completed, Rock and Doris had a falling out. Cary had received progress payments of $3,000 at the time, and had spent $5,000 in labor and materials on the job. Rock was ordered to cease work. Rock promptly ordered Cary to cease work. Two days later, Cary entered into a new contract with Doris to complete the plumbing work at a cost to Doris of $24,000. The plumbing job was finished in due course at a cost of $22,000. Doris paid Cary $24,000. Would you advise Cary that it would be worthwhile to sue Rock for breach of contract?

PEEVYHOUSE v. GARLAND COAL & MINING CO.

Supreme Court of Oklahoma, 1962.
382 P.2d 109.

JACKSON, JUSTICE. In the trial court, plaintiffs Willie and Lucille Peevyhouse sued the defendant, Garland Coal and Mining Company, for damages for breach of contract. Judgment was for plaintiffs in an amount considerably less than was sued for. Plaintiffs appeal and defendant cross-appeals. . . .

Briefly stated, the facts are as follows: plaintiffs owned a farm containing coal deposits, and in November, 1954, leased the premises to defendant for a period of five years for coal mining purposes. A "strip-mining" operation was contemplated in which the coal would be taken from pits on the surface of the ground, instead of from underground mine shafts. In addition to the usual covenants found in a coal mining lease, defendant specifically agreed to perform certain restorative and remedial work at the end of the lease period. It is unnecessary to set out the details of the work to be done, other than to say that it would involve the moving of many thousands of cubic yards of dirt, at a cost estimated by expert witnesses at about $29,000.00. However, plaintiffs sued for only $25,000.00.

During the trial, it was stipulated that all covenants and agreements in the lease contract had been fully carried out by both parties, except the remedial work mentioned above; defendant conceded that this work had not been done.

Plaintiffs introduced expert testimony as to the amount and nature of the work to be done, and its estimated cost. Over plaintiffs' objections, defendant thereafter introduced expert testimony as to the "diminution in value" of plaintiffs' farm resulting from the failure of defendant to render performance as agreed in the contract—that is, the difference between the present value of the farm, and what its value would have been if defendant had done what it agreed to do.

At the conclusion of the trial, the court instructed the jury that it must return a verdict for plaintiffs, and left the amount of damages for jury determination. On the measure of damages, the court instructed the jury that it might consider the cost of performance of the work defendant agreed to do, "together with all of the evidence offered on behalf of either party."

It thus appears that the jury was at liberty to consider the "diminution in value" of plaintiffs' farm as well as the cost of "repair work" in determining the amount of damages.

It returned a verdict for plaintiffs for $5,000.00—only a fraction of the "cost of performance," *but more than the total value of the farm even after the remedial work is done.*

On appeal, the issue is sharply drawn. Plaintiffs contend that the true measure of damages in this case is what it will cost plaintiffs to obtain performance of the work that was not done because of defendant's default. Defendant argues that the measure of damages is the cost of performance "limited, however, to the total difference in the market value before and after the work was performed."

It appears that this precise question has not heretofore been presented to this court. In Ardizonne v. Archer, 72 Okl. 70, 178 P. 263, this court held that the measure of damages for breach of a contract to drill an oil well was the reasonable cost of drilling the well, but here a slightly different factual situation exists. The drilling of an oil well will yield valuable geological information, even if no oil or gas is found, and of course if the well is a producer, the value of the premises increases. In the case before us, it is argued by defendant with some force that the performance of the remedial work defendant agreed to do will add at the most only a few hundred dollars to the value of plaintiffs' farm, and that the damages should be limited to that amount because that is all plaintiffs have lost.

Plaintiffs rely on Groves v. John Wunder Co., 205 Minn. 163, 286 N.W. 235, 123 A.L.R. 502. In that case, the Minnesota court, in a substantially similar situation, adopted the "cost of performance" rule as opposed to the "value" rule. The result was to authorize a jury to give plaintiff damages in the amount of $60,000, where the real estate concerned would have been worth only $12,160, even if the work contracted for had been done.

It may be observed that Groves v. John Wunder Co., supra, is the only case which has come to our attention in which the cost of performance rule has been followed under circumstances where the cost of performance greatly exceeded the diminution in value resulting from the breach of contract. Incidentally, it appears that this case was decided by a plurality rather than a majority of the members of the court.

Defendant relies principally upon Sandy Valley & E. R. Co. v. Hughes, 175 Ky. 320, 194 S.W. 344; Bigham v. Wabash–Pittsburg Terminal Ry. Co., 223 Pa. 106, 72 A. 318; and Sweeney v. Lewis Const. Co., 66 Wash. 490, 119 P. 1108. These were all cases in which, under similar circumstances, the appellate courts followed the "value" rule instead of the "cost of performance" rule. Plaintiff points out that in the earliest of these cases (Bigham) the court cites as authority on the measure of damages an earlier Pennsylvania *tort* case, and that the other two cases follow the first, with no explanation as to why a measure of damages ordinarily followed in cases sounding in tort should be used in contract cases. Nevertheless, it is of some significance that three out of four appellate courts have followed the diminution in value rule under circumstances where, as here, the cost of performance greatly exceeds the diminution in value.

The explanation may be found in the fact that the situations presented are artificial ones. It is highly unlikely that the ordinary property owner would agree to pay $29,000 (or its equivalent) for the construction of "improvements" upon his property that would increase its value only about ($300) three hundred dollars. The result is that we are called upon to apply principles of law theoretically based upon reason and reality to a situation which is basically unreasonable and unrealistic. . . .

[T]he authorities are not in agreement as to the factors to be considered in determining whether the cost of performance rule or the value rule should be applied. The American Law Institute's Restatement of the Law, Contracts, Volume 1, Sections 346(1)(a)(i) and (ii) submits the proposition that the cost of performance is the proper measure of damages "if this is possible and does not involve *unreasonable economic waste*;" and that the diminution in value caused by the breach is the proper measure "if construction and completion in accordance with the contract would involve *unreasonable economic waste*." (Emphasis supplied.) In an explanatory comment immediately following the text, the Restatement makes it clear that the "economic waste" referred to consists of the destruction of a substantially completed building or other structure. Of course no such destruction is involved in the case now before us.

On the other hand, in McCormick, Damages, Section 168, it is said with regard to building and construction contracts that ". . . in cases where the defect is one that can be repaired or cured without *undue expense*" the cost of performance is the proper measure of damages, but where ". . . the defect in material or construction is one that cannot be remedied without *an expenditure for reconstruction disproportionate to the end to be attained*" (emphasis supplied) the value rule should be followed. The same idea was expressed in Jacob & Youngs, Inc. v. Kent, 230 N.Y. 239, 129 N.E. 889, 23 A.L.R. 1429, as follows:

"The owner is entitled to the money which will permit him to complete, unless the cost of completion is grossly and unfairly out of proportion to the good to be attained. When that is true, the measure is the difference in value."

It thus appears that the prime consideration in the Restatement was "economic waste;" and that the prime consideration in McCormick, Damages, and in Jacob & Youngs, Inc. v. Kent, supra, was the relationship between the expense involved and the "end to be attained"—in other words, the "relative economic benefit."

In view of the unrealistic fact situation in the instant case, . . . we are of the opinion that the "relative economic benefit" is a proper consideration here. This is in accord with the recent case of Mann v. Clowser, 190 Va. 887, 59 S.E.2d 78, where, in applying the cost rule, the Virginia court specifically noted that ". . . the defects are remediable from a practical standpoint and the costs *are not grossly disproportionate to the results to be obtained*" (Emphasis supplied). . . .

We therefore hold that where, in a coal mining lease, lessee agrees to perform certain remedial work on the premises concerned at the end of the lease period, and thereafter the contract is fully performed by both parties except that the remedial work is not done, the measure of damages in an action by lessor against lessee for damages for breach of contract is ordinarily the reasonable cost of performance of the work; however, where the contract provision breached was merely incidental to the main purpose in view, and where the economic benefit which would result to lessor by full performance of the work is grossly disproportionate to the cost of performance, the damages which lessor may recover are limited to the diminution in value resulting to the premises because of the non-performance.

We believe the above holding is in . . . harmony with the better-reasoned cases from the other jurisdictions where analogous fact situations have been considered. It should be noted that the rule as stated does not interfere with the property owner's right to "do what he will with his own" (Chamberlain v. Parker, 45 N.Y. 569), or his right, if he chooses, to contract for "improvements" which will actually have the effect of reducing his property's value. Where such result is in fact contemplated by the parties, and is a main or principal purpose of those contracting, it would seem that the measure of damages for breach would ordinarily be the cost of performance. . . .

Under the most liberal view of the evidence herein, the diminution in value resulting to the premises because of non-performance of the remedial work was $300.00. After a careful search of the record, we have found no evidence of a higher figure, and plaintiffs do not argue in their briefs that a greater diminution in value was sustained. It thus appears that the judgment was clearly excessive, and that the amount for which judgment should have been rendered is definitely and satisfactorily shown by the record. . . .

We are of the opinion that the judgment of the trial court for plaintiffs should be, and it is hereby, modified and reduced to the sum of $300.00, and as so modified it is affirmed.

IRWIN, JUSTICE (dissenting). By the specific provisions in the coal mining lease under consideration, the defendant agreed as follows:

" . . .

"7b Lessee agrees to make fills in the pits dug on said premises on the property line in such manner that fences can be placed thereon and access had to opposite sides of the pits.

"7c Lessee agrees to smooth off the top of the spoil banks on the above premises.

"7d Lessee agrees to leave the creek crossing the above premises in such a condition that it will not interfere with the crossings to be made in pits as set out in 7b.

"7f Lessee further agrees to leave no shale or dirt on the high wall of said pits. . . ."

Following the expiration of the lease, plaintiffs made demand upon defendant that it carry out the provisions of the contract and to perform those covenants contained therein.

Defendant admits that it failed to perform its obligations that it agreed and contracted to perform under the lease contract and there is nothing in the record which indicates that defendant could not perform its obligations. Therefore, in my opinion defendant's breach of the contract was wilful and not in good faith.

Although the contract speaks for itself, there were several negotiations between the plaintiffs and defendant before the contract was executed. Defendant admitted in the trial of the action, that plaintiffs insisted that the above provisions be included in the contract and that they would not agree to the coal mining lease unless the above provisions were included.

In consideration for the lease contract, plaintiffs were to receive a certain amount as royalty for the coal produced and marketed and in addition thereto their land was to be restored as provided in the contract.

Defendant received as consideration for the contract, its proportionate share of the coal produced and marketed and in addition thereto, the *right to use* plaintiffs' land in the furtherance of its mining operations.

The cost for performing the contract in question could have been reasonably approximated when the contract was negotiated and executed and there are no conditions now existing which could not have been reasonably anticipated by the parties. Therefore, defendant had knowledge, when it prevailed upon the plaintiffs to execute the lease, that the cost of performance might be disproportionate to the value or benefits received by plaintiff for the performance.

Defendant has received its benefits under the contract and now urges, in substance, that plaintiffs' measure of damages for its failure to perform should be the economic value of performance to the plaintiffs and not the cost of performance.

If a peculiar set of facts should exist where the above rule should be applied as the proper measure of damages, (and in my judgment those facts do not exist in the instant case) before such rule should be applied, consideration should be given to the benefits received or contracted for by the party who asserts the application of the rule.

Defendant did not have the right to mine plaintiffs' coal or to use plaintiffs' property for its mining operations without the consent of plaintiffs. Defendant had knowledge of the benefits that it would receive under the contract and the approximate cost of performing the contract. With this knowledge, it must be presumed that defendant thought that it would be to its economic advantage to enter into the contract with plaintiffs and that it would reap benefits from the contract, or it would have not entered into the contract.

Therefore, if the value of the performance of a contract should be considered in determining the measure of damages for breach of a contract, the value of the benefits received under the contract by a party who breaches a contract should also be considered. However, in my judgment, to give consideration to either in the instant action, completely rescinds and holds for naught the solemnity of the contract before us and makes an entirely new contract for the parties. . . .

In my judgment, we should follow the case of Groves v. John Wunder Company, 205 Minn. 163, 286 N.W. 235, 123 A.L.R. 502, which defendant agrees "that the fact situation is apparently similar to the one in the case at bar," and where the Supreme Court of Minnesota held:

> "The owner's or employer's damages for such a breach (i.e. breach hypothesized in 2d syllabus) are to be measured, not in respect to the value of the land to be improved, but by the reasonable cost of doing that which the contractor promised to do and which he left undone."

The hypothesized breach referred to states that where the contractor's breach of a contract is wilful, that is, in bad faith, he is not entitled to any benefit of the equitable doctrine of substantial performance.

In the instant action defendant has made no attempt to even substantially perform. The contract in question is not immoral, is not tainted with fraud, and was not entered into through mistake or accident and is not contrary to public policy. It is clear and unambiguous and the parties understood the terms thereof, and the approximate cost of fulfilling the obligations could have been approximately ascertained. There are no conditions existing now which could not have been reasonably anticipated when the contract was negotiated and executed. The defendant could have performed the contract if it desired. It has accepted and reaped the benefits of its contract and now urges that plaintiffs' benefits under the contract be denied. If plaintiffs' benefits are denied, such benefits would inure to the direct benefit of the defendant.

Therefore, in my opinion, the plaintiffs were entitled to specific performance of the contract and since defendant has failed to perform, the proper measure of damages should be the cost of performance. Any other measure of damage would be holding for naught the express provisions of the contract; would be taking from the plaintiffs the benefits of the contract and placing those benefits in defendant which has failed to perform its obligations; would be granting benefits to defendant without a resulting obligation; and would be completely rescinding the solemn obligation of the contract for the benefit of the defendant to the detriment of the plaintiffs by making an entirely new contract for the parties.

I therefore respectfully dissent to the opinion promulgated by a majority of my associates.

SUPPLEMENTAL OPINION ON REHEARING

JACKSON, JUSTICE. In a Petition for Rehearing, plaintiffs Peevyhouse have raised certain questions not presented in the original briefs on appeal.

They insist that the trial court excluded evidence as to the total value of the premises concerned, and, in effect, that they have not had their "day in court." This argument arises by reason of the fact that their farm consists not merely of the 60 acres covered by the coal mining lease, but includes other lands as well. . . .

Numbered paragraph 2 of plaintiffs' petition alleges that they own and live upon 60 acres of land which are specifically described. *This is the only land described in the petition, and there is no allegation as to the ownership or leasing of any other lands.*

Page 4 of the transcript of evidence reveals that near the beginning of the trial, plaintiff Peevyhouse was asked a question concerning improvements he had made to his property. His answer was, "For one thing I built a new home on the place in 1951, and along about that time I was building a pasture. And I would say *ninety percent of this 120 acres is in good grass.*" (Emphasis supplied.) Mr. Watts, defense counsel, then objected "to any testimony about the property, other than the 160 acres." (It is obvious that he means "60" instead of "160.") Further proceedings were as follows:

> "The Court: The objection will be sustained as to any other part. Go ahead.

> "Mr. McCornell (attorney for plaintiffs): Comes now the plaintiff and dismisses the second cause of action without prejudice."

It thus appears that plaintiffs made no complaint as to the court's exclusion of evidence concerning lands other than the 60 acres described in their petition. . . .

The defendant offered the testimony of five witnesses in the trial court; four of them testified as to "diminution in value." They were not cross examined by plaintiffs.

In their motion for new trial, plaintiffs did not complain that they had been prevented from offering evidence as to the diminution in value of their lands; on the contrary, they affirmatively complained of the trial court's action in admitting evidence of the *defendant* on that point.

In the original brief of plaintiffs in error (Peevyhouse) filed in this court there appears the following language at page 4:

"... Near the outset of the trial plaintiffs dismissed their second cause of action without prejudice: ... It was further stipulated that the *only issue remaining in the lawsuit* was the proof and *measure of damages* to which plaintiffs were entitled...."

(Emphasis supplied.)

In the answer brief of Garland Coal & Mining Co., at page 3, there appears the following language:

"Defendant offered evidence that the total value of the property involved before the mining operation would be $60.00 per acre, and $11.00 per acre after the mining operation (60 acres at $49.00 per acre is $2,940.00). Other evidence was that the property was worth $5.00 to $15.00 per acre after the mining, but before the repairs; and would be worth an increase of $2.00 to $5.00 per acre after the repairs had been made (60 acres at $5.00 per acre is $300.00) [citations to transcript omitted]."

At page 18 of the same brief there is another statement to the effect that the "amount of diminution in value of the land" was $300.00.

About two months after the answer brief was filed in this court, plaintiffs filed a reply brief. The reply brief makes no reference at all to the language of the answer brief above quoted and *does not deny that the diminution in value shown by the record amounts to $300.00.* On the contrary, it contains the following language at page 5:

"... Plaintiffs in error pointed out in their initial brief that this evidence concerning land values was objectionable as being incompetent and refused to cross-examine or offer rebuttal for the reason that they did not choose to waive their objections to the competency of the evidence by disproving defendant in error's allegations as to land values. We strongly urged at the trial below, and still do, that market value of the land has no application...."

Our extended reference to the pleadings, testimony and prior briefs in this case has not been solely for the purpose of showing that plaintiffs failed to complain of the court's rulings. Our purpose, rather, has been to demonstrate the plan and theory upon which plaintiffs tried their case below, and upon which they argued it in the prior briefs on appeal.

The whole record in this case justifies the conclusion that plaintiffs tried their case upon the theory that the "cost of performance" would be the sole measure of damages and that they would recognize no other. In view of the whole record in this case and the original briefs on appeal, we conclude that they so tried it *with notice* that defendant would contend for the "diminution in value" rule. The testimony to which they specifically refer in the petition for rehearing shows that the trial court properly excluded defendant's evidence concerning lands other than the 60 acres described in the petition because such evidence was *not within the scope of the pleadings*. At no time did plaintiffs ask permission to amend their petition, either with or without prejudice to trial, so as to describe *all* of the lands they own or lease, and no evidence was admitted which could broaden the scope of the petition.

Plaintiffs' petition described 60 acres of land only; plaintiffs offered no evidence on the question of "diminution in value" and objected to similar evidence offered by the defendant; their motion for new trial contained no allegation that they had been prevented from offering evidence on this question; in their reply brief they did not controvert the allegation in defendant's answer brief that the record showed a "diminution in value" of only $300.00; and in view of the stipulation they admittedly made in the trial court, their statement in petition for rehearing that the court's instructions on the measure of damages came as a "complete surprise" and "did not afford them the opportunity to prepare and introduce evidence under the 'diminution in value' rule" is not supported by the record.

We think plaintiffs' present position is that of a plaintiff in any damage suit who has failed to prove his damages—opposed by a defendant who has proved plaintiff's damages; and that plaintiffs' complaint that the record does not show the total "diminution in value" to their lands comes too late. It is well settled that a party will not be permitted to change his theory of the case upon appeal. Knox v. Eason Oil Co., 190 Okl. 627, 126 P.2d 247.

Also, plaintiffs' expressed fear that by introducing evidence on the question of "diminution in value" they would have waived their objection to similar evidence by defendant was not justified. Vogel v. Fisher et al., 203 Okl. 657, 225 P.2d 346; 53 Am.Jur. Trial, Sec. 144....

The petition for rehearing is denied.

Questions

1. Were the Peevyhouses put in the position they would have been in had the contract been performed? What was their contractual expectation interest? What was the harm to that interest when Garland breached? Should it matter whether the breach was willful?

2. Why does the court write, "it is of some significance that three out of four appellate courts have followed the diminution in value rule" under similar circumstances? Do you agree that counting precedents is significant in legal reasoning? Is a "majority rule" more authoritative than a "minority rule"?

3. Based on the facts reported in the main appellate opinion, what do you think the Peevyhouses would do with the money if they were awarded $25,000? If they would pocket it without actually restoring the land, what does that say about their contractual interest? If they would restore the land, what does that say about their interest?

4. Does the main appellate opinion provide all of the facts needed to answer the foregoing questions? Does the opinion on rehearing supply the needed facts? What went wrong for the Peevyhouses? Is their disappointment due to the law of contracts?

5. *Problems.*

a. The facts are as reported in the main opinion in *Peevyhouse*, except that the contract contained a clause in a Preamble reading: "*Whereas* the land owned by Willie and Lucille Peevyhouse has been in the family for three generations, having been staked by Willie's grandfather in the Great Oklahoma Land Rush, and *whereas* fourteen members of the Peevyhouse family are buried on the land, making restoration of the land extraordinarily important to the Peevyhouses...." Same result?

b. The facts are as reported in the main opinion in *Peevyhouse*, except that, in addition, Garland Coal Co. ceased excavations earlier than expected because the land ran out of coal. Completion would have required bringing in much fill dirt, at unexpected expense. Garland performed some remedial work, but concluded that the remainder would be useless due to the early termination of the work. Same result?

c. The facts are as reported in the main opinion in *Peevyhouse*, except that the Peevyhouses prove at trial that they sought restoration of the land to preserve the environment. Their lawyer argues that, as a matter of public policy, damages should reflect the cost of restoration. Same result?

c. Limitations on Damages

Special or consequential damages compensate for losses peculiar to the nonbreaching party, in addition to any general damages to which it is entitled. For example, when a seller breaches by nondelivery, the buyer will probably spend time and money searching for an alternative supplier and contracting for substitute goods ("covering"). Transportation costs may be higher under the cover contract. Such losses are caused by the breach and are compensable as incidental damages. RESTATEMENT (SECOND) OF CONTRACTS § 347(b); U.C.C. § 2–715(1). In addition, the nonbreaching party may suffer special losses as a consequence of the breach. For example, when a seller fails to deliver a piece of machinery on time, the buyer may suffer a delay in production. It may lose customers and hence profits. Or it may be liable for breach of its contracts for sale of its product. Such damages are compensable as consequential damages, provided that certain limitations are not applicable.

Prominent among the limitations are legal requirements that damages be reasonably foreseeable and proven with reasonable certainty.

Both requirements in practice affect mainly claims for lost profits sought as special damages.

———

RESTATEMENT (SECOND) OF CONTRACTS § 352

———

LOCKE v. UNITED STATES

United States Court of Claims, 1960.
151 Ct.Cl. 262, 283 F.2d 521.

JONES, CHIEF JUDGE. This is a suit, first, for lost profits resulting from an alleged breach of a requirements contract held by plaintiff with the General Services Administration. The contract covered the repair of typewriters in the San Diego, California, area. . . .

The plaintiff, Harvey Ward Locke, was the owner of a typewriter-repair company doing business variously under the names "Ward's Typewriter Repair" and "Allied Typewriter Company." As Ward's Typewriter Repair, of San Diego, California, plaintiff was awarded GSA Federal Supply Schedule Contract GS–09S–1329. The contract covered the repair, maintenance and reconditioning of manual typewriters in the San Diego area for the period July 1, 1955, through June 30, 1956. Similar typewriter-repair contracts were awarded to three other local companies covering the same period of time. These contracts provided that upon an acceptable bid and a showing of responsibility the contractor's name, address, and telephone number would be placed in a Federal Supply Schedule which was widely distributed to Government installations in the area. Apart from certain exceptional conditions not pertinent here, it was mandatory upon on the various departments of the Executive Branch of the Federal Government in the area to use contractors whose names appeared in this schedule when typewriter-repair services were desired. (The Department of Defense was specifically excluded.) However, these agencies were at liberty to choose *any* name from the schedule and were not bound to proceed in the schedule in a given order. In addition to "mandatory use" all agencies of the Federal Government, particularly the Department of Defense, optionally might order repair services from contractors appearing in the schedule. Each bidder whose bid was accepted and whose name was listed in the schedule was obligated to perform all the services for which he contracted that resulted from the "mandatory" provisions of the contract. However, contractors were at liberty to decline those progressive awards which arose from the "optional" provisions of the contract.

Plaintiff operated under his contract for several months and received some business from the Government. But on February 2, 1956, the Government's contracting officer terminated the contract for default and plaintiff's name was stricken from the schedule. Other contractors in the schedule continued to receive Government business until the expiration of their contracts. Plaintiff filed an appeal with the Board of Review, General Services Administration, and following a full hearing, the board rendered the following decision:

"1. Contract No. GS–09S–1329 was terminated for default on February 2, 1956, without proper cause.

"2. The Appellant's claim for the payment of $30,000 as compensation for lost profits is denied.

"3. The Appellant's claim for the payment of $60,000 as compensation for alleged defamation of character and loss of other business is denied."

Following this denial of relief the plaintiff filed his appeal to this court.

The question brought to this court for determination is what if any compensable damage did plaintiff suffer as a direct result of the Government's improper termination of plaintiff's contract. The Government says no damage has occurred and has moved to dismiss the complaint for failure to state a cause of action upon which relief can be granted. The plaintiff, appearing *pro se*, has alleged in his jumble of testimony, less explicitly but no less expressively, that various forms of damages have occurred. He has asked "this Court to assist him to see that justice does not suffer miscarriage under American Jurisprudence."

Simply phrased, the defendant takes the position that while the contract may have been improperly terminated no loss of profits is recoverable because the contract was a "requirements contract" and did not guarantee that *any* minimum requirement would exist. Furthermore, where a requirement did in fact occur, the contract by its terms did not guarantee that the Government would give all or any part of this requirement to the plaintiff. The contract merely provided that plaintiff's name would appear in a Federal Supply Schedule along with other typewriter-repair contractors. Certain Federal agencies could select typewriter-repair companies from the schedule to fulfill their requirements, if any. Furthermore, since plaintiff could not have demanded business while he remained in the schedule, he cannot now be heard to complain that he received no business, albeit he may have been improperly removed from the schedule. With this we cannot agree.

It is now beyond question that contracts for requirements do not lack mutuality and are enforceable. In every case it is the reasonable expectation by both parties that there will be requirements on which the bargain is grounded. Ready–Mix Concrete Co., Ltd. v. United States, 130 F.Supp. 390, 131 Ct.Cl. 204. . . . The facts, as alleged, show that plaintiff in the past had received substantially all of his business from Government agencies under similar contracts. We cannot believe that in this instance plaintiff bargained merely to have his name printed in the supply schedule. It appears more important that being in the schedule created a reasonable probability that business would be obtained. Particularly is this so when it is noted that among the four San Diego repair companies originally put in the schedule plaintiff was the low bidder.

We agree that nothing in the contract would have prevented the Government from enlarging its own repair facilities to fill completely its needs. This would have left nothing to be awarded under the Federal Supply Schedule contracts. But the facts as alleged show that the Government did have some service requirements beyond its own capacity. Presumably, these requirements were awarded to contractors in the schedule. Plaintiff's chance of obtaining some of these awards, by being in the schedule and competing with the other contractors, had *value* in a business sense. The Government by its breach deprived plaintiff of this value.

The defendant further takes the position that the fact of damage as well as the amount that resulted from the removal of plaintiff's name from the schedule is too speculative to permit of proof. But the constant tendency of the courts is to find some way in which damages can be awarded where a wrong has been done. Bigelow et al. v. RKO Radio Pictures, 327 U.S. 251, 265, 66 S.Ct. 574, 90 L.Ed. 652. Difficulty of ascertainment is not to be confused with right of recovery. Nor does it exonerate the defendant that his misconduct, which has made necessary the inquiry into the question of harm, renders that inquiry difficult. Eastman Kodak Co. v. Southern Photo Materials Co., 273 U.S. 359, 379, 47 S.Ct. 400, 71 L.Ed. 684. The defendant who has wrongfully broken a contract should not be permitted to reap advantage from his own wrong by insisting on proof which by reason of his breach is unobtainable. Crichfield v. Julia, 2 Cir., 147 F. 65. It remains true, however, that the plaintiff must meet a higher standard of proof to establish that he has sustained *some* injury than to fix the amount. Story Parchment Co. v. Paterson Parchment Paper Co., 282 U.S. 555, 51 S.Ct. 248, 75 L.Ed. 544.

If a reasonable probability of damage can be clearly established, uncertainty as to the amount will not preclude recovery. Story Parchment Co., supra. The amount may be approximated if a reasonable basis of computation is afforded. Eastman Kodak Co., supra.... "All that the law requires is that such damage be allowed as, in the judgment of fair men, directly and naturally resulted from the breach of the contract for which the suit is brought." Needles et al. v. United States, 101 Ct.Cl. 535, 618.... Certainty is sufficient if the evidence adduced enables the court to make a fair and reasonable approximation of the damages. Stern v. Dunlap Co., 10 Cir., 228 F.2d 939. In circumstances such as these we may act upon probable and inferential as well as direct and positive proof. Bigelow et al. v. RKO Radio Pictures, supra.

> "Any other rule would enable the wrongdoer to profit by his wrongdoing at the expense of his victim. It would be an inducement to make wrongdoing so effective and complete in every case as to preclude any recovery by rendering the measure of damages uncertain. Failure to apply [this rule] would mean that the more grievous the wrong done, the less likelihood there would be of a recovery.

"The most elementary conceptions of justice and public policy require that the wrongdoer shall bear the risk of the uncertainty which his own wrong has created." Bigelow v. RKO Radio Pictures, supra, 327 U.S. at page 264, 66 S.Ct. at page 580.

We are here concerned with the value of a chance for obtaining business and profits. The last time this question of recovery for a lost chance at business was put to this court, recovery was denied. Zephyr Aircraft Corp. v. United States, 104 F.Supp. 990, 122 Ct.Cl. 523, certiorari denied 344 U.S. 878, 73 S.Ct. 165, 97 L.Ed. 680. However, that case is not governing for there the court expressly found that the plaintiff never had *any* chance to obtain business. Here it appears that the plaintiff did have a chance of obtaining at least one-fourth of the total typewriter-repair business let by the Government. It is true that plaintiff's reasonable expectations might have been disappointed by the happening of diverse contingencies. We should not, however, overlook the fact that the plaintiff gave valuable consideration for the promise of a performance which would have given him a chance at business and profit. We believe that where the value of a chance for profit is not outweighed by a countervailing risk of loss, and where it is fairly measurable by calculable odds and by evidence bearing specifically on the probabilities that the court should be allowed to value that lost opportunity.

Therefore, we direct the trial commissioner to determine the following facts:

1. The total amount of typewriter-repair business let by the Government for which plaintiff would have been eligible under his contract but for the Government's breach. (This should be easily obtained from the Government's records.)

2. Whether there were any material facts that would have tended to prevent plaintiff from receiving his proportionate share of such business.

3. The average per unit cost normally incurred in performing repair work of the type here involved.

4. Expenses plaintiff necessarily incurred in preparing to fulfill his obligations under the contract. The expense of preparing the bid should not be included.

In view of the small amounts involved it is suggested that most of the above facts may be stipulated by the parties....

It is so ordered.

KENFORD CO., INC. v. COUNTY OF ERIE

Court of Appeals of New York, 1986.
67 N.Y.2d 257, 502 N.Y.S.2d 131, 493 N.E.2d 234.

PER CURIAM. The issue in this appeal is whether a plaintiff, in an action for breach of contract, may recover loss of prospective profits for its contemplated 20–year operation of a domed stadium which was to be constructed by defendant County of Erie (County).

On August 8, 1969, pursuant to a duly adopted resolution of its legislature, the County of Erie entered into a contract with Kenford Company, Inc. (Kenford) and Dome Stadium, Inc. (DSI) for the construction and operation of a domed stadium facility near the City of Buffalo. The contract provided that construction of the facility by the County would commence within 12 months of the contract date and that a mutually acceptable 40–year lease between the County and DSI for the operation of said facility would be negotiated by the parties and agreed upon within three months of the receipt by the County of preliminary plans, drawings and cost estimates. It was further provided that in the event a mutually acceptable lease could not be agreed upon within the three-month period, a separate management contract between the County and DSI, as appended to the basic agreement, would be executed by the parties, providing for the operation of the stadium facility by DSI for a period of 20 years from the completion of the stadium and its availability for use.

Although strenuous and extensive negotiations followed, the parties never agreed upon the terms of a lease, nor did construction of a domed facility begin within the one-year period or at any time thereafter. A breach of the contract thus occurred and this action was commenced in June 1971 by Kenford and DSI.

Prolonged and extensive pretrial and preliminary proceedings transpired throughout the next 10 years, culminating with the entry of an order which affirmed the grant of summary judgment against the County on the issue of liability and directed a trial limited to the issue of damages (*Kenford Co. v. County of Erie*, 88 A.D.2d 758, 451 N.Y.S.2d 1021, *lv dismissed* 58 N.Y.2d 689). The ensuing trial ended some nine months later with a multimillion dollar jury verdict in plaintiffs' favor. An appeal to the Appellate Division resulted in a modification of the judgment. That court reversed portions of the judgment awarding damages for loss of profits and for certain out-of-pocket expenses incurred, and directed a new trial upon other issues (*Kenford Co. v. County of Erie*, 108 A.D.2d 132, 489 N.Y.S.2d 939). On appeal to this court, we are concerned only with that portion of the verdict which awarded DSI money damages for loss of prospective profits during the 20–year period of the proposed management contract, as appended to the basic contract. That portion of the verdict was set aside by the Appellate Division and the cause of action dismissed. The court concluded that the use of expert opinion to present statistical projections of future business operations involved the use of too many variables to provide a rational basis upon which lost profits could be calculated and, therefore, such projections were insufficient as a matter of law to support an award of lost profits. We agree with this ultimate conclusion, but upon different grounds.

Loss of future profits as damages for breach of contract have been permitted in New York under long-established and precise rules of law. First, it must be demonstrated with certainty that such damages have been caused by the breach and, second, the alleged loss must be capable of proof with reasonable certainty. In other words, the damages may not be merely speculative, possible or imaginary, but must be reasonably certain and directly traceable to the breach, not remote or the result of other intervening causes (*Wakeman v. Wheeler & Wilson Mfg. Co.*, 101 N.Y. 205, 4 N.E. 264). In addition, there must be a showing that the particular damages were fairly within the contemplation of the parties to the contract at the time it was made (*Witherbee v. Meyer*, 155 N.Y. 446, 50 N.E. 58). If it is a new business seeking to recover for loss of future profits, a stricter standard is imposed for the obvious reason that there does not exist a reasonable basis of experience upon which to estimate lost profits with the requisite degree of reasonable certainty (*Cramer v. Grand Rapids Show Case Co.*, 223 N.Y. 63, 119 N.E. 227; 25 C.J.S. Damages, § 42[b]).

These rules must be applied to the proof presented by DSI in this case. We note the procedure for computing damages selected by DSI was in accord with contemporary economic theory and was presented through the testimony of recognized experts. Such a procedure has been accepted in this State and many other jurisdictions (*see, De Long v. County of Erie*, 60 N.Y.2d 296, 469 N.Y.S.2d 611, 457 N.E.2d 717). DSI's economic analysis employed historical data, obtained from the operation of other domed stadiums and related facilities throughout the country, which was then applied to the results of a comprehensive study of the marketing prospects for the proposed facility in the Buffalo area. The quantity of proof is massive and, unquestionably, represents business and industry's most advanced and sophisticated method for predicting the probable results of contemplated projects. Indeed, it is difficult to conclude what additional relevant proof could have been submitted by DSI in support of its attempt to establish, with reasonable certainty, loss of prospective profits. Nevertheless, DSI's proof is insufficient to meet the required standard.

The reason for this conclusion is twofold. Initially, the proof does not satisfy the requirement that liability for loss of profits over a 20–year period was in the contemplation of the parties at the time of the execution of the basic contract or at the time of its breach (*see, Chapman v. Fargo*, 223 N.Y. 32, 119 N.E. 76; 36 N.Y.Jur.2d, Damages, §§ 39, 40, at 66–70). Indeed, the provisions in the contract providing remedy for a default do not suggest or provide for such a heavy responsibility on the part of the County. In the absence of any provision for such an eventuality, the common-sense rule to apply is to consider what the parties would have concluded had they considered the subject. The evidence here fails to demonstrate that liability for loss of profits over the length of the contract would have been in the contemplation of the parties at the relevant times.

Next, we note that despite the massive quantity of expert proof submitted by DSI, the ultimate conclusions are still projections, and as employed in the present day commercial world, subject to adjustment and modification. We of course recognize that any projection cannot be absolute, nor is there any such requirement, but it is axiomatic that the degree of certainty is dependent upon known or unknown factors which form the basis of the ultimate conclusion. Here, the foundations upon which the economic model was created undermine the certainty of the projections. DSI assumed that the facility was completed, available for use and successfully operated by it for 20 years, providing professional sporting events and other forms of entertainment, as well as hosting meetings, conventions and related commercial gatherings. At the time of the breach, there was only one other facility in this country to use as a basis of comparison, the Astrodome in Houston. Quite simply, the multitude of assumptions required to establish projections of profitability over the life of this contract require speculation and conjecture, making it beyond the capability of even the most sophisticated procedures to satisfy the legal requirements of proof with reasonable certainty.

The economic facts of life, the whim of the general public and the fickle nature of popular support for professional athletic endeavors must be given great weight in attempting to ascertain damages 20 years in the future. New York has long recognized the inherent uncertainties of predicting profits in the entertainment field in general (*see, Broadway Photoplay Co. v. World Film Corp.*, 225 N.Y. 104, 121 N.E. 756) and, in this case, we are dealing, in large part, with a new facility furnishing entertainment for the public. It is our view that the record in this case demonstrates the efficacy of the principles set forth by this court in Cramer v. Grand Rapids Show Case Co., 223 N.Y. 63, 119 N.E. 227, *supra*, principles to which we continue to adhere. In so doing, we specifically reject the "rational basis" test enunciated in *Perma Research & Dev. Co. v. Singer Co.*, ((2nd Cir.), 542 F.2d 111, *cert. denied* 429 U.S. 987, 97 S.Ct. 507, 50 L.Ed.2d 598), and adopted by the Appellate Division.

Accordingly, that portion of the order of the Appellate Division being appealed from should be affirmed.

Questions

1. In *Locke*, what was the government's breach of contract? What harm did it cause? What should the plaintiff's counsel prove on remand? What standard of certainty does the court employ?

2. In *Kenford*, what was the procedure employed by DSI for computing damages? If it was, as the court said, "in accord with contemporary economic theory" and "massive," why should the court decide that it was not good enough to sustain DSI's claim for damages? What standard of certainty does the court employ?

3. Would the *Kenford* court have decided *Locke* as *Locke* was decided by the Court of Claims? Is *Kenford* soundly decided? Is *Locke* soundly decided? What are the relevant principles and interests at stake? Do courts have an institutional interest in the nonarbitrariness of their judgments, in addition to the parties' contractual interests?

RESTATEMENT (SECOND) OF CONTRACTS § 351

———

U.C.C. § 2–715(2)

———

HADLEY v. BAXENDALE

In the Court of Exchequer, 1854.
9 Exch. 341.

. . . At the trial before Crompton, J., at the last Gloucester Assizes, it appeared that the plaintiffs carried on an extensive business as millers at Gloucester; and that, on the 11th of May, their mill was stopped by a breakage of the crank shaft by which the mill was worked. The steam-engine was manufactured by Messrs. Joyce & Co., the engineers, at Greenwich, and it became necessary to send the shaft as a pattern for a new one to Greenwich. The fracture was discovered on the 12th, and on the 13th the plaintiffs sent one of their servants to the office of the defendants, who are the well known carriers trading under the name of Pickford & Co., for the purpose of having the shaft carried to Greenwich. The plaintiffs' servant told the clerk that the mill was stopped, and that the shaft must be sent immediately; and in answer to the inquiry when the shaft would be taken, the answer was, that if it was sent up by twelve o'clock any day, it would be delivered at Greenwich on the following day. On the following day the shaft was taken by the defendants, before noon, for the purpose of being conveyed to Greenwich, and the sum of £ 2, 4s. was paid for its carriage for the whole distance; at the same time the defendants' clerk was told that a special entry, if required, should be made to hasten its delivery. The delivery of the shaft at Greenwich was delayed by some neglect; and the consequence was, that the plaintiffs did not receive the new shaft for several days after they would otherwise have done, and the working of their mill was thereby delayed, and they thereby lost the profits they would otherwise have received.

On the part of the defendants, it was objected that these damages were too remote, and that the defendants were not liable with respect to them. The learned Judge left the case generally to the jury, who found a verdict with £ 25 damages beyond the amount paid into Court.

WHATELEY, in last Michaelmas Term, obtained a rule nisi for a new trial, on the ground of misdirection.

KEATING and DOWDESWELL [counsel for the Hadleys] showed cause. The plaintiffs are entitled to the amount awarded by the jury as damages. These damages are not too remote, for they are not only the natural and necessary consequence of the defendants' default, but they are the only loss which the plaintiffs have actually sustained. The principle upon which damages are assessed is founded upon that of rendering compensation to the injured party....

WHATLEY, WILLES, and PHIPSON [counsel for Baxendale], in support of the rule. It has been contended, on the part of the plaintiffs, that the damages found by the jury are a matter fit for their consideration; but still the question remains, in what way ought the jury to have been directed? It has been also urged, that, in awarding damages, the law gives compensation to the injured individual. But it is clear that complete compensation is not to be awarded; for instance, the non-payment of a bill of exchange might lead to the utter ruin of the holder, and yet such damage could not be considered as necessarily resulting from the breach of contract, so as to entitle the party aggrieved to recover in respect of it. Take the case of the breach of a contract to supply a rick-cloth, whereby and in consequence of bad weather the hay, being unprotected, is spoiled, that damage would not be recoverable. Many similar cases might be added.... Sedgwick says [p. 38], "In regard to the quantum of damages, instead of adhering to the term compensation, it would be far more accurate to say, in the language of Domat, which we have cited above, 'that the object is to discriminate between that portion of the loss which must be borne by the offending party and that which must be borne by the sufferer.' The law, in fact, aims not at the satisfaction but at a division of the loss." ... This therefore is a question of law, and the jury ought to have been told that these damages were too remote; and that, in the absence of the proof of any other damage, the plaintiffs were entitled to nominal damages only....

The judgment of the Court was now delivered by

ALDERSON, B. We think that there ought to be a new trial in this case; but, in so doing, we deem it to be expedient and necessary to state explicitly the rule which the Judge, at the next trial, ought, in our opinion, to direct the jury to be governed by when they estimate the damages.

It is, indeed, of the last importance that we should do this; for, if the jury are left without any definite rule to guide them, it will, in such cases as these, manifestly lead to the greatest injustice.... "There are certain established rules," this Court says, in Alder v. Keighley, 15 M. & W. 117, "according to which the jury ought to find." And the Court, in that case, adds: "and here there is a clear rule, that the amount which would have been received if the contract had been kept, is the measure of damages if the contract is broken."

Now we think the proper rule in such a case as the present is this:– Where two parties have made a contract which one of them has broken, the damages which the other party ought to receive in respect of such breach of contract should be such as may fairly and reasonably be considered either arising naturally, i.e., according to the usual course of things, from such breach of contract itself, or such as may reasonably be supposed to have been in the contemplation of both parties, at the time they made the contract, as the probable result of the breach of it. Now, if the special circumstances under which the contract was actually made were communicated by the plaintiffs to the defendants, and thus known to both parties, the damages resulting from the breach of such a contract, which they would reasonably contemplate, would be the amount of injury which would ordinarily follow from a breach of contract under these special circumstances so known and communicated. But, on the other hand, if these special circumstances were wholly unknown to the party breaking the contract, he, at the most, could only be supposed to have had in his contemplation the amount of injury which would arise generally, and in the great multitude of cases not affected by any special circumstances, from such a breach of contract. For, had the special circumstances been known, the parties might have specially provided for the breach of contract by special terms as to the damages in that case; and of this advantage it would be very unjust to deprive them. Now the above principles are those by which we think the jury ought to be guided in estimating the damages arising out of any breach of contract.... Now, in the present case, if we are to apply the principles above laid down, we find that the only circumstances here communicated by the plaintiffs to the defendants at the time the contract was made, were, that the article to be carried was the broken shaft of a mill, and that the plaintiffs were the millers of that mill. But how do these circumstances show reasonably that the profits of the mill must be stopped by an unreasonable delay in the delivery of the broken shaft by the carrier to the third person? Suppose the plaintiffs had another shaft in their possession put up or putting up at the time, and that they only wished to send back the broken shaft to the engineer who made it; it is clear that this would be quite consistent with the above circumstances, and yet the unreasonable delay in the delivery would have no effect upon the intermediate profits of the mill. Or, again, suppose that, at the time of the delivery to the carrier, the machinery of the mill had been in other respects defective, then, also, the same results would follow. Here it is true that the shaft was actually sent back to serve as a model for a new one, and that the want of a new one was the only cause of the stoppage of the mill, and that the loss of profits really arose from not sending down the new shaft in proper time, and that this arose from the delay in delivering the broken one to serve as a model. But it is obvious that, in the great multitude of cases of millers sending off broken shafts to third persons by a carrier under ordinary circumstances, such consequences would not, in all probability, have occurred; and these special circumstances were here never communicated by the plaintiffs to the defendants. It follows, therefore, that the loss of profits here cannot reasonably be considered such a consequence of the breach of contract as could have been fairly and reasonably contemplated by both the parties when they made this contract. For such loss would neither have flowed naturally from the breach of this contract in the great multitude of such cases occurring under ordinary circumstances, nor were the special circumstances, which, perhaps, would have made it a reasonable and natural consequence of such breach of contract, communicated to or known by the defendants. The Judge ought, therefore, to have told the jury, that, upon the facts then before them, they ought not to take the loss of profits into consideration at all in estimating the damages. There must therefore be a new trial in this case.

Rule absolute.

Questions

1. What does the plaintiff claim? What is the rule of law established by *Hadley v. Baxendale*? How does that rule apply here? Is there anything left to be decided in the lower court? Was the court's reasoning persuasive for applying the rule as it did?

2. Does the rule in *Hadley* produce undercompensatory expectation damages awards? Does a requirement of reasonable certainty in proving lost profits result in undercompensatory expectation damages? Is either limit consistent with the efficient breach hypothesis? If not, what justifies these limitations?

3. *Problems.*

a. The facts are as in *Hadley v. Baxendale*, except that the Hadleys' clerk said that the mill would lose profits every day until the shaft was returned. Baxendale's clerk took the package. Same result?

b. The facts are as in *Kenford Co., Inc. v. County of Erie*, above at p. 342, except that a clause in the contract expressly made the County liable for lost profits. Same result?

c. The facts are as in *Kenford Co., Inc. v. County of Erie*, except that the plaintiff brings the action for anticipated losses resulting from Kenford Co.'s purchase of land adjacent to the stadium site. Kenford Co. claims that these losses include a decline in the market value of the land due to cancellation of the stadium project and also lost profits that would have been earned had the adjacent land been developed as planned to take advantage of the new neighbor. Real estate appraisers provide ample proof of the loss in the market value of the land at the time of cancellation. Economists provide clear proof of lost profits. Can Kenford Co. recover for this loss? See Kenford Co., Inc. v. County of Erie, 73 N.Y.2d 312, 540 N.Y.S.2d 1, 537 N.E.2d 176 (1989).

NOTE ON FORESEEABILITY

"Foreseeability" is a legal concept that appears in several contexts, especially in tort and contract. In negligence law, the doctrine of proximate cause generally requires that the harm and the person harmed be reasonably foreseeable to the tortfeasor. See, e.g., Palsgraf v. Long Island R.R. Co., 248 N.Y. 339, 162 N.E. 99 (1928). In that context, foreseeability is marked from the time of the wrong. In contract, however, foreseeability is marked from the time of contract formation, not the time of breach. Why this difference?

In an interesting article, Professor Melvin A. Eisenberg argues that the rule of *Hadley v. Baxendale*, venerable as it has been, should be jettisoned in favor of a regime of proximate cause drawn from tort. Elaborating on Lord Denning's suggestion in *Parsons (Livestock) Ltd. v. Uttley Ingham & Co.*, [1978] 1 Q.B. 791, 798–804, he proposes to mark foreseeability from the time of breach and to abandon any doctrinal distinction between tort and contract damages on this point. Thus, subject to the parties' agreement otherwise, the standard of foreseeability might vary depending on the nature of the interest invaded and the wrong involved. In torts, he points out, foreseeability requirements vary in negligence cases involving personal injuries and property damage, on one hand, and economic loss on the other; so, too, as between negligence and intentional torts. See Melvin A. Eisenberg, *The Principle of* Hadley v. Baxendale, 80 CALIF. L. REV. 563 (1992).

Arguments can be made for either time marking foreseeability in contract. On one hand, the obligation undertaken autonomously by a party does not extend to risks that were unforeseeable at formation; consequently, it can be argued, the liability should be limited accordingly unless grounds other than the autonomy principle justify imposing an obligation. Moreover, a foreseeability limitation might limit liability in a way that encourages trade. It can also be argued that one party has no reason to know of risks faced by the other when the other's situation is unusual; limiting liability encourages the party in unusual circumstances to disclose those circumstances at formation, allowing the parties to allocate them by agreement. On the other hand, Professor Eisenberg suggests, facilitating an optimum level of contracting depends importantly on maintaining an efficient rate of performance and breach. Perhaps contract law should aim to discourage only inefficient breaches. If so, it seems, foreseeability should be marked at the time of breach. A party decides to breach mainly when circumstances change after formation and the party regrets having made the contract. It is implausible to suppose that a party contemplating breach will more accurately identify the parties' joint costs of breach when damages are limited to those foreseeable at the earlier time.

SECTION 3. RELIANCE REMEDIES

SECURITY STOVE & MFG. CO. v. AMERICAN RY. EXPRESS CO.

Kansas City Court of Appeals, Missouri, 1932.
227 Mo.App. 175, 51 S.W.2d 572.

BLAND, JUDGE. This is an action for damages for the failure of defendant to transport, from Kansas City to Atlantic City, New Jersey, within a reasonable time, a furnace equipped with a combination oil and gas burner. The cause was tried before the court without the aid of a jury, resulting in a judgment in favor of plaintiff in the sum of $801.50 and interest, or in a total sum of $1,000.00. Defendant has appealed.

The facts show that plaintiff manufactured a furnace equipped with a special combination oil and gas burner it desired to exhibit at the

American Gas Association Convention held in Atlantic City in October, 1926. The president of plaintiff testified that plaintiff engaged space for the exhibit for the reason "that the Henry L. Dougherty Company was very much interested in putting out a combination oil and gas burner; we had just developed one, after we got through, better than anything on the market and we thought this show would be the psychological time to get in contact with the Dougherty Company;" that "the thing wasn't sent there for sale but primarily to show;" that at the time the space was engaged it was too late to ship the furnace by freight so plaintiff decided to ship it by express, and, on September 18th, 1926, wrote the office of the defendant in Kansas City, stating that it had engaged a booth for exhibition purposes at Atlantic City, New Jersey, from the American Gas Association, for the week beginning October 11th; that its exhibit consisted of an oil burning furnace, together with two oil burners which weighed at least 1,500 pounds; that, "In order to get this exhibit in place on time it should be in Atlantic City not later than October the 8th. What we want you to do is to tell us how much time you will require to assure the delivery of the exhibit on time."

Mr. Bangs, chief clerk in charge of the local office of the defendant, upon receipt of the letter, sent Mr. Johnson, a commercial representative of the defendant, to see plaintiff. Johnson called upon plaintiff taking its letter with him. Johnson made a notation on the bottom of the letter giving October 4th, as the day that defendant was required to have the exhibit in order for it to reach Atlantic City on October 8th.

On October 1st, plaintiff wrote the defendant at Kansas City, referring to its letter of September 18th, concerning the fact that the furnace must be in Atlantic City not later than October 8th, and stating what Johnson had told it, saying: "Now Mr. Bangs, we want to make doubly sure that this shipment is in Atlantic City not later than October 8th and the purpose of this letter is to tell you that you can *have your truck call for the shipment between 12 and 1 o'clock on Saturday, October 2nd for this.*" (Italics plaintiff's.) On October 2d, plaintiff called the office of the express company in Kansas City and told it that the shipment was ready. Defendant came for the shipment on the last mentioned day, received it and delivered the express receipt to plaintiff. The shipment contained 21 packages. Each package was marked with stickers backed with glue and covered with silica of soda, to prevent the stickers being torn off in shipping. Each package was given a number. They ran from 1 to 21.

Plaintiff's president made arrangements to go to Atlantic City to attend the convention and install the exhibit, arriving there about October 11th. When he reached Atlantic City he found the shipment had been placed in the booth that had been assigned to plaintiff. The exhibit was set up, but it was found that one of the packages shipped was not there. This missing package contained the gas manifold, or that part of the oil and gas burner that controlled the flow of gas in the burner. This was the most important part of the exhibit and a like burner could not be obtained in Atlantic City.

Wires were sent and it was found that the stray package was at the "over and short bureau" of defendant in St. Louis. Defendant reported that the package would be forwarded to Atlantic City and would be there by Wednesday, the 13th. Plaintiff's president waited until Thursday, the day the convention closed, but the package had not arrived at the time, so he closed up the exhibit and left. About a week after he arrived in Kansas City, the package was returned by the defendant....

Plaintiff asked damages, which the court in its judgment allowed as follows: $147.00 express charges (on the exhibit); $45.12 freight on the exhibit from Atlantic City to Kansas City; $101.39 railroad and pullman fares to and from Atlantic City, expended by plaintiff's president and a workman taken by him to Atlantic City; $48.00 hotel room for the two; $150.00 for the time of the president; $40.00 for wages of plaintiff's other employee and $270.00 for rental of booth, making a total of $801.51.

Defendant contends ... that the court erred in allowing plaintiff's expenses as damages; that the only damages, if any, that can be recovered in cases of this kind, are for loss of profits and that plaintiff's evidence is not sufficient to base any recovery on this ground....

We think, under the circumstances in this case, that it was proper to allow plaintiff's expenses as its damages. Ordinarily the measure of damages where the carrier fails to deliver a shipment at destination within a reasonable time is the difference between the market value of the goods at the time of the delivery and the time when they should have been delivered. But where the carrier has notice of peculiar circumstances under which the shipment is made, which will result in an unusual loss by the shipper in case of delay in delivery, the carrier is responsible for the real damage sustained from such delay if the notice given is of such character, and goes to such extent, in informing the carrier of the shipper's situation, that the carrier will be presumed to have contracted with reference thereto....

Defendant contends that plaintiff "is endeavoring to achieve a return of the status quo in a suit based on a breach of contract. Instead of seeking to recover what he would have had, had the contract not been broken, plaintiff is trying to recover what he would have had, had there never been any contract of shipment;" that the expenses sued for would have been incurred in any event. It is no doubt, the general rule that where there is a breach of contract the party suffering the loss can recover only that which he would have had, had the contract not been broken.... But this is merely a general statement of the rule and is not inconsistent with the holdings that, in some instances, the injured party may recover expenses incurred in relying upon the contract, although such expenses would have been incurred had the contract not been breached....

In Sperry et al. v. O'Neill–Adams Co. (C.C.A.) 185 F. 231, the court held that the advantages resulting from the use of trading stamps as a means of increasing trade are so contingent that they cannot form a basis on which to rest a recovery for a breach of contract to supply them. In lieu of compensation based thereon the court directed a recovery in the sum expended in preparation for carrying on business in connection with the use of the stamps. The court said, loc. cit. 239:

> "Plaintiff in its complaint had made a claim for lost profits, but, finding it impossible to marshal any evidence which would support a finding of exact figures, abandoned that claim. Any attempt to reach a precise sum would be mere blind guesswork. Nevertheless a contract, which both sides conceded would prove a valuable one, had been broken and the party who broke it was responsible for resultant damage. In order to carry out this contract, the plaintiff made expenditures which otherwise it would not have made.... The trial judge held, as we think rightly, that plaintiff was entitled at least to recover these expenses to which it had been put in order to secure the benefits of a contract of which defendant's conduct deprived it."

The case at bar was [not] to recover damages for loss of profits by reason of the failure of the defendant to transport the shipment within a reasonable time, so that it would arrive in Atlantic City for the exhibit. There were no profits contemplated. The furnace was to be shown and shipped back to Kansas City. There was no money loss, except the expenses, that was of such a nature as any court would allow as being sufficiently definite or lacking in pure speculation. Therefore, unless plaintiff is permitted to recover the expenses that it went to, which were a total loss to it by reason of its inability to exhibit the furnace and equipment, it will be deprived of any substantial compensation for its loss. The law does not contemplate any such injustice. It ought to allow plaintiff, as damages, the loss in the way of expenses that it sustained, and which it would not have been put to if it had not been for its reliance upon the defendant to perform its contract. There is no contention that the exhibit would have been entirely valueless and whatever it might have accomplished defendant knew of the circumstances and ought to respond for whatever damages plaintiff suffered. In cases of this kind the method of estimating the damages should be adopted which is the most definite and certain and which best achieves the fundamental purpose of compensation.... Had the exhibit been shipped in order to realize a profit on sales and such profits could have been realized, or to be entered in competition for a prize, and plaintiff failed to show loss of profits with sufficient definiteness, or that he would have won the prize, defendant's cases might be in point. But as before stated, no such situation exists here.

While, it is true that plaintiff already had incurred some of these expenses, in that it had rented space at the exhibit before entering into the contract with defendant for the shipment of the exhibit and this part of plaintiff's damages, in a sense, arose out of a circumstance which transpired before the contract was even entered into, yet, plaintiff arranged for the exhibit knowing that it could call upon defendant to perform its common law duty to accept and transport the shipment with reasonable dispatch. The whole damage, therefore, was suffered in contemplation of defendant performing its contract, which it failed to do, and would not have been sustained except for the reliance by plaintiff upon defendant to perform it. It can, therefore, be fairly said that the damages or loss suffered by plaintiff grew out of the breach of the contract, for had the shipment arrived on time, plaintiff would have had the benefit of the contract, which was contemplated by all parties, defendant being advised of the purpose of the shipment.

The judgment is affirmed.

Questions

1. Why were reliance damages the proper remedy in *Security Stove* when the ground for enforcement was a bargain contract?

2. Was Security Stove left undercompensated? What should you propose to do about it, were you counsel to Security Stove?

3. *Problem.*

The facts are as in *Security Stove*, except that American Railways Express Co. proved at trial that, at the time of contracting, Security Stove intended to send only its sales manager to the exhibit. The sales manager was paid at half the rate of the president. Should the damages be reduced by $75 under *Hadley v. Baxendale*?

NOTE ON REMEDIES UNDER SECTION 90

As *Security Stove v. American Railway Express Co.* indicates, the prevailing law does not always award an expectation, reliance, or restitutionary remedy to vindicate the counterpart contractual interest. In that case, recourse to reliance damages for breach of a bargain contract was due to the ban on speculative damages. In principle, however, Security Stove was entitled to its lost profits. The issue also arises when considering the available remedies under RESTATEMENT (SECOND) OF CONTRACTS § 90.

Consider, for example, the following cases:

1. Uncle promises Nephew $10,000 to buy a car. Is Uncle liable for $10,000 when nephew justifiably and foreseeably relies by buying a car for $10,000?

2. Uncle promises Nephew $10,000 to buy a car. Is Uncle liable for $10,000 when nephew justifiably and foreseeably relies by buying a car for $500?

3. Uncle promises Nephew $10,000 to buy a car. Is Uncle liable for $10,000 when nephew justifiably and foreseeably relies by buying a car for $6,000?

In Case #1, expectation and reliance remedies would both give Nephew $10,000, so no practical issue is raised. The two remedies come apart in the other cases, raising the issue whether expectation damages are recoverable for breach of promises made enforceable by the promisee's reliance.

Samuel Williston, the Reporter for the first restatement of contracts, took a doctrinaire position that expectation damages were always the proper remedy for breach of a promise made enforceable for reasons of reliance under RESTATEMENT [FIRST] OF CONTRACTS § 90. This was evident in a famous exchange at a meeting of the American Law Institute in 1926, where Williston favored a $10,000 remedy in Case #3, but met serious skepticism, leaving the law unclear. See 4 A.L.I. Proc. 95–96 (App. 1926). Williston would not have held Uncle liable for $10,000 in Case #2. The original Section 90 allowed recovery only when the reliance induced by the promise was "of a definite and substantial character." Arguably, a $500 reliance expenditure is not substantial in relation to the promise of $10,000. Accordingly, Uncle would not be held liable for anything.

The second restatement allows reliance recoveries under § 90. RESTATEMENT (SECOND) OF CONTRACTS § 90, Comment d. According to the Reporter, "[t]he principal change from former § 90 [was] the recognition of the possibility of partial enforcement. . . . Partly because of that change, the requirement that the action or forbearance have 'a definite and substantial character' [was] deleted." Id., Reporter's Note. So both restatements agree that Nephew should not get $10,000 in Case #2. Nephew could recover $500 in Case #2 under RESTATEMENT (SECOND). In all likelihood, Nephew would recover $6,000 in Case #3 under RESTATEMENT (SECOND).

The more topical question now is whether expectation damages are ever recoverable for breach of a promise made enforceable by reliance. (Williston would be most chagrined!) The following two cases take contrasting positions.

GOODMAN v. DICKER

United States Court of Appeals, District of Columbia, 1948.
83 U.S.App.D.C. 353, 169 F.2d 684.

PROCTOR, ASSOCIATE JUSTICE. This appeal is from a judgment of the District Court in a suit by appellees for breach of contract.

Appellants are local distributors for Emerson Radio and Phonograph Corporation in the District of Columbia. Appellees, with the knowledge and encouragement of appellants, applied for a "dealer franchise" to sell Emerson's products. The trial court found that appellants by their representations and conduct induced appellees to incur expenses in preparing to do business under the franchise, including employment of salesmen and solicitation of orders for radios. Among other things, appellants represented that the application had been accepted; that the franchise would be granted, and that appellees would receive an initial delivery of thirty to forty radios. Yet, no radios were delivered, and notice was finally given that the franchise would not be granted.

The case was tried without a jury. The court held that a contract had not been proven but that appellants were estopped from denying the same by reason of their statements and conduct upon which appellees relied to their detriment. Judgment was entered for $1,500, covering cash outlays of $1,150 and loss of $350, anticipated profits on sale of thirty radios.

The main contention of appellants is that no liability would have arisen under the dealer franchise had it been granted because, as understood by appellees, it would have been terminable at will and would have imposed no duty upon the manufacturer to sell or appellees to buy any fixed number of radios. From this it is argued that the franchise agreement would not have been enforceable (except as to acts performed thereunder) and cancellation by the manufacturer would have created no liability for expenses incurred by the dealer in preparing to do business. Further, it is argued that as the dealer franchise would have been unenforceable for failure of the manufacturer to supply radios appellants would not be liable to fulfill their assurance that radios would be supplied.

We think these contentions miss the real point of this case. We are not concerned directly with the terms of the franchise. We are dealing with a promise by appellants that a franchise would be granted and radios supplied, on the faith of which appellees with the knowledge and encouragement of appellants incurred expenses in making preparations to do business. Under these circumstances we think that appellants cannot now advance any defense inconsistent with their assurance that the franchise would be granted. Justice and fair dealing require that one who acts to his detriment on the faith of conduct of the kind revealed here should be protected by estopping the party who has brought about the situation from alleging anything in opposition to the natural consequences of his own course of conduct. Dair v. United States, 1872, 16 Wall. 1, 4, 21 L.Ed. 491. In Dickerson v. Colgrove, 100 U.S. 578, 580, 25 L.Ed. 618, the Supreme Court, in speaking of equitable estoppel, said: "The law upon the subject is well settled. The vital principle is that he who by his language or conduct leads another to do what he would not otherwise have done, shall not subject such person to loss or injury by disappointing the expectations upon which he acted. Such a change of position is sternly forbidden.... This remedy is always so applied as to promote the ends of justice." See also Casey v. Galli, 94 U.S. 673, 680, 24 L.Ed. 168....

In our opinion the trial court was correct in holding defendants liable for moneys which appellees expended in preparation to do business under the promised dealer franchise. These items aggregated $1,150. We think, though, the court erred in adding the item of $350 for loss of profits on radios promised under an initial order. The true measure of damage is the loss sustained by expenditures made in reliance upon the assurance of a dealer franchise. As thus modified, the judgment is

Affirmed.

WALTERS v. MARATHON OIL CO.

United States Court of Appeals, Seventh Circuit, 1981.
642 F.2d 1098.

SPEARS, DISTRICT JUDGE. This action arose as a result of the Iranian revolution and the uncertainty of oil supplies. Marathon Oil Company, the appellant, is engaged in the business of reselling and distributing petroleum products. The appellee, Dennis E. Walters, contacted appellant in late December, 1978, about the possibility of locating a combination foodstore and service station on a vacant gasoline service station site in Indianapolis. Appellees (husband and wife) purchased the service station in February, 1979, and continued to make improvements upon it, based upon promises made, and the continuing negotiations with representatives from appellant. Paper work apparently proceeded normally, and appellees' proposal was delivered to appellant along with a three-party agreement, signed by appellees and Time Oil Company, the previous supplier to the service station site appellees had purchased. Before appellees' proposal was accepted by appellant, but after it was received at the office, appellant placed a moratorium on the consideration of new applications for dealerships and seller arrangements, and refused to sign the three-party agreement.

After a bench trial, the court found for appellees and against appellant on the theory of promissory estoppel. This finding has not been challenged. The two issues presented for review in this appeal pertain only to the award of damages in the form of lost profits, and the alleged failure of appellees to take reasonable steps to mitigate their damages. We affirm the judgment of the district court....

The appellant next argues that the trial court's computation of damages is clearly erroneous and contrary to the law. The trial court found that appellees lost anticipated profits of six cents per gallon for the 370,000 gallons they were entitled to receive under their allocation for the first year's gasoline sales, totalling $22,200.00, and awarded this amount in damages. The appellant insists that since appellees succeeded at trial solely on a promissory estoppel theory, and the district court so found, loss of profits is not a proper measure of damages. It contends that appellees' damages should have been the amount of their expenditures in reliance on the promise, measured by the difference between their expenditures and the present value of the property. Using this measure of damages, appellees would have received no award, for the present value of the real estate and its improvements is slightly more than the amount expended by appellees in reliance upon the promise. As a consequence, the appellant says that because appellees can recoup all they spent in reliance on appellant's promise, they would be in the same position they would have been in had the promise not been made.

However, in reliance upon appellant's promise to supply gasoline supplies to them, appellees purchased the station, and invested their funds and their time. It is unreasonable to assume that they did not anticipate a return of profits from this investment of time and funds, but, in reliance upon appellant's promise, they had foregone the opportunity to make the investment elsewhere. As indicated, the record reflects that had appellant performed according to its promise, appellees would have received the anticipated net profit of $22,200.00. The findings of the trial court in this regard were fully supported by the evidence. For example, it was shown that the 19⁷⁷/₈ base period for this particular station was 375,450 gallons. The appellant's own exhibit reflected the same amount. The testimony of the previous owner showed that the location pumped 620,000 gallons in 1972, and that he pumped 375,450 gallons in 1978. Furthermore, an expert witness testified that the site would pump 360,000 gallons a year. Appellant's own witness testified that all of its dealers received 100% of their base period allocation for the time in question. Thus, the trial court was not clearly erroneous in its finding that appellees would have sold 370,000 gallons of gasoline had appellant's promise been performed.

An equity court possesses some discretionary power to award damages in order to do complete justice. *Albemarle Paper Co. v. Moody*, 422 U.S. 405, 95 S.Ct. 2362, 45 L.Ed.2d 280 (1975).... Furthermore, since it is the historic purpose of equity to secure complete justice, the courts are able to adjust the remedies so as to grant the necessary relief, *Equal Employment Opportunity Commission v. General Tel. Co. of Northwest, Inc.*, 599 F.2d 322 (9th Cir.1979), *affirmed*, 446 U.S. 318, 100 S.Ct. 1698, 64 L.Ed.2d 319 (1980), and a district court sitting in equity may even devise a remedy which extends or exceeds the terms of a prior agreement between the parties, if it is necessary to make the injured party whole. *Levitt Corp. v. Levitt*, 593 F.2d 463 (2d Cir.1979).

Since promissory estoppel is an equitable matter, the trial court has broad power in its choice of a remedy, and it is significant that the ancient maxim that "equity will not suffer a wrong to be without a remedy" has long been the law in the State of Indiana. *King v. City of Bloomington*, 239 Ind. 548, 159 N.E.2d 563 (Ind.1959)....

In this case the promissory estoppel finding of the district court is not challenged. Moreover, it is apparent that the appellees suffered a loss of profits as a direct result of their reliance upon the promise made by appellant, and the amount of the lost profits was ascertained with reasonable certainty.[1] In addition, appellees took reasonable steps to mitigate their damages, and an award of damages based upon lost profits was appropriate in order to do complete justice.

Under the circumstances, and concluding, as we do, that the findings of the district court are not clearly erroneous, we affirm the judgment which awards damages to appellees based upon lost profits.

---

1. In *Goodman v. Dicker*, 169 F.2d 684 (D.C.Cir.1948), relied upon by appellant, the court held that the true measure of damages in that equitable estoppel case was the loss in the sum of $1,150 sustained by expenditures made in reliance on assurances given to the injured parties, and that the trial court had erred in *adding* the item of $350 for lost profits. No reasons were assigned or authorities cited by the court for the action it took, and there was no suggestion that in an appropriate case loss of profits could not be a true measure of damages....

AFFIRMED.

Questions

1. Whatever the court's characterization, should the legal basis for liability in *Goodman* be different from that in *Walters*?

2. Does RESTATEMENT (SECOND) OF CONTRACTS § 90 require that the remedy be limited to reliance losses? Or does it only permit such a limitation in a court's discretion? If the latter, on what basis should a court decide how to exercise its discretion? Are *Goodman* and *Walters* decided consistently? If not, which is the right result?

3. In *Goodman v. Dicker,* would recovery of the anticipated profit on the thirty radios compensate the dealer-franchisee for the forgone opportunity to make an alternate investment? In *Walters v. Marathon Oil Co.,* would a recovery of the lost profit for the first year compensate the dealer for his forgone investment? If not, would the recovery for lost profits in *Walters* function as a reasonable surrogate for the value of the opportunity forgone in reliance on the oil company's promise?

RESTATEMENT (SECOND) OF CONTRACTS §§ 344, 353

SULLIVAN v. O'CONNOR

Supreme Judicial Court of Massachusetts, 1973.
363 Mass. 579, 296 N.E.2d 183.

KAPLAN, JUSTICE. The plaintiff patient secured a jury verdict of $13,500 against the defendant surgeon for breach of contract in respect to an operation upon the plaintiff's nose. The substituted consolidated bill of exceptions presents questions about the correctness of the judge's instructions on the issue of damages.

The declaration was in two counts. In the first count, the plaintiff alleged that she, as patient, entered into a contract with the defendant, a surgeon, wherein the defendant promised to perform plastic surgery on her nose and thereby to enhance her beauty and improve her appearance; that he performed the surgery but failed to achieve the promised result; rather the result of the surgery was to disfigure and deform her nose, to cause her pain in body and mind, and to subject her to other damage and expense. The second count, based on the same transaction, was in the conventional form for malpractice, charging that the defendant had been guilty of negligence in performing the surgery. Answering, the defendant entered a general denial.

On the plaintiff's demand, the case was tried by jury. At the close of the evidence, the judge put to the jury, as special questions, the issues of liability under the two counts, and instructed them accordingly. The jury returned a verdict for the plaintiff on the contract count, and for the defendant on the negligence count. The judge then instructed the jury on the issue of damages.

As background to the instructions and the parties' exceptions, we mention certain facts as the jury could find them. The plaintiff was a professional entertainer, and this was known to the defendant. The agreement was as alleged in the declaration. More particularly, judging from exhibits, the plaintiff's nose had been straight, but long and prominent; the defendant undertook by two operations to reduce its prominence and somewhat to shorten it, thus making it more pleasing in relation to the plaintiff's other features. Actually the plaintiff was obliged to undergo three operations, and her appearance was worsened. Her nose now had a concave line to about the midpoint, at which it became bulbous; viewed frontally, the nose from bridge to midpoint was flattened and broadened, and the two sides of the tip had lost symmetry. This configuration evidently could not be improved by further surgery. The plaintiff did not demonstrate, however, that her change of appearance had resulted in loss of employment. Payments by the plaintiff covering the defendant's fee and hospital expenses were stipulated at $622.65.

The judge instructed the jury, first, that the plaintiff was entitled to recover her out-of-pocket expenses incident to the operations. Second, she could recover the damages flowing directly, naturally, proximately, and foreseeably from the defendant's breach of promise. These would comprehend damages for any disfigurement of the plaintiff's nose—that is, any change of appearance for the worse—including the effects of the consciousness of such disfigurement on the plaintiff's mind, and in this connection the jury should consider the nature of the plaintiff's profession. Also consequent upon the defendant's breach, and compensable, were the pain and suffering involved in the third operation, but not in the first two. As there was no proof that any loss of earnings by the plaintiff resulted from the breach, that element should not enter into the calculation of damages.

By his exceptions the defendant contends that the judge erred in allowing the jury to take into account anything but the plaintiff's out-of-pocket expenses (presumably at the stipulated amount). The defendant excepted to the judge's refusal of his request for a general charge to that effect, and, more specifically, to the judge's refusal of a charge that the plaintiff could not recover for pain and suffering connected with the third operation or for impairment of the plaintiff's appearance and associated mental distress.

The plaintiff on her part excepted to the judge's refusal of a request to charge that the plaintiff could recover the difference in value between the nose as promised and the nose as it appeared after the operations. However, the plaintiff in her brief expressly waives this exception and others made by her in case this court overrules the defendant's exceptions; thus she would be content to hold the jury's verdict in her favor.

We conclude that the defendant's exceptions should be overruled.

It has been suggested on occasion that agreements between patients and physicians by which the physician undertakes to effect a cure or to bring about a given result should be declared unenforceable on grounds of public policy. See Guilmet v. Campbell, 385 Mich. 57, 76, 188 N.W.2d 601 (dissenting opinion). But there are many decisions recognizing and enforcing such contracts, see annotation, 43 A.L.R.3d 1221, 1225, 1229–1233, and the law of Massachusetts has treated them as valid, although we have had no decision meeting head on the contention that they should be denied legal sanction. Small v. Howard, 128 Mass. 131.... These causes of action are, however, considered a little suspect, and thus we find courts straining sometimes to read the pleadings as sounding only in tort for negligence, and not in contract for breach of promise, despite sedulous efforts by the pleaders to pursue the latter theory. See Gault v. Sideman, 42 Ill.App.2d 96, 191 N.E.2d 436.

It is not hard to see why the courts should be unenthusiastic or skeptical about the contract theory. Considering the uncertainties of medical science and the variations in the physical and psychological conditions of individual patients, doctors can seldom in good faith promise specific results. Therefore it is unlikely that physicians of even average integrity will in fact make such promises. Statements of opinion by the physician with some optimistic coloring are a different thing, and may indeed have therapeutic value. But patients may transform such statements into firm promises in their own minds, especially when they have been disappointed in the event, and testify in that sense to sympathetic juries. If actions for breach of promise can be readily maintained, doctors, so it is said, will be frightened into practicing "defensive medicine." On the other hand, if these actions were outlawed, leaving only the possibility of suits for malpractice, there is fear that the public might be exposed to the enticements of charlatans, and confidence in the profession might ultimately be shaken. See Miller, The Contractual Liability of Physicians and Surgeons, 1953 Wash. L. Q. 413, 416–423. The law has taken the middle of the road position of allowing actions based on alleged contract, but insisting on clear proof. Instructions to the jury may well stress this requirement and point to tests of truth, such as the complexity or difficulty of an operation as bearing on the probability that a given result was promised. See annotation, 43 A.L.R.3d 1225, 1225–1227.

If an action on the basis of contract is allowed, we have next the question of the measure of damages to be applied where liability is found. Some cases have taken the simple view that the promise by the physician is to be treated like an ordinary commercial promise, and accordingly that the successful plaintiff is entitled to a standard measure of recovery for breach of contract—"compensatory" ("expectancy") damages, an amount intended to put the plaintiff in the position he would be in if the contract had been performed, or, presumably, at the plaintiff's election, "restitution" damages, an amount corresponding to any benefit conferred by the plaintiff upon the defendant in the performance of the contract disrupted by the defendant's breach. See Restatement: Contracts § 329 and comment a, §§ 347, 384(1). Thus in Hawkins v. McGee, 84 N.H. 114, 146 A. 641, the defendant doctor was taken to have promised the plaintiff to convert his damaged hand by means of an operation into a good or perfect hand, but the doctor so operated as to damage the hand still further. The court, following the usual expectancy formula, would have asked the jury to estimate and award to the plaintiff the difference between the value of a good or perfect hand, as promised, and the value of the hand after the operation. (The same formula would apply, although the dollar result would be less, if the operation had neither worsened nor improved the condition of the hand.) If the plaintiff had not yet paid the doctor his fee, that amount would be deducted from the recovery. There could be no recovery for the pain and suffering of the operation, since that detriment would have been incurred even if the operation had been successful; one can say that this detriment was not "caused" by the breach. But where the plaintiff by reason of the operation was put to more pain that he would have had to endure, had the doctor performed as promised, he should be compensated for that difference as a proper part of his expectancy recovery. It may be noted that on an alternative count for malpractice the plaintiff in the *Hawkins* case had been nonsuited; but on ordinary principles this could not affect the contract claim, for it is hardly a defence to a breach of contract that the promisor acted innocently and without negligence. The New Hampshire court further refined the *Hawkins* analysis in McQuaid v. Michou, 85 N.H. 299, 157 A. 881, all in the direction of treating the patient-physician cases on the ordinary footing of expectancy. . . .

Other cases, including a number in New York, without distinctly repudiating the *Hawkins* type of analysis, have indicated that a different and generally more lenient measure of damages is to be applied in patient-physician actions based on breach of alleged special agreements to effect a cure, attain a stated result, or employ a given medical method. This measure is expressed in somewhat variant ways, but the substance is that the plaintiff is to recover any expenditures made by him and for other detriment (usually not specifically described in the opinions) following proximately and foreseeably upon the defendant's failure to carry out his promise. Robins v. Finestone, 308 N.Y. 543, 546, 127 N.E.2d 330. . . . This, be it noted, is not a "restitution" measure, for it is not limited to restoration of the benefit conferred on the defendant (the fee paid) but includes other expenditures, for example, amounts paid for medicine and nurses; so also it would seem according to its logic to take in damages for any worsening of the plaintiff's condition due to the breach. Nor is it an "expectancy" measure, for it does not appear to contemplate recovery of the whole difference in value between the condition as promised and the condition actually resulting from the treatment. Rather the tendency of the formulation is to put the plaintiff back in the position he occupied just before the parties entered upon the agreement, to compensate him for the detriments he suffered in reliance upon the agreement. This kind of intermediate pattern of recovery for breach of contract is discussed in the suggestive article by Fuller and Perdue, The Reliance Interest in Contract Damages, 46 Yale L.J. 52, 373, where the authors show that, although not attaining the currency of the standard measures, a "reliance" measure has for special reasons been applied by the courts in a variety of settings, including noncommercial settings. See 46 Yale L.J. at 396–401.

For breach of the patient-physician agreements under consideration, a recovery limited to restitution seems plainly too meager, if the agreements are to be enforced at all. On the other hand, an expectancy recovery may well be excessive. The factors, already mentioned, which have made the cause of action somewhat suspect, also suggest moderation as to the breadth of the recovery that should be permitted. Where, as in the case at bar and in a number of the reported cases, the doctor has been absolved of negligence by the trier, an expectancy measure may be thought harsh. We should recall here that the fee paid by the patient to the doctor for the alleged promise would usually be quite disproportionate to the putative expectancy recovery. To attempt, moreover, to put a value on the condition that would or might have resulted, had the treatment succeeded as promised, may sometimes put an exceptional strain on the imagination of the fact finder. As a general consideration, Fuller and Perdue argue that the reasons for granting damages for broken promises to the extent of the expectancy are at their strongest when the promises are made in a business context, when they have to do with the production or distribution of goods or the allocation of functions in the market place; they become weaker as the context shifts from a commercial to a noncommercial field. 46 Yale L.J. at 60–63.

There is much to be said, then, for applying a reliance measure to the present facts, and we have only to add that our cases are not unreceptive to the use of that formula in special situations. We have, however, had no previous occasion to apply it to patient-physician cases.

The question of recovery on a reliance basis for pain and suffering or mental distress requires further attention. We find expressions in the decisions that pain and suffering (or the like) are simply not compensable in actions for breach of contract. The defendant seemingly espouses this proposition in the present case. True, if the buyer under a contract for the purchase of a lot of merchandise, in suing for the seller's breach, should claim damages for mental anguish caused by his disappointment in the transaction, he would not succeed; he would be told, perhaps, that the asserted psychological injury was not fairly foreseeable by the defendant as a probable consequence of the breach of such a business contract. See Restatement: Contracts, § 341, and comment a. But there is no general rule barring such items of damage in actions for breach of contract. It is all a question of the subject matter and background of the contract, and when the contract calls for an operation on the person of the plaintiff, psychological as well as physical injury may be expected to figure somewhere in the recovery, depending on the particular circumstances. The point is explained in Stewart v. Rudner, 349 Mich. 459, 469, 84 N.W.2d 816.... Again, it is said in a few of the New York cases, concerned with the classification of actions for statute of limitations purposes, that the absence of allegations demanding recovery for pain and suffering is characteristic of a contract claim by a patient against a physician, that such allegations rather belong in a claim for malpractice. See Robins v. Finestone, 308 N.Y. 543, 547, 127 N.E.2d 330.... These remarks seem unduly sweeping. Suffering or distress resulting from the breach going beyond that which was envisaged by the treatment as agreed, should be compensable on the same ground as the worsening of the patient's condition because of the breach. Indeed it can be argued that the very suffering or distress "contracted for"–that which would have been incurred if the treatment achieved the promised result–should also be compensable on the theory underlying the New York cases. For that suffering is "wasted" if the treatment fails. Otherwise stated, compensation for this waste is arguably required in order to complete the restoration of the status quo ante.[6]

In the light of the foregoing discussion, all the defendant's exceptions fail: the plaintiff was not confined to the recovery of her out-of-pocket expenditures; she was entitled to recover also for the worsening of her condition,[7] and for the pain and suffering and mental distress involved in the third operation. These items were compensable on either an expectancy or a reliance view. We might have been required to elect between the two views if the pain and suffering connected with the first two operations contemplated by the agreement, or the whole difference in value between the present and the promised conditions, were being claimed as elements of damage. But the plaintiff waives her possible claim to the former element, and to so much of the latter as represents the difference in value between the promised condition and the condition before the operations....

Questions

1. What was the basis for enforcing Dr. O'Connor's promise, if one was made? Was there a bargained-for exchange? Was there foreseeable reliance? Which basis does the court assume?

2. Does the court decide between expectation and reliance damages for medical cases like this one? How much of this opinion is dictum? What would you predict the law would require as damages in a similar case in Massachusetts after this decision?

3. Should expectation damages be denied in cases involving nonmarket values? Do reliance damages better compensate for the harm caused by a

---

6. Recovery on a reliance basis for breach of the physician's promise tends to equate with the usual recovery for malpractice, since the latter also looks in general to restoration of the condition before the injury. But this is not paradoxical, especially when it is noted that the origins of contract lie in tort. See Farnsworth, The Past of Promise: An Historical Introduction to Contract, 69 Col. L. Rev. 576, 594–596....

7. That condition involves a mental element and appraisal of it properly called for consideration of the fact that the plaintiff was an entertainer. Cf. McQuaid v. Michou, 85 N.H. 299, 303–304, 157 A. 881 (discussion of continuing condition resulting from physician's breach).

breach? Reread *Hawkins v. McGee*, above at p. 3. Does *Hawkins* or *Sullivan* offer the better approach to damages recoverable from physicians who fail to keep promises to achieve a specified result?

NOTE ON THE FACTS IN *SULLIVAN v. O'CONNOR*

The record in *Sullivan v. O'Connor* casts doubt on the facts as presented by the Supreme Judicial Court of Massachusetts. It seems there was little evidence that Dr. O'Connor made the promise sued upon or that Ms. Sullivan endured significant pain and suffering after the third operation.

According to excerpts reprinted in RICHARD DANZIG & GEOFFREY R. WATSON, THE CAPABILITY PROBLEM IN CONTRACT LAW 5–47 (2d ed.2004), Dr. O'Connor testified that, before the operations, he had never described how Ms. Sullivan's nose would look after the operations or promised an outcome. Ms. Sullivan testified that Dr. O'Connor had taken a photograph of her face and drawn a line on it, saying that "it would look more or less like that when he finished." Id. at 36. After all three operations, she testified, Dr. O'Connor said that he had given her "a nose like Hedy Lamarr's." Id. at 38. These apparently predictive and descriptive statements do not seem to amount to substantial evidence of a promise. See Chapter 1, § 1 above.

On the question of damages, Dr. O'Connor testified that the third operation was terminated almost at its inception because Ms. Sullivan was not in a psychological condition to accept the procedure. She was given anesthesia and an incision was started, but it took only one stitch to close the incision after Ms. Sullivan apparently panicked. Id. at 41. Ms. Sullivan testified that she refused permission for a third operation. Id. at 44. She gave no evidence of any suffering due to that operation. Moreover, the record includes the following exchange during questioning by Dr. O'Connor's lawyer:

FINNERTY: Now, you do agree, do you not, that your nose, now, is a lot better than it ever was, don't you?

SULLIVAN: It's smaller, but it's distorted, though.

FINNERTY: Remember my asking you this question [while taking your pretrial deposition]? Let me ask you this question in all seriousness, "You agree that it's a lot better than it ever was?"

And your answer: "Yes, but there is a lot wrong with it, too. It isn't what I was supposed to get."

Id.

SECTION 4. RESTITUTION

Restitution is often available to prevent unjust enrichment. Conceptually, a restitutionary recovery differs from expectation and reliance damages in a straightforward way. Expectation damages seek to place the injured party in the position it would have been in had the contract been performed by compensating for both gains prevented and losses sustained as a consequence of the breach. Reliance damages seek to place the injured party in the position it would have been in had the contract not been performed by compensating for losses sustained, including benefits conferred on the party in breach, expenditures made to third parties, and other costs. Restitution seeks to disgorge any unjust enrichment. Restitution differs from reliance because it includes benefits conferred on the party in breach by the nonbreaching party, but excludes expenditures made to third parties by the nonbreaching party and sometimes the costs of preparing to perform. Restitution can also take the form of specific relief, as when a court orders a buyer to return delivered goods to the seller.

Accordingly, restitution is often a component of reliance damages, but the reverse is not the case. Restitution may also be a component of expectation damages for breach of contract. U.C.C. § 2–711(1), for example, makes clear that, for the specified types of breaches, a nonbreaching buyer can recover "so much of the price as has been paid." A buyer in breach has a right to restitution of payments made subject to deductions as provided in U.C.C. § 2–718. On the other hand, a buyer's remedies for a seller's breach differ markedly depending on who has the goods, partly to avoid unjust enrichment when the buyer has them. See U.C.C. § 2–714.

The law of restitution ranges far beyond the law of contracts. See generally I–IV George E. Palmer, The Law of Restitution (1978). The question of special relevance here concerns the availability of restitution as an alternative remedy for breach of contract. Unless the nonbreaching party has fully performed and the party in breach owes only money, it is clear that restitution is an alternative to expectation or reliance damages whenever the breach is a serious one. As we will see in Chapter 6, a serious breach has the legal effect of allowing the nonbreaching party to cancel the contract. Having done so rightfully, the nonbreaching party can pursue restitution "off the contract." Restitution may be more advantageous in circumstances such as those in the cases below.

OLIVER v. CAMPBELL

Supreme Court of California, 1954.
43 Cal.2d 298, 273 P.2d 15.

Carter, Justice. Plaintiff appeals from a judgment for defendant, administratrix of the estate of Roy Campbell, deceased, in an action for attorney's fees.

Plaintiff's cause of action was stated in a common count alleging that Roy Campbell became indebted to him in the sum of $10,000, the reasonable value of services rendered as attorney for Campbell; that no part had been paid except $450. Campbell died after the services were rendered by plaintiff. Plaintiff filed a claim against his estate for the fees which defendant rejected. Defendant in her answer denied the allegations made and as a "further" defense alleged that plaintiff and Campbell entered into an "express written contract" employing plaintiff as attorney for a stated fee of $750, and all work alleged to have been performed by plaintiff was performed under that contract.

According to the findings of the trial court the claim against the estate was founded on the alleged reasonable value of legal services rendered by plaintiff for Campbell in an action for separate maintenance by defendant, Campbell's wife, against Campbell and in which the latter cross complained for a divorce. Plaintiff was not counsel when the pleadings in that action were filed. He came into the case on December 16, 1949, before trial of the action. He and Campbell entered into a written contract that date for plaintiff's representation of Campbell in the action, the contract stating that plaintiff agrees to represent Campbell in the separate maintenance and divorce action which has been set for trial in the superior court for a "total fee" of $750 plus court costs and other incidentals in the sum of $100 making a total of $850. The fees were to be paid after trial. Plaintiff represented Campbell at the trial consuming 29 days and lasting until May, 1950. (Defendant's complaint for separate maintenance was changed to one for divorce.) After the trial ended the court indicated its intention to give Mrs. Campbell a divorce. But while her proposed findings were under consideration by plaintiff and the court, defendant Campbell substituted himself instead of plaintiff and thereby the representation by plaintiff of Campbell was "terminated." The findings in the divorce action were filed in May, 1951. Plaintiff's services were furnished pursuant to the contract. The reasonable value of the services was $5,000. Campbell paid $450 to plaintiff and the $100 costs.

The court concluded that plaintiff should take nothing because neither his claim against the estate nor his action was on the contract but were in quantum meruit and no recovery could be had for the reasonable value of the services because the compensation for those services was covered by the express contract.

According to plaintiff's undisputed testimony Campbell told him after defendant had offered proposed findings in the divorce action that he was dissatisfied with plaintiff as his counsel and would discharge him and asked him if he would sign a substitution of attorneys under which Campbell would represent himself. Plaintiff replied that he recognized Campbell had a right to discharge him but that he was prepared to carry the case to conclusion; that he expected to be paid the reasonable value of his services which would be as much as defendant's counsel in the divorce action received, $9,000, to which Campbell replied he was not going to pay "a cent more." (At that time Campbell had paid $450.) Thereupon the substitution (dated January 25, 1951) was signed and Campbell took plaintiff's file in the divorce case with him.

It seems that the contract of employment contemplated that plaintiff was to continue his services and representation at least until and including final judgment in the divorce action. See Neblett v. Getty, 20 Cal.App.2d 65, 66 P.2d 473. It might thus appear that plaintiff was discharged before he had fully completed his services under the contract and the discharge prevented him from completing his performance. (That question is later discussed.)

One alleged rule of law applied by the trial court and that urged by defendant is that where there is a contract of employment for a definite term which fixes the compensation, there cannot be any recovery for the reasonable value of the services even though the employer discharges the employee—repudiates the contract before the end of the term; that the only remedy of the employee is an action on the contract for the fixed compensation or damages for the breach of the contract. The trial court accepted that theory and rendered judgment for defendant because plaintiff did not state a cause of action on the contract nor for damages for its breach; it was for the reasonable value of the services performed before plaintiff's discharge. Accordingly there is no express finding on whether the discharge was wrongful or whether there was a rescission of the contract by plaintiff because of Campbell's breach of it, or whether plaintiff had substantially performed at the time of this discharge.

The rule applied is not in accord with the general contract law, the law applicable to employment contracts or employment of an attorney by a client. The general rule is stated: "... that one who has been injured by a breach of contract has an election to pursue any of three remedies, to wit: 'He may treat the contract as rescinded and may recover upon a *quantum meruit* so far as he has performed; or he may keep the contract alive, for the benefit of both parties, being at all times ready and able to perform; or, third, he may treat the repudiation as putting an end to the contract for all purposes of performance, and sue for the profits he would have realized if he had not been prevented from performing.' " Alder v. Drudis, 30 Cal.2d 372, 381, 182 P.2d 195, 201.... It is the same in agency or contract for services cases.... And in entire contracts employing an attorney for a fixed fee it has been said that when the client wrongfully discharges the attorney before he has completed the contract, the attorney may recover the reasonable value of the services performed to the time of discharge.... Inasmuch as the contract has been repudiated by the employer before its term is up and after the employee has partly performed and the employee may treat the contract as "rescinded," there is no longer any contract upon which the employer can rely as fixing conclusively the limit of the compensation—the reasonable value of services recoverable by the employee for his part performance. Hence it is stated in Lessing v. Gibbons, ... 6 Cal.App.2d 598, 607, 45 P.2d 258, 262, that: "It is well settled that one who is wrongfully discharged and prevented from further performance of his contract may elect as a general rule to treat the contract as rescinded, may sue upon a *quantum meruit* as if the special contract of employment had never been made and may recover the reasonable value of the services performed even though such reasonable value exceeds the contract price." ...

It should further be noted that under the only evidence on the subject, above mentioned, plaintiff in effect promptly notified Campbell of the rescission of the contract when he advised him that he would execute the substitution of attorneys when he was discharged by Campbell but told Campbell he would hold him for the reasonable value of the services. On the issue of the necessity of restoration or offer to restore the part payment for the services which Campbell had made, the rule applies that such restoration is not necessary where plaintiff would be entitled to it in any event. See Kales v. Houghton, 190 Cal. 294, 212 P. 21.... It is clear that plaintiff was entitled to receive the $450 paid to him either under the contract or for the reasonable value of his services.

The question remains, however, of the application of the foregoing rules to the instant case. Plaintiff had performed practically all of the services he was employed to perform when he was discharged. The trial was at an end. The court had indicated its intention to give judgment against Campbell and all that remained was the signing of findings and judgment. The full sum called for in the contract was payable because the trial had ended. Under these circumstances it would appear that in effect, plaintiff had completed the performance of his services and the rule would apply that: "The remedy of restitution in money is not available to one who has fully performed his part of a contract, if the only part of the agreed exchange for such performance that has not been rendered by the defendant is a sum of money constituting a liquidated debt; but full performance does not make restitution unavailable if any part of the consideration due from the defendant in return is something other than a liquidated debt." Rest. Contracts, § 350.... [T]here being no dispute as to the amount called for in the contract, the services having been in effect fully performed, the court should have rendered judgment for the balance due on the contract which is conceded to be $300.

The judgment is therefore reversed and the trial court is directed to render judgment in favor of plaintiff for the sum of $300.

Questions

1. Did Oliver bring this action for breach of contract? Could he have done so? What would he have recovered had he brought the action for breach of contract? Why might he prefer restitution?

2. What is an action for "quantum meruit"? Is it brought for the defendant's failure to perform a promise? If there had been no contract between Oliver and Campbell, what would Oliver be able to recover in quantum meruit? Why does he recover the contract price less the amount already paid?

3. Why should a recovery in quantum meruit be limited by the contract price when the plaintiff fully performs? Did Oliver fully perform? Is there any less an unjust enrichment on facts like those in *Oliver v. Campbell*? What would be the consequence if nonbreaching parties had an unhindered choice between quantum meruit and contract damages in such cases? Would anything untoward happen?

4. How should the value of Oliver's services be calculated?

5. *Problems.*

a. The facts are otherwise as in *Oliver v. Campbell*, except that the contract called for a fixed fee of $5,000, though the trial took only one day, for which Oliver would normally receive $450. How much should Oliver get in an action on the contract? How much should he get in an action in quantum meruit?

b. The facts are otherwise as in *Oliver v. Campbell*, except that the contract called for a contingency fee of 40% of the amount of any favorable judgment or any settlement reached in the case, to be paid upon Campbell's receipt of the money. Before trial, Campbell discharged Oliver, as was his right under the relevant code of professional responsibility, but in breach of the contract. The reasonable value of services rendered to that point was $5,000, and the trial eventually produced a judgment for Campbell, 40% of which was $750. What can Oliver recover? See Reid, Johnson, Downes, Andrachik & Webster v. Lansberry, 68 Ohio St.3d 570, 629 N.E.2d 431 (1994).

UNITED STATES v. ALGERNON BLAIR, INC.

United States Court of Appeals, Fourth Circuit, 1973.
479 F.2d 638, 26 A.L.R. Fed. 741.

CRAVEN, CIRCUIT JUDGE. May a subcontractor, who justifiably ceases work under a contract because of the prime contractor's breach, recover in quantum meruit the value of labor and equipment already furnished pursuant to the contract irrespective of whether he would have been entitled to recover in a suit on the contract? We think so, and, for reasons to be stated, the decision of the district court will be reversed.

The subcontractor, Coastal Steel Erectors, Inc., brought this action under the provisions of the Miller Act, 40 U.S.C.A. § 270a et seq., in the name of the United States against Algernon Blair, Inc., and its surety, United States Fidelity and Guaranty Company. Blair had entered a contract with the United States for the construction of a naval hospital in Charleston County, South Carolina. Blair had then contracted with Coastal to perform certain steel erection and supply certain equipment in conjunction with Blair's contract with the United States. Coastal commenced performance of its obligations, supplying its own cranes for handling and placing steel. Blair refused to pay for crane rental, maintaining that it was not obligated to do so under the subcontract. Because of Blair's failure to make payments for crane rental, and after completion of approximately 28 percent of the subcontract, Coastal terminated its performance. Blair then proceeded to complete the job with a new subcontractor. Coastal brought this action to recover for labor and equipment furnished.

The district court found that the subcontract required Blair to pay for crane use and that Blair's refusal to do so was such a material breach as to justify Coastal's terminating performance. This finding is not questioned on appeal. The court then found that under the contract the amount due Coastal, less what had already been paid, totaled approximately $37,000. Additionally, the court found Coastal would have lost more than $37,000 if it had completed performance. Holding that any amount due Coastal must be reduced by any loss it would have incurred by complete performance of the contract, the court denied recovery to Coastal. While the district court correctly stated the " 'normal' rule of contract damages,"[1] we think Coastal is entitled to recover in quantum meruit.

In United States for Use of Susi Contracting Co. v. Zara Contracting Co., 146 F.2d 606 (2d Cir.1944), a Miller Act action, the court was faced with a situation similar to that involved here—the prime contractor had unjustifiably breached a subcontract after partial performance by the subcontractor. The court stated:

> For it is an accepted principle of contract law, often applied in the case of construction contracts, that the promisee upon breach has the option to forego any suit on the contract and claim only the reasonable value of his performance.

146 F.2d at 610. . . . Quantum meruit recovery is not limited to an action against the prime contractor but may also be brought against the Miller Act surety, as in this case. Further, that the complaint is not clear in regard to the theory of a plaintiff's recovery does not preclude recovery under quantum meruit. Narragansett Improvement Co. v. United States, 290 F.2d 577 (1st Cir.1961). A plaintiff may join a claim for quantum meruit with a claim for damages from breach of contract.

In the present case, Coastal has, at its own expense, provided Blair with labor and the use of equipment. Blair, who breached the subcontract, has retained these benefits without having fully paid for them. On these facts, Coastal is entitled to restitution in quantum meruit.

> The "restitution interest," involving a combination of unjust impoverishment with unjust gain, presents the strongest case for relief. If, following Aristotle, we regard the purpose of justice as the maintenance of an equilibrium of goods among members of society, the restitution interest presents twice as strong a claim to judicial intervention as the reliance interest, since if A not only causes B to lose one unit but appropriates that unit to himself, the resulting discrepancy between A and B is not one unit but two.

Fuller & Perdue, The Reliance Interest in Contract Damages, 46 Yale L.J. 52, 56 (1936).

The impact of quantum meruit is to allow a promisee to recover the value of services he gave to the defendant irrespective of whether he would have lost money on the contract and been unable to recover in a suit on the contract. Scaduto v. Orlando, 381 F.2d 587, 595 (2d Cir. 1967). The measure of recovery for quantum meruit is the reasonable value of the performance, Restatement of Contracts § 347 (1932); and, recovery is undiminished by any loss which would have been incurred by

---

1. Fuller & Perdue, The Reliance Interest in Contract Damages, 46 Yale L.J. 52   (1936); Restatement of Contracts § 333 (1932).

complete performance. 12 Williston on Contracts § 1485, at 312 (3d ed. 1970). While the contract price may be evidence of reasonable value of the services, it does not measure the value of the performance or limit recovery. Rather, the standard for measuring the reasonable value of the services rendered is the amount for which such services could have been purchased from one in the plaintiff's position at the time and place the services were rendered.

Since the district court has not yet accurately determined the reasonable value of the labor and equipment use furnished by Coastal to Blair, the case must be remanded for those findings.[9] When the amount has been determined, judgment will be entered in favor of Coastal, less payments already made under the contract. Accordingly, for the reasons stated above, the decision of the district court is

Reversed and remanded with instructions.

Questions

1.   Did the subcontractor bring this action for breach of contract? Could it have done so? What would the subcontractor have recovered had the action been brought for breach of contract? Why might the subcontractor prefer restitution?

2.   In the action for quantum meruit, should the subcontractor's recovery be limited by the amount the subcontractor would have made (or lost) had the contract been fully performed? How would that affect the disgorgement of unjust enrichment? How would it affect the efficiency of contract breach behavior? If the subcontractor's recovery should be limited, what result in *United States v. Algernon Blair, Inc.*?

3.   In a contract for services, how should the value of the benefit conferred be calculated? By the cost to the provider of providing the services? By the cost of those services on the market? By the net increase in the recipient's wealth?

4.   *Problems.*

The facts are as in *United States v. Algernon Blair, Inc.*, except that the rental cost of the crane was only $100. Same result?

---

9. Under the view of the case taken by the district court it was unnecessary to precisely appraise the value of services and materials rendered; an approximation was thought to suffice because the hypothetical loss had the contract been fully performed was greater in amount.

Chapter 5

THE AUTONOMY PRINCIPLE
AGAIN

The law empowers people to make and receive enforceable promises when they communicate decisions to act or refrain from acting in some definite way in the future, subject to other principles.

Once we decide that a contract has been formed, a range of questions drops from further consideration and new questions arise. In deciding that a contract has been formed, we decide the relevant questions of capacity, mistake, duress, unconscionability, and public policy. The parties' agreement passes muster. Consequently, except in highly unusual circumstances, the contract is within the realm of private autonomy, where the parties determine their own contractual relations.

The parties determine their contractual relations by agreeing to *terms*—the stated or statable propositions from which contract rights, duties, and powers flow. You will want to identify and interpret the contract terms before determining whether a party is in breach, i.e., has failed to fulfill his or her duty. The next chapter will take up the main consequences of breach, other than the right to money damages or specific performance, which were considered in Chapter 4.

SECTION 1. IDENTIFYING EXPRESS CONTRACT TERMS

We will approach this chapter in four analytical steps, though you should not think that the four steps are entirely distinct in practice. The first step is *to identify the express terms* of the contract. An express term is that portion of the parties' agreement which was stated and relates to a distinct element of performance or enforcement. In oral contracts, this is a matter of identifying what the parties communicated to each other by way of committing themselves to a future course of conduct toward each other. In written contracts, however, the problem is complicated by the fact that many agreed terms are superseded as negotiations evolve into a final written product. Section 1 addresses the bases for identifying operative contract terms in written contracts. The second step is *to interpret the express terms.* For several reasons, the language in which express terms are stated may permit the parties to dispute their specific rights, duties, and powers in the circumstances that actually arise. Section 2 aims at selecting the intended or reasonably expected meaning of express terms from among all possible meanings of the language as stated. The third step is *to identify and interpret the implied terms* of the contract. Contract parties often refrain from stating the obvious and fail to govern all possible contingencies. Section 3 examines some of the terms that courts may find to be implicit in a contract. The fourth step is to distinguish between certain kinds of terms thus identified—promises, conditions, and promissory conditions. A breach of contract does not occur until a nonperforming party's duty, arising from a promise, is due. Whether it is due may depend on whether all conditions precedent have occurred. Section 4 introduces the law of conditions.

GIANNI v. R. RUSSEL & CO., INC.

Supreme Court of Pennsylvania, 1924.
281 Pa. 320, 126 A. 791.

SCHAFFER, JUSTICE. Plaintiff had been a tenant of a room in an office building in Pittsburgh wherein he conducted a store, selling tobacco, fruit, candy and soft drinks. Defendant acquired the entire property in which the storeroom was located, and its agent negotiated with plaintiff for a further leasing of the room. A lease for three years was signed. It contained a provision that the lessee should "use the premises only for the sale of fruit, candy, soda water," etc., with the further stipulation that "it is expressly understood that the tenant is not allowed to sell tobacco in any form, under penalty of instant forfeiture of this lease." The document was prepared following a discussion about renting the room between the parties and after an agreement to lease had been reached. It was signed after it had been left in plaintiff's hands and admittedly had been read over to him by two persons, one of whom was his daughter.

Plaintiff sets up that in the course of his dealings with defendant's agent it was agreed that, in consideration of his promises not to sell tobacco and to pay an increased rent, and for entering into the agreement as a whole, he should have the exclusive right to sell soft drinks in the building. No such stipulation is contained in the written lease. Shortly after it was signed defendant demised the adjoining room in the building to a drug company without restricting the latter's right to sell soda water and soft drinks. Alleging that this was in violation of the contract which defendant had made with him, and that the sale of these beverages by the drug company had greatly reduced his receipts and profits, plaintiff brought this action for damages for breach of the alleged oral contract, and was permitted to recover. Defendant has appealed.

Plaintiff's evidence was to the effect that the oral agreement had been made at least two days, possibly longer, before the signing of the instrument, and that it was repeated at the time he signed; that, relying upon it, he executed the lease. Plaintiff called one witness who said he heard defendant's agent say to plaintiff at a time admittedly several days before the execution of the lease that he would have the exclusive right to sell soda water and soft drinks, to which the latter replied if that was the case he accepted the tenancy. Plaintiff produced no witness who was present when the contract was executed to corroborate his statement as to what then occurred. Defendant's agent denied that any such agreement was made, either preliminary to or at the time of the execution of the lease.

Appellee's counsel argues this is not a case in which an endeavor is being made to reform a written instrument because of something omitted as a result of fraud, accident, or mistake, but is one involving the breach of an independent oral agreement which does not belong in the writing at all and is not germane to its provisions. We are unable to reach this conclusion.

"Where parties, without any fraud or mistake, have deliberately put their engagements in writing, the law declares the writing to be not only the best, but the only evidence of their agreement." Martin v. Berens, 67 Pa. 459, 463; Irvin v. Irvin, 142 Pa. 271, 287, 21 A. 816.

"All preliminary negotiations, conversations and verbal agreements are merged in and superseded by the subsequent written contract, . . . and 'unless fraud, accident, or mistake be averred, the writing constitutes the agreement between the parties, and its terms cannot be added to nor subtracted from by parol evidence.' " Union Storage Co. v. Speck, 194 Pa. 126, 133, 45 A. 48, 49; Vito v. Birkel, 209 Pa. 206, 208, 58 A. 127.

The writing must be the entire contract between the parties if parol evidence is to be excluded, and to determine whether it is or not the writing will be looked at, and if it appears to be a contract complete within itself, "couched in such terms as import a complete legal obligation without any uncertainty as to the object or extent of the engagement, it is conclusively presumed that the whole engagement of the parties, and the extent and manner of their undertaking, were reduced to writing." Seitz v. Brewers' Refrigerating Machine Co., 141 U.S. 510, 517, 12 S.Ct. 46, 48, 35 L.Ed. 837.

When does the oral agreement come within the field embraced by the written one? This can be answered by comparing the two, and determining whether parties, situated as were the ones to the contract, would naturally and normally include the one in the other if it were made. If they relate to the same subject-matter, and are so interrelated that both would be executed at the same time and in the same contract, the scope of the subsidiary agreement must be taken to be covered by the writing. This question must be determined by the court.

In the case at bar the written contract stipulated for the very sort of thing which plaintiff claims has no place in it. It covers the use to which the storeroom was to be put by plaintiff and what he was and what he was not to sell therein. He was "to use the premises only for the sale of fruit, candy, soda water," etc., and was not "allowed to sell tobacco in any form." Plaintiff claims his agreement not to sell tobacco was part of the consideration for the exclusive right to sell soft drinks. Since his promise to refrain was included in the writing, it would be the natural thing to have included the promise of exclusive rights. Nothing can be imagined more pertinent to these provisions which were included than the one appellee avers.

In cases of this kind, where the cause of action rests entirely on an alleged oral understanding concerning a subject which is dealt with in a written contract it is presumed that the writing was intended to set forth the entire agreement as to that particular subject.

"In deciding upon this intent [as to whether a certain subject was intended to be embodied by the writing], the chief and most satisfactory index ... is found in the circumstance whether or not the particular element of the alleged extrinsic negotiation is dealt with at all in the writing. If it is mentioned, covered, or dealt with in the writing, then presumably the writing was meant to represent all of the transaction on that element, if it is not, then probably the writing was not intended to embody that element of the negotiation." Wigmore on Evidence (2d Ed.) vol. 5, p. 309.

As the written lease is the complete contract of the parties, and since it embraces the field of the alleged oral contract, evidence of the latter is inadmissible under the parol evidence rule....

We have stated on several occasions recently that we propose to stand for the integrity of written contracts.... We reiterate our position in this regard.

The judgment of the court below is reversed, and is here entered for defendant.

Questions

1. What was the deal in *Gianni*? What is the relevant parol agreement? What is the legal issue before the court?

2. What is the "parol evidence rule"? Insofar as *Gianni* tells you, how might you formulate the parol evidence rule?

3. Was Gianni treated unjustly? Should the law of contracts have a parol evidence rule? Should it be applied even when it would discharge an agreement that was really made? If not, should it be applied, as in *Gianni*, whenever a court looks at the writing only and decides the writing "appears to be a contract complete within itself"?

———

UNIFORM COMMERCIAL CODE § 2–202

———

RESTATEMENT (SECOND) OF CONTRACTS §§ 209–10, 213–16

MASTERSON v. SINE

Supreme Court of California, 1968.
68 Cal.2d 222, 65 Cal.Rptr. 545, 436 P.2d 561.

TRAYNOR, CHIEF JUSTICE. Dallas Masterson and his wife Rebecca owned a ranch as tenants in common. On February 25, 1958, they conveyed it to Medora and Lu Sine by a grant deed "Reserving unto the Grantors herein an option to purchase the above described property on or before February 25, 1968" for the "same consideration as being paid heretofore plus their depreciation value of any improvements Grantees may add to the property from and after two and a half years from this date." Medora is Dallas' sister and Lu's wife. Since the conveyance Dallas has been adjudged bankrupt. His trustee in bankruptcy and Rebecca brought this declaratory relief action to establish their right to enforce the option.

The case was tried without a jury. Over defendants' objection the trial court admitted extrinsic evidence that by "the same consideration as being paid heretofore" both the grantors and the grantees meant the sum of $50,000 and by "depreciation value of any improvements" they meant the depreciation value of improvements to be computed by deducting from the total amount of any capital expenditures made by defendants grantees the amount of depreciation allowable to them under United States income tax regulations as of the time of the exercise of the option.

The court also determined that the parol evidence rule precluded admission of extrinsic evidence offered by defendants to show that the parties wanted the property kept in the Masterson family and that the option was therefore personal to the grantors and could not be exercised by the trustee in bankruptcy.

The court entered judgment for plaintiffs, declaring their right to exercise the option, specifying in some detail how it could be exercised, and reserving jurisdiction to supervise the manner of its exercise and to determine the amount that plaintiffs will be required to pay defendants for their capital expenditures if plaintiffs decide to exercise the option.

Defendants appeal. They contend that the option provision is too uncertain to be enforced and that extrinsic evidence as to its meaning should not have been admitted. The trial court properly refused to frustrate the obviously declared intention of the grantors to reserve an option to repurchase by an overly meticulous insistence on completeness and clarity of written expression.... It properly admitted extrinsic evidence to explain the language of the deed ... to the end that the consideration for the option would appear with sufficient certainty to permit specific enforcement.... The trial court erred, however, in excluding the extrinsic evidence that the option was personal to the grantors and therefore nonassignable.

When the parties to a written contract have agreed to it as an "integration"—a complete and final embodiment of the terms of an agreement—parol evidence cannot be used to add to or vary its terms. . . . When only part of the agreement is integrated, the same rule applies to that part, but parol evidence may be used to prove elements of the agreement not reduced to writing. . . .

The crucial issue in determining whether there has been an integration is whether the parties intended their writing to serve as the exclusive embodiment of their agreement. The instrument itself may help to resolve that issue. It may state, for example, that "there are no previous understandings or agreements not contained in the writing," and thus express the parties' "intention to nullify antecedent understandings or agreements." (See 3 Corbin, Contracts (1960) § 578, p. 411.) Any such collateral agreement itself must be examined, however, to determine whether the parties intended the subjects of negotiation it deals with to be included in, excluded from, or otherwise affected by the writing. Circumstances at the time of the writing may also aid in the determination of such integration. . . .

California cases have stated that whether there was an integration is to be determined solely from the face of the instrument . . . and that the question for the court is whether it "appears to be a complete . . . agreement. . . ." . . . Neither of these strict formulations of the rule, however, has been consistently applied. The requirement that the writing must appear incomplete on its face has been repudiated in many cases where parol evidence was admitted "to prove the existence of a separate oral agreement as to any matter on which the document is silent and which is not inconsistent with its terms"—even though the instrument appeared to state a complete agreement. . . . Even under the rule that the writing alone is to be consulted, it was found necessary to examine the alleged collateral agreement before concluding that proof of it was precluded by the writing alone. (See 3 Corbin, Contracts (1960) § 582, pp. 444–446.) It is therefore evident that, "The conception of a writing as wholly and intrinsically self-determinative of the parties' intent to make it a sole memorial of one or seven or twenty-seven subjects of negotiation is an impossible one." (9 Wigmore, Evidence (3d ed. 1940) § 2431, p. 103.) For example, a promissory note given by a debtor to his creditor may integrate all their present contractual rights and obligations, or it may be only a minor part of an underlying executory contract that would never be discovered by examining the face of the note.

In formulating the rule governing parol evidence, several policies must be accommodated. One policy is based on the assumption that written evidence is more accurate than human memory. . . . This policy, however, can be adequately served by excluding parol evidence of agreements that directly contradict the writing. Another policy is based on the fear that fraud or unintentional invention by witnesses interested in the outcome of the litigation will mislead the finder of facts.... McCormick has suggested that the party urging the spoken as against the written word is most often the economic underdog, threatened by severe hardship if the writing is enforced. In his view the parol evidence rule arose to allow the court to control the tendency of the jury to find through sympathy and without a dispassionate assessment of the probability of fraud or faulty memory that the parties made an oral agreement collateral to the written contract, or that preliminary tentative agreements were not abandoned when omitted from the writing. (See McCormick, Evidence (1954) § 210.) He recognizes, however, that if this theory were adopted in disregard of all other considerations, it would lead to the exclusion of testimony concerning oral agreements whenever there is a writing and thereby often defeat the true intent of the parties. (See McCormick, op. cit. supra, § 216, p. 441.)

Evidence of oral collateral agreements should be excluded only when the fact finder is likely to be misled. The rule must therefore be based on the credibility of the evidence. One such standard, adopted by section 240(1)(b) of the Restatement of Contracts, permits proof of a collateral agreement if it "is such an agreement as might *naturally* be made as a separate agreement by parties situated as were the parties to the written contract." (Italics added; see McCormick, Evidence (1954) § 216, p. 441; see also 3 Corbin, Contracts (1960) § 583, p. 475, § 594, pp. 568–569; 4 Williston, Contracts (3d ed. 1961) § 638, pp. 1039–1045.) The draftsmen of the Uniform Commercial Code would exclude the evidence in still fewer instances: "If the additional terms are such that, if agreed upon, they would *certainly* have been included in the document in the view of the court, then evidence of their alleged making must be kept from the trier of fact." (Com. 3, § 2–202, italics added.)

The option clause in the deed in the present case does not explicitly provide that it contains the complete agreement, and the deed is silent on the question of assignability. Moreover, the difficulty of accommodating the formalized structure of a deed to the insertion of collateral agreements makes it less likely that all the terms of such an agreement were included. (See 3 Corbin, Contracts (1960) § 587; 4 Williston, Contracts (3d ed. 1961) § 645; 70 A.L.R. 752, 759 (1931); 68 A.L.R. 245 (1930).) The statement of the reservation of the option might well have been placed in the recorded deed solely to preserve the grantors' rights against any possible future purchasers and this function could well be served without any mention of the parties' agreement that the option was personal. There is nothing in the record to indicate that the parties to this family transaction, through experience in land transactions or otherwise, had any warning of the disadvantages of failing to put the whole agreement in the deed. This case is one, therefore, in which it can be said that a collateral agreement such as that alleged "might naturally be made as a separate agreement." A *fortiori*, the case is not one in which the parties "would certainly" have included the collateral agreement in the deed.

It is contended, however, that an option agreement is ordinarily presumed to be assignable if it contains no provisions forbidding its transfer or indicating that its performance involves elements personal to the parties.... The fact that there is a written memorandum, however, does not necessarily preclude parol evidence rebutting a term that the law would otherwise presume. In American Industrial Sales Corp. v. Airscope, Inc., supra, 44 Cal.2d 393, 397–398, 282 P.2d 504, we held it proper to admit parol evidence of a contemporaneous collateral agreement as to the place of payment of a note, even though it contradicted the presumption that a note, silent as to the place of payment, is payable where the creditor resides....

In the present case defendants offered evidence that the parties agreed that the option was not assignable in order to keep the property in the Masterson family. The trial court erred in excluding that evidence.

The judgment is reversed.

BURKE, JUSTICE. I dissent. The majority opinion:

(1) Undermines the parol evidence rule as we have known it in this state since at least 1872 by declaring that parol evidence should have been admitted by the trial court to show that a written option, absolute and unrestricted in form, was intended to be limited and nonassignable;

(2) Renders suspect instruments of conveyance absolute on their face;

(3) Materially lessens the reliance which may be placed upon written instruments affecting the title to real estate; and

(4) Opens the door, albeit unintentionally to a new technique for the defrauding of creditors.

The opinion permits defendants to establish by parol testimony that their grant to their brother (and brother-in-law) of a written option, absolute in terms, was nevertheless agreed to be nonassignable by the grantee (now a bankrupt), and that therefore the right to exercise it did not pass, by operation of the bankruptcy laws, to the trustee for the benefit of the grantee's creditors.

And how was this to be shown? By the proffered testimony of the bankrupt optionee himself! Thereby one of his assets (the option to purchase defendants' California ranch) would be withheld from the trustee in bankruptcy and from the bankrupt's creditors. Understandably the trial court, as required by the parol evidence rule, did not allow the bankrupt by parol to so contradict the unqualified language of the written option.

The court properly admitted parol evidence to explain the intended meaning of the "same consideration" and "depreciation value" phrases of the written option to purchase defendants' land, as the intended meaning of those phrases was not clear. However, there was nothing ambiguous about the *granting* language of the option and not the slightest suggestion in the document that the option was to be nonassignable. Thus, to permit such words of limitation to be added by parol is to *contradict* the absolute nature of the grant, and to directly violate the parol evidence rule.

Just as it is unnecessary to state in a deed to "lot X" that the house located thereon goes with the land, it is likewise unnecessary to add to "I grant an option to Jones" the words *"and his assigns"* for the option to be assignable.... California statutes expressly declare that it *is* assignable, and only if I add language in writing showing my intent to withhold or restrict the right of assignment may the grant be so limited. Thus, to seek to restrict the grant by parol is to *contradict* the written document in violation of the parol evidence rule....

At the outset the majority in the present case reiterate that the rule against contradicting or varying the terms of a writing remains applicable when only part of the agreement is contained in the writing, and parol evidence is used to prove elements of the agreement not reduced to writing. But having restated this established rule, the majority opinion inexplicably proceeds to subvert it....

Options are property, and are widely used in the sale and purchase of real and personal property. One of the basic incidents of property ownership is the right of the owner to sell or transfer it. The author of the present majority opinion, speaking for the court in Farmland Irrigation Co. v. Dopplmaier (1957) 48 Cal.2d 208, 222, 308 P.2d 732, 740, 66 A.L.R.2d 590, put it this way: "The statutes in this state clearly manifest a policy in favor of the free transferability of all types of property, including rights under contracts." (Citing Civ.Code, §§ 954, 1044, 1458; see also 40 Cal.Jur.2d 289–291, and cases there cited.) These rights of the owner of property to transfer it, confirmed by the cited code sections, are elementary rules of substantive law and not the mere disputable presumptions which the majority opinion in the present case would make of them....

This new rule, not hitherto recognized in California, provides that proof of a claimed collateral oral agreement is admissible if it is such an agreement as might *naturally* have been made a separate agreement by the parties under the particular circumstances. I submit that this approach opens the door to uncertainty and confusion. Who can know what its limits are? Certainly I do not. For example, in its application to this case who could be expected to divine as "natural" a separate oral agreement between the parties that the assignment, absolute and unrestricted on its face, was intended by the parties to be limited to the Masterson family?

Or, assume that one gives to his relative a promissory note and that the payee of the note goes bankrupt. By operation of law the note becomes an asset of the bankruptcy. The trustee attempts to enforce it. Would the relatives be permitted to testify that by a separate oral agreement made at the time of the execution of the note it was understood that should the payee fail in his business the maker would be excused from payment of the note, or that, as here, it was intended that the benefits of the note would be *personal* to the payee? I doubt that trial judges should be burdened with the task of conjuring whether it would have been "natural" under those circumstances for such a separate agreement to have been made by the parties. Yet, under the application of the proposed rule, this is the task the trial judge would have, and in essence the situation presented in the instant case is no different. . . .

In an effort to provide justification for applying the newly pronounced "natural" rule to the circumstances of the present case, the majority opinion next attempts to account for the silence of the writing in this case concerning assignability of the option, by asserting that "the difficulty of accommodating the formalized structure of a deed to the insertion of collateral agreements makes it less likely that all the terms of such an agreement were included." What difficulty would have been involved here, to add the words "this option is nonassignable"? The asserted "formalized structure of a deed" is no formidable barrier. . . .

Comment hardly seems necessary on the convenience to a bankrupt of such a device to defeat his creditors. He need only produce parol testimony that any options (or other property, for that matter) which he holds are subject to an oral "collateral agreement" with family members (or with friends) that the property is nontransferable "in order to keep the property in the family" or in the friendly group. In the present case the value of the ranch which the bankrupt and his wife held an option to purchase has doubtless increased substantially during the years since they acquired the option. The initiation of this litigation by the trustee in bankruptcy to establish his right to enforce the option indicates his belief that there is substantial value to be gained for the creditors from this asset of the bankrupt. Yet the majority opinion permits defeat of the trustee and of the creditors through the device of an asserted collateral oral agreement that the option was "personal" to the bankrupt and nonassignable "in order to keep the property in the family"! . . .

I would hold that the trial court ruled correctly on the proffered parol evidence, and would affirm the judgment.

Questions

1. What is the parol evidence offered by plaintiff in *Masterson*? Why is the trial court's admission of plaintiff's offered parol evidence affirmed? What is the parol evidence offered by defendant? Why do you suppose the trial court excluded that agreement?

2. What was the deal in *Masterson*? What is the deal if one looks at the writing only? What is the deal if one looks also at the parol evidence?

3. Why does Chief Justice Traynor reverse the trial court and order the parol agreement admitted? On what point do the majority and dissent most importantly disagree? What is Justice Traynor's concept of "the contract"? Of "the intentions of the parties"? Whose contractual interests is he most keen to protect? Which opinion better supports the parties' autonomy?

4. How would *Gianni* and *Masterson* be decided under the RESTATEMENT (SECOND) provisions assigned above? Is there anything left of a parol evidence rule in California after *Masterson*?

INTERFORM CO. v. MITCHELL

United States Court of Appeals, Ninth Circuit, 1978.
575 F.2d 1270.

SNEED, C. J. The appellant Mitchell Construction Company used certain forms which belonged to Interform Company for molding concrete on two construction jobs it performed as prime contractor for the State of Idaho. Interform received $32,000 from Mitchell which Mitchell contended was the purchase price of the forms. Interform contended the $32,000 was a rental payment for use of the forms on Mitchell's first job. Consequently, in the district court Interform sought payment for Mitchell's use of its forms on the second job, and the return of its forms. Mitchell sought a decision giving it ownership of the forms and general and punitive damages for abuse of process.

The district court in a trial without a jury found that the parties had in fact entered into a contract in September 1971 for the rental of the forms for use in Mitchell's first job. It found that no oral or written agreement had been entered into for use of the forms in the second job; rather, Mitchell had used the forms "despite knowledge on his part that Interform was claiming ownership . . . and claimed a right to payment by Mitchell of additional rentals for further use of the forms." The use of the forms in the second job, the court found, benefited Mitchell and caused detriment to Interform. Finding also that Interform had not "volunteered" the free use of its forms, the court concluded that Mitchell had been unjustly enriched by its use of the forms. It found the fair rental value for the second job to have been $29,250 and, after deducting certain expenditures by Mitchell, awarded $26,750 to Interform. It denied Mitchell's counterclaim and declined to award attorney's fees to Interform. We affirm in all respects except as to attorney's fees. As to these we believe the trial court erred. We reverse and remand for further proceedings with respect to these.

Many of the pertinent facts were sharply disputed by the parties. Our statement of the facts will indicate the major areas of conflict. Preliminary negotiations in the spring and summer of 1971 without question centered entirely upon the rental of forms. On September 8, Mitchell, President of Mitchell Construction Company, and Miller, a salesman for Interform, drove around Seattle in order to observe some of Interform's concrete forms in use. As Miller was driving the group to a restaurant, Mitchell stated that he would be interested in purchasing the forms. Miller was surprised at this comment and testified that he "thought at first he was kidding, because up to that point no one had mentioned anything about a sale, and all of our quotes had been straight rental." (Tr.78).

Mitchell contends that the contract of sale was agreed to orally at that time, and was confirmed by a document which Mitchell sent to Interform. That document, admittedly backdated to September 8, was written between September 13 and 17 and was received by Interform on September 21. Entitled "Purchase Order," it requested Interform to "furnish" forms according to size and quantity specifications set forth therein. It also set price, time and payment terms, and contained the condition that "[i]f Mitchell Construction Company does the hauling, which is their option, there will be an allowance of $.43 per loaded mile."

Mitchell asserts that this sales agreement reflected an agreement arrived at during the tour of September 8. Miller, on the other hand, testified that he did not have authority to set a sales price, and that his attempt that day to contact Dashew, the President of Interform, by telephone to receive instructions was unsuccessful. Miller's version, which the trial judge chose to accept, was supported by testimony of the pilot who had flown Mitchell to Seattle and accompanied him on the tour. The trial judge also agreed with Interform that the contract was arrived at during a telephone conversation on September 13 between Mitchell and Dashew, at which time a rental agreement as to quantity and price was reached.

On September 14, a "speed memo" was sent from Mitchell's general superintendent to Miller asking: Jim, Have you ordered the Pans? What is the delivery date? Are you sending shape drawings? Are you sending Freight rate allowance? When we get this information we will send a P.O. for proper amount. We wish to check this frieght [sic] first." The freight issue was settled shortly thereafter, because the "purchase order" discussed above, drawn between September 13 and 17, sets forth a resolution of the question.

Several days after Mitchell's purchase order was dispatched, a confirmation was sent by Interform, set forth on a second sheet of Mitchell's standard purchase form and also containing the word "furnish." Three bills of lading and three invoices from Interform followed, each specifically referring to the "rental" of the forms. No one at Mitchell objected to these six documents. At trial Mitchell, his general supervisor and his jobs supervisor testified that they had never seen or checked the invoices or bills of lading.

The trial court judge chose not to believe this, nor did he find credible other inconsistent testimony offered by Mitchell. He did, however, accept Interform's evidence of a custom within the construction trade by which builders would order equipment for rental on purchase forms. . . .

Appellant's contention regarding the two purchase orders brings to the fore principles of contract law pertaining to the integration of writings and the interpretation of written contracts, the formal statement of which provides inadequate warning of the complexity that attends their application. Thus, the Idaho Supreme Court many years ago observed:

"In the construction of a contract, the court will endeavor to arrive at the real intention of the parties, and will consider the facts and circumstances out of which the contract arose, and will construe the contract in the light of such facts and circumstances."

Wood River Power Co. v. Arkoosh, 37 Idaho 348, 215 P. 975 (1923).

Also in determining whether the intention of the parties is to be ascertained only from the written agreement that Court has stated:

"Where preliminary negotiations are consummated by written contract, the writing supersedes all previous understandings and the intent of the parties must be ascertained from the writing."

Nuquist v. Bauscher, 71 Idaho 89, 94, 227 P.2d 83 (1951). These pronouncements, by no means unique or complex, obscure more than reveal the existence of a fundamental difference concerning the manner in which integration and interpretation should be approached. That difference relates to how a writing is to be viewed and the respective roles of the judge and jury.

One view is to treat the writing as having a unique and quite compelling force. Under that approach a writing "supersedes all previous undertakings" when the writing taken as a whole appears complete and the alleged additional terms ordinarily and naturally would have been included in the writing by reasonable parties situated as were the parties to the writing. See Calamari and Perillo, *Contracts*, 103–111 (1977) (hereinafter Calamari & Perillo). Also a writing which so supersedes all previous undertakings, i. e., which is integrated, means what a reasonably intelligent person, "acquainted with all the operative usages and knowing all the circumstances prior to and contemporaneous with the making of the integration[,] other than the oral statements made by the parties to each other as to what they intended it to mean," would understand it to mean. Id. at 118. 4 *Williston on Contracts* §§ 607, 631 (1961) (hereinafter Williston); *Restatement, Contracts* § 230. The writing becomes the focus of attention and the judge by assuming the function of a reasonable person determines whether the writing did supersede all previous undertakings and, if so, its meaning to a reasonable person situated as described above. Williston §§ 616–17. An integrated writing clear in meaning to the reasonable person constitutes the contract between the parties. In this manner the judge can fix the legal relations of the parties without aid of a jury and provide a measure of security to written agreements. *McCormick on Evidence* §§ 214–16 (1954); Calamari & Perillo 100; Williston §§ 616, 633.

Another, and opposing view, imparts to the writing no unique or compelling force. A writing is integrated when the parties intend it to be and it means what they intended it to mean. *Corbin on Contracts* § 581 at 442, § 582 at 448–57, § 583 at 485 (1960) (hereinafter Corbin); *Restatement (Second), Contracts* § 21A; Williston § 605; *Restatement, Contracts* § 240(b), comment a; § 238, comments a, b. In theory, therefore, integration may be lacking even if the additional terms ordinarily and naturally would have been included in the writing and an integrated writing can have a meaning to which a reasonably intelligent person, situated as described above, could not subscribe. Corbin § 544 at 145–46. Again, in theory, this view accords the jury, when the trial employs one, a potentially larger role in the process of fixing contractual relations and provides somewhat less security to written agreements.

In practice, however, the difference between the two views is less significant than one might imagine. A writing, which ordinarily and naturally would be an integrated one, generally is one the parties thereto intended to be integrated. Also, the meaning to which the reasonably intelligent person would subscribe generally is that to which the parties did subscribe. Under both views, the judge makes the initial determinations; if the writing is integrated, evidence of an alleged collateral agreement is excluded, and, if the meaning is clear or unambiguous, evidence tending to show a different meaning will not be received. Where the writing is not integrated or its meaning not unambiguous, parol evidence is admissible under both views. . . .

There are, however, significant differences between the two views. To suggest none exist would reduce the debate between their respective leading protagonists, Williston with regard to the first and Corbin the second, to a triviality. The debate is not that. It relates, as indicated, to the attitude with which judges should approach written contracts. Williston requires the judge to ascertain the legal relations between the parties by reference to those associated with the "forms" . . . to which they should adhere and from which they depart at their peril. Calamari & Perillo 104–05; Williston §§ 633, 638–39. Corbin, on the other hand, directs the judge to fix the legal relations between the parties in accordance with their intention even when the "forms" they employed suggest otherwise. Corbin §§ 538–42A. A judge, guided by Williston, in the case before us would impose upon the parties the terms of the "purchase orders" as understood by the reasonably intelligent person if the "purchase orders" appear complete and any additional terms ordinarily and naturally would have been included therein. Williston §§ 638–39; Calamari & Perillo 105. A judge, guided by Corbin, would impose upon the parties the agreement that the evidence indicates they in fact reached. It is understandable that Mitchell urges us to proceed as Williston would have us; it is equally clear why Interform prefers Corbin's way.

It is unlikely that any jurisdiction will inflexibly adopt one approach to the exclusion of the other; each is likely to influence the conduct of judges and the disposition of cases. However, it must be acknowledged that the influence of Corbin's way is stronger now, id. at 111, than when he and Williston grappled during the drafting of the American Law Institute's first Restatement of Contracts. . . .

Moreover, Idaho Code § 28–2–202, a provision of Idaho's version of Article II of the Uniform Commercial Code, reflects Corbin's influence. It precludes contradiction of "confirmatory memoranda" by prior or contemporaneous oral agreements when the writing was "*intended* by the parties as a final expression of their agreement" and permits the introduction of consistent additional terms "unless the court finds the writing to have been *intended* also as a complete and exclusive statement of the terms of the agreement." (Italics added). The focus plainly is on the intention of the parties, not the integration practices of reasonable persons acting normally and naturally. This is Corbin's focus. . . .

Idaho law being, in its relevant parts, infused with Corbin's spirit, the trial judge in this case was acting within both its spirit and letter when he admitted evidence extrinsic to the purchase orders to determine whether the transaction was a sale or a lease. Of particular importance to the trial judge's determination was the exchange of correspondence and quotations prior to September 8, the six invoices and bills of lading, as well as evidence of a trade custom indicating that builders normally used purchase order forms when requesting rentals. This evidence enabled him to derive the contract from the September 13 phone conversation between Dashew and Mitchell, the speed memo of September 14 from Mitchell which corroborates the existence of an agreement regarding the forms while evidencing uncertainty as to freight terms, and the purchase order of Mitchell which Interform confirmed and which resolved the freight issue.

We find no error under Idaho law in the evidence the trial judge considered or the conclusions he reached. It is clear that Mitchell's and Interform's purchase orders were not "intended by the parties as a final expression of their agreement," Idaho Code 28–2–202, and that the intent of the parties must be derived from all the documents employed, the circumstances surrounding their execution, and the subsequent conduct of the parties. Moreover, under Idaho law we believe there exists no compulsion that the intent of the parties be only what a reasonably intelligent person would have understood their intent to be after examining only Mitchell's and Interform's purchase orders. . . .

Questions

1. What are the important facts in *Interform*? What does Interform Co. think are the important facts? What does Mitchell think are the important facts? What does the court think are the important facts? What makes the facts important in each one's view?

2. How do Williston's and Corbin's views of the parol evidence rule differ, as their views are presented in *Interform*? Which view does *Gianni* better represent? Which view does *Masterson* better represent? What is the jury's role under Williston's view? What is the jury's role under Corbin's view? Which view makes better sense to you in a case like *Interform*? Why?

3. What was Idaho law before the decision in *Interform*? On what basis does the court in *Interform* conclude that Idaho law is "infused with Corbin's spirit"? Does it decide this point on the basis of precedent, statute or principle? Does U.C.C. § 2–202 apply in this case?

LEE v. JOSEPH E. SEAGRAM & SONS, INC.

United States Court of Appeals, Second Circuit, 1977.
552 F.2d 447.

GURFEIN, CIRCUIT JUDGE. This is an appeal by defendant Joseph E. Seagram & Sons, Inc. ("Seagram") from a judgment entered by the District Court, Hon. Charles H. Tenney, upon the verdict of a jury in the amount of $407,850 in favor of the plaintiffs on a claim asserting common law breach of an oral contract. The court also denied Seagram's motion under Rule 50(b), Fed.R.Civ.P., for judgment notwithstanding the verdict. *Harold S. Lee, et al. v. Joseph E. Seagram and Sons*, 413 F.Supp. 693 (S.D.N.Y.1976). It had earlier denied Seagram's motion for summary judgment. The plaintiffs are Harold S. Lee (now deceased) and his two sons, Lester and Eric ("the Lees"). Jurisdiction is based on diversity of citizenship. We affirm.

The jury could have found the following. The Lees owned a 50% interest in Capitol City Liquor Company, Inc. ("Capitol City"), a wholesale liquor distributorship located in Washington, D.C. The other 50% was owned by Harold's brother, Henry D. Lee, and his nephew, Arthur Lee. Seagram is a distiller of alcoholic beverages. Capitol City carried numerous Seagram brands and a large portion of its sales were generated by Seagram lines.

The Lees and the other owners of Capitol City wanted to sell their respective interests in the business and, in May 1970, Harold Lee, the father, discussed the possible sale of Capitol City with Jack Yogman ("Yogman"), then Executive Vice President of Seagram (and now President), whom he had known for many years. Lee offered to sell Capitol City to Seagram but conditioned the offer on Seagram's agreement to relocate Harold and his sons, the 50% owners of Capitol City, in a new distributorship of their own in a different city.

About a month later, another officer of Seagram, John Barth, an assistant to Yogman, visited the Lees and their co-owners in Washington and began negotiations for the purchase of the assets of Capitol City by Seagram on behalf of a new distributor, one Carter, who would take it over after the purchase. The purchase of the assets of Capitol City was consummated on September 30, 1970 pursuant to a written agreement. The promise to relocate the father and sons thereafter was not reduced to writing.

Harold Lee had served the Seagram organization for thirty-six years in positions of responsibility before he acquired the half interest in the Capitol City distributorship. From 1958 to 1962, he was chief executive officer of Calvert Distillers Company, a wholly-owned subsidiary. During this long period he enjoyed the friendship and confidence of the principals of Seagram.

In 1958, Harold Lee had purchased from Seagram its holdings of Capitol City stock in order to introduce his sons into the liquor distribution business, and also to satisfy Seagram's desire to have a strong and friendly distributor for Seagram products in Washington, D.C. Harold Lee and Yogman had known each other for 13 years.

The plaintiffs claimed a breach of the oral agreement to relocate Harold Lee's sons, alleging that Seagram had had opportunities to procure another distributorship for the Lees but had refused to do so. The Lees brought this action on January 18, 1972, fifteen months after the sale of the Capitol City distributorship to Seagram. They contended that they had performed their obligation by agreeing to the sale by Capitol City of its assets to Seagram, but that Seagram had failed to perform its obligation under the separate oral contract between the Lees and Seagram. The agreement which the trial court permitted the jury to find was "an oral agreement with defendant which provided that if they agreed to sell their interest in Capitol City, defendant in return, within a reasonable time, would provide the plaintiffs a Seagram distributorship whose price would require roughly an amount equal to the capital obtained by the plaintiffs for the sale of their interest in Capitol City, and which distributorship would be in a location acceptable to plaintiffs." No specific exception was taken to this portion of the charge. By its verdict for the plaintiffs, we must assume—as Seagram notes in its brief—that this is the agreement which the jury found was made before the sale of Capitol City was agreed upon.[2]

Appellant urges several grounds for reversal. It contends that, as a matter of law, (1) plaintiffs' proof of the alleged oral agreement is barred by the parol evidence rule; and (2) the oral agreement is too vague and indefinite to be enforceable. Appellant also contends that plaintiffs' proof of damages is speculative and incompetent.

I.

Judge Tenney, in a careful analysis of the application of the parol evidence rule, decided that the rule did not bar proof of the oral agreement. We agree.

The District Court, in its denial of the defendant's motion for summary judgment, treated the issue as whether the written agreement for the sale of assets was an "integrated" agreement not only of all the mutual agreements concerning the sale of Capitol City assets, but also of *all* the mutual agreements of the parties. Finding the language of the sales agreement "somewhat ambiguous," the court decided that the determination of whether the parol evidence rule applies must await the taking of evidence on the issue of whether the sales agreement was

---

2. The complaint alleged that Seagram agreed to "obtain" or "secure" or "provide" a "similar" distributorship within a reasonable time, and plaintiffs introduced some testimony to that effect. Although other testimony suggested that Seagram agreed merely to provide an opportunity for the Lees to negotiate with third parties, and Judge Tenney indicated in his denial of judgment n.o.v. that Seagram merely agreed "to notify plaintiffs as they learned of distributors who were considering the sale of their businesses," 413 F.Supp. at 698–99, the jury was permitted to find that the agreement was in the nature of a commitment to provide a distributorship. There was evidence to support such a finding, and the jury so found.

intended to be a complete and accurate integration of all of the mutual promises of the parties.

Seagram did not avail itself of this invitation. It failed to call as witnesses any of the three persons who negotiated the sales agreement on behalf of Seagram regarding the intention of the parties to integrate all mutual promises or regarding the failure of the written agreement to contain an integration clause.

Appellant contends that, as a matter of law, the oral agreement was "part and parcel" of the subject-matter of the sales contract and that failure to include it in the written contract barred proof of its existence. *Mitchill v. Lath*, 247 N.Y. 377, 380, 160 N.E. 646 (1928). The position of appellant, fairly stated, is that the oral agreement was either an inducing cause for the sale or was a part of the consideration for the sale, and in either case, should have been contained in the written contract. In either case, it argues that the parol evidence rule bars its admission.

Appellees maintain, on the other hand, that the oral agreement was a collateral agreement and that, since it is not contradictory of any of the terms of the sales agreement, proof of it is not barred by the parol evidence rule. Because the case comes to us after a jury verdict we must assume that there actually was an oral contract, such as the court instructed the jury it could find. The question is whether the strong policy for avoiding fraudulent claims through application of the parol evidence rule nevertheless mandates reversal on the ground that the jury should not have been permitted to hear the evidence. *See Fogelson v. Rackfay Constr. Co.*, 300 N.Y. 334 at 337–38, 90 N.E.2d 881 (1950).

The District Court stated the cardinal issue to be whether the parties "intended" the written agreement for the sale of assets to be the complete and accurate integration of all the mutual promises of the parties. If the written contract was not a complete integration, the court held, then the parol evidence rule has no application.[3] We assume that the District Court determined intention by objective standards. *See* 3 Corbin on Contracts §§ 573–574. The parol evidence rule is a rule of substantive law. *Fogelson v. Rackfay Constr. Co.*, *supra* . . . .

The law of New York is not rigid or categorical, but is in harmony with this approach. As Judge Fuld said in *Fogelson*:

> "Decision in each case must, of course, turn upon the type of transaction involved, the scope of the written contract and the content of the oral agreement asserted."

300 N.Y. at 338, 90 N.E.2d at 883. And the Court of Appeals wrote in *Ball v. Grady*, 267 N.Y. 470, 472, 196 N.E. 402, 403 (1935):

---

3. Though the parties have not urged the particular choice of law applicable, both parties appear to assume that New York law governs. We note that in cases of this type, which depend so much on their partic- ular facts and for which direct precedent is therefore so sparse, virtually all jurisdictions would be expected to follow general common law principles.

"In the end, the court must find the limits of the integration as best it may by reading the writing in the light of surrounding circumstances."

Accord, Fogelson, supra, 300 N.Y. at 338, 90 N.E.2d 881. Thus, certain oral collateral agreements, even though made contemporaneously, are not within the prohibition of the parol evidence rule "because [if] they are separate, independent, and complete contracts, although relating to the same subject, ... [t]hey are allowed to be proved by parol, because they were made by parol, and no part thereof committed to writing." *Thomas v. Scutt,* 127 N.Y. 133, 140–41, 27 N.E. 961, 963 (1891).

Although there is New York authority which in general terms supports defendant's thesis that an oral contract inducing a written one or varying the consideration may be barred, *see, e.g., Fogelson v. Rackfay Constr. Co., supra,* 300 N.Y. at 340, 90 N.E.2d 881, the overarching question is whether, in the context of the particular setting, the oral agreement was one which the parties would ordinarily be expected to embody in the writing.... For example, integration is most easily inferred in the case of real estate contracts for the sale of land, *e.g., Mitchill v. Lath, supra,* 247 N.Y. 377, 160 N.E. 646, or leases, *Fogelson, supra....* In more complex situations, in which customary business practice may be more varied, an oral agreement can be treated as separate and independent of the written agreement even though the written contract contains a strong integration clause....

Thus, as we see it, the issue is whether the oral promise to the plaintiffs, as individuals, would be an expectable term of the contract for the sale of assets by a corporation in which plaintiffs have only a 50% interest, considering as well the history of their relationship to Seagram.

Here, there are several reasons why it would *not* be expected that the oral agreement to give Harold Lee's sons another distributorship would be integrated into the sales contract. In the usual case, there is an identity of parties in both the claimed integrated instrument and in the oral agreement asserted. Here, although it would have been physically possible to insert a provision dealing with only the shareholders of a 50% interest, the transaction itself was a *corporate* sale of assets. Collateral agreements which survive the closing of a corporate deal, such as employment agreements for particular shareholders of the seller or consulting agreements, are often set forth in separate agreements. *See Gem Corrugated Box Corp. v. National Kraft Container Corp.,* 427 F.2d at 503 ("it is ... plain that the parties ordinarily would not embody the stock purchase agreement in a writing concerned only with box materials purchase terms"). It was expectable that such an agreement as one to obtain a new distributorship for certain persons, some of whom were not even parties to the contract, would not necessarily be integrated into an instrument for the sale of *corporate* assets. As with an oral condition precedent to the legal effectiveness of an otherwise integrated written contract, which is not barred by the parol evidence rule if it is not directly contradictory of its terms, *Hicks v. Bush,* 10 N.Y.2d 488, 225

N.Y.S.2d 34, 180 N.E.2d 425 (1962); *cf.* 3 Corbin on Contracts § 589, "it is certainly not improbable that parties contracting in these circumstances would make the asserted oral agreement. . . ." 10 N.Y.2d at 493, 225 N.Y.S.2d at 39, 180 N.E.2d at 428.

Similarly, it is significant that there was a close relationship of confidence and friendship over many years between two old men, Harold Lee and Yogman, whose authority to bind Seagram has not been questioned. It would not be surprising that a handshake for the benefit of Harold's sons would have been thought sufficient. In point, as well, is the circumstance that the negotiations concerning the provisions of the sales agreement were not conducted by Yogman but by three other Seagram representatives, headed by John Barth. The two transactions may not have been integrated in their minds when the contract was drafted.[4]

Finally, the written agreement does not contain the customary integration clause, even though a good part of it (relating to warranties and negative covenants) is boilerplate. The omission may, of course, have been caused by mutual trust and confidence, but in any event, there is no such strong presumption of exclusion because of the existence of a detailed integration clause, as was relied upon by the Court of Appeals in *Fogelson, supra,* 300 N.Y. at 340, 90 N.E. 881.

Nor do we see any contradiction of the terms of the sales agreement. *Mitchill v. Lath, supra,* 247 N.Y. at 381, 160 N.E. 646; 3 Corbin on Contracts § 573, at 357. The written agreement dealt with the sale of corporate assets, the oral agreement with the relocation of the Lees. Thus, the oral agreement does not vary or contradict the money consideration recited in the contract as flowing to the selling corporation. That is the only consideration recited, and it is still the only consideration to the corporation.

We affirm Judge Tenney's reception in evidence of the oral agreement and his denial of the motion under Rule 50(b) with respect to the parol evidence rule. . . .

Questions

1. What was the deal in *Lee*?

2. What is the (doctrinal) legal issue in *Lee*? Why does the appellate court allow the agreement on relocating the Lees to be legally operative? Should it?

3. Is there an important difference between finding (1) partial integration and an additional agreement, or (2) complete integration and a collateral agreement? What is a collateral agreement? Which was the proper

---

4. Barth in a confidential memorandum dated June 12, 1970 to Yogman and Edgar Bronfman stated that "he [Harold Lee] would very much like to have another distributorship in another area for his two sons." Apparently Barth, who was not present at Harold Lee's meeting with Yogman, assumed that this was a desire on the part of Lee rather than a promise made by Yogman for Seagram.

finding in *Lee*? List the reasons given by the court for its finding. For each one, why is it a *reason*?

4. *Problems.*

a. Mellon and Frick negotiated an agreement for the sale of Tyrol Steel Co. It has a tightly drawn merger clause. As they are about to sign the writing, Mellon's lawyer has a heart attack and is taken to the hospital. Because it is so difficult for Mellon and Frick to get together, they orally agree to sign the documents, but that it will not take effect until Mellon's lawyer approves the deal. They sign. Mellon's lawyer disapproves the deal and Frick sues on the written contract. Can Mellon introduce evidence of the oral agreement?

b. Builder contracts in writing to build a house for Olner, with a well-drawn merger clause providing: "This contract represents the complete and final agreement of the parties, who agree that there are no collateral agreements that add to or vary the terms of this writing." The parties subsequently agree orally that the Builder will add a fireplace in the bedroom, which was not mentioned in the written contract. Is the oral agreement operative? See Universal Builders, Inc. v. Moon Motor Lodge, Inc., 430 Pa. 550, 244 A.2d 10 (1968).

NELSON v. ELWAY

Supreme Court of Colorado, 1995.
908 P.2d 102.

VOLLACK, C.J. . . . Mel T. Nelson (Nelson) was the president and sole shareholder of two car dealerships, Metro Auto and Metro Toyota, Inc. General Motors Acceptance Corporation (GMAC) provided all the financing for both dealerships. In the first half of 1990, both dealerships were experiencing financial difficulties. In July of 1990, Nelson retained John J. Pico and the Aspen Brokerage Company (Pico) to represent him in the selling or refinancing of one or both of the Dealerships.

In early 1991, Pico, acting on behalf of Nelson and Metro Toyota, began negotiations with John A. Elway, Jr. (Elway) and Rodney L. Buscher (Buscher) regarding the sale of Metro Toyota and the property upon which it was situated. On March 14, 1991, pursuant to those negotiations, Elway and Buscher signed a "Buy–Sell Agreement" and a separate real estate contract to purchase Metro Toyota. The closing was scheduled for April 15, 1991.

Soon after the signing of these documents, Pico asked Nelson if he would be willing to sell both Metro Auto and Metro Toyota to Elway. Nelson stated that he would be willing to sell both dealerships along with the land upon which they were located if he received sufficient personal remuneration. Pico then began negotiating with Elway and Buscher regarding the sale of both dealerships. Through these negotiations it became apparent that Elway and Buscher were unwilling or unable to pay the full purchase price for the dealerships and the land upon which they were located.

In order to consummate the transaction, Pico suggested to Nelson that Elway and Buscher reimburse Nelson for his interest in Metro Toyota by paying Nelson $50 per vehicle sold by both dealerships for a period of seven years commencing on May 1, 1991. In exchange for this compensation arrangement, Elway and Buscher would purchase Metro Auto from Nelson at a greatly reduced purchase price. These terms, referred to by the parties as the "Service Agreement," were reduced to writing but never signed by the parties. Subsequently, on March 16, 1991, the parties signed a "Buy–Sell Agreement" and a separate real estate contract for the purchase of Metro Auto. This written, signed agreement did not incorporate the terms of the Service Agreement.

By early 1991, the dealerships owed GMAC over $3 million. In order to protect its security interests, on April 3, 1991, GMAC required Nelson to execute agreements referred to as "keeper letters," allowing GMAC significant control over the dealerships. GMAC imposed this requirement as consideration for its agreement to pay in excess of $890,000 in debt owed by Metro Auto and Metro Toyota at the closing of the sale of the dealerships to Elway and Buscher. Nelson knew that execution of these letters would preclude his ability to file for bankruptcy protection and proceed through re-organization. He alleges that he thus sought and received assurances from Elway and Buscher that the orally agreed upon, but as yet unsigned, Service Agreement would be honored.

On April 8, 1991, after the execution of the keeper letters, Pico, Elway, and Buscher met at Pico's office. During this meeting, GMAC telephoned Pico's office and informed Pico, Elway, and Buscher that as a condition to its agreement to finance the acquisition of the land and assets of the dealerships by Elway and Buscher, Nelson was not to receive any proceeds from the sale of the dealerships. The respondents then informed Nelson they would not be able to enter into the Service Agreement with him, and the Service Agreement was therefore not executed at the closing on April 12, 1991. After closing, Nelson demanded that the respondents honor the Service Agreement. When the respondents refused, Nelson filed the instant action.

In his complaint, Nelson sought damages from Elway and Buscher for breach of contract, promissory estoppel, fraud, conspiracy, and dual agency. Additionally, Nelson sought exemplary damages. The respondents then moved the trial court for summary judgment, which the court granted as to all counts. The court of appeals affirmed with respect to all counts. . . .

The first issue with regard to the breach of contract claim is whether the merger clauses in the Buy–Sell Agreements precluded the consideration of evidence that the parties intended the Service Agreement to be part of the overall agreement to sell the dealerships.[1] The

---

1. Paragraph 14 of both of the Buy–Sell Agreements (the "Merger Clauses") for Metro Toyota and Metro Auto, both signed on March 16, 1991, by Nelson, Elway, and Buscher, states: This Agreement constitutes the entire Agreement between the parties pertaining to the subject matter contained herein, and supersedes all prior agree-

petitioners argue that the court of appeals erred by ruling that the merger clauses precluded the consideration of the intent of the contracting parties. The respondents assert that the merger clauses wholly manifest the intention of the parties that only those terms of the transaction reduced to writing and signed at the closing would be enforceable terms of the agreement.

We agree with the court of appeals that the merger clauses preclude consideration of extrinsic evidence to ascertain the intent of the parties. Integration clauses generally allow contracting parties to limit future contractual disputes to issues relating to the express provisions of the contract. *Keller v. A.O. Smith Harvestore Prods.*, 819 P.2d 69, 72 (Colo.1991). Therefore, the terms of a contract intended to represent a final and complete integration of the agreement between the parties are enforceable, and extrinsic evidence offered to prove the existence of prior agreements is inadmissible. Id.... Even when extrinsic evidence is admissible to ascertain the intent of the parties, such evidence may not be used to demonstrate an intent that contradicts or adds to the intent expressed in the writing. *KN Energy, Inc. v. Great Western Sugar Co.*, 698 P.2d 769, 777 n. 9 (Colo.1985).

In this case, the merger clauses plainly and unambiguously manifest the intent of the parties that the Buy–Sell Agreements executed on March 16, 1991 constitute the entire agreement between the parties pertaining to the subject matter contained therein. Where, as here, sophisticated parties who are represented by counsel have consummated a complex transaction and embodied the terms of that transaction in a detailed written document, it would be improper for this court to rewrite that transaction by looking to evidence outside the four corners of the contract to determine the intent of the parties.

The petitioners and respondents signed the March 16, 1991 Buy–Sell Agreements after extensive negotiation and numerous drafts of documents. By doing so, all parties expressly agreed, pursuant to the merger clauses, that the terms of those Buy–Sell Agreements would control the transaction and that all other agreements, oral or written, would be void. We will not step into a commercial transaction after the fact and attempt to ascertain the intent of the parties when that intent is clearly manifested by an express term in a written document. We thus conclude that the merger clauses in the March 16, 1991, Buy–Sell Agreements are dispositive as to the intent of the parties in this case. As there is no dispute as to any material fact with regard to this issue, the court of appeals correctly affirmed the trial court's order of summary judgment in favor of the respondents on this issue.

Lohr, J. dissenting. Petitioners Mel T. Nelson and Metro Auto, Inc. (collectively "Nelson") appealed a trial court ruling dismissing their claims on summary judgment grounds. The Colorado Court of Appeals

ments, representations and understandings of the parties. No modification or amendment of this Agreement shall be binding unless in writing and signed by the parties....

affirmed the trial court's dismissal of all of Nelson's claims except a claim based on promissory estoppel. *Nelson v. Elway*, No. 93CA0629 (Colo.App. May 26, 1994) (not selected for official publication). On certiorari review in this court, the majority holds that Nelson's civil conspiracy, breach of contract, and promissory estoppel claims were all properly dismissed by the trial court on summary judgment.

I respectfully dissent....

... Merger clauses preclude consideration of extrinsic evidence only where the parties intend that the document containing the merger is exclusive. *ARB, Inc. v. E–Systems, Inc.*, 663 F.2d 189, 199 (D.C.Cir. 1980).... The very essence of this case is a dispute regarding whether the parties intended the service agreement to be part and parcel of the overall deal. Because Nelson's position is adequately supported in the record, the intention of the parties regarding the exclusivity of the document containing the merger agreement is a disputed issue of material fact. As a result, this case is inappropriate for summary judgment disposition....

Although I believe that merger and integration clauses are presumptively valid, in keeping with the honored tenets of contract law there is an exception such that "[w]here giving effect to the merger clause would frustrate and distort the parties' true intentions and understanding regarding the contract, the clause will not be enforced." *Zinn v. Walker*, 87 N.C.App. 325, 361 S.E.2d 314, 319 (1987). In particular, where the parties intend that both a written contract and an alleged oral agreement constitute components of an overall agreement, a merger clause does not preclude consideration of extrinsic evidence. See Coulter v. Anderson, 144 Colo. 402, 410, 357 P.2d 76, 80 (1960)....

The parties' intention that the buy-sell agreements constituted entire contracts, allegedly evidenced by the merger clauses within, was by no means clearly manifested. *See Sierra Diesel Injection Serv. v. Burroughs Corp.*, 874 F.2d 653, 657 (9th Cir.1989) ("the presence of a merger clause while often taken as a strong sign of the parties' intent is not conclusive in all cases"). In this case, despite the disclaimer in both merger clauses that each buy-sell agreement constituted the entire agreement, the overall deal involved two buy-sell agreements and two real estate contracts. Furthermore, each buy-sell agreement made reference to the real estate contracts despite the exclusivity disclaimer. Regardless of the standard merger and integration language in the buy-sell agreements, it is clear that the parties intended their ultimate bargain to encompass other agreements, although the substantive weight of the alleged service agreement remains unclear. *See Gem Corrugated Box Corp. v. National Kraft Container Corp.*, 427 F.2d 499, 502–03 (2d Cir.1970).

When the parties disagree as to whether a document expresses the complete agreement of the parties, and a court subsequently finds that the evidence is conflicting or admits of more than one inference, the resolution of the parties' dispute requires a factual determination....

Questions

1. What is the "buy-sell agreement"? What is the "service agreement"? What are the important facts in *Nelson*, according to the majority? Does the dissenting judge think different or additional facts are important? What distinguishes the two opinions?

2. Do the majority and the dissent differ on the effect of the merger clause along the lines of the dispute between Williston and Corbin, discussed in *Interform*? Should a well-drawn merger clause make a difference as to how the written contract is regarded? If one should make a difference, should a well-drawn merger clause be conclusive or presumptive? Or should it be merely evidence of the parties' intention to integrate their agreement?

3. Would the majority give a merger clause the same effect in a standard form contract between a sophisticated and an unsophisticated party? Should it? If not, why should sophisticated parties be treated differently? Should a court follow Restatement (Second) of Contracts § 211(3) (1979) in the case of an unsophisticated party?

SECTION 2. INTERPRETING CONTRACT TERMS

The cases in the preceding section reflect a tension that will reappear often in the next three chapters in many contexts. Some courts follow the *Gianni* approach by treating "the contract" as the express terms assented to by the parties. For these courts, the express terms take on a life of their own, independently of the parties' subjective intentions or reasonable expectations. Other courts follow the *Masterson* approach by treating the express terms as a window to the parties' intentions or reasonable expectations. For these courts, intentions and expectations constitute "the contract;" express terms will not be given a meaning that neither party intended or expected. This tension is readily apparent in the law of contract interpretation, as indicated by the following cases. As you read them, consider which concept of "the contract" better implements the autonomy principle.

NOTE ON INTERPRETATION

Problems of contract interpretation can arise in any contract—whether or not the terms are in writing and whether or not a writing is partially or totally integrated. Indeed, interpretive problems probably are of more frequent concern to practicing lawyers than any other contract law problems. Negotiating and drafting contracts, for example, requires forecasting how the parties and the courts will later interpret linguistic formulations put into the contract. Good drafters prefer the formulation that will best protect the client's foreseeable interests.

What is a problem of interpretation? To say that interpretation is ascertaining the meaning of language does little more than restate the question in a different form: What is meaning? Academic treatments of interpretation ("hermeneutics" and "semantics") suggest great controversy over this elementary starting point. But lawyers and judges generally follow a conventional understanding while the academics pursue their theories. In principle, the terms of a contract are all stated (orally or in writing) or statable in language. Language generally *refers* to ideas, actions, events, or states of affairs. In general, lawyers and judges treat a problem of contract interpretation as a *failure of language* to clearly refer to the actions that the contract authorizes, permits, or requires of the parties in specified circumstances at a later time.

Language may fail for two main reasons. First, all language (except proper names) is general and indeterminate; that is, each meaningful term refers to at least one *class* of things in the world, not to one and only one particular thing. Language would be useless for communication if it was so fine-grained as to have a separate word for each bit of sand on each beach in the world: Even two neighbors would be unlikely to share much of a vocabulary. Second, the knowledge, foresight, and attention span of the parties are limited. They tend to communicate in detail only about the most salient actions, events, and states of affairs that might occur under their contract. As the possibilities seem more remote, the parties tend to express themselves with less clarity and completeness.

Language tends to fail in one or more of three ways:

1. *Vagueness.* A word or phrase is vague when it has no distinct boundaries between its range of application and the range of neighboring words. For example, the range of application for "orange" shades into that for "yellow" and "red" with no line of demarcation. Rather, there is a band in which reasonable people may differ over the use of the term. A contract that calls for delivery of goods of "fair and average quality" may lead to a dispute due to vagueness.

2. *Term Ambiguity.* Technically, a word or phrase is ambiguous when it has two or more distinct meanings. It then can refer to two or more distinct actions, events, or states of affairs in the world, laying the groundwork for an interpretative dispute. For example, the word "bank" refers to distinct things when it is used in descriptions of rivers or financial arrangements. Colloquially, "ambiguity" may be used to refer to any failure of language. Consequently, "ambiguity" is ambiguous.

3. *Sentence ambiguity.* It is worth highlighting problems of sentence ambiguity because they so plague the contract drafter. Consider: "The house had a gazebo in the yard which was white." Is it the house, or the gazebo, or the yard that was white? In a land sale contract, the seller may commit to "put in gas and electricity lines at no cost to buyer; property also to be surveyed at once." Must the seller put the gas and electricity in "at once"?

See generally, E. Allan Farnsworth, *"Meaning" in the Law of Contracts,* 76 YALE L.J. 939, 952–57 (1967). Most of what we say and write is to some extent truncated; that is, it is less than fully explicated because we take for granted that the listener or reader will fill in the obvious. What is obvious to one party, however, may not be obvious to the other; moreover, unscrupulous people may take advantage of truncation in bad faith.

The lawyer who sets out to draft a contract faces choices about how detailed the contract should be. Clients use lawyers to draft contracts in part because lawyers should have a richer sense of what might go wrong (in part from reading many cases) and a special skill at guarding against unwanted contingencies by writing contract terms. Some lawyers would say that they try to deal with all imaginable contingencies, however remote, and to avoid all possible failures of language. Their motto is, "If you write at all, write it all." This is bluster. The lawyer should offer the client a service that adds something valuable that the client needs: The lawyer should anticipate more and draft better than the client could on his or her own. But the ideal of a "fully-specified contract" is never realized in fact; the question is how far to fall short. It may do a client a disservice to overlawyer a transaction, as by piling up legal fees disproportionate to the stakes or by breaking up a deal by injecting controversial, remote contingencies into the negotiation. In many circumstances, it is most appropriate to call for goods of "fair and average quality" and then trust to commercial practices and the law of contract interpretation.

When failures of language occur and a contract dispute materializes, however, the lawyers and the court must find a way to decide to what the contract terms refer. In general, judges most often say that they look to the "intention of the parties" to interpret their language. But "intention" is a tricky concept. In ordinary conversation, we think of a *speaker's intention* as whatever she had in mind when speaking. But that is not the same as *the meaning of the language* spoken. Thus, we can fail to say what we meant to say; we may use language that has a meaning different from what we meant. This distinction is crucial to understanding the standards of interpretation employed by the law of contracts.

As a first approximation, we might distinguish between three possible standards of contract interpretation. One associates the meaning of the agreed language with what the speaker had in mind when speaking; problems arise when the parties had different things in mind even though they used the same words. The second associates the meaning with what the listener had in mind when the speaker uttered the words; problems arise in an analogous fashion. The third associates meaning with what a reasonable person, under the circumstances of the parties, would understand the language to mean. Furthermore, there is a question whether meaning is established at the time the contract is formed or later. In general, courts look to the time of formation when they call upon the "intention of the parties." But, as you will see, it would be a mistake to think that this requires a psychological inquiry into the parties' minds at that time. See Note on Subjective and Objective Theories, above at p. ___.

Problems of contract interpretation will concern us throughout the remainder of this casebook.

PACIFIC GAS AND ELECTRIC CO. v. G.W. THOMAS DRAYAGE & RIGGING CO.

Supreme Court of California, 1968.
69 Cal.2d 33, 69 Cal.Rptr. 561, 442 P.2d 641.

Traynor, Chief Justice. Defendant appeals from a judgment for plaintiff in an action for damages for injury to property under an indemnity clause of a contract.

In 1960 defendant entered into a contract with plaintiff to furnish the labor and equipment necessary to remove and replace the upper metal cover of plaintiff's steam turbine. Defendant agreed to perform the work "at [its] own risk and expense" and to "indemnify" plaintiff "against all loss, damage, expense and liability resulting from . . . injury to property, arising out of or in any way connected with the performance of this contract." Defendant also agreed to procure not less than $50,000 insurance to cover liability for injury to property. Plaintiff was to be an additional named insured, but the policy was to contain a cross-liability clause extending the coverage to plaintiff's property.

During the work the cover fell and injured the exposed rotor of the turbine. Plaintiff brought this action to recover $25,144.51, the amount it subsequently spent on repairs. During the trial it dismissed a count based on negligence and thereafter secured judgment on the theory that the indemnity provision covered injury to all property regardless of ownership.

Defendant offered to prove by admissions of plaintiff's agents, by defendant's conduct under similar contracts entered into with plaintiff, and by other proof that in the indemnity clause the parties meant to cover injury to property of third parties only and not to plaintiff's property. Although the trial court observed that the language used was "the classic language for a third party indemnity provision" and that "one could very easily conclude that . . . its whole intendment is to indemnify third parties," it nevertheless held that the "plain language" of the agreement also required defendant to indemnify plaintiff for injuries to plaintiff's property. Having determined that the contract had a plain meaning, the court refused to admit any extrinsic evidence that would contradict its interpretation.

When a court interprets a contract on this basis, it determines the meaning of the instrument in accordance with the " . . . extrinsic evidence of the judge's own linguistic education and experience." (3 Corbin on Contracts (1960 ed.) (1964 Supp. § 579, p. 225, fn. 56).) The exclusion of testimony that might contradict the linguistic background of the judge reflects a judicial belief in the possibility of perfect verbal expression. (9 Wigmore on Evidence (3d ed. 1940) § 2461, p. 187.) This belief is a remnant of a primitive faith in the inherent potency and inherent meaning of words.

The test of admissibility of extrinsic evidence to explain the meaning of a written instrument is not whether it appears to the court to be plain and unambiguous on its face, but whether the offered evidence is relevant to prove a meaning to which the language of the instrument is reasonably susceptible....

A rule that would limit the determination of the meaning of a written instrument to its four-corners merely because it seems to the court to be clear and unambiguous, would either deny the relevance of the intention of the parties or presuppose a degree of verbal precision and stability our language has not attained.

Some courts have expressed the opinion that contractual obligations are created by the mere use of certain words, whether or not there was any intention to incur such obligations.[4] Under this view, contractual obligations flow, not from the intention of the parties but from the fact that they used certain magic words. Evidence of the parties' intention therefore becomes irrelevant.

In this state, however, the intention of the parties as expressed in the contract is the source of contractual rights and duties. A court must ascertain and give effect to this intention by determining what the parties meant by the words they used. Accordingly, the exclusion of relevant, extrinsic evidence to explain the meaning of a written instrument could be justified only if it were feasible to determine the meaning the parties gave to the words from the instrument alone.

If words had absolute and constant referents, it might be possible to discover contractual intention in the words themselves and in the manner in which they were arranged. Words, however, do not have absolute and constant referents. "A word is a symbol of thought but has no arbitrary and fixed meaning like a symbol of algebra or chemistry...." (Pearson v. State Social Welfare Board (1960) 54 Cal.2d 184, 195, 5 Cal.Rptr. 553, 559, 353 P.2d 33, 39.) The meaning of particular words or groups of words varies with the "... verbal context and surrounding circumstances and purposes in view of the linguistic education and experience of their users and their hearers or readers (not excluding judges).... A word has no meaning apart from these factors; much less does it have an objective meaning, one true meaning." (Corbin, The Interpretation of Words and the Parol Evidence Rule (1965) 50 Cornell L.Q. 161, 187.) Accordingly, the meaning of a writing "... can only be found by interpretation in the light of all the circumstances that reveal the sense in which the writer used the words. The exclusion of parol evidence regarding such circumstances merely because

---

4. "A contract has, strictly speaking, nothing to do with the personal, or individual, intent of the parties. A contract is an obligation attached by the mere force of law to certain acts of the parties, usually words, which ordinarily accompany and represent a known intent." (Hotchkiss v. National City Bank of New York (S.D.N.Y.1911) 200 F. 287, 293....)

the words do not appear ambiguous to the reader can easily lead to the attribution to a written instrument of a meaning that was never intended. (Citations omitted.)" . . .

Although extrinsic evidence is not admissible to add to, detract from, or vary the terms of a written contract, these terms must first be determined before it can be decided whether or not extrinsic evidence is being offered for a prohibited purpose. The fact that the terms of an instrument appear clear to a judge does not preclude the possibility that the parties chose the language of the instrument to express different terms. That possibility is not limited to contracts whose terms have acquired a particular meaning by trade usage,[6] but exists whenever the parties' understanding of the words used may have differed from the judge's understanding.

Accordingly, rational interpretation requires at least a preliminary consideration of all credible evidence offered to prove the intention of the parties.[7] (Civ.Code, § 1647; Code Civ.Proc. § 1860; see also 9 Wigmore on Evidence, op. cit. supra, § 2470, fn. 11, p. 227.) Such evidence includes testimony as to the "circumstances surrounding the making of the agreement . . . including the object, nature and subject matter of the writing . . ." so that the court can "place itself in the same situation in which the parties found themselves at the time of contracting." (Universal Sales Corp. v. Cal. Press Mfg. Co., . . . 20 Cal.2d 751, 761, 128 P.2d 665, 671; Lemm v. Stillwater Land & Cattle Co., . . . 217 Cal. 474, 480–481, 19 P.2d 785.) If the court decides, after considering this evidence, that the language of a contract, in the light of all the circumstances, is "fairly susceptible of either one of the two interpretations contended for. . . ." (Balfour v. Fresno C. & I. Co. (1895) 109 Cal. 221, 225, 41 P. 876, 877. . . .) extrinsic evidence relevant to prove either of such meanings is admissible.[8]

---

6. Extrinsic evidence of trade usage or custom has been admitted to show that the term "United Kingdom" in a motion picture distribution contract included Ireland (Ermolieff v. R.K.O. Radio Pictures (1942) 19 Cal.2d 543, 549–552, 122 P.2d 3); that the word "ton" in a lease meant a long ton or 2,240 pounds and not the statutory ton of 2,000 pounds (Higgins v. Cal. Petroleum, etc., Co. (1898) 120 Cal. 629, 630–632, 52 P. 1080); that the word "stubble" in a lease included not only stumps left in the ground but everything "left on the ground after the harvest time" (Callahan v. Stanley (1881) 57 Cal. 476, 477–479); that the term "north" in a contract dividing mining claims indicated a boundary line running along the "magnetic and not the true meridian" (Jenny Lind Co. v. Bower & Co. (1858) 11 Cal. 194, 197–199) and that a form contract for purchase and sale was actually an agency contract (Body–Steffner Co. v. Flotill Products (1944) 63 Cal.App.2d 555, 558–562, 147 P.2d 84). (See also Code

Civ. Proc. § 1861; Annot., 89 A.L.R. 1228; Note (1942) 30 Cal.L.Rev. 679.)

7. When objection is made to any particular item of evidence offered to prove the intention of the parties, the trial court may not yet be in a position to determine whether in the light of all of the offered evidence, the item objected to will turn out to be admissible as tending to prove a meaning of which the language of the instrument is reasonably susceptible or inadmissible as tending to prove a meaning of which the language is not reasonably susceptible. In such case the court may admit the evidence conditionally by either reserving its ruling on the objection or by admitting the evidence subject to a motion to strike. (See Evid.Code, § 403.)

8. Extrinsic evidence has often been admitted in such cases on the stated ground that the contract was ambiguous (e.g., Universal Sales Corp. v. Cal. Press Mfg. Co., supra, 20 Cal.2d 751, 761, 128 P.2d 665).

In the present case the court erroneously refused to consider extrinsic evidence offered to show that the indemnity clause in the contract was not intended to cover injuries to plaintiff's property. Although that evidence was not necessary to show that the indemnity clause was reasonably susceptible of the meaning contended for by defendant, it was nevertheless relevant and admissible on that issue. Moreover, since that clause was reasonably susceptible of that meaning, the offered evidence was also admissible to prove that the clause had that meaning and did not cover injuries to plaintiff's property.[9] Accordingly, the judgment must be reversed. . . .

W.W.W. ASSOCIATES, INC. v. GIANCONTIERI

Court of Appeals of New York, 1990.
77 N.Y.2d 157, 565 N.Y.S.2d 440, 566 N.E.2d 639.

KAYE, J. In this action for specific performance of a contract to sell real property, the issue is whether an unambiguous reciprocal cancellation provision should be read in light of extrinsic evidence, as a contingency clause for the sole benefit of plaintiff purchaser. Applying the principle that clear, complete writings should generally be enforced according to their terms, we reject plaintiff's reading of the contract and dismiss its complaint.

Defendants, owners of a two-acre parcel in Suffolk County, on October 16, 1986 contracted for the sale of the property to plaintiff, a real estate investor and developer. The purchase price was fixed at $750,000–$25,000 payable on contract execution, $225,000 to be paid in cash on closing (to take place "on or about December 1, 1986"), and the $500,000 balance secured by a purchase-money mortgage payable two years later.

The parties signed a printed form Contract of Sale, supplemented by several of their own paragraphs. Two provisions of the contract have particular relevance to the present dispute–a reciprocal cancellation provision (para 31) and a merger clause (para 19). Paragraph 31, one of the provisions the parties added to the contract form, reads: "The parties acknowledge that Sellers have been served with process instituting an action concerned with the real property which is the subject of this agreement. In the event the closing of title is delayed by reason of such litigation it is agreed that closing of title will in a like manner be adjourned until after the conclusion of such litigation provided, *in the event such litigation is not concluded, by or before 6–1–87 either party*

This statement of the rule is harmless if it is kept in mind that the ambiguity may be exposed by extrinsic evidence that reveals more than one possible meaning.

9. The court's exclusion of extrinsic evidence in this case would be error even under a rule that excluded such evidence when the instrument appeared to the court to be clear and unambiguous on its face.

The controversy centers on the meaning of the word "indemnify" and the phrase "all loss, damage, expense and liability." The trial court's recognition of the language as typical of a third party indemnity clause and the double sense in which the word "indemnify" is used in statutes and defined in dictionaries demonstrate the existence of an ambiguity. . . .

shall have the right to cancel this contract whereupon the down payment shall be returned and there shall be no further rights hereunder." (Emphasis supplied.) Paragraph 19 is the form merger provision, reading: "All prior understandings and agreements between *seller* and *purchaser* are merged in this contract [and it] completely expresses their full agreement. It has been entered into after full investigation, neither party relying upon any statements made by anyone else that are not set forth in this contract."

The Contract of Sale, in other paragraphs the parties added to the printed form, provided that the purchaser alone had the unconditional right to cancel the contract within 10 days of signing (para. 32), and that the purchaser alone had the option to cancel if, at closing, the seller was unable to deliver building permits for 50 senior citizen housing units (para. 29).

The contract in fact did not close on December 1, 1986, as originally contemplated. As June 1, 1987 neared, with the litigation still unresolved, plaintiff on May 13 wrote defendants that it was prepared to close and would appear for closing on May 28; plaintiff also instituted the present action for specific performance. On June 2, 1987, defendants canceled the contract and returned the down payment, which plaintiff refused. Defendants thereafter sought summary judgment dismissing the specific performance action, on the ground that the contract gave them the absolute right to cancel.

Plaintiff's claim to specific performance rests upon its recitation of how paragraph 31 originated. Those facts are set forth in the affidavit of plaintiff's vice-president, submitted in opposition to defendants' summary judgment motion.

As plaintiff explains, during contract negotiations it learned that, as a result of unrelated litigation against defendants, a lis pendens had been filed against the property. Although assured by defendants that the suit was meritless, plaintiff anticipated difficulty obtaining a construction loan (including title insurance for the loan) needed to implement its plans to build senior citizen housing units. According to the affidavit, it was therefore agreed that paragraph 31 would be added for plaintiff's sole benefit, as contract vendee. As it developed, plaintiff's fears proved groundless—the lis pendens did not impede its ability to secure construction financing. However, around March 1987, plaintiff claims it learned from the broker on the transaction that one of the defendants had told him they were doing nothing to defend the litigation, awaiting June 2, 1987 to cancel the contract and suggesting the broker might get a higher price.

Defendants made no response to these factual assertions. Rather, its summary judgment motion rested entirely on the language of the Contract of Sale, which it argued was, under the law, determinative of its right to cancel.

The trial court granted defendants' motion and dismissed the complaint, holding that the agreement unambiguously conferred the right to cancel on defendants as well as plaintiff. The Appellate Division, however, reversed and, after searching the record and adopting the facts alleged by plaintiff in its affidavit, granted summary judgment to plaintiff directing specific performance of the contract. We now reverse and dismiss the complaint.

Critical to the success of plaintiff's position is consideration of the extrinsic evidence that paragraph 31 was added to the contract solely for its benefit. . . .

We conclude . . ., however, that the extrinsic evidence tendered by plaintiff is not material. In its reliance on extrinsic evidence to bring itself within the "party benefited" cases, plaintiff ignores a vital first step in the analysis: before looking to evidence of what was in the parties' minds, a court must give due weight to what was in their contract.

A familiar and eminently sensible proposition of law is that, when parties set down their agreement in a clear, complete document, their writing should as a rule be enforced according to its terms. Evidence outside the four corners of the document as to what was really intended but unstated or misstated is generally inadmissible to add to or vary the writing. . . . That rule imparts "stability to commercial transactions by safeguarding against fraudulent claims, perjury, death of witnesses . . . infirmity of memory . . . [and] the fear that the jury will improperly evaluate the extrinsic evidence." (Fisch, New York Evidence § 42, at 22 [2d ed].) Such considerations are all the more compelling in the context of real property transactions, where commercial certainty is a paramount concern.

Whether or not a writing is ambiguous is a question of law to be resolved by the courts (*Van Wagner Adv. Corp. v. S & M Enters.*, 67 NY2d 186, 191). In the present case, the contract, read as a whole to determine its purpose and intent (*see, e.g., Rentways, Inc. v. O'Neill Milk & Cream Co.*, 308 NY 342, 347), plainly manifests the intention that defendants, as well as plaintiff, should have the right to cancel after June 1, 1987 if the litigation had not concluded by that date; and it further plainly manifests the intention that all prior understandings be merged into the contract, which expresses the parties' full agreement (*see*, 3 Corbin, Contracts § 578, at 402–403). . . .

Thus, we conclude there is no ambiguity as to the cancellation clause in issue, read in the context of the entire agreement, and that it confers a reciprocal right on both parties to the contract.

The question next raised is whether extrinsic evidence should be considered in order to *create* an ambiguity in the agreement. That question must be answered in the negative. It is well settled that "extrinsic and parol evidence is not admissible to create an ambiguity in a written agreement which is complete and clear and unambiguous upon its face." (*Intercontinental Planning v. Daystrom, Inc.*, 24 NY2d 372, 379....)

. . .

Finally, plaintiff's conclusory assertion of bad faith is supported only by its vice-president's statement that one of the defendants told the broker on the transaction, who then told him, that defendants were doing nothing to defend the action, waiting for June 2 to cancel, and suggesting that the broker might resell the property at a higher price. Where the moving party "has demonstrated its entitlement to summary judgment, the party opposing the motion must demonstrate by admissible evidence the existence of a factual issue requiring a trial of the action or tender an acceptable excuse for his failure so to do." (*Zuckerman v. City of New York*, 49 NY2d 557, 560.) Even viewing the burden of a summary judgment opponent more generously than that of the summary judgment proponent, plaintiff fails to raise a triable issue of fact (*see, Friends of Animals v. Associated Fur Mfrs.*, 46 NY2d 1065, 1068).

Accordingly, the Appellate Division order should be reversed, with costs, defendants' motion for summary judgment granted, and the complaint dismissed.

Questions

1. What is a problem of interpretation? How is it different from identifying the express terms to be interpreted? What was the language to be interpreted in *W.W.W. Associates*? Was it unambiguous? What was the language to be interpreted in *Pacific Gas and Electric*? Was it unambiguous? What does it mean for language to be "ambiguous"? How does a judge tell?

2. Does *W.W.W. Associates, Inc.* manifest the kind of interpretive method that Justice Traynor criticizes in *Pacific Gas and Electric*? Would the trial judge in *Pacific Gas and Electric* have decided *W.W.W. Associates, Inc.* differently from the New York Court of Appeals? Would Chief Justice Traynor decide *W.W.W. Associates, Inc.* differently?

3. What is it about the trial court's action that Justice Traynor objects to in *Pacific Gas and Electric*? What should a trial judge in California do after *Pacific Gas and Electric* when a parol interpretation issue comes up?

4. *Problem.*

Smiley and Bond agree on a written contract for the sale of trade secrets contained in certain documents "to be delivered at Lincoln Memorial." However, Smiley showed up at the Lincoln Memorial while Bond was at the Washington Monument. At trial, after Bond claims nondelivery by Smiley, Bond offers to prove that the parties were concerned about industrial espionage and so orally agreed when signing the contract that "Lincoln Memorial" shall mean Washington Monument. What should the trial judge do? Why?

———

RESTATEMENT (SECOND) OF CONTRACTS
§§ 200–203, 206–207

BRINDERSON–NEWBERG JOINT VENTURE
v. PACIFIC ERECTORS, INC.

United States Court of Appeals, Ninth Circuit, 1992.
971 F.2d 272, cert. denied 507 U.S. 914, 113 S.Ct. 1267, 122 L.Ed.2d 663 (1993).

WIGGINS, CIRCUIT JUDGE. This appeal stems from a contract dispute between a general contractor, Brinderson–Newberg Joint Venture (Brinderson), a subcontractor, Pacific Erectors (Pacific), and the bonding company that issued Pacific's performance bond, Hartford Accident & Indemnity Company (Hartford). Brinderson appeals the district court's denial of Brinderson's motions for a directed verdict and for JNOV. Brinderson argues that a directed verdict or JNOV was necessary because the jury verdicts on Brinderson's contract claim and Pacific's fraud claim were dependent on inadmissible parol evidence....

In May 1985, the United States Navy awarded Brinderson a contract to construct a coal-fired power plant at the Puget Sound Naval Shipyard in Bremerton, Washington. In June 1985, Brinderson entered into negotiations with Pacific, one of the subcontractors who had submitted a low bid for certain erection work. Part of these negotiations focused on the erection of the Flue Gas System (FGS), a large pollution control system. As part of its $1.54 million pre-contract bid, Pacific offered to erect the support steel for the FGS for $257,000. Brinderson, however, wanted Pacific to erect the large steel FGS components along with the support steel.

The negotiations between Brinderson and Pacific took place in three meetings, the first in late June 1985, the second on July 29, 1985, and the third on August 16, 1985.... After the second meeting, Brinderson drafted a contract reflecting the parties' agreement and sent a copy to Pacific for review. Article 1(e)I.A., section 15603 of the contract required Pacific to "erect complete" the FGS equipment. Article 33, paragraph 16 of the contract stated that Pacific "shall erect complete the Government Furnished Flue Gas System including Bag Houses, Scrubbers, I.D. Fans, Breeching and Dampers, Steel Gratings and appurtenances to make a complete installation." Pacific reviewed these provisions along with the other parts of the contract in preparation for the final negotiations and signing of the contract on August 16, 1985....

At the August 16 meeting, Pacific and Brinderson reviewed the contract line by line and negotiated a number of changes or clarifications concerning Pacific's scope of work. Both parties remember that Pacific requested that Brinderson change article 1(e)I.A. section 15603 and article 33, paragraph 16 to limit Pacific's work on the FGS components to picks and sets. Brinderson contends that it refused to make the change because it expected Pacific to erect the components and that Pacific agreed to erect the FGS components. Pacific and Hartford contend that no change was made because Brinderson assured Pacific that the language only required picks and sets for the FGS components and that article 1(a) limited the scope of work to jobs that Pacific customarily performed. According to Pacific and Hartford, Brinderson claimed that it just did not want to take the time to write the pick and set agreement into the contract. Pacific signed the contract at the end of the August 16 meeting. Pacific admits that it understood the effect of the integration clause in the contract and that the contract was a completely integrated agreement.

Brinderson and Pacific performed under the contract until the summer of 1986, when a dispute arose concerning the erection of the FGS components. Brinderson claimed that Pacific was required to erect the components under the contract. Pacific contended that it was only required to pick and set the components while Brinderson erected the components. . . .

I.   Brinderson's Contract Claim

The contract required Pacific to "erect complete" the FGS. Pacific interpreted the phrases "erect complete" and "make a complete installation" to mean that the contract required Pacific to complete the structural and miscellaneous steel, such as steel gratings and appurtenances, but required only pick and sets for the components of the FGS. Under Pacific's understanding, Pacific only had to complete the work to the extent that it had customarily completed similar work as a subcontractor. In other words, Pacific was required to "erect complete" only a portion of the FGS, not the entire system.

To advance its interpretation of the contract, Pacific introduced parol evidence at trial alleging that, before the contract was signed, Brinderson orally assured Pacific that the phrases "erect complete" and "make a complete installation" only meant that Pacific had to complete the structural and miscellaneous steel work for the FGS. Brinderson denies making such representations and contends it was clear that Pacific was required to erect and install the entire FGS. Brinderson argues that the district court erred by allowing the jury to hear and consider this parol evidence.

A.   The Law

Under California contract law, the parol evidence analysis governing this case is divided into two initial inquiries: "1) was the writing intended to be an integration, i.e. a complete and final expression of the parties' agreement, precluding any evidence of collateral agreements . . . ; and 2) is the agreement susceptible of the meaning contended for by the party offering the evidence?" *Gerdlund v. Electronic Dispensers Int'l,* 190 Cal.App.3d 263, 235 Cal.Rptr. 279, 282 (Ct.App.1987) (citing *Masterson v. Sine*, 68 Cal.2d 222, 65 Cal.Rptr. 545, 436 P.2d 561 (Cal.1968) and

Pacific Gas & Elec. Co. v. G.W. Thomas Drayage & Rigging Co., 69 Cal.2d 33, 69 Cal.Rptr. 561, 442 P.2d 641 (Cal.1968))....

The first inquiry is easily resolved. All the parties agree that the written contract is a completely integrated agreement. Thus, parol evidence of terms not specifically included in the written contract is not admissible. *Masterson*, 65 Cal.Rptr. at 547, 436 P.2d at 563.... However, California also recognizes one of the broad exceptions to the parol evidence rule. Because "[n]o contract should ever be interpreted and enforced with a meaning that neither party gave it," 3 Arthur L. Corbin, *Corbin on Contracts* § 572B (rule no. 2) (West Supp. 1991), parol evidence may be introduced to show the meaning of the express terms of the written contract. *See, e.g.*, Pacific Gas & Elec., 69 Cal.Rptr. at 563–565, 442 P.2d at 643–45.

To avoid completely eviscerating the parol evidence rule, however, there must be reasonable harmony between the parol evidence and the integrated contract for the evidence to be admissible. Thus, the parol evidence issues in this case turn on the second inquiry—whether the written contract is susceptible of the meaning that Pacific gives to it. "The test of admissibility of extrinsic evidence to explain the meaning of a written instrument is ... whether the offered evidence is relevant to prove a meaning to which the language of the instrument is reasonably susceptible." *Gerdlund*, 235 Cal.Rptr. at 283 (quoting *Pacific Gas & Elec.*, 69 Cal.Rptr. at 564, 442 P.2d at 644)....

The precise issue is whether the terms "erect complete" and "make a complete installation," when read in context with the rest of the contract, are reasonably susceptible of the meaning Pacific attempts to advance through its parol evidence. "If the court finds after considering this preliminary evidence that the language of the contract is not reasonably susceptible of [the proffered] interpretation and is unambiguous, extrinsic evidence cannot be received for the purpose of varying the terms of the contract." *Brobeck, Phleger & Harrison v. Telex Corp.*, 602 F.2d 866, 871 (9th Cir.) (applying California law), *cert. denied*, 444 U.S. 981 (1979).

B. Standard of Review

Whether the written contract is reasonably susceptible of a proffered meaning is a matter of law that is reviewed de novo. *See, e.g., United States v. King Features Entertainment*, 843 F.2d 394, 398 (9th Cir.1988) ("Interpretation of a contract is a matter of law, including whether the contract is ambiguous.")....

C. The Contract Is Not Susceptible of Pacific's Interpretation

The contract language is not reasonably susceptible of the meaning proffered by Pacific. We find as a matter of law that the contract is unambiguous and required Pacific to erect both the structural and miscellaneous steel *and* the FGS components.

Even if all of Pacific's evidence is accepted as fact and all reasonable inferences are drawn in favor of Pacific, Pacific merely shows that the parties orally agreed before the contract was signed that they would both interpret the phrases "erect complete" and "make a complete installation" to mean something else, despite the plain language of the contract itself. If Pacific did indeed make such an oral agreement with Brinderson, it did so at its own peril because the completely integrated contract negates any such agreement. The law recognizes the written integrated contract as the final word on the actual agreement of the parties and requires that the contract itself be reasonably susceptible of Pacific's proffered meaning.

Article 33, paragraph 16 of the contract sets forth the work that is expressly included in the contract:

> Subcontractor shall erect complete the Government Furnished Flue Gas System including Bag Houses, Scrubbers, I.D. Fans, Breeching and Dampers, Steel Gratings and appurtenances to make a complete installation.

By Pacific's own admission, the normal meaning of "erect complete" and "make a complete installation" in the construction industry includes field assembly, picking and setting, and bolting and welding the relevant components into permanent position. Pacific argues that the phrase "erect complete" applies only to the steel gratings and appurtenances, while the phrase "pick and set" applies to the FGS components. Simply put, the language of article 33, paragraph 16 is not susceptible of such a construction.

Pacific's construction of the contract rests primarily upon article 1(a) which states

> the work includes the following: (a) Any item of labor, service, and/or material reasonably inferred by the plans and/or specifications *or* customarily furnished by a subcontractor performing work in this line;

(emphasis added). Pacific argues that this language limited the scope of its contractual obligations to work Pacific had customarily performed. This construction of the contract is implausible for four reasons.

First, article 1(a) is phrased in the disjunctive and requires Pacific to perform work inferred by the specifications "or" work inferred by customary practices of subcontractors who perform such work. Pacific cannot refuse to perform work inferred by the specifications by claiming that Pacific did not customarily perform such work. To limit the scope of work to jobs Pacific customarily performed, article 33 would have to be phrased in the conjunctive, requiring Pacific to perform work only if inferred by the specifications *and* "customarily furnished by a subcontractor performing work in this line." Fairly read, article 1(a) requires Pacific to perform any "customarily furnished" work in addition to the work explicitly set out in the contract.

Moreover, even if the word "or" could be read as "and," the scope of the work would not be limited to work that Pacific customarily performs, but to work "customarily furnished by a subcontractor performing work in this line." By agreeing to "erect complete" the FGS, Pacific agreed to perform work customarily performed by contractors who "erect complete" similar structures. In other words, the work that is "customarily furnished by a subcontractor performing work in this line" can only be evaluated by comparing the work that Pacific agreed to perform in the contract with similar work performed by subcontractors in that line. Whether Pacific had customarily performed similar work is irrelevant to whether Pacific agreed to perform certain work under the contract.

Second, Pacific's interpretation of article 1(a) violates a fundamental rule of contract interpretation because it would render other portions of the contract meaningless. It is well settled that a contract should be interpreted so as to give meaning to each of its provisions: "Since an agreement is interpreted as a whole, it is assumed in the first instance that no part of it is superfluous." *Restatement (Second) of Contracts* § 203(a) cmt. b (1979)....

Article 1(e) is actually entitled "Scope of Work" and states that the "Subcontractor agrees to make the entire project complete in every respect insofar as this subcontract is concerned ... in strict accordance with the Plans and Specifications ... and Submittals as approved by the Owner." Under article 1(e)I.A. section 15603, Pacific is required to "erect complete" the FGS. Pacific's interpretation of article 1(a) would render this language useless.[3] Moreover, Pacific's interpretation conflicts with the detailed description of included work set forth in article 33, paragraph 16, and renders that provision meaningless.

Third, Pacific's interpretation stands the usual rules of interpretation on their head by arguing that a general provision governs more specific provisions. It is well settled that "[w]here there is an inconsistency between general provisions and specific provisions, the specific provisions ordinarily qualify the meaning of the general provisions." *Restatement of Contracts* § 236(c) (1932).... Thus, even if article 1(a) could be viewed as ambiguous and therefore inconsistent with the specific descriptions of work in article 33, paragraph 16, and article 1(e)I.A., the more specific descriptions requiring Pacific to "erect complete" the FGS must control.

Fourth and finally, "[w]here written provisions are inconsistent with printed provisions, an interpretation is preferred which gives effect to the written provisions." *Restatement of Contracts* § 236(e) (1932).... Article 1(a) is a boilerplate provision that is part of the printed form, while articles 1(e)I.A. and 33 are specific, typewritten additions to the standard form.

Indeed, Pacific does little to show how the contract itself is reasonably susceptible of Pacific's proffered interpretation.... At bottom,

---

3. The requirements of section 15603 are stated succinctly: "Flue Gas Cleaning Equipment Installation (Government Furnished Property)—erect complete."

Pacific's argument is that its construction of article 1(a) and the rest of the contract is reasonable because Brinderson promised that the contract would be interpreted in such a manner. This is not the issue before the court; the issue is whether the contract itself is susceptible of Pacific's proffered interpretation.

If strained interpretations are accepted as reasonable, the parol evidence rule will be completely eviscerated, and integrated contracts will be unenforceable. Parties would always be able to introduce parol evidence by arguing that they are advancing an alternative interpretation of the contract, despite the language of the integrated contract itself. Thus, California requires that the language of the instrument is reasonably susceptible of the proffered meaning before parol evidence may be introduced. *Pacific Gas & Elec.*, 442 P.2d at 644; *Gerdlund*, 235 Cal.Rptr. at 283.

Pacific's proffered interpretation stretches the contractual language beyond reasonable limits and violates most applicable rules of contract construction. Therefore, we find (1) that the district court erred in allowing the jury to hear parol evidence supporting Pacific's proffered interpretation and (2) that as a matter of law Pacific's work under the contract included the field assembly, picking and setting, and bolting and welding of the FGS components into permanent position. . . .

Questions

1. Did the court reach the right result under California law, represented by *Masterson v. Sine*, above at p. 363, and *Pacific Gas and Electric Co. v. G.W. Thomas Drayage & Rigging Co.*, above at p. 386? Would the *Brinderson* court have decided *W.W.W. Associates, Inc. v. Giaucontieri* as the New York Court of Appeals did?

2. Is the admissibility of parol evidence for purposes of interpretation an "exception" to the parol evidence rule, as this opinion suggests? How would the parol evidence rule have to be stated in order for this to be an "exception"?

3. Consider the rules of interpretation employed in Part I(C) of the *Brinderson–Newberg* opinion and the similar rules in RESTATEMENT (SECOND) OF CONTRACTS §§ 202–203. Why should the law favor interpretations supported by those rules? Do they treat the words uttered by the parties as the sole text to be interpreted? Do they interpret those utterances by the meanings found in a dictionary?

———

UNIFORM COMMERCIAL CODE §§ 1–205, 2–208

———

FRIGALIMENT IMPORTING CO. v. B.N.S. INTERNATIONAL SALES CORP.

United States District Court, Southern District of New York, 1960.
190 F.Supp. 116.

FRIENDLY, CIRCUIT JUDGE. The issue is, what is chicken? Plaintiff says "chicken" means a young chicken, suitable for broiling and frying. Defendant says "chicken" means any bird of that genus that meets contract specifications on weight and quality, including what it calls "stewing chicken" and plaintiff pejoratively terms "fowl." Dictionaries give both meanings, as well as some others not relevant here. To support its, plaintiff sends a number of volleys over the net; defendant essays to return them and adds a few serves of its own. Assuming that both parties were acting in good faith, the case nicely illustrates Holmes' remark "that the making of a contract depends not on the agreement of two minds in one intention, but on the agreement of two sets of external signs—not on the parties' having *meant* the same thing but on their having *said* the same thing." The Path of the Law, in Collected Legal Papers, p. 178. I have concluded that plaintiff has not sustained its burden of persuasion that the contract used "chicken" in the narrower sense.

The action is for breach of the warranty that goods sold shall correspond to the description, New York Personal Property Law, McKinney's Consol. Laws, c. 41, 95. Two contracts are in suit. In the first, dated May 2, 1957, defendant, a New York sales corporation, confirmed the sale to plaintiff, a Swiss corporation, of

US Fresh Frozen Chicken, Grade A, Government Inspected, Eviscerated

2½–3 lbs. and 1½–2 lbs. each

all chicken individually wrapped in cryovac, packed in secured fiber cartons or wooden boxes, suitable for export

75,000 lbs. 2½–3 lbs	@$33.00
25,000 lbs. 1½–2 lbs	@$36.50

scheduled May 10, 1957 pursuant to instructions from Penson & Co., New York.[1]

The second contract, also dated May 2, 1957, was identical save that only 50,000 lbs. of the heavier "chicken" were called for, the price of the smaller birds was $37 per 100 lbs., and shipment was scheduled for May 30. The initial shipment under the first contract was short but the balance was shipped on May 17. When the initial shipment arrived in Switzerland, plaintiff found, on May 28, that the 2½–3 lbs. birds were not

---

1. The Court notes the contract provision whereby any disputes are to be settled by arbitration by the New York Produce Exchange; it treats the parties' failure to avail themselves of this remedy as an agreement eliminating that clause of the contract.

young chicken suitable for broiling and frying but stewing chicken or "fowl;" indeed, many of the cartons and bags plainly so indicated. Protests ensued. Nevertheless, shipment under the second contract was made on May 29, the 2½–3 lbs. birds again being stewing chicken. Defendant stopped the transportation of these at Rotterdam.

This action followed. Plaintiff says that, notwithstanding that its acceptance was in Switzerland, New York law controls under the principle of Rubin v. Irving Trust Co., 1953, 305 N.Y. 288, 305, 113 N.E.2d 424, 431; defendant does not dispute this, and relies on New York decisions. I shall follow the apparent agreement of the parties as to the applicable law.

Since the word "chicken" standing alone is ambiguous, I turn first to see whether the contract itself offers any aid to its interpretation. Plaintiff says the 1½–2 lbs. birds necessarily had to be young chicken since the older birds do not come in that size, hence the 2½–3 lbs. birds must likewise be young. This is unpersuasive—a contract for "apples" of two different sizes could be filled with different kinds of apples even though only one species came in both sizes. Defendant notes that the contract called not simply for chicken but for "US Fresh Frozen Chicken, Grade A, Government Inspected." It says the contract thereby incorporated by reference the Department of Agriculture's regulations, which favor its interpretation; I shall return to this after reviewing plaintiff's other contentions.

The first hinges on an exchange of cablegrams which preceded execution of the formal contracts. The negotiations leading up to the contracts were conducted in New York between defendant's secretary, Ernest R. Bauer, and a Mr. Stovicek, who was in New York for the Czechoslovak government at the World Trade Fair. A few days after meeting Bauer at the fair, Stovicek telephoned and inquired whether defendant would be interested in exporting poultry to Switzerland. Bauer then met with Stovicek, who showed him a cable from plaintiff dated April 26, 1957, announcing that they "are buyer" of 25,000 lbs. of chicken 2½–3 lbs. weight, Cryovac packed, grade A Government inspected, at a price up to 33¢ per pound, for shipment on May 10, to be confirmed by the following morning, and were interested in further offerings. After testing the market for price, Bauer accepted, and Stovicek sent a confirmation that evening. Plaintiff stresses that, although these and subsequent cables between plaintiff and defendant, which laid the basis for the additional quantities under the first and for all of the second contract, were predominantly in German, they used the English word "chicken;" it claims this was done because it understood "chicken" meant young chicken whereas the German word, "Huhn," included both "Brathuhn" (broilers) and "Suppenhuhn" (stewing chicken), and that defendant, whose officers were thoroughly conversant with German, should have realized this. Whatever force this argument might otherwise have is largely drained away by Bauer's testimony that he asked Stovicek what kind of chickens were wanted, received the answer "any kind of chickens," and then, in German, asked whether the cable meant "Huhn" and received an affirmative response. . . .

Plaintiff's next contention is that there was a definite trade usage that "chicken" meant "young chicken." Defendant showed that it was only beginning in the poultry trade in 1957, thereby bringing itself within the principle that "when one of the parties is not a member of the trade or other circle, his acceptance of the standard must be made to appear" by proving either that he had actual knowledge of the usage or that the usage is "so generally known in the community that his actual individual knowledge of it may be inferred." 9 Wigmore, Evidence (3d ed. 1940) 2464. Here there was no proof of actual knowledge of the alleged usage; indeed, it is quite plain that defendant's belief was to the contrary. In order to meet the alternative requirement, the law of New York demands a showing that "the usage is of so long continuance, so well established, so notorious, so universal and so reasonable in itself, as that the presumption is violent that the parties contracted with reference to it, and made it a part of their agreement." Walls v. Bailey, 1872, 49 N.Y. 464, 472–473.

Plaintiff endeavored to establish such a usage by the testimony of three witnesses and certain other evidence. Strasser, resident buyer in New York for a large chain of Swiss cooperatives, testified that "on chicken I would definitely understand a broiler." However, the force of this testimony was considerably weakened by the fact that in his own transactions the witness, a careful businessman, protected himself by using "broiler" when that was what he wanted and "fowl" when he wished older birds. Indeed, there are some indications, dating back to a remark of Lord Mansfield, Edie v. East India Co., 2 Burr. 1216, 1222 (1761), that no credit should be given "witnesses to usage, who could not adduce instances in verification." 7 Wigmore, Evidence (3d ed. 1940), 1954; see McDonald v. Acker, Merrall & Condit Co., 2d Dept.1920, 192 App.Div. 123, 126, 182 N.Y.S. 607. While Wigmore thinks this goes too far, a witness' consistent failure to rely on the alleged usage deprives his opinion testimony of much of its effect. Niesielowski, an officer of one of the companies that had furnished the stewing chicken to defendant, testified that "chicken" meant "the male species of the poultry industry. That could be a broiler, a fryer or a roaster," but not a stewing chicken; however, he also testified that upon receiving defendant's inquiry for "chickens," he asked whether the desire was for "fowl or frying chickens" and, in fact, supplied fowl, although taking the precaution of asking defendant, a day or two after plaintiff's acceptance of the contracts in suit, to change its confirmation of its order from "chickens," as defendant had originally prepared it, to "stewing chickens." Dates, an employee of Urner–Barry Company, which publishes a daily market report on the poultry trade, gave it as his view that the trade meaning of "chicken" was "broilers and fryers." In addition to this opinion testimony, plaintiff relied on the fact that the Urner–Barry service, the Journal of Commerce, and Weinberg Bros. & Co. of Chicago, a large supplier of poultry, published quotations in a manner which, in one way or another, distinguish between "chicken," comprising broilers, fryers and certain other categories, and "fowl," which, Bauer acknowledged, included stewing chickens. This material would be impressive if there were nothing to the contrary. However, there was, as will now be seen.

Defendant's witness Weininger, who operates a chicken eviscerating plant in New Jersey, testified "Chicken is everything except a goose, a duck, and a turkey. Everything is a chicken, but then you have to say, you have to specify which category you want or that you are talking about." Its witness Fox said that in the trade "chicken" would encompass all the various classifications. Sadina, who conducts a food inspection service, testified that he would consider any bird coming within the classes of "chicken" in the Department of Agriculture's regulations to be a chicken. The specifications approved by the General Services Administration include fowl as well as broilers and fryers under the classification "chickens." Statistics of the Institute of American Poultry Industries use the phrases "Young chickens" and "Mature chickens," under the general heading "Total chickens," and the Department of Agriculture's daily and weekly price reports avoid use of the word "chicken" without specification.

Defendant advances several other points which it claims affirmatively support its construction. Primary among these is the regulation of the Department of Agriculture, 7 C.F.R. 70.300–70.370, entitled, "Grading and Inspection of Poultry and Edible Products Thereof," and in particular 70.301 which recited:

> *Chickens*. The following are the various classes of chickens: (a) Broiler or fryer ... (b) Roaster ... (c) Capon ... (d) Stag ... (e) Hen or stewing chicken or fowl ... (f) Cock or old rooster....

Defendant argues, as previously noted, that the contract incorporated these regulations by reference. Plaintiff answers that the contract provision related simply to grade and Government inspection and did not incorporate the Government definition of "chicken," and also that the definition in the Regulations is ignored in the trade. However, the latter contention was contradicted by Weininger and Sadina; and there is force in defendant's argument that the contract made the regulations a dictionary, particularly since the reference to Government grading was already in plaintiff's initial cable to Stovicek.

Defendant makes a further argument based on the impossibility of its obtaining broilers and fryers at the 33¢ price offered by plaintiff for the 2½–3 lbs. birds. There is no substantial dispute that, in late April, 1957, the price for 2½–3 lbs. broilers was between 35 and 37¢ per pound, and that when defendant entered into the contracts, it was well aware of this and intended to fill them by supplying fowl in these weights. It claims that plaintiff must likewise have known the market since plaintiff had reserved shipping space on April 23, three days before plaintiff's cable to Stovicek, or, at least, that Stovicek was chargeable with such knowledge. It is scarcely an answer to say, as plaintiff does in its brief, that the 33¢ price offered by [sic] the 2½–3 lbs. "chickens" was closer to the prevailing 35 price for broilers than to the 30 at which defendant procured fowl. Plaintiff must have expected defendant to make some profit—certainly it could not have expected defendant deliberately to incur a loss.

Finally, defendant relies on conduct by the plaintiff after the first shipment had been received. On May 28 plaintiff sent two cables complaining that the larger birds in the first shipment constituted "fowl." Defendant answered with a cable refusing to recognize plaintiff's objection and announcing "We have today ready for shipment 50,000 lbs. chicken 2½–3 lbs. 25,000 lbs. broilers 1½–2 lbs.," these being the goods procured for shipment under the second contract, and asked immediate answer "whether we are to ship this merchandise to you and whether you will accept the merchandise." After several other cable exchanges, plaintiff replied on May 29, "Confirm again that merchandise is to be shipped since resold by us if not enough pursuant to contract chickens are shipped the missing quantity is to be shipped within ten days stop we resold to our customers pursuant to your contract chickens grade A you have to deliver us said merchandise we again state that we shall make you fully responsible for all resulting costs."[2] Defendant argues that if plaintiff was sincere in thinking it was entitled to young chickens, plaintiff would not have allowed the shipment under the second contract to go forward, since the distinction between broilers and chickens drawn in defendant's cablegram must have made it clear that the larger birds would not be broilers. However, plaintiff answers that the cables show plaintiff was insisting on delivery of young chickens and that defendant shipped old ones at its peril. Defendant's point would be highly relevant on another disputed issue—whether if liability were established, the measure of damages should be the difference in market value of broilers and stewing chicken in New York or the larger difference in Europe, but I cannot give it weight on the issue of interpretation. Defendant points out also that plaintiff proceeded to deliver some of the larger birds in Europe, describing them as "poulets;" defendant argues that it was only when plaintiff's customers complained about this that plaintiff developed the idea that "chicken" meant "young chicken." There is little force in this in view of plaintiff's immediate and consistent protests.

When all the evidence is reviewed, it is clear that defendant believed it could comply with the contracts by delivering stewing chicken in the 2½–3 lbs. size. Defendant's subjective intent would not be significant if this did not coincide with an objective meaning of "chicken." Here it did coincide with one of the dictionary meanings, with the definition in the Department of Agriculture Regulations to which the contract made at least oblique reference, with at least some usage in the trade, with the realities of the market, and with what plaintiff's spokesman had said. Plaintiff asserts it to be equally plain that plaintiff's own subjective intent was to obtain broilers and fryers; the only evidence against this is

2. These cables were in German; "chicken," "broilers" and, on some occa- sions, "fowl," were in English.

the material as to market prices and this may not have been sufficiently brought home. In any event it is unnecessary to determine that issue. For plaintiff has the burden of showing that "chicken" was used in the narrower rather than in the broader sense, and this it has not sustained. . . .

Questions

1. What is the language to be interpreted in *Frigaliment*? In what sense is the legal issue in the case, as Judge Friendly famously put it, "What is chicken?" Can *the* answer be found in a dictionary? Can *an* answer be found in a dictionary? When a farmer tells the farmhand to "feed the chickens," is he to feed only the young ones? Is he to feed the rooster? If so, could the seller in *Frigaliment* satisfy its obligations by shipping rooster to the buyer? See Corbin, *Interpretation of Words and the Parole Evidence Rule*, 50 Cornell L.Q. 161, 168 (1965).

2. What is the problem of interpretation here? What resources are available to solve that problem? Why should a judge interpret the language of the contract in light of the usages of the trade, any course of dealing, and any course of performance?

3. Does either party persuade you that both meant the same thing by "chicken"? Was one party more justified in interpreting the term as it did?

4. *Problems.*

    a. Otherwise on the facts of *Frigaliment*, assume that the buyer sent a letter to seller before delivery insisting that all shipments be of broilers only. Assume further that seller held the broader meaning and refused to ship, claiming that the buyer had breached the contract by repudiation. Seller sues buyer for its profit. Does the seller now have the burden of showing that the contract meant "chicken" in the broader rather than the narrower sense? See U.C.C. § 2–607(4); E. Farnsworth, Contracts § 7.9 (2d ed. 1990).

    b. The U.S. Government awarded Coz, a minority subcontractor, his first contract to install carpeting under an affirmative action construction contract for a government building. His bid had not included a sum for the cost of carpet padding which, by usage in the government construction contracting industry, was always borne by the subcontractor. Coz seeks compensation for the cost of carpet padding. Should he be bound by the usage? See United States ex rel. Union Building Materials Corp. v. Haas & Haynie Corp., 577 F.2d 568 (9th Cir.1978).

NANAKULI PAVING AND ROCK CO. v. SHELL OIL CO., INC.

United States Court of Appeals, Ninth Circuit, 1981.
664 F.2d 772.

Hoffman, District Judge. Appellant Nanakuli Paving and Rock Company (Nanakuli) initially filed this breach of contract action against appellee Shell Oil Company (Shell) in Hawaiian State Court in February,

1976. Nanakuli, the second largest asphaltic paving contractor in Hawaii, had bought all its asphalt requirements from 1963 to 1974 from Shell under two long-term supply contracts; its suit charged Shell with breach of the later 1969 contract. The jury returned a verdict of $220,800 for Nanakuli on its first claim, which is that Shell breached the 1969 contract in January, 1974, by failing to price protect Nanakuli on 7,200 tons of asphalt at the time Shell raised the price for asphalt from $44 to $76. Nanakuli's theory is that price-protection, as a usage of the asphaltic paving trade in Hawaii, was incorporated into the 1969 agreement between the parties, as demonstrated by the routine use of price protection by suppliers to that trade, and reinforced by the way in which Shell actually performed the 1969 contract up until 1974. Price protection, appellant claims, required that Shell hold the price on the tonnage Nanakuli had already committed because Nanakuli had incorporated that price into bids put out to or contracts awarded by general contractors and government agencies. The District Judge set aside the verdict and granted Shell's motion for judgment n.o.v., which decision we vacate. We reinstate the jury verdict because we find that, viewing the evidence as a whole, there was substantial evidence to support a finding by reasonable jurors that Shell breached its contract by failing to provide protection for Nanakuli in 1974. . . .

Nanakuli . . . argues [that] all material suppliers to the asphaltic paving trade in Hawaii followed the trade usage of price protection and thus it should be assumed, under the U.C.C., that the parties intended to incorporate price protection into their 1969 agreement. This is so, Nanakuli continues, even though the written contract provided for the price to be "Shell's Posted Price at time of delivery," F.O.B. Honolulu. . . .

The key to price protection being so prevalent in 1969 that both parties would intend to incorporate it into their contract is found in one reality of the Oahu asphaltic paving market: the largest paving contracts were let by government agencies and none of the three levels of government—local, state, or federal—allowed escalation clauses for paving materials. If a paver bid at one price and another went into effect before the award was made, the paving company would lose a great deal of money, since it could not pass on increases to any government agency or to most general contractors. Extensive evidence was presented that, as a consequence, aggregate suppliers routinely price protected paving contractors in the 1960's and 1970's, as did the largest asphaltic supplier in Oahu, Chevron. Nanakuli presented documentary evidence of routine price protection by aggregate suppliers as well as two witnesses. . . . Both testified that price protection to their knowledge had always been practiced. . . . Such protection consisted of advance notices of increases, coupled with charging the old price for work committed at that price or for enough time to order the tonnage committed. The smallness of the Oahu market led to complete trust among suppliers and pavers. . . .

Two important factors form the backdrop for the 1974 failure by Shell to price protect Nanakuli: the Arab oil embargo and a complete change of command and policy in Shell's asphalt management. The jury was read a page or so from the World Book about the events and effect of the partial oil embargo, which shortened supplies and increased the price of petroleum, of which asphalt is a byproduct. The federal government imposed direct price controls on petroleum, but not on asphalt. Despite the international importance of those events, the jury may have viewed the second factor as of more direct significance to this case. The structural changes at Shell offered a possible explanation for why Shell in 1974 acted out of step with, not only the trade usage and commercially reasonable practices of all suppliers to the asphaltic paving trade on Oahu, but also with its previous agreement with, or at least treatment of, Nanakuli.

Bohner [Shell's Hawaiian representative] testified to a big organizational change at Shell in 1973 when asphalt sales were moved from the construction sales to the commercial sales department. In addition, by 1973 the top echelon of Shell's asphalt sales had retired. Lewis and Blee, who had negotiated the 1969 contract with Nanakuli, were both gone. Their duties were taken over by three men: Fuller in San Mateo, California, District Manager for Shell Sales, Lawson, and Chippendale, who was Shell's regional asphalt manager in Houston. When the philosophy toward asphalt pricing changed, apparently no one was left who was knowledgeable about the peculiarities of the Hawaiian market or about Shell's long-time relations with Nanakuli or its 1969 agreement, beyond the printed contract. . . .

We conclude that the decision to deny Nanakuli price protection was made by new Houston management without a full understanding of Shell's 1969 agreement with Nanakuli or any knowledge of its past pricing practices toward Nanakuli. If Shell did commit itself in 1969 to price protect Nanakuli, the Shell officials who made the decisions affecting Nanakuli in 1974 knew nothing about that commitment. Nor did they make any effective effort to find out. They acted instead solely in reliance on the 1969 contract's express price term, devoid of the commercial context that the Code says is necessary to an understanding of the meaning of the written word. Whatever the legal enforceability of Nanakuli's right, Nanakuli officials seem to have acted in good faith reliance on its right, as they understood it, to price protection and rightfully felt betrayed by Shell's failure to act with any understanding of its past practices toward Nanakuli.

SCOPE OF TRADE USAGE

The validity of the jury verdict in this case depends on four legal questions. First, how broad was the trade to whose usages Shell was bound under its 1969 agreement with Nanakuli: did it extend to the Hawaiian asphaltic paving trade or was it limited merely to the purchase and sale of asphalt, which would only include evidence of practices by Shell and Chevron? [Second question omitted.] Third, could the jury have construed an express contract term of Shell's posted price at delivery as reasonably consistent with a trade usage, . . . which consisted of charging the old price at times of price increases, either for a period of time or for specific tonnage committed at a fixed price in non-escalating contracts? . . . [Fourth question omitted.]

We approach the first issue in this case mindful that an underlying purpose of the U.C.C. as enacted in Hawaii is to allow for liberal interpretation of commercial usages. The Code provides, "This chapter shall be liberally construed and applied to promote its underlying purposes and policies." Haw.Rev.Stat. § 490:1–102(1). Only three purposes are listed, one of which is "[t]o permit the continued expansion of commercial practices through custom, usage and agreement of the parties. . . ." *Id.* § 490:1–102(2)(b). . . . *In this connection*, Section 1–205 incorporating into the agreement *prior course of dealing and usages of trade is of particular importance. Id.,* Comments 1 & 2 (emphasis supplied). We read that to mean that courts should not stand in the way of new commercial practices and usages by insisting on maintaining the narrow and inflexible old rules of interpretation. We seek the definition of trade usage not only in the express language of the Code but also in its underlying purposes, defining it liberally to fit the facts of the particular commercial context here.

The Code defines usage of trade as "any practice or method of dealing having such regularity of observance in a *place, vocation or trade* as to justify an expectation that it will be observed with respect to the transaction in question." *Id.* § 490:1–205(2) (emphasis supplied). We understand the use of the word "or" to mean that parties can be bound by a usage common to the *place* they are in business, even if it is not the usage of their particular vocation or trade. . . . This language indicates that Shell would be bound not only by usages of sellers of asphalt but by more general usages on Oahu, as long as those usages were so regular in their observance that Shell should have been aware of them. This reading of the Code, in our opinion, achieves an equitable result. A party is always held to conduct generally observed by members of his chosen trade because the other party is justified in so assuming unless he indicates otherwise. He is held to more general business practices to the extent of his actual knowledge of those practices or to the degree his ignorance of those practices is not excusable: they were so generally practiced he should have been aware of them.

No U.C.C. cases have been found on this point, but the court's reading of the Code language is similar to that of two of the best-known commentators on the U.C.C.:

> Under pre-Code law, a trade usage was not operative against a party who *was not a member of the trade unless* he actually knew of it or *the other party could reasonably believe he knew of it.*

J. White & R. Summers, *Uniform Commercial Code,* § 12–6 at 371 (1972) (emphasis supplied) . . . White and Summers add (emphasis supplied):

> This view has been carried forward by 1–205(3), . . . [U]sage of the trade is only binding on *members of the trade* involved *or persons*

> who know or *should know about it*. Persons who should be aware of the trade usage doubtless *include those who regularly deal with members of the relevant trade*, and also members of a second trade that commonly deals with members of a relevant trade (for example, farmers should know something of seed selling).

White & Summers, *supra*, § 12–6 at 371. Using that analogy, even if Shell did not "regularly deal" with aggregate supplies, it did deal constantly and almost exclusively on Oahu with one asphalt paver. It therefore should have been aware of the usage of Nanakuli and other asphaltic pavers to bid at fixed prices and therefore receive price protection from their materials suppliers due to the refusal by government agencies to accept escalation clauses. Therefore, we do not find the lower court abused its discretion or misread the Code as applied to the peculiar facts of this case in ruling that the applicable trade was the asphaltic paving trade in Hawaii. An asphalt seller should be held to the usages of trade in general as well as those of asphalt sellers and common usages of those to whom they sell. Certainly, under the unusual facts of this case it was not unreasonable for the judge to extend trade usages to include practices of other material suppliers toward Shell's primary and perhaps only customer on Oahu. . . .

Shell argued not only that the definition of trade was too broad, but also that the practice itself was not sufficiently regular to reach the level of a usage. . . . The extent of a usage is ultimately a jury question. The Code provides, "The existence and scope of such a usage are to be proved as facts." Haw. Rev. Stat. § 490:1–205(2). The practice must have "such regularity of observance . . . as to justify an expectation that it will be observed. . . ." *Id*. The Comment explains:

> The ancient English tests for "custom" are abandoned in this connection. Therefore, it is not required that a usage of trade be "ancient or immemorial," "universal" or the like. . . . [F]ull recognition is thus available for new usages and for usages currently observed by the great majority of decent dealers, even though dissidents ready to cut corners do not agree.

Id., Comment 5. The Comment's demand that "not universality but only the described 'regularity of observance' " is required reinforces the provision only giving "effect to usages of which the parties 'are or should be aware'. . . ." *Id.*, Comment 7. A "regularly observed" practice of protection, of which Shell "should have been aware," was enough to constitute a usage that Nanakuli had reason to believe was incorporated into the agreement.

Nanakuli went beyond proof of a regular observance. It proved and offered to prove that price protection was probably a universal practice by suppliers to the asphaltic paving trade in 1969. It had been practiced by H.C. & D. since at least 1962, by P.C. & A. since well before 1960, and by Chevron routinely for years, with the last specific instance before the contract being March, 1969, as shown by documentary evidence. The only usage evidence missing was the behavior by Shell, the only other asphalt supplier in Hawaii, prior to 1969. That was because its only major customer was Nanakuli and the judge ruled prior course of dealings between Shell and Nanakuli inadmissible. Shell did not point in rebuttal to one instance of failure to price protect by any supplier to an asphalt paver in Hawaii before its own 1974 refusal to price protect Nanakuli. Thus, there clearly was enough proof for a jury to find that the practice of price protection in the asphaltic paving trade existed in Hawaii in 1969 and was regular enough in its observance to rise to the level of a usage that would be binding on Nanakuli and Shell. . . .

WAIVER OR COURSE OF PERFORMANCE

[The court held that Shell's acts to price protect Nanakuli were not ambiguous and therefore indicated Shell's understanding of the agreement, rather than constituting a waiver of its written terms.]

EXPRESS TERMS AS REASONABLY CONSISTENT WITH
USAGE IN COURSE OF PERFORMANCE

Perhaps one of the most fundamental departures of the Code from prior contract law is found in the parol evidence rule and the definition of an agreement between two parties. Under the U.C.C., an agreement goes beyond the written words on a piece of paper. " 'Agreement' means the bargain of the parties in fact as found in their language or by implication from other circumstances including course of dealing or usage of trade or course of performance as provided in this chapter (sections 490:1–205 and 490:2–208)." *Id.* § 490:1–201(3). Express terms, then, do not constitute the entire agreement, which must be sought also in evidence of usages, dealings, and performance of the contract itself. The purpose of evidence of usages, which are defined in the previous section, is to help to understand the entire agreement. . . . Course of dealings is more important than usages of the trade, being specific usages between the two parties to the contract. "[C]ourse of dealing controls usage of trade." *Id.* § 490:1–205(4). . . .

A commercial agreement, then, is broader than the written paper and its meaning is to be determined not just by the language used by them in the written contract but "by their action, read and interpreted in the light of commercial practices and other surrounding circumstances. The measure and background for interpretation are set by the commercial context, which may explain and supplement even the language of a formal or final writing." *Id.*, Comment 1. Performance, usages, and prior dealings are important enough to be admitted always, even for a final and complete agreement; only if they cannot be reasonably reconciled with the express terms of the contract are they not binding on the parties. "The express terms of an agreement and an applicable course of dealing or usage of trade shall be construed wherever reasonable as consistent with each other; but when such construction is unreasonable express terms control both course of dealing and usage of trade and course of dealing controls usage of trade." *Id.* § 490:1–205(4). . . .

Our study of the Code provisions and Comments, then, form the first basis of our holding that a trade usage to price protect pavers at times of price increases for work committed on nonescalating contracts could reasonably be construed as consistent with an express term of seller's posted price at delivery. Since the agreement of the parties is broader than the express terms and includes usages, which may even add terms to the agreement, and since the commercial background provided by those usages is vital to an understanding of the agreement, we follow the Code's mandate to proceed on the assumption that the parties have included those usages unless they cannot reasonably be construed as consistent with the express terms. . . .

Here the evidence was overwhelming that all suppliers to the asphaltic paving trade price protected customers under the same types of circumstances. Chevron's contract with H.B. was a similar long-term supply contract between a buyer and seller with very close relations, on a form supplied by the seller, covering sales of asphalt, and setting the price at seller's posted price, with no mention of price protection. . . . *Levie,* [*Trade Usage and Custom Under the Common Law and the Uniform Commercial Code,* 40 N.Y.U.L.Rev. 1101 (1965)] at 1112, writes, "Astonishing as it will seem to most practicing attorneys, under the Code it will be possible in some cases to use custom to contradict the written agreement. . . . Therefore usage may be used to 'qualify' the agreement, which presumably means to 'cut down' express terms although not to negate them entirely." Here, the express price term was "Shell's Posted Price at time of delivery." A total negation of that term would be that the buyer was to set the price. It is a less than complete negation of the term that an unstated exception exists at times of price increases, at which times the old price is to be charged, for a certain period or for a specified tonnage, on work already committed at the lower price on nonescalating contracts. Such a usage forms a broad and important exception to the express term, but does not swallow it entirely. Therefore, we hold that, under these particular facts, a reasonable jury could have found that price protection was incorporated into the 1969 agreement between Nanakuli and Shell and that price protection was reasonably consistent with the express term of seller's posted price at delivery. . . .

Because the jury could have found for Nanakuli on its price protection claim . . ., we reverse the judgment of the District Court and reinstate the jury verdict for Nanakuli in the amount of $220,800, plus interest according to law.

Questions

1. What is the role of trade usage in Nanakuli's claim? What are Shell's two arguments in defense? Why does the court reject both of Shell's arguments?

2. Did the Court make a contract term for the parties in *Nanakuli*? Did it interpret the express language of the contract? Did it interpret "the

agreement"? What is this court's concept of "the agreement"? Is it equated with the written document? With the intention of the parties? With the parties' "relationship"? Or does the court base its decision in justice, independently of the parties' autonomous undertakings?

3. Were the express, written terms ambiguous? Should the parol evidence rule have led the court to a different result? See U.C.C. § 2–202. Should the express terms have taken priority over the commercial context? See U.C.C. §§ 1–205(3), 2–208(2).

CORENSWET, INC. v. AMANA REFRIGERATION, INC.

United States Court of Appeals, Fifth Circuit, 1979.
594 F.2d 129.

WISDOM, CIRCUIT JUDGE. Consolidated appeals in this diversity litigation arise from the termination of a distributorship. Corenswet, Inc., headquartered in New Orleans, has been an authorized, exclusive distributor of certain home appliances manufactured by Amana Refrigeration, Inc. ("Amana"). Corenswet sued to prevent Amana from terminating the relationship, on the ground that Amana's attempted termination was arbitrary and capricious. The district court found that the termination was arbitrary and was therefore in breach of the distributorship agreement as well as of the Uniform Commercial Code's general "good faith" principle. Amana challenges the district court's finding that the termination was arbitrary and without cause. We hold that the finding is not clearly erroneous. That is far from settling the dispute. The court issued a preliminary injunction forbidding the termination. . . .

The basic question at the heart of these appeals is whether Amana was entitled to terminate the distributorship arbitrarily. Amana assails the district court's interpretation of the contract to forbid an arbitrary termination, as well as the court's alternative rationale that the attempted termination is barred by the Iowa U.C.C.'s "good faith" principle. We hold that an arbitrary termination is permissible under both the contract and the law of Iowa. We reverse the district court's judgments.

I.

The primary facts are not disputed.

The plaintiff, Corenswet, Inc., is an independent wholesale distributor of appliances, dishware, and similar products. Since 1969, Corenswet has been the exclusive distributor of Amana refrigerators, freezers, room air conditioners, and other merchandise in southern Louisiana. Amana is a Delaware corporation domiciled in Iowa. Under the Amana system, products manufactured by Amana are sold to wholesale distributors such as Corenswet and to Amana's factory wholesale branches. The independent distributors and the factory branches then resell the merchandise to retail dealers who, in turn, sell to the public. The first distributorship agreement executed between Amana and Corenswet was of indefinite duration, but terminable by either party at any time "with or without cause" on ten days' notice to the other party. According to the record, the agreement was modified twice, in 1971 and again in July 1975, before the institution of this lawsuit. The 1975 agreement modified the termination provision to allow termination by either party "at any time for any reason" on ten days' notice.

As is so often the case with franchise and distributorship relationships, the termination clause in the standard form contract was of little interest or concern to the parties so long as things were going well between them. At the hearing before the district court, Corenswet introduced testimony that it understood, in the early 1970's, that the relationship would be a lasting one, a relationship that would continue so long as Corenswet performed satisfactorily. According to Corenswet, it developed an organization for wholesale distribution of Amana merchandise: it hired a manager and salesmen for the line, as well as specially trained repairmen. Corenswet also expanded its physical plant. In all, Corenswet contended, it invested over $1.5 million over the period of 1969 to 1976 in developing the market for Amana products in the southern Louisiana area. The parties stipulated in district court that the annual sales of Amana products in the distributorship area increased from $200,000 in 1969 to over $2.5 million in 1976. The number of retail outlets selling Amana products in the area increased from six in 1969 to seventy-two in 1976. Corenswet, in short, developed an important new market for Amana products. And Amana became as important to Corenswet as Corenswet became to Amana: sales of Amana products as a percentage of Corenswet's total sales of all products swelled from six percent in 1969 to nearly twenty-six percent in 1976. Over the seven and one-half year period, Amana representatives repeatedly praised Corenswet for its performance.

At the 1976 mid-year meeting of Amana distributors, however, George Foerstner, Amana's president, informed Corenswet that Amana would soon terminate its relationship with Corenswet because Corenswet was underfinanced. The parties agree that in early 1976 Corenswet had exceeded its credit limit with Amana, and that Amana at that time indicated that it might have to take a security interest in Corenswet's Amana inventory. According to a January communication from Amana, however, the "problem" was viewed by Amana as "a good kind of problem," reflecting, as it did, the growth of Corenswet's sales and hence purchases of Amana products. It is Corenswet's contention that the problem was not a serious one. Amana executives, the record reflects, assured Corenswet at the 1976 mid-year meeting that "satisfactory arrangements would be made" and that, Foerstner's statement notwithstanding, Corenswet would retain its distributorship.

There followed a complicated sequence of negotiations concerning Amana's security for credit extended. Amana sought a security interest in Corenswet's Amana inventory, to which Corenswet agreed. Amana asked also that Corenswet obtain more working capital from its parent corporation, Select Brands, Inc., as well as a bank letter of credit or line of credit. There is ample evidence in the record that Corenswet responded adequately to each Amana request, but that Amana persisted in changing its requirements as quickly as Corenswet could respond to its requests.... In September, Sam Corenswet ... informed [Amana] that Corenswet was ready and able to meet Amana's latest request.... Within a week Corenswet received a letter ... notifying it of the decision to terminate....

In October 1976, Corenswet filed suit for damages and injunctive relief in state court alleging that Amana had breached the distributorship agreement by terminating it arbitrarily. The reasons given by Amana for the termination, it contended, were pretextual. [The state court issued a temporary restraining order barring termination and the defendant had the case removed to federal court.]

The district court conducted a three-day hearing on Corenswet's prayer for a preliminary injunction. The court concluded that Amana had indeed acted arbitrarily in deciding to terminate Corenswet. The record reflects that in early 1976, well before the mid-year distributor meeting, Amana began negotiating with another New Orleans concern, George H. Lehleitner & Co., about transferring its area distributorship to Lehleitner. The beginning of Amana's alleged concern over Corenswet's finances corresponded neatly with its Lehleitner negotiations. There was ample evidence in the record, moreover, to support the district court's conclusion that the real factor motivating Foerstner's decision was animosity towards Fred Schoenfeld, the president of Corenswet's parent corporation, Select Brands, Inc. That animosity dated back to 1972, when Schoenfeld's action in protesting to Raytheon Corporation, Amana's parent, aborted Amana's attempt to transfer the distributorship from Corenswet to Corenswet's then Amana sales manager.

The district court ruled that the arbitrary termination was a breach of the distributorship agreement. The court rejected Amana's argument that the termination clause, which permitted either party to terminate the contract "for any reason," permitted termination for any reason be that reason good, bad, or indifferent. Although unwilling to accept Corenswet's position that the term "for any reason" imported a good or just cause limitation, the court ruled that the term means "for some reason, not for no reason ... for something that appeals to the reason, to the mind, to the judgment, not for something that is arbitrary, capricious or wanton." ...

II.

Amana appeals both the entry and the modification of the preliminary injunction. It contests the district court's interpretation of the contract and its view of applicable Iowa law and urges that even "bad faith" or "arbitrary" terminations are permitted by the contract and applicable law.... In assessing the district court's interpretation of the contract we must look to the appropriate rules of construction found in applicable state law in this case, as the parties have stipulated, the law of Iowa. Although most distributorship agreements, like franchise agreements, are more than sales contracts, the courts have not hesitated to apply the Uniform Commercial Code to cases involving such agreements. . . .

The starting point under the Code is the express terms of the agreement. U.C.C. §§ 1–205, 2–208(2); Iowa Code Ann. §§ 554.1205, 554.2208 (2). Under the contract, Amana was free to terminate the relationship "at any time and for any reason." The district court did not expressly rely on record evidence concerning the parties' understanding or the common understanding of the term "any reason" in concluding that the term means "something that appeals to the reason, to the mind." In the common understanding, it seems to us, the phrase "for any reason" means "for any reason that the actor deems sufficient." The phrase, that is, is ordinarily used not to limit a power, but to free it from implied limitations of "cause." That this is the intendment of the phrase becomes all the more clear when it is read in conjunction with the immediately preceding phrase "at any time." That phrase plainly frees the termination power from limitations as to timing. The exact parallelism of the two phrases reinforces the interpretation of the "any reason" language as negating any limitations whatsoever. In Webster's New International Dictionary (2d Ed. 1939) the first definition of reason is "An expression or statement offered as an explanation of a belief or an assertion or as a justification of an act or procedure." The second of nine definitions given for the word is "a ground or a cause; that in the reality which makes any fact intelligible." Id. We consider that this is the usual sense of the word when used in the phrase "for any reason." . . .

. . . Even if it is assumed that Amana needed "some reason" to terminate the contract, that reason is supplied by its evident desire to give the New Orleans distributorship to the Lehleitner company, just as we think that Corenswet would, under the contract, be entitled to terminate the relationship by reason, to take an example, of its wish to handle Kelvinator, rather than Amana, products.

There is no evidence in the record that the parties understood the phrase otherwise. There is testimony that Corenswet officials "understood" that the contract would not be terminated arbitrarily. That, however, is evidence not of Corenswet's understanding of the termination clause as written, but of its expectations about Amana's behavior, that is, its belief that Amana would never use the termination language to Corenswet's detriment. Corenswet has made much of certain testimony given by Amana's president, George Foerstner. Foerstner testified that Amana does "not cancel a distributor without a reason, without a good reason." When asked whether Amana then needed a reason to cancel Corenswet, Foerstner replied: "We needed a reason, yes, but we do not cancel distributors without a reason." This, too, we take not to be evidence of an understanding of the written contractual provision at issue, but as evidence of Amana's usual practice or, at best, of Amana's understanding of how it ought to treat its distributors. The questions posed to Foerstner did not direct his attention to the written contract, much less to the disputed clause. The district court, significantly, did not in its opinion advert to the Foerstner testimony.

We take Corenswet to be arguing that the contractual language must be interpreted in light of Amana's historical treatment of Corenswet and its other distributors. Although Amana's past dealing with Corenswet does not fit the Code categories of sources relevant to contract interpretation—usage of trade, course of dealing, and course of performance—we may assume that it is a source sufficiently similar to the Code categories to be relevant in construing the contract. Courses of commercial conduct "may not only supplement or qualify express [contract] terms, but in appropriate circumstances may even override express terms." J. White & R. Summers, *Handbook of the Law under the Uniform Commercial Code* § 3–3 at 84 (1972). The Code commands that express contract terms and "an applicable course of dealing or usage of trade shall be construed wherever reasonable as consistent with each other." U.C.C. § 1–205, Iowa Code Ann. § 554.1205; *see also* U.C.C. § 2–208(2), Iowa Code Ann. § 554.2208(2). In this case, however, no reasonable construction can reconcile the contract's express terms with the interpretation Corenswet seeks to glean from the conduct of the parties. The conflict could not be more complete: Amana's past conduct, with regard both to Corenswet and to its other distributors, may have created a reasonable expectation that Amana would not terminate a distributor arbitrarily, yet the contract expressly gives Amana the right to do so. We can find no justification, except in cases of conduct of the sort giving rise to promissory estoppel, for holding that a contractually reserved power, however distasteful, may be lost through nonuse. The express contract term cannot be construed as Corenswet would constitute it, and it therefore controls over any allegedly conflicting usage or course of dealing. U.C.C. §§ 1–205, 2–208(2), Iowa Code Ann. §§ 554.1205, 554.2208(2)....

The district court's alternative rationale was that arbitrary termination of a distributorship agreement contravenes the Code's general obligation of good faith dealing. Section 1–203 states: "Every contract or duty within this Act imposes an obligation of good faith in its performance or enforcement." Iowa Code Ann. § 554.1203. The good faith obligation is one of those obligations that § 1–102 of the Code says "may not be disclaimed by agreement." Iowa Code Ann. § 554.1102(3). As courts and scholars have become increasingly aware of the special problems faced by distributors and franchisees, and of the inadequacy of traditional contract and sales law doctrines to the task of protecting the reasonable expectations of distributors and franchisees, commentators have debated the utility of the Code's general good faith obligation as a tool for curbing abuse of the termination power. *See, e.g.*, E. Gellhorn, *Limitations on Contract Termination Rights—Franchise Cancellations*, 1967 Duke L.J. 465; Hewitt, *Good Faith or Unconscionability Franchise Remedies for Termination*, 29 Bus.Law 227 (1973)....

We do not agree with Corenswet that the § 1–203 good faith obligation, like the Code's unconscionability provision, can properly be used to override or strike express contract terms. According to Professor Farnsworth, "[T]he chief utility of the concept of good faith performance has always been as a rationale in a process ... of implying contract terms...." Farnsworth, *Good Faith Performance and Commercial Reasonableness under the Uniform Commercial Code*, 30 U. Chi. L. Rev. 666, 672 (1963). He defines the Code's good faith obligation as "an implied term of the contract requiring cooperation on the part of one party to the contract so that another party will not be deprived of his reasonable expectations." Id. at 666. When a contract contains a provision expressly sanctioning termination without cause there is no room for implying a term that bars such a termination. In the face of such a term there can be, at best, an expectation that a party will decline to exercise his rights.

As a tool for policing distributorship terminations, moreover, the good faith test is erratic at best. It has been observed that the good faith approach

> is analytically unsound because there is no necessary correlation between bad motives and unfair terminations.... The terminated dealer seeks relief against the harsh effects of termination which may be unfairly placed on him, not against the manufacturer's ill will.

E. Gellhorn, *supra*, at 521. The better approach, endorsed by Professor Gellhorn, is to test the disputed contract clause for unconscionability under § 2–302 of the Code. The question these cases present is whether public policy forbids enforcement of a contract clause permitting unilateral termination without cause. Since a termination without cause will almost always be characterizable as a "bad faith" termination, focus on the terminating party's state of mind will always result in the invalidation of unrestricted termination clauses. We seriously doubt, however, that public policy frowns on any and all contract clauses permitting termination without cause. Such clauses can have the salutary effect of permitting parties to end a soured relationship without consequent litigation. Indeed when, as here, the power of unilateral termination without cause is granted to both parties, the clause gives the distributor an easy way to cut the knot should he be presented with an opportunity to secure a better distributorship from another manufacturer. What public policy does abhor is economic overreaching—the use of superior bargaining power to secure grossly unfair advantage. That is the precise focus of the Code's unconscionability doctrine; it is not at all the concern of the Code's good faith performance provision. It is the office of the unconscionability concept, and not of the good faith concept, to strike down "unfair" contract terms....

III.

It follows from what we have said that the preliminary injunction was erroneously entered.... Although Corenswet alleged in its complaint that the contract term was unconscionable, it never pressed that issue, and the district court made no finding in that regard, as indeed it could not on the state of the record.

Corenswet's rights with respect to termination extend only to a right to notice. . . .

Questions

1. What were the express terms of the contract regarding termination? What was the meaning of those terms urged by Corenswet? On what grounds did Corenswet urge that meaning? Why did the court reject Corenswet's argument?

2. What are the practical differences between Corenswet's "just cause" standard, the trial court's "for some reason" standard, and the appellate court's "for any reason" standard? Does Amana necessarily lose under the trial court's view of the law? What were Amana's reasons for terminating the contract? Were they all "bad motives"?

3. Would the *Nanakuli* court have decided *Corenswet* as the Fifth Circuit did? What is the role of the commercial context in *Corenswet*? Is the result in *Corenswet* unjustified? Does the *Nanakuli* or *Corenswet* court have the better approach to express contract terms? Or can the two cases be reconciled?

4. *Problem.*

   a. Edward G. and Jimmy agreed on a contract for Edward G. to buy a quantity of horse-meat scraps specified to be "minimum 50% protein." Jimmy delivered scraps that were mostly between 49.53% to 49.96% protein. When Edward G. objected, Jimmy argued that "minimum 50% protein," within the contract, required "minimum 49.5% protein" according to a trade usage that was widely understood by dealers in horse-meat. What would you advise Edward G.? Does it matter whether the language "minimum 50% protein" is ambiguous? See Hurst v. W. J. Lake & Co., 141 Or. 306, 16 P.2d 627 (1932).

   b. The facts are as stated in paragraph a above, except that Jimmy delivers scraps with 46% protein. Can Jimmy argue successfully that 46% should be rounded up to 50%?

SECTION 3.   IMPLICATION OF TERMS

Let us pause briefly to review the overall strategy of this chapter thus far. Recall that the main goal is to learn how to ascertain the rights and duties of the parties under a contract, understood as a legally enforceable agreement. In general, we begin by *identifying the express terms* of the contract. The parol evidence rule controls the identification of contract terms when there is a writing that is at least in part the final expression of the parties' agreement. Then we must *interpret the express terms*. The express terms were all stated (orally or in writing) in language by the parties. When the express terms are unclear, the courts generally will interpret to find a meaning shared by both parties, if possible. Otherwise, the courts will give the express terms a reasonable meaning as indicated by the objective theory of contract interpretation.

We now turn to a third technique—*identifying and interpreting implied terms.*

Terms are implied for two main reasons. First, the agreement may say nothing relevant because the parties presupposed agreement on the point in issue, as when they did not trouble to state the obvious. The law may then imply presupposed terms to implement the parties' intentions or to protect their reasonable expectations. This kind of implication is supposed to implement the autonomy principle. Second, contract disputes can arise when the parties' agreement says nothing relevant and, in truth, the parties at formation had no intentions or reasonable expectations about their resolution. The law's function in providing final and peaceful settlements of disputes then may justify implying a term to resolve the controversy, whether or not it impinges on party autonomy. In addition, courts will imply terms on occasion to prevent unjust enrichment, forfeiture, or to protect important public policies.

RESTATEMENT (SECOND) OF CONTRACTS § 204

SPAULDING v. MORSE

Supreme Judicial Court of Massachusetts, 1947.
322 Mass. 149, 76 N.E.2d 137.

DOLAN, JUSTICE. By this bill in equity the plaintiff, as he is succeeding trustee under an instrument in writing entered into by the defendant and Ruth D. Morse, with one Baldwin, as original trustee, seeks to enforce the provisions made therein for the maintenance and education of Richard, the minor son of said Ruth D. Morse and the defendant.

The case was heard by the judge upon a statement of agreed facts which incorporated therein a copy of the trust instrument. Its pertinent provisions will be recited hereinafter. The other agreed facts are that "the ... [plaintiff] is the succeeding trustee in accordance with the terms of said agreement. That the ... [defendant] has paid the ... [plaintiff] and his predecessor, C. Harold Baldwin, one hundred dollars ($100) per month in accordance with the terms of said agreement up to February 1, 1946, and that he ceased making payments at that time. That Richard D. Morse, the beneficiary under said agreement, completed his high school grades on February 5, 1946, and he was inducted into the United States Army on February 6, 1946, and has been continuously in the service and that he has not yet entered any college, university or higher institution of learning." The statement of agreed facts concludes thus: "The sole question before the court is whether or not the ... [defendant] is excused from performance under the agreement while the beneficiary is in the armed services of the United States." After hearing, the judge in findings and order for decree found the facts to be as set forth in the statement of agreed facts and in accordance with his order for decree a final decree was entered: "1. That the . . . [defendant] pay to the . . . [plaintiff] forthwith the sum of fifteen hundred dollars ($1,500). 2. That the . . . [defendant] pay to the . . . [plaintiff], beginning May 1, 1947, the sum of one hundred dollars ($100) per month until such time, if any as the beneficiary enters college, and, thereupon, and for a period not to exceed four (4) years thereafter, to pay the sum of twenty-two hundred dollars ($2,200) per year to the . . . [plaintiff] payable in monthly payments."

The trust agreement was executed on July 30, 1937. It appears from its recitals that the defendant and Ruth D. Morse were married on March 26, 1921; that on June 14, 1932, Mrs. Morse obtained a decree of divorce from the defendant in the Second Judicial District Court of the State of Nevada, in which decree provision was made for the "care, custody, maintenance and support" of their two children, Merilyn Morse, born July 25, 1923, and Richard D. Morse, born October 11, 1927; and that disputes had arisen between the defendant and Mrs. Morse, as a result of which they entered into the agreement in question with the trustee named. . . .

The question before us for determination is concerned solely with the provisions made therein for the custody, maintenance, and education of the son Richard. The trust instrument provided that his mother was to have the care and custody of Richard, "unlimited so far as any interference with the same by the said George D. Morse is concerned, and the said George D. Morse shall have the right to visit Richard at all reasonable times and places, and the said Ruth D. Morse shall not be restricted in the care and custody of her son Richard, and may take him for any period and keep him at any place within the continental limits of the United States. The said George D. Morse shall and will pay to the said trustee in trust for his said minor son Richard the sum of twelve hundred dollars ($1,200) per year, payable in equal monthly installments on the first day of each month until the entrance of Richard D. Morse into some college, university or higher institution of learning beyond the completion of the high school grades, and thereupon, instead of said payments, amounting to twelve hundred dollars ($1,200) yearly, he shall and will then pay to the trustee payments in the sum of twenty-two hundred dollars ($2,200) per year for a period of said higher education but not more than four years, upon such installments, in amounts and at times as is required by the trustee to meet the general provisions of this paragraph. The said trustee shall turn over said trust payments to the said Ruth D. Morse or to such guardian or legal representative of the said Richard D. Morse as may be appointed, to be applied by her or the trustee upon or toward the maintenance and education and benefit of said Richard, so long as she shall maintain and educate said Richard to the satisfaction of the said trustee," and that "This agreement is intended to supersede in so far as the provisions herein contained are concerned, provisions made for the benefit of Ruth D. Morse, said minor children Merilyn and Richard Morse in a decree of divorce in the Second

Judicial District Court of the State of Nevada in and for the County of Washoe dated, June 14, 1932, so far as it is lawful and competent on the part of the parties so to do...." The defendant's appeal from the decree entered by the judge brings the case before us.

"Every instrument in writing is to be interpreted, with a view to the material circumstances of the parties at the time of the execution, in the light of the pertinent facts within their knowledge and in such manner as to give effect to the main end designed to be accomplished.... [The] instrument is to be so construed as to give effect to the intent of the ... [parties] as manifested by the words used illumined by all the attendant factors, unless inconsistent with some positive rule of law or repugnant to other terms of the instrument. An omission to express an intention cannot be supplied by conjecture. But if the instrument as a whole produces a conviction that a particular result was fixedly desired although not expressed by formal words, that defect may be supplied by implication and the underlying intention ... may be effectuated, provided it is sufficiently declared by the entire instrument." Dittemore v. Dickey, 144 N.E. 57, 60 (1924) ...

Examining the instrument before us, guided by the settled rule[s] of interpretation set forth above, it is manifest that the main purpose of the parents of Richard was to arrive at an agreement for his maintenance and education and to provide security therefor. At the time of the execution of the agreement he was almost ten years of age. His custody had already been awarded to his mother by the decree of divorce of the Nevada court, concerning the validity of which no question is raised. This being so, it is a fair inference that in so far as Richard was concerned his maintenance and education were the main purposes sought to be accomplished by the trust agreement, the parties to the agreement having in mind his age and recognizing the necessity of his being supported during the years to come, and of his being properly educated in a manner appropriate to the defendant's financial ability and station in life. The instrument specifically provided that the payments to be made by the defendant to the trustee for Richard's benefit should "be applied by ... [his mother] or the trustee upon or toward the maintenance and education and benefit of said Richard, so long as she shall maintain and educate said Richard to the satisfaction of the said trustee." But, as appears by the agreed facts and the record, the education of Richard was interrupted by the second World War and his induction into the armed forces of the United States on February 6, 1946, the day following the completion of high school grades on February 5, 1946. Since then he had been continuously, and at the time of the hearing and order for decree in the court below was, in the service of the armed forces of the nation. Thus he was actually under the command of his superior officers in that service, his maintenance was provided for during the period here involved by the government, and he was not in the actual custody of his mother and was not a student in any higher institution of learning. Thus neither of the main objects for which the defendant had bound himself to provide existed within the meaning of the trust instrument during the period for which the plaintiff claims payment. In these circumstances we are of opinion that the proper construction of the trust instrument is that the defendant is not required under its terms to perform provisions for the maintenance and education of Richard while he was or is in the armed service of the United States. . . .

It follows from what we have said that the decree entered by the judge must be reversed and that instead a final decree must be entered after rescript dismissing the bill with costs of the appeal.

Questions

1. What is the language to be interpreted in *Spaulding*? How did the trial court interpret it? Can you give a legal argument supporting the trial court's interpretation of the agreement?

2. Is the relevant language of the contract unclear on its face? Is it unclear in its application? Why does the appellate court reverse the trial court? Is the appellate court *interpreting* the agreement of the parties? Did they have any intentions with respect to the contingency that occurred? Or did the court supply an omitted term? Should the trial court's decision have been upheld?

3. *Problems.*

a. Paul gave Jean a "right of first refusal" on a parcel of real estate under which Paul retained the right to sell to another if, upon receipt of an offer to the seller, Jean did not exercise an option to purchase the parcel "at a value equivalent to the market value of the premises according to the assessment rolls as maintained by the County." Ten years later, Paul received offers of $150,000 and $172,000 for the property and so notified Jean. The County tax rolls at that time showed the assessed value of the parcel at $35,000. Must Paul sell to Jean for $35,000? See Steuart v. McChesney, 498 Pa. 45, 444 A.2d 659 (1982).

b. Suppose that, the facts otherwise being as given in *Spaulding*, Mr. and Mrs. Morse had reached an oral understanding when signing the trust instrument that Richard should receive some funds even if he went into the Army. Same result?

WOOD v. LUCY, LADY DUFF–GORDON

Court of Appeals of New York, 1917.
222 N.Y. 88, 118 N.E. 214.

[The text of this opinion will be found above at p. 153.]

Questions

1. What was the deal in *Wood*? What were the express terms? Did the express terms include anything that, properly interpreted, resolved the dispute before the court? Or did Judge Cardozo imply a term?

2. On what basis does Judge Cardozo hold that Wood promised to use "reasonable efforts" to market Lady Duff–Gordon's fashions? Why would

Lady Duff–Gordon otherwise be left at Wood's mercy? What is the "business efficacy" to which Cardozo makes reference?

3. *Problem.*

Assume that Mr. Wood made no effort to sell Lady Duff–Gordon's fashions. When she sues him, he retains you as his lawyer. Prepare to interview him to begin developing the facts of the case. Are there any facts you might develop to establish that your client was not in breach?

BLOOR v. FALSTAFF BREWING CORP.

United States Court of Appeals, Second Circuit, 1979.
601 F.2d 609.

FRIENDLY, CIRCUIT JUDGE: This action, wherein federal jurisdiction is predicated on diversity of citizenship, 28 U.S.C. § 1332, was brought in the District Court for the Southern District of New York, by James Bloor, Reorganization Trustee of Balco Properties Corporation, formerly named P. Ballantine & Sons (Ballantine), a venerable and once successful brewery based in Newark, N.J. He sought to recover from Falstaff Brewing Corporation (Falstaff) for breach of a contract dated March 31, 1972, wherein Falstaff bought the Ballantine brewing labels, trademarks, accounts receivable, distribution systems and other property except the brewery. The price was $4,000,000 plus a royalty of fifty cents on each barrel of the Ballantine brands sold between April 1, 1972 and March 31, 1978. Although other issues were tried, the appeals concern only two provisions of the contract. These are:

8. *Certain Other Covenants of Buyer.*

(a) After the Closing Date the [Buyer] will use its best efforts to promote and maintain a high volume of sales under the Proprietary Rights.

2(a)(v) [The Buyer will pay a royalty of $.50 per barrel for a period of 6 years], provided, however, that if during the Royalty Period the Buyer substantially discontinues the distribution of beer under the brand name "Ballantine" (except as the result of a restraining order in effect for 30 days issued by a court of competent jurisdiction at the request of a governmental authority), it will pay to the Seller a cash sum equal to the years and fraction thereof remaining in the Royalty Period times $1,100,000, payable in equal monthly installments on the first day of each month commencing with the first month following the month in which such discontinuation occurs. . . .

Bloor claimed that Falstaff had breached the best efforts clause, 8(a), and indeed that its default amounted to the substantial discontinuance that would trigger the liquidated damage clause, 2(a)(v). In an opinion that interestingly traces the history of beer back to Domesday Book and beyond, Judge Brieant upheld the first claim and awarded damages but dismissed the second. Falstaff appeals from the former ruling, Bloor from the latter. Both sides also dispute the court's measurement of damages for breach of the best efforts clause.

... Ballantine had been a family owned business, producing low-priced beers primarily for the northeast market, particularly New York, New Jersey, Connecticut and Pennsylvania. Its sales began to decline in 1961, and it lost money from 1965 on. On June 1, 1969, Investors Funding Corporation (IFC), a real estate conglomerate with no experience in brewing, acquired substantially all the stock of Ballantine for $16,290,000. IFC increased advertising expenditures, levelling off in 1971 at $1 million a year. This and other promotional practices, some of dubious legality, led to steady growth in Ballantine's sales despite the increased activities in the northeast of the "nationals"[1] which have greatly augmented their market shares at the expense of smaller brewers. However, this was a profitless prosperity; there was no month in which Ballantine had earnings and the total loss was $15,500,000 for the 33 months of IFC ownership.

After its acquisition of Ballantine, Falstaff continued the $1 million a year advertising program, IFC's pricing policies, and also its policy of serving smaller accounts not solely through sales to independent distributors, the usual practice in the industry, but by use of its own warehouses and trucks—the only change being a shift of the retail distribution system from Newark to North Bergen, N.J., when brewing was concentrated at Falstaff's Rhode Island brewery. However, sales declined and Falstaff claims to have lost $22 million in its Ballantine brand operations from March 31, 1972 to June 1975. Its other activities were also performing indifferently, although with no such losses as were being incurred in the sale of Ballantine products, and it was facing inability to meet payrolls and other debts. In March and April 1975, control of Falstaff passed to Paul Kalmanovitz, a businessman with 40 years experience in the brewing industry. After having first advanced $3 million to enable Falstaff to meet its payrolls and other pressing debts, he later supplied an additional $10 million and made loan guarantees, in return for which he received convertible preferred shares in an amount that endowed him with 35% of the voting power and became the beneficiary of a voting trust that gave him control of the board of directors.

Mr. Kalmanovitz determined to concentrate on making beer and cutting sales costs. He decreased advertising, with the result that the Ballantine advertising budget shrank from $1 million to $115,000 a year. In late 1975, he closed four of Falstaff's six retail distribution centers, including the North Bergen, N.J. depot, which was ultimately replaced by two distributors servicing substantially fewer accounts. He also discontinued various illegal practices that had been used in selling Ballantine products.[3] What happened in terms of sales volume is shown in

1. Miller's, Schlitz, Anheuser-Busch, Coors and Pabst.

3. There were two kinds of illegal practices, the testimony on both of which is, unsurprisingly, rather vague. Certain "na-

plaintiff's exhibit 114 J, set out in the margin.[4] With 1974 as a base, Ballantine declined 29.72% in 1975 and 45.81% in 1976, as compared with a 1975 gain of 2.24% and a 1976 loss of 13.08% for all brewers excluding the top 15. Other comparisons are similarly devastating, at least for 1976.[5] Despite the decline in the sale of its own labels as well as Ballantine's, Falstaff, however, made a substantial financial recovery. In 1976, it had net income of $8.7 million and its year-end working capital had increased from $8.6 million to $20.2 million and its cash and certificates of deposit from $2.2 million to $12.1 million.

Seizing upon remarks made by the judge during the trial that Falstaff's financial standing in 1975 and thereafter "is probably not relevant" and a footnote in the opinion, 454 F.Supp. at 267 n. 7,[6] appellate counsel for Falstaff contend that the judge read the best efforts clause as requiring Falstaff to maintain Ballantine's volume by any sales methods having a good prospect of increasing or maintaining sales or, at least, to continue lawful methods in use at the time of purchase, no matter what losses they would cause. Starting from this premise, counsel reason that the judge's conclusion was at odds with New York law, stipulated by the contract to be controlling, as last expressed by the Court of Appeals in *Feld v. Henry S. Levy & Sons, Inc.*, 37 N.Y.2d 466, 373 N.Y.S.2d 102, 335 N.E.2d 320 (1975). The court was there dealing with a contract whereby defendant agreed to sell and plaintiff to purchase all bread crumbs produced by defendant at a certain factory.

tional accounts," i.e. large draught beer buyers, were gotten or retained by "black bagging," the trade term for commercial bribery. On a smaller scale, sales to taverns were facilitated by the salesman's offering a free round for the house of Ballantine if it was available ("retention"), or the customer's choice ("solicitation"). Both practices seem to have been indulged in by many brewers, including Falstaff before Kalmanovitz took control.

4. Percentage Increase or Decline in Sales Volume of Ballantine Beer, Falstaff Beer and Comparable Brewers for Years Ending December 31, 1972–76.

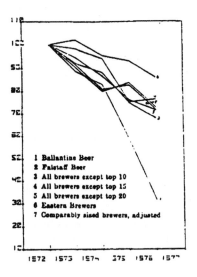

1 Ballantine Beer
2 Falstaff Beer
3 All brewers except top 10
4 All brewers except top 15
5 All brewers except top 20
6 Eastern Brewers
7 Comparably sized brewers, adjusted

1972 1973 1974 1975 1976 1977

5. Falstaff argues that a trend line projecting the declining volume of Ballantine's sales since 1966, before IFC's purchase, would show an even worse picture. We agree with plaintiff that the percentage figures since 1974 are more significant; at least the judge was entitled to think so.

6. "Even if Falstaff's financial position had been worse in mid–1975 than it actual-

During the term of the agreement defendant ceased producing bread crumbs because production with existing facilities was "very uneconomical," and the plaintiff sued for breach. The case was governed by § 2–306 of the Uniform Commercial Code.... Affirming the denial of cross-motions for summary judgment, the court said that, absent a cancellation on six months' notice for which the contract provided:

> Defendant was expected to continue to perform in good faith and could cease production of the bread crumbs, a single facet of its operation, only in good faith. Obviously, a bankruptcy or genuine imperiling of the very existence of its entire business caused by the production of the crumbs would warrant cessation of production of that item; the yield of less profit from its sale than expected would not. Since bread crumbs were but a part of defendant's enterprise and since there was a contractual right of cancellation, good faith required continued production until cancellation, even if there be no profit. In circumstances such as these and without more, defendant would be justified, in good faith, in ceasing production of the single item prior to cancellation only if its losses from continuance would be more than trivial, which, overall, is a question of fact.

37 N.Y.2d 471–72, 373 N.Y.S.2d 106, 335 N.E.2d 323. Falstaff argues from this that it was not bound to do anything to market Ballantine products that would cause "more than trivial" losses.

We do not think the judge imposed on Falstaff a standard as demanding as its appellate counsel argues that he did. Despite his footnote 7, he did not in fact proceed on the basis that the best efforts clause required Falstaff to bankrupt itself in promoting Ballantine products or even to sell those products at a substantial loss. He relied rather on the fact that Falstaff's obligation to "use its best efforts to promote and maintain a high volume of sales" of Ballantine products was not fulfilled by a policy summarized by Mr. Kalmanovitz as being:

> We sell beer and you pay for it. . . .

> We sell beer, F.O.B. the brewery. You come and get it.

—however sensible such a policy may have been with respect to Falstaff's other products. Once the peril of insolvency had been averted, the drastic percentage reductions in Ballantine sales as related to any possible basis of comparison, ... required Falstaff at least to explore whether steps not involving substantial losses could have been taken to stop or at least lessen the rate of decline. The judge found that, instead of doing this, Falstaff had engaged in a number of misfeasances and

---

ly was, and even if Falstaff had continued in that state of impecuniosity during the term of the contract, performance of the contract is not excused where the difficulty of performance arises from financial difficulty or economic hardship. As the New York Court of Appeals stated in *407 E. 61st St. Garage, Inc. v. Savoy Corp.*, 23 N.Y.2d 275, 281, 296 N.Y.S.2d 338, 344, 244 N.E.2d 37, 41 (1968):

> '[W]here impossibility or difficulty of performance is occasioned only by financial difficulty or economic hardship, even to the extent of insolvency or bankruptcy, performance of a contract is not excused.' (Citations omitted.)"

nonfeasances which could have accounted in substantial measure for the catastrophic drop in Ballantine sales shown in the chart, see 454 F.Supp. at 267–72. These included the closing of the North Bergen depot which had serviced "Mom and Pop" stores and bars in the New York metropolitan area; Falstaff's choices of distributors for Ballantine products in the New Jersey and particularly the New York areas, where the chosen distributor was the owner of a competing brand; its failure to take advantage of a proffer from Guinness–Harp Corporation to distribute Ballantine products in New York City through its Metrobeer Division; Falstaff's incentive to put more effort into sales of its own brands which sold at higher prices despite identity of the ingredients and were free from the $.50 a barrel royalty burden; its failure to treat Ballantine products evenhandedly with Falstaff's; its discontinuing the practice of setting goals for salesmen; and the general Kalmanovitz policy of stressing profit at the expense of volume. In the court's judgment, these misfeasances and nonfeasances warranted a conclusion that, even taking account of Falstaff's right to give reasonable consideration to its own interests, Falstaff had breached its duty to use best efforts....

... While [the best efforts] clause clearly required Falstaff to treat the Ballantine brands as well as its own, it does not follow that it required no more. With respect to its own brands, management was entirely free to exercise its business judgment as to how to maximize profit even if this meant serious loss in volume. Because of the obligation it had assumed under the sales contract, its situation with respect to the Ballantine brands was quite different. The royalty of $.50 a barrel on sales was an essential part of the purchase price. Even without the best efforts clause Falstaff would have been bound to make a good faith effort to see that substantial sales of Ballantine products were made, unless it discontinued under clause 2(a)(v) with consequent liability for liquidated damages. Cf. *Wood v. Duff–Gordon*, 222 N.Y. 88, 118 N.E. 214 (1917) (Cardozo, J.). Clause 8 imposed an added obligation to use "best efforts to promote and maintain a *high* volume of sales...." (emphasis supplied). Although we agree that even this did not require Falstaff to spend itself into bankruptcy to promote the sales of Ballantine products, it did prevent the application to them of Kalmanovitz' philosophy of emphasizing profit *über alles* without fair consideration of the effect on Ballantine volume. Plaintiff was not obliged to show just what steps Falstaff could reasonably have taken to maintain a high volume for Ballantine products. It was sufficient to show that Falstaff simply didn't care about Ballantine's volume and was content to allow this to plummet so long as that course was best for Falstaff's overall profit picture, an inference which the judge permissibly drew. The burden then shifted to Falstaff to prove there was nothing significant it could have done to promote Ballantine sales that would not have been financially disastrous.

Having correctly concluded that Falstaff had breached its best efforts covenant, the judge was faced with a difficult problem in computing what the royalties on the lost sales would have been. There is no need to rehearse the many decisions that, in a situation like this, certainty is not required; "[t]he plaintiff need only show a 'stable foundation for a reasonable estimate of royalties he would have earned had defendant not breached.'" . . . After carefully considering other possible bases, the court arrived at the seemingly sensible conclusion that the most nearly accurate comparison was with the combined sales of Rheingold and Schaefer beers. . . .

[The court also rejected the plaintiff's claim regarding the liquidated damages clause.]

Questions

1. What was the deal in *Bloor*? Was the "best efforts" requirement an express or implied term? Would it make a legal difference here if the parties had said nothing about "best efforts"?

2. What did Falstaff do that constituted a breach of contract? Would the result differ if Clause 8 of the contract had based the royalty on a percentage of profits, or a percentage of gross receipts, for Ballantine sales?

3. Is enforcement of the "best efforts" clause in *Bloor* justified by the autonomy principle? If the contract had not contained clause 8(a) but the same obligation were implied, would that be justified by the autonomy principle?

4. *Problems*.

a. Mitchum Properties Co. leased a store in its shopping center to Grace's Food Stores, Inc. for 20 years. Rental was to be $12,000 per month plus 3% of Grace's revenues at the store in excess of $375,000. After seven years, during which Grace's regularly paid substantial rent as a percentage of revenues, Grace's opened a new store one mile away. It shut down operations at Mitchum's shopping center, continued to pay the base rent of $12,000 per month, and left the store empty. Mitchum Properties seeks advice from your law firm. What might you suggest?

b. The facts are the same as in paragraph a above, except that the contract provided for no base rental and required a rent of 7% of Grace's revenues at the store. Does this make a difference in the advice you should give? See Fifth Avenue Shopping Center, Inc. v. Grand Union Co., 491 F.Supp. 77 (N.D.Ga.1980).

NOTE ON IMPLICATION

All terms of a contract in principle are either stated, and thus express, *or statable*. That is, some terms of a contract are not expressed by the parties together, or by either of them. They are *presupposed* and left implicit in the agreement. Fuller and Braucher explained the idea as follows:

> Words like "intention," "assumption," "expectation" and "understanding" all seem to imply a *conscious* state involving an awareness of alternatives and a deliberate choice among them. It is, however, plain that there is a psychological state which can be described as a

"tacit assumption" that does not involve a consciousness of alternatives. The absent-minded professor stepping from his office into the hall as he reads a book "assumes" that the floor of the hall will be there to receive him. His conduct is conditioned and directed by this assumption, even though the possibility that the floor has been removed does not "occur" to him, that is, is not present in his conscious mental processes.

L. Fuller & R. Braucher, Basic Contract Law 555 (2d ed. 1964).

Looking to the context and common sense, Judge Cardozo in *Wood* sought to understand and state the agreement as reasonable business people, in the circumstances of Wood and Lady Duff–Gordon, would state it. His fuller *statement* of the agreement thus added a term to the express agreement of the parties. In other words, he implied a term.

Is such an implied term in furtherance of the autonomy principle? The answer may be complicated by different conceptions of autonomy. Consider whether Cardozo imposed upon Wood by construing Wood's assent in light of the business context in which it was given. We might think that he was imposed upon if we think of autonomy as a liberty of choice that can be limited only by a deliberate and express consent. A moment's reflection will suggest, however, that no one ever acts outside of a social, economic, and historical environment that constrains the available opportunities. We cannot live the life of an honored cannibal! Since there is no point to complaining that someone did not act as no one ever acts in the relevant circumstances, there is no point in criticizing Cardozo just because he found a contract term to which Wood had not deliberately and expressly consented. See also Randy Barnett, *The Sounds of Silence: Default Rules and Contractual Consent*, 78 Va. L. Rev. 821 (1992).

Perhaps, then, autonomy requires only that a person enjoy a range of reasonable opportunities among which to choose. See Note on Autonomy in Context, above at p. 151. Suppose that, under the circumstances in which Wood contracted with Lady Duff–Gordon, he had at least four alternative opportunities: (1) not to contract with Lady Duff–Gordon at all, (2) to gain her agreement to an express term leaving him discretion to market her fashions as he saw fit, subject to the conventional obligations of an exclusive dealing arrangement, (3) to gain her agreement to an express term leaving him unbridled discretion, including the option of taking her wares off the market, or (4) to contract with her as he did, leaving some contingencies unspecified. These alternatives may be sufficient to treat the choice he made—to enter a conventional exclusive dealing arrangement—as an autonomous decision to accept the conventionally understood (default) obligations of exclusive dealing arrangements in general. On this understanding of autonomy, Wood would have been imposed upon if Cardozo got the business practices wrong or if Lady Duff–Gordon did something wrongful when making the contract.

But his autonomy was not infringed upon just because he was bound to comply with ordinary business practices for the *kind* of deal he struck.

———

RESTATEMENT (SECOND) OF CONTRACTS § 205

———

UNIFORM COMMERCIAL CODE §§ 1–102(3), 1–201(19), 1–203, 2–103(1)(b)

———

GREER PROPERTIES, INC. v. LaSALLE NATIONAL BANK

United States Court of Appeals, Seventh Circuit, 1989.
874 F.2d 457.

Wood, Jr., Circuit Judge. This is a contracts case arising from efforts to develop a piece of commercial real estate located near the Edens Expressway in Skokie, Illinois. Four local developers formed a partnership called Old Orchard West Venture ("Old Orchard") and acquired the real estate parcel in 1984. Legal title to the real estate is held in the name of LaSalle National Bank ("LaSalle"), as trustee. In 1987, Old Orchard and LaSalle ("Sellers") entered into a contract to sell the property to plaintiff-appellant Greer Properties, Inc. ("Greer"), a wholly-owned subsidiary of the Marriott Corporation. The Sellers terminated the contract prior to the closing and Greer brought this action in federal district court, claiming the termination was improper. The district court entered summary judgment for the defendants and Greer appeals. . . .

I. Factual Background

William Hoag, Albert Scherb, Jr., Kyle Ahrberg, and Michael Klonoski are the four developers who formed Old Orchard. The affairs of the partnership were managed primarily by William Hoag. Old Orchard purchased the property in January, 1984 for $700,721.70, intending to develop the parcel by constructing, leasing, and managing a building on it. In 1986, unable to fulfill its development plan, Old Orchard commenced efforts to sell the property outright or to construct a building on it for a predetermined tenant. Two buyers expressed serious interest in the property: G.D. Searle Co. ("Searle"), which maintained its corporate headquarters on the adjoining real estate, and Marriott Corporation, which wanted to construct a motel on the property.

The Sellers agreed to sell the property to Searle and entered into a contract on February 16, 1987. Searle promised to pay approximately $1,100,000. The contract between Searle and the Sellers allowed Searle to terminate the agreement if the soil of the property was contaminated by environmental waste. Searle hired an environmental consulting firm to study the condition of the property. The firm reported that cleaning up the contamination would cost in excess of $500,000. Because of the extensive contamination, Searle requested that the Sellers reduce the contract price. The Sellers refused and Searle exercised its right to terminate the contract.

The Sellers then began negotiating with Marriott Corporation through its real estate subsidiary, Greer. The parties entered into a contract on July 31, 1987. The Sellers agreed to sell the property to Greer for $1,250,000. As part of the contract, the Sellers were required to remove the environmental contamination at their own expense. The Sellers were also allowed to terminate the contract if the cost of the clean-up became "economically impracticable." The pertinent section of the contract states:

> Seller is currently having a study conducted to determine the existing soil condition ("Soils Study").... Seller further agrees to take all action recommended by the Soils Study and the Illinois Environmental Protection Agency to bring the soil into compliance with all local, state and federal ordinances, laws or regulations and shall use its best efforts to have all such work completed prior to closing; provided, however, that if the cost of such clean-up work will, in Seller's best business judgment, be economically impracticable, then Seller, at its option, may terminate this Contract....

Greer had been advised that Searle had found contaminants on the property, but Greer was not told of the cost estimates contained in the Searle report. In September 1987, after the contract had been signed, Hoag informed Greer of his own cost estimates for the clean-up between $60,000 and $100,000. Hoag testified that he did not believe the estimate made in the Searle study; he felt the high estimate of the clean-up cost was a negotiating tactic used by Searle to get the Sellers to lower their price.

The Sellers retained a soil consultant to study the nature and extent of the contamination. In mid-September, the consultant estimated the cost of the clean-up at between $100,000 and $200,000. The parties disagree about whether the Sellers informed Greer at that time of their conclusion that the contract had been rendered economically impracticable by the escalating cost of the clean-up. Without formally notifying Greer that they intended to terminate the contract, the Sellers entered into a new round of negotiations with Searle following the receipt of the consultant's report and a purchase price of $1,455,000 was proposed. A draft contract containing this price was sent by Searle to the Sellers on October 7, 1987. On that same date, Sellers received a final report from their soil consultant, estimating the clean-up costs at between $190,000 and $240,000. On October 8, 1987, the Sellers formally terminated the contract with Greer by sending the required written notice. After the termination, the Sellers indicated to Greer that Greer could still buy the property if it increased the purchase price by $250,000. Greer never made the higher offer. After terminating the contract, the Sellers cleaned up the property at a cost of $251,825.

On December 31, 1987, Greer filed a complaint in the United States District Court for the Northern District of Illinois, Eastern Division, seeking specific performance of the contract and money damages. The Sellers answered the complaint and filed a counterclaim seeking a declaratory judgment that their termination of the contract was proper. The Sellers also filed a motion for summary judgment on their counterclaim. The district court granted the Sellers' motion for summary judgment, concluding that no genuine issue of material fact existed and that Sellers were entitled to judgment as a matter of law. The district court found that, under Illinois law, the language of the contract gave the Sellers broad discretion to terminate upon receipt of the soil consultant's study. The court rejected Greer's contention that the Sellers terminated the contract in bad faith so they could sell the property to Searle, finding that the Sellers had decided to end their contract with Greer before reopening negotiations with Searle. Greer appeals this entry of summary judgment, arguing that the district court erred in finding that the clean-up cost made performance economically impracticable. Greer also states that genuine issues of material fact exist as to whether the Sellers were acting in bad faith when they terminated the contract.

II. DISCUSSION

Summary judgment was entered by the district court in favor of the Sellers. Summary judgment shall be entered if "the pleadings, depositions, answers to interrogatories, and admissions on file, together with the affidavits, if any, show that there is no genuine issue as to any material fact and that the moving party is entitled to a judgment as a matter of law." Fed. R. Civ. P. 56(c)....

Applying this standard to the district court's decision, we address Greer's first contention. Greer argues that the district court erred by finding that the contract's termination provision gave the Sellers broad discretion in determining whether the cost of the clean-up made the sale economically impracticable. The district court found that the Sellers effectively exercised their option to terminate the contract, noting that the use of the term "best business judgment" gave the Sellers much discretion in determining economic impracticability....

... [T]he use of the phrase "best business judgment" is critical to understanding the discretion given to the Sellers by this contract. "Best business judgment" reserved to the Sellers the ultimate determination of whether the cost increase was large enough to warrant cancellation. "Economic impracticability" must be read together with "best business judgment" to understand the breadth of discretion given to the Sellers. The district court's analysis of the termination clauses was correct; the Sellers were vested with broad discretion to terminate the contract.

Nonetheless, Greer argues that, even if the Sellers had that broad discretion, they acted in bad faith in terminating the contract as they did. Greer claims that the Sellers terminated the contract to get a better price from Searle. The district court found that the Sellers acted in good faith, discounting the fact that Searle made an offer to the Sellers one day before the Sellers notified Greer of the termination. The district court determined that the Sellers had decided to end the contract with Greer long before they opened negotiations with Searle, and the court placed great weight on the Sellers offer to convey the property to Greer if Greer would add $250,000 to the purchase price.

Under Illinois law, "every contract implies good faith and fair dealing between the parties to it." *Martindell v. Lake Shore Nat'l Bank*, 15 Ill.2d 272, 286, 154 N.E.2d 683, 690 (1958)…. This implied obligation of good faith and fair dealing in the performance of contracts acts as a limit on the discretion possessed by the parties. In Illinois, "a party vested with contractual discretion must exercise his discretion reasonably and may not do so arbitrarily or capriciously." *Foster Enterprises, Inc. v. Germania Fed. Savings and Loan Ass'n*, 97 Ill.App.3d 22, 30, 52 Ill.Dec. 303, 309, 421 N.E.2d 1375, 1381 (1981). See generally Burton, *Breach of Contract and the Common Law Duty To Perform in Good Faith*, 94 Harv. L. Rev. 369 (1980); *see also* Andersen, *Good Faith in the Enforcement of Contracts*, 73 Iowa L. Rev. 299 (1988). If discretion is exercised in bad faith, a breach of contract occurs and the court must grant relief to the aggrieved party. *Foster Enterprises*, 97 Ill.App.3d at 30, 421 N.E.2d at 1381.

With this limitation on the discretion of the Sellers in mind, their decision to terminate the contract must be analyzed to determine if they acted in good faith. If the Sellers terminated the contract to obtain a better price from Searle, their action would have been in bad faith. When the Sellers entered the contract with Greer and Greer agreed to pay them a specific price for the property, the Sellers gave up their opportunity to shop around for a better price. By using the termination clause to recapture that opportunity, the Sellers would have acted in bad faith.

The district court's determination that, as a matter of law, the Sellers terminated the contract in good faith was not correct. There are questions of material fact that remain. As we have noted, in a summary judgment situation doubts should be resolved in favor of the nonmoving party. *DeValk Lincoln Mercury*, 811 F.2d at 329. The timing of the negotiations with Searle raises many questions. Although the district court insisted that the Sellers did not contact Searle until after they had decided unequivocally to cancel the deal with Greer, the evidence on this point is far from clear, and the only uncontroverted point is that the actual notice of termination was not sent to Greer until October 8, 1987, the day after Searle made an offer to buy the property for $1,455,000. There is a question of whether the estimate of the clean-up costs was foreseeable by the Sellers when they entered the contract with Greer, since during the earlier negotiations with Searle, Searle's consultants had estimated the clean-up would cost more than $500,000.

The circumstances of this termination raise many questions of fact concerning the motive behind the termination. These questions go directly to the issue of whether the Sellers breached their duty of good faith and fair dealing by terminating the contract. The conflicting testimony found in the depositions does not eliminate all questions of material fact in relation to this issue. The district court's entry of summary judgment on the issue of whether the Sellers terminated the contract in good faith must be reversed. . . .

Questions

1.　What did the buyer allege was the act constituting a breach? What promise was allegedly broken?

2.　If the seller's discretion were held to be limitless and final, would the contract be enforceable? Would that construction best protect the parties' stated and unstated intentions and reasonable expectations? Would it be fair? In what way should the seller's discretion be limited?

3.　If you were representing the buyer on remand, what would you argue was the seller's reason for terminating? How would you argue that the seller's termination was invalid such that the seller breached? How would you argue on behalf of the seller? Would the matter be decided by judge or jury? If the latter, how should the jury be instructed?

NOTE ON GOOD FAITH PERFORMANCE

The obligation to perform a contract in good faith emerged in recent decades as a central part of the law of contract performance. Contracting parties often want flexibility in their agreement. One way to provide flexibility is to leave a decision affecting the parties' rights and duties to the *discretion* of one of them. Thus, in *Greer Properties, Inc. v. LaSalle National Bank*, the sellers were allowed to assess the cost of environmental cleanup after the contract was concluded. They could terminate if, in their "best business judgment," cleanup costs would be economically impracticable. Good faith is typically employed by the courts to constrain such discretion, which may concern points of quality, quantity, price, time, conditions within the control of one party, and other matters too varied to catalogue. This much is settled law.

It is less settled exactly what good faith permits or requires of a party with contractual discretion. The comments to RESTATEMENT (SECOND) OF CONTRACTS § 205 indicate that good faith requires

> faithfulness to an agreed common purpose and consistency with the justified expectations of the other party; it excludes a variety of types of conduct characterized as involving 'bad faith' because they violate community standards of decency, fairness or reasonableness.

See also Robert S. Summers, *"Good Faith" in General Contract Law and the Sales Provisions of the Uniform Commercial Code*, 54 VA. L. REV. 195 (1968); Robert S. Summers, *The General Duty of Good Faith—Its Recog-*

nition and Conceptualization, 67 CORNELL L. REV. 810 (1982). Most courts, however, take a more focused approach.

Both at common law and under the U.C.C., most courts hold that good faith requires a discretion-exercising party to act for *reasons* allowed by the parties' agreement, in order to protect justifiable expectations arising from their agreement, understood in the context in which it was made. When we identify and interpret most contract terms, we focus on the *acts* that are permitted or required within the world of the contract. A party with discretion, however, is permitted to act in a variety of ways if the act is done for a contractually permitted reason. Accordingly, the seller in *Greer Properties* could terminate, and thereby act, without liability, if it did so because the cost of environmental cleanup was too great. It could not terminate because a better deal had come along. The latter reason is outside the world of the contract. As the court said, "the Sellers gave up their opportunity to shop around for a better price. By using the termination clause to recapture that opportunity, the Sellers would have acted in bad faith." See generally STEVEN J. BURTON & ERIC G. ANDERSEN, CONTRACTUAL GOOD FAITH: FORMATION, PERFORMANCE, BREACH AND ENFORCEMENT (1995).

UNIFORM COMMERCIAL CODE § 2–306

EASTERN AIR LINES, INC. v. GULF OIL CORP.

United States District Court, Southern District of Florida, 1975.
415 F.Supp. 429.

JAMES LAWRENCE KING, DISTRICT JUDGE. Eastern Air Lines, Inc., hereafter Eastern, and Gulf Oil Corporation, hereafter Gulf, have enjoyed a mutually advantageous business relationship involving the sale and purchase of aviation fuel for several decades.

This controversy involves the threatened disruption of that historic relationship and the attempt, by Eastern, to enforce the most recent contract between the parties. On March 8, 1974, the correspondence and telex communications between the corporate entities culminated in a demand by Gulf that Eastern must meet its demand for a price increase or Gulf would shut off Eastern's supply of jet fuel within fifteen days.

Eastern responded by filing its complaint with this court, alleging that Gulf had breached its contract and requesting preliminary and permanent mandatory injunctions requiring Gulf to perform the contract in accordance with its terms. By agreement of the parties, a preliminary injunction preserving the status quo was entered on March 20, 1974, requiring Gulf to perform its contract and directing Eastern to pay in accordance with the contract terms, pending final disposition of the case. . . .

THE CONTRACT

On June 27, 1972, an agreement was signed by the parties which, as amended, was to provide the basis upon which Gulf was to furnish jet fuel to Eastern at certain specific cities in the Eastern system. Said agreement supplemented an existing contract between Gulf and Eastern which, on June 27, 1972, had approximately one year remaining prior to its expiration.

The contract is Gulf's standard form aviation fuel contract and is identical in all material particulars with the first contract for jet fuel, dated 1959, between Eastern and Gulf and, indeed, with aviation fuel contracts antedating the jet age. It is similar to contracts in general use in the aviation fuel trade. The contract was drafted by Gulf after substantial arm's length negotiation between the parties. Gulf approached Eastern more than a year before the expiration of the then-existing contracts between Gulf and Eastern, seeking to preserve its historic relationship with Eastern. Following several months of negotiation, the contract, consolidating and extending the terms of several existing contracts, was executed by the parties in June, 1972, to expire January 31, 1977.

The parties agreed that this contract, as its predecessor, should provide a reference to reflect changes in the price of the raw material from which jet fuel is processed, i.e., crude oil, in direct proportion to the cost per gallon of jet fuel.

Both parties regarded the instant agreement as favorable, Eastern, in part, because it offered immediate savings in projected escalations under the existing agreement through reduced base prices at the contract cities; while Gulf found a long term outlet for a capacity of jet fuel coming on stream from a newly completed refinery, as well as a means to relate anticipated increased cost of raw material (crude oil) directly to the price of the refined product sold. The previous Eastern/Gulf contracts contained a price index clause which operated to pass on to Eastern only one-half of any increase in the price of crude oil. Both parties knew at the time of contract negotiations that increases in crude oil prices would be expected, were "a way of life," and intended that those increases be borne by Eastern in a direct proportional relationship of crude oil cost per barrel to jet fuel cost per gallon.

Accordingly, the parties selected an indicator (West Texas Sour); a crude which is bought and sold in large volume and was thus a reliable indicator of the market value of crude oil. From June 27, 1972 to the fall of 1973, there were in effect various forms of U.S. government imposed price controls which at once controlled the price of crude oil generally, West Texas Sour specifically, and hence the price of jet fuel. As the government authorized increased prices of crude those increases were in turn reflected in the cost of jet fuel. Eastern has paid a per gallon increase under the contract from 11 cents to 15 cents (or some 40%).

The indicator selected by the parties was "the average of the posted prices for West Texas sour crude, 30.0–30.9 gravity of Gulf Oil Corporation, Shell Oil Company, and Pan American Petroleum Corporation." The posting of crude prices under the contract "shall be as listed for these companies in Platts Oilgram Service-Crude Oil Supplement...."

"Posting" has long been a practice in the oil industry. It involves the physical placement at a public location of a price bulletin reflecting the current price at which an oil company will pay for a given barrel of a specific type of crude oil. Those posted price bulletins historically have, in addition to being displayed publicly, been mailed to those persons evincing interest therein, including sellers of crude oil, customers whose price of product may be based thereon, and, among others, Platts Oilgram, publishers of a periodical of interest to those related to the oil industry.

In recent years, the United States has become increasingly dependent upon foreign crude oil, particularly from the "OPEC" nations most of which are in the Middle East. OPEC was formed in 1970 for the avowed purpose of raising oil prices, and has become an increasingly cohesive and potent organization as its member nations have steadily enhanced their equity positions and their control over their oil production facilities. Nationalization of crude oil resources and shutdowns of production and distribution have become a way of life for oil companies operating in OPEC nations, particularly in the volatile Middle East. The closing of the Suez Canal and the concomitant interruption of the flow of Mid-East oil during the 1967 "Six-Day War," and Libya's nationalization of its oil industry during the same period, are only some of the more dramatic examples of a trend that began years ago. By 1969, "the handwriting was on the wall" in the words of Gulf's foreign oil expert witness, Mr. Blackledge.

During 1970, domestic United States oil production "peaked;" since then it has declined while the percentage of imported crude oil has been steadily increasing. Unlike domestic crude oil, which has been subject to price control since August 15, 1971, foreign crude oil has never been subject to price control by the United States Government.... It was during late 1973 that the Mid-East exploded in another war, accompanied by an embargo (at least officially) by the Arab oil-producing nations against the United States and certain of its allies. World prices for oil and oil products increased.

Mindful of that situation ..., the United States government began a series of controls affecting the oil industry culminating, in the fall of 1973, with the implementation of price controls known as "two-tier": taking as the bench mark the number of barrels produced from a given well in May of 1972, that number of barrels is deemed "old" oil. The price of "old" oil then is frozen by the government at a fixed level. To the extent that the productivity of a given well can be increased over the May, 1972, production, that increased production is deemed "new" oil. For each barrel of "new" oil produced, the government authorized the release from price controls of an equivalent number of barrels from those theretofore designated "old" oil. For example, from a well which in

May of 1972, produced 100 barrels of oil; all of the production of that well would, since the imposition of "two-tier" in August of 1973, be "old" oil. Increased productivity to 150 barrels would result in 50 barrels of "new" oil and 50 barrels of "released" oil; with the result that 100 barrels of the 150 barrels produced from the well would be uncontrolled. . . .

The implementation of "two-tier" was completely without precedent in the history of government price control action. Its impact, however, was nominal, until the imposition of an embargo. . . .

Following closely after the embargo, OPEC (Oil Producing Export Countries) unilaterally increased the price of their crude to the world market some 400% between September, 1973, and January 15, 1974. Since the United States domestic production was at capacity, it was dependent upon foreign crude to meet its requirements. New and released oil (uncontrolled) soon reached parity with the price of foreign crude, moving from approximately $5 to $11 a barrel from September, 1974 to January 15, 1974.

Since imposition of "two-tier," the price of "old oil" has remained fixed by government action, with the oil companies resorting to postings reflecting prices they will pay for the new and released oil, and subject to government controls. Those prices, known as "premiums," are the subject of supplemental bulletins which are likewise posted by the oil companies and furnished to interested parties, including Platts Oilgram. . . .

The information which has appeared in Platts since the implementation of "two-tier" with respect to the price of West Texas Sour crude oil has been the price of "old" oil subject to government control.

Under the court's restraining order, Eastern has been paying for jet fuel from Gulf on the basis of the price of "old" West Texas Sour crude oil as fixed by government price control action, i.e., $5 a barrel. Approximately 40 gallons of finished jet fuel product can be refined from a barrel of crude.

THE "REQUIREMENTS" CONTRACT

Gulf has taken the position in this case that the contract between it and Eastern is not a valid document in that it lacks mutuality of obligation; it is vague and indefinite; and that it renders Gulf subject to Eastern's whims respecting the volume of jet fuel Gulf would be required to deliver to the purchaser Eastern.

The contract talks in terms of fuel "requirements."[4] The parties have interpreted this provision to mean that any aviation fuel purchased by Eastern at one of the cities covered by the contract, must be bought from Gulf. Conversely, Gulf must make the necessary arrangements to

---

4. 'Gulf agrees to sell and deliver to Eastern, and Eastern agrees to purchase, receive and pay for their requirements of Gulf Jet A and Gulf Jet A—1 at the locations listed. . . .'

supply Eastern's reasonable good faith demands at those same locations. This is the construction the parties themselves have placed on the contract and it has governed their conduct over many years and several contracts.

In early cases, requirements contracts were found invalid for want of the requisite definiteness, or on the grounds of lack of mutuality. 14 A.L.R. 1300.... [W]ell prior to the adoption of the Uniform Commercial Code, case law generally held requirements contracts binding. See 26 A.L.R.2d 1099, 1139. The Uniform Commercial Code, adopted in Florida in 1965, specifically approves requirements contracts in F.S. 672.306 (U.C.C. § 2–306(1)).... The court concludes that the document is a binding and enforceable requirements contract.

BREACH OF CONTRACT

Gulf suggests that Eastern violated the contract between the parties by manipulating its requirements through a practice known as "fuel freighting" in the airline industry. Requirements can vary from city to city depending on whether or not it is economically profitable to freight fuel. This fuel freighting practice in accordance with price could affect lifting from Gulf stations by either raising such liftings or lowering them. If the price was higher at a Gulf station, the practice could have reduced liftings there by lifting fuel in excess of its actual operating requirements at a prior station....

The court however, finds that Eastern's performance under the contract does not constitute a breach of its agreement with Gulf and is consistent with good faith and established commercial practices as required by U.C.C. § 2–306.

"Good Faith" means "honesty in fact in the conduct or transaction concerned" U.C.C. § 1–201(19). Between merchants, "good faith" means "honesty in fact and the observance of reasonable commercial standards of fair dealing in the trade;" U.C.C. § 2–103(1)(b) and Official Comment 2 of U.C.C. § 2–306. The relevant commercial practices are "courses of performance," "courses of dealing" and "usages of trade."

Throughout the history of commercial aviation, including 30 years of dealing between Gulf and Eastern, airlines' liftings of fuel by nature have been subject to substantial daily, weekly, monthly and seasonal variations, as they are affected by weather, schedule changes, size of aircraft, aircraft load, local airport conditions, ground time, availability of fueling facilities, whether the flight is on time or late, passenger convenience, economy and efficiency of operation, fuel taxes, into-plane fuel service charges, fuel price, and ultimately, the judgment of the flight captain as to how much fuel he wants to take.

All these factors are, and for years have been, known to oil companies, including Gulf, and taken into account by them in their fuel contracts. Gulf's witnesses at trial pointed to certain examples of numerically large "swings" in monthly liftings by Eastern at various Gulf stations. Gulf never complained of this practice and apparently accepted it as normal procedure....

The court concludes that fuel freighting is an established industry practice.... If a customer's demands under a requirements contract become excessive, U.C.C. § 2–306 protects the seller and, in the appropriate case, would allow him to refuse to deliver unreasonable amounts demanded (but without eliminating his basic contract obligation); similarly, in an appropriate case, if a customer repeatedly had no requirements at all, the seller might be excused from performance if the buyer suddenly and without warning should descend upon him and demand his entire inventory, but the court is not called upon to decide those cases here.

Rather, the case here is one where the established courses of performance and dealing between the parties, the established usages of the trade, and the basic contract itself all show that the matters complained of for the first time by Gulf after commencement of this litigation are the fundamental given ingredients of the aviation fuel trade to which the parties have accommodated themselves successfully and without dispute over the years....

The court concludes that Eastern has not violated the contract....

ORANGE AND ROCKLAND UTILITIES, INC. v. AMERADA HESS CORP.

Supreme Court of New York, Appellate Division, Second Department, 1977.
59 A.D.2d 110, 397 N.Y.S.2d 814.

MARGETT, JUSTICE. This action, for damages as a result of an alleged breach of a requirements contract, raises related but distinctly separate issues as to whether the plaintiff buyer's requirements occurred in good faith and whether those requirements were unreasonably disproportionate to the estimates stated in the contract.

In a fuel oil supply contract executed in early December, 1969, defendant Amerada Hess Corporation (Hess) agreed to supply the requirements of plaintiff Orange and Rockland Utilities, Inc. (O & R) at plaintiff's Lovett generating plant in Tompkins Cove, New York. A fixed price of $2.14 per barrel for No. 6 fuel oil, with a sulphur content of 1% or less, was to continue at least through September 30, 1974, with the price subject to renegotiation at that time. Estimates of the amounts required by plaintiff were included in the contract clause entitled "Quantity." Insofar as those estimates are relevant to the instant controversy, they were as follows:

1970—1,750,000 barrels

1971—1,380,000 barrels

1972—1,500,000 barrels

1973—1,500,000 barrels

The estimates had been prepared by plaintiff on December 30, 1968, as part of a five-year budget projection. The estimates anticipated that gas would be the primary fuel used for generation during the period in question. This was a result of the lower cost of gas and of the fact that gas became readily available for power generation during the warmer months of the year as a result of decreased use by gas customers. Plaintiff expressly reserved its right to burn as much gas as it chose by the inclusion, in the "Quantity" provision of the requirements contract, of a clause to the effect that "[n]othing herein shall preclude the use by Buyer of … natural gas in such quantities as may be or become available."

Within five months of the execution of the requirements contract, the price of fuel oil began to ascend rapidly. On April 24, 1970, the market price of the oil supplied to plaintiff stood at between $2.65 and $2.73 per barrel. On May 1, 1970, the price was in excess of $3 per barrel. The rise continued and was in excess of $3.50 per barrel by mid-August, and more than $4 per barrel by the end of October, 1970. By March, 1971, the lowest market price was $4.30 per barrel, more than double the price set forth in the subject contract.

Coincident with the earliest of these increases in the cost of oil, O & R proceeded to notify Hess, on four separate dates, of increases in the fuel oil requirements estimates for the year. By letter dated April 16, 1970, O & R notified Hess that it was expected that over 1,460,000 barrels of oil would be consumed over the period April–December, 1970. Since well over 600,000 barrels of oil had been consumed during the first three months of the year, the total increase anticipated at that time was well in excess of 300,000 barrels over the estimate given in the contract.

Eight days later, by letter dated April 24, 1970, O & R furnished Hess with a revised estimate for the period May through December, 1970. The figure given was nearly 1,580,000 barrels which, when combined with quantities which had already been delivered or were in the process of delivery during the month of April, exceeded the contract estimate by over 700,000 barrels, a 40% increase.

The following month the estimates were again increased this time to nearly one million barrels above the contract estimate. Hess was so notified by letter dated May 22, 1970. Finally, a letter dated June 19, 1970 indicates a revised estimate of more than one million barrels in excess of the 1,750,000 barrels mentioned in the contract; an increase of about 63%.

On May 22, 1970, the date of the third of the revised estimates, representatives of the two companies met to discuss the increased demands. At that meeting O & R's president allegedly attributed the increased need for oil to the fact that O & R could make more money *selling* gas than burning it for power generation. Hess refused to meet the revised requirements, but offered to supply the amount of the contract estimate for the year 1970, plus an additional 10 percent.

The June 19, 1970 letter referred to above recited that the Hess position was "wholly unacceptable" to O & R. It attributed the vastly increased estimates to (a) an inability to burn as much natural gas as had been planned and (b) the fact that O & R had been "required" to meet higher electrical demands on its "own system" and to furnish "more electricity to interconnected systems" than had been anticipated.

Thereafter, for the remainder of 1970, Hess continued to supply the amount of the contract estimates plus 10 percent. A proposal by Hess, in October, 1970, to modify the existing contract by setting minimum and maximum quantities, and by setting a price keyed to market prices, was ignored by O & R. Although the proposed modification set a price 65 cents lower than the market price, it was more advantageous for O & R to insist on delivery of the estimated amounts in the December, 1969 contract (at $2.14 per barrel) and to purchase additional amounts required at the full market price.

During the remainder of the contract period Hess continued to deliver quantities approximately equal to the estimates stated in the subject contract. O & R purchased additional oil for its Lovett plant from other suppliers. The contract between Hess and O & R terminated one year prematurely by reason of an environmental regulation which took effect on October 1, 1973 and which necessarily curtailed the use of No. 6 fuel oil with a sulphur content as high as 1%. During the period 1971 through September, 1973, O & R consistently used more than double its contract estimates of oil at Lovett.

This action was commenced in mid–1972. O & R's complaint seeks damages consisting of the difference between its costs for fuel oil during the period in question and the cost it would have incurred had Hess delivered the total amount used by O & R at the fixed contract price of $2.14 per barrel. The trial was conducted in September, 1975 before Mr. Justice Donohoe, sitting without a jury. In an opinion dated March 8, 1976, Trial Term held that plaintiff should be denied any recovery on the ground that its requirements were not incurred in good faith. Specifically, Trial Term found that plaintiff's greatly increased oil consumption was due primarily to (a) increases in sales of electricity to other utilities and (b) a net shift from other fuels, primarily gas, to oil. The former factor was condemned on the premise that "[i]ndirectly, O & R called upon Hess to supply the demands for electricity to the members of the [New York Power] Pool. O & R then shared the savings in the cost of fuel with the other members of the Pool." The latter factor was not elaborated on to any great degree. Trial Term did, however, infer that O & R seized "the opportunity to release its reserve commitment of gas" and thereby reaped very substantial profits.

Although Trial Term stated in its opinion that one of the questions before it was whether plaintiff's demands were unreasonably disproportionate to the estimates set forth in the contract, it failed to reach this question in the light of its conclusion that plaintiff had failed to act in good faith. Plaintiff contends on this appeal (1) that Trial Term's finding of an absence of good faith is unsupported by the record and (2) that since its requirements for the entire term of the contract were less than twice total contract estimates, its demands were not "unreasonably disproportionate" as a matter of law. We reject both contentions upon the facts of this case and affirm Trial Term's dismissal of the complaint. . . .

There is, as Trial Term observed, a good deal of pre-Code case law on the requirement of "good faith." It is well settled that a buyer in a rising market cannot use a fixed price in a requirements contract for speculation (*New York Cent. Ironworks Co. v. United States Radiator Co.*, 174 N.Y. 331, 335–336, 66 N.E. 967, 968). . . . Nor can a buyer arbitrarily and unilaterally change certain conditions prevailing at the time of the contract so as to take advantage of market conditions at the seller's expense (*C.A. Andrews Coal Co. v. Board of Directors of Public Schools, Parish of Orleans*, 151 La. 695, 92 So. 303). . . .

[T]here was ample evidence to justify a finding of lack of good faith on plaintiff's part. Even through the thicket of divergent and contrasting figures entered into exhibit at trial, the following picture emerges: non-firm sales from plaintiff's Lovett plant, presumably in large part to the New York Power Pool, increased nearly sixfold from 67,867 megawatt hours in 1969 to 390,017 megawatt hours in 1970. The significance of that increase in non-firm sales lies in the fact that such sales did not enter into the budget calculations which formed the basis of the estimates included in the contract. Even assuming that a prudent seller of oil could anticipate some additional requirements generated by non-firm sales, an increase of the magnitude which occurred in 1970 is unforeseeable. That increase, of 322,150 megawatt hours, translates into the equivalent of over 500,000 barrels of oil. The conclusion is inescapable that this dramatic change in plaintiff's relationship with the New York Power Pool came about as a result of the subject requirements contract, which insured it a steady flow of cheap oil despite swiftly rising prices. O & R's use of the subject contract to suddenly and dramatically propel itself into the position of a large seller of power to other utilities evidences a lack of good faith dealing. . . .

Thus it appears that in May, 1970, Hess refused an O & R demand of roughly one million barrels in excess of the contract estimate, which demand was occasioned by greatly increased sales to other utilities and a proposed release of gas which might otherwise normally have been burned for power generation. The former factor is tantamount to making the other utilities in the State silent partners to the contract (cf. *City of Lakeland, Florida v. Union Oil Co. of California*, 352 F.Supp. 758), while the latter factor amounts to a unilateral and arbitrary change in the conditions prevailing at the time of the contract so as to take advantage of market conditions at the seller's expense (*C.A. Andrews Coal v. Board of Directors of Public Schools, Parish of Orleans*, 151 La. 695, 92 So. 303, supra). Hess was therefore justified in 1970 in refusing to meet plaintiff's demands, by reason of the fact that plaintiff's "requirements" were not incurred in good faith. . . .

[The court held also that "under the circumstances of this case, any demand by plaintiff for more than double its contract estimates, was, as a matter of law, 'unreasonably disproportionate' (UCC, § 2–306, subd. [1]) to those estimates." The court declined to adopt the factor of more than double the contract estimates as any sort of an inflexible yardstick.]

Questions

1. What was the deal in *Eastern Air Lines*? What was the deal in *Orange & Rockland*? In what ways are the two cases alike on their facts?

2. What is the distinction between the good faith in *Eastern Air Lines* and the bad faith in *Orange & Rockland*? Were both cases decided correctly? If not, which is in error?

3. Review the definitions of "good faith" in U.C.C. §§ 1–201(19), 2–103(1)(b). Are they helpful in understanding any of the above three cases? In *Eastern Air Lines* and *Orange & Rockland*, was either buyer "dishonest"? How are reasonable commercial standards of fair dealing in the trade different from trade usage, course of dealing, and course of performance?

4. *Problem.*

   A buyer rejected a fourth shipment of potatoes tendered by a grower under a contract requiring that the potatoes be satisfactory for making potato chips. The buyer had accepted the first three shipments under the contract when the market and contract prices were equal. The market price then fell to less than half the contract price, and the buyer rejected all further shipments, saying that the potatoes would not "chip" satisfactorily. The buyer told the seller that he would turn down any further shipments because he could buy all the potatoes he wanted at the lower market price. Was the buyer in bad faith under the U.C.C.? See Neumiller Farms, Inc. v. Cornett, 368 So.2d 272 (Ala.1979).

NOTE ON LAWFUL PERFORMANCE OF A CONTRACT

It is commonly said to be a "fundamental principle" of our law that

> [a]ll contracts are made subject to any law prescribing their effect, or the conditions to be observed in their performance; and hence the [law] is as much a part of the contract in question as if it had been actually written into it, or made a part of the stipulations.

In re Estate of Havemeyer, 17 N.Y.2d 216, 219, 217 N.E.2d 26, 27, 270 N.Y.S.2d 197, 199 (1966). As Judge Cardozo had earlier explained, "[s]tatutes [existing at the time of contract formation] are read into the contract. They enter by implication into its terms. They do not change the obligation. They make it what it is." People ex rel. City of New York v. Nixon, 229 N.Y. 356, 361, 128 N.E. 245, 247 (1920). A few recent cases have used this principle to find parties in breach of contract for violating a statute or ordinance governing the performance under the contract.

For example, a warranty of habitability, measured by the standards in a housing code, may be implied by operation of law into leases of urban dwelling units covered by those regulations. Breach of this warranty may give rise to the usual remedies for breach of contract. Javins v. First Nat'l Realty Corp., 428 F.2d 1071 (D.C.Cir.1970), cert. denied, 400 U.S. 925, 91 S.Ct. 186, 27 L.Ed.2d 185 (1970). A state statute, requiring the supplier to repurchase inventory upon termination of a distributorship agreement, may be imported into a contract so that a supplier's refusal to repurchase inventory is a breach to be remedied by contract damages. Hall GMC, Inc. v. Crane Carrier Co., 332 N.W.2d 54 (N.D.1983). A stock option agreement may be augmented by additional terms to maintain its conformity with state law. General Dev. Corp. v. Catlin, 139 So.2d 901 (Fla.Dist.Ct.App.1962). And a consumer protection statute requiring automobile repair shops to tender defective parts upon replacing them may result in a contractual obligation, the breach of which relieves the consumer of any duty to pay for the repairs. Design and Funding, Inc. v. Betz Garage, Inc., 292 Md. 265, 438 A.2d 1316 (1981). In each case of this kind, a statutory law becomes a term of the contract and the ground of a breach, for which the injured party is awarded normal contract remedies to protect her expectation interest.

What is the legal basis for importing a statutory or similar obligation into a contract? In the foregoing cases, it would not seem to be the legislature's authority. Statutes generally provide remedies for violations. In none of these cases did the statute expressly require that the contract contain the relevant term, nor was there an implied right of action under the statute. It is doubtful that the importation is justified by party autonomy in all such cases. Consider, for example, whether a court would or should enforce an agreement by parties to a construction contract that violations of the building code are permitted. Rather, it seems, the legal basis is a doctrine of the common law that has been dubbed the "lawful performance doctrine." Though not yet widely recognized, and of uncertain scope, recent cases have increasingly applied it in situations like those mentioned above.

CITIZENS FOR PRESERVATION OF WATERMAN LAKE v. DAVIS

Supreme Court of Rhode Island, 1980.
420 A.2d 53.

BEVILACQUA, C.J. This is a civil action heard before a justice of the Superior Court sitting without a jury. Judgments were entered for the defendants, William Davis (Davis) and John Coyne (Coyne). The plaintiffs appealed from the judgments to this court....

In September of 1974, the town of Glocester (the town) and Davis entered into a contract that, *inter alia*, granted Davis the right to use certain property as a commercial dump. This property, which Davis has designated as the Glocester Smithfield Regional Landfill (GSRL), is located partly in Glocester and partly in Smithfield. Shortly after Davis had begun to operate the GSRL dump under his contract with the town, he contracted with third parties to accept for disposal there refuse originating outside Glocester. Moreover, contrary to his representations to the then Department of Natural Resources (DNR) and the Department of Health, Davis apparently deposited refuse in wetlands located on the GSRL property.

On May 29, 1975, Citizens for Preservation of Waterman Lake, plaintiffs, a nonprofit Rhode Island corporation, and several individually named persons,[2] filed the instant complaint. In its complaint, the Citizens group alleged, *inter alia*, that Davis, in the course of operating the GSRL dump, violated the Fresh Water Wetlands Act (wetlands act), as enacted by P.L. 1971, ch. 213 § 1, now G.L. 1956 (1976 Reenactment) § 2–1–18 to § 2–1–25, by dumping trash and fill in a wetlands area without a permit; that he caused a nuisance to occur by polluting the waters of Nine Foot Brook, which is a tributary of Waterman Lake and which apparently runs through Glocester and Smithfield; that the trucks hauling refuse constituted a nuisance by virtue of the loud noise attending their operation; that Davis and Coyne conspired to violate certain ordinances of the town by permitting the disposal, within Glocester, of refuse originating outside Glocester; and that the September, 1974 contract between the town and Davis was illegal and invalid. The Citizens group prayed for injunctive and declaratory relief and for money damages. Prior to trial the town was permitted under Super.R.Civ.P. 24 to intervene as a plaintiff. In its complaint, as amended, the town alleged that Davis had breached the terms of the September, 1974 contract by disposing, at the GSRL dump, refuse originating outside Glocester, in violation of local ordinances. In addition, the town also claimed that Davis had violated the wetlands act. The town prayed for injunctive and declaratory relief. After hearing the claims asserted by the Citizens group and the town, the trial justice found for defendants on all issues; and judgments were entered accordingly. . . .

The first issue that we shall address is the contention put forth by the Citizens group and the town that the trial justice erred when he refused to enjoin Davis's dump operation until Davis had filed an application to alter wetlands in accordance with the wetlands act. The trial justice held that authority to enforce the wetlands act was exclusively vested in the DNR director and that neither the Citizens group nor the town had standing to enforce the wetlands act against Davis.

The Citizens group and the town contend that they are not attempting to enforce the wetlands act but that they are guaranteed certain rights under [the] wetlands act and that they have a private cause of action for injunctive relief to secure those rights. *See generally Cort v. Ash,* 422 U.S. 66, 74–85, 95 S.Ct. 2080, 2086–91, 45 L.Ed.2d 26, 34–40 (1975). . . . It is well-settled that when the language of a statute is clear

---

2. Citizens for Preservation of Waterman Lake is a nonprofit Rhode Island corporation dedicated to preserving the ecology of Waterman Lake and its tributary waters. The persons individually named in the instant complaint are members of Citizens for Preservation of Waterman Lake and are landowners, residents, and taxpayers of either Glocester or Smithfield. The group of plaintiffs shall hereinafter be referred to as "the Citizens group."

and unambiguous, the statute may not be construed or extended but must be applied literally. *Brier Mfg. Co. v. Norberg*, 377 A.2d 345, 348 (R.I.1977). . . .

Under the wetlands act all powers necessary to enforce its provisions are expressly vested in the DNR director. The director, in the first instance, determines which areas are to be designated as wetlands. Section 2–1–20.2. He has the authority to approve or disapprove applications, subject to the city or town wherein the area is located, for altering of wetlands. Section 2–1–21. He has broad powers to remedy any violation of the wetlands act. Sections 2–1–23 and 2–1–24. Significantly, he is authorized to obtain relief in equity or by prerogative writ whenever such relief is necessary to the proper performance of his duties under the wetlands act. Section 2–1–24. In view of the express statutory scheme of enforcement, we conclude that all enforcement powers are vested in the director. Moreover, nothing in the legislation indicates either expressly or implicitly an intent to create a remedy for a private citizen or a town or city to enforce the provisions of the wetlands act. Until the director acts, no other individual is authorized under the wetlands act to initiate any proceedings pursuant to the provisions of the wetlands act.

Similarly, we reject the town's contention that because existing law is a part of its contract with Davis, it may treat the wetlands act as a term of that contract which may be enforced through injunctive relief. We do not dispute the well-settled principle that existing law is an implied term of every contract. *Sterling Engineering & Construction Co. v. Burrillville Housing Authority*, 108 R.I. 723, 726, 279 A.2d 445, 447 (1971). This principle is, however, not applicable to the case before us. Neither is this a case in which we are called upon to construe an ambiguous contract; in such a case existing law is an extrinsic aid to discerning the contracting parties' intent, see, e.g., *Deerhurst Estates v. Meadow Homes, Inc.*, 64 N.J.Super. 134, 152, 165 A.2d 543, 552–53 (1960). Nor is this a case in which an existing statute expressly creates a specific obligation between the contracting parties; in such a case the "statute is as much a part of the contract as if the statute had been actually written into the contract," see, e.g., *Sterling Engineering & Construction Co. v. Burrillville Housing Authority*, 108 R.I. at 726, 279 A.2d at 447. . . .

We agree also with the trial justice's denial of the town's claim for injunctive relief to remedy Davis's alleged violations of the refuse ordinances. We have several times made clear that in the absence of a cause of action at common law or a specific grant of authority, a town may not resort to the equitable powers of the Superior Court in every case in which there has been a violation of some local ordinance. Rather, the town must resort to the penal sanctions contained in the applicable ordinance. . . . We will not permit the town to use its contract with Davis to enhance its rights under the local ordinance when its rights under the ordinance are limited strictly to a criminal action in the District Court. . . .

Questions

1. Why does the court refuse to allow the Citizens Group to enforce the law? Does the court do more than pay lip service to the "well-settled principle that existing law is an implied term of every contract"?

2. Should the court in *Citizens* have given greater weight to the public interest in environmental protection? Can you develop a better argument that contract law should vindicate that interest in a case like this? What is the counterargument? Which is stronger?

3. *Problems.*

    a. In a separation agreement, a husband promised to pay his former wife a sum of money each month until he dies. He then committed suicide, which was a crime in the jurisdiction. Should the wife recover damages for breach of contract from the husband's estate? See Wilmington Trust Co. v. Clark, 289 Md. 313, 424 A.2d 744 (1981).

    b. A contract for the construction of a home expressly required the builder to conform to plans and specifications attached to the contract. The plans said nothing about the use of horizontal steel reinforcements, which nonetheless were required by the local building code. That code provided that failure to conform to its requirements precludes the City Housing Authority from issuing a certification for occupancy. When the builder omits horizontal steel, should the owner have an action for breach of contract? See Quedding v. Arisumi Bros., Inc., 66 Haw. 335, 661 P.2d 706 (1983); Bruffett v. Warner Communications, Inc., 692 F.2d 910 (3d Cir.1982).

SECTION 4. PROMISES AND CONDITIONS

The terms of a contract can be classified along two dimensions. On one, terms are express or implied, as in the foregoing sections. On another, to be introduced here and explored further in Chapter 6, they may be promises, conditions, or promissory conditions. In general, a promise creates an obligation, the breach of which entitles the non-breaching party to damages and other remedies for breach. Conditions have a different legal consequence: they determine when a party's obligation to perform her promise is *due*. Thus, Hepburn might promise Tracy that she will pay for lunch, on condition that Tracy show up on time. If Tracy is late, the condition to Hepburn's obligation (here, a moral one) does not occur, and her obligation does not come due. Tracy, however, is not in breach of contract. He will have an obligation that can be breached only when he also *promises* to show up on time, which in this case he did not do. When a term is both a promise and a condition, it may be called a "promissory condition."

RESTATEMENT (SECOND) OF CONTRACTS §§ 224–27, 229

Problem

In Constable v. Cloberie, 81 Eng.Rep. 1141 (K.B. 1626), a cargo owner wanted a ship owner to carry his cargo from England to Cadiz (in Spain). The ship owner promised to do so in return for the cargo owner's promise to pay the freight. Moreover, the cargo owner also wanted the ship owner to "sail with the next wind," as it was then put when time was of the essence. They agreed on language stating, "[ship owner] to sail with the next wind," leaving it unclear whether sailing with the next wind was a promise, a condition, or both.

Imagine that the cargo owner had sought your advice on how to draft the contract to protect his interest in a quick departure. Should you draft a condition or a promise that the ship sail with the next wind? Come to class prepared to interview the client to decide upon a legal strategy, with proposed language to effectuate whatever strategy you settle on at the end of the interview. Think about your goals in interviewing the client carefully: The client is a capable businessperson who seeks the special contribution that a lawyer can make to his or her project. The client, in particular, knows little or no law, and does not want to learn it. You must imagine what might happen with adverse effects on the client's interests and develop a protective legal strategy. (RESTATEMENT (SECOND) OF CONTRACTS §§ 224–25 should be a sufficient legal basis for this exercise.)

JUNGMANN & CO., INC. v. ATTERBURY BROTHERS, INC.

Court of Appeals of New York, 1928.
249 N.Y. 119, 163 N.E. 123.

LEHMAN, J. In February, 1923, the plaintiff entered into a written contract with the defendant for the sale of thirty tons of casein. The contract contained a clause: "Shipment: May–June from Europe. Advice of shipment to be made by cable immediately goods are dispatched." Fifteen tons of casein were shipped on June 9th, 1923. No notice of shipment was given to the defendant. Tender of this shipment by the plaintiff was refused by the defendant on June 20th. On June 21st the defendant wrote to the plaintiff that the plaintiff "failed to make any May delivery under the contract and also failed to advise us of shipment as required to do by your contract." The plaintiff declined an offer of the defendant "to take this shipment as the June quota on your . . . contract and call the contract filled." On June 26th the plaintiff shipped the remaining fifteen tons of casein. The defendant received no advice of shipment "by cable" immediately after the goods were shipped. It did receive a letter from the plaintiff dated June 23d, that the plaintiff had received advice by cable that these fifteen tons would be shipped per steamship Magnolia sailing on June 26th, and another letter from the plaintiff on June 28th stating that upon the arrival of the steamship Magnolia "which sailed on June 26th with the balance of your order on board, we will deliver to you the full 30 tons of Casein in conformity with our contract." On the arrival of the steamship Magnolia the plaintiff tendered to the defendant the thirty tons of casein. The defendant refused the tender.

.   .   .

Upon the demand of the defendant the parties agreed to the insertion in the contract of the clause, "Advice of shipment to be made by cable immediately goods are dispatched." Concededly until the goods shipped on June 9th arrived, no notice of any kind was given to the plaintiff that they had been shipped. Notice that the remainder of the goods was shipped on June 26th was given by letter from the plaintiff, not by cable. It is said that since the defendant received notice when the steamship Magnolia sailed with fifteen tons that upon its arrival the plaintiff would tender to the defendant the entire thirty tons, the defendant is in no worse position than if it had received the stipulated "advice of shipment by cable immediately the goods are dispatched." Even if that be true, the fact remains that the plaintiff was obligated under its contract to see that defendant obtained advice of shipment by cable. That it failed to do. It may be that the defendant would have been satisfied to enter into a contract which required the plaintiff only to notify the defendant of intention to make delivery a definite time before actual delivery. It stipulated for another kind of notice. It may have believed that certainty of delivery would be greater if it received advice of actual shipment by cable. We may not weigh the benefit it might receive from other notice. The plaintiff may not recover upon its contract without proof that it has performed all conditions precedent required of it. (Van Iderstine Co., Inc. v. Barnet L. Co., Inc., 242 N. Y. 425; . . . The plaintiff is barred from recovery here by failure to give notice according to the terms of the contract. . . .

Questions

1.   What is the legal issue in *Jungmann & Co.*? What does the buyer argue? What does the seller argue? Why does the seller lose?

2.   Does the result make commercial sense? Does it implement the intentions of the parties, interpreted in light of the commercial realities? Or, insofar as the opinion suggests, is the buyer relying on a technicality to get out of the contract? Should the buyer be able to get out just because of the literal meaning of the contract term? Does it have any legitimate interests in receiving notice by cable upon shipment of the goods (by sea)? If it does not, would that matter to the New York Court of Appeals?

3.   Given the result in *Jungmann & Co.*, might the seller have been treated too harshly? Where are the goods after the buyer declines to take shipment? Could the seller easily resell them? If the buyer was treated harshly, should the law do something about it? Should the buyer have to show that it was harmed by the seller's failure to send notice according to the contract, taken literally?

4. *Problem.*

Otherwise on the facts of *Jungman & Co.*, assume that the contract called for notice by telegram upon shipment. The buyer sent notice by e-mail and by telephone upon shipment. Would the New York Court of Appeals reach the same result? Should it? See W.W.W. Associates, Inc. v. Giancontieri, 77 N.Y.2d 157, 565 N.Y.S.2d 440, 566 N.E.2d 639 (1990).

PEACOCK CONSTRUCTION CO., INC. v. MODERN AIR CONDITIONING, INC.

Supreme Court of Florida, 1977.
353 So.2d 840.

BOYD, ACTING CHIEF JUSTICE. We issued an order allowing certiorari in these two causes because the decisions in them of the District Court of Appeal, Second District, conflict with the decision in *Edward J. Gerrits, Inc. v. Astor Electric Service, Inc.*, 328 So.2d 522 (Fla. 3d DCA 1976). The two causes have been consolidated for all appellate purposes in this Court because they involve the same issue. That issue is whether the plaintiffs, Modern Air Conditioning and Overly Manufacturing, were entitled to summary judgments against Peacock Construction Company in actions for breaches of identical contractual provisions.

Peacock Construction was the builder of a condominium project. Modern Air Conditioning subcontracted with Peacock to do the heating and air conditioning work and Overly Manufacturing subcontracted with Peacock to do the "rooftop swimming pool" work. Both written subcontracts provided that Peacock would make final payment to the subcontractors,

> "within 30 days after the completion of the work included in this sub-contract, written acceptance by the Architect and full payment therefor by the Owner."

Modern Air Conditioning and Overly Manufacturing completed the work specified in their contracts and requested final payment. When Peacock refused to make the final payments the two subcontractors separately brought actions in the Lee County Circuit Court for breach of contract. In both actions it was established that no deficiencies had been found in the completed work. But Peacock established that it had not received from the owner full payment for the subcontractors' work. And it defended on the basis that such payment was a condition which, by express term of the final payment provision, had to be fulfilled before it was obligated to perform under the contract. On motions by the plaintiffs, the trial judges granted summary judgments in their favor. The orders of judgment implicitly interpreted the contract not to require payment by the owner as a condition precedent to Peacock's duty to perform.

The Second District Court of Appeal affirmed the lower court's judgment in the appeal brought by Modern Air Conditioning. In so doing it adopted the view of the majority of jurisdictions in this country that provisions of the kind disputed here do not set conditions precedent but rather constitute absolute promises to pay, fixing payment by the owner as a reasonable time for when payment to the subcontractor is to be made. When the judgment in the *Overly Manufacturing* case reached the Second District Court, *Modern Air Conditioning* had been decided and the judgment, therefore, was affirmed on the authority of the latter decision. These two decisions plainly conflict with *Gerrits,* supra.

In *Gerrits,* the Court had summarily ordered judgment for the plaintiff/subcontractor against the defendant/general contractor on a contractual provision for payment to the subcontractor which read,

> "The money to be paid in current funds and at such times as the General Contractor receives it from the Owner." Id. at 523.

In its review of the judgment, the Third District Court of Appeal referred to the fundamental rule of interpretation of contracts that it be done in accordance with the intention of the parties. Since the defendant had introduced below the issue of intention, a material issue, and since the issue was one that could be resolved through a factual determination by the jury, the Third District reversed the summary judgment and remanded for trial.

Peacock urges us to adopt *Gerrits* as the controlling law in this State. It concedes that the Second District's decisions are backed by the weight of authority. But it argues that they are incorrect because the issue of intention is a factual one which should be resolved after the parties have had an opportunity to present evidence on it. Peacock urges, therefore, that the causes be remanded for trial. If there is produced no evidence that the parties intended there be condition precedents, only then, says Peacock, should the judge, by way of a directed verdict for the subcontractors, be allowed to take the issue of intention from the jury.

The contractual provisions in dispute here are susceptible to two interpretations. They may be interpreted as setting a condition precedent or as fixing a reasonable time for payment. The provision disputed in *Gerrits* is susceptible to the same two interpretations. The questions presented by the conflict between these decisions, then, are whether ambiguous contractual provisions of the kind disputed here may be interpreted only by the factfinder, usually the jury, or if they should be interpreted as a matter of law by the court, and if so what interpretation they should be given.

Although it must be admitted that the meaning of language is a factual question, the general rule is that interpretation of a document is a question of law rather than of fact. 4 Williston on Contracts, 3rd Ed., § 616. If an issue of contract interpretation concerns the intention of parties, that intention may be determined from the written contract, as a matter of law, when the nature of the transaction lends itself to judicial interpretation. A number of courts, with whom we agree, have recognized that contracts between small subcontractors and general contractors on large construction projects are such transactions. Cf. *Thos. J. Dyer Co. v. Bishop International Engineering Co.,* 6 Cir., 303 F.2d 655

(1962). The reason is that the relationship between the parties is a common one and usually their intent will not differ from transaction to transaction, although it may be differently expressed.

That intent in most cases is that payment by the owner to the general contractor is not a condition precedent to the general contractor's duty to pay the subcontractors. This is because small subcontractors, who must have payment for their work in order to remain in business, will not ordinarily assume the risk of the owner's failure to pay the general contractor. And this is the reason for the majority view in this country, which we now join.

Our decision to require judicial interpretation of ambiguous provisions for final payment in subcontracts in favor of subcontractors should not be regarded as anti-general contractor. It is simply a recognition that this is the fairest way to deal with the problem. There is nothing in this opinion, however, to prevent parties to these contracts from shifting the risk of payment failure by the owner to the subcontractor. But in order to make such a shift the contract must unambiguously express that intention. And the burden of clear expression is on the general contractor.

The decisions of the Second District Court of Appeal to affirm the summary judgments were correct. We adopt, therefore, these two decisions as the controlling law in Florida and we overrule *Gerrits*, to the extent it is inconsistent with this opinion.

Questions

1. What is the problem of interpretation in *Peacock Construction*? What are the key legal issues before the court? Is the court faced with a question of interpretation, or of construction?

2. Why does the court conclude that payment by the owner to the general contractor is not a condition precedent to the general contractor's duty to pay the subcontractors? Would this always be the case? If not, when would it not be the case?

3. If the general contractor's duty to pay were clearly conditional on payment from the owner, should the condition be excused?

4. *Problems.*

    a. The facts are as in *Peacock Construction*, except that the prime contractor introduced evidence that it was a small, family-run business with average annual gross income for the preceding five years of $2.2 million. The subcontractor's project manager admitted on cross-examination that the subcontractor was the largest heating and air conditioning firm in Florida with average annual gross income for the same period of over $22 million. Should the result change?

    b. On February 18, 1992, during a deep recession in the local construction business, Leopold contracted with Mickey, a general contractor, to erect the concrete walls required under a contract between Mickey and Village Apartments. The contract provided: "Payments to be made as received from Owner." Before the contract was concluded with Leopold, an officer of Mickey's company explained to Leopold that the contract would be contingent upon Mickey's contract with Village Apartments. Leopold then delayed signing the contract so that he could check into the worth of the owner. The subcontract was signed and Leopold fully performed. Village apartments, however, failed to pay Mickey. Mickey refused to pay Leopold, citing the quoted clause. What would you advise Leopold? See Mascioni v. I.B. Miller, Inc., 261 N.Y. 1, 184 N.E. 473 (1933).

BURGER KING CORP. v. FAMILY DINING, INC.

United States District Court, Eastern District of Pennsylvania, 1977.
426 F.Supp. 485, affirmed mem. 566 F.2d 1168 (3d Cir.1977).

MEMORANDUM AND ORDER

HANNUM, DISTRICT JUDGE. Presently before the Court is defendant's motion for an involuntary dismissal in accordance with Rule 41(b), Federal Rules of Civil Procedure, advanced at the close of plaintiff's case. The trial is before the Court sitting without a jury.

In bringing the suit plaintiff seeks a determination under the Declaratory Judgment Act, Title 28, United States Code § 2201, that a contract between the parties, by its own terms, is no longer of any force and effect. A request for declaratory relief is appropriate in a case such as this where the primary question is whether such a termination has occurred. See: Wright and Miller, *Federal Practice and Procedure: Civil* § 2765, n.35.

Jurisdiction of the parties is based on diversity of citizenship in accordance with Title 28, United States Code § 1332(a).

FACTS ESTABLISHED IN PLAINTIFF'S CASE

Plaintiff Burger King Corporation (hereinafter "Burger King") is a Florida corporation engaged in franchising the well-known Burger King Restaurants. In 1954, James W. McLamore, founder of Burger King Restaurants, Inc. (the corporate predecessor of Burger King) built the first Burger King Restaurant in Miami, Florida. In 1961, the franchise system was still relatively modest [in] size having only about 60 or 70 restaurants in operation outside of Florida. By 1963, however, Burger King began to experience significant growth and was building and operating, principally through franchisees, 24 restaurants per year. It was also at this time that Burger King's relationship with defendant Family Dining, Inc., (hereinafter "Family Dining") was created.

Family Dining is a Pennsylvania corporation which at the present time operates ten Burger King Restaurants (hereinafter "Restaurant") in Bucks and Montgomery Counties in Pennsylvania. Family Dining was founded and is currently operated by Carl Ferris who had been a close personal friend of McLamore's for a number of years prior to 1963. In fact they had attended Cornell University together in the late 1940's. It would seem that this friendship eventually led to the business relationship between Burger King and Family Dining which was conceived in the "Burger King Territorial Agreement" (hereinafter "Territorial Agreement") entered on May 10, 1963.

In accordance with the Territorial Agreement Burger King agreed that Family Dining would be its sole licensee, and thus have an "exclusive territory," in Bucks and Montgomery Counties provided Family Dining operated each Restaurant pursuant to Burger King license agreements and maintained a specified rate of development. Articles I and II of the Territorial Agreement (Plaintiff's Exhibit P–2) are pertinent to this dispute. They provide as follows:

I.

For a period of one year, beginning on the date hereof, Company will not operate or license others for the operation of any BURGER KING restaurant within the following described territory hereinafter referred to as "exclusive territory," to-wit:

> The counties of Bucks and Montgomery, all in the State of Pennsylvania

as long as licensee operates each BURGER KING restaurant pursuant to BURGER KING restaurant licenses with Company and faithfully performs each of the covenants contained.

This agreement shall remain in effect and Licensee shall retain the exclusive territory for a period of ninety (90) years from the date hereof, provided that at the end of one, two, three, four, five, six, seven, eight, nine and ten years from the date hereof, and continuously thereafter during the next eighty years, Licensee has the following requisite number of BURGER KING restaurants in operation or under active construction, pursuant to Licenses with Company:

> One (1) restaurant at the end of one year;
>
> Two (2) restaurants at the end of two years;
>
> Three (3) restaurants at the end of three years;
>
> Four (4) restaurants at the end of four years;
>
> Five (5) restaurants at the end of five years;
>
> Six (6) restaurants at the end of six years;
>
> Seven (7) restaurants at the end of seven years;
>
> Eight (8) restaurants at the end of eight years;
>
> Nine (9) restaurants at the end of nine years;
>
> Ten (10) restaurants at the end of ten years;

and continually maintains not less than ten (10) restaurants during the next eighty (80) years. . . .

II.

If at the end of either one, two, three, four, five, six, seven, eight, nine or ten years from the date hereof, or anytime thereafter during the next eighty (80) years, there are less than the respective requisite number of BURGER KING operations or under active construction in the "exclusive territory" pursuant to licenses by Company, this agreement shall terminate and be of no further force and effect. Thereafter, Company may operate or license others for the operation of BURGER KING Restaurants anywhere within the exclusive territory, so long as such restaurants are not within the "Protected Area," as set forth in any BURGER KING Restaurant License to which the Licensee herein is a party.

The prospect of exclusivity for ninety years was clearly intended to be an inducement to Family Dining to develop the territory as prescribed and it appears that it had exactly this effect as Family Dining was to become one of Burger King's most successful franchisees. While Burger King considered Carl Ferris to be somewhat of a problem at various times and one who was overly meticulous with detail, it was nevertheless through his efforts which included obtaining the necessary financing and assuming significant risks, largely without assistance from Burger King, that enabled both parties to benefit from the arrangement.

On August 16, 1963, Family Dining opened the First Restaurant at 588 West DeKalb Pike in King of Prussia, Pennsylvania. The second Restaurant was opened on July 2, 1965, at 409 West Ridge Pike, Conshohocken, Pennsylvania, and the third Restaurant was opened October 19, 1966, at 2561 West Main Street, Norristown, Pennsylvania.

However, by April, 1968, Family Dining had not opened or begun active construction on a fourth Restaurant which, in accordance with the development rate, should have been accomplished by May 10, 1967, and it was apparent that a fifth Restaurant would not be opened by May 10, 1968, the date scheduled. On May 1, 1968, the parties entered into a Modification of the Territorial Agreement (hereinafter "Modification") whereby Burger King agreed to waive Family Dining's failure to comply with the development rate. (Plaintiff's Exhibit P–4). There is nothing contained in the record which indicates that Burger King received anything of value in exchange for entering this agreement. However, McLamore testified that if the fourth and fifth Restaurants would be built nearly in compliance with the development rate for the fifth year he would overlook the year or so default in the fourth Restaurant. (N.T. 39). This attitude seems to be consistent with his overall view toward the development rate with respect to which, he testified, was "designed to insure the company of an orderly process of growth which would also enable the company to produce a profit on the sale of its franchises and through the collection of royalties that the restaurants would themselves produce." (N.T. 35).

The fourth Restaurant was opened on July 1, 1968, at 1721 North DeKalb Pike, Norristown, Pennsylvania, and the fifth Restaurant was opened on October 17, 1968, at 1035 Bustleton Pike in Feasterville, Pennsylvania.

On April 18, 1969, Ferris forwarded a letter to McLamore pertaining to certain delays in site approval and relating McLamore's earlier statement that there would be no problem in waiving the development schedule for the sixth Restaurant. (Plaintiff's Exhibit P–5). The letter expressed Ferris' concern regarding compliance with the development rate. By letter dated April 26, 1969, from Howard Walker of Burger King, Ferris was granted a month extension in the development rate. (Plaintiff's Exhibit P–6). With respect to this extension McLamore testified that "it never crossed my mind to call a default of this agreement on a technicality." (N.T. 47).

On October 1, 1969, the sixth Restaurant was opened at 1515 East High Street in Pottstown, Pennsylvania. The seventh Restaurant was opened on February 2, 1970, ahead of schedule, at 560 North Main Street in Doylestown, Pennsylvania.

At this point in time Burger King was no longer a modest sized franchise system. It had became a wholly owned subsidiary of the Pillsbury Company and had, in fact, evolved into a complex corporate entity. McLamore was elevated to Chairman of the Board of Burger King and, while he remained the chief executive officer for a time, Arthur A. Rosewall was installed as Burger King's President. Ferris was no longer able to expect the close, one to one relationship with McLamore that had previously obtained in his dealings with the company. It seems clear that as a result Family Dining began to experience difficulties in its day to day operations with Burger King.

One of the problem areas which arose concerned site selection. In a typical situation when a franchisee would seek approval for a building site an application would be submitted to the National Development Committee comprised of various Burger King officials. Based on Ferris' prior showing regarding site selection it could be expected that he would have little difficulty in obtaining their approval. In McLamore's view, Ferris was an exceptionally fine franchisee whose ability to choose real estate locations was exceptional. (N.T. 61). However, in August, 1970, a Frankford Avenue location selected by Ferris was rejected by the National Development Committee. The reasons offered in support of the decision to reject are not entirely clear and it seems that for the most part it was an exercise of discretion. The only plausible reason, given Ferris' expertise, was that the site was 2.7 miles from another Burger King franchise operated by Pete Miller outside Family Dining's exclusive territory. Yet Burger King chose not to exercise its discretion in similar circumstances when it permitted another franchisee to build a Restaurant in Devon, Pennsylvania, approximately 3 miles away from an existing Family Dining Restaurant.

In his August 25, 1970, memo to the Carl Ferris file McLamore observed that Burger King "had sloppy real estate work involved in servicing him and that [Burger King was] guilty of many follow up delinquencies." (Defendant's Exhibit D–7). This was during a time, as Burger King management was well aware, where it was one thing to select a location and quite another to actually develop it. That is, local governing bodies were taking a much stricter view toward allowing this type of development. It was also during this time, as McLamore's memo points out, Burger King realized that the Bucks-Montgomery territory was capable of sustaining substantially more Restaurants than originally thought.

Amidst these circumstances, the eighth Restaurant was opened ahead of schedule on October 7, 1970, at 601 South Broad Street in Lansdale, Pennsylvania. And in December, 1971, Burger King approved Family Dining's proposed sites for two additional Restaurants in Ambler, Pennsylvania and Levittown, Pennsylvania.

In early 1972, Arthur Rosewell became the chief executive officer of Burger King. At this time it also became apparent that the ninth Restaurant would not be opened or under construction by May 10, 1972. On April 27, 1972, in a telephone conversation with McLamore, Ferris once again expressed his concern to Burger King regarding compliance with the development rate. Burger King's position at that time is evidenced by McLamore's Memo to the Carl Ferris file dated April 28, 1972, wherein he provides that "Ferris' territorial arrangement with the company is such that he must have his ninth store (he has eight open now) under construction next month. I indicated to him that, due to the fact that he was in the process of developing four sites at this time, the company would consider he had met, substantially, the requirements of exclusivity." (Plaintiff's Exhibit P–7). McLamore testified that at that time he had in mind a further delay of 3 to 6 months. (N.T. 55).

In April, 1973, Burger King approved Family Dining's proposed site for a Restaurant in Warminster, Pennsylvania. However, as of May 10, 1973, neither the ninth or the tenth Restaurant had been opened or under active construction.

A letter dated May 23, 1973, from Helen D. Donaldson, Franchise Documents Administrator for Burger King, was sent to Ferris. (Plaintiff's Exhibit P–10). The letter provides as follows:

Dear Mr. Ferris:

During a periodic review of all territorial agreements we note that as of this date your development schedule requiring ten restaurants to be open or under construction by May 10, 1973, has not been met. Our records reflect eight stores open in Bucks and/or Montgomery County, and one site approved but not manned.

Under the terms of your territorial agreement failure to have the required number of stores in operation or under active construction constitutes a default of your agreement.

If there are extenuating circumstances about which this office is not aware, we would appreciate your earliest advice.

It is doubtful that the Donaldson letter was intended to communicate to Ferris that the Territorial Agreement was terminated. The testimony of both Rosewall (N.T. 187) and Leslie W. Paszat (N.T. 256), an executive of Burger King, who worked closely with Rosewall on the Family Dining matter indicates that even Burger King had not settled its position at this time. Ferris' letter dated July 27, 1973, to Rosewall (Defendant's Exhibit D–10), and Rosewall's reply dated August 3, 1973 (Plaintiff's Exhibit P–11) also fail to demonstrate any understanding that the Territorial Agreement was terminated.

It seems that throughout this period Burger King treated the matter as something of a "hot potato" subjecting Ferris to contact with several different Burger King officials. Much of Ferris' contact with Rosewall was interrupted by Rosewall's month long vacation and a meat shortage crisis to which he had to devote a substantial amount of his time. Ultimately Paszat was given responsibility for Family Dining and it appears that he provided Ferris with the first clear indication that Burger King considered the Territorial Agreement terminated in his letter of November 6, 1973 (Plaintiff's Exhibit P–14). Burger King's corporate structure had become so complex that the question of who, when or where the decision was made could not be answered. The abrupt manner in which Burger King's position was communicated to Family Dining, under the circumstances, was not straightforward.

From November, 1973, until some point early in 1975, the parties attempted to negotiate their differences with no success. The reason for the lack of success is understandable given that Burger King from the outset considered exclusivity a non-negotiable item. It was during this period on September 7, 1974, that Family Dining began actual construction of the ninth Restaurant in Warminster, Pennsylvania.

Several months before the instant litigation was begun Family Dining informed Burger King that it intended to open a ninth Restaurant on or about May 15, 1975, on Street Road, Warminster, Pennsylvania. In February, 1975, Burger King notified Family Dining that a franchise agreement (license) had to be entered for the additional Restaurant without which Family Dining would be infringing Burger King's trademarks. A similar notice was given in April, 1975, in which Burger King indicated it would retain counsel to protect its rights. Nevertheless Family Dining proceeded with its plans to open the Warminster Restaurant.

In May, 1975, Burger King filed a complaint, which was the inception of this lawsuit, seeking to enjoin the use of Burger King trademarks by Family Dining at the Warminster Restaurant. The Court granted a Temporary Restraining Order until a hearing on the complaint could be held. On May 13, 1975, the parties reached an agreement on terms under which the Burger King trademarks could be used at the Warminster Restaurant. Pursuant to the agreement Burger King filed an amended complaint seeking the instant declaratory relief. Subsequently and also pursuant to this agreement Family Dining opened its tenth Restaurant in Willow Grove, Pennsylvania, the construction of which began on March 28, 1975.

DISCUSSION

Family Dining raises several arguments in support of its motion pursuant to Rule 41(b). One of its principal arguments is that the termination provision should be found inoperative because otherwise it would result in a forfeiture to Family Dining. For reasons which have become evident during the presentation of Burger King's case the Court finds Family Dining's position compelling both on legal and equitable grounds and is thus persuaded that the Territorial Agreement should not be declared terminated. . . .

In bringing this suit Burger King maintains that . . . since Family Dining clearly failed to perform its promises the Court must, in accordance with the express language of Article II, declare the contract terminated. Burger King further argues that because Family Dining did not earn exclusivity beyond the ninth year, upon termination, it could not be found that Family Dining would forfeit anything in which it had an interest.

Contrary to the analysis offered by Burger King, the Court considers the development rate a condition subsequent, not a promise, which operates to divest Family Dining of exclusivity. Where words in a contract raise no duty in and of themselves but rather modify or limit the promisee's right to enforce the promise such words are considered to be a condition. Whether words constitute a condition or a promise is a matter of the intention of the parties to be ascertained from a reasonable construction of the language used, considered in light of the surrounding circumstances. *Feinberg v. Automobile Banking Corporation*, 353 F.Supp. 508, 512 (E.D.Pa.1973). . . . It seems clear that the true purpose of the Territorial Agreement was to create a long term promise of exclusivity to act as an inducement to Family Dining to develop Bucks and Montgomery Counties within a certain time frame. A careful reading of the agreement indicates that it raises no duties, as such, in Family Dining. Both Article I and Article II contain language which refers to ninety years of exclusivity subject to limitation. For instance, Article I provides in part that "[t]his Agreement shall remain in effect and licensee shall retain the exclusive territory for a period of ninety (90) years from the date hereof, provided that at the end of one, two . . ." Failure to comply with the development rate operates to defeat liability on Burger King's promise of exclusivity. . . .

The question arises whether Burger King has precluded itself from asserting Family Dining's untimeliness on the basis that Burger King did not demand literal adherence to the development rate throughout most of the first ten years of the contract. Nothing is commoner in contracts than for a promisor to protect himself by making his promise conditional. Ordinarily a party would be entitled to have such an agreement strictly enforced, however, before doing so the Court must consider not only the written contract but also the acts and conduct of the parties in carrying out the agreement. As Judge Kraft, in effect, provided in *Dempsey v. Stauffer*, 182 F.Supp. 806, 810 (E.D.Pa.1960), after one party by conduct indicates that literal performance will not be required, he cannot without notice and a reasonable time begin demanding literal performance.

In the early going Burger King did not demand that Family Dining perform in exact compliance with the development schedule. It failed to introduce any evidence indicating that a change in attitude had been communicated to Family Dining. At the time of the Donaldson letter Family Dining's non-compliance with the development rate was no worse than it was with respect to the fourth and fifth Restaurants. The letter itself was sent by a documents administrator rather than a Burger King official and it seems to imply that the Territorial Agreement would not be terminated. Assuming that at some point between May and November, or even at the time of the Donaldson letter, Ferris realized literal performance would be required, the circumstances of this type of development are such that Burger King was unreasonable in declaring a termination such a short time after, if not concurrent with, notice that literal performance would be required....

Based on the foregoing the Court concludes that Burger King is not entitled to have the condition protecting its promise strictly enforced.

Moreover and more important, even though a suit for declaratory relief can be characterized as neither legal nor equitable, *United States Fidelity & Guaranty Co. v. Koch*, 102 F.2d 288, 290 (3d Cir.1939), giving strict effect to the termination provision involves divesting Family Dining of exclusivity, which, in the Court's view, would amount to a forfeiture. As a result the Court will not ignore considerations of fairness and believes that equitable principles, as well, ought to govern the outcome of this suit. *Barraclough v. Atlantic Refining*, 230 Pa.Super. 276, 326 A.2d 477 (1974).

The Restatement, Contracts, § 302 provides:

"A condition may be excused without other reason if its requirement

"(a) will involve extreme forfeiture or penalty, and

"(b) its existence or occurrence forms no essential part of the exchange for the promisor's performance."

Taking the latter consideration first, it seems clear that throughout the early duration of the contract Burger King was more concerned with a general development of the territory than it was with exact compliance with the terms of the development rate. Burger King offered no evidence that it ever considered literal performance to be critical. In fact, the evidence indicates quite the contrary. Even though McLamore testified that he never contemplated a delay of the duration which occurred with the ninth and tenth Restaurants, he felt a total delay of approximately 19 months with respect to the fourth and fifth Restaurants was nearly in compliance. On the basis of his prior conduct and his testimony considered in its entirety his comments on this point command little weight.

Clearly Burger King's attitude with respect to the development rate changed. Interestingly enough it was sometime after Burger King realized Bucks and Montgomery Counties could support substantially more than ten Restaurants as had been originally thought. It was also at a time after Rosewall replaced McLamore as chief executive officer.

... In short, the evidence fails to establish that either Burger King or Family Dining considered the development rate critical. If it eventually did become critical it was not until very late in the first ten years and in such a way that, in conscience, it cannot be used to the detriment of Family Dining.

... [T]he Court believes that if the right of exclusivity were to be extinguished by termination it would constitute a forfeiture. In arguing that by termination Family Dining will lose nothing that it earned, Burger King overlooks the risks assumed and the efforts expended by Family Dining, largely without assistance from Burger King, in making the venture successful in the exclusive territory. While it is true that Family Dining realized a return on its investment, certainly part of this return was the prospect of continued exclusivity. Moreover, this is not a situation where Burger King did not receive any benefit from the relationship.

In making the promise of exclusivity Burger King intended to induce Family Dining to develop its Restaurants in the exclusive territory. There is no evidence that the failure to fulfill the time feature of this inducement was the result of any intentional or negligent conduct on the part of Family Dining. And at the present time there are ten Restaurants in operation which was all the inducement was intended to elicit. Assuming all ten were built on time Burger King would have been able to expect some definable level of revenue, a percentage of which it lost due to the delay. Burger King did not, however, attempt to establish the amount of this loss at trial.

In any event if Family Dining were forced to forfeit the right of exclusivity it would lose something of incalculable value based on its investment of time and money developing the area, the significant risks assumed and the fact that there remains some 76 years of exclusivity under the Territorial Agreement. Such a loss would be without any commensurate breach on its part since the injury caused to Burger King by the delay is relatively modest and within definable limits. Thus a termination of the Territorial Agreement would result in an extreme forfeiture to Family Dining.

In accordance with the foregoing the Court finds that under the law and based upon the facts adduced in Burger King's case, it is not entitled to a declaration that the Territorial Agreement is terminated. Therefore, Family Dining's Rule 41(b) motion for an involuntary dismissal is granted.

Questions

1. What was the contractual condition upon which the case turns? What was Burger King's argument based on this condition? Was it well-founded in the express language of the contract? Why did it fail?

2. A "waiver" generally is defined as the intentional relinquishment of a known right. Did Burger King waive its rights to rely on the condition? If so, for how long? What facts might establish a waiver? Does the possibility of a waiver further or retard the autonomy principle?

3. What facts would establish an excuse due to "disproportionate forfeiture" under RESTATEMENT (SECOND) OF CONTRACTS § 229? Is a disproportionate forfeiture just any big loss that the court can't stomach without doing something about it? Disproportion is a relationship between two things. If Family Dining's loss of its exclusive territory is a forfeiture, what must be disproportionate to that loss to make out an excuse? What are the relevant contractual interests in *Burger King*?

4. Could Burger King have recovered damages for its lost revenue due to the delayed opening of the last restaurant?

NOTE ON CONDITIONS WITHIN A PARTY'S CONTROL

A fully-specified contract is one that fixes the rights and duties of the parties with particularity in all possible circumstances. It should be obvious by now that no contract is fully-specified; the press of time, and limitations of language and human foresight render all contracts to some extent incomplete. In many contracts, moreover, the parties do not even want to settle everything at once. A developer putting together a shopping center, for example, must conclude dozens of interrelated contracts. The developer may not want to conclude a construction contract until some number of tenants have signed on; they may not want to sign on until a builder has committed to a completion date and other tenants have been secured. Networks of contracts can be linked by conditions so that all deals fall through unless all come through.

In such situations (and others) the occurrence of a condition may be within the control of one of the parties, as in the two cases that follow. Control over a condition to one's own duty to perform creates a moral hazard. The party in control can ensure that the condition does not occur, thereby allowing him to claim that he is not bound to perform. The courts seek to prevent that result by implying a duty of good faith on such a party.

Especially in this context, the question arises whether a party's good faith is to be judged by subjective or objective standards. When a contract is subject to one party's satisfaction with another's performance, for example, the standard litany distinguishes between matters of "commercial value or quality, operative fitness, or mechanical utility," which are judged objectively, and those of "fancy, taste, or judgment," which are judged subjectively. Mattei v. Hopper, 51 Cal.2d 119, 330 P.2d

625 (1958) (en banc). Under the objective standard, a court or jury considers only whether the party in control exercised its discretion reasonably, commercially reasonably, or for a reason within the justifiable expectations of the parties. Under a subjective standard, by contrast, the question is whether the discretion-exercising party was *motivated* by the right kinds of reasons. The difference is in whether it matters what the party had in mind that caused it to claim that it was dissatisfied. Consider how this issue should be resolved in the following pair of cases.

FRY v. GEORGE ELKINS CO.

District Court of Appeal, Second District, California, 1958.
162 Cal.App.2d 256, 327 P.2d 905.

Fox, Presiding Justice. Plaintiff brought this action to recover a deposit of $4,250 that he made in connection with his contemplated purchase of a home from defendants Miller. The court, however, awarded him a judgment for only $937.50. Plaintiff has appealed.

On May 20, 1956, plaintiff made an offer in writing, through defendant George Elkins Company, real estate broker, to purchase the Miller home for $42,500. Plaintiff put up his check for $4,250. The offer contained this provision: "This offer is further conditioned upon the buyer obtaining $20,000.00 loan at 5% for 20 years." The buyer was advised at that time that there was a 5 per cent loan on the property on which there was a balance of $16,650.00; that this loan was held by Western Mortgage Co.; that arrangements could likely be made to refinance the loan in line with the buyer's desire but that a loan upon the required terms could not be obtained from a bank. The owners immediately accepted Fry's offer and agreed in writing to pay the broker a 5 per cent commission, or one half of the deposit in the event the same was forfeited by the purchaser. A 30–day escrow was opened the next day. It recited the loan above mentioned and then provided: "The completion of this escrow is subject to buyer being able to refinance said loan to $20,000.00 at 5% per annum, maturing over a period of 20 years."

The buyer did not contact Western Mortgage either personally or by telephone relative to refinancing the loan. At the instance, however, of a representative of the Elkins organization, Mr. Reed, on behalf of Western Mortgage, mailed a loan application on May 28th to Fry, together with a letter stating that his company would consider a $20,000 loan at 5 per cent over a 15–year period. Reed contacted Fry twice regarding this loan by telephone but at no time did the latter ask whether Western Mortgage would make the loan for a 20–year term. He did, however, complain about the 2 per cent prepayment provision in the loan application in the event of payment within the first three years. On June 11th, Reed, having been told by the broker's representative, that a 20–year loan was essential to a sale, sent Fry another letter stating that Western would consider making the loan for that term. During the early part of

June Mrs. Lynch, of the Elkins organization, with whom Fry had had his initial dealings for the purchase of the house, assured him there was a $20,000 loan at 5 per cent for 20 years waiting for him at Western Mortgage and advised him to get down as quickly as he could and sign the papers. Fry was also told about the same time by both Mr. and Mrs. Miller that the required loan on the stated terms was available at Western Mortgage if he would just file the application papers. Fry, however, failed to file any application therefor. Reed's testimony indicates that if such application had been made by Fry the loan would have been made. It was approximately at this time that Fry told Mrs. Lynch, according to her testimony, that he had lost all interest in the house; that he had changed his plans; and that he was going to Hawaii as he had planned originally. Fry had in the meantime applied to two banks where he was known for the desired loan. Both banks, however, had rejected his application. Fry thereupon wrote the Millers attempting to rescind the deal because of his inability to obtain the loan on which the transaction was conditioned.

A couple of days after the expiration of the Fry escrow the Millers entered into another escrow with the Rothschilds for the sale of their home for $40,375 without a broker's commission. But in order to make the sale the Millers had to include certain items of personal property valued at $937.50. The transaction was concluded on June 27. Western Mortgage made a loan to the new purchasers on the property for $20,000 at 5 per cent for 20 years. Mr. Rothschild had requested Western Mortgage by telephone on June 14th to send him an application for a loan on this property. In order to get the escrow closed quickly (it was closed in 5 days) the Millers employed an attorney to handle the deal and paid him $250 for his services. A brokerage commission of $2,125 on the Fry transaction was retained by Elkins. The trial court deducted the total of these last three items ($3,312.50) from plaintiff's deposit of $4,250 and rendered judgment for plaintiff for the difference, viz., for $937.50. Being dissatisfied with the amount of this award plaintiff has appealed.

In seeking a reversal plaintiff argues that the evidence is insufficient to support certain findings and that the findings do not support the judgment. . . .

Plaintiff first challenges the finding to the effect that he did not in good faith attempt to refinance the encumbrance on the property by obtaining a $20,000, 5 per cent, 20–year loan. He bases his argument primarily on the fact that his application for such a loan was rejected by two banks. It is a matter of common knowledge that the lending policies of different classes of financial institutions vary greatly. This is particularly true with respect to the period for which a loan may be made. The fact that a bank is unwilling to make 20–year loans on residential property in a particular locality does not necessarily justify an inference that other lending institutions will not make such a loan. At the initial stage of this transaction plaintiff was advised of the unlikelihood of obtaining the requisite loan from a bank but that it probably could be obtained from Western Mortgage, which already had a substantial loan on the property. Notwithstanding this advice, plaintiff contented himself with making applications only at the banks and made no application or inquiry of Western Mortgage for such a loan and declined to contact that institution when told that the required loan was available upon his signing the application and other necessary papers. Furthermore, there was evidence that plaintiff had changed his plans and was no longer interested in buying the property. From the foregoing evidence the trial court reasonably could infer that plaintiff did not in good faith try to refinance the loan in question.

Plaintiff seeks to justify his position on the ground that the loan application from Western Mortgage contained a two per cent prepayment privilege in the event the loan was paid during the first three years. The simple answer to this argument is that no such restriction was placed on the conditions of the loan by the plaintiff either in the deposit receipt or in the escrow agreement. He was therefore not entitled to reject the loan because of the inclusion of such a prepayment privilege.

Plaintiff's next contention is that the evidence is not sufficient to support the finding that he refused to perform all the obligations on his part to be performed under the agreement and thereby was guilty of a breach of the agreement. Implicit in the refinancing of the loan in question was the obligation of the plaintiff to put forth a good faith effort to obtain such refinancing on the terms he had specified. The court found, on substantial evidence as we have pointed out, that plaintiff did not in good faith carry out that obligation, which was essential to the consummation of the deal. This was obviously a breach of the agreement between the parties....

Plaintiff argues that the Millers were not obligated to pay the Elkins Company, as broker, a commission of $2,125. By the terms of the deposit agreement the Millers promised to pay the broker a commission of 5 per cent or one half of the deposit ($2,125.00) in the event the same was forfeited by the purchaser, provided the same did not exceed the full amount of the commission. The deposit was $4,250, one half thereof ($2,125) was equal to 5 per cent of the purchase price. It is clear from the record that the Millers were at all times ready, able and willing to convey the property on the agreed terms. It is also clear that the deal fell through because plaintiff was at fault. Under these circumstances the Millers became obligated to the broker for the agreed commission of $2,125....

The judgment is affirmed.

PANNONE v. GRANDMAISON

Connecticut Superior Court, Judicial District of Waterbury, 1990.
1990 WL 265273.

McWEENY, JUDGE. In this action, the plaintiffs seek the return of an $18,000 real estate deposit with interest. The deposit was pursuant to a contract entered into between the parties to this litigation; in which the plaintiffs were the buyers and defendants the sellers. The contract contained a contingency clause which provided in pertinent part: "Offer is contingent upon Purchaser's approval of the result of a home inspection, a termite inspection and a radon gas inspection."

The plaintiffs retained a home building inspector who performed the home and radon gas inspection. The inspector provided a report to plaintiff (Exhibit #7) indicating that the results were "well below the level that concerns the EPA." The report also indicated that as to the radon level found:

"Exposures in this range (1 to 4pCi/L) do present some risk, to the more sensitive occupants, of contracting lung cancer. However, reductions of concentration this low may be difficult, and sometimes impossible, to achieve. If the screening measurement result is less than 4pCi/L, a follow up measurement is not necessary...."

The plaintiffs' inspector indicated at trial that it would be unlikely to get a lower reading in Connecticut.

The plaintiffs offered evidence of their preparation for the closing. (Exhibits 4, 5, 6 and testimony of Joseph Pannone) and of their intent to close until their receipt of the radon test result on September 23, 1988.

Mr. Pannone also testified concerning his sensitivity to anything connected to radioactivity; resulting from his exposure to radiation during the Korean War service in the U.S. Air Force. The service included missions as an airplane radio operator, monitoring radiation levels resulting from Soviet atomic testing. Evidence was also introduced to demonstrate that his concern was long standing (Exhibits 8, 9, and 10), though Mr. Pannone currently enjoys good health.

The plaintiffs, by letter of September 26, 1988, cancelled the contract and demanded the return of the deposit.

The plaintiffs have never tested their current residence for radon gas, though they have resided there for four years. Plaintiffs had on two occasions prior to the September 26, 1988, cancellation attempted to cancel the agreement because of perceived failure of the defendant-sellers to perform conditions under the contract.

The parties had a verbal dispute on the premises on September 26, 1988, prior to the cancellation letter being transmitted.

The authority which directs the court's resolution of this difficult case is found in our Supreme Court's decision in Warner v. Konover, 210 Conn. 150 (1989) and Central New Haven Development Corporation v. LaCrepe, 177 Conn. 212 (1979). The cases rely on the Restatement (Second) of Contracts which provides: "Every contract imposes upon each party a duty of good faith and fair dealing in its performance and its enforcement." 210 Conn. at 154, 177 Conn. at 217.

The plaintiffs were thus obligated to exercise this discretion in reviewing the radon gas inspection results in good faith and fair dealing. . . .

In the instant case, the plaintiffs exercised their discretion in a manner which they could not justify in terms of objective reasonableness. It was, however, within the contemplation of the parties that the inspection contingencies were subject to "Purchaser's approval," and thus involved an element of personal satisfaction with results.

The court finds that under the circumstances of this case, the plaintiffs' exercise of discretion was subject to a standard of subjective good faith.

The long history of the plaintiff Joseph Pannone's perception of his cancer risk and phobia concerning radiation meets by the barest preponderance the burden of a rational though subjective good faith exercise of discretion.

The prior difficulties in the contract negotiations are attributable to the plaintiff Joseph Pannone's extremely exacting and difficult nature, and not as evidence of a desire to break the contract.

The court's conclusion is reinforced by the evidence that the plaintiffs have not subsequently purchased another home, or sought to renegotiate price with the defendants. . . .

The plaintiffs seek, in addition to the return of their deposit other damages, but have failed to meet their burden of proof as to such claims. . . .

Questions

1. What was the condition in *Fry*? Did it occur? Why, then, was Fry held to be in breach of contract? Does the court employ an objective or subjective standard of good faith? Was Fry treated unjustly?

2. What was the condition in *Pannone*? Should the court employ an objective or subjective standard of good faith? Was Grandmaison treated unjustly?

3. *Problems.*

     a. Alec entered into a contract to purchase a country home where he could keep horses. The contract contained the standard condition that the buyer obtain financing, in this case specifying a 30 year fixed rate mortgage at not more than 8% interest. Three days after concluding the deal, Alec decided he'd rather get a home on the ocean. He visits your law office to find out if he can get out of the deal. Prepare to interview Alec with a view to determining whether you can advise him that he can get out of the deal without liability for breach of contract. What questions would you ask? Are there any legitimate reasons for getting this client out of the deal? See Ide Farm & Stable, Inc. v. Cardi, 110 R.I. 735, 297 A.2d 643 (1972).

b. George, a broker, contracted to purchase cherries from a grower, Gracie, throughout the season, "provided that all cherries tendered shall be satisfactory for making candies." George accepted the first three shipments under the contract, but rejected the fourth and several thereafter, saying that they would not make satisfactory candies. As counsel for Gracie, what facts would you want to develop to determine whether or not the broker rejected the cherries in good faith? Would good faith here be governed by a subjective or objective standard? What difference would it make? See Devoine Co. v. International Co., 151 Md. 690, 136 A. 37 (1927).

GODBURN v. MESERVE

Supreme Court of Connecticut, 1944.
130 Conn. 723, 37 A.2d 235.

Action by Lulu Godburn and another against George Meserve and another, executors of the estate of Carrie J. Wells, deceased, to recover damages for breach of a contract by defendants' decedent and for value of services rendered to her, which action was tried to a jury.

Brown, Judge. In this action based on an agreement by the plaintiffs to provide and care for the defendants' decedent in her house in Stratford in consideration of her promise to leave the property to them by will, the jury rendered a verdict for the plaintiffs which, it was undisputed, was predicated upon the decedent's breach of an express agreement alleged in the first count. There was a second count based on quantum meruit. The defendants have appealed from the court's denial of their motion to set aside the verdict and from the judgment, assigning error in the court's charge to the jury. In the view which we take of the case it is necessary to consider only the claimed error in the court's denial of the motion.

For more than three years prior to February 21, 1936, the plaintiffs had lived as tenants of the decedent in a house owned by her in Stratford. As of the above date, the decedent, seventy-six years of age, was living alone in the house next door, which she also owned. On that date, the parties entered into an express written agreement which provided that for the remainder of the decedent's life they were to live together in her homestead, she occupying the front upstairs room and they furnishing her with board, heat, light and laundry, providing care for her in case of any minor ailments or sickness not requiring a nurse or hospital service, and paying ten dollars per month rent. It further provided that the plaintiffs' family was to be limited to themselves and daughter, and that the decedent was to leave the property to them by will at her death. The decedent made a will in accordance with the agreement and the plaintiffs occupied the house with the decedent and provided for her as stipulated until on or about August 5, 1941, when the plaintiffs moved out and did nothing further in performance of the contract. Thereupon the decedent revoked her will. She died May 21, 1942, at the age of eighty-three. During the first two years that the parties lived together their relations were generally harmonious and mutually agreeable, but thereafter increasing friction developed. Just before the plaintiffs moved out Mr. Godburn proposed a modification of the agreement whereby the decedent would have two rooms, get her own meals and do her own laundry, and the plaintiffs would make an increased cash payment monthly. The decedent refused to modify the agreement. These facts are undisputed.

The jury could reasonably have further found that the plaintiffs faithfully and fully performed their part of the contract up to the time they left; that the decedent objected to the plaintiffs' having their grandchildren and others stay in the home as their guests; that she objected to being left alone in the house at night and thus prevented the plaintiffs from going out or away on vacation; that she constantly found fault with many minor things around the house; that she, without reason, objected to the amount of water used by the plaintiffs which she had to pay for; that she, likewise without reason, demanded food other than that which the plaintiffs provided; constantly objected to the manner in which Mrs. Godburn cooked food and at times refused to eat it, developed a habit of tapping her foot on the floor while eating, and once when Mr. Godburn was seriously ill made a disturbance because her meal was not served on time; and that this course of conduct so disturbed the plaintiffs' home life that they became very nervous, and rendered it very disagreeable and difficult for them to continue to reside with her.

The contract was bilateral containing mutual and dependent covenants demanding of each of the parties readiness and willingness to perform. It therefore required, "as a condition of judicial enforcement or redress for breach at the complaint of either such readiness and willingness on his part or a showing of sufficient excuse for their absence. Phillips v. Sturm, 91 Conn. 331, 335, 99 A. 689." ... Therefore here, if the plaintiffs on their part were prevented by the decedent from completing the contract, they were entitled to bring their action for damages for her breach of it. Valente v. Weinberg, 80 Conn. 134, 135, 67 A. 369, 13 L.R.A., N.S., 448.... However, "In order to amount to a prevention of performance by the adversary party, the conduct on the part of the party who is alleged to have prevented performance must be wrongful, and, accordingly, in excess of his legal rights." 5 Page, Contracts, § 2919, p. 5145; Landsdowne v. Reihmann, Ky., 124 S.W. 353. Although " 'where a party stipulates that another shall do a certain thing, he thereby impliedly promises that he will himself do nothing which will hinder or obstruct that other in doing that thing' " (3 Williston, Contracts, Rev. Ed., § 677, p. 1956), manifestly this principle has no application where the hindrance is due to some action of the promisor which he was permitted to take under either the express or implied terms of the contract. See Restatement, 1 Contracts, § 295. The mere fact that permitted conduct of this nature by one promisor renders unpleasant or inconvenient performance by the other of his agreement effects no discharge of that obligation. See 5 Page, Contracts, § 2919, p. 5146; Smoot's Case, 15 Wall. 36, 46, 82 U.S. 36, 46, 21 L.Ed. 107....

Accordingly, the question for determination is whether the decedent's conduct complained of was wrongful in the sense of being violative of her obligations under the contract. In other words, was it or was it not conduct which must be said to have been fairly within the contemplation of the parties when the agreement was entered into? See Huminsky v. Gary Nat. Bank, 107 W.Va. 658, 150 S.E. 9. In addition to the facts already mentioned, the undisputed testimony was that for twenty years prior to the agreement Mr. Godburn had known the decedent as a customer in the grocery store where he was employed, that during the last three and one-half years of this period, while he and his family were living next door as her tenants, the plaintiffs came to know the decedent very well, that she was regularly and frequently in their home as a guest and ate meals there, and that they knew she was an elderly lady apparently about seventy-six or seven years of age. It is a matter of common knowledge that a gradually increasing impairment of powers and a not unusual tendency to more or less eccentricity naturally are to be expected as incident to the advancing years of one of that age, and under the circumstances the only reasonable conclusion upon the record before us is that the decedent's conduct was fairly within the contemplation of the parties under their contract as made. The gist of the situation is apparently well summarized by Mr. Godburn's testimony that "the only thing she complained about was the eats," which everybody else thought were all right, that her conduct was upsetting and disturbing to the plaintiffs and that they "didn't have to take it" and they "wouldn't." It follows from what we have said that not only is there no evidence that the decedent "forced the plaintiffs to leave said premises in violation of the terms of the contract," as alleged in the complaint, but furthermore there is none that what she did was "wrongful, and, accordingly, in excess of [her] legal rights" within the principle quoted above. The defendants' motion to set aside the verdict should therefore have been granted.

There is error, the judgment is set aside, and a new trial is ordered.

Questions

1. What is the plaintiff's doctrinal argument? What is the defendant's doctrinal response? Exactly how do they join issue?

2. Did Ms. Wells breach the contract? Why not? What would it take for her to breach?

3. *Problem.*

Altgeld, a broker of railroad supplies, contracted to sell Gompers 2,600 tons of iron rails, to be delivered in New York harbor on an agreed schedule at a price of $410 per ton. Altgeld failed to deliver any rails. Gompers claimed that he had to cover elsewhere at an average price of $500 per ton. Altgeld visits your law office to complain that Gompers was dealing dirty. Altgeld said that there were only three suppliers of iron rails in the East and that the supply was pretty tight. He is angry because, before he could contract for the rails he had committed to Gompers, Gompers had gone to his suppliers and bought up all the rails that they could supply within the contract period. He says that he failed to deliver because it would have cost him about $1,500 per ton to bring rails in from Europe. What do you advise him? See Iron Trade Products Co. v. Wilkoff Co., 272 Pa. 172, 116 A. 150 (1922).

Chapter 6

THE SECURITY PRINCIPLE

The law requires each party to a contract formation or performance to do its part to respect the other party's reasonable expectations and reliance.

Recall the Note on "Interests," "Rights," and "Duties," above at p. 7. It was there suggested that a person has an *interest* when he or she has a stake in how another person conducts him- or herself. As reflected most obviously in the law of contract damages, the law protects three main contractual interests—the expectation, reliance, and restitution interests. Even when one party to a contract has one or more of these contractual interests, however, it does not follow that it will be vindicated in a lawsuit. As the following cases often illustrate, both parties may have contractual interests that conflict in a case. It may fall to the law to sort out which of the interests in a particular case are the more deserving of legal protection. The more deserving ("stronger") interest then is described as a "contract right." This signifies that the interest is strong enough under the circumstances to justify imposing a "contract duty" on the other party.

We will see in this Chapter that the expectation interest can be divided between an interest in present performance and an interest in future performance. The idea of an interest in performance not yet due, and which may be harmed before performance is due, implements the security principle.

SECTION 1. INTERESTS OF THE PARTIES IMPAIRED BY A BREACH

The security principle implies that a contract "imposes an obligation on each party that the other's expectation of receiving due performance will not be impaired." U.C.C. § 2–609(1) (quoted in RESTATEMENT (SECOND) OF CONTRACTS § 251, com. a). A party thus has an expectation interest in performance as and when promised and also in "a continuing sense of reliance and security that the promised performance will be forthcoming when due." U.C.C. § 2–609, com. 1 (quoted in RESTATEMENT

(SECOND) OF CONTRACTS § 251, com. a). This interest in security during the executory phase of a contract is protected by the law of breach by anticipatory repudiation and related doctrines. It may, however, be qualified by the interests of the party in breach, much as a nonbreaching party's damages may be qualified to minimize avoidable losses to the party in breach. In this section, we concentrate on how the doctrinal law accommodates these contractual interests when possible, giving priority of course to the nonbreaching party when accommodation is not feasible. The next section, on material breach, builds upon the groundwork laid here.

———

RESTATEMENT (SECOND) OF CONTRACTS § 238

———

KINGSTON v. PRESTON

Court of King's Bench, 1773.
99 Eng.Rep. 606.

[The plaintiff joined the defendant's silk business as an apprentice. The covenant on articles called for the defendant to retire after a year and a quarter. The plaintiff was to continue the business with a person to be nominated by the defendant. The plaintiff promised to pay £ 250 per month for his stake in the business. The plaintiff also agreed to give the defendant sufficient security for these payments, to be approved by the defendant before transferring the business. The defendant refused to surrender the business as promised. In an action by the plaintiff alleging the foregoing facts, the defendant pleaded that the plaintiff failed to give sufficient security. The following account of the case is from the argument of counsel in Jones v. Barkley, 2 Dougl. 684, 99 Eng.Rep. 434, 437 38 (K.B. 1781), which is far clearer than the original (unofficial) report.]

"On the part of the plaintiff, the case was argued by Mr. Buller, who contended that the covenants were mutual and independent, and therefore a plea of the breach of one of the covenants to be performed by the plaintiff was no bar to an action for a breach by the defendant of one which he had bound himself to perform, but that the defendant might have his remedy for the breach by the plaintiff in a separate action. On the other side, Mr. Gross insisted that the covenants were dependent in their nature, and therefore performance must be alleged: the security to be given for the money was manifestly the chief object of the transaction, and it would be highly unreasonable to construe the agreement so as to oblige the defendant to give up a beneficial business, and valuable stock-in-trade, and trust to the plaintiff's personal security (who might, and, indeed was admitted to be worth nothing), for the performance of his part.

"In delivering the judgment of the Court, Lord Mansfield expressed himself to the following effect: There are three kinds of covenants: 1. Such as are called mutual and independent, where either party may recover damages from the other for the injury he may have received by a breach of the covenants in his favor, and where it is no excuse for the defendant to allege a breach of the covenants on the part of the plaintiff. 2. There are covenants which are conditions and dependent, in which the performance of one depends on the prior performance of another, and, therefore, till this prior condition is performed, the other party is not liable to an action on his covenant. 3. There is also a third sort of covenants, which are mutual conditions to be performed at the same time; and in these, if one party was ready and offered to perform his part, and the other neglected or refused to perform his, he who was ready and offered has fulfilled his engagement, and may maintain an action for the default of the other; though it is not certain that either is obliged to do the first act. His Lordship then proceeded to say, that the dependence or independence of covenants was to be collected from the evident sense and meaning of the parties, and that, however transposed they might be in the deed, their precedency must depend on the order of time in which the intent of the transaction requires their performance. That, in the case before the Court, it would be the greatest injustice if the plaintiff should prevail: the essence of the agreement was, that the defendant should not trust to the personal security of the plaintiff, but, before he delivered up his stock and business, should have good security for the payment of the money. The giving of such security, therefore, must necessarily be a condition precedent. Judgment was accordingly given for the defendant, because the part to be performed by the plaintiff was clearly a condition precedent."

Questions

1. Why would one party want the other party to go first? Wouldn't both want the other to go first? Can one party do something less than full performance that should be sufficient to require the other to perform?

2. Why should the law presume that mutual promises are conditioned on each other?

3. *Problems.*

     a. Dr. Gene is a plastic surgeon who worked for Dr. Will under a one year written contract. It provided that, upon termination, Dr. Gene would not offer or perform plastic surgery within a 50–mile radius of Dr. Will's clinic. Six months into the contract, the two doctors had a falling out, generating considerable distrust between them. Dr. Will now solicits your advice on whether he can discharge Dr. Gene without exposing himself to competition from her within the 50–mile radius. What should you advise him? See RESTATEMENT (SECOND) OF CONTRACTS § 232, Ill. 3.

     b. Gabby bought Roy's muffler shop for $52,000. The contract required Gabby to pay $20,000 immediately and then installments of $10,000 on July 1 of each of the next three years. The contract also obligated Roy not to compete with Gabby by operating a muffler shop within a 50–mile radius of Gabby's shop for a period of five years. After receiving the first installment of $10,000, Roy opened a muffler shop in a town 22 miles from Gabby's shop. Gabby brought suit to enjoin Roy from operating the shop. Before that suit was concluded, the next installment came due. Should you advise Gabby to make the payment?

RESTATEMENT (SECOND) OF CONTRACTS §§ 250–57

UNIFORM COMMERCIAL CODE §§ 2–609–2–611

HOCHSTER v. DE LA TOUR

Court of Queen's Bench, 1853.
2 E. & B. 678, 118 Eng.Rep. 922.

This was an action for breach of contract. On the trial before Erle, J., at the London sittings in last Easter term, it appeared that plaintiff was a courier, who in April, 1852, was engaged by defendant to accompany him on a tour, to commence on 1st June, 1852, on the terms mentioned in the declaration. On the 11th May, 1852, defendant wrote to plaintiff that he had changed his mind, and declined his services. He refused to make him any compensation. The action was commenced on 22d May. The plaintiff, between the commencement of the action and the 1st of June, obtained an engagement with Lord Ashburton, on equally good terms, but not commencing till 4th July. The defendant's counsel objected that there could be no breach of the contract before the 1st of June. The learned judge was of contrary opinion, but reserved leave to enter a nonsuit on this objection. The other questions were left to the jury, who found for plaintiff. . . .

LORD CAMPBELL, CHIEF JUSTICE., now delivered the judgment of the court. On this motion in arrest of judgment, the question arises, whether, if there be an engagement between A. and B., whereby B. engages to employ A. on and from a future day for a given period of time, to travel with him into a foreign country as a courier, and to start with him in that capacity on that day, A. being to receive a monthly salary during the continuance of such service, B. may, before the day, refuse to perform the agreement and break and renounce it, so as to entitle A. before the day to commence an action against B. to recover damages for breach of the agreement; A. having been ready and willing to perform it, till it was broken and renounced by B. The defendant's counsel very powerfully contended that, if the plaintiff was not contented to dissolve the contract, and to abandon all remedy upon it, he was bound to remain ready and willing to perform it till the day when the actual employment as courier in the service of the defendant was to begin; and that there could be no breach of the agreement, before that day, to give a right of action. But it cannot be laid down as a universal rule that, where by agreement an act is to be done on a future day, no action can be brought for a breach of the agreement till the day for doing the act has arrived. If a man promises to marry a woman on a future day, and before that day marries another woman, he is instantly liable to an action for breach of promise of marriage. *Short v. Stone* (8 Q.B. 358). If a man contracts to execute a lease on and from a future day for a certain term, and, before that day, executes a lease to another for the same term, he may be immediately sued for breaking the contract. *Ford v. Tiley* (7 B. & C. 325). So if a man contracts to sell and deliver specific goods on a future day, and before the day he sells and delivers them to another he is immediately liable to an action at the suit of the person with whom he first contracted to sell and deliver them. *Bowdell v. Parsons* (10 East, 359). One reason alleged in support of such an action is, that the defendant has, before the day, rendered it impossible for him to perform the contract at the day; but this does not necessarily follow; for, prior to the day fixed for doing the act, the first wife may have died, a surrender of the lease executed might be obtained, and the defendant might have repurchased the goods so as to be in a situation to sell and deliver them to the plaintiff. Another reason may be that, where there is a contract to do an act on a future day, there is a relation constituted between the parties in the meantime by the contract, and that they impliedly promise that in the meantime neither will do anything to the prejudice of the other inconsistent with that relation. As an example, a man and woman engaged to marry are affianced to one another during the period between the time of the engagement and the celebration of the marriage. In this very case of traveller and courier, from the day of the hiring till the day when the employment was to begin, they were engaged to each other; and it seems to be a breach of an implied contract if either of them renounced the engagement. This reasoning seems in accordance with the unanimous decisions of the Exchequer Chamber in *Elderton v. Emmens* (6 C.B. 160), which we have followed in subsequent cases in this court. The declaration in the present case, in alleging a breach, states a great deal more than a passing intention on the part of the defendant which he may repent of, and could only be proved by evidence that he had utterly renounced the contract, or done some act which rendered it impossible for him to perform it. If the plaintiff has no remedy for breach of the contract unless he treats the contract as in force, and acts upon it down to the 1st June, 1852, it follows that, till then, he must enter into no employment which will interfere with his promise "to start with the defendant on such travels on the day and year," and that he must then be properly equipped in all respects as a courier for a three months tour on the continent of Europe. But it is surely much more rational, and more for the benefit of both parties, that, after the renunciation of the agreement by the defendant, the plaintiff should be at liberty to consider himself absolved from any future performance of it, retaining his right to sue for any damage he has suffered from the breach of it. Thus, instead of remaining idle and laying out money in preparations which must be useless, he is at liberty to seek service under another employer, which would go in mitigation of the damages to which he would otherwise be entitled for a breach of the contract. It seems strange that the defendant, after renouncing the contract, and absolutely declaring that he will never act under it, should be permitted to object that faith is given to his assertion, and that an opportunity is not left to him of changing his mind. If the plaintiff is barred of any remedy by entering into an engagement inconsistent with starting as a courier with the defendant on the 1st June, he is prejudiced by putting faith in the defendant's assertion; and it would be more consistent with principle if the defendant were precluded from saying that he had not broken the contract when he declared that he entirely renounced it. Suppose that the defendant, at the time of his renunciation, had embarked on a voyage for Australia, so as to render it physically impossible for him to employ the plaintiff as a courier on the continent of Europe in the months of June, July and August, 1852; according to decided cases, the action might have been brought before the 1st June; but the renunciation may have been founded on other facts, to be given in evidence, which would equally have rendered the defendant's performance of the contract impossible. The man who wrongfully renounces a contract into which he has deliberately entered cannot justly complain if he is immediately sued for a compensation in damages by the man whom he has injured; and it seems reasonable to allow an option to the injured party, either to sue immediately, or to wait till the time when the act was to be done, still holding it as prospectively binding for the exercise of this option, which may be advantageous to the innocent party, and cannot be prejudicial to the wrongdoer. An argument against the action before the 1st of June is urged from the difficulty of calculating the damages; but this argument is equally strong against an action before the 1st of September, when the three months would expire. In either case, the jury in assessing the damages would be justified in looking to all that happened, or was likely to happen, to increase or mitigate the loss of the plaintiff down to the day of trial....

If it should be held that, upon a contract to do an act on a future day, a renunciation of the contract by one party dispenses with a condition to be performed in the meantime by the other, there seems no reason for requiring that other to wait till the day arrives before seeking his remedy by action; and the only ground on which the condition can be dispensed with seems to be, that the renunciation may be treated as a breach of the contract.

Upon the whole, we think that the declaration in this case is sufficient. It gives us great satisfaction to reflect that, the question being on the record, our opinion may be reviewed in a Court of Error. In the meantime we must give judgment for the plaintiff.

Judgment for plaintiff.

Questions

1. What is the sequence of key events? What does the plaintiff want in this case of first impression? Is he interested only in damages? Why does he want it at the time he makes his claim? Why does the defendant oppose his claim? Why does the court give the plaintiff what he wants? Should a court give it to him?

2. Does it matter when suit is brought? Assume that, the facts being otherwise the same, Hochster brought suit after returning from the trip with Lord Ashburton. Same result?

3. *Problems*.

    a. On May 10, Alice contracted to sell and Gleason to buy land for a honeymooner's resort, with the closing scheduled for July 10. On June 1, Alice told Gleason, "I am not sure that I can perform, and I don't intend to do so unless I am legally required to do it." Did Alice breach by anticipatory repudiation?

    b. The facts are the same as in a., but Alice told Norton that she was sure she would not perform the contract with Gleason. Did Alice breach by anticipatory repudiation?

    c. The facts are the same as in a., but on June 1, Gleason learned that Alice mortgaged the land to Norton as security for a loan that was not due and payable for six more months. Did Alice breach by anticipatory repudiation?

    d. The facts are the same as in a., but on June 1 Gleason defaulted on a loan payment then due to someone else and Alice learned of the default from the local newspaper. Did Gleason breach by anticipatory repudiation?

UNITED STATES v. SEACOAST GAS CO.

United States Court of Appeals, Fifth Circuit, 1953.
204 F.2d 709.

HUTCHESON, CHIEF JUDGE. Brought against Seacoast Gas Company and the surety on its performance bond, the suit was for damages alleged to have resulted from the anticipatory breach by the Gas Company of its contract with plaintiff to supply gas to a federal housing project during the period from April 15, 1947, to June 15, 1948. The claim was: that on October 7, 1947, while performance of the contract was in progress, Seacoast anticipatorily breached the contract by writing plaintiff unequivocally that, because of plaintiff's breach of the contract, Seacoast intended to cancel same as of November 15, 1947; that the plaintiff immediately notified Seacoast that it did not recognize any right in it to cease performance and that it proposed to advertise for bids to insure a continued supply of gas if Seacoast's breach persisted; that, thereafter, having advertised for bids and on November 6th, having received the low bid from Trion Company, it on that date notified Seacoast by letter that unless it retracted its repudiation of the contract within three days from the letter date, Trion's bid would be accepted and Seacoast and its surety would be held liable for breach of contract; and that thereafter Seacoast not having retracted within the time fixed, plaintiff on November 10, accepted Trion's bid and, pursuant thereto, began its preparations to execute with Trion a contract for a price in excess of that provided in the Seacoast contract, and Seacoast is liable to plaintiff for this excess.

Defendant Seacoast, admitting in its pleading and its testimony that the facts were substantially as claimed by plaintiff, defended on the ground: that it had retracted its notice of repudiation and given assurance of its intention to continue to perform before the plaintiff had actually signed the new contract; and that, since, as it claimed, plaintiff had not then substantially changed its position or suffered any damages as a result of Seacoast's notice to terminate the contract and cease performance under it, the retraction was timely and healed the breach.

Upon the issue thus joined, the cause was tried to the court without a jury, and the court stating the question for decision thus, "The question in this case is as to whether Seacoast Gas Company, Inc. withdrew its notice of cancellation of its contract prior to the rendering of the contract to the Trion Gas Company," found that it had done so. On the basis of this finding and a further finding that on November 13, two days before the termination date which Seacoast had fixed in its notice, Zell, who was president both of Seacoast and of Trion Company, to whom the new contract was awarded, notified the regional counsel for the Public Housing Authority that Seacoast admitted it had no right to cancel the contract and was rescinding its notice, the court held that the anticipatory breach had been healed and plaintiff could not recover.

Appealing from this judgment, plaintiff is here insisting that under the settled law governing anticipatory breaches not only as it is laid down in Georgia but generally, Seacoast's retraction came too late to heal the breach, and the judgment must be reversed.

Appellees, on their part, insist that the judgment appealed from was soundly based in law and in fact and must be affirmed.

We do not think so. The undisputed facts establish: that Zell, president of both companies, was present at the opening of the new bids on November 6, 1947, and upon being asked to withdraw Seacoast's notice that it would cease performing the contract, refused to do so; that on that date the Public Housing Administration regional counsel wrote Seacoast by registered mail, addressed "Attention Zell," advising of the steps the government had taken and stating that unless Seacoast retracted its repudiation within three days from the date of the letter, Trion's bid would be accepted and Seacoast and its sureties would be held liable for breach of contract; and that having received no response from Seacoast within the three days specified, and Zell again asked on November 10th, to retract the notice of repudiation having refused to do so, the government accepted Trion's bid and proceeded with the execution of the contract. The record standing thus, under settled law not only of Georgia but generally elsewhere, the breach was not healed, the judgment was wrong, and it must be reversed.

A comparison of the briefs and arguments of appellant and appellees will show that the case is in quite small compass. Both agree that Seacoast's letter of October 24th operated as an anticipatory breach and that unless effectively withdrawn during the *locus poenitentiae* it operated to put Seacoast in default and to render it liable for the loss to the government of the difference in price between the old and the new contract.

Appellees, after quoting from Anson on Contracts, 6th Ed. Sec. 385, p. 444:

> "The repudiator has the power of retraction prior to any change of position by the other party, but not afterwards."

go on to say:

> "So we see that the authorities seem to be unanimous that a person who gives notice of his intention not to perform a contract may withdraw such notice and offer to perform prior to the time the other party acted or relied thereon."

Based upon these premises, they insist that "the undisputed evidence is that appellant did not 'accept the bid of Trion Gas' until November 17th, which was after the notice of cancellation had been withdrawn in writing."

We think: that this statement is erroneous; that it represents the crucial difference between the parties; and that the error of the statement lies in the fact that it confuses the acceptance of the bid with the signing of the contract.

It is true that the contract was not signed until the 17th, after Seacoast had retracted its notice and if appellees were correct in its position that the date of the signing of the new contract was determinative of this case, they would be correct in their conclusion that the judgment should be affirmed.

But that position is not correct. In fact and in law, when the government took bids and notified Seacoast that unless it retracted within three days it would proceed to accept the Trion bid and award the contract to it, the *locus poenitentiae* ended with these three days. The fact that Seacoast claims that it did not receive the notice is completely immaterial both because it was not necessary for the government to give any notice or fix any time and because Zell, on November 10th, repeated to the Regional Counsel his refusal to retract.

All that is required to close the door to repentance is definite action indicating that the anticipatory breach has been accepted as final, and this requisite can be supplied either by the filing of a suit or a firm declaration, as here, that unless within a fixed time the breach is repudiated, it will be accepted.

Here, in addition to this firm declaration, the record shows the taking of bids and the awarding of the contract to the lowest bidder. The error of the district judge lies, we think, in holding that the *locus poenitentiae* was extended until the 17th, when the contract was signed, and that Seacoast having repented before the signing of the contract, had healed the breach and restored the contract to its original vitality.

Whatever of doubt there may be, and we have none with respect to this view, as a matter of strict law, there can be none with respect to the justice or equity of this determination when it is considered; that Zell, the president and practically sole owner of Seacoast, was the organizer, the president and practically sole owner of Trion; that he organized Trion for the sole purpose of the bidding; and that on the date the bids were opened and later on the date the contract was awarded, he, though requested to do so, refused to withdraw Seacoast's repudiation and continued in that refusal until a day or two before the contract was signed.

The evidence showing, as it does, without contradiction, that the signing of the contract was not delayed because of a purpose on the part of the government to extend the time for Seacoast's repentance, but because until that date Trion had not furnished his bond, we think it clear that, in entering judgment for the defendants, the court erred. The judgment is, therefore, reversed and the cause is remanded with directions to enter judgment for plaintiff for the loss Seacoast's breach of contract has caused it.

Questions

1. What is the legal issue in *Seacoast*? What is the seller's argument? What does the court hold? Would the result differ if the case were governed by the U.C.C.? *See* U.C.C. § 2–611.

2. Why does Seacoast think its retraction was effective? Why does the United States Government think it ineffective? Why might the court prefer the U.S.G.? Does it give a good reason for its preference?

3. Should the result differ if Seacoast had retracted after the 3–day period but before the U.S. had called for any bids? What balance of interests justifies your answer?

––––––––

PITTSBURGH–DES MOINES STEEL CO. v. BROOKHAVEN MANOR WATER CO.

United States Court of Appeals, Seventh Circuit, 1976.
532 F.2d 572.

PELL, CIRCUIT JUDGE. This is an appeal by the Pittsburgh–Des Moines Steel Company (hereinafter PDM) from the district court's entry of a judgment notwithstanding the verdict against PDM on its complaint for repudiation of contract and for Brookhaven Manor Water Company (hereinafter Brookhaven) on its counterclaim for breach of contract and from the district court's subsequent adjudgment of damages. The questions raised on appeal are whether the district court erred in entering judgment notwithstanding the verdict in favor of Brookhaven on the liability issue and whether error was committed in the district court's subsequent assessment of damages against PDM.

The record discloses the following series of events. On July 24, 1968, PDM, a designer, fabricator, and engineer of steel products, submitted a proposal to Brookhaven for the construction of a one-million-gallon water tank for $175,000. The original proposal incorporated, as terms of payment, 60 percent upon receipt of materials in PDM's plant, 30 percent upon completion of erection, and 10 percent upon completion of testing, or within 30 days after the tank had been made ready for testing. The original terms were not satisfactory to Brookhaven's president, Irving Betke, and were subsequently changed. The altered payment term provided that 100% of the contract price was due and payable within 30 days after the tank had been tested and accepted. The altered proposal was signed and accepted by Brookhaven on November 26, 1968.

Sometime during the following month Norman Knuttel, PDM's district manager who had prepared and signed the original and revised proposals, talked to a representative of the Arbanas Construction Company which company had contracted with Brookhaven for the construction of the tank foundation. Knuttel was informed that Brookhaven had received a loan from Diversified Finance Corporation. Although this information as to the receipt of the loan was incorrect, Brookhaven had negotiated with Diversified for a loan for the purpose of the construction which negotiations continued into the following year. Under date of January 3, 1969, PDM's credit manager wrote Diversified with a copy to Betke which letter in part was as follows:

> "[We] hereby request a letter assuring that $175,000.00 for payment of the referenced project will be held in escrow and fully committed to payment to us upon completion of referenced elevated tank.
>
> "As a matter of good business we are holding this order in abeyance until receipt of such notification."

The contract contained no provision for escrow financing. Brookhaven, through Betke, took no action upon the receipt of the copy of the letter. Subsequently, after further correspondence and meetings, resulting primarily from Brookhaven's not having secured a planned loan of $275,000.00 from Diversified Finance, PDM's credit manager sent an air mail, special delivery letter to Betke, dated March 19, 1969, which suggested that Betke "mail us your personal guarantee of payment of $175,000.00 as per the contract, to protect us in the interim between now and the time your loan is completed."

While the contract specified the payment of the amount mentioned no later than 30 days after completion of the tank, it was silent as to any reference to a personal guarantee by Betke. The letter concluded as follows:

"Upon receipt of such guarantee, we could immediately set in motion our shop fabrication which would result in earlier completion of your new tank.

"When your loan is completed we will still require a letter of instructions to be forwarded from you to your bank, or other financial institution which extends this loan, that $175,000.00 is to be held in escrow for disbursement only to Pittsburgh–Des Moines Steel Company in accordance with our contract."

The construction of the water tower was scheduled to begin on April 15, 1969. A crew had been scheduled for the site three months previously, and a crew was ready to appear there on April 15, 1969. As matters transpired, however, the tank was never installed at Brookhaven's site. On March 31, 1969, Betke sent PDM Comptroller Harry Kelly his personal financial statement, but he did not send PDM his personal guarantee for the loan. After Betke failed to provide his personal guarantee of the $175,000.00 contract price, PDM took no further steps toward performance.[1] On April 22, 1969, Kelley, PDM Secretary–Treasurer Tom Morris, PDM Sales Manager Dwight Long, and Betke attended a meeting on the Brookhaven premises. Although the record reveals somewhat inconsistent versions of the details of that meeting, it appears that Morris told Betke that PDM would complete the fabrication of the tank and deliver it to the job site within a matter of weeks but that Betke replied that he had no need for the tank until the following year.

Further efforts to implement the contract broke down completely after April 22, 1969. Brookhaven's installation of the reinforced concrete foundation for the tank had been accomplished at a cost to it of $18,895. Subsequent to the March meeting, Brookhaven purchased additional land and developed two wells which provided an adequate water supply. Brookhaven later sold all its assets, including both equipment and land, to the City of Darien. At the trial of the damages issue, an expert in demolition testified that the cost of removing the reinforced concrete foundation would be about $7,000. On the basis of this testimony, which was proffered upon the legal theory that Brookhaven had a right to recover the cost of the removal, the district court found that the total amount of damages sustained by Brookhaven was the sum of $25,895.00 and entered judgment in its favor for that amount. . . .

II. CLAIMED BASES OF LIABILITY

Under the contract as executed, into which prior negotiations had been merged, Brookhaven's performance of its principal obligation to pay

---

1. The record indicates that as of April 22, 1969, the foundation, the construction of which was the obligation of Brookhaven, had been completed and two-thirds of the required tankage parts, which were the obligation of PDM, had been fabricated. However, it is also noted that as late as March 19, 1969, PDM had written Betke that upon the receipt of the guarantee, the shop could immediately set in motion fabrication. It is not clear whether PDM did anything to dispel the clear inference to Betke that there would be no fabrication, or at least further fabrication, until the guarantee had been received.

the purchase price was not due until after the completion of construction. Nevertheless within a period of time shortly more than one month after the contract became effective, PDM was requesting that a prospective lender of the funds to Brookhaven should hold the entire $175,000.00 in escrow. This was not a request that a lending institution give a letter of intent or otherwise confirm that it would make a particular loan when the payment became due after completion of construction. Instead the letter explicitly would, if honored, have required Brookhaven to complete all necessary loan papers and to arrange for the consummation of the loan, the proceeds of which would then be held by Diversified for some months until the work was completed. It is no answer to say that perhaps Brookhaven could have arranged for the escrowed fund to have been invested in some safe, readily liquidable form which might offset in part at least the loss to Brookhaven resulting from having to pay interest on money already borrowed. PDM having purported to agree not to ask for progress payments during the course of construction, more than half of which would have been due before the first act took place by PDM on the construction site, it now was substituting another requirement clearly beyond any requirement contemplated in the contract which would not have put the purchase price in hand but would nevertheless have it where it could be available for the picking at the appropriate time. The contract is silent as to any right of PDM to insist Brookhaven provide any such guarantee during the period before completion of construction. Further, PDM made it quite clear that it was "holding this order in abeyance until receipt of" notification that the money was being so held. We find no basis for an inference that at this time Brookhaven was not ready, willing and able to perform its obligations under the contract nor that it would not be able to pay when it owed. The fact that there had been negotiations for a loan of money that would not be needed for some months, which negotiations had not come to fruition, does not support such an inference. Two months after the letter to Diversified, PDM reaffirmed its lack of retreat from the position of requiring assurance that the money would be forthcoming.

PDM argues that its position was in accordance with Section 2–609 of the Uniform Commercial Code (UCC) enacted into law in Illinois as Ill. Rev. Stat. ch. 26, sec. 2–609.... There appears to be considerable doubt that a seller was entitled to this protection prior to the adoption of the UCC; therefore before deciding that question we address ourselves to whether the UCC is applicable to the present transaction. That determination is primarily dependent upon whether the one-million gallon water tank constitutes "goods" within the meaning of the UCC.... We find ample support in the cases arising under the UCC itself that the scope of coverage of "goods" is not to be given a narrow construction but instead should be viewed as being broad in scope so as to carry out the underlying purpose of the Code of achieving uniformity in commercial transactions. The Code, which by its own terms, § 1–102, is to be liberally construed, should be uniformly applied to achieve its purposes.

We believe Illinois would so decide. In the present case, while the finished tank was scarcely one to be taken off the shelf, we are unaware of any authority that specially manufactured small dies should be goods and a very large tank not so classified. In the words of the UCC this was a "movable" "thing" "specially manufactured." That which PDM agreed to sell and Brookhaven agreed to buy was not services but goods as defined in the UCC.

That determination, however, is not dispositive of the ultimate issue. The question remaining is whether PDM's actions subsequent to the execution of the contract were within the protection provided by § 2–609. We hold that they were not.

The performance to which PDM was entitled was the full payment of the purchase price within a specified time after the completion of the tank. While we have a substantial question as to whether PDM made a written demand as required by the statute, in keeping with our concept that the UCC should be liberally construed, we do not desire to rest our decision on a formalistic approach. Letters were written which conveyed what PDM wanted done before they would pursue their obligations under the contract. The fundamental problem is that these letters, if they be deemed to be in the nature of a demand, demanded more than that to which PDM was entitled and the demand was not founded upon what in our opinion was an actuating basis for the statute's applicability.

We do not construe § 2–609 as being a vehicle without more for an implied term being inserted in a contract when a substantially equivalent term was expressly waived in the contract. The something more to trigger applicability of the statute is that the expectation of due performance on the part of the other party entertained at contracting time no longer exists because of "reasonable grounds for insecurity" arising. We find that PDM's actions in demanding either the escrowing of the purchase price or a personal guarantee lacked the necessary predicate of reasonable grounds for insecurity having arisen. The contract negates the existence of any basis for insecurity at the time of the contract when PDM was willing to wait 30 days beyond completion for payment. The fact that Brookhaven had not completed its loan negotiations does not constitute reasonable grounds for insecurity when the money in question was not to be needed for some months. Reasonable business men prefer in the absence of some compulsive reason not to commence paying interest on borrowed money until the time for the use for that money is at hand. The credit manager's January letter that the order was being held in abeyance until receipt of notification of escrowing was based upon a "matter of good business," but not upon any change of condition bearing upon Brookhaven's ability to discharge its payment obligation under the contract. With regard to the later request for a personal guarantee, it is not uncommon for an individual to decline assuming obligations of a corporation in which he is a shareholder. Indeed, the use of the corporate device frequently has as a principal purpose the limitation on individual exposure to liability. If an unfavorable risk in dealing with a corporation exists at contracting time, good business judgment may well indicate that an assurance be secured before contracting that there will be individual shareholder backup. None of this occurred and the record is silent as to any reasonable grounds for insecurity arising thereafter. . . .

. . . We do not fault Brookhaven for its rejection of various proposals advanced by PDM each of which amounted to a rewriting of the contract in the absence of a proper § 2–609 basis. The fact, if it were a fact, that Brookhaven may not have had a large amount of cash lying in the bank in a checking account, not an unusual situation for a real estate developer, does not support the belief that it, as a company with substantial assets, would fail to meet its obligations as they fell due. Section 2–609 is a protective device when reasonable grounds for insecurity arise; it is not a pen for rewriting a contract in the absence of those reasonable grounds having arisen, particularly when the proposed rewriting involves the very factors which had been waived by the one now attempting to wield the pen. The situation is made no more persuasive for PDM when it is recalled that that company was the original scrivener.

Brookhaven's request to put off the contract for a year clearly came after PDM's repudiation of the contract and was indicative of nothing more than that Brookhaven was willing to undertake a new arrangement with PDM a year hence. Pursuant to § 2–610 of the UCC, Brookhaven was entitled to suspend its own performance by virtue of the anticipatory repudiation by PDM and to resort to available remedies, including damages pursuant to § 2–711 of the Code. . . .

For the reasons hereinbefore set out the judgment of the district court is AFFIRMED.

Cummings, Circuit Judge (concurring). Although I agree with the result reached in the majority opinion, I differ with the reasoning. Reasonable men could certainly conclude that PDM had legitimate grounds to question Brookhaven's ability to pay for the water tank. When the contract was signed, the parties understood that Brookhaven would obtain a loan to help pay for the project. When the loan failed to materialize, a prudent businessman would have "reasonable grounds for insecurity." I disagree that there must be a fundamental change in the financial position of the buyer before the seller can invoke the protection of UCC § 2–609. Rather, I believe that the section was designed to cover instances where an underlying condition of the contract, even if not expressly incorporated into the written document, fails to occur. See Comment 3 to UCC § 2–609. Whether, in a specific case, the breach of the condition gives a party "reasonable grounds for insecurity" is a question of fact for the jury.

UCC § 2–609, however, does not give the alarmed party a right to redraft the contract. Whether the party invoking that provision is merely requesting an assurance that performance will be forthcoming or whether he is attempting to alter the contract is a mixed question of law and fact, depending in part upon the court's interpretation of the obligations imposed on the parties. In this case, PDM would have been assured only if significant changes in the contract were made, either by receiving Betke's personal guarantee, by attaining escrow financing or by purchasing an interest in Brookhaven. The district court could properly conclude as a matter of law that these requests by PDM demanded more than a commercially "adequate assurance of due performance."

Questions

1. How does the deal break down in *Pittsburgh–Des Moines Steel Co.*? What is the contractor's defense to the counterclaim by the owner? Why does that defense fail?

2. Does PDM ask for more than it bargained for? Doesn't *any* request for assurances ask for something more? Why was this request more than that to which PDM was entitled? On what point does the concurrence differ?

3. *Problems.*

   a. Reconsider Problem d, above at p. 489.

   b. Willie borrowed $100,000 from Duke's Bank to buy a home in San Francisco. Duke's Bank took a mortgage on the property and a promise from Willie to repay the loan by monthly payments over 30 years. After making payments as required for two years, Willie's home was destroyed by an earthquake. Willie repudiated the contract, telling Duke's it could have the property. Duke's wants to sue Willie to collect the entire balance due, though the contract did not contain an "acceleration clause." What do you advise? See RESTATEMENT (SECOND) OF CONTRACTS § 243.

NOTE ON INTERESTS OF PARTIES IN BREACH

Perhaps surprisingly, understanding the law of contract performance requires special attention to the contractual interests of the party in breach. These may be expectation, reliance, or restitutionary in nature. No doubt the expectation interest of the nonbreaching party, including the interest in reasonable security, has a claim to legal protection that is superior to any contractual interest of the party in breach. There may, however, be a variety of ways to fully protect the nonbreaching party's expectation interest while protecting the contractual interests of the party in breach to some extent. Here, as in the law of contract damages, the law refrains from punishing the party in breach and seeks to minimize its losses from breach.

———

UNITED NATIONS CONVENTION ON THE INTERNATIONAL SALE OF GOODS, Art. (1)

———

COSDEN OIL & CHEMICAL CO. v. KARL O. HELM AKTIENGESELLSCHAFT

United States Court of Appeals, Fifth Circuit, 1984.
736 F.2d 1064.

REAVLEY, CIRCUIT JUDGE. We must address one of the most difficult interpretive problems of the Uniform Commercial Code—the appropriate time to measure buyer's damages where the seller anticipatorily repudiates a contract and the buyer does not cover. The district court applied the Texas version of Article 2 and measured buyer's damages at a commercially reasonable time after seller's repudiation. We affirm....

I. CASE HISTORY

This contractual dispute arose out of events and transactions occurring in the first three months of 1979, when the market in polystyrene, a petroleum derivative used to make molded products, was steadily rising. During this time Iran, a major petroleum producer, was undergoing political turmoil. Karl O. Helm Aktiengesellschaft (Helm or Helm Hamburg), an international trading company based in Hamburg, West Germany, anticipated a tightening in the world petrochemical supply and decided to purchase a large amount of polystyrene. Acting on orders from Helm Hamburg, Helm Houston, a wholly-owned subsidiary, initiated negotiations with Cosden Oil & Chemical Company (Cosden), a Texas-based producer of chemical products, including polystyrene.

Rudi Scholtyssek, general manager of Helm Houston, contacted Ken Smith, Cosden's national sales coordinator, to inquire about the possibility of purchasing quantities of polystyrene. Negotiating over the telephone and by telex, the parties agreed to the purchase and sale of 1,250 metric tons of high impact polystyrene at $.2825 per pound and 250 metric tons of general purpose polystyrene at $.265 per pound. The parties also discussed options on each polystyrene type. On January 18, 1979, Scholtyssek met with Smith in Dallas, leaving behind two purchase confirmations. Purchase confirmation 04 contained the terms for high impact and 05 contained the terms for general purpose. Both confirmations contained the price and quantity terms listed above, and specified the same delivery and payment terms. The polystyrene was to be delivered during January and February in one or more lots, to be called for at Helm's instance. Confirmation 04 specified that Helm had an option for an additional 1,000 metric tons of high impact, and confirmation 05 expressed a similar option for 500 metric tons of general purpose. The option amounts were subject to the same terms, except that delivery was to be during February and March. The options were to be declared, at the latest, by January 31, 1979.

On January 22, Helm called for the first shipment of high impact under order 04, to be delivered FAS at a New Jersey port to make a January 29 shipping date for a trans-Atlantic voyage. On January 23, Helm telexed Cosden to declare the options on purchase orders 04 and

05, designating the high impact option quantity as order 06 and the general purpose option quantity as order 07. After exercising the options, Helm sent purchase confirmations 06 and 07, which Cosden received on January 29. That same day Helm Houston received confirmations 04 and 05, which Smith had signed.

Cosden shipped 90,000 pounds of high impact polystyrene to Helm on or about January 26. Cosden then sent an invoice for that quantity to Helm Houston on or about January 31.... As Helm had expected, polystyrene prices began to rise in late January, and continued upward during February and March. Cosden also experienced problems at two of its plants in late January. Normally, Cosden supplied its Calumet City, Illinois, production plant with styrene monomer, the "feed stock" or main ingredient of polystyrene, by barges that traveled from Louisiana up the Mississippi and Illinois Rivers to a canal that extended to Cosden's plant. Due to the extremely cold winter of 1978–79, however, the Illinois River and the canal froze, suspending barge traffic for a few weeks. A different problem beset Cosden's Windsor, New Jersey, production plant. A new reactor, used in the polystyrene manufacturing process, had recently been installed at the Windsor plant. A manufacturing defect soon became apparent, however, and Cosden returned the reactor to the manufacturer for repair, which took several weeks. At the time of the reactor breakdown, Cosden was manufacturing only general purpose at the Windsor plant. Cosden had planned on supplying Helm's high impact orders from the Calumet City plant.

Late in January, Cosden notified Helm that it was experiencing problems at its production facilities and that the delivery under 04 might be delayed. On February 6, Smith telephoned Scholtyssek and informed him that Cosden was cancelling orders 05, 06, and 07 because two plants were "down" and it did not have sufficient product to fill the orders. Cosden, however, would continue to honor order 04. Smith confirmed the cancellation in a letter dated February 8, which Scholtyssek received on or about February 12. After Helm Hamburg learned of Cosden's cancellation, Wolfgang Gordian, a member of Helm's executive board, sent an internal memorandum to Helm Houston outlining a strategy. Helm would urge that Cosden continue to perform under 04 and, after receiving the high impact polystyrene, would offset amounts owing under 04 against Helm's damages for nondelivery of the balance of polystyrene. Gordian also instructed Helm Houston send a telex to Cosden. Following instructions, Scholtyssek ... urged Cosden to deliver immediately several hundred metric tons of high impact to meet two February shipping dates for which Helm had booked shipping space.

In mid-February, Cosden shipped approximately 1,260,000 pounds of high impact to Helm under order 04. This shipment's invoice, which also included the force majeure provision on the reverse side, specified that Helm owed $355,950, due by March 15 or 16. After this delivery Helm requested that Cosden deliver the balance under order 04 for shipment on a vessel departing March 16. Cosden informed Helm that a March 16 delivery was not possible. On March 15, citing production problems with the 04 balance, Cosden offered to sell 1,000 metric tons of styrene monomer at $.41 per pound. Although Cosden later lowered the price on the styrene monomer, Helm refused the offer, insisting on delivery of the balance of 04 polystyrene by March 31 at the latest. Around the end of March, Cosden informed Scholtyssek by telephone that it was cancelling the balance of order 04.

Cosden sued Helm, seeking damages for Helm's failure to pay for delivered polystyrene. Helm counterclaimed for Cosden's failure to deliver polystyrene as agreed. The jury found on special verdict that Cosden had agreed to sell polystyrene to Helm under all four orders. The jury also found that Cosden anticipatorily repudiated orders 05, 06, and 07 and that Cosden cancelled order 04 before Helm's failure to pay for the second 04 delivery constituted a repudiation. The jury fixed the per pound market prices for polystyrene under each of the four orders at three different times: when Helm learned of the cancellation, at a commercially reasonable time thereafter, and at the time for delivery.

The district court, viewing the four orders as representing one agreement, determined that Helm was entitled to recover $628,676 in damages representing the difference between the contract price and the market price at a commercially reasonable time after Cosden repudiated its polystyrene delivery obligations and that Cosden was entitled to an offset of $355,950 against those damages for polystyrene delivered, but not paid for, under order 04.

II.   TIME FOR MEASURING BUYER'S DAMAGES

Both parties find fault with the time at which the district court measured Helm's damages for Cosden's anticipatory repudiation of orders 05, 06, and 07.[5] Cosden argues that damages should be measured when Helm learned of the repudiation. Helm contends that market price as of the last day for delivery—or the time of performance—should be used to compute its damages under the contract-market differential. We reject both views, and hold that the district court correctly measured damages at a commercially reasonable point after Cosden informed Helm that it was cancelling the three orders.

Article 2 of the Code has generally been hailed as a success for its comprehensiveness, its deference to mercantile reality, and its clarity. Nevertheless, certain aspects of the Code's overall scheme have proved troublesome in application. The interplay among sections 2.610, 2.711, 2.712, 2.713, 2.723, Tex. Bus. & Com. Code Ann. (Vernon 1968), represents one of those areas, and has been described as "an impossible legal thicket." J. White & R. Summers, *Uniform Commercial Code* §§ 6–7 at 242 (2d ed. 1980). The aggrieved buyer seeking damages for seller's anticipatory repudiation presents the most difficult interpretive problem. Section 2.713 describes the buyer's damages remedy:

5. The damages measurement problem does not apply to Cosden's breach of order 04, which was not anticipatorily repudiated. The time Helm learned of Cosden's intent to deliver no more polystyrene under 04 was the same time as the last date of performance, which had been extended to the end of March.

Buyer's Damages for Non-Delivery or Repudiation

(a) Subject to the provisions of this chapter with respect to proof of market price (Section 2.723), the measure of damages for non-delivery or repudiation by the seller is the difference between the market price *at the time when the buyer learned of the breach* and the contract price together with any incidental and consequential damages provided in this chapter (Section 2.715), but less expenses saved in consequence of the seller's breach.

(emphasis added).

Courts and commentators have identified three possible interpretations of the phrase "learned of the breach." If seller anticipatorily repudiates, buyer learns of the breach:

(1) When he learns of the repudiation;

(2) When he learns of the repudiation plus a commercially reasonable time; or

(3) When performance is due under the contract.

See, e.g., *First National Bank of Chicago v. Jefferson Mortgage Co.*, 576 F.2d 479 (3d Cir.1978). . . .

We do not doubt, and Texas law is clear, that market price at the time buyer learns of the breach is the appropriate measure of section 2.713 damages in cases where buyer learns of the breach at or after the time for performance. This will be the common case, for which section 2.713 was designed. *See* Peters, *Remedies for Breach of Contracts Relating to the Sale of Goods Under the Uniform Commercial Code: A Roadmap for Article Two*, 73 Yale L.J. 199, 264 (1963). In the relatively rare case where seller anticipatorily repudiates and buyer does not cover, . . . the specific provision for anticipatory repudiation cases, section 2.610, authorizes the aggrieved party to await performance for a commercially reasonable time before resorting to his remedies of cover or damages.

In the anticipatory repudiation context, the buyer's specific right to wait for a commercially reasonable time before choosing his remedy must be read together with the general damages provision of section 2.713 to extend the time for measurement beyond when buyer learns of the breach. Comment 1 to section 2.610 states that if an aggrieved party "awaits performance beyond a commercially reasonable time he cannot recover resulting damages which he should have avoided." This suggests that an aggrieved buyer can recover damages where the market rises during the commercially reasonable time he awaits performance. To interpret 2.713's "learned of the breach" language to mean the time at which seller first communicates his anticipatory repudiation would undercut the time that 2.610 gives the aggrieved buyer to await performance.

The buyer's option to wait a commercially reasonable time also interacts with section 2.611, which allows the seller an opportunity to retract his repudiation. Thus, an aggrieved buyer "learns of the breach" a commercially reasonable time after he learns of the seller's anticipatory repudiation. The weight of scholarly commentary supports this interpretation. See J. Calamari & J. Perillo, *Contracts* §§ 14–20 (2d ed. 1977); Sebert, *Remedies Under Article Two of the Uniform Commercial Code: An Agenda for Review*, 130 U. Pa. L. Rev. 360, 372–80 (1981); Wallach, *Anticipatory Repudiation and the UCC*, 13 U.C.C. L. J. 48 (1980); Peters, *supra*, at 263–68.

Typically, our question will arise where parties to an executory contract are in the midst of a rising market. To the extent that market decisions are influenced by a damages rule, measuring market price at the time of seller's repudiation gives seller the ability to fix buyer's damages and may induce seller to repudiate, rather than abide by the contract. By contrast, measuring buyer's damages at the time of performance will tend to dissuade the buyer from covering, in hopes that market price will continue upward until performance time.

Allowing the aggrieved buyer a commercially reasonable time, however, provides him with an opportunity to investigate his cover possibilities in a rising market without fear that, if he is unsuccessful in obtaining cover, he will be relegated to a market-contract damage remedy measured at the time of repudiation. The Code supports this view. While cover is the preferred remedy, the Code clearly provides the option to seek damages. See § 2.712(c) & comment 3. If "[t]he buyer is always free to choose between cover and damages for non-delivery," and if 2.712 "is not intended to limit the time necessary for [buyer] to look around and decide as to how he may best effect cover," it would be anomalous, if the buyer chooses to seek damages, to fix his damages at a time before he investigated cover possibilities and before he elected his remedy. See id. comment 2 & 3; *Dura-Wood Treating Co. v. Century Forest Industries*, Inc., 675 F.2d 745, 754 (5th Cir.), *cert. denied*, 459 U.S. 865, 103 S.Ct. 144, 74 L.Ed.2d 122 (1982) ("buyer has some time in which to evaluate the situation"). Moreover, comment 1 to section 2.713 states, "The general baseline adopted in this section uses as a yardstick the market in which the buyer would have obtained cover had he sought that relief." See § 2.610 comment 1. When a buyer chooses not to cover, but to seek damages, the market is measured at the time he could have covered—a reasonable time after repudiation. See §§ 2.711 & 2.713.

Persuasive arguments exist for interpreting "learned of the breach" to mean "time of performance," consistent with the pre-Code rule. *See* J. White & R. Summers, *supra*, §§ 6–7; Anderson, *supra*. If this was the intention of the Code's drafters, however, phrases in section 2.610 and 2.712 lose their meaning. If buyer is entitled to market-contract damages measured at the time of performance, it is difficult to explain why the anticipatory repudiation section limits him to a commercially reasonable time to await performance. *See* § 2.610 comment 1. Similarly, in a rising market, no reason would exist for requiring the buyer to act "without unreasonable delay" when he seeks to cover following an anticipatory repudiation. *See* § 2.712(a).

The interplay among the relevant Code sections does not permit, in this context, an interpretation that harmonizes all and leaves no loose ends. We therefore acknowledge that our interpretation fails to explain the language of section 2.723(a) insofar as it relates to aggrieved buyers. We note, however, that the section has limited applicability—cases that come to trial before the time of performance will be rare. Moreover, the comment to section 2.723 states that the "section is not intended to exclude the use of any other reasonable method of determining market price or of measuring damages...." In light of the Code's persistent theme of commercial reasonableness, the prominence of cover as a remedy, and the time given an aggrieved buyer to await performance and to investigate cover before selecting his remedy, we agree with the district court that "learned of the breach" incorporates section 2.610's commercially reasonable time....

Questions

1. If you are representing the seller in a case like *Cosden Oil*, what result would you advocate under the U.C.C.? Why? If you are representing the buyer, what result would you advocate under the U.C.C.? Why? Which of the arguments under the U.C.C. is the stronger? See U.C.C. §§ 2–610, 2–711, 2–713(1), 2–723(1).

2. Would the United Nations' Convention on Contracts for the International Sale of Goods apply to this transaction were it to occur today? How would the dispute be resolved under that law?

3. As a matter of good policy, when a seller anticipatorily repudiates a contract for the sale of goods, should damages be measured with reference to the market price at the time of the repudiation, a reasonable time thereafter, or at the time for performance, or should the buyer have an election? What is the buyer's interest? What is the seller's? Which should have priority in the law? Why?

BRITTON v. TURNER

Superior Court of Judicature of the State of New Hampshire, 1834.
6 N.H. 481.

PARKER, JUDGE. It may be assumed that the labor performed by the plaintiff, and for which he seeks to recover a compensation in this action, was commenced under a special contract to labor for the defendant the term of one year, for the sum of one hundred and twenty dollars, and that the plaintiff has labored but a portion of that time, and has voluntarily failed to complete the entire contract.

It is clear, then that he is not entitled to recover upon the contract itself, because the service, which was to entitle him to the sum agreed upon, has never been performed.

But the question arises, can the plaintiff, under these circumstance, recover a reasonable sum for the service he has actually performed, under the count in *quantum meruit*?

Upon this, and questions of a similar nature, the decisions to be found in the books are not easily reconciled.

It has been held, upon contracts of this kind for labor to be performed at a specified price, that the party who voluntarily fails to fulfill the contract, by performing the whole labor contracted for, is not entitled to recover anything for the labor actually performed, however much he may have done towards the performance, and this has been considered the settled rule of law upon this subject. . . .

That such rule in its operation may be very unequal, not to say unjust, is apparent.

A party who contracts to perform certain specified labor, and who breaks his contract in the first instance, without any attempt to perform it, can only be made liable to pay the damages which the other party has sustained by reason of such non-performance, which in many instances may be trifling—whereas a party who, in good faith, has entered upon the performance of his contract, and nearly completed it, and then abandoned the further performance—although the other party has had the full benefit of all that has been done, and has perhaps sustained no actual damage—is in fact subjected to a loss of all which has been performed, in the nature of damages for the nonfulfillment of the remainder, upon the technical rule, that the contract must be fully performed, in order to a recovery of any part of the compensation.

By the operation of this rule, then, the party who attempts performance may be placed in a much worse situation than he who wholly disregards his contract, and the other party may receive much more, by the breach of the contract, than the injury which he has sustained by such breach, and more than he could be entitled to were he seeking to recover damages by an action.

The case before us presents an illustration. Had the plaintiff in this case never entered upon the performance of his contract, the damage could not probably have been greater than some small expense and trouble incurred in procuring another to do the labor which he had contracted to perform. But having entered upon the performance, and labored nine and a half months, the value of which labor to the defendant, as found by the jury, is ninety-five dollars, if the defendant can succeed in this defense, he in fact receives nearly five sixths of the value of a whole year's labor, by reason of the breach of contract by the plaintiff, a sum not only utterly disproportionate to any probable, not to say possible damage, which could have resulted from the neglect of the plaintiff to continue the remaining two and a half months, but altogether beyond any damage which could have been recovered by the defendant, had the plaintiff done nothing towards the fulfillment of his contract. . . .

In case of a failure to perform such special contract by the default of the party contracting to do the service, if the money is not due by the terms of the special agreement, he is not entitled to recover for his labor, or for the materials furnished, unless the other party receives what has been done or furnished, and upon the whole case derives a benefit from it.

But if, where a contract is made of such a character, a party actually receives labor or materials, and thereby derives a benefit and advantage, over and above the damage which has resulted from the breach of the contract by the other party, the labor actually done and the value received furnish a new consideration, and the law thereupon raises a promise to pay to the extent of the reasonable worth of such excess. This may be considered as making a new case, one not within the original agreement, and the party is entitled to "recover on his new case, for the work done, not as agreed, but yet accepted by the defendant." 1 Dane Abr. 224.

If on such failure to perform the whole, the nature of the contract be such that the employer can reject what has been done, and refuse to receive any benefit from the part performance, he is entitled so to do, and in such case is not liable to be charged, unless he has before assented to and accepted of what has been done, however much the other party may have done towards the performance. He has in such case received nothing, and having contracted to receive nothing but the entire matter contracted for, he is not bound to pay, because his express promise was only to pay on receiving the whole, and having actually received nothing the law can not and ought not to raise an implied promise to pay. But where the party received value—takes and uses the materials, or has advantage from the labor he is liable to pay the reasonable worth of what he has received. . . . And the rule is the same, whether it was received and accepted by the assent of the party prior to the breach, under a contract by which, from its nature, he was to receive labor, from time to time, until the completion of the whole contract; or whether it was received and accepted by an assent subsequent to the performance of all which was in fact done. If he received it under such circumstances as precluded him from rejecting it afterwards, that does not alter the case—it has still been received by his assent.

In fact we think the technical reasoning, that the performance of the whole labor is a condition precedent, and the right to recover anything dependent upon it;—that the contract being entire, there can be no apportionment;—and that there being an express contract no other can be implied, even upon the subsequent performance of service, is not properly applicable to this species of contract, where a beneficial service has been actually performed; for we have abundant reason to believe, that the general understanding of the community is, that the hired laborer shall be entitled to compensation for the service actually performed, though he do not continue the entire term contracted for, and such contracts must be presumed to be made with reference to that understanding, unless an express stipulation shows the contrary.

. . .

It is easy, if parties so choose, to provide by an express agreement that nothing shall be earned, if the laborer leaves his employer without having performed the whole service contemplated, and then there can be no pretense for a recovery if he voluntarily deserts the service before the expiration of the time.

The amount, however, for which the employer ought to be charged, where the laborer abandons his contract, is only the reasonable worth, or the amount of advantage he receives upon the whole transaction, . . . and, in estimating the value of the labor, the contract price for the service can not be exceeded.

If, under such circumstances, he actually receives a benefit from the labor performed, over and above the damage occasioned by the failure to complete, there is as much reason why he should pay the reasonable worth of what has thus been done for his benefit, as there is when he enters and occupies the house which has been built for him, but not according to the stipulations of the contract, and which he perhaps enters, not because he is satisfied with what has been done, but because circumstances compel him to accept it such as it is, that he should pay for the value of the house. . . .

We hold, then, that where a party undertakes to pay upon a special contract for the performance of labor or the furnishing of materials, he is not to be charged upon such special agreement, until the money is earned according to the terms of it; and where the parties have made an express contract, the law will not imply and raise a contract different from that which the parties have entered into, except upon some farther transaction between the parties.

If a person makes a contract fairly, he is entitled to have it fully performed, and if this is not done, he is entitled to damages. He may maintain a suit to recover the amount of damage sustained by the non-performance.

The benefit and advantage which the party takes by the labor, therefore, is the amount of value which he receives, if any, after deducting the amount of damage; and if he elects to put this in defense he is entitled so to do, and the implied promise which the law will raise, in such case, is to pay such amount of the stipulated price for the whole labor, as remains after deducting what it would cost to procure a completion of the residue of the service, and also any damage which has been sustained by reason of the non-fulfillment of the contract.

If, in such case, it be found that the damages are equal to, or greater than the amount of the labor performed, so that the employer, having a right to the full performance of the contract, has not upon the whole case received a beneficial service, the plaintiff can not recover.

This rule, by binding the employer to pay the value of the service he actually receives, and the laborer to answer in damages where he does not complete the entire contract, will leave no temptation to the former to drive the laborer from his service near the close of his term, by ill-treatment, in order to escape from payment; nor to the latter to desert his service before the stipulated time, without a sufficient reason; and it will, in most instances, settle the whole controversy in one action, and prevent a multiplicity of suits and cross actions. . . .

Applying the principles thus laid down to this case, the plaintiff is entitled to judgment on the verdict.

The defendant sets up a mere breach of the contract in defense of the action, but this can not avail him. He does not appear to have offered evidence to show that he was damnified by such breach, or to have asked that a deduction should be made upon that account. The direction to the jury was therefore correct, that the plaintiff was entitled to recover as much as the labor performed was reasonably worth; and the jury appear to have allowed a pro rata compensation for the time which the plaintiff labored in the defendant's service. . . .

Judgment on the verdict.

Questions

1. In *Britton*, is the action one "in contract" or in "quantum meruit"? What is the difference? Why did the plaintiff not bring an action in contract? Why should the alternative action be allowed?

2. Should a plaintiff in breach be able to recover something "off the contract" when its breach was "willful"? When it did nothing in part performance of its duties under the contract? When it substantially performed? When it completely performed? What is the breaching plaintiff's interest that might be deserving of legal protection in some such cases? Should that interest also be protected in actions "on the contract"?

3. *Problems*.

a. Charlie agreed to make certain repairs and improvements on Oona's house in return for $27,000. Charlie's anticipated profit was $3,300. Oona paid $5,000 when Charlie began. After working for two months and completing work worth $6,500, Charlie quit without just cause. Should Charlie recover his profit on the contract? Should he recover $1,500? See Kirkland v. Archbold, 113 N.E.2d 496 (Ohio Ct.App. 1953).

b. A client who had a contract to sell 100 widgets for a total of $5,000 tells you that the buyer has wrongfully refused to take delivery or make further payment after making a down payment of $2,500. The market value of the widgets has fallen; the seller sells them for $4,000 in a manner satisfying the requirements of U.C.C. § 2–706. Assume the seller has no incidental losses and that he has saved no expenses as a consequence of the buyer's breach. The contract does not contain a liquidated damages clause. The buyer now wants her money back. How much money, if any, does the seller have to return to the breaching buyer?

SECTION 2. CANCELLATION IN RESPONSE TO BREACH

When a contract does not specify remedies, a breach generally entitles its victim to compensatory damages. An additional remedy is sometimes available. *Cancellation* brings the contract to an end, discharging all executory duties of both parties. The event triggering the power to cancel is a "material breach." Any breach that is not material is considered "partial" or "immaterial." Put otherwise, one party may cancel when the other does not substantially perform. Any case of material breach is a case of insubstantial performance; any case of substantial performance is a case of immaterial breach. The criteria for determining the materiality of a breach are unsettled, as the next four cases illustrate. As you read them, identify the test or criterion employed by each court and evaluate its adequacy in light of the parties' contractual interests, the principles of contract law, and the practicalities of advising clients, advocating before courts, and judging cases.

———

RESTATEMENT (SECOND) OF CONTRACTS
§§ 235, 237–39, 241–42

———

JACOB & YOUNGS v. KENT

Court of Appeals of New York, 1921.
230 N.Y. 239, 129 N.E. 889.

CARDOZO, JUDGE. The plaintiff built a country residence for the defendant at a cost of upwards of $77,000, and now sues to recover a balance of $3,483.46, remaining unpaid. The work of construction ceased in June, 1914, and the defendant then began to occupy the dwelling. There was no complaint of defective performance until March, 1915. One of the specifications for the plumbing work provides that

> "All wrought-iron pipe must be well galvanized, lap welded pipe of the grade known as 'standard pipe' of Reading manufacture."

The defendant learned in March, 1915, that some of the pipe, instead of being made in Reading, was the product of other factories. The plaintiff was accordingly directed by the architect to do the work anew. The plumbing was then encased within the walls except in a few places where it had to be exposed. Obedience to the order meant more than the substitution of other pipe. It meant the demolition at great expense of substantial parts of the completed structure. The plaintiff left the work untouched, and asked for a certificate that the final payment was due. Refusal of the certificate was followed by this suit.

The evidence sustains a finding that the omission of the prescribed brand of pipe was neither fraudulent nor willful. It was the result of the oversight and inattention of the plaintiff's subcontractor. Reading pipe is distinguished from Cohoes pipe and other brands only by the name of the manufacturer stamped upon it at intervals of between six and seven feet. Even the defendant's architect, though he inspected the pipe upon arrival, failed to notice the discrepancy. The plaintiff tried to show that the brands installed, though made by other manufacturers, were the same in quality, in appearance, in market value, and in cost as the brand stated in the contract—that they were, indeed, the same thing, though manufactured in another place. The evidence was excluded, and a verdict directed for the defendant. The Appellate Division reversed, and granted a new trial.

We think the evidence, if admitted, would have supplied some basis for the inference that the defect was insignificant in its relation to the project. The courts never say that one who makes a contract fills the measure of his duty by less than full performance. They do say, however, that an omission, both trivial and innocent, will sometimes be atoned for by allowance of the resulting damage, and will not always be the breach of a condition to be followed by a forfeiture. Spence v. Ham, 163 N.Y. 220, 57 N.E. 412, 51 L. R. A. 238. . . . The distinction is akin to that between dependent and independent promises, or between promises and conditions. Anson on Contracts (Corbin's Ed.) § 367; 2 Williston on Contracts, § 842. Some promises are so plainly independent that they can never by fair construction be conditions of one another. (Rosenthal Paper Co. v. Nat. Folding Box & Paper Co., 226 N.Y. 313, 123 N.E. 766. . . .) Others are so plainly dependent that they must always be conditions. Others, though dependent and thus conditions when there is departure in point of substance, will be viewed as independent and collateral when the departure is insignificant. 2 Williston on Contracts, §§ 841, 842; Eastern Forge Co. v. Corbin, 182 Mass. 590, 592, 66 N.E. 419. . . . Considerations partly of justice and partly of presumable intention are to tell us whether this or that promise shall be placed in one class or in another. The simple and the uniform will call for different remedies from the multifarious and the intricate. The margin of departure within the range of normal expectation upon a sale of common chattels will vary from the margin to be expected upon a contract for the construction of a mansion or a "skyscraper." There will be harshness sometimes and oppression in the implication of a condition when the thing upon which labor has been expended is incapable of surrender because united to the land, and equity and reason in the implication of a like condition when the subject-matter, if defective, is in shape to be returned. From the conclusion that promises may not be treated as dependent to the extent of their uttermost minutiae without a sacrifice of justice, the progress is a short one to the conclusion that they may not be so treated without a perversion of intention. Intention not otherwise revealed may be presumed to hold in contemplation the reasonable and probable. If something else is in view, it must not be left to implication. There will be no assumption of a purpose to visit venial faults with oppressive retribution.

Those who think more of symmetry and logic in the development of legal rules than of practical adaptation to the attainment of a just result will be troubled by a classification where the lines of division are so wavering and blurred. Something, doubtless, may be said on the score of consistency and certainty in favor of a stricter standard. The courts have balanced such considerations against those of equity and fairness, and found the latter to be the weightier. The decisions in this state commit us to the liberal view, which is making its way, nowadays, in jurisdictions slow to welcome it. Dakin & Co. v. Lee, 1916, 1 K. B. 566, 579. Where the line is to be drawn between the important and the trivial cannot be settled by a formula. "In the nature of the case precise boundaries are impossible." 2 Williston on Contracts, § 841. The same omission may take on one aspect or another according to its setting. Substitution of equivalents may not have the same significance in fields of art on the one side and in those of mere utility on the other. Nowhere will change be tolerated, however, if it is so dominant or pervasive as in any real or substantial measure to frustrate the purpose of the contract. Crouch v. Gutman, 134 N.Y. 45, 51, 31 N.E. 271, 30 Am. St. Rep. 608. There is no general license to install whatever, in the builder's judgment, may be regarded as "just as good." Easthampton L. & C. Co., Ltd. v. Worthington, 186 N.Y. 407, 412, 79 N.E. 323. The question is one of degree, to be answered, if there is doubt, by the triers of the facts . . . and, if the inferences are certain, by the judges of the law. . . . We must weigh the purpose to be served, the desire to be gratified, the excuse for deviation from the letter, the cruelty of enforced adherence. Then only can we tell whether literal fulfillment is to be implied by law as a condition. This is not to say that the parties are not free by apt and certain words to effectuate a purpose that performance of every term shall be a condition of recovery. That question is not here. This is merely to say that the law will be slow to impute the purpose, in the silence of the parties, where the significance of the default is grievously out of proportion to the oppression of the forfeiture. The willful transgressor must accept the penalty of his transgression. Schultze v. Goodstein, 180 N.Y. 248, 251, 73 N.E. 21. . . . For him there is no occasion to mitigate the rigor of implied conditions. The transgressor whose default is unintentional and trivial may hope for mercy if he will offer atonement for his wrong. Spence v. Ham, supra.

In the circumstances of this case, we think the measure of the allowance is not the cost of replacement, which would be great, but the difference in value, which would be either nominal or nothing. Some of the exposed sections might perhaps have been replaced at moderate expense. The defendant did not limit his demand to them, but treated the plumbing as a unit to be corrected from cellar to roof. In point of fact, the plaintiff never reached the stage at which evidence of the extent of the allowance became necessary. The trial court had excluded evidence that the defect was unsubstantial, and in view of that ruling there was no occasion for the plaintiff to go farther with an offer of proof. We think, however, that the offer, if it had been made, would not of necessity have been defective because directed to difference in value. It is true that in most cases the cost of replacement is the measure. Spence v. Ham, supra. The owner is entitled to the money which will permit him to complete, unless the cost of completion is grossly and unfairly out of proportion to the good to be attained. When that is true, the measure is the difference in value. Specifications call, let us say, for a foundation built of granite quarried in Vermont. On the completion of the building, the owner learns that through the blunder of a subcontractor part of the foundation has been built of granite of the same quality quarried in New Hampshire. The measure of allowance is not the cost of reconstruction. "There may be omissions of that which could not afterwards be supplied exactly as called for by the contract without taking down the building to its foundations, and at the same time the omission may not affect the value of the building for use or otherwise, except so slightly as to be hardly appreciable." Handy v. Bliss, 204 Mass. 513, 519, 90 N.E. 864, 134 Am. St. Rep. 673.... The rule that gives a remedy in cases of substantial performance with compensation for defects of trivial or inappreciable importance has been developed by the courts as an instrument of justice. The measure of the allowance must be shaped to the same end.

The order should be affirmed, and judgment absolute directed in favor of the plaintiff upon the stipulation, with costs in all courts.

McLaughlin, Judge. I dissent. The plaintiff did not perform its contract. Its failure to do so was either intentional or due to gross neglect which, under the uncontradicted facts, amounted to the same thing, nor did it make any proof of the cost of compliance, where compliance was possible....

I am of the opinion the trial court was right in directing a verdict for the defendant. The plaintiff agreed that all the pipe used should be of the Reading Manufacturing Company. Only about two-fifths of it, so far as appears, was of that kind. If more were used, then the burden of proving that fact was upon the plaintiff, which it could easily have done, since it knew where the pipe was obtained. The question of substantial performance of a contract of the character of the one under consideration depends in no small degree upon the good faith of the contractor. If the plaintiff had intended to, and had, complied with the terms of the contract except as to minor omissions, due to inadvertence, then he might be allowed to recover the contract price, less the amount necessary to fully compensate the defendant for damages caused by such omissions. Woodward v. Fuller, 80 N.Y. 312.... But that is not this case. It installed between 2,000 and 2,500 feet of pipe, of which only 1,000 feet at most complied with the contract. No explanation was given why pipe called for by the contract was not used, nor that any effort made to show what it would cost to remove the pipe of other manufacturers and install that of the Reading Manufacturing Company. The defendant had a right to contract for what he wanted. He had a right before making payment to get what the contract called for. It is no answer to this suggestion to say that the pipe put in was just as good as that made by the Reading Manufacturing Company, or that the difference in value between such pipe and the pipe made by the Reading Manufacturing Company would be either "nominal or nothing." Defendant contracted for pipe made by the Reading Manufacturing Company. What his reason was for requiring this kind of pipe is of no importance. He wanted that and was entitled to it. . . . The rule, therefore, of substantial performance, with damages for unsubstantial omissions, has no application. . . .

Questions

1. Why should the defendant in *Jacob and Youngs* argue that the plaintiff had not substantially performed the contract? What is the legal consequence of insubstantial performance? Would the measure of contract damages due to the defendant differ depending on whether the plaintiff had or had not substantially performed? If it does not affect the measure of damages, does it nonetheless have a remedial consequence?

2. What is the contract term on which the case turns? Is it a promise, a condition, or a promissory condition? If it is a promissory condition, is there any difference in its content *qua* promise and *qua* condition?

3. What is Judge Cardozo's test of substantiality? Is it an effective test? Should it matter whether the breach was "willful," as Judge McLaughlin suggests? Should it matter that, as Judge McLaughlin suggests, only about two fifths of the pipe was of Reading manufacture?

4. *Problem.*

    a. Otherwise on the facts of *Jacob and Youngs v. Kent,* what result if a clause in the contract expressly made compliance with all specifications a condition?

    b. Paulette employed Charlie to construct an addition to her home. To do so required some grading work. Paulette made it very clear to Charlie that her prize rose garden must not be disturbed. While operating a bulldozer in the back yard, one of Charlie's employees backed it into the rose garden, destroying several rare bushes. Paulette wants to fire Charlie. What should you advise her under the law in *Jacob & Youngs*?

PLANTE v. JACOBS

Supreme Court of Wisconsin, 1960.
10 Wis.2d 567, 103 N.W.2d 296.

HALLOWS, JUSTICE. The defendants argue the plaintiff cannot recover any amount because he has failed to substantially perform the contract. The plaintiff conceded he failed to furnish the kitchen cabinets, gutters and downspouts, sidewalk, closet clothes poles, and entrance seat amounting to $1,601.95. This amount was allowed to the defendants. The defendants claim some 20 other items of incomplete or faulty performance by the plaintiff and no substantial performance because the cost of completing the house in strict compliance with the plans and specifications would amount to 25 or 30 per cent of the contract price. The defendants especially stress the misplacing of the wall between the living room and the kitchen, which narrowed the living room in excess of one foot. The cost of tearing down this wall and rebuilding it would be approximately $4,000. The record is not clear why and when this wall was misplaced, but the wall is completely built and the house decorated and the defendants are living therein. Real estate experts testified that the smaller width of the living room would not affect the market price of the house.

The defendants rely on Manitowoc Steam Boiler Works v. Manitowoc Glue Co., 1903, 120 Wis. 1, 97 N.W. 515, for the proposition there can be no recovery on the contract as distinguished from *quantum meruit* unless there is substantial performance. This is undoubtedly the correct rule at common law. For recovery on *quantum meruit*, see Valentine v. Patrick Warren Construction Co., 1953, 263 Wis. 143, 56 N.W.2d 860. The question here is whether there has been substantial performance. The test of what amounts to substantial performance seems to be whether the performance meets the essential purpose of the contract. In the Manitowoc case the contract called for a boiler having a capacity of 150 per cent of the existing boiler. The court held there was no substantial performance because the boiler furnished had a capacity of only 82 per cent of the old boiler and only approximately one-half of the boiler capacity contemplated by the contract. In Houlahan v. Clark, 1901, 110 Wis. 43, 85 N.W. 676, the contract provided the plaintiff was to drive pilings in the lake and place a boat house thereon parallel and in line with a neighbor's dock. This was not done and the contractor so positioned the boat house that it was practically useless to the owner. Manthey v. Stock, 1907, 133 Wis. 107, 113 N.W. 443, involved a contract to paint a house and to do a good job, including the removal of the old paint where necessary. The plaintiff did not remove the old paint, and blistering and roughness of the new paint resulted. The court held that the plaintiff failed to show substantial performance. The defendants also cite Manning v. School District No. 6, 1905, 124 Wis. 84, 102 N.W. 356. However, this case involved a contract to install a heating and ventilating plant in the school building which would meet certain tests which the heating apparatus failed to do. The heating plant was practically a total failure to accomplish the purposes of the contract. See also Nees v. Weaver, 1936, 222 Wis. 492, 269 N.W. 266, 107 A.L.R. 1405 (roof on a garage).

Substantial performance as applied to construction of a house does not mean that every detail must be in strict compliance with the specifications and the plans. Something less than perfection is the test of specific [substantial?] performance unless all details are made the essence of the contract. This was not done here. There may be situations in which features or details of construction of special or of great personal importance, which if not performed, would prevent a finding of substantial performance of the contract. In this case the plan was a stock floor plan. No detailed construction of the house was shown on the plan. There were no blueprints. The specifications were standard printed forms with some modifications and additions written in by the parties. Many of the problems that arose during the construction had to be solved on the basis of practical experience. No mathematical rule relating to the percentage of the price, of cost of completion or of completeness can be laid down to determine substantial performance of a building contract. Although the defendants received a house with which they are dissatisfied in many respects, the trial court was not in error in finding the contract was substantially performed.

The next question is what is the amount of recovery when the plaintiff has substantially, but incompletely, performed. For substantial performance the plaintiff should recover the contract price less the damages caused the defendant by the incomplete performance. Both parties agree. Venzke v. Magdanz, 1943, 243 Wis. 155, 9 N.W.2d 604, states the correct rule for damages due to faulty construction amounting to such incomplete performance, which is the difference between the value of the house as it stands with faulty and incomplete construction and the value of the house if it had been constructed in strict accordance with the plans and specifications. This is the diminished-value rule. The cost of replacement or repair is not the measure of such damage, but is an element to take into consideration in arriving at value under some circumstances. The cost of replacement or the cost to make whole the omissions may equal or be less than the difference in value in some cases and, likewise, the cost to rectify a defect may greatly exceed the added value to the structure as corrected. The defendants argue that under the Venzke rule their damages are $10,000. The plaintiff on review argues the defendants' damages are only $650. Both parties agree the trial court applied the wrong rule to the facts.

The trial court applied the cost-of-repair or replacement rule as to several items, relying on Stern v. Schlafer, 1943, 244 Wis. 183, 11 N.W.2d 640, 12 N.W.2d 678, wherein it was stated that when there are a number of small items of defect or omission which can be remedied without the reconstruction of a substantial part of the building or a great sacrifice of work or material already wrought in the building, the reasonable cost of correcting the defect should be allowed. However, in Mohs v. Quarton, 1950, 257 Wis. 544, 44 N.W.2d 580, the court held when the separation of defects would lead to confusion, the rule of diminished value could apply to all defects.

In this case no such confusion arises in separating the defects. The trial court disallowed certain claimed defects because they were not proven. This finding was not against the great weight and clear preponderance of the evidence and will not be disturbed on appeal. Of the remaining defects claimed by the defendants, the court allowed the cost of replacement or repair except as to the misplacement of the living-room wall. Whether a defect should fall under the cost-of-replacement rule or be considered under the diminished-value rule depends upon the nature and magnitude of the defect. This court has not allowed items of such magnitude under the cost-of-repair rule as the trial court did. Viewing the construction of the house as a whole and its cost we cannot say, however, that the trial court was in error in allowing the cost of repairing the plaster cracks in the ceilings, the cost of mud jacking and repairing the patio floor, and the cost of reconstructing the non-weight-bearing and nonstructural patio wall. Such reconstruction did not involve an unreasonable economic waste.

The item of misplacing the living room wall under the facts of this case was clearly under the diminished-value rule. There is no evidence that defendants requested or demanded the replacement of the wall in the place called for by the specifications during the course of construction. To tear down the wall now and rebuild it in its proper place would involve a substantial destruction of the work, if not all of it, which was put into the wall and would cause additional damage to other parts of the house and require replastering and redecorating the walls and ceilings of at least two rooms. Such economic waste is unreasonable and unjustified. The rule of diminished value contemplates the wall is not going to be moved. Expert witnesses for both parties, testifying as to the value of the house, agreed that the misplacement of the wall had no effect on the market price. The trial court properly found that the defendants suffered no legal damage, although the defendants' particular desire for specified room size was not satisfied. For a discussion of these rules of damages for defective or unfinished construction and their application see Restatement, 1 Contracts, pp. 572–573, sec. 346(1)(a) and illustrations.

. . .

It would unduly prolong this opinion to detail and discuss all the disputed items of defects of workmanship or omissions. We have reviewed the entire record and considered the points of law raised and believe the findings are supported by the great weight and clear preponderance of the evidence and the law properly applied to the facts.

Questions

1. Did the builder in *Plante* materially breach? What is this court's test of materiality? What legal consequence follows upon a finding of materiality?

2. Is it relevant that "the cost of completing the house in strict compliance with the plans and specifications would amount to 25 or 30 per cent of the contract price"? What is the "essential purpose" of the contract in *Plante*? Was it met or not? Is the "essential purpose" test an improvement over Judge Cardozo's approach in *Jacob & Youngs*?

3. *Problems.*

   a. Reconsider Problem b, above at p. 514, under the law in *Plante v. Jacobs*.

   b. The facts are as stated in *Plante v. Jacobs*, except that, during the negotiations, the owners informed the builder that the living room had to be 16' wide in order to accommodate a door and their 9' Steinway grand piano. Further, when the studs were up, the owners measured the width of the living room and discovered that it was 1' too narrow and so informed the builder, who told them that the wall would not be moved. The owners want to fire the builder but consult you first. What should you advise them? Is their unusual interest in the width of the living room part of the "essential purpose of the contract"?

WALKER & CO. v. HARRISON

Supreme Court of Michigan, 1957.
347 Mich. 630, 81 N.W.2d 352.

SMITH, JUSTICE. This is a suit on a written contract. The defendants are in the dry-cleaning business. Walker & Company, plaintiff, sells, rents, and services advertising signs and billboards. These parties entered into an agreement pertaining to a sign. The agreement is in writing and is termed a "rental agreement." It specifies in part that:

"The lessor agrees to construct and install, at its own cost, one 18'9" high x 8'8" wide pylon type d.f. neon sign with electric clock and flashing lamps.... The lessor agrees to and does hereby lease or rent unto the said lessee the said SIGN for the term, use and rental and under the conditions, hereinafter set out, and the lessee agrees to pay said rental....

"(a) The term of this lease shall be 36 months....

"(b) The rental to be paid by lessee shall be $148.50 per month for each and every calendar month during the term of this lease; ...

"(d) Maintenance. Lessor at its expense agrees to maintain and service the sign together with such equipment as supplied and installed by the lessor to operate in conjunction with said sign under the terms of this lease; this service is to include cleaning and repainting of sign in original color scheme as often as deemed necessary by lessor to keep sign in first class advertising condition and make all necessary repairs to sign and equipment installed by lessor...."

At the "expiration of this agreement," it was also provided, "title to this sign reverts to lessee." This clause is in addition to the printed form of agreement and was apparently added as a result of defendants' concern over title, they having expressed a desire "to buy for cash" and the salesman, at one time, having "quoted a cash price."

The sign was completed and installed in the latter part of July, 1953. The first billing of the monthly payment of $148.50 was made August 1, 1953, with payment thereof by defendants on September 3, 1953. This first payment was also the last. Shortly after the sign was installed, someone hit it with a tomato. Rust, also, was visible on the chrome, complained defendants, and in its corners were "little spider cobwebs." In addition, there were "some children's sayings written down in here." Defendant Herbert Harrison called Walker for the maintenance he believed himself entitled to under subparagraph (d) above. It was not forthcoming. He called again and again. "I was getting, you might say, sorer and sorer.... Occasionally, when I started calling up, I would walk around where the tomato was and get mad again. Then I would call up on the phone again." Finally, on October 8, 1953, plaintiff not having responded to his repeated calls, he telegraphed Walker that:

> "You Have Continually Voided Our Rental Contract By Not Maintaining Signs As Agreed As We No Longer Have A Contract With You Do Not Expect Any Further Remuneration."

Walker's reply was in the form of a letter. After first pointing out that "your telegram does not make any specific allegations as to what the failure of maintenance comprises," and stating that "We certainly would appreciate your furnishing us with such information," the letter makes reference to a prior collateral controversy between the parties, "wondering if this refusal on our part prompted your attempt to void our rental contract," and concludes as follows:

> "We would like to call your attention to paragraph G in our rental contract, which covers procedures in the event of a Breach of Agreement. In the event that you carry out your threat to make no future monthly payments in accordance with the agreement, it is our intention to enforce the conditions outlined under paragraph G[1] through the proper legal channels. We call to your attention that your monthly rental payments are due in advance at our office not later than the 10th day of each current month. You are now approximately 30 days in arrears on your September payment. Unless we receive both the September and October payments by October 25th, this entire matter will be placed in the hands of our attorney for collection in accordance with paragraph G which stipulates that the entire amount is forthwith due and payable."

No additional payments were made and Walker sued in assumpsit for the entire balance due under the contract, $5,197.50, invoking paragraph (g) of the agreement. Defendants filed answer and claim of

---

1. "(g) Breach of Agreement. Lessee shall be deemed to have breached this agreement by default in payment of any installment of the rental herein provided for; abandonment of the sign or vacating premises where the sign is located; termination or transfer of lessee's interest in the premises by insolvency, appointment of a receiver for lessee's business; filing of a voluntary or involuntary petition in bankruptcy with respect to lessee or the violation of any of the other terms or conditions hereof. In the event of such default, the lessor may, upon notice to the lessee, which notice shall conclusively be deemed sufficient if mailed or delivered to the premises where the sign was or is located, take possession of the sign and declare the balance of the rental herein provided for to be forthwith due and payable, and lessee hereby agrees to pay such balance upon any such contingencies. Lessor may terminate this lease and without notice, remove and repossess said sign and recover from the lessee such amounts as may be unpaid for the remaining unexpired term of this agreement. Time is of the essence of this lease with respect to the payment of rentals herein provided for. Should lessee after lessor has declared the balance of rentals due and payable, pay the full amount of rental herein provided, he shall then be entitled to the use of the sign, under all the terms and provisions hereof, for the balance of the term of this lease. No waiver by either party hereto of the nonperformance of any term, condition or obligation hereof shall be a waiver of any subsequent breach of, or failure to perform the same, or any other term, condition or obligation hereof. It is understood and agreed that the sign is especially constructed for the lessee and for use at the premises now occupied by the lessee for the term herein provided; that it is of no value unless so used and that it is a material consideration to the lessor in entering into this agreement that the lessee shall continue to use the sign for the period of time provided herein and for the payment of the full rental for such term."

recoupment, asserting that plaintiff's failure to perform certain maintenance services constituted a prior material breach of the agreement, thus justifying their repudiation of the contract and grounding their claim for damages. The case was tried to the court without a jury and resulted in a judgment for the plaintiff. The case is before us on a general appeal.

Defendants urge upon us again and again, in various forms, the proposition that Walker's failure to service the sign, in response to repeated requests, constituted a material breach of the contract and justified repudiation by them. Their legal proposition is undoubtedly correct. Repudiation is one of the weapons available to an injured party in event the other contractor has committed a material breach. But the injured party's determination that there has been a material breach, justifying his own repudiation, is fraught with peril, for should such determination, as viewed by a later court in the calm of its contemplation, be unwarranted, the repudiator himself will have been guilty of material breach and himself have become the aggressor, not an innocent victim.

What is our criterion for determining whether or not a breach of contract is so fatal to the undertaking of the parties that it is to be classed as "material"? There is no single touchstone. Many factors are involved. They are well stated in section 275 of Restatement of the Law of Contracts in the following terms:

"In determining the materiality of a failure fully to perform a promise the following circumstances are influential:

"(a) The extent to which the injured party will obtain the substantial benefit which he could have reasonably anticipated;

"(b) The extent to which the injured party may be adequately compensated in damages for lack of complete performance;

"(c) The extent to which the party failing to perform has already partly performed or made preparations for performance;

"(d) The greater or less hardship on the party failing to perform in terminating the contract;

"(e) The wilful, negligent or innocent behavior of the party failing to perform;

"(f) The greater or less uncertainty that the party failing to perform will perform the remainder of the contract."

We will not set forth in detail the testimony offered concerning the need for servicing. Granting that Walker's delay (about a week after defendant Herbert Harrison sent his telegram of repudiation Walker sent out a crew and took care of things) in rendering the service requested was irritating, we are constrained to agree with the trial court that it was not of such materiality as to justify repudiation of the contract, and we are particularly mindful of the lack of preponderant evidence contrary to his determination. Jones v. Eastern Michigan

Motorbuses, 287 Mich. 619, 283 N.W. 710. The trial court, on this phase of the case, held as follows:

> "Now Mr. Harrison phoned in, so he testified, a number of times. He isn't sure of the dates but he sets the first call at about the 7th of August and he complained then of the tomato and of some rust and some cobwebs. The tomato, according to the testimony, was up on the clock; that would be outside of his reach, without a stepladder or something. The cobwebs are within easy reach of Mr. Harrison and so would the rust be. I think that Mr. Bueche's argument that these were not materially a breach would clearly be true as to the cobwebs and I really can't believe in the face of all the testimony that there was a great deal of rust seven days after the installation of this sign. And that really brings it down to the tomato. And, of course, when a tomato has been splashed all over your clock, you don't like it. But he says he kept calling their attention to it, although the rain probably washed some of the tomato off. But the stain remained, and they didn't come. I really can't find that that was such a material breach of the contract as to justify rescission. I really don't think so."

Nor, we conclude, do we. There was no valid ground for defendants' repudiation and their failure thereafter to comply with the terms of the contract was itself a material breach, entitling Walker, upon this record, to judgment.

The question of damages remains. The parties, particularly appellants, have discussed at some length whether this contract is one of sale or of lease. Through much of its content it appears merely to be an ordinary lease, but when we come to its end we find that title, without more, is to pass to the "lessee" at the expiration of the agreement. Is the so-called rent merely the payment of a sale price in installments? We need not, in the light of the terms of the particular contract, and upon the record, vex this question, despite illustrious aid offered us by 2 Williston on Sales, § 336, extensive annotations in 17 A.L.R. 1435, 43 A.L.R. 1257, 92 A.L.R. 323, and 175 A.L.R. 1366, and the comprehensive analysis of Dalzell in 1 Oregon Law Review 9, "Lease—Contracts as a Means of Conveying Title to Chattels." For the parties before us have agreed, with particularity, as to remedies in event of breach, the remedy here sought, as provided, being acceleration of "rentals" due. The trial court cut down such sum by the amount that service would have cost Walker during the unexpired portion of the agreement (Restatement, Contracts, § 335) and as to such diminution Walker does not complain or cross-appeal. Judgment was, therefore, rendered for the cash price of the sign, for such services and maintenance as were extended and accepted, and interest upon the amount in default. There was no error.

Questions

1. What is the plaintiff's argument in *Walker & Co.*? What is the defendant's argument? Why does the plaintiff prevail? Should it? Is the

plaintiff's contractual interest more deserving of the legal protection sought by the plaintiff? If so, should the plaintiff recover despite its breach?

2. On the facts reported by the court, did the plaintiff clearly breach?

3. Assuming that the plaintiff breached, what is this court's test for material breach? Is it an improvement over the tests in *Jacob & Youngs* and *Plante*? How effective is the guidance offered by the factors approach of the RESTATEMENT (FIRST) OF CONTRACTS? See also RESTATEMENT (SECOND) OF CON-TRACTS §§ 241, 242.

4. *Problem.*

Reconsider Problem b, above at p. 514 under the law in *Walker & Co. v. Harrison*.

NOTE ON THE DOCTRINE OF MATERIAL BREACH

The tests for material breach in the preceding three cases might seem to do little more than give a court or jury free rein to decide questions of material breach on an ad hoc basis. This should not be satisfactory for two reasons. First, the law is supposed to guide official decisionmakers to keep the use of official coercion within bounds. Second, the law should be reasonably predictable so that people can conduct themselves without running afoul of the law. The latter reason is of special concern to lawyers advising clients in Paulette's situation. If Paulette's lawyer advises her that she can fire Charlie, she does so, and that advice turns out to have been unreliable, Paulette's lawyer will have thrown his client into material breach of contract. Paulette is not likely to thank her lawyer for such advice.

In an important article, Eric G. Andersen, *A New Look at Material Breach in the Law of Contracts*, 21 U.C. DAVIS L. REV. 1073 (1988), Professor Andersen argues that a main reason for the difficulty has been a general failure to recognize that material breach is a remedial concept. The practical consequence of classifying a breach as "material" is that the nonbreaching party gains a power to cancel the contract. The definition of material breach, he argues, should therefore turn on whether cancellation is justified. Accordingly, we should consider under what circumstances a party *should* be entitled to end the contract in response to the other's breach.

The expectation interest of a party to a contract can be divided into two distinct interests that may be impaired by the other's breach. The first is the *interest in present performance*. That interest is harmed when the one in breach fails to perform properly on time. For example, when a landowner contracts to have a commercial building constructed, direct financial interests are impaired if the building is completed late or imperfectly. The owner may lose rent from tenants, be liable to tenants for delays, or be required to spend money repairing defects. Unjustified impairment of the interest in present performance usually is remedied by an award of compensatory damages. The victim of the breach is entitled to a judgment sufficient to pay for the net loss of value that breach causes, such as the amount needed to repair defects or to cover lost rents.

Professor Andersen asked: What is the harm for which cancellation is an appropriate, additional remedy when compensatory damages are available for harms to the interest in present performance? He answered that the interest protected by the cancellation remedy is the *interest in future performance*, which involves a party's security or confidence that the other party will perform duties *not yet due* as and when agreed. To continue the example, long before the building is completed (perhaps before it is even started), the owner may be willing to make commitments to the building's future tenants that would be ill-advised absent a reliable expectation that the builder will perform as promised. The security at the heart of the interest in future performance is one of the most important benefits enjoyed by contracting parties.

A breach of contract may harm either the interest in present performance, the interest in future performance, or both. If, early in the construction, the owner finds that the foundation of a building deviates substantially from the agreed plans in its position and strength, the owner has received a lesser performance than was promised—a harm to the interest in present performance. An award of damages can compensate by enabling the owner to put the defective work right. But the flawed work at the commencement of the project may convince the owner that further shortcomings in workmanship will occur. Such insecurity impairs the interest in future performance. Significantly, damages sufficient to repair the foundation do not remedy that harm. Cancellation, by contrast, remedies that harm by bringing the contract to an end and substituting a right to damages for a right to the builder's pending performance. The damages will be what the owner must spend to get a competent builder to finish the job properly, less the amount not yet paid to the builder in breach. Thus, the law gives the owner the means to replace the builder and restore the security for which it bargained.

Questions

1. Review *Jacob & Youngs*, *Plante*, and *Walker & Co.* in light of the analysis suggested by Professor Andersen. Would the result differ in any one of them? If not, could an opinion be written that would better justify the result and provide better guidance for future cases?

2. *Problem.*

Reconsider Problem b, above at p. 514 in light of your synthesis of the above cases.

PLOTNICK v. PENNSYLVANIA SMELTING & REFINING CO.

United States Court of Appeals, Third Circuit, 1952.
194 F.2d 859.

HASTIE, CIRCUIT JUDGE. This litigation arises out of an installment contract for the sale of quantities of battery lead by a Canadian seller to a Pennsylvania buyer. The seller sued for the price of a carload of lead delivered but not paid for. The buyer counterclaimed for damages caused by the seller's failure to deliver the remaining installments covered by the contract. The district court sitting without a jury allowed recovery on both claim and counterclaim. The ultimate question is whether the buyer had committed such a breach of contract as constituted a repudiation justifying recision by the seller.

Suit was brought in the District Court for the Eastern District of Pennsylvania. Federal Jurisdiction is based on diversity of citizenship. Consequently, the conflict of laws rules of the forum, Pennsylvania, are invoked to solve the choice of law problem. Klaxon Co. v. Stentor Electric Mfg. Co., 1941, 313 U.S. 487, 61 S.Ct. 1020, 85 L.Ed. 1477. . . .

Uncontested findings of fact show that the contract in question was the last of a series of agreements, several of them installment contracts, entered into by the parties between June and October, 1947. Under these contracts, numerous shipments of lead were made by the seller in Canada to the buyer in Philadelphia. The seller frequently complained, and with justification, that payments were too long delayed. On the other hand, several shipments were not made at the times required by the contracts. However, by the end of March 1948, all contracts other than the one in suit had been fully performed by both parties. In this connection, it was the unchallenged finding of the district court that both parties waived the delays which preceded the buyer's breach involved in this suit. The earlier delays are relevant only insofar as they may reasonably have influenced either party in its interpretation of subsequent conduct of the other party.

The contract in suit was executed October 23, 1947 and called for deliveries aggregating 200 tons of battery lead to be completed not later than December 25, 1947. The agreed price was 8.1 cents per pound, or better if quality warranted. The court found that it was the understanding of the parties that at least 63 percent of the price should be paid shortly after each shipment was delivered and the balance within four weeks after that delivery. This finding is not contested.

Under this contract a first carload was delivered November 7, 1947. About 75 percent of the price was paid six days later. A second carload was received January 8, and about 75 percent of the price was paid 10 days later. Final adjustments and payments of small balances due on these two carloads were completed March 30, and these shipments are not now in dispute. The earliest shipment immediately involved in this litigation, the third under the contract, was a carload of lead received by the buyer on March 23, 1948. This delivery followed a March 12 conference of the parties. They disagree on what transpired at that conference. However, about 290,000 pounds of lead were then still to be delivered under the contract which stated December 25, 1947 as the agreed time for the completion of performance. And shortly after the conference, one carload of 43,000 pounds was delivered. No part of the price of this third carload has been paid. It is not disputed that plaintiff is entitled to the price of this shipment and his recovery on his claim in this suit vindicates that right.

On April 7, the buyer, who had been prodding the seller for more lead for some time, notified the seller that unless the balance of the lead should be delivered within thirty days he would buy in the open market and charge the seller any cost in excess of 8.1 cents per pound. On April 10, the seller replied refusing to ship unless the recently delivered third carload should be paid for. On May 12, buyer's attorney threatened suit unless the undelivered lead should be shipped promptly and at the same time promised to pay on delivery 75 percent of the price of this prospective shipment together with the full price of the third installment already received. Seller's solicitor replied on May 22 that seller regarded the contract as "cancelled" as a result of buyer's failure to pay for lead already delivered. At the same time the letter stated the seller's willingness to deliver at the originally agreed price if the overdue payment should be made by return mail and a letter of credit established to cover the price of the lead not yet shipped. Buyer's attorney replied on May 25 that buyer had withheld the price of the third carload "only as a set-off by reason of the failure of your client to deliver" and that buyer would place the overdue payment in escrow and would accept the remaining lead if shipped to Philadelphia "sight draft attached for the full invoice price of each car." On May 27, seller's solicitors reiterated the position stated in their March 22 letter and on June 2 seller notified buyer that the Canadian government had imposed export control on lead. The district court found, and it is here admitted, that between October 1947 and May 1948 the market price of battery lead increased from 8.1 cents to 11½ cents per pound.

The court concluded that the failure of defendant to make a down payment of at least 63 percent of the price of the third carload constituted a breach of contract but "not such a material breach of the contract as to justify plaintiff in refusing to ship the balance due under the contract within the meaning of section 45 of The Sales Act." This was the decisive conclusion of law which the seller has challenged.

Section 45 of the Sales Act as in force in Pennsylvania provides in relevant part as follows: "Where there is a contract to sell goods to be delivered by stated installments, which are to be separately paid for, ... and the buyer neglects or refuses to ... pay for one or more installments, it depends in each case on the terms of the contract, and the circumstances of the case, whether the breach of contract is so material as to justify the injured party in refusing to proceed further ... or whether the breach is severable, giving rise to a claim for compensation, but not to a right to treat the whole contract as broken." Pa. Stat. Ann. Tit. 69, Sec. 255 (Purdon, 1931).

We are dealing, therefore, with a situation in which the controlling statute explicitly makes the circumstances of the particular case determine whether failure to pay the price of one shipment delivered under an installment contract justifies the seller in treating his own obligation with reference to future installments as ended. Our problem is how to determine the legal effect of non-payment in a particular case.

We think the key is to be found in the rational basis of the statute itself. The flexibility of the statute reflects the impossibility of generalization about the consequences of failure to pay promptly for installments as delivered. Yet, the commercial sense of the statute yields two guiding considerations. First, non-payment for a delivered shipment may make it impossible or unreasonably burdensome from a financial point of view for the seller to supply future installments as promised. Second, buyer's breach of his promise to pay for one installment may create such reasonable apprehension in the seller's mind concerning payment for future installments that the seller should not be required to take the risk involved in continuing deliveries. . . .

In this case there is no evidence that the delay in payment for one carload made it difficult to provide additional lead. To the contrary, seller admits that throughout the period in controversy he had sufficient lead on hand for the full performance of this contract. He could have delivered had he chosen to do so. His excuse, if any, must be found in reasonable apprehension as to the future of the contract engendered by buyer's behavior.

The district court's finding number 16, with which seller takes issue, is a direct negation of the claim of reasonable apprehension upon which seller seeks to establish under Section 45 of the Sales Act his asserted "right to treat the whole contract as broken." It reads as follows: "Plaintiff's claim of fear that the defendant would not pay for the balance of battery lead due under Contract No. 5794 at the contract price was without foundation and unreasonable."

In considering the propriety of this finding, it is to be borne in mind that the point here is not the absence of legal justification for the withholding of an overdue payment but rather whether, under the circumstances, that withholding gave the seller reason to believe that there was likelihood of continuing or additional default when and after he should deliver the rest of the lead in accordance with his promise. The substantiality of this alleged apprehension must be judged in the light of the uncontroverted finding that no impairment of buyer's credit had been shown. Moreover, the market was rising and all of the evidence indicates that buyer needed and urgently requested the undelivered lead. Indeed, as early as March 1, before the delivery of the carload for which payment was withheld, the buyer had complained quite urgently of the non-delivery of the entire balance of some 290,000 pounds overdue since

December. Thereafter, when the seller shipped 43,000 pounds, about one-seventh of what was due, the buyer insisted that he was withholding payment because of the delay in delivery of the overdue balance. The court's finding that buyer had waived any claim for damages for delay up to that time does not alter this factual picture or its rational implications. In these circumstances, the trial court was justified in concluding that buyer's explanation of his conduct merited belief and that seller had no valid reason to be fearful that payment would not be forthcoming upon full delivery.

The clincher here is provided by the additional evidence concerning the possibility of delivery with sight draft attached. While there is no specific finding on the point, the evidence, including testimony tendered on behalf of seller, shows without dispute that at the beginning of this series of contracts, the seller had the privilege of shipping on sight draft but elected not to do so. And just before the collapse of the efforts of the parties to work out their difficulties amicably, the buyer specifically proposed that the seller assure himself of prompt payment by the use of sight drafts accompanying shipments. It is again important that at this time the market was substantially higher than the contract price and that seller was advised of buyer's urgent need for lead to meet his own commitments. In such circumstances it is incredible that the buyer would refuse to honor sight drafts for the contract price. These facts considered together leave no basis for reasonable apprehension concerning payment.

There is one other relevant and important fact. Throughout the controversial period the seller, with a stock of lead on hand adequate for the full performance of this contract, was using this lead in a rising market for sales to other purchasers at prices higher than agreed in the present contract. The inference was not only allowable but almost inescapable that desire to avoid a bad bargain rather than apprehension that the buyer would not carry out that bargain caused the seller to renounce the agreement and charge the buyer with repudiation. Rescission for such cause is not permissible. See Truitt v. Guenther Lumber Co., 1920, 73 Pa.Super. 445, 450.

It follows that the seller has failed to establish justification for rescission under Section 45 of the Sales Act and that judgment for the buyer on the counterclaim was proper.

The judgment will be affirmed.

Questions

1. In common law terms, did the buyer materially breach? Why or why not? Which of the tests of material breach makes the most sense here?

2. Would the same result be required under the U.C.C. (which replaced the older Sales Act)? Under the United Nations Convention on the International Sale of Goods (which partially replaces the U.C.C., Art. 2)? Under current law, what would you advise a seller at the time it learns of the buyer's failure to make the payment then due?

McCLOSKEY & CO. v. MINWELD STEEL CO.

United States Court of Appeals, Third Circuit, 1955.
220 F.2d 101.

McLAUGHLIN, CIRCUIT JUDGE. Plaintiff-appellant, a general contractor, sued on three contracts alleging an anticipatory breach as to each. At the close of the plaintiff's case the district judge granted the defense motions for judgment on the ground that plaintiff had not made out a cause of action.

By the contracts involved the principal defendant, a fabricator and erector of steel, agreed to furnish and erect all of the structural steel required on two buildings to be built on the grounds of the Hollidaysburg State Hospital, Hollidaysburg, Pa. and to furnish all of the long span steel joists required in the construction of one of the two buildings. Two of the contracts were dated May 1, 1950 and the third May 26, 1950. By Article V of each of the contracts, "Should the Sub–Contractor [the defendant herein] ... at any time refuse or neglect to supply a sufficiency ... of materials of the proper quality, ... in and about the performance of the work required to be done pursuant to the provisions of this agreement ..., or fail, in the performance of any of the agreements herein contained, the Contractor shall be at liberty, without prejudice to any other right or remedy, on two days' written notice to the Sub-Contractor, either to provide any such ... materials and to deduct the cost thereof from any payments then or thereafter due the Sub-Contractor, or to terminate the employment of the Sub-Contractor for the said work and to enter upon the premises...."

There was no stated date in the contracts for performance by the defendant subcontractor. Article VI provided for completion by the subcontractor of its contract work "by and at the time or times hereafter stated to-wit":

"Samples, Shop Drawings and Schedules are to be submitted in the quantities and manner required by the Specifications, for the approval of the Architects, immediately upon receipt by the Sub-Contractor of the contract drawings, or as may be directed by the Contractor. All expense involved in the submission and approval of these Samples, Shop Drawings and Schedules shall be borne by the Sub-Contractor.

"All labor, materials and equipment required under this contract are to be furnished at such times as may be directed by the Contractor, and in such a manner so as to at no time delay the final completion of the building.

"It being mutually understood and agreed that prompt delivery and installation of all materials required to be furnished under this contract is to be the essence of this Agreement."

Appellee Minweld Steel Co., Inc., the subcontractor, received contract drawings and specifications for both buildings in May, 1950. On

June 8, 1950, plaintiff McCloskey & Co. wrote appellee asking when it might "expect delivery of the structural steel" for the buildings and "also the time estimated to complete erection." Minweld replied on June 13, 1950, submitting a schedule estimate of expecting to begin delivery of the steel by September 1, and to complete erection approximately November 15. On July 20, 1950, plaintiff wrote Minweld threatening to terminate the contracts unless the latter gave unqualified assurances that it had effected definite arrangements for the procurement, fabrication and delivery within thirty days of the required materials. On July 24, 1950, Minweld wrote McCloskey & Co. explaining its difficulty in obtaining the necessary steel. It asked McCloskey's assistance in procuring it and stated that "We are as anxious as you are that there be no delay in the final completion of the buildings or in the performance of our contract,...."[2]

Plaintiff-appellant claims that by this last letter, read against the relevant facts, defendant gave notice of its positive intention not to

---

2. This letter in full is as follows:

Minweld Steel Company Incorporated
Shaler and Wabash Streets
Pittsburgh 20, Pa.
July 24, 1950.

McCloskey & Company

1620 Thompson Street

Philadelphia 21, Penna.

In re: New Hospital Buildings

Hollidaysburg State Hospital

Hollidaysburg, Pennsylvania

Attention of J. C. McCloskey, Vice President

Dear Sir:

This will acknowledge receipt of your letter of July 20th, 1950, which was received by us today.

Upon receipt of the architect's specifications, we completed the engineering and erection plans on the said specifications. Immediately after those details were available, we attempted to place orders for the steel with the Bethlehem Steel Company. Our order was held in the offices of the Bethlehem Steel Company for two weeks before we were notified that it could not be supplied. Since that time, we have tried the U.S. Steel Corporation and Carnegie-Illinois, both companies informing us that they were under contract for approximately one year and could not fulfill the order.

The recent directive by the President of the United States, with which we assume you are familiar, has further tightened up the steel market so that at the present writing we cannot give you any positive promise as to our ability to obtain the steel or delivery dates.

In view of the directive from Washington and the tightening up of the entire steel industry, we solicit your help and that of the General State Authority in aiding us to obtain the steel for these contracts.

We are as anxious as you are that there be no delay in the final completion of the buildings or in the performance of our contract, but we have nowhere else to turn at the present time for the supply of steel necessary under said contracts, unless through your aid and assistance, and that of the General State Authority, a supplier can be induced to give us the materials needed.

The U.S. Steel Corporation informs us that you have discussed this matter with them and are presently aware of our present difficulties.

If steel is to be supplied to these hospital buildings by governmental directive, we feel that the steel should be supplied to us for completion under our contract.

Very truly yours,
Minweld Steel Company, Inc.
J. A. Roberts Sales Manager

JAR/fs
c/c   Travelers Indemnity Co.,
Hartford, Conn.
General State Authority,
Harrisburg, Penna.

perform its contracts and thereby violated same.[3] Some reference has already been made to the background of the July 24th letter. It concerned Minweld's trouble in securing the steel essential for performance of its contract. Minweld had tried unsuccessfully to purchase this from Bethlehem Steel, U.S. Steel and Carnegie-Illinois. It is true as appellant urges that Minweld knew and was concerned about the tightening up of the steel market.[4] And as is evident from the letter it, being a fabricator and not a producer, realized that without the help of the general contractor on this hospital project particularly by it enlisting the assistance of the General State Authority,[5] Minweld was in a bad way for the needed steel. However, the letter conveys no idea of contract repudiation by Minweld. That company admittedly was in a desperate situation. Perhaps if it had moved earlier to seek the steel its effort might have been successful. But that is mere speculation for there is no showing that the mentioned producers had they been solicited sooner would have been willing to provide the material.

Minweld from its written statement did, we think, realistically face the problem confronting it. As a result it asked its general contractor for the aid which the latter, by the nature of the construction, should have been willing to give. Despite the circumstances there is no indication in the letter that Minweld had definitely abandoned all hope of otherwise receiving the steel and so finishing its undertaking. One of the mentioned producers might have relented. Some other supplier might have turned up. It was McCloskey & Co. who eliminated whatever chance there was. That concern instead of aiding Minweld by urging its plea for the hospital construction materials to the State Authority which represented the Commonwealth of Pennsylvania took the position that the subcontractor had repudiated its agreement and then moved quickly to have the work completed. Shortly thereafter, and without the slightest trouble as far as appears, McCloskey & Co. procured the steel from Bethlehem[6] and brought in new subcontractors to do the work contemplated by the agreement with Minweld.

Under the applicable law Minweld's letter was not a breach of the agreement. The suit is in the federal court by reason of diversity of citizenship of the parties. Though there is no express statement to that effect the contracts between the parties would seem to have been executed in Pennsylvania with the law of that state applicable. In McClelland v. New Amsterdam Casualty Co., 1936, 322 Pa. 429, 433, 185 A. 198, 200, the Pennsylvania Supreme Court held in a case where the

---

3. Plaintiff cancelled the contracts on July 26, 1950 on the ground that the July 24th letter constituted an admission of defendant's inability to perform the required work.

4. The Korean War broke out on June 24, 1950.

5. The Pennsylvania state agency which represented and owned the Hollidaysburg State Hospital.

6. Bethlehem had originally submitted a bid in competition with Minweld. Its new proposals were dated July 28, 1950 and were finally accepted by McCloskey & Co. on August 7, 1950. The long span steel joists required by the third contract were procured from the Frederick Grundy Iron Works.

subcontractor had asked for assistance in obtaining credit. "In order to give rise to a renunciation amounting to a breach of contract, there must be an absolute and unequivocal refusal to perform or a distinct and positive statement of an inability to do so." Minweld's conduct is plainly not that of a contract breaker under that test....

Appellant contends that its letter of July 20, requiring assurances of arrangements which would enable appellee to complete delivery in thirty days, constituted a fixing of a date under Article VI of the contracts. The short answer to this is that the thirty day date, if fixed, was never repudiated. Appellee merely stated that it was unable to give assurances as to the preparatory arrangements. There is nothing in the contracts which authorized appellant to demand or receive such assurances.

The district court acted properly in dismissing the actions as a matter of law on the ground that plaintiff had not made out a prima facie case.

The order of the district court of July 14, 1954, denying the plaintiff's motions for findings of facts, to vacate the judgments and for new trials will be affirmed.

Questions

1. What is the general contractor's complaint? What is the factual basis underlying it? What is the subcontractor's response? What is the factual basis underlying it? What is the basis for the court's holding?

2. Is the court's opinion persuasive in its own terms? Would the result differ under RESTATEMENT (SECOND) OF CONTRACTS § 251 or U.C.C. § 2–609?

3. Whatever the soundness of the court's rationale, was the result unjust? Consider: Was the general contractor in a position to mitigate the harm to its interest in future performance? If so, should that bear on a judgment of breach by anticipatory repudiation or material breach?

––––––

RESTATEMENT (SECOND) OF CONTRACTS §§ 236, 243

––––––

K & G CONSTRUCTION CO. v. HARRIS

Court of Appeals of Maryland, 1960.
223 Md. 305, 164 A.2d 451.

PRESCOTT, JUDGE. Feeling aggrieved by the action of the trial judge of the Circuit Court for Prince George's County, sitting without a jury, in finding a judgment against it in favor of a subcontractor, the appellant, the general contractor on a construction project, appealed.

The principal question presented is: Does a contractor, damaged by a subcontractor's failure to perform a portion of his work in a workmanlike manner, have a right, under the circumstances of this case, to withhold, in partial satisfaction of said damages, an installment payment, which, under the terms of the contract, was due the subcontractor, unless the negligent performance of his work excused its payment?

The appeal is presented on a case stated in accordance with Maryland Rule 826g.

The statement, in relevant part, is as follows:

"... K & G Construction Company, Inc. (hereinafter called Contractor), plaintiff and counter-defendant in the Circuit Court and appellant herein, was owner and general contractor of a housing subdivision project being constructed (herein called Project). Harris and Brooks (hereinafter called Subcontractor), defendants and counter-plaintiffs in the Circuit Court and appellees herein, entered into a contract with Contractor to do excavating and earth-moving work on the Project. Pertinent parts of the contract are set forth below:

"Section 3. The Subcontractor agrees to complete the several portions and the whole of the work herein sublet by the time or times following:

" '(a) Without delay, as called for by the Contractor.

" '(b) It is expressly agreed that time is of the essence of this contract, and that the Contractor will have the right to terminate this contract and employ a substitute to perform the work in the event of delay on the part of Subcontractor, and Subcontractor agrees to indemnify the Contractor for any loss sustained thereby, provided, however, that nothing in this paragraph shall be construed to deprive Contractor of any rights or remedies it would otherwise have as to damage for delay.

" 'Section 4. (b) Progress payments will be made each month during the performance of the work. Subcontractor will submit to Contractor, by the 25th of each month, a requisition for work performed during the preceding month. Contractor will pay these requisitions, less a retainer equal to ten per cent (10%), by the 10th of the months in which such requisitions are received.

" '(c) No payments will be made under this contract until the insurance requirements of Sec. 9 hereof have been complied with.

" 'Section 5. The Contractor agrees:

" '(1) That no claim for services rendered or materials furnished by the Contractor to the Subcontractor shall be valid unless written notice thereof is given by the Contractor to the Subcontractor during the first ten days of the calendar month following that in which the claim originated.

" 'Section 8.... All work shall be performed in a workmanlike manner, and in accordance with the best practices.

" 'Section 9. Subcontractor agrees to carry, during the progress of the work, ... liability insurance against ... property damage, in such amounts and with such companies as may be satisfactory to Contractor and shall provide Contractor with certificates showing the same to be in force.' "

"While in the course of his employment by the Subcontractor on the Project, a bulldozer operator drove his machine too close to Contractor's house while grading the yard, causing the immediate collapse of a wall and other damage to the house. The resulting damage to contractor's house was $3,400.00. Subcontractor had complied with the insurance provision (Sec. 9) of the aforesaid contract. Subcontractor reported said damages to their liability insurance carrier. The Subcontractor and its insurance carrier refused to repair damage or compensate Contractor for damage to the house, claiming that there was no liability on the part of the Subcontractor.

"Contractor was generally satisfied with Subcontractor's work and progress as required under Sections 3 and 8 of the contract until September 12, 1958, with the exception of the bulldozer accident of August 9, 1958.

"Subcontractor performed work under the contract during July, 1958, for which it submitted a requisition by the 25th of July, as required by the contract, for work done prior to the 25th of July, payable under the terms of the contract by Contractor on or before August 10, 1958. Contractor was current as to payments due under all preceding monthly requisitions from Subcontractor. The aforesaid bulldozer accident damaging Contractor's house occurred on August 9, 1958. Contractor refused to pay Subcontractor's requisition due on August 10, 1958, because the bulldozer damage to Contractor's house had not been repaired or paid for. Subcontractor continued to work on the project until the 12th of September, 1958, at which time they discontinued working on the project because of Contractor's refusal to pay the said work requisition and notified Contractor by registered letters of their position and willingness to return to the job, but only upon payment. At that time, September 12, 1958, the value of the work completed by Subcontractor on the project for which they had not been paid was $1,484.50.

"Contractor later requested Subcontractor to return and complete work on the Project which Subcontractor refused to do because of nonpayment of work requisitions of July 25 and thereafter. Contractor's house was not repaired by Subcontractor nor compensation paid for the damage.

"It was stipulated that Subcontractor had completed work on the Project under the contract for which they had not been paid in the amount of $1,484.50 and that if they had completed the remaining work to be done under the contract, they would have made a profit of $1,340.00 on the remaining uncompleted portion of the contract. It was further stipulated that it cost the Contractor $450.00 above the contract price to have another excavating contractor complete the remaining work required under the contract. It was the opinion of the Court that if judgment were in favor of the Subcontractor, it should be for the total amount of $2,824.50.

"... Contractor filed suit against the Subcontractor in two counts: (1), for the aforesaid bulldozer damage to Contractor's house, alleging negligence of the Subcontractor's bulldozer operator, and (2) for the $450.00 costs above the contract price in having another excavating subcontractor complete the uncompleted work in the contract. Subcontractor filed a counter-claim for recovery of work of the value of $1,484.50 for which they had not received payment and for loss of anticipated profits on uncompleted portion of work in the amount of $1,340.00. By agreement of the parties, the first count of Contractor's claim, i.e., for aforesaid bulldozer damage to Contractor's house, was submitted to jury who found in favor of Contractor in the amount of $3,400.00. Following the finding by the jury, the second count of the Contractor's claim and the counter-claims of the Subcontractor, by agreement of the parties, were submitted to the Court for determination, without jury. All of the facts recited herein above were stipulated to by the parties to the Court. Circuit Court Judge Fletcher found for counter-plaintiff Subcontractor in the amount of $2,824.50 from which Contractor has entered this appeal."

The $3,400 judgment has been paid.

It is immediately apparent that our decision turns upon the respective rights and liabilities of the parties under that portion of their contract whereby the subcontractor agreed to do the excavating and earth-moving work in "a workmanlike manner, and in accordance with the best practices," with time being of the essence of the contract, and the contractor agreed to make progress payments therefor on the 10th day of the months following the performance of the work by the subcontractor.[3] The subcontractor contends, of course, that when the contractor failed to make the payment due on August 10, 1958, he breached his contract and thereby released him (the subcontractor) from any further obligation to perform. The contractor, on the other hand, argues that the failure of the subcontractor to perform his work in a workmanlike manner constituted a material breach of the contract, which justified his refusal to make the August 10 payment; and, as there was no breach on his part, the subcontractor had no right to cease performance on September 12, and his refusal to continue work on the project constituted another breach, which rendered him liable to the contractor for damages. The vital question, more tersely stated, remains:

---

3. The statement of the case does not show the exact terms concerning the remuneration to be paid the subcontractor. It does not disclose whether he was to be paid a total lump sum, by the cubic yard, by the day, or in some other manner. It does state that the excavation finally cost the contractor $450 more than the "contract price."

Did the contractor have a right, under the circumstances, to refuse to make the progress payment due on August 10, 1958? . . .

Considering the presumption that promises and counter-promises are dependent and the statement of the case, we have no hesitation in holding that the promise and counter-promise under consideration here were mutually dependent, that is to say, the parties intended performance by one to be conditioned on performance by the other; and the subcontractor's promise was, by the explicit wording of the contract, precedent to the promise of payment, monthly, by the contractor. In Shapiro Engineering Corp. v. Francis O. Day Co., 215 Md. 373, 380, 137 A.2d 695, we stated that it is the general rule that where a total price for work is fixed by a contract, the work is not rendered divisible by progress payments. It would, indeed present an unusual situation if we were to hold that a building contractor, who has obtained someone to do work for him and has agreed to pay each month for the work performed in the previous month, has to continue the monthly payments, irrespective of the degree of skill and care displayed in the performance of work, and his only recourse is by way of suit for ill-performance. If this were the law, it is conceivable, in fact, probable, that many contractors would become insolvent before they were able to complete their contracts. As was stated by the Court in Measures Brothers Ltd. v. Measures, 2 Ch. 248: "Covenants are to be construed as dependent or independent according to the intention of the parties and the good sense of the case."

We hold that when the subcontractor's employee negligently damaged the contractor's wall, this constituted a breach of the subcontractor's promise to perform his work in a "workmanlike manner, and in accordance with the best practices." Gaybis v. Palm, 201 Md. 78, 85, 93 A.2d 269. . . . And there can be little doubt that the breach was material: the damage to the wall amounted to more than double the payment due on August 10. Speed v. Bailey, 153 Md. 655, 661, 662, 139 A. 534. 3A Corbin, Contracts, § 708, says: "The failure of a contractor's [in our case, the subcontractor's] performance to constitute 'substantial' performance may justify the owner [in our case, the contractor] in refusing to make a progress payment. . . . If the refusal to pay an installment is justified on the owner's [contractor's] part, the contractor [subcontractor] is not justified in abandoning work by reason of that refusal. His abandonment of the work will itself be a wrongful repudiation that goes to the essence, even if the defects in performance did not." . . . Professor Corbin, in § 954, states further: "The unexcused failure of a contractor to render a promised performance when it is due is always a breach of contract. . . . Such failure may be of such great importance as to constitute what has been called herein a 'total' breach. . . . For a failure of performance constituting such a 'total' breach, an action for remedies that are appropriate thereto is at once maintainable. Yet the injured party is not required to bring such action. He has the option of treating the non-performance as a 'partial' breach only. . . ." In permitting the subcontractor to proceed with work on the project after August 9, the contractor, obviously, treated the breach by the subcontractor as a partial one. As the promises were mutually dependent and the subcontractor had made a material breach in his performance, this justified the contractor in refusing to make the August 10 payment; hence, as the contractor was not in default, the subcontractor again breached the contract when he, on September 12, discontinued work on the project, which rendered him liable (by the express terms of the contract) to the contractor for his increased cost in having the excavating done—a stipulated amount of $450. Cf. Keystone Engineering Corp. v. Sutter, 196 Md. 620, 628, 78 A.2d 191. . . .

Judgment against the appellant reversed; and judgment entered in favor of the appellant against the appellees for $450, the appellees to pay the costs.

Questions

1.   On the facts of *K & G*, after the subcontractor's bulldozer operator bulldozes the wall, the general contractor phones you to ask if he must make the August 10 progress payment to the subcontractor. What do you advise him under the court's view of the law in *K & G*?

2.   Is the court's view of the law sound? Does the general contractor have an interest in performance that would be harmed in a way that justifies withholding payment? Why is it relevant that the damages caused by the bulldozer accident were greater than the amount due on August 10? Can you tell from the facts given by the court whether the subcontractor materially breached? What further facts might you want to know?

3.   *Problems.*

a.   Otherwise on the facts of *K & G*, assume that the bulldozer accident was a material breach and the general contractor filed an action against the subcontractor on August 12. The subcontractor seeks your advice on whether it should continue working. What would you advise?

b.   Otherwise on the facts of *K & G*, assume that the bulldozer accident was an immaterial breach and the general contractor withheld the August 10 payment. What would you advise the subcontractor?

c.   Otherwise on the facts of *K & G*, assume that the bulldozer accident was an immaterial breach and the general contractor withheld the August 10 payment. The subcontractor continued to work for three weeks while demanding the payment and then quits work. What would you advise the general contractor?

RESTATEMENT (SECOND) OF CONTRACTS § 240

GILL v. JOHNSTOWN LUMBER CO.

Supreme Court of Pennsylvania, 1892.
151 Pa. 534, 25 A. 120.

[Action in assumpsit for driving logs under a written contract, the terms of which are described in the opinion. Plaintiff agreed to drive some four million feet of logs, and to begin driving at once, "if sufficient natural water by use of splash dams." Directed verdict for defendant on ground that contract was "entire" and that plaintiff defaulted in that a flood had carried away a considerable proportion of the logs past defendant's boom.]

HEYDRICK, JUDGE. The single question in this cause is whether the contract upon which the plaintiff sued is entire or severable. If it is entire, it is conceded that the learned court below properly directed a verdict for the defendant; if severable, it is not denied that the cause ought to have been submitted to the jury. The criterion by which it is to be determined to which class any particular contract shall be assigned is thus stated in Parsons on Contracts, 29–31: "If the part to be performed by one party consists of several and distinct items, and the price to be paid by the other is apportioned to each item to be performed, or is left to be implied by law, such a contract will generally be held to be severable. . . . But if the consideration to be paid is single and entire, the contract must be held to be entire, although the subject of the contract may consist of several distinct and wholly independent items." . . .

Applying the test of an apportionable or apportioned consideration to the contract in question, it will be seen at once that it is severable. The work undertaken to be done by the plaintiff consisted of several items, viz., driving logs, first, of oak, and, second, of various other kinds of timber, from points upon Stony creek and its tributaries above Johnstown to the defendant's boom at Johnstown, and also driving cross-ties from some undesignated point or points, presumably understood by the parties, to Bethel, in Somerset county, and to some other point or points below Bethel. For this work the consideration to be paid was not an entire sum, but was apportioned among the several items at the rate of $1 per 1,000 feet for the oak logs; 75 cents per 1,000 feet for all other logs; 3 cents each for cross-ties driven to Bethel; and 5 cents each for cross-ties driven to points below Bethel. But while the contract is severable, and the plaintiff entitled to compensation at the stipulated rate for all logs and ties delivered at the specified points, there is neither reason nor authority for the claim for compensation in respect to logs that were swept by the flood to and through the defendant's boom, whether they had been driven part of the way by plaintiff, or remained untouched by him at the coming of the flood. In respect to each particular log the contract in this case is like a contract of common carriage, which is dependent upon the delivery of the goods at the designated place, and, if by *casus* the delivery is prevented, the carrier cannot recover *pro tanto* for freight for part of the route over which the goods were taken. Whart. Cont. § 714. Indeed, this is but an application of the rule already stated. The consideration to be paid for driving each log is an entire sum per 1,000 feet for the whole distance, and is not apportioned to parts of the drive. The judgment is reversed, and a *venire facias de novo* is awarded.

Questions

1. Why was the log owner required to pay for the logs driven all of the way? Why was the plaintiff's claim rejected for logs driven past the defendant's boom?

2. What should be the test for determining whether a contract is severable? What are the contractual interests protected by the division in *Gill*? Does the law of contract severability adequately protect those interests?

3. *Problem.*

The Burma Shave Co. contracted with Adeline's Signs to place five signs at one mile intervals along a country road popular with speeding motorists. Burma Shave agreed to pay $250. The signs were to read, in sequence:

> Don't lose your head
>
> To gain a minute.
>
> You need your head.
>
> Your brains are in it.
>
> Burma Shave

Adeline's Signs put up the first four signs but never put up the fifth sign. Burma Shave refused to pay, and Adeline sued for $200. What result?

UNIFORM COMMERCIAL CODE §§ 2–508, 2–601, 2–602, 2–606, 2–607, 2–608, 2–612

RAMIREZ v. AUTOSPORT

Supreme Court of New Jersey, 1982.
88 N.J. 277, 440 A.2d 1345.

POLLOCK, J. This case raises several issues under the Uniform Commercial Code ("the Code" and "UCC") concerning whether a buyer may reject a tender of goods with minor defects and whether a seller may cure the defects. We consider also the remedies available to the buyer, including cancellation of the contract. The main issue is whether plaintiffs, Mr. and Mrs. Ramirez, could reject the tender by defendant,

Autosport, of a camper van with minor defects and cancel the contract for the purchase of the van.

The trial court ruled that Mr. and Mrs. Ramirez rightfully rejected the van and awarded them the fair market value of their trade-in van. The Appellate Division affirmed in a brief per curiam decision which, like the trial court opinion, was unreported. We affirm the judgment of the Appellate Division.

I

Following a mobile home show at the Meadowlands Sports Complex, Mr. and Mrs. Ramirez visited Autosport's showroom in Somerville. On July 20, 1978, the Ramirezes and Donald Graff, a salesman for Autosport, agreed on the sale of a new camper and the trade-in of the van owned by Mr. and Mrs. Ramirez. Autosport and the Ramirezes signed a simple contract reflecting a $14,100 purchase price for the new van with a $4,700 trade-in allowance for the Ramirez van, which Mr. and Mrs. Ramirez left with Autosport. After further allowance for taxes, title and documentary fees, the net price was $9,902. Because Autosport needed two weeks to prepare the new van, the contract provided for delivery on or about August 3, 1978.

On that date, Mr. and Mrs. Ramirez returned with their checks to Autosport to pick up the new van. Graff was not there so Mr. White, another salesman, met them. Inspection disclosed several defects in the van. The paint was scratched, both the electric and sewer hookups were missing, and the hubcaps were not installed. White advised the Ramirezes not to accept the camper because it was not ready.

Mr. and Mrs. Ramirez wanted the van for a summer vacation and called Graff several times. Each time Graff told them it was not ready for delivery. Finally, Graff called to notify them that the camper was ready. On August 14, Mr. and Mrs. Ramirez went to Autosport to accept delivery, but workers were still touching up the outside paint. Also, the camper windows were open, and the dining area cushions were soaking wet. Mr. and Mrs. Ramirez could not use the camper in that condition, but Mr. Leis, Autosport's manager, suggested that they take the van and that Autosport would replace the cushions later. Mrs. Ramirez counter-offered to accept the van if they could withhold $2,000, but Leis agreed to no more than $250, which she refused. Leis then agreed to replace the cushions and to call them when the van was ready.

On August 15, 1978, Autosport transferred title to the van to Mr. and Mrs. Ramirez, a fact unknown to them until the summer of 1979. Between August 15 and September 1, 1978, Mrs. Ramirez called Graff several times urging him to complete the preparation of the van, but Graff constantly advised her that the van was not ready. He finally informed her that they could pick it up on September 1.

When Mr. and Mrs. Ramirez went to the showroom on September 1, Graff asked them to wait. And wait they did–for one and a half hours.

No one from Autosport came forward to talk with them, and the Ramirezes left in disgust.

On October 5, 1978, Mr. and Mrs. Ramirez went to Autosport with an attorney friend. Although the parties disagreed on what occurred, the general topic was whether they should proceed with the deal or Autosport should return to the Ramirezes their trade-in van. Mrs. Ramirez claimed they rejected the new van and requested the return of their trade-in. Mr. Lustig, the owner of Autosport, thought, however, that the deal could be salvaged if the parties could agree on the dollar amount of a credit for the Ramirezes. Mr. and Mrs. Ramirez never took possession of the new van and repeated their request for the return of their trade-in. Later in October, however, Autosport sold the trade-in to an innocent third party for $4,995. Autosport claimed that the Ramirez' van had a book value of $3,200 and claimed further that it spent $1,159.62 to repair their van. By subtracting the total of those two figures, $4,159.62, from the $4,995.00 sale price, Autosport claimed a $600–700 profit on the sale.

On November 20, 1978, the Ramirezes sued Autosport seeking, among other things, rescission of the contract. Autosport counterclaimed for breach of contract.

II

Our initial inquiry is whether a consumer may reject defective goods that do not conform to the contract of sale. The basic issue is whether under the UCC, adopted in New Jersey as N.J.S.A. 12A:1–101 et seq., a seller has the duty to deliver goods that conform precisely to the contract. We conclude that the seller is under such a duty to make a "perfect tender" and that a buyer has the right to reject goods that do not conform to the contract. That conclusion, however, does not resolve the entire dispute between buyer and seller. A more complete answer requires a brief statement of the history of the mutual obligations of buyers and sellers of commercial goods.

In the nineteenth century, sellers were required to deliver goods that complied exactly with the sales agreement. See Filley v. Pope, 115 U.S. 213, 220, 6 S.Ct. 19, 21, 29 L.Ed. 372, 373 (1885) (buyer not obliged to accept otherwise conforming scrap iron shipped to New Orleans from Leith, rather than Glasgow, Scotland, as required by contract).... That rule, known as the "perfect tender" rule, remained part of the law of sales well into the twentieth century. By the 1920's, the doctrine was so entrenched in the law that Judge Learned Hand declared "(t)here is no room in commercial contracts for the doctrine of substantial performance." Mitsubishi Goshi Kaisha v. J. Aron & Co., Inc., 16 F.2d 185, 186 (2 Cir.1926).

The harshness of the rule led courts to seek to ameliorate its effect and to bring the law of sales in closer harmony with the law of contracts, which allows rescission only for material breaches. LeRoy Dyal Co. v. Allen, 161 F.2d 152, 155 (4 Cir.1947).... The chief objection to the continuation of the perfect tender rule was that buyers in a declining market would reject goods for minor nonconformities and force the loss on surprised sellers. See Hawkland, Sales and Bulk Sales Under the Uniform Commercial Code, 120–122 (1958), cited in N.J.S.A. 12A:2–508, New Jersey Study Comment 3.

To the extent that a buyer can reject goods for any nonconformity, the UCC retains the perfect tender rule. Section 2–106 states that goods conform to a contract "when they are in accordance with the obligations under the contract". N.J.S.A. 12A:2–106. Section 2–601 authorizes a buyer to reject goods if they "or the tender of delivery fail in any respect to conform to the contract". N.J.S.A. 12A:2–601. The Code, however, mitigates the harshness of the perfect tender rule and balances the interests of buyer and seller. See Restatement (Second), Contracts, § 241 comment (b) (1981). The Code achieves that result through its provisions for revocation of acceptance and cure. N.J.S.A. 12A:2–608, 2–508.

Initially, the rights of the parties vary depending on whether the rejection occurs before or after acceptance of the goods. Before acceptance, the buyer may reject goods for any nonconformity. N.J.S.A. 12A:2–601. Because of the seller's right to cure, however, the buyer's rejection does not necessarily discharge the contract. N.J.S.A. 12A:2–508. Within the time set for performance in the contract, the seller's right to cure is unconditional. Id., subsec. (1); see id., Official Comment 1. Some authorities recommend granting a breaching party a right to cure in all contracts, not merely those for the sale of goods. Restatement (Second), Contracts, ch. 10, especially §§ 237 and 241. Underlying the right to cure in both kinds of contracts is the recognition that parties should be encouraged to communicate with each other and to resolve their own problems. Id., Introduction p. 193.

The rights of the parties also vary if rejection occurs after the time set for performance. After expiration of that time, the seller has a further reasonable time to cure if he believed reasonably that the goods would be acceptable with or without a money allowance. N.J.S.A. 12A:2–508(2). The determination of what constitutes a further reasonable time depends on the surrounding circumstances, which include the change of position by and the amount of inconvenience to the buyer. N.J.S.A. 12A:2–508, Official Comment 3. Those circumstances also include the length of time needed by the seller to correct the nonconformity and his ability to salvage the goods by resale to others. See Restatement (Second), Contracts, § 241 comment (d). Thus, the Code balances the buyer's right to reject nonconforming goods with a "second chance" for the seller to conform the goods to the contract under certain limited circumstances. N.J.S.A. 12A:2–508, New Jersey Study Comment 1.

After acceptance, the Code strikes a different balance: the buyer may revoke acceptance only if the nonconformity substantially impairs the value of the goods to him. N.J.S.A. 12A:2–608. See Herbstman v. Eastman Kodak Co., 68 N.J. 1, 9, 342 A.2d 181 (1975). See generally, Priest, "Breach and Remedy for the Tender of Non-Conforming Goods under the Uniform Commercial Code: An Economic Approach," 91 Harv.L.Rev. 960, 971–973 (1978). This provision protects the seller from revocation for trivial defects. Herbstman, supra, 68 N.J. at 9, 342 A.2d 181. It also prevents the buyer from taking undue advantage of the seller by allowing goods to depreciate and then returning them because of asserted minor defects. See White & Summers, Uniform Commercial Code, § 8–3 at 391 (2 ed. 1980). Because this case involves rejection of goods, we need not decide whether a seller has a right to cure substantial defects that justify revocation of acceptance. See Pavesi v. Ford Motor Co., 155 N.J.Super. 373, 378, 382 A.2d 954 (Ch.Div.1978) (right to cure after acceptance limited to trivial defects) and White & Summers, supra, § 8–4 at 319 n.76 (open question as to the relationship between §§ 2–608 and 2–508).

Other courts agree that the buyer has a right of rejection for any nonconformity, but that the seller has a countervailing right to cure within a reasonable time. Marine Mart, Inc. v. Pearce, 252 Ark. 601, 480 S.W.2d 133, 137 (1972).... One New Jersey case, Gindy Mfg. Corp. v. Cardinale Trucking Corp., suggests that, because some defects can be cured, they do not justify rejection. 111 N.J.Super. 383, 387 n. 1, 268 A.2d 345 (Law Div.1970).... Nonetheless, we conclude that the perfect tender rule is preserved to the extent of permitting a buyer to reject goods for any defects. Because of the seller's right to cure, rejection does not terminate the contract. Accordingly, we disapprove the suggestion in *Gindy* that curable defects do not justify rejection.

A further problem, however, is identifying the remedy available to a buyer who rejects goods with insubstantial defects that the seller fails to cure within a reasonable time. The Code provides expressly that when "the buyer rightfully rejects, then with respect to the goods involved, the buyer may cancel." N.J.S.A. 12A:2–711. "Cancellation" occurs when either party puts an end to the contract for breach by the other. N.J.S.A. 12A:2–106(4)....

Although the complaint requested rescission of the contract, plaintiffs actually sought not only the end of their contractual obligations, but also restoration to their pre-contractual position. That request incorporated the equitable doctrine of restitution, the purpose of which is to restore plaintiff to as good a position as he occupied before the contract. Corbin, supra, § 1102 at 455. In UCC parlance, plaintiffs' request was for the cancellation of the contract and recovery of the price paid. N.J.S.A. 12A:2–106(4), 2–711.

General contract law permits rescission only for material breaches, and the Code restates "materiality" in terms of "substantial impairment". See Herbstman v. Eastman Kodak Co., supra, 68 N.J. at 9, 342 A.2d 181; id. at 15, 342 A.2d 181 (Conford, J., concurring). The Code permits a buyer who rightfully rejects goods to cancel a contract of sale. N.J.S.A. 12A:2–711. Because a buyer may reject goods with insubstantial defects, he also may cancel the contract if those defects remain uncured. Otherwise, a seller's failure to cure minor defects would compel a buyer to accept imperfect goods and collect for any loss caused by the nonconformity. N.J.S.A. 12A:2–714.

Although the Code permits cancellation by rejection for minor defects, it permits revocation of acceptance only for substantial impairments. That distinction is consistent with other Code provisions that depend on whether the buyer has accepted the goods. Acceptance creates liability in the buyer for the price, N.J.S.A. 12A:2–709(1), and precludes rejection. N.J.S.A. 12A:2–607(2); N.J.S.A. 12A:2–606, New Jersey Study Comment 1. Also, once a buyer accepts goods, he has the burden to prove any defect. N.J.S.A. 12A:2–607(4); White & Summers, supra, § 8–2 at 297. By contrast, where goods are rejected for not conforming to the contract, the burden is on the seller to prove that the nonconformity was corrected. Miron v. Yonkers Raceway, Inc., 400 F.2d 112, 119 (2 Cir. 1968).

Underlying the Code provisions is the recognition of the revolutionary change in business practices in this century. The purchase of goods is no longer a simple transaction in which a buyer purchases individually-made goods from a seller in a face-to-face transaction. Our economy depends on a complex system for the manufacture, distribution, and sale of goods, a system in which manufacturers and consumers rarely meet. Faceless manufacturers mass-produce goods for unknown consumers who purchase those goods from merchants exercising little or no control over the quality of their production. In an age of assembly lines, we are accustomed to cars with scratches, television sets without knobs and other products with all kinds of defects. Buyers no longer expect a "perfect tender". If a merchant sells defective goods, the reasonable expectation of the parties is that the buyer will return those goods and that the seller will repair or replace them.

Recognizing this commercial reality, the Code permits a seller to cure imperfect tenders. Should the seller fail to cure the defects, whether substantial or not, the balance shifts again in favor of the buyer, who has the right to cancel or seek damages. N.J.S.A. 12A:2–711. In general, economic considerations would induce sellers to cure minor defects. See generally Priest, supra, 91 Harv.L.Rev. 973–974. Assuming the seller does not cure, however, the buyer should be permitted to exercise his remedies under N.J.S.A. 12A:2–711. The Code remedies for consumers are to be liberally construed, and the buyer should have the option of cancelling if the seller does not provide conforming goods. See N.J.S.A. 12A:1–106.

To summarize, the UCC preserves the perfect tender rule to the extent of permitting a buyer to reject goods for any nonconformity. Nonetheless, that rejection does not automatically terminate the contract. A seller may still effect a cure and preclude unfair rejection and cancellation by the buyer. N.J.S.A. 12A:2–508, Official Comment 2; N.J.S.A. 12A:2–711, Official Comment 1.

III

The trial court found that Mr. and Mrs. Ramirez had rejected the van within a reasonable time under N.J.S.A. 12A:2–602. The court found that on August 3, 1978 Autosport's salesman advised the Ramirezes not to accept the van and that on August 14, they rejected delivery and Autosport agreed to replace the cushions. Those findings are supported by substantial credible evidence, and we sustain them. See Rova Farms Resort v. Investors Ins. Co., 65 N.J. 474, 483–484, 323 A.2d 495 (1974). Although the trial court did not find whether Autosport cured the defects within a reasonable time, we find that Autosport did not effect a cure. Clearly the van was not ready for delivery during August, 1978 when Mr. and Mrs. Ramirez rejected it, and Autosport had the burden of proving that it had corrected the defects. Although the Ramirezes gave Autosport ample time to correct the defects, Autosport did not demonstrate that the van conformed to the contract on September 1. In fact, on that date, when Mr. and Mrs. Ramirez returned at Autosport's invitation, all they received was discourtesy.

On the assumption that substantial impairment is necessary only when a purchaser seeks to revoke acceptance under N.J.S.A. 12A:2–608, the trial court correctly refrained from deciding whether the defects substantially impaired the van. The court properly concluded that plaintiffs were entitled to "rescind"—i.e., to "cancel"—the contract.

Because Autosport had sold the trade-in to an innocent third party, the trial court determined that the Ramirezes were entitled not to the return of the trade-in, but to its fair market value, which the court set at the contract price of $4,700. A buyer who rightfully rejects goods and cancels the contract may, among other possible remedies, recover so much of the purchase price as has been paid. N.J.S.A. 12A:2–711. The Code, however, does not define "pay" and does not require payment to be made in cash.

A common method of partial payment for vans, cars, boats and other items of personal property is by a "trade-in". When concerned with used vans and the like, the trade-in market is an acceptable, and perhaps the most appropriate, market in which to measure damages. It is the market in which the parties dealt; by their voluntary act they have established the value of the traded-in article. See Frantz Equipment Co. v. Anderson, 37 N.J. 420, 431–432, 181 A.2d 499 (1962) (in computing purchaser's damages for alleged breach of uniform conditional sales law, trade-in value of tractor was appropriate measure); accord, California Airmotive Corp. v. Jones, 415 F.2d 554, 556 (6 Cir.1969). In other circumstances, a measure of damages other than the trade-in value might be appropriate. . . .

The ultimate issue is determining the fair market value of the trade-in. This Court has defined fair market value as "the price at which the property would change hands between a willing buyer and a willing seller when the former is not under any compulsion to buy and the latter is not under any compulsion to sell, both parties having reasonable knowledge of relevant facts." In re Estate of Romnes, 79 N.J. 139, 144, 398 A.2d 543 (1979). Although the value of the trade-in van as set forth in the sales contract was not the only possible standard, it is an appropriate measure of fair market value.

For the preceding reasons, we affirm the judgment of the Appellate Division.

Questions

1. Define the following terms: tender of delivery, rejection, revocation of acceptance, cure, and installment contract. When does Article 2 employ a perfect tender rule? When does it not? When it does not employ a perfect tender rule, is the standard for calling the deal off always the same? Are cases in which cure is permitted cases in which perfect tender is not required?

2. What is the justification for Article 2's perfect tender rule? Would that rationale require a perfect tender rule in any cases governed by the common law? What is the difference in this respect between a sale of goods and one of services? Would a perfect tender rule be wise in the case of a loan?

3. *Problems.*

a. Otherwise on the facts of *Ramirez*, what if the buyer had made the first complaint of defects 45 days after taking delivery, and upon receiving the bill for the final payment. Must the buyer pay? Why or why not?

b. Shirley, owner of a paint store, decided in the autumn to stock Christmas toys in her store for the upcoming season. She contracted with Bojangles Merchandise Co. for a large quantity of colorful stuffed animals to be delivered before December 15 for a price of $3,500.00. When the first shipment arrived, it was about a quarter of the promised shipment. Shirley phoned Bojangles and said, "I reject. Come get your goods." What should you advise Bojangles?

c. The facts are as stated in Problem b above, except that Bojangles made several shipments to Shirley's store in November, but each contained fewer stuffed animals than Shirley expected. He answered her complaints with the claim that stuffed animals were back-ordered and would be shipped as soon as possible. She received only $1,800.00 worth of animals by December 1. Shirley phoned Bojangles on that day and said, "I reject. Our deal is off because your shipments are short. Come get your goods. Nothing has been opened." What should you advise Bojangles?

d. The facts are as stated in Problem b above, except that Shirley called Bojangles and told him to ship no more. An additional small shipment, worth $200, arrived on December 4, which Shirley kept. Bojangles sent a bill for $2,000.00 in February, which Shirley refused to pay. She then sent the dolls back to Bojangles' warehouse, where he refused delivery and returned them to Shirley. What should you advise Shirley when Bojangles brings an action for $2,000.00 plus interest?

e.   The facts are as stated in Problem b above, except that Shirley phoned Bojangles on November 5, after receiving one short shipment and said, "I reject. Our deal is off because your shipment is short. Come get your goods. Nothing has been opened." What should you advise Bojangles on November 6? See Hays Merchandise, Inc. v. Dewey, 78 Wash.2d 343, 474 P.2d 270 (1970).

NOTE ON PERFORMANCE AND ENFORCEMENT

Article 2 grants important rights and powers to the buyer when the seller makes a nonconforming tender or delivery of goods. The buyer may reject some or all of the goods (§§ 2–601, 2–612), revoke acceptance (§ 2–608), cancel, and/or claim damages (§§ 2–711 et seq.). Of course, acquiring such rights or powers are not the buyer's main purpose in entering the contract. The buyer wants to receive the goods as and when promised. Delivery as and when promised constitutes the seller's performance of the contract. The function of rejection, revocation of acceptance, and damages is to make it more likely that the seller will perform or compensate for nonperformance. Exercising such rights and powers is part of contract *enforcement*.

Statutory enforcement rights and powers are conditioned on the existence of certain facts or events to protect both the performance interests of the buyer and the breaching seller's interest in minimizing the cost of enforcement to him. Imagine a contract for the sale of a computer. Absent agreement to the contrary, any nonconforming tender prior to acceptance triggers the buyer's power to reject, protecting the buyer's interest in performance as promised. Rejection can seem a draconian remedy when the nonconformity is minor. The seller, however, can usually realize the market value of the deficient computer elsewhere. Once acceptance has occurred, the seller is less likely to be able to realize the full value once the computer has been accepted and perhaps used to some extent. See George Priest, *Breach and Remedy for the Tender of Nonconforming Goods Under the Uniform Commercial Code: An Economic Approach*, 91 HARV. L. REV. 960 (1978).

Consequently, the power to revoke acceptance is triggered only when the nonconformity substantially impairs the value of the computer to the buyer. Thus, revocation is restricted to more serious harms, adding to the seller's protection while still providing significant enforcement powers for the buyer. Note that the powers of rejection and revocation are conditioned on giving notice to the seller (§§ 2–602(1), 2–608(2)), a requirement demanding little of the buyer but protecting the seller's interests in cure and in preparing for negotiation or litigation.

SECTION 3.   AGREED ENFORCEMENT TERMS

Enforcement rights and powers provided by law, such as those considered in the preceding two sections, may not be adequate to protect a contract party's interest in future performance. When parties enter into a series of separate contracts, a repudiation or other breach of one contract will not give the nonbreaching party rights or powers to redress resulting insecurity on another contract. Northwest Lumber Sales, Inc. v. Continental Forest Prods., Inc., 261 Or. 480, 495 P.2d 744 (1972). In addition, uncertainties are created by the vagueness in standard doctrinal formulations and confusion among relevant provisions of the U.C.C. These uncertainties may leave a party less secure than the security principle promises.

Enforcement rights and powers provided by law, however, are not exclusive. They are mainly default rules that the parties can vary or supplement by agreement. For example, the law (not without controversy) provides that a nonbreaching party has no claim for damages for total breach when, at the time of a breach involving less than the whole, the only remaining performance duties are those of the party in breach and are for the payment of money in installments. RESTATEMENT (SECOND) OF CONTRACTS § 243(3). Consider an insurer who issued a disability policy requiring monthly payments should the insured be totally and permanently disabled. When the insured suffers the requisite disability and the insurer unjustifiably discontinues payments after a year, the insured cannot recover for future payments. The insured's claim is limited to compensation for missed payments (partial breach), even if the insurer repudiates all future obligations. New York Life Ins. Co. v. Viglas, 297 U.S. 672, 56 S.Ct. 615, 80 L.Ed. 971 (1936). The parties, however, can change the result by writing an "acceleration clause" into the contract. Such a clause may provide that all payments become due at once should the insured so elect upon a breach by the insurer as to any installment. (You will find acceleration clauses more often in mortgage and loan agreements, running in favor of the lenders, than in insurance contracts, running in favor of the insureds.)

In a significant number of cases, the courts decline to make an agreed enforcement right or power available to the party invoking it, despite the occurrence of an event that triggers it according to the express contract terms. Many of these cases can be explained by the law of good faith in enforcement, which is stated in U.C.C. § 1–203 and RESTATEMENT (SECOND) OF CONTRACTS § 205. Bad faith in contract performance is a breach of contract. By contrast, bad faith in contract enforcement disables a party from exercising an enforcement right or power. Put otherwise, good faith is a condition to the valid exercise of remedial rights provided by contract (and, under the U.C.C., by statute). It is not, as such, a breach of contract. The following cases explore this developing area of the law.

––––––

UNIFORM COMMERCIAL CODE §§ 1–208

––––––

BAKER v. RATZLAFF

Court of Appeals of Kansas, 1977.
1 Kan.App.2d 285, 564 P.2d 153.

REES, JUDGE. This is an action for breach of contract. The case was tried to the court and judgment was entered for the plaintiff. Both parties appeal. The defendant asserts that the trial court erred in its finding that he breached the contract. Plaintiff contests the amount of the judgment.

Plaintiff is a buyer and distributor of popcorn. His business office is in Garden City. He operates a plant at Stratford, Texas. Defendant is engaged in farming and it appears that he is the operator of land in Thomas County. The written contract that is the subject of this lawsuit was entered into by the parties in 1973.

It was agreed by the parties that in 1973 defendant would raise 380 acres of popcorn and the plaintiff would buy the crop. Plaintiff was to provide seed popcorn at a stated price. Plaintiff was to purchase the popcorn crop, shelled and delivered by defendant to plaintiff's plant at Stratford, Texas, at a price of $4.75 per hundredweight. The popcorn was to be delivered by defendant upon plaintiff's order. Plaintiff was to order delivery of one-third of the crop by March 30, 1974, one-third by June 30, 1974, and the balance by September 30, 1974. The contract included other terms that dealt with the quality of the popcorn to be delivered, payments to be made by plaintiff to defendant for storage and transportation, interest to be paid by plaintiff on the popcorn held in storage by defendant from the time of harvest to the time of delivery, and other matters. The particular provisions of the contract that give rise to this litigation are as follows:

> "12. Baker agrees to pay Grower for the above corn when delivered and in addition thereto, agrees to pay storage fees, in and out charges, transportation charges, and the accrued interest on each bushel or cwt. of corn as delivered.

> "13. It is further understood and agreed that if Baker, for any reason, fails neglects, or refuses to pay Grower for said popcorn along with the heretofore specified charges at the time of delivery, then, and in that event, the remaining undelivered popcorn in Grower's possession shall, at Grower's option, be released by Baker for Grower to retain or dispose of as he sees fit."

The requirement for payment on delivery was made a part of the contract at defendant's request.

Some time in January, 1974, plaintiff telephoned defendant and asked that he begin delivery to the Stratford plant. The first truckload was delivered at about 5:00 P.M. on Saturday, February 2, by defendant and his employee, Boucher. Plaintiff's plant manager, Martin, gave a weight ticket to defendant. A second truckload was delivered on Monday, February 4, by Boucher. Martin gave a weight ticket to Boucher. On neither occasion did defendant or Boucher ask Martin for payment for the popcorn delivered and Martin did not offer to pay.

During the week of February 4, Martin telephoned defendant and asked when further deliveries would be made. Later that same week, plaintiff telephoned defendant and asked about the delay. Defendant told Martin and plaintiff that he was having equipment problems and that Boucher had been ill. In neither of the telephone conversations was there any discussion of payment. On Monday, February 11, defendant sent a written notice of termination of the contract claiming that plaintiff had breached the contract by failing to pay on delivery as required by paragraphs 12 and 13. Upon receipt of the notice of termination on or within a few days following February 12, plaintiff sent checks to defendant in payment for the two loads that had been delivered. After sending the notice of termination, defendant entered into a contract with a third party for the sale of the balance of the 1973 popcorn at a price of $8.00 per hundredweight. This contract was performed by defendant's delivery of 1,600,000 pounds of popcorn.

Martin testified that he made no payments for popcorn at Stratford. The practice was that copies of weight tickets were sent to plaintiff's Garden City office where checks were written and mailed. At the time of defendant's two deliveries, Martin would accumulate weight tickets and send them to Garden City so that they would arrive on Monday mornings. He did not know when he had sent the weight tickets for the February 2 and 4 deliveries.

Defendant testified that at the time he made his contract to sell the balance of his 1973 crop to the third party, popcorn was selling for $8.00 and the commodity market price was between $7.00 and $7.25. He further testified that after the 1974 harvest popcorn was selling for around $14.00. Plaintiff testified that he had to pay $10.30 for some replacement popcorn. The trial court awarded damages of $52,000. This amount represents the value of 1,600,000 pounds at $3.25 per hundredweight, the difference between the parties' contract price of $4.75 and an $8.00 price.

The trial court's findings were in part as follows:

"2. That the defendant knew or should have known that the plaintiff's business office was located in Garden City, Kansas, and that in the normal course of events payment would be made from that office. That Garden City, Kansas, is on a direct route from the plaintiff's grain receiving facilities in Stratford, Texas, to the defendant's farm and that nothing prevented the defendant or his agents, servants and employees from stopping off on their way back from delivering the grain and requesting payment or obtaining payment from plaintiff's business office in Garden City, Kansas. That the evidence discloses that any request for payment would have been promptly handled and that the plaintiff had ample funds with which to make the payment and the only reason payment was not made was the failure of the defendant to request it.

"3. That between the time that the contract for the production of the popcorn was entered into and the time for delivery the price of popcorn had risen sharply and that it was greatly to the defendant's financial advantage if he could in some way get out of his contract for the sale of popcorn. . . .

"The Court concludes that the parties are under a duty to deal fairly with each other in good faith and that the defendant breached this duty by declaring a termination of the contract upon a technical pretense and that therefore as a matter of law the plaintiff is entitled to recover the damages suffered.

"The Court further concludes that to interpret the contract to require immediate payment without request or demand upon delivery of the grain to the processing facility in Stratford, Texas, would result in an unconscionable and unenforceable contract and that the contract should not be so interpreted. . . ."

Defendant . . . contends that the district court erred in finding that defendant's termination of the agreement was a breach of its duty to perform and enforce the contract in good faith. Defendant argues that it was under no good faith obligation in terminating the contract and, even if it was, the termination was made in good faith. . . .

Defendant maintains the good faith obligation of K.S.A. 84–1–203 [U.C.C. § 1–203] is not applicable because termination of a contract is not "performance" or "enforcement" of a contract. Under the facts of this case, we disagree. The termination clause in paragraph 13 of the contract does not permit termination at will but only upon failure of plaintiff to pay on delivery. Defendant's right to terminate and retain or dispose of undelivered popcorn is an inseparable incident of enforcement of substantive provisions of the contract. We believe that only tortured reasoning could exempt defendant's exercise of the termination clause from the good faith obligation of K.S.A. 84–1–203, and we decline to do so.

There was substantial competent evidence in the record to support the district court's finding that defendant had breached his obligation of good faith. His failure on delivery of either load of popcorn to the Stratford plant to demand payment, his failure in the subsequent telephone conversations with plaintiff and Martin to demand payment, and his hasty resale of the popcorn to another buyer at a price nearly double the contract price, provided the trial court with ample evidence upon which to find an absence of good faith. The finding was one of fact and is not to be overturned where supported by substantial competent evidence. *McGilbray v. Scholfield Winnebago, Inc.,* 221 Kan. 605, 561 P.2d 832 (filed March 5, 1977). . . .

The parties having failed to show prejudicial error, the judgment is affirmed.

Questions

1. What is the key express term in the popcorn contract? Is it a promise or a condition? What is the seller's argument with respect to its implications in the case?

2. What is the legal consequence of bad faith in contract enforcement? How is it different from bad faith in contract performance?

3. Is the court's rationale persuasive? Consider whether the seller used the term requiring cash on delivery for the purpose for which it was included in the agreement. Could a better rationale be developed from that starting point? See Eric G. Andersen, *Good Faith in the Enforcement of Contracts*, 73 Iowa L.Rev. 299 (1988).

BROWN v. AVEMCO INVESTMENT CORP.

United States Court of Appeals, Ninth Circuit, 1979.
603 F.2d 1367.

Ferguson, District Judge. Plaintiffs, citizens of Montana, sued defendant, a Maryland corporation, in a diversity action (28 U.S.C. § 1332) alleging a conversion of an airplane. Defendant counterclaimed for interference with contractual rights. A jury trial was held and verdicts against plaintiffs returned. A final judgment was entered in accordance with the verdicts. The district court denied plaintiffs' motion for new trial and defendant's motion for judgment notwithstanding the verdict. Plaintiffs appeal from the judgment and the denial of the motion for a new trial. This court orders a new trial on the grounds that the trial court gave erroneous instructions on the issue of acceleration and these instructions prejudiced the plaintiffs.

Facts

1. On September 22, 1972, Robert Herriford borrowed $6,500 from AVEMCO and executed a promissory note for $9,607.92 (amount borrowed plus "add-on" interest and credit for insurance).

2. The promissory note was secured by an agreement granting to AVEMCO a security interest in an airplane. The security agreement contained the following language:

> Time is of the essence of this Security Agreement. It is hereby agreed that if default be made in the payment of any part of the principal or interest of the promissory note secured hereby at the time and in the manner therein specified, or if any breach be made of any obligation or promise of debtor herein contained or secured hereby, or *if any or all of the property covered hereby be hereafter sold, leased, transferred, mortgaged, or otherwise encumbered without the written consent of Secured Party first had and obtained*, or in the event of the seizure of the aircraft under execution or other legal process, or if for any reason Secured Party may deem itself insecure, *then the whole principal sum unpaid upon said promissory note,*

with the interest accrued thereon or advanced under the terms of this Security Agreement, or secured hereby, and the interest thereon, *shall immediately become due and payable at the option of Secured Party.* (emphasis added)

The security agreement also provided that the laws of Texas would apply with respect to rights under the agreement.

3. On July 4, 1973, Herriford entered into a lease and option agreement with the three plaintiffs whereby plaintiffs would pay hourly rentals for the plane and contribute equally toward Herriford's debt retirement with AVEMCO. Upon full payment of the mortgage on the airplane, the plaintiffs would have an option to purchase one-fourth ownership (each) of the plane for the sum of one dollar.

4. Plaintiffs became co-insureds with Herriford on the airplane in 1973. Copies of this policy were sent to AVEMCO.

5. On July 9, 1975, the plaintiffs advised AVEMCO that they had exercised their option with Herriford and now tendered to AVEMCO the $4,859.93 still owed by Herriford.

6. On July 18, 1975, AVEMCO refused this offer and wrote to Herriford announcing that because of his failure to comply with the note and security agreement, AVEMCO was accelerating the payments and the entire balance of $5,078.97 was due and payable on or before July 28, 1975. AVEMCO later explained that the additional amount was due to reimburse AVEMCO for its purchase of "Vendor's Single Interest Insurance."

7. On July 25, 1975, plaintiff McAlear advised AVEMCO that plaintiffs did not accept AVEMCO's rejection of their tender and that the money to retire the debt was available to AVEMCO at the First Security Bank of Bozeman, Montana, upon presentation of a satisfaction of the mortgage.

8. On July 29 or 30, 1975, an agent of AVEMCO used a passkey to start the plane and flew it to Seattle.

9. On July 30, 1975, AVEMCO notified Herriford of this repossession and demanded payment of $5,578.97 by August 10, 1975 or the aircraft would be sold with proceeds to be applied first to sale expenses and second to Herriford's account.

10. On September 22, 1975, a bill of sale for the plane was filed by AVEMCO with the Federal Aviation Agency. The consideration was $7,000 and the bill of sale was dated August 25, 1975. (AVEMCO had earlier recorded a sale which was subsequently withdrawn as an error).

11. Plaintiffs filed this action for conversion on August 15, 1975. Defendant counterclaimed charging interference with contract rights. A jury trial was held and the jury returned a verdict for defendant on both the conversion claim and the counterclaim. No damages were assessed, however.

12. Defendant moved for judgment notwithstanding the verdict and plaintiffs moved for a new trial. The district court denied these motions. Plaintiffs appeal from the final judgment and the denial of the motion for a new trial.

This court finds that the court gave erroneous instructions on acceleration and a new trial must be ordered. The court refused to instruct that acceleration could only be done if defendant believed in good faith that its security interest was impaired by the breach of the security agreement. That refusal was prejudicial error.....

ACCELERATION

The facts as established at trial are as follows: The security agreement between the debtor Herriford and the creditor AVEMCO provided that if Herriford leased the plane without the consent of AVEMCO, AVEMCO could, at its option, accelerate full payment of the loan. Herriford leased the plane to plaintiffs in 1973. In that year, plaintiffs became co-insureds on the airplane and copies of the policy were sent to AVEMCO. For two years payments continued to be regularly made on the note. When on July 9, 1975, the plaintiffs contacted AVEMCO and offered what they believed was full payment of the debt, AVEMCO refused to negotiate with them and did not inquire further of either Herriford or the plaintiffs about their intention to pay the debt in full. While plaintiffs' offer of $4,859.93 may not have met the legal requirements of a valid tender, AVEMCO's complete disregard of the offer and eagerness to accelerate payment, repossess the plane and sell it for $7000 should have invoked the concern of the district court and prompted an examination of the fairness of the acceleration.

Both the Uniform Commercial Code (U.C.C.) and equity impose this duty. Plaintiffs sought this protection and proposed jury instructions on acceleration which incorporated a test of reasonableness and fairness: the U.C.C. requirement of good faith belief of security impairment. The district court rejected these and instructed that there could be an automatic enforcement of the acceleration clause if the jury merely found the technical breach of a lease without consent. This instruction was erroneous and prejudicial. A new trial is required.

Acceleration clauses are designed to protect the creditor from actions by the debtor which jeopardize or impair the creditor's security. They are not to be used offensively, e.g., for the commercial advantage of the creditor. Acceleration is a harsh remedy with draconian consequences for the debtor. Acceleration is a matter of equity and the courts, including those of Texas, have historically been careful to evaluate the fairness of acceleration in the particular facts of a case. As the Texas Court of Civil Appeals stated in *Parker v. Mazur*, 13 S.W.2d 174, 175 (Tex.Civ.App.1928), courts of equity "will scan very closely the enforcement of so hard and rigorous a contract."

In performing their equitable duties, Texas courts have long required that acceleration be reasonable in light of the facts. *Warren v.*

Osborne, 97 S.W. 851 (Tex.Civ.App.1906); 125 A.L.R. 318. They would not permit enforcement of acceleration clauses when the debtor's default was due to the debtor's accident or mistake or to the creditor's own fraudulent or inequitable conduct. *Parker v. Mazur, supra.* . . . Nor would they permit acceleration when the facts made its use unjust or oppressive. *Bischoff v. Rearick*, 232 S.W.2d 174, 176 (Tex.Civ.App. 1950). . . .

The provisions of the U.C.C. impose similar requirements on acceleration in the transactions it governs. The U.C.C. requirements are harmonious with the older equitable tests of reasonableness. Section 1–203 of the U.C.C. imposes an obligation of good faith on the performance or enforcement of every contract or duty within the Code. Section 1–208 further defines and applies the good faith obligation to options to accelerate at will and requires that the accelerating party "in good faith believes that the prospect of payment or performance is impaired." . . .

The Fifth Circuit has applied [Texas' version of U.C.C. § 1–208] to acceleration based on a clause authorizing acceleration when the creditor "deemed himself insecure." *Sheppard Federal Credit Union v. Palmer*, 408 F.2d 1369 (5th Cir.1969). Acceleration on this basis clearly falls within the specific language of § 1–208. . . .

The more difficult question presented in this case is whether the statute applies to "default" acceleration clauses as well as to "insecurity" acceleration clauses. When the creditor chooses to accelerate because the debtor violated a specific provision of the security agreement and not because he feels insecure, does § 1–208 apply? Here AVEMCO's agreement with Herriford contains both types of clauses. Yet AVEMCO's asserted basis for the acceleration is breach of the consent-for-lease provision of the security agreement and not the "deem itself insecure" language.

The question of application of § 1–208 to this situation has not been answered. Several courts have confronted security agreements which, like the one here, authorized acceleration both when a specific provision is breached and when the creditor deems itself insecure. In these cases, without much discussion, the courts have applied both the U.C.C. and equity principles. . . . In *Williamson v. Wanlass*, 545 P.2d 1145 (Utah 1976), the Utah Supreme Court applied § 1–208 to acceleration authorized by an agreement which apparently did not even include any "deem itself insecure" language. . . . [T]he Utah court emphasized that "this statute [§ 1–208] is in harmony with the principles of equity. . . . [I]t seems to recognize that acceleration is a harsh remedy which should be allowed only if there is some reasonable justification for doing so, such as a good faith belief that the prospect of payment is impaired." *Williamson v. Wanlass*, 545 P.2d at 1149. . . .

According to its language, § 1–208 applies when a party in interest may accelerate payment "at will" or "when he deems himself insecure" or "in words of similar import." Here the agreement provided that AVEMCO may, *at its option*, accelerate payment when the debtor leases without consent or when AVEMCO deems itself insecure or when various other contingencies occur. The agreement does not require immediate, automatic acceleration upon one of these events but further ties acceleration to the option of AVEMCO. Section 1–208 applies the Code's good faith concept to such acceleration and provides that the creditor has power to exercise the option "only if he in good faith believes that the prospect of payment or performance is impaired."

An option to accelerate when the debtor leases without consent is different, however, than one based on the creditor's feelings of insecurity. The lease is within the control of the debtor; the feelings of insecurity are subject to the whim and caprice of the creditor. As the U.C.C. Comment to § 1–208 suggests, the drafters' greatest concern was with abuse due to the uncontrolled will of the creditor. Some may argue that § 1–208 therefore addresses only "insecurity" clause acceleration. While this type of clause may be the primary focus of § 1–208, this court does not believe it is the only focus. Abuse is possible with "due-on-lease" acceleration as well. The "option" to accelerate based on a lease, like the one based on feelings of insecurity, could be used by AVEMCO as a sword for commercial gain rather than as a shield against security impairment. Section 1–208, growing from and incorporating equitable principles, defines "good faith" in acceleration to provide protection from such abuse.

The trial court gave a general good faith instruction but refused to give plaintiffs' proposed instruction requiring for acceleration the good faith belief that payment or security is impaired. The U.C.C. requires more than a good faith belief that a technical breach occurred but the court's instructions erroneously required no more. . . .

In the instant case, the facts before the trial court . . . sufficiently suggested the possibility that . . . the creditor accelerated not out of a reasonable fear of security impairment but rather from an inequitable desire to take advantage of a technical default. Indeed acceleration because of a lease executed two years earlier is less clearly defensive and is subject to even more suspicion. . . . Here, there was no suggestion that the prospect of payment was impaired. There was some discussion at trial of alleged insurance difficulties but these allegations were never fully developed and the trial court's instruction clearly allowed the jury to find AVEMCO's acceleration lawful solely on the basis of a lease without consent without even considering insurance questions. . . .

For these reasons, this court finds that the trial court erred in refusing to give instructions on acceleration which incorporated the U.C.C. and equitable principles. This error prejudiced the plaintiffs. The judgment of the district court is reversed and the case is remanded to the district court for a new trial.

Questions

1. What is the precise question before the court in *Brown*? Does U.C.C. § 1–208 answer that question? What is the creditor's view? What is the debtor's view? Which is more sound? (Assume that, should the sale of the collateral produce more than the balance of the debt, the debtor is entitled to a deficiency judgment for the difference.)

2. Is the court's rationale persuasive? Should it have relied on U.C.C. § 1–208? Can you construct a better justification for the result it reached? What should "good faith" require in this context?

BURNE v. FRANKLIN LIFE INSURANCE CO.

Supreme Court of Pennsylvania, 1973.
451 Pa. 218, 301 A.2d 799.

ROBERTS, JUSTICE. This is an appeal from the order of the Court of Common Pleas of Lackawanna County denying plaintiff-appellant's motion for summary judgment and from the judgment entered below in favor of defendant-insurance company, upon said defendant's motion for summary judgment. The action below, in assumpsit, was for the recovery of the accidental (double indemnity) death benefits of a life insurance policy, of which appellant is the beneficiary. For the reasons set out below, we reverse.

In 1949, defendant-appellee issued to the insured (appellant's husband) a life insurance policy in the face amount of $15,000. The policy also contained a double indemnity proviso for an additional $15,000 if the death of the insured resulted from purely accidental means. This double indemnity provision, and the exceptions contained therein, are the subject of this appeal.

On January 30, 1959, while the policy was in effect, the insured, Bartholomew Burne, was struck by an automobile while crossing a street in North Miami, Florida. Immediate and extensive brain surgery was required. From the moment of the accident until his death, Mr. Burne's existence was that of a complete and hopeless invalid, unable to speak, subject to seizures and requiring constant nursing and medical care. Vast sums of money were expended by appellant, and the most sophisticated medical techniques utilized, merely to keep her husband medically alive, albeit in a vegetative state, for 4½ years.[1] It is conceded by the appellee insurance company that the injuries sustained were the direct and sole cause of the insured's death. Appellee paid the face amount of the policy, but refused to pay the accidental death benefits.

The life insurance policy under consideration provides for double indemnity liability for death resulting from accident. However, the policy

---

1. It is not inappropriate to observe, in view of this record, that the insurance carrier suffered no prejudice by the retention of the double indemnity death proceeds for these additional 4½ years. What appears in fact is that the appellee enjoyed an economic benefit by having the use of these funds during that period, rather than having to pay out that sum at or near the time of the accident.

states that such accidental death benefits will be payable only if "... such death occurred ... within ninety days from the date of the accident." [A further exception in the double indemnity rider excluded payment of the accidental death benefit "if the death of the insured shall occur while any premium is being waived under any disability benefit attached to or incorporated in said policy...." The portion of the opinion addressing this clause is omitted.] On the basis of these exceptions, the trial court, en banc, granted defendant-appellee's motion for summary judgment. This appeal challenges the validity of these exceptions as applied to the facts of the instant case.

There are strong public policy reasons which militate against the enforceability of the ninety day limitation. The provision has its origins at a much earlier stage of medicine. Accordingly, the leading case construing the provision predates three decades of progress in the field of curative medicine. Advancements made during that period have enabled the medical profession to become startlingly adept at delaying death for indeterminate periods. Physicians and surgeons now stand at the very citadel of death, possessing the awesome responsibility of sometimes deciding whether and what measure should be used to prolong, even though momentarily, an individual's life. The legal and ethical issues attending such deliberations are gravely complex.

The result reached by the trial court presents a gruesome paradox indeed—it would permit double indemnity recovery for the death of an accident victim who dies instantly or within ninety days of an accident, but would deny such recovery for the death of an accident victim who endures the agony of prolonged illness, suffers longer, and necessitates greater expense by his family in hopes of sustaining life even momentarily beyond the ninety day period. To predicate liability under a life insurance policy upon death occurring only on or prior to a specific date, while denying policy recovery if death occurs after that fixed date, offends the basic concepts and fundamental objectives of life insurance and is contrary to public policy. Hence, the ninety day limitation is unenforceable.

All must recognize the mental anguish that quite naturally accompanies these tragic occurrences. Surely that anguish ought not to be aggravated in cases of this kind with concerns of whether the moment of death permits or defeats the double indemnity claim. So too, the decisions as to what medical treatment should be accorded an accident victim should be unhampered by considerations which might have a tendency to encourage something less than the maximum medical care on penalty of financial loss if such care succeeds in extending life beyond the 90th day. All such factors should, wherever possible, be removed from the antiseptic halls of the hospital. Rejection of the arbitrary ninety day provision does exactly that.

Aside from considerations of public policy, the ninety day provision possesses no persuasive decisional support. In granting appellee's motion for summary judgment, the trial court obviously relied upon a single thirty year old case, Sidebothom v. Metropolitan Life Insurance Co., 339 Pa. 124, 14 A.2d 131 (1940). That case, as well as virtually every other case which construed a ninety day limitation provision, is based on considerations which have no pragmatic applicability to the factual situation here. The earlier judicial interpretation of the ninety day provision was that its underlying purpose was to govern situations where there existed some possible uncertainty over whether injuries sustained in an accident would actually result in death. The ninety day provision attempted to delineate a line governing cases where the injuries may or may not cause death. Ninety days was the arbitrary period advanced by the carrier within which to ascertain whether death will in fact result from the accident.

The factual situation in *Sidebothom* is illustrative of the principles underlying a ninety day provision. There the insured suffered injuries from two different exposures to carbon monoxide. While in the hospital he suffered further injuries from a fall from a hospital bed. In two crucial ways that case is distinguishable from the instant one. First, the injury involved in *Sidebothom* was not the type that with any degree of certainty could be regarded as fatal. In addition *Sidebothom* presented distinct causation problems, the deceased having suffered injuries both within and without the ninety day period. The instant case suffers from neither of these infirmities. It was clear from the moment of the accident that the husband would die as a result thereof, the only question being one of time. Nor was there any causation problem, it being conceded by the defendant that the sole cause of death was the injuries suffered by the husband when struck by the car.

It is well settled that if a provision in an insurance policy cannot reasonably be applied to a certain factual situation it should be disregarded. This sound rule of law was succinctly articulated as early as Grandin v. Rochester German Insurance Company, 107 Pa. 26 (1884), where the Court refused to mechanically apply an insurance provision, saying:

> "It will thus be seen that where the reason of a condition does not apply this court has refused to apply it. Other instances of the same might be cited were it necessary. We are not to suppose that conditions involving forfeitures are introduced into policies by insurance companies, which are purely arbitrary and without reason, merely as a trap to the assured or as a means of escape for the company in case of loss. When therefore a general condition has no application to a particular policy; where the reason which alone gives it force is out of the case, the condition itself drops out with it."

Id. at 37. . . . This case is clearly one where "the reason of a condition does not apply." The provision should not be applied to cases where, as this record establishes, no dispute exists as to the cause of death. Surely the ninety day provision was not meant to be "merely . . . a trap to the assured or as a means of escape for the company in case of loss."

POMEROY, JUSTICE (dissenting). This case presents the question whether a contract of life insurance is to be interpreted and performed in accordance with the intent of the contracting parties as expressed in terms which are neither unclear nor ambiguous, or whether it is to be rewritten by this Court through benefit of hindsight to afford a benefit where none was provided. Specifically, the question is whether a 90–day clause in a double indemnity provision means 90 days, or whether, in a "hard" case, it can be stretched beyond that period (in this case to some 1,640 days), or ignored altogether as violative of public policy. It was the opinion of the lower court that the intent of the parties was as expressed in the policy and that no public policy restraints on the freedom of contract had been violated; the majority of this Court holds to the contrary. I believe the court below correct, and I accordingly dissent. . . .

I.   THE 90–DAY PROVISION, THE INTENT OF THE PARTIES, AND PUBLIC POLICY

a.   Intent of the Parties

In construing contracts arguably violative of public policy, we traditionally begin by determining the intent of the parties and only reach the question of public policy if then necessary. . . . The majority, however, first invalidates the 90–day provision of the accidental death benefit endorsement on public policy grounds, and only then advances a "well settled" principle of law that "if a provision in an insurance policy cannot reasonably be applied to a certain factual situation[,] it should be disregarded." In support of this principle, three of our past decisions are cited: Grandin v. Rochester German Ins. Co., 107 Pa. 26 (1884); Tennant v. Hartford Steam Boiler Inspection and Ins. Co., 351 Pa. 102, 40 A.2d 385 (1944); Norlund v. Reliance Life Ins. Co., 282 Pa. 389, 128 A. 93 (1925). An examination of these decisions reveals that in all of them the court sought to interpret the language of a contract to arrive at *the intention of the parties* . . . .

I take no exception to the implicitly stated view of the majority that in interpreting contracts, courts should be careful not to defeat the intention of the parties by applying terms and conditions appearing in the writing to situations in which the parties could not have intended that they apply. Unlike the majority, however, I do not find that proposition of any help in this case. For I have no doubt—indeed, the parties do not argue otherwise—that not only the insurer but the insured *intended* that the additional recovery for an accidental death would be precluded if death in the normal acceptation of the term should occur more than 90 days after the date of the accident. Whatever else this appeal presents, therefore, it does not in my judgment present a problem in determining the intent—as of the time of contracting—of the parties.

b.   Public Policy

The Court's public policy argument itself suffers from an ambiguity. Is the reader to understand (1) that *all* 90–day provisions in accidental death benefit endorsements are invalid as violative of public policy, or (2)

only those found in policies owned by insureds who in fact die outside 90 days but without "some possible uncertainty" as to causation? There is ample support for either reading.

The opinion of the court observes that to enforce the 90–day limitation would permit "a gruesome paradox indeed—it would permit double indemnity recovery for the death of an accident victim who dies instantly or within 90 days of an accident, but would deny such recovery for the death of an accident victim who endures the agony of prolonged illness, suffers longer, and necessitates greater expense...." This type of "gruesome paradox" in no way depends on a distinction between those after 90–day deaths that present "some possible uncertainty" as to causation and those that do not. Neither does the evocation of the specter of human greed shaping medical decisions depend upon whether or not the insured in fact died outside the 90–day period and without uncertainty as to causation....

It is obvious that the Court is here determining the validity of a contract by means of hindsight. In so doing it fails to observe the fundamental principle that the judicial function in determining the validity of contractual terms must be limited to examination of circumstances known to the parties at the time of contracting. Thus the American Law Institute, in its section dealing with unconscionable contracts or terms, provides:

> "If a contract or term thereof is unconscionable *at the time the contract is made* a court may refuse to enforce the contract, or may enforce the remainder of the contract without the unconscionable term, or may limit the application of any unconscionable term as to avoid any unconscionable result." Restatement (Second) of Contracts § 234 (Tent. Draft No. 5, March 31, 1970) (emphasis added).

Contrary to what the Court apparently holds, it is my view that we must allow persons to make contracts which are reasonable in the light of circumstances known to them at the time of contracting. More we cannot ask; more we should not impose. Absent a violation of some external rule limiting freedom of contract, a court should not presume to intervene and redraft contracts which were reasonable at the time they were entered into....

Questions

1. What result if a case like *Sidebothom*, discussed in the majority opinion, were to arise after this opinion?

2. Does the majority or the dissent make the stronger case on the public policy issue? Do you think that courts should decide contracts cases like this one on the basis of public policy, as the majority did in this case? Would the majority's result better be grounded in the unconscionability doctrine?

3. Assume you conclude that the majority's public policy holding is improper, and that the clause is not unconscionable. Does the majority or

the dissent make the stronger case on the remaining contract issues? Can you construct a stronger argument for one or the other view?

Chapter 7

THE BOUNDARIES OF AUTONOMY

It should be clear that the autonomy of the parties plays a central role in the law of contracts: Their choices are the immediate source of the authority of the agreement as a determinant of their contractual rights, duties, and powers in relation to one another. The autonomy of the parties, however, is qualified in two main ways.

First, autonomy is not the ultimate source of the agreement's authority. Party autonomy is given its role by the law, which is the higher authority in any case. The law, accordingly, may limit the agreement's authority, as contract law does for reasons of justice and public policy (Chapter 3), and as many statutes, such as the minimum wage laws, do in many areas. These are ways of supplanting or supplementing the agreement for reasons deemed more important than the parties' legal power to make their own legal relationship by promising. Second, the parties' agreement may "run out" of authority as circumstances change over time. In some cases, the changes are so great that it becomes implausible to say that the parties allocated the relevant risks by agreement. When that is so, the autonomy principle may no longer justify giving agreed language its full semantic scope.

The second of these qualifications concerns the boundaries of autonomy. We can think of these boundaries in different ways. If we conceive the agreement narrowly, by confining it to the shared concrete intentions in the minds of the parties and stated in the contract at the time of formation, the agreement will have run out of authority in many of the cases covered before this chapter. If we conceive the agreement to include the background practices presupposed by most contracting parties, however, its authority would run out much less often. Most implied promises and conditions would be grounded in the parties' autonomy as exercised in a social context. Even on the latter view, however, the agreement will run out of authority in some cases—when enforcing the agreement on the basis of party autonomy would not be justified because circumstances have changed too much.

550

In this chapter, we will look at the law governing agreements that, a party claims, have been overtaken by events. This is currently an unsettled area of contract law. It is, accordingly, difficult to generalize even about the precise issues to be addressed. Not surprisingly, theories that underlie legal doctrines throughout contract law come to the surface here.

In Section 1, we consider traditional doctrines governing one party's claim of excuse due to changed circumstances. We will focus on when a contract has run out of authority, with attention also to the legal consequences of an excuse. In Section 2, we look at some recent developments that may be harbingers of important changes in contract law, conferring a greater judicial warrant to adjust or modify the legal relations of the parties due to changed circumstances. Together, the two sections raise a deeper issue: If a contract has run out of authority based in the autonomy of the parties, what law should govern the settlement of remaining disputes arising from the transaction? Recent scholarship suggests that possibly the law of contracts should turn to the law of torts, requiring just and reasonable conduct according to standards unrelated to the undertakings of the parties. Section 3 will examine some recent cases that consider using tort principles to impose additional duties on the parties.

SECTION 1.   EXCUSE FOR NONPERFORMANCE

RESTATEMENT (SECOND) OF CONTRACTS §§ 261–72

TAYLOR v. CALDWELL

Court of Queen's Bench, 1863.
3 B. & S. 826, 122 Eng.Rep. 309.

BLACKBURN, JUDGE. In this case the plaintiffs and defendants had, on the 27th May, 1861, entered into a contract by which the defendants agreed to let the plaintiffs have the use of the Surrey Gardens and Music Hall on four days then to come, viz., the 17th June, 15th July, 5th August and 19th August, for the purpose of giving a series of four grand concerts, and day and night fetes at the Gardens and Hall on those days respectively; and the plaintiffs agreed to take the Gardens and Hall on those days, and pay £100 for each day.

The parties inaccurately call this a "letting," and the money to be paid, a "rent;" but the whole agreement is such as to show that the defendants were to retain the possession of the Hall and Gardens so that there was to be no demise of them, and that the contract was merely to give the plaintiffs the use of them on those days. Nothing, however, in our opinion, depends on this. The agreement then proceeds to set out various stipulations between the parties as to what each was to supply for these concerts and entertainments, and as to the manner in which they should be carried on. The effect of the whole is to show that the existence of the Music Hall in the Surrey Gardens in a state fit for a concert was essential for the fulfillment of the contract,—such entertainments as the parties contemplated in their agreement could not be given without it.

After the making of the agreement, and before the first day on which a concert was to be given, the Hall was destroyed by fire. This destruction, we must take it on the evidence, was without the fault of either party, and was so complete that in consequence the concerts could not be given as intended. And the question we have to decide is whether, under these circumstances, the loss which the plaintiffs have sustained is to fall upon the defendants. The parties when framing their agreement evidently had not present to their minds the possibility of such a disaster, and have made no express stipulation with reference to it, so that the answer to the question must depend upon the general rules of law applicable to such a contract.

There seems no doubt that where there is a positive contract to do a thing, not in itself unlawful, the contractor must perform it or pay damages for not doing it, although in consequence of unforeseen accidents, the performance of his contract has become unexpectedly burthensome or even impossible. The law is so laid down in 1 Roll.Abr. 450, Condition (G), and in the note (2) to *Walton v. Waterhouse*, 2 Wms. Saund. 421a. 6th Ed., and is recognized as the general rule by all the judges in the much discussed case of *Hall v. Wright* (E.B. & E. 746). But this rule is only applicable when the contract is positive and absolute, and not subject to any condition either express or implied: and there are authorities which, as we think, establish the principle that where, from the nature of the contract, it appears that the parties must from the beginning have known that it could not be fulfilled unless when the time for the fulfillment of the contract arrived some particular specified thing continued to exist, so that, when entering into the contract, they must have contemplated such continuing existence as the foundation of what was to be done; there, in the absence of any express or implied warranty that the thing shall exist, the contract is not to be construed as a positive contract, but as subject to an implied condition that the parties shall be excused in case, before breach, performance becomes impossible from the perishing of the thing without default of the contractor.

There seems little doubt that this implication tends to further the great object of making the legal construction such as to fulfil the intention of those who entered into the contract. For in the course of affairs men in making such contracts in general would if it were brought to their minds, say that there should be such a condition. . . .

There is a class of contracts in which a person binds himself to do something which requires to be performed by him in person; and such promises, e.g. promises to marry, or promises to serve for a certain time, are never in practice qualified by an express exception of the death of the party; and therefore in such cases the contract is in terms broken if the promisor dies before fulfillment. Yet it was very early determined that, if the performance is personal, the executors are not liable; *Hyde v. The Dean of Windsor* (Cro. Eliz. 552, 553). See 2 Wms. Exors, 1560, 5th Ed., where a very apt illustration is given. "Thus," says the learned author, "if an author undertakes to compose a work, and dies before completing it, his executors are discharged from this contract; for the undertaking is merely personal in its nature, and by the intervention of the contractor's death, has become impossible to be performed." . . .

These are instances where the implied condition is of the life of a human being, but there are others in which the same implication is made as to the continued existence of a thing. For example, where a contract of sale is made amounting to a bargain and sale, transferring presently the property in specific chattels, which are to be delivered by the vendor at a future day; there, if the chattels, without the fault of the vendor, perish in the interval, the purchaser must pay the price and the vendor is excused from performing his contract to deliver, which has thus become impossible. . . .

. . . [In *Williams v. Lloyd W. Jones,*] the court, which was in assumpsit, alleged that the plaintiff had delivered a horse to the defendant, who promised to redeliver it on request. Breach, that though requested to redeliver the horse he refused. Plea, that the horse was sick and died, and the plaintiff made the request after its death; and on demurrer it was held a good plea, and the bailee was discharged from his promise by the death of the horse without default or negligence on the part of the defendant. "Let it be admitted," say the Court, "that he promised to deliver it on request, if the horse die before, that is become impossible by the act of God, so the party shall be discharged, as much as if an obligation were made conditioned to deliver the horse on request, and he died before it." . . .

It may, we think, be safely asserted to be now English law, that in all contracts of loan of chattels or bailments if the performance of the promise of the borrower or bailee to return the things lent or bailed, becomes impossible because it [sic] has perished, this impossibility (if not arising from the fault of the borrower or bailee from some risk which he has taken upon himself) excuses the borrower or bailee from the performance of his promise to redeliver the chattel.

The great case of *Coggs v. Bernard* (1 Smith's L.C. 171, 5th ed.; 2 L.Raym. 909) is now the leading case on the law of bailments, and Lord Holt, in that case, referred so much to the Civil Law that it might perhaps be thought that this principle was there delivered direct from the civilians, and was not generally applicable in English law except in the case of bailments; but the case of *Williams v. Lloyd W. Jones,* 179, above cited, shows that the same law had been already adopted by the English law as early as The Book of Assizes. The principle seems to us to be that, in contracts in which the performance depends on the continued existence of a given person or thing, a condition is implied that the impossibility of performance arising from the perishing of the person or thing shall excuse the performance.

In none of these cases is the promise in words other than positive, nor is there any express stipulation that the destruction of the person or thing shall excuse the performance; but that excuse is by law implied, because from the nature of the contract it is apparent that the parties contract on the basis of the continued existence of the particular person or chattel. In the present case, looking at the whole contract, we find that the parties contracted on the basis of the continued existence of the Music Hall at the time when the concerts were to be given; that being essential to their performance.

We think, therefore, that the Music Hall having ceased to exist, without fault of either party, both parties are excused, the plaintiffs from taking the gardens and paying the money, the defendants from performing their promise to give the use of the Hall and Gardens and other things. Consequently the rule must be absolute to enter the verdict for the defendants.

Rule absolute.

Questions

1.   What does the promoter want in *Taylor*? Why does the hall owner think he should not get it? Why does the court excuse the hall owner's performance? What is its test for excusing nonperformance?

2.   Why does the court treat the basis for excusing performance as an "implied condition" in the contract? Did the parties intend for there to be such a condition? If not, what is the court's best argument for implying the condition? Why should the hall owner's promise to let the plaintiffs have the use of the facility not be given effect according to its terms?

3.   *Problems*.

a.   The facts are as in *Taylor* except that the hall owner burned the hall down in an act of arson. Same result?

b.   The facts are as in *Taylor* except that a clause in the contract made the hall owner liable in case of fire. Same result?

c.   Charlie contracted to build a new building for Greta under a standard form construction contract calling for progress payments with a final payment due only upon issuance of a certificate of completion by the architect. When the building was two-thirds complete, and Charlie had received half of the price, the building was completely destroyed by a fire caused by lightning. Charlie comes to see you. Should you advise him that he is legally obligated to rebuild?

d.   Charlie contracted to do extensive repairs on an existing building under a standard form construction contract calling for progress payments with a final payment due only upon issuance of a certificate of completion by the architect. When the repairs were two-thirds complete, and Charlie had received half of the price, the building was completely destroyed by a fire caused by lightning. Charlie comes to see you. Should you advise him that he is legally obligated to rebuild?

e.   The facts are the same as Problem c above except that, instead of a fire, Charlie died. How would you respond to Greta's request for advice?

f.   The facts are as in *Taylor* except that the promoter had given the hall owner a deposit of £100 when concluding the contract. Should the promoter get the deposit back? What if, in addition, the promoter incurred expenses of £50 on promoting the event to be held at the gardens. Should the promoter get £150? Should the promoter get his lost profit, if any?

KRELL v. HENRY

Court of Appeal, 1903.
2 K.B. 740.

[The defendant agreed, by a contract in writing of June 20, 1902, to let from the plaintiff a flat in Pall Mall, London, for June 26 and 27. It had been officially announced that the coronation processions (i.e., to be held in connection with the coronation of Edward VII) would take place and pass along Pall Mall on those days. The contract contained no express reference to any purpose for which the flat was taken, such as for viewing the coronation processions. A deposit was paid when the contract was concluded. Owing to the serious illness of the King, the processions did not take place on the days originally fixed. The defendant refused to pay the balance of the rent.]

VAUGHN WILLIAMS, LORD JUSTICE. The real question in this case is the extent of the application in English law of the principle of the Roman law which has been adopted and acted on in many English decisions, and notably in the case of Taylor v. Caldwell, (3 B. & S. 826). . . . I do not think that the principle of the civil law as introduced into the English law is limited to cases in which the event causing the impossibility of performance is the destruction or non-existence of some thing which is the subject matter of the contract or of some condition or state of things expressly specified as a condition of it. I think that you first have to ascertain, not necessarily from the terms of the contract, but, if required, from necessary inferences, drawn from surrounding circumstances recognized by both contracting parties, what is the substance of the contract, and then to ask the question whether that substantial contract needs for its foundation the assumption of the existence of a particular state of things. If it does, this will limit the operation of the general words, and in such case, if the contract becomes impossible of performance by reason of the non-existence of the state of things assumed by both contracting parties as the foundation of the contract there will be no breach of the contract thus limited. Now what are the facts of the present case? The contract is contained in two letters of June 20 which passed between the defendant and the plaintiff's agent, Mr. Cecil Bisgood. These letters do not mention the coronation, but speak merely of the taking of Mr. Krell's chambers, or, rather, of the use of them, in the daytime of June 26 and 27, for the sum of sum of 75£., 25£. then paid, balance 50£. to be paid on the 24th. But the affidavits, which by agreement between the parties are to be taken as stating the facts of the case, show that the plaintiff exhibited on his premises, third floor, 56A, Pall Mall, an announcement to the effect that windows to view the Royal coronation procession were to be let, and that the defendant was induced by that announcement to apply to the housekeeper on the premises, who said that the owner was willing to let the suite of rooms for the purpose of seeing the Royal procession for both days, but not nights, of June 26 and 27. In my judgment the use of rooms was let and taken for the purpose of seeing the Royal procession. It was not a demise of the rooms, or even an agreement to let and take the rooms. It is a license to use rooms for a particular purpose and none other. And in my judgment the taking place of those processions on the days proclaimed along the proclaimed route, which passed 56A, Pall Mall, was regarded by both contracting parties as the foundation of the contract; and I think that it cannot reasonably be supposed to have been in the contemplation of the contracting parties, when the contract was made, that the coronation would not be held on the proclaimed days, or the processions not take place on those days along the proclaimed route; and I think that the words imposing on the defendant the obligation to accept and pay for the use of the rooms for the named days, although general and unconditional, were not used with reference to the possibility of the particular contingency which afterwards occurred. It was suggested in the course of the argument that if the occurrence, on the proclaimed days, of the coronation and the procession in this case were the foundation of the contract, and if the general words are thereby limited or qualified, so that in the event of the nonoccurrence of the coronation and procession along the proclaimed route they would discharge both parties from further performance of the contract, it would follow that if a cabman was engaged to take someone to Epsom on Derby Day at a suitable enhanced price for such a journey, say 10£., both parties to the contract would be discharged in the contingency of the race at Epsom for some reason becoming impossible; but I do not think this follows, for I do not think that in the cab case the happening of the race would be the foundation of the contract. No doubt the purpose of the engager would be to go to see the Derby, and the price would be proportionately high; but the cab had no special qualification for this particular occasion. Any other cab would have done as well.

Appeal dismissed.

Questions

1. How does the legal issue in *Krell* differ from that in *Taylor v. Caldwell*? What is the relationship between the doctrines of *Taylor* ("impossibility") and *Krell* ("frustration")?

2. Does the court succeed in distinguishing the hypothetical case of the cab ride on Derby Day? Would that case require different treatment if the cabman had not charged an enhanced price?

3. *Problems.*

a. The facts are as in *Krell v. Henry*, except that the lessor waived any claim to the promised rent and sought only reimbursement for expenses he had incurred in fitting the rooms for the tenant's use. Same result?

b. Patton, a new automobile dealer, contracted to lease an automobile lot, showroom, and garage just before the outbreak of war in the Crimea. Shortly after the war began, the U.S. Government imposed restrictions on the manufacture and sale of new cars, requiring allocations of all new cars to dealers on the basis of a 50% cut in contract quantities. Patton believes that he cannot break even without more cars to sell, even though the lessor offered to reduce the rent by 15%. Patton cancelled his plans for the dealership and vacated the premises. Is he excused from his obligation to pay the rent? See Lloyd v. Murphy, 25 Cal.2d 48, 153 P.2d 47 (1944).

———

UNIFORM COMMERCIAL CODE §§ 2–613–2–616

———

NORTHERN INDIANA PUBLIC SERVICE CO. v. CARBON COUNTY COAL CO.

United States Court of Appeals, Seventh Circuit, 1986.
799 F.2d 265.

POSNER, CIRCUIT JUDGE. These appeals bring before us various facets of a dispute between Northern Indiana Public Service Company (NIPSCO), an electric utility in Indiana, and Carbon County Coal Company, a partnership that until recently owned and operated a coal mine in Wyoming. In 1978, NIPSCO and Carbon County signed a contract whereby Carbon County agreed to sell and NIPSCO to buy approximately 1.5 million tons of coal every year for 20 years, at a price of $24 a ton subject to various provisions for escalation which by 1985 had driven the price up to $44 a ton.

NIPSCO's rates are regulated by the Indiana Public Service Commission. In 1983, NIPSCO requested permission to raise its rates to reflect increased fuel charges. Some customers of NIPSCO opposed the increased fuel charges. Some customers of NIPSCO opposed the increase on the ground that NIPSCO could reduce its overall costs by buying more electrical power from neighboring utilities for resale to its customers and producing less of its own power. Although the Commission granted the requested increase, it directed NIPSCO, in orders issued in December 1983 and February 1984 (the "economy purchase orders"), to make a good faith effort to find, and wherever possible buy from, utilities that would sell electricity to it at prices lower than its costs of internal generation. The Commission added ominously that "the adverse effects of entering into long-term coal supply contracts which do not allow for renegotiation and are not requirement contracts, is a burden which must rest squarely on the shoulders of NIPSCO management." Actually the contract with Carbon County did provide for renegotiation of the contract price—but one-way renegotiation in favor of Carbon County; the price fixed in the contract (as adjusted from time to time in accordance with the escalator provisions) was a floor. And the contract was indeed not a requirements contract: it specified the exact amount of coal that NIPSCO must take over the 20 years during which the contract was to remain in effect. NIPSCO was eager to have an assured supply of low-sulphur coal and was therefore willing to guarantee both price and quantity.

Unfortunately for NIPSCO, however, as things turned out it was indeed able to buy electricity at prices below the costs of generating electricity from coal bought under the contract with Carbon County; and because of the "economy purchase orders," of which it had not sought judicial review, NIPSCO could not expect to be allowed by the Public Service Commission to recover in its electrical rates the costs of buying coal from Carbon County. NIPSCO therefore decided to stop accepting coal deliveries from Carbon County, at least for the time being; and on April 24, 1985, it brought this diversity suit against Carbon County in a federal district court in Indiana, seeking a declaration that it was excused from its obligations under the contract either permanently or at least until the economy purchase orders ceased preventing it from passing on the costs of the contract to its ratepayers. In support of this position it argued that ... NIPSCO's performance was excused or suspended—either under the contract's *force majeure* clause or under the doctrines of frustration or impossibility—by reason of the economy purchase orders.

On May 17, 1985, Carbon County counterclaimed for breach of contract and moved for a preliminary injunction requiring NIPSCO to continue taking delivery under the contract. On June 19, 1985, the district judge granted the preliminary injunction, from which NIPSCO has appealed. Also on June 19, rejecting NIPSCO's argument that it needed more time for pretrial discovery and other trial preparations, the judge scheduled the trial to begin on August 26, 1985. Trial did begin then, lasted for six weeks, and resulted in a jury verdict for Carbon County of $181 million. The judge entered judgment in accordance with the verdict, rejecting Carbon County's argument that in lieu of damages it should get an order of specific performance requiring NIPSCO to comply with the contract. Upon entering the final judgment the district judge dissolved the preliminary injunction, and shortly afterward the mine—whose only customer was NIPSCO—shut down. NIPSCO has appealed from the damage judgment, and Carbon County from the denial of specific performance. . . .

The contract permits NIPSCO to stop taking delivery of coal "for any cause beyond [its] reasonable control ... including but not limited to ... orders or acts of civil ... authority ... which wholly or partly prevent ... the utilizing ... of the coal." This is what is known as a *force majeure* clause. See, e.g., *Northern Illinois Gas Co. v. Energy Coop., Inc.,* 122 Ill.App.3d 940, 949–52, 78 Ill.Dec. 215, 223–24, 461 N.E.2d 1049, 1057–58 (1984). NIPSCO argues that the Indiana Public Service Commission's "economy purchase orders" prevented it, in whole or part, from using the coal that it had agreed to buy, and it complains that the district judge instructed the jury incorrectly on the meaning and application of the clause. The complaint about the instructions is immaterial. The judge should not have put the issue of *force majeure* to the jury. It is evident that the clause was not triggered by the orders.

All that those orders do is tell NIPSCO it will not be allowed to pass on fuel costs to its ratepayers in the form of higher rates if it can buy electricity cheaper than it can generate electricity internally using Carbon County's coal. Such an order does not "prevent," whether wholly or in part, NIPSCO from using the coal; it just prevents NIPSCO from shifting the burden of its improvidence or bad luck in having incorrectly forecasted its fuel needs to the backs of the hapless ratepayers. The purpose of public utility regulation is to provide a substitute for competition in markets (such as the market for electricity) that are naturally monopolistic. Suppose the market for electricity were fully competitive, and unregulated. Then if NIPSCO signed a long-term fixed-price fixed-quantity contract to buy coal, and during the life of the contract competing electrical companies were able to produce and sell electricity at prices below the cost to NIPSCO of producing electricity from that coal, NIPSCO would have to swallow the excess cost of the coal. It could not raise its electricity prices in order to pass on the excess cost to its consumers, because if it did they would buy electricity at a lower prices from NIPSCO's competitors. By signing the kind of contract it did, NIPSCO gambled that fuel costs would rise rather than fall over the life of the contract; for if they rose then the contract price would give it an advantage over its (hypothetical) competitors who would have to buy fuel at the current market price. If such a gamble fails, the result is not *force majeure*.

This is all the clearer when we consider that the contract price was actually fixed just on the downside; it put a floor under the price NIPSCO had to pay, but the escalator provisions allowed the actual contract prices to rise above the floor, and they did. This underscores the gamble NIPSCO took in signing the contract. It committed itself to paying a price at or above a fixed minimum and to taking a fixed quantity at that price. It was willing to make this commitment to secure an assured supply of low-sulphur coal, but the risk it took was that the market price of coal or substitute fuels would fall. A *force majeure* clause is not intended to buffer a party against the normal risks of a contract. The normal risk of a fixed-price contract is that the market price will change. If it rises, the buyer gains at the expense of the seller (except insofar as escalator provisions give the seller some protection); if it falls, as here, the seller gains at the expense of the buyer. The whole purpose of a fixed-price contract is to allocate risk in this way. A *force majeure* clause interpreted to excuse the buyer from the consequences of the risk he expressly assumed would nullify a central term of the contract....

If the Commission had ordered NIPSCO to close plant because of a safety or pollution hazard, we would have a true case of *force majeure.* As a regulated firm NIPSCO is subject to more extensive controls than unregulated firms and it therefore wanted and got a broadly worded *force majeure* clause that would protect it fully (hence the reference to partial effects) against government actions that impeded its using the coal. But as the only thing the Commission did was prevent NIPSCO from using its monopoly position to make consumers bear the risk that NIPSCO assumed when it signed a long-term fixed-price fuel contract, NIPSCO cannot complain of *force majeure*; the risk that has come to pass was one that NIPSCO voluntarily assumed when it signed the contract.

The district judge refused to submit NIPSCO's defenses of impracticability and frustration to the jury, ruling that Indiana law does not allow a buyer to claim impracticability and does not recognize the defense of frustration. Some background (on which see Farnsworth, Contracts §§ 9.5–9.7 (1982)) may help make these rulings intelligible. In the early common law a contractual undertaking unconditional in terms was not excused merely because something had happened (such as an invasion, the passage of a law, or a natural disaster) that prevented the undertaking. See *Paradine v. Jane,* Aleyn 26, 82 Eng.Rep. 897 (K.B. 1647). Excuses had to be written into the contract; this is the origin of *force majeure* clauses. Later it came to be recognized that negotiating parties cannot anticipate all the contingencies that may arise in the performance of the contract; a legitimate judicial function in contract cases is to interpolate terms to govern remote contingencies—terms the parties would have agreed on explicitly if they had had the time and foresight to make advance provision for every possible contingency in performance. Later still, it was recognized that physical impossibility was irrelevant, or at least inconclusive; a promisor might want his promise to be unconditional, not because he thought he had superhuman powers but because he could insure against the risk of nonperformance better than the promisee, or obtain a substitute performance more easily than the promisee. See *Field Container Corp. v. ICC,* 712 F.2d 250, 257 (7th Cir.1983); Holmes, The Common Law 300 (1881). Thus the proper question in an "impossibility" case is not whether the promisor could not have performed his undertaking but whether his nonperformance should be excused because the parties, if they had thought about the matter, would have wanted to assign the risk of the contingency that made performance impossible or uneconomical to the promisor or to the promisee; if to the latter, the promisor is excused.

Section 2–615 of the Uniform Commercial Code takes this approach. It provides that "delay in delivery ... by a seller ... is not a breach of his duty under a contract for sale if performance as agreed has been made impracticable by the occurrence of a contingency the non-occurrence of which was a basic assumption on which the contract was made...." Performance on schedule need not be impossible, only infeasible—provided that the event which made it infeasible was not a risk that the promisor had assumed. Notice, however, that the only type of promisor referred to is a seller; there is no suggestion that a buyer's performance might be excused by reason of impracticability. The reason is largely semantic. Ordinarily all the buyer has to do in order to perform his side of the bargain is pay, and while one can think of all sorts of reasons why, when the time came to pay, the buyer might not have the money, rarely would the seller have intended to assume the risk that the buyer might, whether through improvidence or bad luck, be unable to pay for the seller's goods or services. To deal with the rare case where the buyer or (more broadly) the paying party might have a good excuse based on some unforeseen change in circumstances, a new rubric was thought necessary, different from "impossibility" (the common law term) or "impracticability" (the Code term, picked up in Restatement (Second) of Contracts § 261 (1979)), and it received the name "frustration." Rarely is it impracticable or impossible for the payor to pay; but if something has happened to make the performance for which he would be paying worthless to him, an excuse for not paying, analogous to impracticability or impossibility, may be proper. See Restatement, *supra*, § 265, comment a.

The leading case on frustration remains *Krell v. Henry*, [1903] 2 K.B. 740 (C.A.). Krell rented Henry a suite of rooms for watching the coronation of Edward VII, but Edward came down with appendicitis and the coronation had to be postponed. Henry refused to pay the balance of the rent and the court held that he was excused from doing so because his purpose in renting had been frustrated by the postponement, a contingency outside the knowledge, or power to influence, of either party. The question was, to which party did the contract (implicitly) allocate the risk? Surely Henry had not intended to insure Krell against the possibility of the coronation's being postponed, since Krell could always relet the room, at the premium rental, for the coronation's new date. So Henry was excused.

NIPSCO is the buyer in the present case, and its defense is more properly frustration than impracticability; but the judge held that frustration is not a contract defense under the law of Indiana. He relied on an Indiana Appellate Court decision which indeed so states, *Ross Clinic, Inc. v. Tabion*, 419 N.E.2d 219, 223 (Ind.App.1981), but solely on the basis of an old decision of the Indiana Supreme Court, *Krause v. Board of Trustees*, 162 Ind. 278, 283–84, 70 N.E. 264, 265 (1904), that doesn't even discuss the defense of frustration and anyway precedes by years the recognition of the defense by American courts. At all events, the facts of the present case do not bring it within the scope of the frustration doctrine, so we need not decide whether the Indiana Supreme Court would embrace the doctrine in a suitable case....

Whether or not Indiana recognizes the doctrine of frustration, and whether or not a buyer can ever assert the defense of impracticability under section 2–615 of the Uniform Commercial Code, these doctrines, so closely related to each other and to *force majeure* as well, see *International Minerals & Chemical Corp. v. Llano, Inc.*, 770 F.2d 879, 885–87 (10th Cir.1985), cannot help NIPSCO. All are doctrines for shifting risk to the party better able to bear it, either because he is in a better position to prevent the risk from materializing or because he can better reduce the disutility of the risk (as by insuring) if the risk does occur. Suppose a grower agrees before the growing season to sell his crop to a grain elevator, and the crop is destroyed by blight and the grain elevator sues. Discharge is ordinarily allowed in such cases. See, e.g., *Matousek v. Galligan*, 104 Neb. 731, 178 N.W. 510 (1920).... The grower has every incentive to avoid the blight; so if it occurs, it probably could not have been prevented; and the grain elevator, which buys from a variety of growers not all of whom will be hit by blight in the same growing season, is in a better position to buffer the risk of blight than the grower is.

Since impossibility and related doctrines are devices for shifting risk in accordance with the parties' presumed intentions, which are to minimize the costs of contract performance, one of which is the disutility created by risk, they have no place when the contract explicitly assigns a particular risk to one party or the other. As we have already noted, a fixed-price contract is an explicit assignment of the risk of market price increases to the seller and the risk of market price decreases to the buyer, and the assignment of the latter risk to the buyer is even clearer where, as in this case, the contract places a floor under price but allows for escalation. If, as is also the case here, the buyer forecasts the market incorrectly and therefore finds himself locked into a disadvantageous contract, he has only himself to blame and so cannot shift the risk back to the seller by invoking impossibility or related doctrines. See [E. Allen Farnsworth, Contracts 680 and n. 18 (1982)]; White & Summers, Handbook of the Law Under the Uniform Commercial Code 133 (2d ed. 1980). It does not matter that it is an act of government that may have made the contract less advantageous to one party. See, e.g., *Connick v. Teachers Ins. & Annuity Ass'n*, 784 F.2d 1018, 1022 (9th Cir.1986).... Government these days is a pervasive factor in the economy and among the risks that a fixed-price contract allocates between the parties is that of a price change induced by one of government's manifold interventions in the economy. Since "the very purpose of a fixed price agreement is to place the risk of increased costs on the promisor (and the risk of decreased costs on the promisee)," the fact that costs decrease steeply (which is in effect what happened here—the cost of generating electricity turned out to be lower than NIPSCO thought when it signed the fixed-price contract with Carbon County) cannot allow the buyer to walk away from the contract....

Questions

1. What is Judge Posner's test for determining when a party should be excused? Is it adequately rooted in U.C.C. § 2–615?

2. Should the duty to perform promises be excused whenever it would be inefficient to perform them according to their terms? Is that what the parties would "intend"? Should they be bound by a judge's view of what they would have agreed should happen, when they in fact did not agree to it? Should they be bound to do the efficient thing whether or not they agreed or would have agreed to that?

3. *Problem.*

> Assume that Gehrig has $50,000 in a passbook savings account paying 2.25% interest at Ruth's savings bank. He plans to use the money next year for the down payment on a house. Ruth also sells certificates of deposit paying 3.85% interest with a mandatory six month commitment. The conditions are set for a deal that improves efficiency (with rare exception). Gehrig would be better off moving his money to a certificate of deposit, and Ruth would be better off paying Gehrig the higher rate and moving the money to a more highly valued use. The community, therefore, would be better off. But, due to the transaction costs of learning of the better opportunity and taking it, Gehrig leaves his money in the passbook account. Ruth later sues Gehrig for breach of contract. Should he recover? Does Judge Posner's test require that he recover?

TRANSATLANTIC FINANCING CORP. v. UNITED STATES

United States Court of Appeals, District of Columbia Circuit, 1966.
124 U.S.App.D.C. 183, 363 F.2d 312.

J. SKELLY WRIGHT, CIRCUIT JUDGE: This appeal involves a voyage charter between Transatlantic Financing Corporation, operator of the SS CHRISTOS, and the United States covering carriage of a full cargo of wheat from a United States Gulf port to a safe port in Iran. The District Court dismissed a libel filed by Transatlantic against the United States for costs attributable to the ship's diversion from the normal sea route caused by the closing of the Suez Canal. We affirm.

On July 26, 1956, the Government of Egypt nationalized the Suez Canal Company and took over operation of the Canal. On October 2, 1956, during the international crisis which resulted from the seizure, the voyage charter in suit was executed between representatives of Transatlantic and the United States. The charter indicated the termini of the voyage but not the route. On October 27, 1956, the SS CHRISTOS sailed from Galveston for Bandar Shapur, Iran, on a course which would have taken her through Gibraltar and the Suez Canal. On October 29, 1956, Israel invaded Egypt. On October 31, 1956, Great Britain and France invaded the Suez Canal Zone. On November 2, 1956, the Egyptian Government obstructed the Suez Canal with sunken vessels and closed it to traffic.

On or about November 7, 1956, Beckmann, representing Transatlantic, contacted Potosky, an employee of the United States Department of Agriculture, who appellant concedes was unauthorized to bind the Government, requesting instructions concerning disposition of the cargo and seeking an agreement for payment of additional compensation for a voyage around the Cape of Good Hope. Potosky advised Beckmann that Transatlantic was expected to perform the charter according to its terms, that he did not believe Transatlantic was entitled to additional compensation for a voyage around the Cape, but that Transatlantic was free to file such a claim. Following this discussion, the CHRISTOS changed course for the Cape of Good Hope and eventually arrived in Bandar Shapur on December 30, 1956.

Transatlantic's claim is based on the following train of argument. The charter was a contract for a voyage from a Gulf port to Iran. Admiralty principles and practices, especially stemming from the doctrine of deviation, require us to imply into the contract the term that the voyage was to be performed by the "usual and customary" route. The usual and customary route from Texas to Iran was, at the time of contract, via Suez, so the contract was for a voyage from Texas to Iran via Suez. When Suez was closed this contract became impossible to perform. Consequently, appellant's argument continues, when Transatlantic delivered the cargo by going around the Cape of Good Hope, in compliance with the Government's demand under claim of right, it conferred a benefit upon the United States for which it should be paid in *quantum meruit*.

The doctrine of impossibility of performance has gradually been freed from the earlier fictional and unrealistic strictures of such tests as the "implied term" and the parties' "contemplation." Page, *The Development of the Doctrine of Impossibility of Performance*, 18 Mich. L. Rev. 589, 596 (1920). See generally 6 Corbin, Contracts §§ 1320–1372 (rev. ed. 1962); 6 Williston, Contracts §§ 1931–1979 (rev. ed. 1938). It is now recognized that "A thing is impossible in legal contemplation when it is not practicable; and a thing is impracticable when it can only be done at an excessive and unreasonable cost." Mineral Park Land Co. v. Howard, 172 Cal. 289, 293, 156 P. 458, 460, L.R.A. 1916E, 1 (1916). *Accord*, Whelan v. Griffith Consumers Company, D.C.Mun.App., 170 A.2d 229 (1961); Restatement, Contracts § 454 (1932); Uniform Commercial Code (U.L.A.) § 2–615, comment 3. The doctrine ultimately represents the ever-shifting line, drawn by courts hopefully responsive to commercial practices and mores, at which the community's interest in having contracts enforced according to their terms is outweighed by the commercial senselessness of requiring performance. When the issue is raised, the court is asked to construct a condition of performance based on the changed circumstances, a process which involves at least three reasonably definable steps. First, a contingency—something unexpected—must have occurred. Second, the risk of the unexpected occurrence must not have been allocated either by agreement or by custom. Finally, occurrence of the contingency must have rendered performance commercially impracticable.[3] Unless the court finds these three requirements satisfied, the plea of impossibility must fail.

The first requirement was met here. It seems reasonable, where no route is mentioned in a contract, to assume the parties expected performance by the usual and customary route at the time of contract.[4] Since the usual and customary route from Texas to Iran at the time of contract was through Suez, closure of the Canal made impossible the expected method of performance. But this unexpected development raises rather than resolves the impossibility issue, which turns additionally on whether the risk of the contingency's occurrence had been allocated and, if not, whether performance by alternative routes was rendered impracticable.[6]

Proof that the risk of a contingency's occurrence has been allocated may be expressed in or implied from the agreement. Such proof may also be found in the surrounding circumstances, including custom and usages of the trade. See 6 CORBIN, *supra*, § 1339, at 394–397; 6 WILLISTON, *supra*, § 1948, at 5457–5458. The contract in this case does not expressly condition performance upon availability of the Suez route. Nor does it specify "via Suez" or, on the other hand, "via Suez or Cape of Good Hope." Nor are there provisions in the contract from which we may properly imply that the continued availability of Suez was a condition of performance. Nor is there anything in custom or trade usage, or in the surrounding circumstances generally, which would support our constructing a condition of performance. The numerous cases requiring performance around the Cape when Suez was closed, see *e.g.*, Ocean

---

3. Compare UNIFORM COMMERCIAL CODE § 2–615(a), which provides that, in the absence of an assumption of greater liability, delay or non-delivery by a seller is not a breach if performance as agreed is made "impracticable" by the occurrence of a "contingency" the non-occurrence of which was a "basic assumption on which the contract was made." To the extent this limits relief to "unforeseen" circumstances, comment 1, see the discussion below, and compare UNIFORM COMMERCIAL CODE § 2–614(1). There may be a point beyond which agreement cannot go, UNIFORM COMMERCIAL CODE § 2–615, comment 8, presumably the point at which the obligation would be "manifestly unreasonable," § 1–102(3), in bad faith, § 1–203, or unconscionable, § 2–302. For an application of these provisions see Judge Friendly's opinion in United States v. Wegematic Corporation, 2 Cir., 360 F.2d 674 (1966).

4. UNIFORM COMMERCIAL CODE § 2–614, comment 1, states: "Under this Article, in the absence of specific agreement, the normal or usual facilities enter into the agreement either through the circumstances, usage of trade or prior course of dealing." So long as this sort of assumption does not

necessarily result in construction of a condition of performance, it is idle to argue over whether the usual and customary route is an "implied term." The issue of impracticability must eventually be met. One court refused to imply the Suez route as a contract term, but went on to rule the contract had been "frustrated." Carapanayoti & Co. Ltd. v. E. T. Green Ltd., [1959] 1 Q.B. 131. The holding was later rejected by the House of Lords. Tsakiroglou & Co. Ltd. v. Noblee Thorl G.m.b.H., [1960] 2 Q.B. 348.

6. In criticizing the "contemplation" test for impossibility Professor Patterson pointed out:

" 'Contemplation' is appropriate to describe the mental state of philosophers but is scarcely descriptive of the mental state of business men making a bargain. It seems preferable to say that the promisee *expects* performance by [the] means ... the promisor expects to (or which on the facts known to the promisee it is probable that he will) use. It does not follow as an inference of fact that the promisee expects performance by *only* that means...." Patterson, [*Constructive Conditions in Contracts*, 42 COLUM. L. REV. 903 (1942)] at 947.

Tramp Tankers Corp. v. V/O Sovfracht (The Eugenia), [1964] 2 Q.B. 226, and cases cited therein, indicate that the Cape route is generally regarded as an alternative means of performance. So the implied expectation that the route would be via Suez is hardly adequate proof of an allocation to the promisee of the risk of closure. In some cases, even an express expectation may not amount to a condition of performance.[9] The doctrine of deviation supports our assumption that parties normally expect performance by the usual and customary route, but it adds nothing beyond this that is probative of an allocation of the risk.[10]

If anything, the circumstances surrounding this contract indicate that the risk of the Canal's closure may be deemed to have been allocated to Transatlantic. We know or may safely assume that the parties were aware, as were most commercial men with interests affected by the Suez situation, see The Eugenia, *supra*, that the Canal might become a dangerous area. No doubt the tension affected freight rates, and it is arguable that the risk of closure became part of the dickered terms. UNIFORM COMMERCIAL CODE § 2–615, comment 8. We do not deem the risk of closure so allocated, however. Foreseeability or even recognition of a risk does not necessarily prove its allocation.[11] Compare UNIFORM COMMERCIAL CODE § 2–615, Comment 1; RESTATEMENT, CONTRACTS § 457 (1932). Parties to a contract are not always able to provide for all the possibilities of which they are aware, sometimes because they cannot agree, often simply because they are too busy. Moreover, that some abnormal risk was contemplated is probative but does not necessarily establish an allocation of the risk of the contingency which actually occurs. In this case, for example, nationalization by Egypt of the Canal Corporation and formation of the Suez Users Group did not necessarily indicate that the Canal would be blocked even if a confrontation resulted.[12] The surrounding circumstances do indicate, however, a willingness

---

9. UNIFORM COMMERCIAL CODE § 2–614(1) provides: "Where without fault of either party . . . the *agreed* manner of delivery . . . becomes commercially impracticable but a commercially reasonable substitute is available, such substitute performance must be tendered and accepted." [emphasis added.] Compare Mr. Justice Holmes' observation: "You can give any conclusion a logical form. You always can imply a condition in a contract. But why do you imply it? It is because of some belief as to the practice of the community or of a class, or because of some opinion as to policy. . . ." Holmes, *The Path of the Law*, 10 HARV. L. REV. 457, 466 (1897).

10. The deviation doctrine, drawn principally from admiralty insurance practice, implies into all relevant commercial instruments naming the termini of voyages the usual and customary route between those points. 1 ARNOULD, MARINE INSURANCE AND AVERAGE § 376, at 522 (10th ed. 1921). Insurance is cancelled when a ship unreasonably "deviates" from this course, for example by extending a voyage or by putting in

at an irregular port, and the shipowner forfeits the protection of clauses of exception which might otherwise have protected him from his common law insurer's liability to cargo. See GILMORE & BLACK, [THE LAW OF ADMIRALTY] § 2–6, at 59–60 [(1957)]. This practice, properly qualified, see *id.* § 3–41, makes good sense, since insurance rates are computed on the basis of the implied course, and deviations in the course increasing the anticipated risk make the insurer's calculations meaningless. ARNOULD, *supra*, § 14, at 26. Thus the route, so far as insurance contracts are concerned, is crucial, whether express or implied. . . .

11. See Note, *The Fetish of Impossibility in the Law of Contracts*, 53 Colum. L. Rev. 94, 98 n. 23 (1953), suggesting that foreseeability is properly used "as a *factor* probative of assumption of the risk of impossibility." [emphasis added.]

12. Sources cited in the briefs indicate formation of the Suez Canal Users Association on October 1, 1956, was viewed in

by Transatlantic to assume abnormal risks, and this fact should legitimately cause us to judge the impracticability of performance by an alternative route in stricter terms than we would were the contingency unforeseen.

We turn then to the question whether occurrence of the contingency rendered performance commercially impracticable under the circumstances of this case. The goods shipped were not subject to harm from the longer, less temperate Southern route. The vessel and crew were fit to proceed around the Cape.[13] Transatlantic was no less able than the United States to purchase insurance to cover the contingency's occurrence. If anything, it is more reasonable to expect owner-operators of vessels to insure against the hazards of war. They are in the best position to calculate the cost of performance by alternative routes (and therefore to estimate the amount of insurance required), and are undoubtedly sensitive to international troubles which uniquely affect the demand for and cost of their services. The only factor operating here in appellant's favor is the added expense, allegedly $43,972.00 above and beyond the contract price of $305,842.92, of extending a 10,000 mile voyage by approximately 3,000 miles. While it may be an overstatement to say that increased cost and difficulty of performance never constitute impracticability, to justify relief there must be more of a variation between expected cost and the cost of performing by an available alternative than is present in this case, where the promisor can legitimately be presumed to have accepted some degree of abnormal risk, and where impracticability is urged on the basis of added expense alone.[15]

We conclude, therefore, as have most other courts considering related issues arising out of the Suez closure, that performance of this contract was not rendered legally impossible. Even if we agreed with appellant, its theory of relief seems untenable. When performance of a contract is deemed impossible it is a nullity. In the case of a charter party involving carriage of goods, the carrier may return to an appropriate port and unload its cargo, The Malcolm Baxter, Jr., 277 U.S. 323, 48 S.Ct. 516, 72 L.Ed. 901 (1928), subject of course to required steps to minimize damages. If the performance rendered has value, recovery in

some quarters as an implied threat of force. See N.Y. Times, Oct. 2, 1956, p. 1, col. 1, noting, on the day the charter in this case was executed, that "[B]ritain has declared her freedom to use force as a last resort if peaceful methods fail to achieve a satisfactory settlement." Secretary of State Dulles was able, however, to view the statement as evidence of the canal users' "dedication to a just and peaceful solution." THE SUEZ PROBLEM 369–370 (Department of State Pub. 1956).

13. The issue of impracticability should no doubt be "an objective determination of whether the promise can reasonably be performed rather than a subjective inquiry into the promisor's capability of performing as

agreed." Symposium, *The Uniform Commercial Code and Contract Law: Some Selected Problems*, 105 U. PA. L. REV. 836, 880, 887 (1957). Dealers should not be excused because of less than normal capabilities. But if both parties are aware of a dealer's limited capabilities, no objective determination would be complete without taking into account this fact.

15. See UNIFORM COMMERCIAL CODE § 2–615, comment 4: "Increased cost alone does not excuse performance unless the rise in cost is due to some unforeseen contingency which alters the essential nature of the performance." See also 6 CORBIN, *supra*, § 1333; 6 WILLISTON, *supra*, 1952, at § 5468.

quantum meruit for the entire performance is proper. But here Transatlantic has collected its contract price, and now seeks *quantum meruit* relief for the additional expense of the trip around the Cape. If the contract is a nullity, Transatlantic's theory of relief should have been *quantum meruit* for the entire trip, rather than only for the extra expense. Transatlantic attempts to take its profit on the contract, and then force the Government to absorb the cost of the additional voyage. When impracticability without fault occurs, the law seeks an equitable solution, see 6 CORBIN, *supra*, § 1321, and *quantum meruit* is one of its potent devices to achieve this end. There is no interest in casting the entire burden of commercial disaster on one party in order to preserve the other's profit. Apparently the contract price in this case was advantageous enough to deter appellant from taking a stance on damages consistent with its theory of liability. In any event, there is no basis for relief.

Questions

1. In *Transatlantic Financing*, what is the plaintiff's claim and argument? What is the court's holding?

2. What is this court's preferred test for finding an excuse when performance becomes more burdensome due to changed circumstances? How does this court's test differ from the one in *Taylor v. Caldwell*? How does it differ from Judge Posner's test in *NIPSCO*? Does it require the court to decide what the parties would have agreed to concerning a contingency, when they did not agree in fact?

3. *Problems.*

   a. Borgnine Gearbox, a U.S. manufacturer, contracted to design and supply special equipment for Fields Machinery of Ohio. Although Borgnine Gearbox was unaware of it, Fields was under contract to supply the equipment to a buyer in Iraq. Before delivery, hostilities broke out between Iraq and Kuwait, leading to a United Nations embargo on trade with Iraq. Fields Machinery cancelled the contract. Should Borgnine Gearbox bring an action against Fields Machinery? See Power Eng'r. & Mfg., Ltd. v. Krug International, 501 N.W.2d 490 (Iowa 1993).

   b. Assume that a written contract required a homeowner to repay a mortgage at the rate of $1,000 each month for thirty years, which sum was to be applied first to interest on the remaining balance, second to the property taxes, and only then to decrease the remaining balance. After twelve years, the property taxes on the property rose to $1,050. What should you advise the lender? See Miller v. Campello Co-op. Bank, 344 Mass. 76, 181 N.E.2d 345 (1962).

Problem

In 1987, Bush Machinery, Inc. of Texas contracted to sell six textile machines to Saddam Textiles Co., located in Baghdad, Iraq, for a price of

$87,550, delivery during January, 1991. Saddam Textiles Co. paid $12,550 upon conclusion of the contract; the balance was due upon delivery. Bush Machinery soon began manufacture of the machines, which were to be manufactured to Saddam's specifications. In August, 1990, Iraq invaded Kuwait, and the United Nations imposed an embargo on trade with Iraq. The embargo continued well past the January, 1991 delivery date. As of August, 1990, Bush had expended $8,000 in unrecoverable costs building the machines. It continued manufacture, expending $17,000 more by January, 1991, at which time United Nations allies began air strikes on Iraq, leading Bush to cease manufacture. Meanwhile, Saddam textiles had rebuilt a part of its plant to receive the machines, at a cost of US $14,000. How should the law allocate the losses when delivery becomes illegal? See Restatement (Second) of Contracts § 272; Fibrosa Spolka Akcyjna v. Fairbairn Lawson Combe Barbour, Ltd., [1943] A.C. 32, 144 A.L.R. 1298 (House of Lords); Law Reform (Frustrated Contracts) Act of 1943, 6 & 7 Geo. 6 c. 40.

SECTION 2.   ADJUSTMENT OF CONTRACTUAL RELATIONS

It would be a mistake to think that the rights and obligations of the parties to a contract are fixed at formation in terms that exclusively govern the course of events thereafter. Even when there is no excuse for nonperformance due to commercial impracticability or frustration. Traditional contract law allows the parties' agreement to be modified in light of changes in their relationship as it unfolds. The pre-existing duty rule once was a barrier of sorts to contractual adjustments by mutual agreement, though the point can be overstated by downplaying the exceptions which were often manipulated to facilitate reasonable modifications unsupported by consideration. More significantly, several well-established legal doctrines facilitate adjustments in various circumstances after formation. Waiver, estoppel, and election, for example, allow adjustment of the legal relations due to the words and acts of the parties after formation. One way to understand the tradition: The law treats the agreement of the parties as dispositive of their rights and obligations *only on the assumption that* there are no overriding legal considerations in the case. Facts that materialize after formation can be of overriding importance due to principles of autonomy, justification, justice, and security that stand independently of the parties' agreement.

Professor Ian MacNeil has argued that traditional contract law, represented by the RESTATEMENTS, should be superseded by a distinct alternative called "relational contract law." *E.g.*, Ian R. Macneil, *Contracts: Adjustment of Long-Term Economic Relations Under Classical, Neoclassical, and Relational Contract Law*, 72 Nw. U. L. REV. 854 (1978). The hallmark of traditional contract law, according to MacNeil, is the centrality of consent at formation time to a discrete and presentiated contract. "Discreteness" refers to a way of understanding the contract and its performance in isolation from the broader relationship of the parties, which also may generate expectations about what each will do. "Presentiation" refers to the habit of viewing the performance of the contract as it is supposed to have been understood at the time of formation, when the promises of the parties are supposed to have brought the future into the present and embodied it in the terms of the agreement. Relational contract law, by contrast, emphasizes the broader context in which a contract is situated. As Professor Stewart Macaulay's empirical studies suggest, parties in ongoing relationships have little incentive to insist on agreed contract terms because they were agreed; rather, they tend to adjust their relationships as they go on with little reliance on the legalisms of lawyers. *E.g.*, Stewart Macaulay, *Non-Contractual Relations in Business: A Preliminary Study*, 28 AM. SOC'Y REV. 55 (1963). Relational contract law downgrades the role of consent at formation to a place equal or subordinate to "the relationship" as a ground of legal rights and duties.

Professor Richard E. Speidel has reduced these daunting abstractions to a concrete proposal that parties in some circumstances should have a duty to accept certain modifications proposed by their contract partners or to fulfill new duties imposed by the courts. Richard E. Speidel, *The New Spirit of Contract*, 2 J. L. & COMM. 193 (1982); Richard E. Speidel, *Court-Imposed Price Adjustments Under Long-Term Supply Contracts*, 76 NW. U. L. REV. 369 (1981). First, Professor Speidel would require that the disadvantaged party propose a modification that would be enforceable if accepted by the advantaged party, under the criteria set forth in RESTATEMENT (SECOND) OF CONTRACTS § 89. Second, he would require that it be clear that the disadvantaged party did not assume the risk of the unanticipated event by agreement or under the test set forth in U.C.C. § 2–615(a). As of yet, the courts have given little support to this and other similar proposals. As you read the following cases, consider whether the dynamics of contract performance require some such new doctrine of contract law.

In thinking about "relational contract law," consider also *what kind of a relationship* should matter for legal purposes. In one sense, the most traditional link between promisor and promisee is a legal "relationship." There are a number of other possibilities. First, as Macaulay's empirical studies suggest, contract practices may reveal that parties often deal repeatedly with each other and conduct themselves with a view to maintaining the pattern. What implications might this description of contract practices have for the prescriptions called "law"? Second, perhaps as suggested by Judge Posner's opinion in *Northern Indiana Public Service Co.*, above at p. 557, parties to long-term contracts might be deemed to have agreed to a default rule requiring a court to resolve disputes on the assumption that the parties intended to maximize the joint value of the contract. Should economic efficiency be the principle governing adjustment of contractual relations? Third, some scholars have suggested that parties or the courts have a distinct interest in keeping the deal together, maintaining the connection between the people. Robert A. Hillman, *Court Adjustment of Long-Term Contracts: An Analysis Under Modern Contract Law*, 1987 DUKE L. J. 1. Should adjudication focus on legal rights and duties or begin transforming itself into a mediational institution? Fourth, the "relationship" can be conceived in purposive terms, perhaps as in the *J.J. Brooksbank Co.* case, below at p. 580. On this view, the stated or statable terms of the contract do not constitute the rights and duties of the parties; rather, they evidence more general agreed purposes that can warrant adjustment in the terms to further the agreed purpose. Again, this is an area of great intellectual ferment. Future trends in contract law might find their birthplace here.

BURGER KING CORP. v. FAMILY DINING, INC.

United States District Court, Eastern District of Pennsylvania, 1977.
426 F.Supp. 485, affirmed mem. 566 F.2d 1168 (3d Cir.1977).

[The opinion will be found above at p. 453.]

BAK–A–LUM CORP. OF AMERICA v. ALCOA BLDG. PRODS., INC.

Supreme Court of New Jersey, 1976.
69 N.J. 123, 351 A.2d 349.

CONFORD, P.J.A.D., Temporarily Assigned. Plaintiff corporation ("BAL" hereinafter) sued defendant ("ALCOA" hereinafter) for an injunction and damages for alleged breach of an exclusive distributorship of aluminum siding and related products manufactured by ALCOA. It was denied an injunction but awarded damages for breach of contract; at the same time the trial court granted defendant judgment on a counter-claim for merchandise sold to plaintiff, together with interest thereon. Plaintiff appealed on the ground the damages awarded were inadequate; the defendant cross-appealed, asserting its conduct was not actionable. The Appellate Division affirmed. We granted plaintiff's petition for certification and defendant's cross-petition. . . .

We find the record to support the trial court's finding of fact that in or about 1962 or 1963 BAL entered into a verbal agreement with ALCOA whereby BAL would be exclusive distributor in Northern New Jersey for ALCOA's aluminum siding and certain related products. Although the agreement did not preclude BAL handling other lines of siding, the understanding was that it would maintain an adequate organization and exert its best efforts to promote the sales of the ALCOA products, and the evidence and trial findings were that BAL produced to the satisfaction of ALCOA, even meeting fixed quotas of sales set by ALCOA during the latter phase of the relationship.

ALCOA terminated the "exclusive" in January 1970 by appointing four additional distributors to share the North Jersey territory with plaintiff, thereby precipitating the controversy that gave rise to this action. The trial court, although refusing a request for a preliminary injunction against the termination of the exclusive distributorship, held after trial that there was a binding agreement between the parties terminable only after a reasonable period of time and on reasonable notice. It found that a reasonable period of time had passed before termination but that a reasonable period of notice of termination would be seven months. It established plaintiff's damages at $5,000 per month and entered judgment in plaintiff's favor for $35,000 together with interest from September 1, 1970.

In addition to a complaint that it established losses in sales profits as a result of the termination of the exclusive at a rate of $10,000 per month rather than at the $5,000 rate determined by the court, plaintiff's major grievance is that in the Spring of 1969, at a time when defendant had already decided upon the termination of the distributorship but was secreting that plan from plaintiff, the latter undertook a major expansion of its warehouse facilities at substantial added operating expense. Plaintiff asserts that defendant knew of and encouraged this step, leading plaintiff to believe it was well warranted in view of the expected enlargement of the business of both of the contracting parties. On the basis of defendant's concealment of its intentions in the face of plaintiff's incurrence of a five year lease obligation for the new space, plaintiff asserts it is entitled to additional damages from defendant for the excess of its expense for the period of the lease over its operating expenses in its former headquarters—a loss allegedly attributable directly to defendant's breach of contract.

The trial court found that if ALCOA'S decision, made in January or February of 1969, to enlarge the number of North Jersey distributors, had been promptly communicated to BAL's president, "it is unlikely that he would have signed the lease [for the new quarters] in April [1969] without first getting from [ALCOA] the assurance of continuance of the distributorship which he sought to get after the lease was signed." The court further found that all the circumstances surrounding the defendant's attitude to and treatment of plaintiff preceding and attending the disruption of the contractual arrangement "bespeak a certain hypocrisy as well as ruthlessness on the part of [ALCOA] toward its distributor of many years." The court further "surmised" that the reason defendant had concealed during the year 1969 its intention to terminate plaintiff's exclusive even though it had arrived at that intent before plaintiff entered into the new lease in 1969 was "that the men at [ALCOA] in charge of sales thought a period of secrecy ending with a sudden announcement to Mr. Diamond [plaintiff's president] of the accomplished fact of new distributors would avoid any risk of cooling plaintiff's interest in selling ALCOA products during the several months before the new distributors were named and made ready to go." Indeed, defendant's salesman induced plaintiff in January 1970, just before the announcement of the termination of the exclusive, to order $150,000 worth of merchandise—a very heavy order for that time of year.

In fixing seven months as a reasonable period of notice of termination of the exclusive agreement the trial court stated that the criterion for such a period of notice is the amount of time the notified party needs to make adjustments and to plan and arrange for business activities to replace those which are to be eliminated. However, the court apparently placed little if any weight on the circumstances of the new lease as an element going to the reasonableness of the period for notice of termination, although it stated that the lease was a "factor" for consideration. It pointed out that the decision to undertake the lease was plaintiff's and that plaintiff was able to use the space to store merchandise other than that purchased from defendant as well as defendant's lines.

Our review of the record leads us to concur in the trial court's holding that there was a valid distributorship agreement terminable only on reasonable notice. . . .

However, we are constrained to differ with the trial court's assessment of seven months as an adequate period for notice of termination of this agreement. It may be true that defendant ordinarily would be under no strictly legal obligation to inform plaintiff that it was about to terminate its exclusive distributorship although it knew that in all probability plaintiff was enlarging its plant upon an assumption of the continuation of the business arrangement for the indefinite future. However, we have been at pains recently to point out that "[i]n every contract there is an implied covenant that 'neither party shall do anything which will have the effect of destroying or injuring the right of the other party to receive the fruits of the contract; in other words, in every contract there exists an implied covenant of good [faith] and fair dealing.' " *Association Group Life, Inc. v. Catholic War Vets. of U.S.*, 61 N.J. 150, 153, 293 A.2d 382, 384 (1972). . . .

. . . While the contractual relation of manufacturer and exclusive territorial distributor continued between the parties an obligation of reciprocal good-faith dealing similarly persisted between them. In such circumstances defendant's selfish withholding from plaintiff of its intention seriously to impair its distributorship although knowing plaintiff was embarking on an investment substantially predicated upon its continuation constituted a breach of the implied covenant of dealing in good faith of which we have spoken. As such it must be given substantial weight in determining the reasonableness of a period of notice of termination of the distributorship.

We cannot, however, agree with plaintiff that the period should encompass the remaining 4½ years of the lease as of the date of breach. The evidence justifies the conclusion that the prospects were fair for ultimate utilization to a substantial extent of the expanded warehouse space for new business plaintiff was able to obtain after defendant's breach or for other means of mitigating that phase of the damage attributable to defendant's conduct.

Exercising our original fact finding jurisdiction in order to bring this litigation to a close, it is our determination that a reasonable period of notice of termination of the distributorship, under all the circumstances, would have been 20 months.

Moreover, we find unwarranted the trial court's determination of plaintiff's monthly losses of profits of sales at $5,000 in the face of apparently unchallenged proofs by plaintiff, accepted by the court, that the damage figures were about $10,000 monthly. . . .

On defendant's appeal the judgment is affirmed, with costs. On plaintiff's appeal the judgment is modified in accordance with this opinion, with costs to plaintiff.

Questions

1. Does the court's use of the implied covenant of good faith and fair dealing fit with the good faith performance cases in Chapter 5, § 3?

2. Did the legal relations of the parties change due to a specific event during the performance stage of the contract? What was that event? Was it outside the control of the parties? Or was it a voluntary act of one of the parties? If the latter, could it constitute a waiver, an estoppel, or an equitable adjustment of the parties' relationship?

3. Is the result in *Bak–A–Lum* justified by the autonomy principle? By some other principle?

BADGETT v. SECURITY STATE BANK

Supreme Court of Washington, 1991.
116 Wash.2d 563, 807 P.2d 356.

DURHAM, JUSTICE. Raymond and Audrey Badgett (the Badgetts) brought an action for damages against Security State Bank (the Bank) after the Bank refused to restructure their agricultural loans. The trial court granted summary judgment in favor of the Bank and dismissed the claims. It also granted the Bank summary judgment on its counterclaims for monies due and entered a decree of foreclosure. The Court of Appeals reversed and remanded for trial, holding that the Bank may have had a good faith duty to consider the Badgetts' proposals for restructuring the loan. We reverse the Court of Appeals and reinstate the trial court's dismissal of the damages claims and entry of the decree of foreclosure.

In 1981, the Badgetts borrowed $476,000 from the Bank for their dairy operation. $336,000 of this amount was an intermediate term loan, and the remaining $140,000 was for operating expenses. The contract for the term loan had a 1–year call or maturity date, but was amortized over 5 to 10 years. According to the Badgetts' first loan officer, it was a fairly typical practice for agricultural loans to be re-examined yearly to recap collateral positions, update financial statements, and make projections for the coming year.

In 1984, the Badgetts decided to quit the dairy business. They asked the Bank for assistance in restructuring their loans so they could liquidate their assets and participate in a government diversion program. After a series of negotiations, the parties agreed to a liquidation plan, evidenced by a new promissory note, a security agreement and general pledge, and a security agreement for crops, livestock, and farm products.

In May 1985, the Badgetts decided to re-enter the dairy business and they requested new financing. The Bank sent a letter to the Badgetts asking for additional financial information and indicating that, in the event new financing was agreed to, a written loan agreement would be required. On September 5, 1985, after a series of negotiations, the parties executed a loan agreement and new promissory note in the amount of $1,050,000. The loan agreement was secured by livestock, equipment, feed inventories, and junior liens on all real estate. It expressly provided that "[a]dditional advances or increased commitments for any purpose *are not contemplated* at this time" (italics ours), and that the written agreement "contains the entire loan agreement between Borrower and Security State Bank with respect to the loan transaction." Clerk's Papers, at 134–35.

In early 1986, the Badgetts again decided to retire from the dairy business and considered participating in the federal government's Dairy Termination Program (DTP). Under this program, participants were selected on the basis ... of bids, and they were required to keep their milk facilities out of production for 5 years. The Badgetts had considered entering a bid of $18 per hundred weight of milk production, for which they could have expected to receive $1,600,000.

On March 3, 1986, the Badgetts and their attorney, Rene Remund, met with their current loan officer, Joe Cooke, and the Bank's attorney, John Hall. The Badgetts initially proposed that the Bank accept $1,300,000, part of the amount they expected to receive through participation in the DTP, in satisfaction of the $1,500,000 debt and forgive the remaining $200,000. Cooke declined to accept this proposal. The parties then discussed the possibility of sale of the cattle at auction. They also discussed the possibility of deferring payment of $200,000, with the Bank releasing its existing collateral and accepting unspecified real estate to secure the remaining debt. No specific parcel was proposed, and neither terms of repayment nor interest rate were discussed. Cooke was to meet with the loan committee and get back to the Badgetts with an answer. The Badgetts left the meeting knowing that an agreement had not been reached and further negotiations were necessary.

Cooke then met with the loan committee of the Bank. The Bank did not accept the Badgetts' proposal and did not make an offer. The Badgetts contend that Cooke misrepresented their offer by presenting it to the committee as non-negotiable. Gail Shaw, who was a member of the loan committee, stated that his impression, which he got from Cooke, although "[n]ot by specific words," was that the Badgetts' proposal was non-negotiable. His impression was based in part on the fact that the Badgetts were operating under a tight time frame because bids for participation in the DTP were due by March 7. Thus, there was not really time to negotiate about the $18 bid underlying the proposal. Shaw also stated that he was disappointed that the Badgetts had not made a formal proposal because the proposal was "not conveyed clearly to [Cooke]," and Shaw "ha[d] to admit [from reading the notes of the meeting] that it appears that [Cooke] didn't understand [the proposal]." On March 7, the Badgetts submitted a bid to the DTP of $25.89 per hundred weight.

On March 28, 1986, they learned that their bid to the DTP was not accepted. Prior to that time, the Badgetts had made their loan payments according to the terms of the note. However, on April 3, 1986, their loan payment was for less than the agreed amount and they stopped making payments thereafter. On April 14, 1986, the Badgetts and the Bank entered into a written agreement to auction certain collateral. The sale of the herd and machinery realized net proceeds of $374,447.85.

On September 11, 1986, the Badgetts filed a complaint against the Bank for $2,000,000 in damages alleging, in part, that the Bank had unreasonably refused permission for the Badgetts to participate in the DTP. They also made a Consumer Protection Act (CPA) claim. The Bank filed a counterclaim for payment of monies due and foreclosure. The trial court granted summary judgment to the Bank, dismissing the Badgetts' claims, ruling that the Bank was under no duty to negotiate and that a prior course of conduct cannot create a new obligation on the part of the Bank. The court also granted the Bank summary judgment on its counterclaims and entered a decree of foreclosure.

The Court of Appeals reversed and remanded for trial stating that there was "enough evidence to support a reasonable inference that the parties' course of dealing had created a good faith obligation on the part of the Bank to consider the Badgetts' proposals" and that the existence of a course of dealing and good faith are issues of fact. *Badgett v. Security State Bank*, 56 Wash.App. 872, 878, 786 P.2d 302 (1990). The court cautioned that its holding was "not to be construed as imposing an obligation to modify this or any contract. Rather, the Bank's freedom to reject the Badgetts' proposals is relevant to the question of whether the failure to consider them was the proximate cause of the Badgetts' losses." *Badgett*, at 878 n. 4, 786 P.2d 302. This court granted the Bank's petition for review.

. . . The Badgetts contend that the Bank had a duty to consider their proposal and that the Bank breached that duty because Cooke inaccurately relayed their proposal to the loan committee. Thus, the threshold question is whether or not, as a matter of law, the Bank had a duty to consider the proposal. If not, the manner in which the proposal was conveyed or considered is not a material fact. . . .

The Badgetts do not contend that any express term in the loan agreement required the Bank to consider their proposal. Nor do they argue that the Bank was under any obligation to modify the agreement. Rather, they assert that the Bank was obligated by the duty of good faith implicit in every contract to affirmatively cooperate with them in their efforts to participate in the DTP and restructure their loan. The duty of good faith is not as broad as the Badgetts suggest.

There is in every contract an implied duty of good faith and fair dealing. This duty obligates the parties to cooperate with each other so that each may obtain the full benefit of performance. *Metropolitan Park Dist. of Tacoma v. Griffith*, 106 Wash.2d 425, 437, 723 P.2d 1093 (1986). . . . However, the duty of good faith does not extend to obligate a party to accept a material change in the terms of its contract. *Betchard–Clayton, Inc. v. King*, 41 Wash.App. 887, 890, 707 P.2d 1361, *review denied*, 104 Wash.2d 1027 (1985). Nor does it "inject substantive terms into the parties' contract." Rather, it requires only that the parties perform in good faith the obligations imposed by their agreement. *Barrett v. Weyerhaeuser Co. Severance Pay Plan*, 40 Wash.App. 630, 635 n. 6, 700 P.2d 338 (1985). Thus, the duty arises only in connection with terms agreed to by the parties. *See Matson v. Emory*, 36 Wash.App. 681, 676 P.2d 1029 (1984)....

By urging this court to find that the Bank had a good faith duty to affirmatively cooperate in their efforts to restructure the loan agreement, in effect the Badgetts ask us to expand the existing duty of good faith to create obligations on the parties in addition to those contained in the contract—a free-floating duty of good faith unattached to the underlying legal document. This we will not do. The duty to cooperate exists only in relation to performance of a specific contract term. *See Cavell v. Hughes*, 29 Wash.App. 536, 629 P.2d 927 (1981).... As a matter of law, there cannot be a breach of the duty of good faith when a party simply stands on its rights to require performance of a contract according to its terms. *Allied Sheet Metal*, 10 Wash.App. at 535–36, 518 P.2d 734.... The Badgetts received the full benefit of their contract when they received the amount of money they bargained for at the agreed rate of interest for the agreed period of time....

The Bank and the Badgetts entered into a written loan agreement. While the parties may choose to renegotiate their agreement, they are under no good faith obligation to do so.[3] The duty of good faith implied in every contract does not exist apart from the terms of the agreement.

The Badgetts next contend that because the Bank had anticipated changes in the Badgetts' financial situation and had been flexible in dealing with them in the past, the parties' course of dealing had created a good faith obligation on the part of the Bank to consider the Badgetts' proposals. However, a course of dealing does not override express terms in a contract or add additional obligations. Rather, it is a tool for interpreting the provisions of a contract.

The concept of relying on the parties' course of dealing to interpret contract provisions is found in the Uniform Commercial Code (U.C.C.). The U.C.C. has been applied by analogy to contracts not explicitly covered by its provisions. *See Liebergesell v. Evans*, 93 Wash.2d 881, 892, 613 P.2d 1170 (1980).... Under RCW 62A.1–205(4) [U.C.C. § 1–205(4)], the express terms of an agreement and an applicable course of dealing "shall be construed wherever reasonable as consistent with each other."

---

3. As pointed out in the amicus brief filed by counsel on behalf of the Washington Bankers Association and the American Bankers Association, a duty to consider proposals might easily lead to a duty to negotiate such proposals. This, in turn, will increase transaction costs for the parties and decrease economic efficiency. More importantly, it may operate to relieve a party of its obligations under an otherwise valid contract. Any request for modification would impose a duty to negotiate, which would then open the door for factual allegations of a lack of good faith in negotiating.

However, when such construction is unreasonable, express terms control.... Thus, the trial court was correct in concluding that [a] prior course of conduct cannot create a new obligation on the part of the bank. *Report of Proceedings, at 50.*

Because the Badgetts are not asking this court to interpret any provision in the loan agreement as imposing a duty on the Bank to consider their proposals, facts relating to prior dealings between the Badgetts and the Bank are not material for the purpose of defeating the Bank's motion for summary judgment.

Finally, the Badgetts contend that a duty on the part of the Bank to consider their proposals may have arisen as a result of Cooke's promise to relay their proposal to the loan committee. However, the Badgetts acknowledge that their proposal was just that—a proposal, not an agreement—and further negotiations were necessary. Cooke's presentation to the loan committee was a step in the negotiation process. "[A]n agreement to do something which requires a further meeting of the minds of the parties and without which it would not be complete is unenforcible [*sic*]." *Sandeman v. Sayres,* 50 Wash.2d 539, 541–42, 314 P.2d 428 (1957).... If Cooke's promise to negotiate is unenforceable, it follows that it cannot give rise to a contractual duty.

In sum, we hold that the implied duty of good faith in every contract did not give rise to a duty on the part of the Bank to consider the Badgetts' proposal.... Because there is no duty to consider the proposal, the Bank is entitled to summary judgment as a matter of law. Accordingly, we reverse the Court of Appeals and reinstate the trial court's granting of summary judgment dismissing the Badgetts' claims.

BADGETT v. SECURITY STATE BANK

Court of Appeals of Washington, 1990.
56 Wash.App. 872, 786 P.2d 302.

PETRICH, J. ... The requirement of good faith dealing is the single most important concept intertwined throughout the entire Uniform Commercial Code. Schroeder v. Fageol Motors, Inc., 86 Wash.2d 256, 262, 544 P.2d 20 (1975). A bank has a duty of good faith to its customers, including borrowers. *Warren v. Washington Trust Bank,* 19 Wash.App. 348, 367, 575 P.2d 1077 (1978), *modified on other grounds,* 92 Wash.2d 381, 598 P.2d 701 (1979). As Security State maintains, this duty of good faith does not require a party to accept a material change in the terms of its contracts. *Betchard-Clayton, Inc. v. King,* 41 Wash.App. 887, 890, 707 P.2d 1361 (1985). However, the scope of the good faith obligation can be expanded by the conduct of a contracting party which gives rise to reasonable expectations on the part of the other party. *See Liebergesell v. Evans,* 93 Wash.2d 881, 891–92, 613 P.2d 1170 (1980). Such expectations can result from a course of dealing, defined in 62A.1–205(1) [U.C.C. § 1–205(1)] ....

In this case, there was evidence that the Bank anticipated changes in its clients' situation and routinely restructured agricultural loans to meet the requirements of these changing circumstances. There was evidence that this had been the pattern of its relationship with the Badgetts for six years, even resulting in the Bank's agreement to a similar liquidation proposal in 1984. The final loan agreement, itself, indicated the possibility of amendments.[3] This was enough evidence to support a reasonable inference that the parties' course of dealing had created a good faith obligation on the part of the Bank to consider the Badgetts' proposals.[4] The existence of a course of dealing or performance is a question of fact. *Central Wash. Production Credit Ass'n v. Baker*, 11 Wash.App. at 20–21, 521 P.2d 226. It should have been submitted to a jury.

The existence of good faith is likewise a jury question. . . .

There was substantial evidence in the record indicating that Joe Cooke and Security's attorney told the Badgetts that their proposals would be presented to the loan committee; that Cooke had, in fact, paid very little attention to the discussion of those proposals,[5] had taken no notes, and had told the loan committee that the Badgetts wanted 20 percent of their loan forgiven and were not willing to negotiate the matter. There was also some indication of hostility between Cooke and the Badgetts. This was clearly enough evidence to raise a question of fact concerning whether or not Cooke had conducted his dealings with the Badgetts in good faith. Summary judgment was thus improper. . . .

Questions

1. What did the Badgetts argue was the bank's obligation in these circumstances? What was the basis of that obligation? Why does the court reject it? If the Supreme Court had approved the Court of Appeals decision, what should be the remedy for a breach of the obligation to consider proposals for modifications?

2. Should the Badgetts have argued that the bank was under an obligation to modify the contract? An obligation to negotiate a modification in good faith? If so, what would be the basis of such an obligation? What should be the remedy when it is breached?

3. Should an evolving relationship of lender and borrower, like the one in *Badgett*, result in a lender's liability for arbitrarily refusing to make a

3. The 1985 agreement stated, in part:

Additional advancements or increased commitments for any purpose are not contemplated at this time. However, if such advances or commitments are made within the duration of this Agreement, each such advance or commitment shall be subject to the terms and conditions of this Agreement *as may be amended* . . . . (Emphasis ours.)

4. This determination is not to be construed as imposing an obligation to modify this or any contract. Rather, the Bank's freedom to reject the Badgetts' proposals is relevant to the question of whether the

failure to consider them was the proximate cause of the Badgetts' losses. This is also a question for the jury. *Lettengarver v. Port of Edmonds*, 40 Wash.App. 577, 581, 699 P.2d 793 (1985).

5. According to Cooke's own deposition, he "got tired of listening" because the lawyers were exceeding the scope as far as he was concerned. He said the other proposals "must have flown clear by [him]." However, he also said that he remembered a discussion of additional real estate liens to cover the other 20 percent of the loan.

further loan? Would a reasonable borrower have expectations the lender would continue a pattern of loan adjustments? Would such expectations arise from promises? If not, should the law of contracts protect them nonetheless?

J.J. BROOKSBANK CO. v. BUDGET RENT–A–CAR CORP.

Supreme Court of Minnesota, 1983.
337 N.W.2d 372.

PETERSON, JUSTICE. Plaintiff, J.J. Brooksbank Co., entered into a licensing agreement with defendant, Budget Rent–A–Car Corporation, in 1962. Certain provisions of the agreement outlined the parties' arrangement for allocating reservation system obligations. The reservation system for Budget and its franchisees has changed over time, creating the present dispute between Budget and Brooksbank over each party's respective obligations. Brooksbank brought a declaratory judgment action to determine the extent of Budget's obligations under the 1962 licensing agreement.

The issue presented is whether the trial court erred in its interpretation and construction of the agreement entered into between Brooksbank and Budget. Both parties alleged error by the trial court—Brooksbank by notice of appeal, Budget by notice of review.

Before examining the trial court's conclusions of law, a brief review of the facts and the agreement is necessary. We essentially paraphrase the trial court's findings of fact, which are supported by the evidence introduced at trial. Budget commenced an automobile rental franchising business in 1960. Brooksbank, by entering into a franchise agreement early in the history of the business, received a licensing agreement more favorable in many respects than later licensees. In particular, the licensing agreement provided for lower monthly per-car service charges, initial franchise fees, and reservation costs than the agreements offered to later licensees. Relevant to each party's obligations are the following provisions:

a. Budget's obligations (Article I):

C. To spend a minimum of FIFTY PERCENT (50%) of the gross monthly per car service charge paid by all Licensees for advertising, promotion, and reservations for the benefit of all Licensees, allocated on a reasonable basis nationally and locally.

D. To maintain reservations offices in New York City, Los Angeles and Chicago.

E. To forward to LICENSEE all applicable reservations made at BUDGET'S reservations office at no charge to LICENSEE.

b. Brooksbank's obligations (Article II):

C. To take and transmit reservations for all other Licensees at no charge to the recipient except for the cost of transmission by telephone or telegraph.

The obligations were to continue "during the existence of the [agreement]," which was automatically renewable every 5 years, subject to conditions not relevant to the present dispute. The agreement also specified other rights and obligations which have no impact on this declaratory judgment action.

During the 1960's, the reservation system operated on a two-tier network, dependent upon the efforts of both Budget and its licensees. Local licensees would take and transmit reservations to other licensees, generally at the cost of telephone or telegraph charges. Budget would forward reservations received by its offices in Chicago, Los Angeles, and New York to applicable licensees. As the automobile rental business grew, Budget increasingly centralized its operations in Chicago, hiring additional staff, adding in- and out-bound WATS lines, and lengthening hours and days of service to the public. The number of licensees grew from approximately 15–20 in 1962 to approximately 350 in 1970. In this time period, Brooksbank received approximately one-third of its out-of-town reservations from Budget's reservation offices in the three designated cities.

Problems developed as both the franchise system and the number of reservations grew. It became common for licensees to fail to transmit reservations, to transmit incomplete information, and to ask customers calling for reservations to call back when counter personnel were not busy. In response to these problems, Budget considered the development of a central computerized reservation system, featuring a single 800 number for taking and transmitting reservations. Other competitors in the automobile rental business were developing similar systems. Two firms, Telemax Corporation and International Reservation Corp., approached Budget, each offering to set up a central reservation system.

Budget received the endorsement of its advisory committee and licensees to proceed with such a system. Many licensees were already paying Budget for reservations received from its reservation offices. Telemax operated the central computerized reservation system from June 1970 to July 1971, when it declared bankruptcy. IRC took over operations in October 1971 and continued to perform reservation services until 1974, when it ceased operations due to large financial losses. Budget then decided to run the reservation system itself, operating it originally from Omaha, Nebraska, and later, in 1981, from Carrollton, Texas.

Throughout the process of centralization and computerization, Brooksbank insisted that it should receive, without charge, all reservations from any Budget reservation office, pursuant to the 1962 licensing agreement. Budget, to the contrary, insisted that its obligation to provide free reservations to Brooksbank was limited to the two-tier, telephone-based reservation system and is not applicable to the more sophisticated computerized system. To avoid litigation over this dispute, the parties entered into two trial agreements in 1970 and 1974, whereby Brooksbank paid the standard reservation charges applicable to all franchisees but was compensated for advertising and promotion expenditures in an amount approximating one-third of its costs relating to computerized reservations. Both parties agreed that Brooksbank could retain its rights under the 1962 agreement. When the 1974 agreement expired, Budget refused to extend any further reservation cost reductions to Brooksbank, contending that Brooksbank had had full opportunity to assess the benefits of the computerized reservation system and that other licensees were paying their full cost for reservations from the system. If Budget was obligated to provide cost-free reservations from a reservation system as it existed in 1962, a system using manually operated telephones with offices located in the three designated cities, Budget suggested that it was ready to operate such a system exclusively for Brooksbank, to satisfy what it perceived to be its obligations under the 1962 agreement. Brooksbank refused to accept such treatment and brought the declaratory judgment action to ascertain its rights under the 1962 licensing agreement.

The case proceeded through trial on theories essentially tracking the parties' positions since 1970. Brooksbank believed that interpretation and practical construction of the 1962 agreement mandated that it receive all of its reservations cost free from Budget reservation offices. At a minimum, it contended that both practical construction and the evidence supported a position that it receive, cost free, at least one-third of its reservations, the one-third figure comporting with the historical percentage of reservations coming from the three designated cities. Budget, in contrast, argued that the agreement allowed for free reservations from the two-tier telephone system in place in 1962; given technological changes since that time, Budget's obligations under the 1962 agreement were properly excused, and Brooksbank was therefore obligated, like all franchisees, to pay the standard reservation charges.

The trial court neither entirely excused Budget from providing Brooksbank with lower reservation charges nor allowed Brooksbank the minimum one-third percentage it thought it deserved by virtue of the 1962 agreement. Rather, the trial court concluded that the central computerized reservation system was not within the purview of the agreement relating to the reservation system and that the technology giving rise to the sophisticated system was not foreseeable in 1962. However, it concluded that Budget, as an incentive for Brooksbank to become a licensee, did intend to give Brooksbank free reservations from offices located in the three designated cities. The trial court finally concluded that Brooksbank was entitled to a 10% reduction in its computer reservation charges in lieu of its contract rights. This result was based upon a finding of fact which assessed the benefits each party had received from the central computerized reservation system and which determined that Brooksbank deserved a 10% reduction in reservation costs. This figure, the trial court concluded, was "equitable in light of all the evidence presented at trial."

From our review of the 1962 agreement and the practical construction placed upon it by the parties, we conclude that Brooksbank is entitled to a one-third reduction in reservation costs. A question of interpretation and practical construction, necessary to a declaratory judgment action, begins with the language of the 1962 agreement (previously set forth) pertaining to the reservation system setup.

The language expresses no agreement on what should happen during the course of the contract relationship with regard to technological changes. That such should be the case is not unusual, because parties form expectations with respect to only a limited number of situations, and only some of these expectations are in turn formulated as terms and reduced to contract language. Budget issued a standard form licensing agreement to Brooksbank, one which in 1962 contemplated the use of a two-tier telephone network to facilitate reservations.

What omissions in language pose for interpretative duties of courts was cogently expressed by Judge Learned Hand: "[I]nterpretation more and more involves an imaginative projection of the expressed purpose upon situations arising later, for which the parties did not provide and which they did not have in mind." *L.N. Jackson & Co. v. Royal Norwegian Government*, 177 F.2d 694, 702 (2d Cir.1949) (dissenting opinion), *cert. denied*, 339 U.S. 914, 70 S.Ct. 574, 94 L.Ed. 1340 (1950); see generally, Farnsworth, *Disputes Over Omission in Contacts*, 68 Colum. L. Rev. 860 (1968). The process of interpretation, moreover, can be supplemented by a practical construction of a contract, which has been defined as:

[The parties'] conduct during the course of performance [which] may support *inferences* as to the meaning of language in the contract, or as to their intentions with respect to gaps or omissions in the contract.

Patterson, *The Interpretation and Construction of Contracts*, 64 Colum. L. Rev. 833, 836 (1964) (emphasis supplied).

Ascertaining the intentions of the parties with respect to reservation costs is necessarily difficult when the parties are involved in a long-term contract which does not specify the parties' agreement on the effect of changed circumstances. As one court has commented:

Of course, where intent, though obscure, is nevertheless discernible, it must be followed; but a certain sophistication must be recognized—if we are to approach the matter frankly—where we are dealing with changed circumstances ... with respect to a contract which does not touch this exact point and which has at most only points of departure for more or less pressing analogies.

Parev Products Co. v. I. Rokeach & Sons, Inc., 124 F.2d 147, 149 (2d Cir.1941).

With these principles in mind, we can examine the parties' various positions with respect to allocation of reservation costs. The most balanced review of the 1962 licensing agreement and the parties' performance under the agreement supports a one-third reduction for Brooksbank on its reservation costs for reservations coming from Budget's reservation center. This result reflects the bargain struck in 1962. In return for Brooksbank's participation in the franchise system, Budget offered free reservations from areas where it already had reservation offices: Chicago, New York, and Los Angeles. Since significant business traffic comes from these geographic areas, this is not an inconsiderable bargain. And, in fact, Brooksbank has historically received one-third of its reservations from these areas, which were to be serviced by Budget reservation offices. From other geographic zones, Budget was to pay the costs of reservations (*i.e.*, telephone charges in transmitting reservations) received from other licensees like Brooksbank. Even as Budget increasingly centralized its operations from 1962 to 1970, Brooksbank continued to receive free reservations from these geographic zones. It is this geographic, practical construction of the 1962 agreement that most closely comports with what we perceive to be the parties' intentions in entering into it.

Necessarily, then, we reject Brooksbank's contention that it is entitled to cost-free reservations from Budget's reservation center in Carrollton, Texas. This contention takes a simple view of the contract language outlined above and ignores the geographic, practical construction placed upon this language by the parties since the inception of their relationship. Allowing Brooksbank a 100% reduction in reservation costs would distort the bargain struck in the 1962 agreement, wherein the parties allocated reservation obligations according to markets serviced by each party.

Equally, however, we reject Budget's contention that it is entirely excused from giving Brooksbank any percentage reduction in reservation costs. This argument ignores the language of the agreement that each parties' [sic] obligations were to continue "during the existence of the [agreement]." From this language, and from the good faith covenant implied in contracts, we consider the agreement as one requiring continued cooperation regarding the allocation of obligations and the performance standards associated with a reservation system. Surely Budget could not let its reservation system stagnate over time. Budget did, in fact, work to improve its system by developing computerized operations. Brooksbank, in turn, operated a successful franchise, benefiting the Budget franchise system as a whole. Although the 1962 agreement may have omitted particular agreement about the effect of technological change on the franchise relationship, that the parties were still bound by the agreement to preserve the bargain struck in 1962 cannot be disregarded. *See,* Burton, *Breach of Contract and the Common Law Duty to Perform in Good Faith,* 94 Harv. L. Rev. 369, 380 n.44 (1980).

To preserve Brooksbank's bargain, Budget remained bound to provide a continuing proportion of cost-free reservations, based upon the practical, geographic construction placed by the parties upon the 1962 agreement. New technology may have altered the mode in which reservations were placed within the franchise system, but it did not alter the parties' essential bargain in apportioning reservation obligations based upon geographic markets.

We reject Budget's contentions that it is excused from performance under either a doctrine of impracticability of performance or frustration of purpose. These doctrines have at their core a requirement that some event must occur, the nonoccurrence of which was a basic assumption of the contract at the time it was made. *See*, Restatement (Second) of Contracts, §§ 261, 265 (1981). In this case, that requirement is not met. Budget did not limit its obligations to the reservation system in place at the time of the 1962 agreement, as our discussion on interpretation and practical construction of the agreement indicates.

Having determined that Brooksbank is not entitled to entirely cost-free reservations from Budget's reservation center and that Budget is not excused from delivering a percentage of cost-free reservations to Brooksbank, we now examine the trial court's conclusion that Brooksbank is entitled to a 10% reduction in reservation costs paid to budget. The 10% figure derived from a judicial estimate of the benefit accruing to each party from the central computerized reservation system. The trial court apparently assessed the advantages of the computerized system and the release of Brooksbank from its obligation to forward reservations to other licensees in determining that Brooksbank, although entitled to some percentage reduction in reservation charges, should only receive a reduction proportionate to its lessened obligation.

The trial court, in so doing, has taken the position that interpretation of the agreement and the parties' course of performance entitled Brooksbank to a percentage reduction in some reservation costs. Although the trial court properly recognized that Brooksbank should receive a percentage reduction in some reservation costs, the court ordered only a 10% reduction, based solely on the statement that the figure was "equitable in light of all the evidence presented at trial." Absent any explanatory memorandum by the trial court, we are at a loss to understand how the trial court estimated the apportionment of reservation system costs under the changed circumstances of the parties.

The trial court's findings of fact do provide a more factually consistent way in which to analyze the proportionate discount in reservation costs to which Brooksbank is entitled. Historically, Brooksbank received approximately one-third of its reservations from those markets in which Budget promised to maintain reservation offices. The centralization and computerization of the reservation system worked to the benefit of both parties in expanding the desirability of Budget franchises, in increasing the efficiency of operations, and in solving problems encountered in the earlier reservation system. Both Budget and Brooksbank obviously benefit from these changes. Although Brooksbank may now have to place fewer reservations for other licensees, it must nevertheless pay Budget for those reservations it would have received at cost from other licensees. In this sense, the essential bargain of the parties remains intact: Budget pays for reservations which would have come from markets it promised Brooksbank to serve, and Brooksbank pays for reservations that it would have had to pay for at cost. A one-third reduction in reservation costs is more consistent with the evidence found by the trial court and with the essential agreement of the parties regarding reservation system obligations. The trial court's declaratory judgment is accordingly modified....

SIMONETT, JUSTICE (dissenting). I respectfully dissent. Since 1970, the provision in the 1962 contract that Brooksbank is to receive cost-free reservations from Budget Rent–A–Car's offices in New York City, Chicago and Los Angeles has been irrelevant to the manner in which the franchisees have handled reservations, and the contract clause cannot, in any meaningful sense, be implemented. In 1962, the parties never foresaw nor made allowance for a conversion to a centralized computer reservation system.

Can the 1962 contract clause nevertheless be enforced in some equivalent fashion? I do not see how this can be done by applying rules for construction of contract language. None of the rules apply, including the rule of practical construction. It may be that over the past 20 years some 30% of Brooksbank's reservations have continued to originate from the three designated cities, but this tells us nothing as to whether the parties intended those reservations to be cost-free. If we look to the "practical construction" the parties gave to the disputed contract clause, we find that the parties emphatically agreed to disagree.

There are strong, competing equities. Brooksbank points to his "sweat equity" and his contribution to making an initial risky enterprise stable and successful. Budget points out that in 1970, when it was essential to the survival of the business to convert to a central computer system, Brooksbank, unlike other major franchisees, refused to make concessions on the cost-free reservations clause in its contract.

It seems to me we are being asked not so much to construe a 1962 document as to arbitrate a dispute between business associates, both with substantial investments in an ongoing business of some 20 years and each needing the other. If the rules of contract construction can be applied, they should be; but where they are of no help, as here, and the parties refuse to bargain their differences, I believe a court may apply equitable principles. This is what the trial court apparently did here, granting a 10% reduction in reservation charges, but without giving its reasons. The majority of this court, applying rules of contract construction, believe a one-third reduction is proper. I agree a reduction is due Brooksbank. I would reverse and remand to the trial court with instructions to determine what should be a proper reduction in the reservation charges, considering the equities of the entire relationship, and, of course, to set out the reasons for its determination.

Questions

1. Did the court in *J.J. Brooksbank* impose a modification on one of the parties? What law permits the court to do so? Was this an "omitted case"? Did the contract, properly interpreted, require the change in fees charged to J.J. Brooksbank under the circumstances? Was Budget acting in bad faith?

2.   Does the court's solution "reflect[ ] the bargain struck in 1962" as it urges? Does the court work from the plain meaning of the text, the text understood in its context at the time of formation, the text understood in its context at the time for performance, or some other view of the bargain struck in 1962? Is the court's solution consistent with the autonomy principle?

3.   Assuming the court is correct to modify the contract, what is the court's reason for giving J.J. Brooksbank a one-third reduction in reservation costs? Why did the trial court give a 10% reduction? According to the dissent, what should happen on remand?

4.   *Problems.*

a.   Reconsider *NIPSCO, Transatlantic Financing,* and *Eastern Air Lines,* in Section 1 of this Chapter. Should the contracts in any of those cases have been adjusted to meet changed circumstances?

b.   Buddy owns a tract of land in West Virginia. In 1893, his predecessor in interest granted an oil and gas lease to Granma Oil Co. with rights of perpetual renewal at Granma's request. The lease required Granma to pay Buddy $100 per year. The well stopped gas production in 1912, but Granma continued to send Buddy $100 every year. In 1988, Granma used a new technique to begin oil production. When Buddy demanded a 12.5% royalty on oil production, Granma sent Buddy his $100 for that year. Does Buddy have recourse? See McGinnis v. Cayton, 173 W.Va. 102, 312 S.E.2d 765 (1984).

NOTE ON EQUITABLE ADJUSTMENT

"Equity" is a confusing word with many meanings. Equity secured a major place in Anglo-American legal history when the courts of law were supplemented with courts of equity in response to the rigidities of the old English writ system and limitations on the remedies it could award. The courts of equity initially were to do justice in cases where the law failed of its purpose; in time, equity courts developed their own rigid rules, though they could issue nonmonetary legal orders. Courts of equity today do not have a general license to do justice on the particulars of each case. They generally do not make equitable adjustments in contracts. (Reformation is available in equity but, it is regularly said, only to correct scrivener's errors to bring a writing into conformity with the parties' agreement.)

Should the law allow courts to do equity by adjusting contractual relations? The answer would seem to depend on the concept of equity one has in mind. The arguments for and against equitable adjustment would surely differ accordingly.

Broadly, the idea of equity, is traced to Aristotle, who offered it as a corrective to a well-known vice of stated legal rules. In his terms, "about some things it is not possible to make a universal statement which will be correct." Aristotle, "Nicomachaen Ethics," in THE BASIC WORKS OF ARISTOTLE 1019–20 (1137b) (Richard McKeon ed. 1941). (In contemporary terms, we would say that rules as stated tend to be over- and underinclusive with respect to the just result and with respect to their own background justifications.) When a case arises "which is not covered by the universal statement," Aristotle wrote, "then it is right ... to say what the legislator himself would have said had he been present, and would have put into his law if he had known." *Id.* at 1019–20 (1137b). In cases like *Badgett* and *J.J. Brooksbank*, however, the parties' agreements covered the situation from which the dispute arose. Equitable adjustments in contract cases are sought only when one party wants to change her rights or duties from those provided by the agreement. So Aristotelian equity would not seem to justify changing the law to permit results like that in *J.J. Brooksbank*.

In ordinary usage, equity is often a virtual synonym for simple fairness or reasonableness in one's conduct toward others, as when one refrains *ex gratia* from insisting on her rights for reasons of fairness, compassion, or gratitude. Surely the bank in *Badgett* and the licensee in *J.J. Brooksbank* were free to modify their contracts for reasons of equity in this sense. Had they done so, we might say they acted equitably. It is another matter, however, for a judge to order a party to act equitably in this way. A judge adjudicates the rights of others and is supposed to apply the law, not to shape admirable characters.

A related notion is that equity dispenses with the application of rules, like the terms of a contract, in favor of doing particularized justice. On this approach, judges would have discretion to decide contracts cases with no obligation to follow the rules of contract law or to hold the parties to their contracts unless, in the circumstances, that seemed best on the whole. Would that be more desirable than the current web of legal doctrines, which to many seems more tattered than seamless?

Whatever the difficulties in fitting equitable adjustments into our conceptions of the judicial role, no such problems arise when a case is brought to arbitration or mediation. The flexibility of arbitration clearly allows the parties to agree that the arbitrator shall decided according to justice. Some well-established forms of arbitration permit the arbitrators to fix a fair price when the parties cannot agree. In mediation, a neutral third party assists the disputing parties in reaching a settlement agreement. Mediators may urge the parties to split the difference. Parties who want an available means toward equitable adjustments should consider arbitration and mediation alternatives.

SECTION 3. TORTIOUS CONDUCT IN CONTRACT PERFORM-ANCE

NOTE ON "CONTORTS"

In 1974, Professor Grant Gilmore published a highly controversial book with the provocative title, *The Death of Contract*. His major thesis was that the boundary between contract and tort was dissolving into a single field that he called "contorts." The focus of his attention was on the development of legal doctrine concerning the promises that should be enforced. The requirement of consideration (as a bargained-for exchange), he claimed, was the hallmark of the classical contract law that dominated during the heyday of laissez faire capitalism in the late nineteenth century. The enforcement of promises that were relied upon or implied to prevent unjust enrichment, however, were presented as later developments reflecting the rejection of that mode of social organization with the advent of a welfare state. Most reviewers of the book thought that Gilmore's thesis was much overstated. But few doubted that RESTATEMENT (SECOND) OF CONTRACTS § 90 represented a tort-like idea that challenged the exclusivity of bargain contracts as the model for contract law.

With respect to the performance stage of a contract, traditional doctrine holds that a breach of contract as such is not a tort, but that the same act may constitute both a breach of contract and an independent tort. Consider a typical medical malpractice case against a surgeon. The tort action is for negligence in the course of surgery, for which the surgeon is paid under a contract to perform services. In principle, an action for breach of contract is also available, though a plaintiff at some point must choose its remedy to avoid a double recovery. The advantages that lead most plaintiffs to proceed in tort center on the more liberal remedies, especially for pain and suffering and emotional distress, and for punitive damages in appropriate cases. There is also a subtle but sometimes important difference in the foreseeability limitations in tort and contract. Under *Hadley v. Baxendale*, above at p. 332, contract damages must be foreseeable at the time of contract formation. As indicated by the opinions in *Palsgraf v. Long Island R.R.*, 248 N.Y. 339, 162 N.E. 99 (1928), foreseeability in tort may not be a limit; when it is, it is marked from the time of the wrongful conduct (the time of breach). On the other hand, the statute of limitations is often longer in contract, most often when the contract is in writing.

A few recent cases, almost always involving insurance contracts, have held that breach of the implied covenant of good faith and fair dealing may be a tort, for which emotional distress and punitive damages might be available. Several very large awards, mostly in California before *Foley v. Interactive Data Corp.*, 47 Cal.3d 654, 254 Cal.Rptr. 211, 765 P.2d 373 (1988), stimulated a huge volume of litigation. As you read the next cases, consider the conditions under which tort damages should be available for a breach of contract that is not an independent tort.

Problem

Mickey has a policy with Judy Insurance Co. for liability to third parties for claims of a certain kind up to a policy limit of $30,000. The policy gives Judy the sole right, in her discretion, to defend any action and to settle any claims within the policy. Stone makes a covered claim against Mickey for $100,000. Mickey and Judy both estimate the odds of losing for that amount after a trial at 50–50. Stone offers to settle for $22,000.

Should Mickey settle? Should Judy Insurance Co.? If Judy controls the decision and refuses to settle, Mickey suffers a $100,000 judgment, Judy pays $30,000 and Mickey $70,000, should Mickey have an action against Judy for refusing to settle? Should that action be in tort?

GRUENBERG v. AETNA INSURANCE CO.

Supreme Court of California, In Bank. 1973.
9 Cal.3d 566, 108 Cal.Rptr. 480, 510 P.2d 1032.

Sullivan, Justice. Plaintiff appeals from a judgment of dismissal entered upon an order sustaining, with leave to amend, defendants' general demurrers to plaintiff's complaint, plaintiff having thereafter declined to amend.[1]

Plaintiff's complaint, containing only one count, alleged in substance the following: On and after April 7, 1969, plaintiff was the owner of a cocktail lounge and restaurant business in Los Angeles known as the Brass Rail. The business premises were insured against fire loss in the aggregate sum of $35,000 by the three defendant insurers, Aetna Insurance Company (Aetna), Yosemite Insurance Company (Yosemite), and American Home Assurance Company (American).

In the early hours of the morning of November 9, 1969, a fire occurred at the Brass Rail. Plaintiff was notified and immediately went to the scene. While there, he became involved in an argument with a member of the arson detail of the Los Angeles Fire Department and was placed under arrest.

On November 10, 1969, defendant insurers, upon being informed of the fire, engaged the services of defendant P. E. Brown and Company (Brown). Carl Busching, a claims adjuster employed by Brown, went to the Brass Rail to investigate the fire and inspect the premises. While he was there, he stated to an arson investigator of the Los Angeles Fire Department that plaintiff had excessive coverage under his fire insurance policies. Eventually the premises were locked and nothing was removed until November 14, 1969, when Busching authorized the removal of the rubble and debris.

About November 13, 1969, plaintiff was charged in a felony complaint with the crimes of arson (Pen. Code § 448a) and defrauding an insurer (Pen. Code § 548). A preliminary hearing was set for January 12, 1970.

Defendant insurance companies also retained defendant law firm Cummins, White, Briedenbach & Alphson (Cummins) to represent them in the matter of plaintiff's claim of fire loss. On November 25, 1969, defendant Donald Ricketts, an attorney-employee of Cummins, demanded in writing that plaintiff appear at the offices of said firm on December

---

1. Defendants are the following: (a) Three insurance companies: Aetna Insurance Company, Yosemite Insurance Company and American Home Assurance Company; (b) P. E. Brown and Company, a corporation engaged in the business of investigating and adjusting insurance claims for insurance companies and Carl H. Busching its staff adjuster; and (c) Cummins, White, Briedenbach and Alphson, a copartnership engaged in the practice of law, attorneys for the insurance companies designated in (a) and Donald W. Ricketts, an attorney-employee of such law firm.

12, 1969, to submit to an examination under oath and to produce certain documents. On November 26, 1969, plaintiff's attorney responded by letter to Ricketts explaining that he had advised plaintiff not to make any statements concerning the fire loss while criminal charges were pending. The letter also requested that the insurers waive the requirement of an examination until the criminal charges lodged against plaintiff were concluded. Ricketts refused the request and warned that failure to appear for the examination would void coverage under the policies. On December 16, 1969, Ricketts, on behalf of the Cummins law firm, advised plaintiff's attorney in writing that defendant insurers were denying liability under the policies because of plaintiff's failure to submit to an examination under oath and to produce documents.

On January 12, 1970, a preliminary hearing was held on the complaint charging plaintiff with arson and defrauding an insurer. Busching appeared as a witness for the prosecution and restated his belief that plaintiff had excessive fire insurance coverage for his business. The charges were dismissed by the magistrate for lack of probable cause.

On January 26, 1970, plaintiff's attorney advised defendant insurers that plaintiff was now prepared to submit himself for an examination. However, the insurers reaffirmed their position that they were denying liability because of plaintiff's failure to appear.

According to the allegations of the complaint, all defendants other than the insurance company defendants were the agents and employees of the three defendant companies and were acting within the scope of such agency and employment when the acts attributed to them were committed. It was further alleged that "the defendants and each of them joined together and acted in concert to falsely imply that the plaintiff had a motive to deliberately set fire to and burn down his place of business [and that] [t]he purpose of the defendants in creating such false implication was to establish a grounds [sic] upon which the defendant Insurers could avoid paying the amounts due to plaintiff under the policies of insurance issued by the defendant Insurers." To carry out their purpose, defendants "conducted themselves in the following manner": (a) defendant Busching stated to an arson investigator that plaintiff had acquired excessive fire insurance coverage; (b) defendant insurers demanded that plaintiff submit to an examination under oath and to produce certain documents "in order to enable them to secure further evidence to support the false implication that plaintiff was guilty of arson;" and (c) defendant Busching, appearing as a witness for the People at the preliminary hearing on the felony complaint, reaffirmed his statement made to the arson investigator.

As a "direct and proximate result of the outrageous conduct and bad faith of the defendants," plaintiff suffered "severe economic damage," "severe emotional upset and distress," loss of earnings and various special damages. Plaintiff sought both compensatory and punitive damages.

Defendants filed general demurrers to the complaint which were sustained with leave to amend. Plaintiff elected to stand on his complaint and an order of dismissal was entered. This appeal followed.

We proceed to examine the complaint for its legal sufficiency according to the familiar well settled principles. . . .

Plaintiff contends that he has stated sufficient facts to constitute a cause of action in tort against defendants for breach of an implied duty of good faith and fair dealing. The duty of an insurer to deal fairly and in good faith with its insured is governed by our decisions in Crisci v. Security Ins. Co. (1967) 66 Cal.2d 425, 58 Cal.Rptr. 13, 426 P.2d 173, and Comunale v. Traders & General Ins. Co. (1958) 50 Cal.2d 654, 328 P.2d 198, 68 A.L.R.2d 883. We explained that this duty, the breach of which sounds in both contract and tort, is imposed because "[t]here is an implied covenant of good faith and fair dealing in every contract [including insurance policies] that neither party will do anything which will injure the right of the other to receive the benefits of the agreement." (*Comunale, supra*, at p. 658, 328 P.2d at p. 200.) Therefore, "an insurer . . . who refuses to accept a reasonable settlement within the policy limits in violation of its duty to consider in good faith the interest of the insured in the settlement, is liable for the entire judgment against the insured even if it exceeds the policy limits." (*Id.* at p. 661, 328 P.2d at p. 202.)

Thus in *Comunale* and *Crisci* we made it clear that "[l]iability is imposed [on the insurer] not for a bad faith breach of the contract but for failure to meet the duty to accept reasonable settlements, a duty included within the implied covenant of good faith and fair dealing." (*Crisci, supra*, at p. 430, 58 Cal.Rptr. at p. 17, 426 P.2d at 177.) In those two cases, we considered the duty of the insurer to act in good faith and fairly in handling the claims of third persons against the insured, described as a "duty to accept reasonable settlements;" in the case before us we consider the duty of an insurer to act in good faith and fairly in handling the claim of an insured, namely a duty not to withhold unreasonably payments due under a policy. These are merely two different aspects of the same duty. That responsibility is not the requirement mandated by the terms of the policy itself—to defend, settle, or pay. It is the obligation, deemed to be imposed by the law, under which the insurer must act fairly and in good faith in discharging its contractual responsibilities. Where in so doing, it fails to deal *fairly and in good faith* with its insured by refusing, without proper cause, to compensate its insured for a loss covered by the policy, such conduct may give rise to a cause of action in tort for breach of an implied covenant of good faith and fair dealing. . . .

In the case at bench plaintiff has alleged in essence that defendants wilfully and maliciously entered into a scheme to deprive him of the benefits of the fire policies in that they encouraged criminal charges by falsely implying that he had a motive to commit arson, and in that, knowing plaintiff would not appear for an examination during the pendency of criminal charges against him, they used his failure to appear as a pretense for denying liability under the policies. We conclude therefore that while the complaint is far from a model pleading, it does allege in substance a breach on the part of defendant insurance companies of their duty of good faith and fair dealing which they owed plaintiff. We emphasize that we are passing only upon the sufficiency of these allegations which of course must be sustained by proper proof.

With regard to the defendants other than the three insurance companies, we reach a different result. Plaintiff alleges that Brown, the insurance adjusting firm, and its employee, Busching, and Cummins, the law firm, and its employee, Ricketts, were the agents and employees of defendant insurers and of each other and were acting within the scope of that agency and employment when they committed the acts attributed to them. However, plaintiff contends that these non-insurer defendants breached only the duty of good faith and fair dealing; therefore, we need not consider the possibility that they may have committed another tort in their respective capacities as total strangers to the contracts of insurance. Obviously, the non-insurer defendants were not parties to the agreements for insurance; therefore, they are not, as such, subject to an implied duty of good faith and fair dealing. Moreover, as agents and employees of the defendant insurers, they cannot be held accountable on a theory of conspiracy. (Wise v. Southern Pacific Co. (1963) 223 Cal. App.2d 50, 72, 35 Cal.Rptr. 652.) This rule, as was explained in *Wise* (at pp. 72–73, Cal.Rptr. at p. 665) "derives from the principle that ordinarily corporate agents and employees acting for and on behalf of the corporation cannot be held liable for inducing a breach of the corporation's contract since being in a confidential relationship to the corporation their action in this respect is privileged." (See also Mallard v. Boring (1960) 182 Cal.App.2d 390, 393, 6 Cal.Rptr. 171.) Accordingly, the judgment of dismissal in favor of the non-insurer defendants must be affirmed.

Defendant insurance companies contend that plaintiff's failure to appear at their attorneys' office in order to submit to an examination under oath and to produce certain documents is a bar to the action since (1) the clause in the contracts requiring the insured to appear is a condition precedent to legal action (see fn. 2, *ante*) and that plaintiff must allege that he has complied with it; (2) the allegations in plaintiff's complaint demonstrate that he has failed to comply with the "cooperation and notice" clause; (3) the demand for appearance was adequate; and (4) even if the demand for appearance were defective, plaintiff may not complain of it for the first time on appeal (see Restina v. Aetna Casualty & Surety Company, *supra*, 306 N.Y.S.2d 219, 222).

Plaintiff responds that his failure to appear at the requested time is of no consequence for the following reasons: (1) the insurers must show, by way of defense, that his failure to appear substantially prejudiced their investigation of his claim; (2) although plaintiff failed to appear on December 12, 1969, he complied with the provisions of the policy requiring his appearance; and (3) the demand to appear on December 12,

1969, was insufficient in that defendants failed to specify the person who would conduct the examination.

All parties appear to assume that plaintiff's contractual duty is a dependent condition (whether precedent or subsequent) to defendants' covenant of good faith and fair dealing. In other words, the underlying premise of their arguments is that if plaintiff's failure to appear on December 12, 1969, constituted a breach of plaintiff's obligation under the policies, then defendants' duty of good faith and fair dealing was excused. We do not think, however, that the controlling issue here is the nature of *plaintiff's* duty, i.e., whether his dependent duty is precedent or subsequent; rather, the crucial issue is the nature of *defendants'* duty, i.e., whether their duty of good faith and fair dealing is absolute or conditional. Therefore, we need not consider the aforementioned contentions of the parties.

Defendants' duty, as we have explained, arises from a contractual relationship existing between the parties. This duty has been characterized as an "implied covenant" that "neither party will do anything which will injure the right of the other to receive the benefits of the agreement." (Comunale v. Traders & General Ins. Co., *supra*, 50 Cal.2d 654, 658, 328 P.2d 198, 200.) While it might be argued that defendants would be excused from their contractual duties (e.g., obligation to indemnify) if plaintiff breached his obligations under the policies, we do not think that plaintiff's alleged breach excuses defendants from their duty, implied by law, of good faith and fair dealing. In other words, the insurer's duty is unconditional and independent of the performance of plaintiff's contractual obligations. . . . [9]

We conclude, therefore, that the duty of good faith and fair dealing on the part of defendant insurance companies is an absolute one. At the same time, we do not say that the parties cannot define, by the terms of the contract, their respective obligations and duties. We say merely that no matter how those duties are stated, the nonperformance by one party of its contractual duties cannot excuse a breach of the duty of good faith and fair dealing by the other party while the contract between them is in effect and not rescinded. . . .

In summary, we conclude that plaintiff has stated facts sufficient to constitute a cause of action in tort against defendant insurance companies for breach of their implied duty of good faith and fair dealing; that plaintiff's failure to appear at the office of the insurers' counsel in order to submit to an examination under oath and to produce certain documents, as appearing from the allegations of the complaint, is not fatal to the statement of such cause of action; and that plaintiff has stated facts

---

9. Even if defendants' duty were construed as a *dependent* condition, i.e., dependent on plaintiff's performance of his obligations under the policies, we think that plaintiff's failure to appear would still not be fatal to his cause of action. That is, the allegations of the complaint demonstrate that plaintiff's failure to appear was induced by defendants' conduct, in breach of their duty of good faith and fair dealing. Therefore, plaintiff's obligation to appear may be seen as excused by defendants' alleged breach. (See 3 Witkin, [Cal. Procedure] § 406, pp. 2063–2064 [2d ed. 1977].)

sufficient for the recovery of damages for mental distress whether or not these facts constitute "extreme" or "outrageous" conduct. On the other hand, since the remaining defendants were not subject to the implied duty arising from the contractual relationship, we conclude that the complaint does not state sufficient facts to constitute a cause of action against them and that the judgment of dismissal in their favor was proper.

As to defendants Aetna Insurance Company, Yosemite Insurance Company and American Home Assurance Company, the judgment is reversed and the cause is remanded to the trial court with directions to overrule the demurrers and to allow said defendants a reasonable time within which to answer. As to the remaining defendants, the judgment is affirmed. Plaintiff shall recover his costs on appeal from defendants, Aetna Insurance Company, Yosemite Insurance Company, and American Home Assurance Company; the other defendants shall recover their costs on appeal from plaintiff.

BECK v. FARMERS INSURANCE EXCHANGE

Supreme Court of Utah, 1985.
701 P.2d 795.

ZIMMERMAN, JUSTICE: Plaintiff Wayne Beck appeals from a summary judgment dismissing his claim against Farmers Insurance Exchange, his automobile insurance carrier, alleging that Farmers had refused in bad faith to settle a claim for uninsured motorist benefits. We hold that on the record before us, Beck stated a claim for relief and a summary judgment was inappropriate. We reverse and remand for further proceedings consistent with this opinion.

Beck injured his knee in a hit-and-run accident on January 16, 1982, when his car was struck by a car owned by Ann Kirkland. Ms. Kirkland asserted that her car had been stolen and denied any knowledge of or responsibility for the accident. Beck filed a claim with Kirkland's insurer, but liability was denied on April 20, 1982.

At the time of the accident, Beck carried automobile insurance with Farmers. Under that policy, Beck was provided with both no-fault and uninsured motorist insurance benefits. On February 23, 1982, while his claim against Kirkland was pending, Beck filed a claim with Farmers for no-fault benefits. Sometime prior to May 26, 1982, Farmers paid Beck $5,000 for medical expenses (the no-fault policy limit) and $1,299.43 for lost wages.

On June 23, 1982, Beck's counsel filed a claim with Farmers for uninsured motorist benefits, demanding the policy limit, $20,000, for general damages suffered as a result of the accident. His counsel alleges that the brochure documenting Beck's damages, submitted to Farmers with the June 23rd settlement offer, established that his claim was worth substantially more than $20,000. Farmers' adjuster rejected the settlement offer without explanation on July 1, 1982.

Beck filed this lawsuit one month later, on August 2, 1982, alleging three causes of action: first, that by refusing to pay his uninsured motorist claim, Farmers had breached its contract of insurance with him; second, that by acting in bad faith in refusing to investigate the claim, bargain with Beck, or settle the claim, Farmers had breached an implied covenant of good faith and fair dealing; and third, that Farmers had acted oppressively and maliciously toward Beck with the intention of, or in reckless disregard of the likelihood of, causing emotional distress. Under the first claim, Beck sought damages for breach of contract in the amount of the policy limits; under the second, he asked for compensatory damages in excess of the policy limits for additional injuries, including mental anguish; and under the third, he sought punitive damages of $500,000.

Sometime in August of 1982, Beck's counsel contacted Farmers' counsel and offered to settle the whole matter for $20,000. This offer was rejected. Farmers filed an answer on September 1, 1982, and at the same time, moved to strike the prayer for punitive damages on the ground that they were unavailable for a breach of contract. Farmers' motion was granted. On September 29th, the trial court bifurcated the case and agreed to try the claim for failure to pay uninsured motorist benefits independent of Beck's claim alleging breach of an implied covenant of good faith and fair dealing.

Immediately after the trial judge bifurcated the case, Beck's counsel expressly revoked the previously rejected offer to settle the whole matter for $20,000. Instead, Beck offered to settle only the failure to pay the uninsured motorist benefits claim for $20,000, reserving the implied covenant or "bad faith" claim for separate resolution.

On October 20, 1982, Farmers apparently counter-offered, negotiations proceeded, and sometime in late November, the parties agreed to settle the uninsured motorist claim for $15,000. On December 6, 1982, the parties stipulated to dismissal of that claim and specifically reserved the bad faith claim for later disposition.

In mid-December, Farmers moved to dismiss the reserved bad faith claim on two theories. First, Farmers asserted that under *Lyon v. Hartford Accident and Indemnity Co.*, 25 Utah 2d 311, 480 P.2d 739 (1971), it "had no duty to bargain with or settle plaintiff's uninsured motorist claim and, therefore, [could not] be held liable" for breach of contract or bad faith. Second, Farmers argued that even if it had some duty to bargain or to settle the claim, the facts set forth in the pleadings on file did not establish that it had breached the duty. No memoranda or factual affidavits supported this motion.

Farmers' motion was opposed by affidavits of Beck, his counsel, and a former insurance adjuster who worked for Beck's counsel as a paralegal. In his affidavit, Beck's counsel recited the dates and terms of the various settlement offers and the fact that they had been rejected without counteroffer. Beck's affidavit stated that he had accepted the $15,000 offer only because of financial pressures caused by the substantial expenses he had incurred in the ten months since the accident. The paralegal's affidavit stated that he had been an insurance adjuster for 19 years and that he had reviewed the settlement documentation submitted to Farmers in June when the claim was first filed. He expressed the opinion that a reasonable and prudent insurance company would have valued the claim at between $30,000 and $40,000 and attempted to settle the matter within weeks after the initial offer. The paralegal charged that the "only reason for such a substantial delay in settling this claim would be to put Mr. Beck in a situation of financial need and stress so that he would accept the first settlement offer," a tactic he characterized as acting in bad faith. Farmers filed no rebuttal affidavits, and the trial court granted Farmers' motion without specifying the basis for its holding.

Beck asks this Court to overrule *Lyon* and permit an insured to sue for an insurer's bad faith refusal to bargain or settle. He points out that many states now allow a tort action for breach of an insurer's duty to deal fairly and in good faith with its insured. Assuming that we abandon *Lyon*, Beck argues that the affidavits submitted in opposition to Farmers' motion for summary judgment were sufficient to create a genuine issue of material fact as to whether Farmers breached an implied covenant of good faith and fair dealing.

Farmers does not now contend, as it did below, that it had no duty to bargain or settle. Instead, it argues that under *Lyon*, an insurer cannot be held liable for bad faith simply because it refused to bargain or to settle a claim; rather, it argues, to sustain such a claim a plaintiff must produce evidence of bad faith wholly apart from the "mere failure" to bargain or settle.

Our ruling in *Lyon* left an insured without any effective remedy against an insurer that refuses to bargain or settle in good faith with the insured. An insured who has suffered a loss and is pressed financially is at a marked disadvantage when bargaining with an insurer over payment for that loss. Failure to accept a proffered settlement, although less than fair, can lead to catastrophic consequences for an insured who, as a direct consequence of the loss, may be peculiarly vulnerable, both economically and emotionally. The temptation for an insurer to delay settlement while pressures build on the insured is great, especially if the insurer's exposure cannot exceed the policy limits....

In light of these considerations, we now conclude that an insured should be provided with a remedy. However, we do not agree with plaintiff that a tort action is appropriate. Instead, we hold that the good faith duty to bargain or settle under an insurance contract is only one aspect of the duty of good faith and fair dealing implied in all contracts and that a violation of that duty gives rise to a claim for breach of contract.[1] In addition, we do not adopt the limitation suggested by

---

1. The Court in *Lyon* considered only the question of whether a claim of bad faith gave rise to a tort cause of action; however, to the extent that *Lyon* is philosophically inconsistent with our recognition today of a cause of action in contract, it is overruled.

Farmers, but hold that the refusal to bargain or settle, standing alone, may, under appropriate circumstances, be sufficient to prove a breach.

We recognize that a majority of states permit an insured to institute a tort action against an insurer who fails to bargain in good faith in a "first- party" situation,[2] adopting the approach first announced by the California Supreme Court in *Gruenberg v. Aetna Insurance Co.*, 9 Cal.3d 566, 510 P.2d 1032, 108 Cal.Rptr. 480 (1973).... Apparently, these courts have taken this step as a matter of policy in order to provide what they perceive to be an adequate remedy for an insured wronged by an insurer's recalcitrance. These courts have reasoned that under contract law principles, an insurer who improperly refuses to settle a first-party claim may be liable only for damages measured by the maximum dollar amount of the insurance provided by the policy, and such a damage measure provides little or no incentive to an insurer to promptly and faithfully fulfill its contractual obligations. Accordingly, these courts have adopted a tort approach in order to allow an insured to recover extensive consequential and punitive damages, which they consider to be unavailable in an action based solely on a breach of contract. *See Availability of Excess Damages, supra*, at 168–77; *First Party Bad Faith, supra*, at 158.

We conclude that the tort approach adopted by these courts is without a sound theoretical foundation and has the potential for distorting well-established principles of contract law. Moreover, the practical end of providing a strong incentive for insurers to fulfill their contractual obligations can be accomplished as well through a contract cause of action, without the analytical straining necessitated by the tort approach and with far less potential for unforeseen consequences to the law of contracts.

The analytical weaknesses of the tort approach are easily seen. In *Gruenberg*, the California court held that an insurer has a duty to deal in good faith with its insured and that an insured can bring an action in tort, rather than contract, for breach of that duty because the duty is imposed by law and, being nonconsensual, does not arise out of the contract. Glossing over any distinctions between first- and third-party situations, the court concluded that the duty imposed upon the insurer when bargaining with its insured in a first-party situation is merely another aspect of the fiduciary duty owed in the third-party context. *Gruenberg v. Aetna Insurance Co.*, 9 Cal.3d at 573–74, 510 P.2d at 1037, 108 Cal.Rptr. at 485.

Although this Court, in *Ammerman v. Farmers Insurance Exchange*, 19 Utah 2d 261, 430 P.2d 576 (1967), recognized a tort cause of action for breach of an insurer's obligation to bargain in a third-party context,

---

2. We use the term "first-party" to refer to an insurance agreement where the insurer agrees to pay claims submitted to it by the insured for losses suffered by the insured. The present case involves such a first-party situation. In contrast, a "third-party" situation is one where the insurer contracts to defend the insured against claims made by third parties against the insured and to pay any resulting liability, up to the specified dollar limit.

we cannot agree with the *Gruenberg* court that the considerations which compel the recognition of a tort cause of action in a third-party context are present in the first-party situation. In *Ammerman*, we stated that because a third-party insurance contract obligates the insurer to defend the insured, the insurer incurs a fiduciary duty to its insured to protect the insured's interests as zealously as it would its own; consequently, a tort cause of action is recognized to remedy a violation of that duty. 19 Utah 2d at 265–66, 430 P.2d at 578–79.

However, in *Lyon v. Hartford Accident and Indemnity Co.*, we held that a tort cause of action did not arise in a first-party insurance contract situation because the relationship between the insurer and its insured is fundamentally different than in a third-party context:

> In the [third-party] situation, the insurer must act in good faith and be as zealous in protecting the interests of the insured as it would be in regard to its own. In the [first-party] situation, the insured and the insurer are in effect and practically speaking, adversaries.

25 Utah 2d at 319, 480 P.2d at 745 (citations omitted). . . .

This distinction is of no small consequence. In a third-party situation, the insurer controls the disposition of claims against its insured, who relinquishes any right to negotiate on his own behalf. *Craft v. Economy Fire & Casualty Co.*, 572 F.2d at 569. An insurer's failure to act in good faith exposes its insured to a judgment and personal liability in excess of the policy limits. *Santilli v. State Farm Life Insurance Co.*, 278 Or. 53, 61–62, 562 P.2d 965, 969 (1977). In essence, the contract itself creates a fiduciary relationship because of the trust and reliance placed in the insurer by its insured. Cf. *Hal Taylor Associates v. UnionAmerica, Inc.*, Utah, 657 P.2d 743, 748–49 (1982). The insured is wholly dependent upon the insurer to see that, in dealing with claims by third parties, the insured's best interests are protected. In addition, when dealing with third parties, the insurer acts as an agent for the insured with respect to the disputed claim. Wholly apart from the contractual obligations undertaken by the parties, the law imposes upon all agents a fiduciary obligation to their principals with respect to matters falling within the scope of their agency. *Id.* at 748; *see generally* 3 Am. Jur.2d *Agency* § 199 (1962).

In the first-party situation, on the other hand, the reasons for finding a fiduciary relationship and imposing a corresponding duty are absent. No relationship of trust and reliance is created by the contract; it simply obligates the insurer to pay claims submitted by the insured in accordance with the contract. *Santilli v. State Farm Life Insurance Co.*, 278 Or. at 61–62, 562 P.2d at 969. Furthermore, none of the indicia of agency are present. *See generally Duncan v. Andrew County Mutual Insurance Co.*, Mo., 665 S.W.2d 13, 18–20 (1983).

Clearly, then, it is difficult to find a theoretically sound basis for analogizing the duty owed in a third-party context to that owed in a first-party context. And wholly apart from any theoretical problems, tailoring the tort analysis to first-party insurance contract cases has proven difficult. The pragmatic reason for adopting the tort approach is that it exposes insurers to consequential and punitive damages awards in excess of the policy limits. However, the courts appear to have had difficulty in developing a sound rationale for limiting the tort approach to insurance contract cases. This may be because there is no sound theoretical difference between a first-party insurance contract and any other contract, at least no difference that justifies permitting punitive damages for the breach of one and not the other. In any event, the tort approach and the accompanying punitive damages have moved rather quickly into areas far afield from insurance. . . .

Furthermore, the courts adopting the tort approach have had some difficulty in determining what degree of bad faith is necessary to sustain a claim. *E.g., Anderson v. Continental Insurance Co.*, 85 Wis.2d 675, 692–94, 271 N.W.2d 368, 376–77 (1978). From a practical standpoint, the state of mind of the insurer is irrelevant; even an inadvertent breach of the covenant of good faith implied in an insurance contract can substantially harm the insured and warrants a remedy.

We therefore hold that in a first-party relationship between an insurer and its insured, the duties and obligations of the parties are contractual rather than fiduciary. Without more, a breach of those implied or express duties can give rise only to a cause of action in contract, not one in tort.[3] This position has not been widely adopted by other courts, although a "respectable body of authority" is developing. *See Duncan v. Andrew County Mutual Insurance Co.*, 665 S.W.2d at 18–19, and cases cited therein. . . . We further hold that as parties to a contract, the insured and the insurer have parallel obligations to perform the contract in good faith, obligations that inhere in every contractual relationship. *State Automobile & Casualty Underwriters v. Salisbury*, 27 Utah 2d 229, 232, 494 P.2d 529, 531 (1972). . . .

Few cases define the implied contractual obligation to perform a first-party insurance contract in good faith. However, because the considerations are similar, we freely look to the tort cases that have described the incidents of the duty of good faith in the context of first-party insurance contracts. From those cases and from our own analysis of the obligations undertaken by the parties, we conclude that the implied obligation of good faith performance contemplates, at the very least, that the insurer will diligently investigate the facts to enable it to determine whether a claim is valid, will fairly evaluate the claim, and will thereafter act promptly and reasonably in rejecting or settling the claim. *See Anderson v. Continental Insurance Co.*, 85 Wis.2d at 692–93, 271 N.W.2d at 377. . . . The duty of good faith also requires the insurer to "deal with laymen as laymen and not as experts in the subtleties of

---

3. We recognize that in some cases the acts constituting a breach of contract may also result in breaches of duty that are independent of the contract and may give rise to causes of action in tort. Hal Taylor Assoc. v. Unionamerica, 657 P.2d at 750; Lawton v. Great Southwest Fire Ins. Co., 392 A.2d at 580. For example, the law of this state recognizes a duty to refrain from intentionally causing severe emotional distress to others. Samms v. Eccles, 11 Utah 2d 289, 358 P.2d 344 (1961). . . .

law and underwriting" and to refrain from actions that will injure the insured's ability to obtain the benefits of the contract. *MFA Mutual Insurance Co. v. Flint*, 574 S.W.2d at 720, quoting *Merchants Indemnity Corp. v. Eggleston*, 37 N.J. 114, 122, 179 A.2d 505, 509 (1962).... These performances are the essence of what the insured has bargained and paid for, and the insurer has the obligation to perform them. When an insurer has breached this duty, it is liable for damages suffered in consequence of that breach.

In adopting the contract approach, we are not ignoring the principal reason for the adoption of the tort approach—to provide damage exposure in excess of the policy limits and thus remove any incentive for breaching the duty of good faith. Despite what some courts have suggested, *e.g.*, *Santilli v. State Farm Insurance Co.*, 562 P.2d at 969, and what some commentators have asserted, *e.g.*, J. Appleman, *Insurance Law & Practice* § 8878.15 at 424–26 (1981), there is no reason to limit damages recoverable for breach of a duty to investigate, bargain, and settle claims in good faith to the amount specified in the insurance policy. Nothing inherent in the contract law approach mandates this narrow definition of recoverable damages. Although the policy limits define the amount for which the insurer may be held responsible in performing the contract, they do not define the amount for which it may be liable upon a breach. *Lawton v. Great Southwest Fire Insurance Co.*, 392 A.2d at 579.

Damages recoverable for breach of contract include both general damages, i.e., those flowing naturally from the breach, and consequential damages, *i.e.*, those reasonably within the contemplation of, or reasonably foreseeable by, the parties at the time the contract was made. *Pacific Coast Title Insurance Co. v. Hartford Accident & Indemnity Co.*, 7 Utah 2d 377, 379, 325 P.2d 906, 907 (1958), *citing Hadley v. Baxendale*, 9 Exch. 341, 156 Eng.Rep. 145 (1854). We have repeatedly recognized that consequential damages for breach of contract may reach beyond the bare contract terms. *See, e.g., Pacific Coast Title Insurance Co. v. Hartford Accident & Indemnity*, 7 Utah 2d at 379, 325 P.2d at 908 (attorney fees incurred for settling and defending claims were foreseeable result of contractor's default); *Bevan v. J.H. Construction Co.*, Utah, 669 P.2d 442, 444 (1983) (home purchasers entitled to damages for loss of favorable mortgage interest rate resulting from builder's breach of contract).

In an action for breach of a duty to bargain in good faith, a broad range of recoverable damages is conceivable, particularly given the unique nature and purpose of an insurance contract. An insured frequently faces catastrophic consequences if funds are not available within a reasonable period of time to cover an insured loss; damages for losses well in excess of the policy limits, such as for a home or a business, may therefore be foreseeable and provable. *See, e.g., Reichert v. General Insurance Co.*, 59 Cal.Rptr. 724, 728, 428 P.2d 860, 864 (1967), *vacated on other grounds*, 68 Cal.2d 822, 442 P.2d 377 (1968) (because bankruptcy was a foreseeable consequence of fire insurer's failure to pay, insurer was liable for consequential damages flowing from bankruptcy). Furthermore, it is axiomatic that insurance frequently is purchased not only to provide funds in case of loss, but to provide peace of mind for the insured or his beneficiaries. Therefore, although other courts adopting the contract approach have been reluctant to allow such an award, *Lawton v. Great Southwest Fire Insurance Co.*, 392 A.2d at 581–82, we find no difficulty with the proposition that, in unusual cases, damages for mental anguish might be provable. *See Kewin v. Massachusetts Mutual Life Insurance Co.*, 409 Mich. at 440–55, 295 N.W.2d at 64–72 (Williams, J., dissenting).... The foreseeability of any such damages will always hinge upon the nature and language of the contract and the reasonable expectations of the parties. J. Calamari & J. Perillo, *Contracts* § 14–5 at 523–25 (2d ed. 1977).

With the foregoing principles in mind, we return to a consideration of the present case. The trial court granted summary judgment for the insurer in the face of affidavits of the insured, his counsel, and a paralegal who has been an adjuster for many years. In the absence of any responsive affidavits, we take the assertions of the affidavits as true and view all unexplained facts in a light most favorable to Beck. It appears that the insurer was served with Beck's claim on June 23, 1982. On July 1st, the claim was rejected without explanation and without any request for additional facts. The insured heard nothing more from the insurer until after August 2d, when this suit was filed. The affidavits state that the insured accepted the settlement offered by the insurer in late October because of the financial pressure caused by the delay in resolving the matter. Affidavits also offer the opinion of the expert adjuster turned paralegal that the delay was in bad faith.

From January until late June, Beck was apparently negotiating with the car owner's carrier and not with Farmers, for no claim was filed with Farmers until June 23rd. Therefore, none of the delay between January and June 23rd can be attributed to Farmers. The unexplained delay thereafter, however, together with a flat rejection of plaintiff's offer, provides a factual basis for this cause of action sufficient to withstand summary judgment. Farmers had an obligation to diligently investigate and evaluate Beck's claim. It rejected the claim in one week, and we must infer that the insurer did nothing to investigate or evaluate the claim during the following month.

Under these circumstances and resolving all doubts in Beck's favor, we cannot say that an jury could not find that Farmers breached its duty of good faith in rejecting Beck's claim without explanation and in failing to further investigate the matter. Therefore, we remand the matter to the trial court for further proceedings.

Questions

1. If you were representing the plaintiff in a case like *Gruenberg* or *Beck*, what advantages would you see in a tort action? Should the tort action for bad faith be available in cases like these? Why or Why not?

2. The *Beck* court's holding regarding the insurer's duty to negotiate and settle is unusual. Do you think it is sound? How is the practical effect of *Beck* different from that of *Gruenberg*?

3. Are insurance contracts, by contrast with other kinds of contracts, in need of special treatment? Should a tort action be available for other kinds of contract breaches? For all contract breaches? If not, how would you distinguish between those in which a breach is tortious and those in which it is only contractual?

3. *Problems.*

a. Silvers Banking Services Co. markets computer-based decision-support services to banks. Silvers hired Zazu in 1982; by 1989, Zazu had been promoted to branch manager of the Phoenix office. She had no explicit contract of employment. In that year, Zazu learned that she was in line for promotion to Vice President for Sales, though others were also in line, including Simon LeGrand. Zazu learned from an old friend that LeGrand was under investigation by the Federal Bureau of Investigation for embezzlement from his former employer, a bank in St. Louis. She revealed this information to the president of Silvers Banking, who promptly fired her. Zazu visits your law office for advice on her legal options. Prepare the main questions you would want to ask Zazu before providing legal advice. See Foley v. Interactive Data Corp., 47 Cal.3d 654, 254 Cal.Rptr. 211, 765 P.2d 373 (1988).

b. The basic facts are the same as in Problem a above, except that Zazu was fired for filing a workers' compensation claim after she was injured in a motor accident while driving the company car on business. Such a claim could result in higher insurance premiums for Silvers Banking Services Co. Should Zazu have an action in contract, tort, or both? See Frampton v. Central Indiana Gas Co., 260 Ind. 249, 297 N.E.2d 425, 428 (1973).

c. The basic facts are the same as in Problem a above, except that Zazu was fired for volunteering to serve on a jury, which could have required her absence from work for some weeks. Should Zazu have an action in contract, tort, or both? See Nees v. Hocks, 272 Or. 210, 536 P.2d 512, 514–15 (1975).

d. The basic facts are the same as in Problem a above, except that Zazu was fired for refusing to date her supervisor. Should Zazu have an action in contract, tort, or both? See Monge v. Beebe Rubber Co., 114 N.H. 130, 316 A.2d 549 (1974) (modified by Howard v. Dorr Woolen Co., 120 N.H. 295, 297, 414 A.2d 1273, 1274 (1980)).

Chapter 8

RIGHTS OF THIRD PARTIES

We now turn to problems involving the rights of third parties to contracts. There are three main ways in which a third party issue may arise. First, a third party may in some circumstances have a right to enforce a contract. This depends on the law of third party beneficiaries, to be studied in Section 1. Second, a party to whom a contractual duty is owed may transfer the right to performance to a third person. This possibility is governed by the law of assignments, covered in Section 2. Third, a party under a duty of performance may delegate that duty to a third person, whose performance then satisfies the delegating party's duty to the other party. This matter is governed by the law of delegation, also covered in Section 2. The problems raised by these three legal possibilities are more complex than the familiar two-party problems for three main reasons: (1) the transactions are more complicated, requiring intense scrutiny of the facts to see the legal issue; (2) it is easy to mistake the legal issue by confusing the three kinds of third-party claims; and (3) any of the legal issues covered in the preceding seven chapters may also arise in a case with a third-party issue, and not always in the familiar way.

All of the principles of contract law studied in this course have a place in the study of this chapter. In addition, the problems in Section 2 introduce an additional policy—free alienability of intangible property rights. Be forewarned: The following materials will challenge your skill at legal analysis. As ever, concentrate on the transaction pattern before attempting to understand the legal doctrine and then to evaluate its justification in principle.

SECTION 1. THIRD PARTY BENEFICIARIES

A commentator, after reviewing the cases involving the rights of third parties who benefit from a contract, concluded that the cases "have typically been conclusory rather than reasoned, and the conclusions have been insecurely rooted and often wrong." Melvin A. Eisenberg, *Third Party Beneficiaries*, 92 COLUM. L. REV. 1358, 1428 (1992). In his view, this

604

area of contract law has suffered more than most from the rigidities of classical contract law. Under that law, prevalent in the late nineteenth century, courts placed greater emphasis on doctrinal stability—even doctrinal purity—than on reformulating the law to maintain its congruence with those principles, policies, and lessons of experience that justify the evolving common law. The doctrine of privity, which held that only parties to contracts could bring actions to enforce them, was a salient feature of classical contract law.

Some cases, however, call for third party rights so strongly that privity was destined to die. A life insurance policy, for example, is concluded between the insured and the insurer. It provides for payments to a beneficiary upon the insured's death. Not allowing the beneficiary to sue an insurer who fails to pay as promised seems perverse. Yet the beneficiary is rarely in privity of contract with the insurer.

The problem is that the doctrine of privity served a valuable function, though overbroadly: It limited the exposure of a promisor to unforeseeable and sometimes crushing liabilities. If it seems clear that the life insurance beneficiary should have a contract right, it seems just as clear that many people may benefit from a contract in remote ways but should not be able to enforce the promise. When Fox fails to pay Lawrence some money as promised, Lawrence will not be able to buy things he could have bought with that money. Should Lawrence's tailor, for example, be allowed to sue Fox because, but for the breach, the tailor would have sold another suit?

The following cases exemplify a number of efforts by courts and Restatement drafters to draw a distinction between third party beneficiaries who should and should not enjoy rights under a contract. Consider, as you read them, whether any have drawn a workable and defensible distinction.

LAWRENCE v. FOX

Court of Appeals of New York, 1859.
20 N.Y. 268.

Appeal from the Superior Court of the City of Buffalo. On the trial before Mr. Justice Masten, it appeared by the evidence of a bystander, that one Holly, in November, 1857, at the request of the defendant, loaned and advanced to him $300, stating at the time that he owed that sum to the plaintiff for money borrowed of him, and had agreed to pay it to him the then next day; that the defendant, in consideration thereof, at the time of receiving the money, promised to pay to the plaintiff the then next day. Upon this state of facts the defendant moved for a nonsuit, upon three several grounds, viz.: That there was no proof tending to show that Holly was indebted to the plaintiff; that the agreement by the defendant with Holly to pay the plaintiff was void for want of consideration, and that there was no privity between the plaintiff and defendant. The court overruled the motion, and the counsel for the defendant excepted. The cause was then submitted to the jury, and they found a verdict for the plaintiff for the amount of the loan and interest, $344.66, upon which judgment was entered; from which the defendant appealed to the Superior Court, at general term, where the judgment was affirmed, and the defendant appealed to this court. The cause was submitted on printed arguments.

GRAY, JUDGE. . . . But it is claimed that notwithstanding this promise was established by competent evidence, it was void for the want of consideration. It is now more than a quarter of a century since it was settled by the Supreme Court of this State—in an able and painstaking opinion by the late Chief Justice SAVAGE, in which the authorities were fully examined and carefully analysed—that a promise in all material respects like the one under consideration was valid; and the judgment of that court was unanimously affirmed by the Court for the Correction of Errors. (*Farley v. Cleveland*), 4 *Cow.* 432, 15 Am.Dec. 387; *s.c. in error*, 9 *Cow.* 639. In that case one Moon owed Farley and sold to Cleveland a quantity of hay, in consideration of which Cleveland promised to pay Moon's debt to Farley; and the decision in favor of Farley's right to recover was placed upon the ground that the hay received by Cleveland from Moon was a valid consideration for Cleveland's promise to pay Farley, and that the subsisting liability of Moon to pay Farley was no objection to the recovery. The fact that the money advanced by Holly to the defendant was a loan to him for a day, and that it thereby became the property of the defendant, seemed to impress the defendant's counsel with the idea that because the defendant's promise was not a trust fund placed by the plaintiff [?] in the defendant's hands, out of which he was to realize money as from the sale of a chattel or the collection of a debt, the promise although made for the benefit of the plaintiff could not inure to his benefit. The hay which [Moon] delivered to [Cleveland] was not to be paid to Farley, but the debt incurred by Cleveland for the purchase of the hay, like the debt incurred by the defendant for money borrowed, was what was to be paid. That case has been often referred to by the courts of this State, and has never been doubted as sound authority for the principle upheld by it. (*Barker v. Bucklin*, 2 *Denio*, 45, 43 Am.Dec. 726. . . .) It puts to rest the objection that the defendant's promise was void for want of consideration. The report of that case shows that the promise was not only made to Moon but to the plaintiff Farley. In this case the promise was made to Holly and not expressly to the plaintiff; and this difference between the two cases presents the question, raised by the defendant's objection, as to the want of privity between the plaintiff and defendant. As early as 1806 it was announced by the Supreme Court of this State, upon what was then regarded as the settled law of England, "That where one person makes a promise to another for the benefit of a third person, that third person may maintain an action upon it." *Schemerhorn v. Vanderheyden*, (1 John. R., 140, 3 Am.Dec. 304) has often been reasserted by our courts and never departed from. . . .

. . . But it is urged that because the defendant was not in any sense a trustee of the property of Holly for the benefit of the plaintiff, the law will not imply a promise. I agree that many of the cases where a promise was implied were cases of trusts, created for the benefit of the promisor [?]. The case of *Felton v. Dickinson*, (10 Mass., 287, 290), and others that might be cited are of that class; but concede them all to have been cases of trusts, and it proves nothing against the application of the rule to this case. The duty of the trustee to pay the *cestui que trust*, according to the terms of the trust, implies his promise to the latter to do so. In this case the defendant, upon ample consideration received from Holly, promised Holly to pay his debt to the plaintiff; the consideration received and the promise to Holly made it as plainly his duty to pay the plaintiff as if the money had been remitted to him for that purpose, and as well implied a promise to do so as if he had been made a trustee of property to be converted into cash with which to pay. The fact that a breach of the duty imposed in the one case may be visited, and justly, with more serious consequences than in the other, by no means disproves the payment to be a duty in both. The principle illustrated by the example so frequently quoted (which concisely states the case in hand) "that a promise made to one for the benefit of another, he for whose benefit it is made may bring an action for its breach," has been applied to trust cases, not because it was exclusively applicable to those cases, but because it was a principle of law, and as such applicable to those cases. It was also insisted that Holly could have discharged the defendant from his promise, though it was intended by both parties for the benefit of the plaintiff, and, therefore, the plaintiff was not entitled to maintain this suit for the recovery of a demand over which he had no control. It is enough that the plaintiff [?] did not release the defendant from his promise, and whether he could or not is a question not now necessarily involved; but if it was, I think it would be found difficult to maintain the right of Holly to discharge a judgment recovered by the plaintiff upon confession or otherwise, for the breach of the defendant's promise; and if he could not, how could he discharge the suit before judgment, or the promise before suit, made as it was for the plaintiff's benefit and in accordance with legal presumption accepted by him (*Berly v. Taylor*, 5 Hill, 577–584 *et seq*.), until his dissent was shown.

The case cited, and especially that of *Farley v. Cleveland*, established the validity of a parol promise; it stands then upon the footing of a written one. Suppose the defendant had given his note in which for value received of Holly, he had promised to pay the plaintiff and the plaintiff had accepted the promise, retaining Holly's liability. Very clearly Holly could not have discharged that promise, be the right to release the defendant as it may. No one can doubt that he owes the sum of money demanded of him, or that in accordance with his promise it was his duty to have paid it to the plaintiff; nor can it be doubted that whatever may be the diversity of opinion elsewhere, the adjudications in this State, from a very early period, approved by experience, have established the defendant's liability; if, therefore, it could be shown that a more strict and technically accurate application of the rules applied, would lead to a different result (which I by no means concede), the effort should not be made in the face of manifest justice.

The judgment should be affirmed.

COMSTOCK, JUDGE (dissenting). The plaintiff had nothing to do with the promise on which he brought this action. It was not made to him, nor did the consideration proceed from him. If he can maintain the suit, it is because an anomaly has found its way into the law on this subject. In general, there must be privity of contract. The party who sues upon a promise must be the promisee, or he must have some legal interest in the undertaking. In this case, it is plain that Holly, who loaned the money to the defendant, and to whom the promise in question was made, could at any time have claimed that it should be performed to himself personally. He had lent the money to the defendant, and at the same time directed the latter to pay the sum to the plaintiff. This direction he could countermand, and if he had done so, manifestly the defendant's promise to pay according to the direction would have ceased to exist. The plaintiff would receive a benefit by a complete execution of the arrangement, but the arrangement itself was between other parties, and was under their exclusive control. If the defendant had paid the money to Holly, his debt would have been discharged thereby. So Holly might have released the demand or assigned it to another person, or the parties might have annulled the promise now in question, and designated some other creditor of Holly as the party to whom the money should be paid. It has never been claimed that in a case thus situated the right of a third person to sue upon the promise rested on any sound principle of law. We are to inquire whether the rule has been so established by positive authority. . . .

The cases in which some trust was involved are also frequently referred to as authority for the doctrine now in question, but they do not sustain it. . . . If A delivers money or property to B, which the latter accepts upon a trust for the benefit of C, the latter can enforce the trust by an appropriate action for that purpose. (*Berly v. Taylor*, 5 *Hill*, 577.) If the trust be of money, I think the beneficiary may assent to it and bring the action for money had and received to his use. If it be of something else than money, the trustee must account for it according to the terms of the trust, and upon principles of equity. There is some authority even for saying that an express promise founded on the possession of a trust fund may be enforced by an action at law in the name of the beneficiary, although it was made to the creator of the trust. Thus, in *Comyn's Digest (Action on the Case upon Assumpsit, B,* 15), it is laid down that if a man promise a pig of lead to A, and his executor give lead to make a pig to B., who assumes to deliver it to A., an assumpsit lies by A. against him. The case of *Delaware & H. Canal Co. v. Westchester County Bank*, (4 Denio, 97), involved a trust because the defendants had received from a thirty party a bill of exchange under an agreement that they would endeavor to collect it, and would pay over the proceeds when collected to the plaintiffs. A fund received under such an agreement does not belong to the person who receives it. He must account for it specifically; and perhaps there is no gross violation of principle in permitting the equitable owner of it to sue upon an express promise to pay it over. Having a specific interest in the thing, the undertaking to account for it may be regarded as in some sense made with him through the author of the trust. But further than this we cannot go without violating plain rules of law. In the case before us there was nothing in the nature of a trust or agency. The defendant borrowed the money of Holly and received it as his own. The plaintiff had no right in the fund, legal or equitable. The promise to repay the money created an obligation in favor of the lender to whom it was made and not in favor of any one else. . . .

The judgment of the court below should, therefore, be reversed, and a new trial granted.

Questions

1. What are the terms of the contract sued upon in *Lawrence*? Who is the promisor to the promise sued upon? Who is the promisee? Who claims rights as a third party beneficiary to that promise? Why did the court, in this landmark case, recognize such rights?

2. What are the arguments against recognizing the rights of third party beneficiaries? Should a privity requirement preclude Lawrence from recovering? What is the "manifest justice" of Lawrence's claim against Fox? Are there drawbacks to recognizing that claim?

3. *Problem.*

Uncle Lionel wanted to give Nephew John a new car for his birthday, but wanted John to pick out the color and the extras himself. On John's birthday, Lionel gave him a birthday card with a handwritten note saying: "I promise to buy you a new Chevrolet Corvette Coupe, as ordered by you from Ethel Motors, as your 21st birthday present. All you must do is promise to give me your old car in return." John promised. He soon went to Ethel Motors, told them of his generous uncle, and began the process of picking out a new Corvette. Lionel then found out that John was using cocaine and repudiated his promise. Can Ethel Motors recover as a third party beneficiary to Lionel's promise?

SEAVER v. RANSOM

Court of Appeals of New York, 1918.
224 N.Y. 233, 120 N.E. 639.

Action by Marion E. Seaver against Matt C. Ransom and another, as executors, etc., of Samuel A. Beman, deceased. From a judgment of the Appellate Division (180 App.Div. 734, 168 N.Y. Supp. 454), affirming judgment for plaintiff, defendants appeal. Affirmed.

POUND, JUDGE. Judge Beman and his wife were advanced in years. Mrs. Beman was about to die. She had a small estate, consisting of a house and lot in Malone and little else. Judge Beman drew his wife's will according to her instructions. It gave $1,000 to plaintiff, $500 to one sister, plaintiff's mother, and $100 each to another sister and her son, the use of the house to her husband for life, and remainder to the American Society for the Prevention of Cruelty to Animals. She named her husband as residuary legatee and executor. Plaintiff was her niece, 34 years old, in ill health, sometimes a member of the Beman household. When the will was read to Mrs. Beman, she said that it was not as she wanted it. She wanted to leave the house to plaintiff. She had no other objection to the will, but her strength was waning, and, although the judge offered to write another will for her, she said she was afraid she would not hold out long enough to enable her to sign it. So the judge said, if she would sign the will, he would leave plaintiff enough in his will to make up the difference. He avouched the promise by his uplifted hand with all solemnity and his wife then executed the will. When he came to die, it was found that his will made no provision for the plaintiff.

This action was brought, and plaintiff recovered judgment in the trial court, on the theory that Beman had obtained property from his wife and induced her to execute the will in the form prepared by him by his promise to give plaintiff $6,000, the value of the house, and that thereby equity impressed his property with a trust in favor of plaintiff. Where a legatee promises the testator that he will use property given him by the will for a particular purpose, a trust arises. O'Hara v. Dudley, 95 N.Y. 403, 47 Am. Rep. 53. . . . Beman received nothing under his wife's will but the use of the house in Malone for life. Equity compels the application of property thus obtained to the purpose of the testator, but equity cannot so impress a trust, except on property obtained by the promise. Beman was bound by his promise, but no property was bound by it; no trust in plaintiff's favor can be spelled out.

An action on the contract for damages, or to make the executors trustees for performance, stands on different ground. Farmers' Loan & Trust Co. v. Mortimer, 219 N.Y. 290, 294, 295, 114 N.E. 389. The Appellate Division properly passed to the consideration of the question whether the judgment could stand upon the promise made to the wife, upon a valid consideration, for the sole benefit of plaintiff. The judgment of the trial court was affirmed by a return to the general doctrine laid down in the great case of Lawrence v. Fox, 20 N.Y. 268, which has since been limited as herein indicated.

Contracts for the benefit of third persons have been the prolific source of judicial and academic discussion. Williston, Contracts for the Benefit of a Third Person, 15 Harvard Law Review, 767; Corbin, Contracts for the Benefit of Third Persons, 27 Yale Law Review, 1008. The general rule, both in law and equity (Phalen v. United States Trust Co., 186 N.Y. 178, 186, 78 N.E. 943, 7 L. R. A. [N.S.] 734, 9 Ann. Cas. 595), was that privity between a plaintiff and a defendant is necessary to the maintenance of an action on the contract. The consideration must be furnished by the party to whom the promise was made. The contract cannot be enforced against the third party, and therefore it cannot be enforced by him. On the other hand, the right of the beneficiary to sue on a contract made expressly for his benefit has been fully recognized in many American jurisdictions, either by judicial decision or by legislation, and is said to be "the prevailing rule in this country." Hendrick v. Lindsay, 93 U.S. 143, 23 L.Ed. 855; Lehow v. Simonton, 3 Colo. 346. It has been said that "the establishment of this doctrine has been gradual, and is a victory of practical utility over theory, of equity over technical subtlety." Brantly on Contracts (2d Ed.) p. 253. The reasons for this view are that it is just and practical to permit the person for whose benefit the contract is made to enforce it against one whose duty it is to pay. Other jurisdictions still adhere to the present English rule (7 Halsbury's Laws of England, 342, 343; Jenks' Digest of English Civil Law, § 229) that a contract cannot be enforced by or against a person who is not a party (Exchange Bank v. Rice, 107 Mass. 37, 9 Am. Rep. 1). But see, also, Forbes v. Thorpe, 209 Mass. 570, 95 N.E. 955; Gardner v. Denison, 217 Mass. 492, 105 N.E. 359, 51 L. R. A. (N. S.) 1108.

In New York the right of the beneficiary to sue on contracts made for his benefit is not clearly or simply defined. It is at present confined: First. To cases where there is a pecuniary obligation running from the promisee to the beneficiary, "a legal right founded upon some obligation of the promisee in the third party to adopt and claim the promise as made for his benefit." Farley v. Cleveland, 4 Cow. 432, 15 Am. Dec. 387; Lawrence v. Fox, supra; ... Secondly. To cases where the contract is made for the benefit of the wife (Buchanan v. Tilden, 158 N.Y. 109, 52 N.E. 724, 44 L. R. A. 170, 70 Am. St. Rep. 454; ..., affianced wife (De Cicco v. Schweizer, 221 N.Y. 431, 117 N.E. 807, Ann. Cas. 1918C, 816), or child (Todd v. Weber, 95 N.Y. 181, 193, 47 Am. Rep. 20; ...) of a party to the contract. The close relationship cases go back to the early King's Bench case (1677), long since repudiated in England, of Dutton v. Poole, 2 Lev. 211 (S.C., 1 Ventris, 318, 332). See Schemerhorn v. Vanderheyden, 1 Johns. 139, 3 Am. Dec. 304. The natural and moral duty of the husband or parent to provide for the future of wife or child sustains the action on the contract made for their benefit. "This is the farthest the cases in this state have gone," says Cullen, J., in the marriage settlement case of Borland v. Welch, 162 N.Y. 104, 110, 56 N.E. 556.

The right of the third party is also upheld in, thirdly, the public contract cases (Little v. Banks, 85 N.Y. 258; ...), where the municipality seeks to protect its inhabitants by covenants for their benefit; and, fourthly, the cases where, at the request of a party to the contract, the promise runs directly to the beneficiary although he does not furnish the consideration (Rector, etc. v. Teed, 120 N.Y. 583, 24 N.E. 1014; ...). It may be safely said that a general rule sustaining recovery at the suit of the third party would include but few classes of cases not included in these groups, either categorically or in principle.

The desire of the childless aunt to make provision for a beloved and favorite niece differs imperceptibly in law or in equity from the moral duty of the parent to make testamentary provision for a child. The contract was made for the plaintiff's benefit. She alone is substantially damaged by its breach. The representatives of the wife's estate have no interest in enforcing it specifically. It is said in Buchanan v. Tilden that the common law imposes moral and legal obligations upon the husband and the parent not measured by the necessaries of life. It was, however, the love and affection or the moral sense of the husband and the parent that imposed such obligations in the cases cited, rather than any common-law duty of husband and parent to wife and child. If plaintiff had been a child of Mrs. Beman, legal obligation would have required no testamentary provision for her, yet the child could have enforced a covenant in her favor identical with the covenant of Judge Beman in this case. De Cicco v. Schweizer, supra. The constraining power of conscience is not regulated by the degree of relationship alone. The dependent or faithful niece may have a stronger claim than the affluent or unworthy son. No sensible theory of moral obligation denies arbitrarily to the former what would be conceded to the latter. We might consistently either refuse or allow the claim of both, but I cannot reconcile a decision in favor of the wife in Buchanan v. Tilden, based on the moral obligations arising out of near relationship, with a decision against the niece here on the ground that the relationship is too remote for equity's ken. No controlling authority depends upon so absolute a rule. In Sullivan v. Sullivan, [161 N.Y. 554, 56 N.E. 116 (1900)], the grandniece lost in a litigation with the aunt's estate, founded on a certificate of deposit payable to the aunt "or in case of her death to her niece;" but what was said in that case of the relations of plaintiff's intestate and defendant does not control here, any more than what was said in Durnherr v. Rau, [135 N.Y. 219, 32 N.E. 49 (1892)], on the relation of husband and wife, and the inadequacy of mere moral duty, as distinguished from legal or equitable obligation, controlled the decision in Buchanan v. Tilden. Borland v. Welch, supra, deals only with the rights of volunteers under a marriage settlement not made for the benefit of collaterals. Kellogg, P.J., writing for the court below well said:

> "The doctrine of Lawrence v. Fox is progressive, not retrograde. The course of the late decisions is to enlarge, not to limit, the effect of that case."

The court in that leading case attempted to adopt the general doctrine that any third person, for whose direct benefit a contract was intended, could sue on it. The headnote thus states the rule. Finch, J., in Gifford v. Corrigan, 117 N.Y. 257, 262, 22 N.E. 756, 6 L. R. A. 610, 15 Am. St. Rep. 508, says that the case rests upon that broad proposition; Edward T. Bartlett, J., in Pond v. New Rochelle Water Co., 183 N.Y. 330, 337, 76 N.E. 211, 213 (1 L. R. A. [N.S.] 958, 5 Ann. Cas. 504), calls it "the general principle;" but Vrooman v. Turner, [69 N.Y. 280, 25 Am. Rep. 195], confined its application to the facts on which it was decided. "In every case in which an action has been sustained," says Allen, J., "there has been a debt or duty owing by the promisee to the party claiming to sue upon the promise." 69 N.Y. 285, 25 Am. Rep. 195. As late as Townsend v. Rackham, 143 N.Y. 516, 523, 38 N.E. 731, 733, we find

Peckham, J., saying that, "to maintain the action by the third person, there must be this liability to him on the part of the promisee." Buchanan v. Tilden went further than any case since Lawrence v. Fox in a desire to do justice rather than to apply with technical accuracy strict rules calling for a legal or equitable obligation. In Embler v. Hartford Steam Boiler Inspection & Ins. Co., 158 N.Y. 431, 53 N.E. 212, 44 L.R.A. 512, it may at least be said that a majority of the court did not avail themselves of the opportunity to concur with the views expressed by Gray, J., who wrote the dissenting opinion in Buchanan v. Tilden, to the effect that an employee could not maintain an action on an insurance policy issued to the employer, which covered injuries to employees.

In Wright v. Glen Telephone Co., 48 Misc.Rep. 192, 195, 95 N.Y. Supp. 101, the learned presiding justice who wrote the opinion in this case said at Trial Term:

> "The right of a third person to recover upon a contract made by other parties for his benefit must rest upon the peculiar circumstances of each case rather than upon the law of some other case."

> "The case at bar is decided upon its peculiar facts."

Edward T. Bartlett, J., in Buchanan v. Tilden.

But, on principle, a sound conclusion may be reached. If Mrs. Beman had left her husband the house on condition that he pay the plaintiff $6,000, and he had accepted the devise, he would have become personally liable to pay the legacy, and plaintiff could have recovered in an action at law against him, whatever the value of the house. Gridley v. Gridley, 24 N.Y. 130.... That would be because the testatrix had in substance bequeathed the promise to plaintiff, and not because close relationship or moral obligation sustained the contract. The distinction between an implied promise to a testator for the benefit of a third party to pay a legacy and an unqualified promise on a valuable consideration to make provision for the third party by will is discernible, but not obvious. The tendency of American authority is to sustain the gift in all such cases and to permit the donee beneficiary to recover on the contract. Matter of Edmundson's Estate (1918, Pa.) 103 Atl. 277, 259 Pa. 429. The equities are with the plaintiff, and they may be enforced in this action, whether it be regarded as an action for damages or an action for specific performance to convert the defendants into trustees for plaintiff's benefit under the agreement.

The judgment should be affirmed, with costs.

Questions

1. Who is the promisor to the promise sued upon? Who is the promisee? Who claims rights as a third party beneficiary?

2. Why does the court recognize the beneficiary's claimed rights? How does it distinguish between beneficiaries who have contract rights and those

who do not? Would you expect the law to be stable after the opinion in *Seaver*?

———

RESTATEMENT [FIRST] OF CONTRACTS § 133

§ 133. Definition of Donee Beneficiary, Creditor Beneficiary, Incidental Beneficiary.

(1) Where performance of a promise in a contract will benefit a person other than the promisee, that person is . . . :

(a) a donee beneficiary if it appears from the terms of the promise in view of the accompanying circumstances that the purpose of the promisee in obtaining the promise of all or part of the performance thereof is to make a gift to the beneficiary or to confer upon him a right against the promisor to some performance neither due nor supposed or asserted to be due from the promisee to the beneficiary;

(b) a creditor beneficiary if no purpose to make a gift appears from the terms of the promise in view of the accompanying circumstances and performance of the promise will satisfy an actual or supposed or asserted duty of the promisee to the beneficiary, or a right of the beneficiary against the promisee which has been barred by the Statute of Limitations or by a discharge in bankruptcy, or which is unenforceable because of the Statute of Frauds;

(c) an incidental beneficiary if neither of the facts stated in Clause (a) nor those stated in Clause (b) exist.

———

RESTATEMENT (SECOND) OF CONTRACTS §§ 302, 304, 315

———

BAIN v. GILLISPIE
Court of Appeals of Iowa, 1984.
357 N.W.2d 47.

SNELL, PRESIDING JUDGE. James C. Bain serves as a referee for college basketball games. During a game which took place on March 6, 1982, Bain called a foul on a University of Iowa player which permitted free throws to a Purdue University player. That player scored the point that gave Purdue a last-minute victory. Some fans of the University of Iowa team blamed Bain for their team's loss, asserting that the foul call was clearly in error.

John and Karen Gillispie operate a novelty store in Iowa City, specializing in University of Iowa sports memorabilia. The store is known as Hawkeye John's Trading Post. Gillispie's business is a private enterprise for profit having no association with the University of Iowa or its sports program.

A few days after the controversial game, Gillispies began marketing T-shirts bearing a reference to Bain. It showed a man with a rope around his neck and was captioned "Jim Bain Fan Club." On learning of it, Bain sued Gillispies for injunctive relief, actual and punitive damages. Gillispies counterclaimed, alleging that Bain's officiating the game was below the standard of competence required of a professional referee. As such, it constituted malpractice which entitles Gillispies to $175,000 plus exemplary damages. They claim these sums because Iowa's loss of the game to Purdue eliminated Iowa from the championship of the Big Ten Basketball Conference. This in turn destroyed a potential market for Gillispies' memorabilia touting Iowa as a Big Ten champion. Their claim for actual damages is for loss of earnings and business advantage, emotional distress and anxiety, loss of good will, and expectancy of profits. Exemplary damages are asked because Bain's calls as a referee were baneful, outrageous, and done with a heedless disregard for the rights of the Gillispies.

The trial court found the Gillispies had no rights and sustained a motion for summary judgment dismissing Gillispies' counterclaim. They appeal, contending the trial court erred in finding no genuine issue of material fact. The triable issues claimed are: 1) that Gillispies' damages were a reasonably foreseeable consequence of Bain's acts as a referee, or 2) that Gillispies are beneficiaries of an employment contract between Bain and the Big Ten Athletic Conference.

In reviewing the propriety of granting summary judgment as to the counterclaim, our task on appeal is to determine only whether a genuine issue of material fact exists and whether the law was correctly applied. *Frohwein v. Haesemeyer*, 264 N.W.2d 792, 796 (Iowa 1978). We are to view the underlying facts in the light most favorable to the party opposing the motion and to reverse if it appears from the record that there is an unresolved issue of material fact. Id. at 795–96.

In addition to the parties' briefs, the National Association of Sports Officials (NASO) has filed a motion to appear as amicus curiae and to file a brief on behalf of appellee Bain. NASO is an association of sports officials who officiate sports at all levels of competition. It has approximately 9,000 members residing in all 50 states. We have granted the motion and considered the brief.

Turning first to the negligence claim, the Gillispies argue that there was an issue of material fact of whether their damages were the reasonably foreseeable consequence of Bain's action. A prerequisite to establishing a claim of negligence is the existence of a duty. *Larsen v. United Fed. Sav. & Loan Ass'n.*, 300 N.W.2d 281, 285 (Iowa 1981); *Wilson v. Nepstad*, 282 N.W.2d 664, 667 (Iowa 1979). Negligence is the breach of legal duty or obligation recognized by the law, requiring the actor to conform to a certain standard of conduct, for the protection of others against unreasonable risks. *Lewis v. State*, 256 N.W.2d 181, 188 (Iowa 1977). It has been defined as conduct which falls below the standard established by law for the protection of others against unreasonable risk of harm. Restatement, (Second) of Torts §§ 281, 286. The standard established by the law is foreseeability of harm or probability of injury. "The risk reasonably to be perceived defines the duty to be obeyed, and risk imports relation; it is risk to another or to others within the range of apprehension." Justice Cardozo in *Palsgraf v. Long Island R. Co.*, 248 N.Y. 339, 344, 162 N.E. 99, 100 (1928). The law's standard is one of reasonable foresight, not prophetic vision. *See* 57 Am. Jur.2d *Negligence*, §§ 57–62 (1971).

"The question of whether a duty arises out of a parties' relationship is always a matter of law for the courts." *Soike v. Evan Matthews and Co.*, 302 N.W.2d 841, 843 (Iowa 1981). Applying these maxims to Gillispies' tort claim, we find the trial court properly granted the summary judgment against the claim. It is beyond credulity that Bain, while refereeing a game, must make his calls at all times perceiving that a wrong call will injure Gillispies' business or one similarly situated and subject him to liability.... As the trial court properly reasoned:

> This is a case where the undisputed facts are of such a nature that a rational fact finder could only reach one conclusion—no foreseeability, no duty, no liability. Heaven knows what uncharted morass a court would find itself in if it were to hold that an athletic official subjects himself to liability every time he might make a questionable call. The possibilities are mind boggling. If there is a liability to a merchandiser like the Gillispies, why not to the thousands upon thousands of Iowa fans who bleed Hawkeye black and gold every time the whistle blows? It is bad enough when Iowa loses without transforming a loss into a litigation field day for "Monday Morning Quarterbacks." There is no tortious doctrine of athletic official's malpractice that would give credence to Gillispie's counterclaim.

The trial court also found that there was no issue of material fact on the Gillispies' claim that they were beneficiaries under Bain's contract with the Big 10.... By deposition Gillispies answered that there was no contract between them and Bain, the Big 10 Athletic Conference, the University of Iowa, the players, coaches, or with any body regarding this issue. Thus, even if [a letter from the Big 10 to Bain defining their "working relationship"] were considered a contract, Gillispies would be considered third-party beneficiaries. Because Gillispies would not be privy to the contract, they must be direct beneficiaries to maintain a cause of action, and not merely incidental beneficiaries. *Khabbaz v. Swartz*, 319 N.W.2d 279, 284 (Iowa 1982).

A direct beneficiary is either a donee beneficiary or a creditor beneficiary. *Id.* In *Olney v. Hutt*, 251 Iowa 1379, 105 N.W.2d 515 (1960), the Iowa Supreme Court defined these terms as follows:

(1) Where performance of a promise in a contract will benefit a person other than the promisee that person is, ... (a) a donee beneficiary if it appears from the terms of the promise in view of the accompanying circumstances that the purpose of the promisee in obtaining the promise of all or part of the performance thereof is to make a gift to the beneficiary or to confer upon him a right against the promisor to some performance neither due nor supposed or asserted to be due from the promisee to the beneficiary; (b) a creditor beneficiary if no purpose to make a gift appears from the terms of the promise in view of the accompanying circumstances and performance of the promise will satisfy an actual or supposed or asserted duty of the promisee to the beneficiary.

Id. at 1386, 105 N.W.2d at 519.

Gillispies make no claim that they are creditor beneficiaries of Bain, the Big 10 Athletic Conference, or the University of Iowa. "The real test is said to be whether the contracting parties intended that a third person should receive a benefit which might be enforced in the courts." *Bailey v. Iowa Beef Processors, Inc.*, 213 N.W.2d 642, 645 (Iowa 1973), *cert. denied* 419 U.S. 830, 95 S.Ct. 52, 42 L.Ed.2d 55 (1974). It is clear that the purpose of any promise which Bain might have made was not to confer a gift on Gillispies. Likewise, the Big 10 did not owe any duty to the Gillispies such that they would have been creditor beneficiaries. If a contract did exist between Bain and the Big 10, Gillispies can be considered nothing more than incidental beneficiaries and as such are unable to maintain a cause of action. *Olney v. Hutt*, 251 Iowa 1379, 1386, 105 N.W.2d 515, 518 (1960).

Consequently, there was no genuine issue for trial which could result in Gillispies obtaining a judgment under a contract theory of recovery. The ruling of the trial court sustaining the summary judgment motion and dismissing the counterclaim is affirmed.

Questions

1. Who is the promisor to the promise sued upon? Who is the promisee? Who claims rights as a third party beneficiary?

2. Using the Restatement (First) terminology (which remains embedded in the law of many jurisdictions well after the promulgation of the Restatement (Second)), why do the Gillispies have no rights to enforce Bain's promise? Using the Restatement (Second) terminology, which is gaining acceptance, why do the Gillispies have no rights to enforce Bain's promise? Would *Lawrence v. Fox* or *Seaver v. Ransom* be decided differently under either Restatement?

3. Why would the authors of the Restatement (Second) have shifted the terminology? Is the new terminology better? Whose "intention to benefit" matters? What does the "intent to benefit" test require?

4. *Problems*

a. Ackroyd conveyed land to Belushi in consideration of Belushi's promise to pay $15,000 as follows: $5,000 to Cloris, Ackroyd's wife, on whom Ackroyd wishes to confer a gift, $5,000 to Doris to whom Ackroyd is indebted in that amount, and $5,000 to Eustis, a life insurance company, to purchase an annuity payable to Ackroyd during his life. Are Cloris, Doris, and Eustice intended or incidental beneficiaries? See RESTATEMENT (SECOND) OF CONTRACTS § 302, Ill. 8.

b. Belushi promises Ackroyd to pay whatever debts Ackroyd may incur while trying to become an actor. Ackroyd incurs in the undertaking debts to Cloris, Doris, and Eustice. Are Cloris, Doris and Eustice intended or incidental beneficiaries? See RESTATEMENT (SECOND) OF CONTRACTS § 302, Ill. 3.

LONSDALE v. CHESTERFIELD

Supreme Court of Washington, En Banc, 1983.
99 Wash.2d 353, 662 P.2d 385.

WILLIAMS, CHIEF JUSTICE. Petitioners, Robert Lonsdale, et al., are assignees of the vendors' interests in certain real estate contracts. They appeal the unpublished decision of the Court of Appeals, Division One, which upheld the dismissal of their class action for rescission and damages. *Lonsdale v. Chesterfield*, 31 Wash.App.1003 (1982). We reverse and remand to the trial court.

In 1968, Chesterfield Land, Inc. (Chesterfield) platted a portion of a development known as Sansaria on land along the Oregon coast near Coos Bay, Oregon. It then sold 81 lots to various purchasers by real estate contracts. In each sales contract Chesterfield agreed to install a water system for the use of the plat. In turn, each purchaser agreed to pay a portion of the cost of installation and to use the water system.

Chesterfield subsequently sold its vendor's interest in some of these real estate contracts to members of the petitioner class who purchased them for investment purposes. The class members paid Chesterfield money and received in return an assignment of the vendor's interest together with a deed to the land corresponding to that particular real estate contract. The deed was intended to secure payment of the outstanding balance on each real estate contract.

In 1969, Jack Chesterfield, the sole owner of Chesterfield, died. Susan Chesterfield, his widow, then sold the remaining undeveloped portion of the development to Sansaria, Inc. (Sansaria), one of the respondents in this case. As part of the consideration for the sale Sansaria assumed Chesterfield's obligation to install a water system for the entire development, including that portion already sold via the real estate contracts. Chesterfield was later dissolved and its assets distributed to Susan Chesterfield. Despite the terms of this contract, neither party installed the system. In a declaratory judgment action brought by Chesterfield against Sansaria, the Superior Court found Sansaria in default on this obligation.

In that action, the trial court found that as a result of failure of both Sansaria and Chesterfield to install the system, many of the original contract purchasers defaulted. Others defaulted for financial reasons and others continued to make the scheduled payments. Some of these purchasers brought suit in Oregon and obtained judgment against both Chesterfield and the individual investors. Thus, the vendors' interests in those contracts became worthless.

In August 1973, petitioners brought suit against Chesterfield to recover for the failure to install the water system. They also sued Sansaria claiming to be third party beneficiaries of the contract between Chesterfield and Sansaria. At the close of petitioners' case, the trial court granted respondents' motion to dismiss, holding Chesterfield's obligation to supply water did not run to petitioners and petitioners were not third party beneficiaries.

Following some procedural confusion, the nature of which is no longer material, petitioners moved to vacate and reenter judgment to allow appeal. This motion was denied on jurisdictional grounds. On appeal, the Court of Appeals reversed on the issue of vacation of judgment but proceeded to decide the case on the merits of petitioners' claim. In so doing the court held: (1) Chesterfield's obligation did run to petitioners and (2) the petitioners were third party beneficiaries of the contract between Chesterfield and Sansaria. *Lonsdale v. Chesterfield*, 19 Wash.App. 27, 573 P.2d 822 (1978).

On review, this court agreed with the Court of Appeals decision on the jurisdiction issue but reversed and remanded the issues on the merits, since respondents had not been given an opportunity to present evidence at trial. *Lonsdale v. Chesterfield*, 91 Wash.2d 189, 588 P.2d 217 (1978). On remand, the trial court reaffirmed its earlier decision. On appeal, a different panel of Division One reversed the prior holding and affirmed. We granted review to decide ...: Are petitioners third party beneficiaries of Sansaria's promise to Chesterfield to install the system? We answer ... in the affirmative.

. . .

II.   THIRD PARTY BENEFICIARIES

Whether Sansaria is liable to petitioners depends upon whether petitioners were third party beneficiaries of the contract between Sansaria and Chesterfield. This in turn depends upon whether the parties to the contract intended that Sansaria assume a direct obligation to petitioners. *Burke & Thomas, Inc. v. International Organization of Masters*, 92 Wash.2d 762, 767, 600 P.2d 1282 (1979).... In *Burke & Thomas, Inc.*, this court observed:

> The creation of a third-party beneficiary contract requires that the parties intend that the promisor assume a direct obligation to the intended beneficiary at the time they enter into the contract.

Burke & Thomas, Inc., at 767, 600 P.2d 1282. In the case of *Vikingstad v. Baggott*, 46 Wash.2d 494, 496–97, 282 P.2d 824 (1955), this court defined the intent required to create a third party beneficiary contract:

> If the terms of the contract *necessarily require the promisor to confer a benefit upon a third person*, then the contract, and hence the parties thereto, *contemplate a benefit to the third person....* The 'intent' which is a prerequisite of the beneficiary's right to sue is 'not a desire or purpose to confer a particular benefit upon him,' nor a desire to advance his interests, but an *intent that the promisor shall assume a direct obligation to him.* (Some italics ours.)

In paragraph 3 of their contract, Sansaria assumed Chesterfield's obligation to construct a water system for the entire development. As noted previously, this part of the agreement was later the subject of a declaratory judgment action brought by Chesterfield wherein Sansaria was found to be in default of its obligation to install the water system. The Court of Appeals found no third party beneficiary contract:

> In his oral opinion, the trial judge succinctly stated: "[N]othing was further from the minds of the two contracting parties than intending ... [a] benefit [to] the plaintiffs...." This is fatal to plaintiffs' claim against Sansaria, Inc.

Lonsdale v. Chesterfield, at 7.

This interpretation constitutes a misreading of *Vikingstad*. In defining intent this court further stated:

> So long as the contract necessarily and directly benefits the third person, it is immaterial that this protection was afforded ..., not as an end in itself, but for the sole purpose of securing to the promisee some consequent benefit or immunity. *In short, the motive, purpose, or desire of the parties is a quite different thing from their intention.*

(Italics ours.) *Vikingstad*, at 497, 282 P.2d 824.

We, unlike the trial court, may not examine the minds of the parties, searching for evidence of their motives or desires. Rather, we must look to the terms of the contract to determine whether performance under the contract would necessarily and directly benefit the petitioners. The fact that representatives of neither Sansaria nor Chesterfield subjectively intended to benefit the petitioners is not determinative of this issue.

Our interpretation of the meaning of intent in no way departs from the reasoning in our earlier case of *Burke & Thomas, Inc.* There, members of the public claimed standing to sue a union for breach of a collective bargaining agreement. They claimed to be third party beneficiaries of the employment agreement between the union and the public employer. We then noted: "Petitioners point to no language in the contract which indicates such an intent. Nor do they put forward any other evidence tending to show that the parties here intended any consequence other than the normal agreement to the terms and conditions of employment." *Burke & Thomas, Inc.*, 92 Wash.2d at 767–68, 600

P.2d 1282. We therefore concluded that under the facts presented, the petitioners could not be third party beneficiaries of the contract.

The petitioners in this case present quite different facts. It is not doubted that the contracting parties were motivated by something other than altruism towards the petitioners. Sansaria possibly viewed its promise to install the system merely as additional consideration for gaining ownership of the development. On the other hand, we can assume that Chesterfield only sought release from this obligation. Notwithstanding these motives, paragraph three of the contract necessarily required Sansaria, as the promisor, to confer a benefit upon petitioners. Under the terms of the contract, Sansaria could not fully perform its promise to install the water system without directly benefitting the petitioners as deeded owners of the lots. Petitioners were thus intended third party beneficiaries of the performance due under the contract.

We therefore reverse the Court of Appeals and remand to the trial court for resolution consistent with this holding.

Questions

1.   Why did Sansaria make the promise sued upon? Why did Chesterfield secure the promise sued upon? Why does the court conclude that Lonsdale, *et al.*, were intended beneficiaries?

2.   Does the court persuade you that its holding here is consistent with *Burke & Thomas*? In that case, the International Organization of Masters, Mates, and Pilots called a strike in breach of a contract with the Washington State Ferry System. The ferries ceased running to several offshore islands. Residents of the islands brought the action against the union. If the two cases are not consistent, which one was wrongly decided?

3.   What does this case suggest about the meaning of a "direct benefit" test? An "intention to benefit" test? Are they effective in drawing a justifiable distinction between third party beneficiaries with and without rights?

THE CRETEX COMPANIES, INC.
v. CONSTRUCTION
LEADERS, INC.

Supreme Court of Minnesota, 1984.
342 N.W.2d 135.

SIMONETT, JUSTICE. We conclude that unpaid materialmen, plaintiff-respondents on this appeal, are not intended third-party beneficiaries under the defaulting general contractor's performance bond and, therefore, are not entitled to recover from the defendant-appellant surety. We reverse the trial court.

Northland Mortgage Company owns property in Maple Grove and Plymouth, Minnesota. It engaged defendant Construction Leaders, Inc., as its general contractor, to do the utilities construction for the development projects on the two properties. Defendant-appellant Travelers Indemnity Company wrote the performance bonds for the construction projects. There were two construction contracts and, since the work was to be done in five phases, five performance bonds. For each performance bond Travelers was the surety, Construction Leaders, Inc., as general contractor, was the principal, and Northland Mortgage Company, as owner of the projects, was the obligee.

Thereafter, during the course of its work, Construction Leaders defaulted and is now apparently insolvent. Travelers stepped in and hired another contractor, who completed the work. Some of Construction Leader's suppliers and subcontractors, however, were left unpaid, including plaintiff-respondents, The Cretex Companies, Inc., and Ess Brothers & Sons, Inc. Although Cretex and Ess Brothers could have filed mechanic's liens against Northland's property, they failed to do so; apparently they assumed their materials were to be used by the general contractor on public projects and they did not discover otherwise until it was too late to file liens. Having lost their lien rights, Cretex and Ess Brothers brought this action against Travelers in an attempt to collect on the performance bonds. In addition, plaintiffs sued the general contractor, Construction Leaders, for breach of their subcontracts.

On cross-motions for summary judgment, the trial court granted summary judgment in favor of the plaintiff suppliers against both the surety and the general contractor on the issue of liability. The parties then stipulated to the amount of damages. Travelers alone appeals, raising only the issue whether plaintiffs are entitled to recover their unpaid claims under the performance bonds.

The issue is whether unpaid materialmen are third-party intended beneficiaries under Travelers' bonds. First of all, it should be noted that the two construction contracts between Northland (the owner) and Construction Leaders (the general contractor) plainly call for a performance rather than a payment bond. The contracts require:

> A good and sufficient *performance bond* in the sum of not less than the full amount of the Contract, payable to the Owner, as provided by law, shall be made and delivered. . . .

> The *Performance Bond* shall guarantee the Contractors: [sic] performance as required by these Contract Documents, satisfaction of all lein [sic] rights of Sub-contractors and materials suppliers. . . .

(Emphasis added.)

Pursuant to this contract requirement, Travelers, as surety, issued its "Contract Bond" with Construction Leaders as principal and Northland as obligee, providing:

> NOW, THEREFORE, the condition of this obligation is such, that if the Principal shall faithfully perform the contract on his part, free and clear of all liens arising out of claims for labor and materials entering into the construction, and indemnify and save harmless the Obligee from all loss, cost or damage which he may

suffer by reason of the failure so to do, then this obligation shall be void; otherwise to remain in full force and effect.

It seems clear enough, at least so far, that the contracting parties intended to have only a performance bond. The purpose of a performance bond is to ensure that the principal or his surety will perform the contract for an agreed price. Because performance of the work alone is not sufficient to protect the owner-obligee, the surety also agrees to indemnify the owner-obligee for any loss from liens filed against the property by reason of the contractor-principal's default in payment of his materialmen. Thus Travelers claims here that its bonds were intended for the exclusive use and benefit of its obligee, Northland, and afford no contractual rights to third-party subcontractors or suppliers.

Travelers points out that if the owner and general contractor had wished to protect third-party materialmen they could have purchased, for a separate premium, a "labor and material payment bond," a bond which Travelers also sells and which is usually issued simultaneously with the performance bond. A "payment" bond expressly provides for the surety to pay the claims of third-party subcontractors and materialmen if the general contractor fails to do so.[1] The distinction between performance bonds and payment bonds is well recognized in the construction industry; the two bonds cover different risks and premiums are set accordingly. *See, e.g., Scales–Douwes Corp. v. Paulaura Realty Corp.*, 24 N.Y.2d 724, 301 N.Y.S.2d 980, 249 N.E.2d 760 (1969); J. Calamari & J. Perillo, *Contracts* § 17–7 (2d ed. 1977); A. Corbin, *Contracts* § 798 (Supp. 1982).

Plaintiff-respondents argue, however, that though Travelers' bond may be in form a "performance" bond, intended for the protection of the owner-obligee, it is also in fact a "payment" bond, intended for the benefit of third persons who are not parties to the surety's contract. To reach this conclusion, respondents rely on the third-party contract beneficiary doctrine.

The trial court found, and Travelers does not dispute, that the provisions of the underlying construction contracts are incorporated by reference into the bonds, and apparently not just for identification purposes. Each bond identifies the construction contract between Northland and Construction Leaders and adds "a copy of which is by reference made a part hereof." Among other things, section 9 of the construction contract reads that "the Contractor shall provide and pay for all materials, labor, water, tools, equipment, light, power, transportation and other facilities necessary for the execution and completion of the work." Other sections provide that if the contractor fails to pay subcontractors or materialmen, the owner may terminate the contract or withhold payments. From this respondents argue as follows: the bond is conditioned

---

1. Thus Travelers' form of "labor and material payment bond" reads that the surety is bound to the owner-obligee "for the use and benefit of claimants as herein-below defined," and the bond then defines claimants as those having a contract with the principal to provide materials and services.

on full and faithful performance of the construction contract by the principal-general contractor; performance of the contract by the contractor includes payment by the contractor of the claims of his subcontractors and materialmen; therefore, the surety has agreed that if the contractor does not pay his suppliers, the surety will do it for him, thus making the suppliers third-party intended beneficiaries of the bond. The trial court accepted this argument, relying also on Restatement of Securities, § 165 (1940), and two cases, *Westinghouse Electric Corp. v. Mill & Elevator Co.*, 254 Iowa 874, 118 N.W.2d 528 (1962), and *Iowa Sheet Metal Contractors, Inc. v. Knab Co.*, 17 Wis.2d 493, 117 N.W.2d 682 (1962).

The parties all cite *Buchman Plumbing Co. v. Regents of the University of Minnesota*, 298 Minn. 328, 215 N.W.2d 479 (1974), as setting out the controlling test or tests for a third-party contract beneficiary. There we described two tests: first, an "intent to benefit" test, *i.e.*, the contract must express some intent by the parties to benefit the third party through contractual performance; and, second, a "duty owed" test, *i.e.*, that the promisor's performance under the contract must discharge a duty otherwise owed the third party by the promisee. Respondents contend that the "duty owed" requirement is satisfied in this case where payment of their claims by the surety would discharge a duty owed them by Northland, as owner of the project improved at their expense. We disagree. Clearly, Northland has no legal responsibility to pay the subcontractors and materialmen who made their own separate contracts with the general contractor. *Duluth Lumber & Plywood Co. v. Delta Development, Inc.*, 281 N.W.2d 377, 384 (Minn.1979). Indeed, plaintiffs seem to concede as much because they have not sued Northland. Consequently, if plaintiffs are to recover on the bonds, they must do so under the "intent to benefit" test. Travelers, however, reads *Buchman* to require that *both* the "duty owed" and the "intent to benefit" tests must be met before a third party obtains rights in the contract. Although the language in *Buchman* is somewhat opaque, we do not think this is what *Buchman* requires or says.

At this point, it may be helpful to review briefly the status of our third-party contract beneficiary law. By 1940, this court, relying on Restatement of Contracts § 133 (1932), was recognizing three kinds of third-party contract beneficiaries: creditor, donee, and incidental. In *Northern National Bank v. Northern Minnesota National Bank*, 244 Minn. 202, 209, 70 N.W.2d 118, 124 (1955), we defined, in dictum, a donee beneficiary as "one to whom the promisee intends to make a gift." In *Buchman, supra,* we observed in a footnote that the then tentative draft of the second edition of the Restatement of Contracts proposed to substitute the term "intended" beneficiary for both "creditor" and "donee" beneficiary. *Id.*, 298 Minn. at 333–34 n.2, 215 N.W.2d at 483 n.2. This proposed change was, indeed, incorporated into Restatement (Second) of Contracts in 1979 and appears at section 302. The Reporter's note explains that the new classification between "intended" and "incidental" beneficiaries eliminates the subclass of "donee beneficiary" which has proved confusing in the many instances where the promisee's purpose is not "to make a gift" but "to confer a right." In *Duluth Lumber & Plywood Co. v. Delta Development, Inc.*, 281 N.W.2d 377 (1979), we used the new "intended-incidental" analysis. There a materialman sued as a third-party beneficiary under a Housing and Urban Development contract made with the Housing Authority of the Indian reservation for construction work to be performed on the Indian reservation. Because the property was public, no liens could be filed. We found no duty owed by the owner to pay the materialman but nevertheless found that the materialman was an "intended beneficiary" under the HUD contract. For an earlier use of an "intended beneficiary" test in a setting similar to this appeal, see *Hedberg & Sons Co. v. Galvin*, 274 Minn. 422, 144 N.W.2d 263 (1966).

We hereby adopt the intended beneficiary approach outlined in Restatement (Second) of Contracts § 302 (1979). Under this approach, if recognition of third-party beneficiary rights is "appropriate" and *either* the duty owed *or* the intent to benefit test is met, the third party can recover as an "intended beneficiary." For the third party to recover, there is no need to satisfy *both* the duty owed and the intent to benefit tests, and, contrary to Travelers' contention, the language in *Buchman* does not so require. Consequently, even though respondent materialmen have failed to meet the "duty owed" test here, they may still recover if they can show an intent by the contracting parties to confer on them a benefit. We conclude, however, that the requisite intent to make subcontractors and materialmen third-party intended beneficiaries of Travelers' bonds is not shown here and that plaintiff-respondents are, at best, incidental third-party beneficiaries.

Travelers' performance bond, read alone, evidences an intent to protect and benefit only the owner-obligee. Plaintiff-respondent argues, however, that if the underlying construction contract is read as part of the bond, a further intent to confer a benefit on materialmen appears, notwithstanding that the construction contract itself expressly states that the general contractor need furnish only a performance bond. Because the contractor promises in the construction contract to "pay for all materials [and] labor," respondents contend that the surety's "guaranty" of this promise shows an intent by the parties to the bond to confer a benefit on those who have furnished the materials and labor. We do not think this conclusion necessarily follows, for while in fact the materialmen receive a benefit when paid by the surety, the issue is whether that benefit was intended by the contracting parties.

Other courts have reached differing results on whether materialmen can recover on a performance bond, the result often depending on the particular facts of the case, particularly the wording of the bond....

The contract must be read in the light of all the circumstances and it is pertinent, in ascertaining intent, to inquire to whom performance is to be rendered. *Buchman*, 298 Minn. at 334, 215 N.W.2d at 483. Here we are dealing with a contract of suretyship and, it seems to us, the fair import of this contract is that the contracting parties intended the surety's performance to be rendered to Northland, the owner-obligee, not to the materialmen. The language of the bond, quite clearly, intends to make certain (1) that the contract will be performed; (2) that the property will be "free and clear of all liens arising out of claims for labor and materials entering into the construction;" and (3) that the owner-obligee will be indemnified and saved harmless from all loss "which he may suffer by reason of the failure so to do." In other words, if the contractor-principal defaults, the surety is obligated to complete the project. If there are any liens filed, the surety is obligated to satisfy them—and the lienholders, quite plainly, would be third-party intended beneficiaries of the bond. If, finally, there are any materialmen left unpaid by the defaulting contractor who have failed to file liens, the surety need only pay these claims to the extent necessary to save the owner-obligee harmless from loss by reason of the contractor-principal's failure "so to do." These obligations the surety must perform to the amount of the bond. If unpaid, non-lienholding subcontractors can collect under the bond, the fund provided by the bond might be so depleted as to jeopardize completion of the project, which would surely be contrary to the intent of the contracting parties.

Another circumstance to be considered in ascertaining the intent of the parties is whether the suretyship contract is for a private or public construction project. There would seem to be no reason for the contracting parties to intend to confer a benefit on materialmen who can protect their own interests by filing liens against the property. In *Hedberg & Sons Co. v. Galvin*, 274 Minn. 422, 144 N.W.2d 263 (1966), the surety issued a bond to a cement contractor, guaranteeing, as required by a city ordinance licensing contractors, that the contractor would pay for any materials used by him in his construction projects "for the benefit of and to protect any person for whom such cement work shall be done." It was held that the bond was not intended for the protection of the unpaid materialmen but for the owner, for whom the "work shall be done." We stated that if unpaid materialmen wanted to be protected their recourse was to file a lien on the owner's property, whereupon the owner would have the surety bond for protection. We think these same considerations are relevant here. . . .

While we acknowledge that third-party recovery is warranted in cases where the surety bond explicitly or by reasonable implication expresses an intent to benefit third-party subcontractors and material-men, we do not believe an "intent to benefit" third parties should be imputed to a surety on the basis of a private construction contract to which that surety was not a party, when the language of the surety's bond, though incorporating the construction contract by reference, evinces no more than an incidental intent to benefit those third parties. We hold that plaintiff-respondents, as unpaid subcontractors and material-men, are not third-party intended beneficiaries of Travelers' surety bonds covering performance of this private construction project.

Reversed.

YETKA, JUSTICE (dissenting). Travelers' bond obligates it "faithfully [to] perform the contract." The majority unnecessarily restricts this language when it holds that the surety is only obligated to "complete the project." Here, the Travelers' bond incorporated portions of the general contract between Northland and Construction Leaders. Section 9 of that contract contained language, as the majority acknowledges, which read as follows: "The Contractor shall provide and pay for all materials, labor, water, tools, equipment, light, power, transportation and other facilities necessary for the execution and completion of the work." Under this language, the contract is not "performed" until all materials provided thereunder are paid for.

Construction jobs are not negotiated in a vacuum. Almost all of the parties, including subcontractors, are experienced people and are aware of the conditions of the general contract. If Travelers wanted to limit their obligation under the bond to completion of the project only, it should have clearly stated so. It did not; therefore, in my opinion, the subcontractors had a right to rely on the conditions of the general contract as guaranteed by the bond.

I would affirm the trial court.

Questions

1. What is a performance bond? What is a payment bond? What is the legal issue in the *Cretex Companies* case? Why was there no "intent to benefit" here?

2. Do you read RESTATEMENT (SECOND) OF CONTRACTS § 302 as the majority does? Why does the majority reject the dissenting view? Which is the stronger opinion? Why?

3. Was the result unjust? In Minnesota after this case, what would you advise a materialman to do to protect his or her interest in similar circumstances?

4. *Problem.*

On the facts of *Cretex Companies*, could the subcontractors recover restitution from the owners?

RESTATEMENT (SECOND) OF CONTRACTS § 313

MARTINEZ v. SOCOMA COMPANIES, INC.

Supreme Court of California, In Bank, 1974.
11 Cal.3d 394, 113 Cal.Rptr. 585, 521 P.2d 841.

WRIGHT, CHIEF JUSTICE. Plaintiffs brought this class action on behalf of themselves and other disadvantaged unemployed persons, alleging that defendants failed to perform contracts with the United States Government under which defendants agreed to provide job training and at least one year of employment to certain numbers of such persons. Plaintiffs claim that they and the other such persons are third party beneficiaries of the contracts and as such are entitled to damages for defendants' nonperformance. General demurrers to the complaint were sustained without leave to amend, apparently on the ground that plaintiffs lacked standing to sue as third party beneficiaries. Dismissals were entered as to the demurring defendants, and plaintiffs appeal.

We affirm the judgments of dismissal. As will appear, the contracts nowhere state that either the government or defendants are to be liable to persons such as plaintiffs for damages resulting from the defendants' nonperformance. The benefits to be derived from defendants' performance were clearly intended not as gifts from the government to such persons but as a means of executing the public purposes stated in the contracts and in the underlying legislation. Accordingly, plaintiffs were only incidental beneficiaries and as such have no right of recovery.

The complaint names as defendants Socoma Companies, Inc. ("Socoma"), Lady Fair Kitchens, Incorporated ("Lady Fair"), Monarch Electronics International, Inc. ("Monarch"), and eleven individuals of whom three are alleged officers or directors of Socoma, four of Lady Fair, and four of Monarch. Lady Fair and the individual defendants associated with it, a Utah corporation and Utah residents respectively, did not appear in the trial court and are not parties to this appeal.

The complaint alleges that under 1967 amendments to the Economic Opportunity Act of 1964 (81 Stat. 688–690, 42 U.S.C. §§ 2763–2768, repealed by 86 Stat. 703 (1972)), "the United States Congress instituted Special Impact Programs with the intent to benefit the residents of certain neighborhoods having especially large concentrations of low income persons and suffering from dependency, chronic unemployment and rising tensions." Funds to administer these programs were appropriated to the United States Department of Labor. The department subsequently designated the East Los Angeles neighborhood as a "Special Impact area" and made federal funds available for contracts with local private industry for the benefit of the "hard-core unemployed residents" of East Los Angeles.

On January 17, 1969, the corporate defendants allegedly entered into contracts with the Secretary of Labor, acting on behalf of the Manpower Administration, United States Department of Labor (hereinafter referred to as the "Government"). Each such defendant entered into a separate contract and all three contracts are made a part of the complaint as exhibits. Under each contract the contracting defendant agreed to lease space in the then vacant Lincoln Heights jail building owned by the City of Los Angeles, to invest at least $5,000,000 in renovating the leasehold and establishing a facility for the manufacture of certain articles, to train and employ in such facility for at least 12 months, at minimum wage rates, a specified number of East Los Angeles residents certified as disadvantaged by the Government, and to provide such employees with opportunities for promotion into available supervisorial-managerial positions and with options to purchase stock in their employer corporation. Each contract provided for the lease of different space in the building and for the manufacture of a different kind of product. As consideration, the Government agreed to pay each defendant a stated amount in installments. Socoma was to hire 650 persons and receive $950,000; Lady Fair was to hire 550 persons and receive $999,000; and Monarch was to hire 400 persons and receive $800,000. The hiring of these persons was to be completed by January 17, 1970.

Plaintiffs were allegedly members of a class of no more than 2,017 East Los Angeles residents who were certified as disadvantaged and were qualified for employment under the contracts. Although the Government paid $712,500 of the contractual consideration to Socoma, $299,700 to Lady Fair, and $240,000 to Monarch, all of these defendants failed to perform under their respective contracts, except that Socoma provided 186 jobs of which 139 were wrongfully terminated, and Lady Fair provided 90 jobs, of which all were wrongfully terminated.

The complaint contains 11 causes of action.... Each cause of action alleges that the "express purpose of the [Government] in entering into [each] contract was to benefit [the] certified disadvantaged hard-core unemployed residents of East Los Angeles [for whom defendants promised to provide training and jobs] and none other, and those residents are thus the express third party beneficiaries of [each] contract."

The general demurrers admitted the truth of all the material factual allegations of the complaint, regardless of any possible difficulty in proving them (Alcorn v. Anbro Engineering, Inc. (1970) 2 Cal.3d 493, 496, 86 Cal.Rptr. 88, 468 P.2d 216).... Thus, we must determine whether the pleaded written contracts support plaintiffs' claim either on their face or under any interpretation to which the contracts are reasonably susceptible and which is pleaded in the complaint or could be pleaded by proper amendment. This determination must be made in light of applicable federal statutes and other matters we must judicially notice. (Evid. Code, §§ 451, 459, subd. (a).)

Plaintiffs contend they are third party beneficiaries under Civil Code section 1559, which provides: "A contract, made expressly for the benefit of a third person, may be enforced by him at any time before the parties thereto rescind it." This section excludes enforcement of a contract by persons who are only incidentally or remotely benefited by it. (Lucas v. Hamm (1961) 56 Cal.2d 583, 590, 15 Cal.Rptr. 821, 364 P.2d 685.) American law generally classifies persons having enforceable rights under contracts to which they are not parties as either creditor beneficiaries or donee beneficiaries.... California decisions follow this classification. (Southern Cal. Gas Co. v. ABC Construction Co. (1962) 204

Cal.App.2d 747, 752, 22 Cal.Rptr. 540; 1 Witkin, Summary of Cal. Law (8th ed. 1973) Contracts, § 500.)

A person cannot be a creditor beneficiary unless the promisor's performance of the contract will discharge some form of legal duty owed to the beneficiary by the promisee. (Hartman Ranch Co. v. Associated Oil Co. (1937) 10 Cal.2d 232, 244, 73 P.2d 1163; Rest., Contracts, § 133, subd. (1)(b).) Clearly the Government (the promisee) at no time bore any legal duty toward plaintiffs to provide the benefits set forth in the contracts and plaintiffs do not claim to be creditor beneficiaries.

A person is a donee beneficiary only if the promisee's contractual intent is either to make a gift to him or to confer on him a right against the promisor. (Rest., Contracts, § 133, subd. (1)(a).) If the promisee intends to make a gift, the donee beneficiary can recover if such donative intent must have been understood by the promisor from the nature of the contract and the circumstances accompanying its execution. (Lucas v. Hamm, supra, 56 Cal.2d at pp. 590–591, 15 Cal.Rptr. 821, 364 P.2d 685.) This rule does not aid plaintiffs, however, because, as will be seen, no intention to make a gift can be imputed to the Government as promisee.

Unquestionably plaintiffs were among those whom the Government intended to benefit through defendants' performance of the contracts which recite that they are executed pursuant to a statute and a presidential directive calling for programs to furnish disadvantaged persons with training and employment opportunities. However, the fact that a Government program for social betterment confers benefits upon individuals who are not required to render contractual consideration in return does not necessarily imply that the benefits are intended as gifts. Congress' power to spend money in aid of the general welfare (U.S. Const., art. I, § 8) authorizes federal programs to alleviate national unemployment. (Helvering v. Davis (1937) 301 U.S. 619, 640–645, 57 S.Ct. 904, 81 L.Ed. 1307, 1314–1317, 109 A.L.R. 1319.) The benefits of such programs are provided not simply as gifts to the recipients but as a means of accomplishing a larger public purpose. The furtherance of the public purpose is in the nature of consideration to the Government, displacing any governmental intent to furnish the benefits as gifts. . . .

Even though a person is not the intended recipient of a gift, he may nevertheless be "a donee beneficiary if it appears from the terms of the promise in view of the accompanying circumstances that the purpose of the promisee in obtaining the promise . . . is . . . to *confer upon him a right against the promisor* to some performance neither due nor supposed or asserted to be due from the promisee to the beneficiary." (Rest., Contracts, § 133, subd. (1)(a) (italics supplied)). . . . The Government may, of course, deliberately implement a public purpose by including provisions in its contracts which expressly confer on a specified class of third persons a direct right to benefits, or damages in lieu of benefits, against the private contractor. But a governmental intent to confer such a direct right cannot be inferred simply from the fact that the third persons were intended to enjoy the benefits. The Restatement of Contracts makes this clear in dealing specifically with contractual promises of the Government to render services to members of the public: "A promisor bound to the United States or to a State or municipality by contract to do an act or render a service to some or all of the members of the public, *is subject to no duty* under the contract to such members to give compensation for the injurious consequences of performing or attempting to perform it, or of failing to do so, unless, . . . *an intention is manifested in the contract*, as interpreted in the light of the circumstances surrounding its formation, *that the promisor shall compensate members of the public for such injurious consequences.* . . ." (Rest., Contracts, § 145 (italics supplied); see City & County of San Francisco v. Western Air Lines, Inc. (1962) 204 Cal.App.2d 105, 121, 22 Cal.Rptr. 216.) . . .

The present contracts manifest no intent that the defendants pay damages to compensate plaintiffs or other members of the public for their nonperformance. To the contrary, the contracts' provisions for retaining the Government's control over determination of contractual disputes and for limiting defendants' financial risks indicate a governmental purpose to exclude the direct rights against defendants claimed here.

Each contract provides that any dispute of fact arising thereunder is to be determined by written decision of the Government's contracting officer, subject to an appeal to the Secretary of Labor, whose decision shall be final unless determined by a competent court to have been fraudulent, capricious, arbitrary, in bad faith, or not supported by substantial evidence. These administrative decisions may include determinations of related questions of law although such determinations are not made final. The efficiency and uniformity of interpretation fostered by these administrative procedures would tend to be undermined if litigation such as the present action, to which the Government is a stranger, were permitted to proceed on the merits.

In addition to the provisions on resolving disputes each contract contains a "liquidated damages" provision obligating the contractor to refund all amounts received from the Government, with interest, in the event of failure to acquire and equip the specified manufacturing facility, and, for each employment opportunity it fails to provide, to refund a stated dollar amount equivalent to the total contract compensation divided by the number of jobs agreed to be provided. This liquidated damages provision limits liability for the breaches alleged by plaintiffs to the refunding of amounts received and indicates an absence of any contractual intent to impose liability directly in favor of plaintiffs, or, as claimed in the complaint, to impose liability for the value of the promised performance. To allow plaintiffs' claim would nullify the limited liability for which defendants bargained and which the Government may well have held out as an inducement in negotiating the contracts. . . .

In providing for special impact programs, Congress declared that such programs were directed to the solution of critical problems existing in particular neighborhoods having especially large concentrations of low-income persons, and that the programs were intended to be of sufficient size and scope to have an appreciable impact in such neighborhoods in arresting tendencies toward dependency, chronic unemployment and rising community tensions. (41 U.S.C. former § 2763.) Thus the contracts here were designed not to benefit individuals as such but to utilize the training and employment of disadvantaged persons as a means of improving the East Los Angeles neighborhood. Moreover, the means by which the contracts were intended to accomplish this community improvement were not confined to provision of the particular benefits on which plaintiffs base their claim to damages—one year's employment at minimum wages plus $1,000 worth of training to be provided to each of 650 persons by one defendant, 400 by another, and 550 by another. Rather the objective was to be achieved by establishing permanent industries in which local residents would be permanently employed and would have opportunities to become supervisors, managers and part owners. The required minimum capital investment of $5,000,000 by each defendant and the defendants' 22–year lease of the former Lincoln Heights jail building for conversion into an industrial facility also indicates the broad, long-range objective of the program. Presumably, as the planned enterprises prospered, the quantity and quality of employment and economic opportunity that they provided would increase and would benefit not only employees but also their families, other local enterprises and the government itself through reduction of law enforcement and welfare costs. . . .

For the reasons above stated we hold that plaintiffs and the class they represent have no standing as third party beneficiaries to recover the damages sought in the complaint under either California law or the general contract principles which federal law applies to government contracts.[10]

The judgments of dismissal are affirmed.

BURKE, JUSTICE (dissenting). I dissent. The certified hard-core unemployed of East Los Angeles were the express, not incidental, beneficiaries of the contracts in question and, therefore, have standing to enforce those contracts.

10. In the absence of controlling provisions in the federal Constitution, statutes or regulations, the United States government's rights and obligations under its contracts are ordinarily construed according to general contract law rather than the law of any particular state. (Priebe & Sons v. United States (1947) 332 U.S. 407, 411, 68 S.Ct. 123, 92 L.Ed. 32, 38; Clearfield Trust Co. v. U.S. (1943) 318 U.S. 363 [87 L.Ed. 838, 63 S.Ct. 573].) In disputes between private parties over conflicting claims stemming from United States government contracts, the applicability of federal law to particular issues is generally held to depend on the degree to which the outcome will affect the government's interests. (Bank of America v. Parnell (1956) 352 U.S. 29, 77 S.Ct. 119, 1 L.Ed.2d 93 . . . .) In view of our holding it is unnecessary for us to decide whether or to what extent federal law applies in the present case.

As the majority point out, we must reverse the order sustaining the demurrer in this case if we determine the written contracts incorporated into the complaint support plaintiffs' claim either on their face or under any interpretation to which the contracts are reasonably susceptible. (maj. opn., p. 588) Furthermore, at this stage of the proceedings, the question of plaintiffs' ability to prove these allegations does not concern us, for plaintiffs need only plead facts showing they may be entitled to some relief. (Alcorn v. Anbro Engineering, Inc., 2 Cal.3d 493, 496, 86 Cal.Rptr. 88, 468 P.2d 216). . . .

The majority contend that the congressional purpose in enacting the Economic Opportunity Act of 1964 (including the subsequent amendments thereto creating the Special Impact Program), and the government's purpose in executing the instant contracts with defendants pursuant to the act, was to benefit only the general public and particularly the local neighborhoods where these programs were to be implemented. Although members of plaintiffs' class "were among those whom the Government intended to benefit . . .," (maj. opn. p. 589) the benefits accruing to plaintiffs' class, according to the majority, were merely "*means* of executing the public purposes stated in the contracts and in the underlying legislation." (p. 587, italics added.)

The majority err in the above conclusion because the congressional purpose was to benefit *both* the communities in which the impact programs are established and the individual impoverished persons in such communities.[1] The benefits from the instant contracts were to accrue directly to the members of plaintiffs' class, as a reading of the contracts clearly demonstrates.[2] These direct benefits to members of plaintiffs' class were not merely the "*means* of executing the public purposes" as the majority contend . . ., but were the *ends* in themselves and one of the public purposes to which the legislation and subsequent contracts were addressed. Accordingly, I cannot agree with the majority that "the contracts here were designed *not* to benefit individuals as such but to utilize the training and employment of disadvantaged persons as a *means* of improving the East Los Angeles neighborhood." (pp. 542, 543, italics added.)

---

1. Evidence of Congress' purpose to aid the *individual* impoverished persons in such communities can be gleaned from 42 United States Code Annotated section § 2701, wherein Congress declared that if our country is to achieve its full potential, "every individual" must be given "the opportunity for education and training, the opportunity to work, and the opportunity to live in decency and dignity." Congress implemented this general policy of assisting our impoverished citizens in various ways, including the Special Impact Program involved in this case. Yet, contrary to the majority, nothing indicates that Congress' *exclusive* purpose in doing so was to assist the neighborhoods and communities in which these persons live. It seems clear that Congress intended *both* the communities and the individuals to be direct beneficiaries of the program. It is incorrect to label one as an intended *direct* beneficiary and the other as merely *incidental*.

2. In the contracts, the defendants agreed to provide training and jobs to a specified class of persons, whom plaintiffs represent. The government's express intent, therefore, was to confer a benefit, namely training and jobs, upon an ascertainable identifiable class and not simply the general public itself.

The intent of the contracts themselves is expressed in their preambles: "WHEREAS, the Secretary of Labor is authorized ... to enter into contracts to provide for Special Impact Programs ... directed to the solution of the critical problems existing in particular communities and neighborhoods within urban areas of the Nation having especially large concentrations of low-income persons; and [¶] WHEREAS, the President of the United States on October 2, 1967, launched a major test program to mobilize the resources of private industry and the Federal Government *to help find jobs and provide training for thousands of the Nation's hardcore unemployed, or underemployed,* by inviting private industry throughout the country to join with the agencies and departments of the Federal Government in assuming responsibility *for providing training and work opportunities for such seriously disadvantaged persons.* [¶] NOW THEREFORE, pursuant to the aforesaid statutory authority, and the directive of the President, the parties hereto, in consideration of the mutual promises herein expressed, agree as follows...." (Italics added.) By these provisions, the contracting parties clearly state as one of their purposes their intent to find jobs for the hard-core unemployed....

Although the contracts may also benefit particular communities and neighborhoods, this fact does not preclude the maintenance of the action by plaintiffs as intended beneficiaries of the contracts. It is not necessary under Civil Code section 1559, *supra,* that a contract be exclusively for the benefit of a third party to give him a right to enforce its provisions. (Hartman Ranch Co. v. Associated Oil Co., 10 Cal.2d 232, 247, 73 P.2d 1163....) ... All that is necessary is that the third party show he is a member of a class for whose benefit the contract was made. (Shell v. Schmidt, *supra*; Ralph C. Sutro Co. v. Paramount, *supra*.) Thus, plaintiffs have standing to bring an action for the breach of defendants' contracts with the government....

Questions

1. State the applicable law in *Martinez.*

2. Why does the majority refuse to recognize contract rights held by the hard-core unemployed of East Lost Angeles? Does the statute require a contrary result?

3. Does it make sense, as the majority urges, to hold the unemployed to be incidental beneficiaries because they were a means to a social end? Is there a better argument to support the majority's conclusion?

4. *Problems.*

a. Assume that the facts are as in *Martinez,* except that the federal statute did not contain exclusive dispute settlement procedures or a liquidated damages clause. Would the result be the same under the court's opinion? Under the RESTATEMENT (SECOND) OF CONTRACTS?

b. Tenant had an apartment building that was financed with a federally insured mortgage in excess of $5,000,000 under the National Housing Act. That Act of Congress puts a ceiling on rents that Landlord may charge to tenants in buildings built with federal assistance under the Act. Landlord exceeded the ceiling. Under *Martinez,* should Tenant have standing to sue as a third party to the contract between Landlord and the United States Government? See *Zigas v. Superior Court,* 120 Cal.App.3d 827, 174 Cal.Rptr. 806 (1981).

RESTATEMENT (SECOND) OF CONTRACTS §§ 309, 311

ROUSE v. UNITED STATES

United States Court of Appeals, District of Columbia Circuit, 1954.
94 U.S.App.D.C. 386, 215 F.2d 872.

EDGERTON, CIRCUIT JUDGE. Bessie Winston gave Associated Contractors, Inc., her promissory note for $1,008.37, payable in monthly installments of $28.01, for a heating plant in her house. The Federal Housing Administration guaranteed the note and the payee endorsed it for value to the lending bank, the Union Trust Company.

Winston sold the house to Rouse. In the contract of sale Rouse agreed to assume debts secured by deeds of trust and also 'to assume payment of $850 for heating plant payable $28 per Mo.' Nothing was said about the note.

Winston defaulted on her note. The United States paid the bank, took an assignment of the note, demanded payment from Rouse, and sued him for $850 and interest.

Rouse alleged as defenses (1) that Winston fraudulently misrepresented the condition of the heating plant and (2) that Associated Contractors did not install it satisfactorily. The District Court struck these defenses and granted summary judgment for the plaintiff. The defendant Rouse appeals.

Since Rouse did not sign the note he is not liable on it. D.C. Code 1951, Sec. 28–119; N.I.L. Sec. 18. He is not liable to the United States at all unless his contract with Winston makes him so. The contract says the parties to it are not 'bound by any terms, conditions, statements, warranties or representation, oral or written' not contained in it. But this means only that the written contract contains the entire agreement. It does not mean that fraud cannot be set up a defense to a suit on the contract. Rouse's promise to 'assume payment of $850 for heating plant' made him liable to Associated Contractors, Inc., only if and so far as it made him liable to Winston; one who promises to make a payment to the promisee's creditor can assert against the creditor any defense that the promisor could assert against the promisee. Accordingly Rouse, if he had been sued by the corporation, would have been entitled to show fraud on the part of Winston. He is equally entitled to do so in this suit by an assignee of the corporation's claim. It follows that the court erred in striking the first defense. We do not consider whether Winston's alleged fraud, if shown, would be a complete or only a partial defense to this suit, since that question has not arisen and may not arise.

We think the court has right in striking the second defense. 'If the promisor's agreement is to be interpreted as a promise to discharge whatever liability the promisee is under, the promisor must certainly be allowed to show that the promisee was under no enforceable liability.... On the other hand, if the promise means that the promisor agrees to pay a sum of money to A, to whom the promisee says he is indebted, it is immaterial whether the promisee is actually indebted to that amount or at all.... Where the promise is to pay a specific debt ... this interpretation will generally be the true one.' [3 Williston, Contracts § 399 (Rev. ed. 1936).]

The judgment is reversed and the cause remanded with instructions to reinstate the first defense.

Questions

1.   Why could Rouse raise the first defense but not the second?

2.   Assuming that there was no fraud by Winston, is it just for Rouse to be left to pay for a faulty furnace? Should the law be different, assuming that all relevant facts are given in the opinion?

3.   Should Rouse have rights as a third party beneficiary to the contract between Associated Contractors and Winston? See U.C.C. § 2–318.

UNITED STATES v. WOOD

United States Court of Appeals, Sixth Circuit, 1989.
877 F.2d 453.

JONES, CIRCUIT JUDGE. Defendant-appellant Jane Wood appeals from the district court's order granting summary judgment in favor of plaintiff-appellee United States, 658 F.Supp. 1561. The district court held that, since the Government was a third-party beneficiary to a property settlement between Ms. Wood and her then-husband, it therefore was entitled to judgment against Wood for breaching her promise to apply the proceeds of the sale of her marital residence to a federal tax lien against her former husband. For the reasons that follow, we affirm the judgment of the district court....

[On March 30, 1984, the Woods executed a property settlement agreement (the Agreement) in contemplation of their impending divorce. It required Mr. Wood to convey their residence, "Berry Hill," to Ms. Wood, who promised to sell the property and pay Mr. Wood's taxes from the proceeds. Further, the agreement stipulated that upon selling the property, Ms. Wood would be entitled to any sale proceeds remaining after the existing encumbrances were paid off. Those encumbrances included a mortgage to the Bank of Louisville and a federal tax lien stemming from Mr. Wood's underpayment of taxes for the tax years 1980 through 1983. Shortly after the execution of the agreement, Mr. Wood informed IRS Officer Roy Wyatt of the terms of the property settlement. The IRS accepted Mr. Wood's representation regarding Ms. Wood's obligations under the Agreement.

[On July 9, 1984, the bank obtained a judgment ordering the sale of Berry Hill in order to satisfy the Woods' mortgage obligations. On the same date, Mr. Wood conveyed Berry Hill to Ms. Wood. Berry Hill was sold at a public auction on August 21, 1984. Because the sale price was less than two-thirds of Berry Hill's appraised value, the sale created a right of redemption under Ky. Rev. Stat. ("KRS") § 426.530(1): "If real property sold in pursuance of a judgment or order of a court, other than an execution, does not bring two-thirds of its appraised value, the defendant and his representatives may redeem it within a year from the day of sale, by paying the original purchase money and ten percent per annum interest thereon. . . ."

[The Woods executed an addendum ("Addendum") to the Agreement on December 10, 1984. The Addendum provided that Mr. Wood would quitclaim his right of redemption arising out of the judicial sale and waive his interest in any proceeds realized upon Ms. Wood's sale of that property. Thereafter, on February 12, 1985, Ms. Wood, having exercised the right of redemption, contracted to sell Berry Hill for the sum of $575,000.

[On April 19, 1985, the Government served Ms. Wood with a Notice of Levy on all property and rights to property which belonged to her husband and which were then in her possession, and demanded payment of his tax liabilities. In August of 1985, the Government initiated this action against the Woods. The district court entered its final judgment on May 7, 1987, holding, *inter alia,* that the Government was a direct creditor beneficiary of the property settlement agreement and ordered judgment against Ms. Wood for $126,471.01 plus interest. Although Ms. Wood moved to alter or amend that portion of the judgment adverse to her and to stay execution of the judgment, the district court denied both post judgment motions. She then filed this timely appeal.]

Wood's . . . claim is that the district court erred in determining that the Government was an intended third party beneficiary of the March 1984 property settlement agreement, rather than an incidental beneficiary of that Agreement. She argues that the Government cannot maintain an action for breach of the Agreement because the language contained therein provided no express indication that it was intended to benefit the Government. Wood further claims that the express purpose of the Agreement was not to benefit the Government, but rather to effect an amiable adjustment and settlement of certain property rights, in light of her impending divorce. Relying on the December 1984 Addendum to the Agreement, wherein Mr. Wood waived any and all rights he had to the subsequent sale of Berry Hill, Ms. Wood asserts that the Agreement did not obligate her as a promisor to Mr. Wood's tax liability.

Under Kentucky law, which we must apply to this question of contract interpretation, "all that is necessary for an enforceable contract for the benefit of a third party 'is that there be consideration for the agreement flowing to the promisor and that the promisee intends to extract a promise directly benefiting the third party.' " *Simpson v. JOC Coal, Inc.*, 677 S.W.2d 305, 309 (Ky.1984). Thus, *Simpson* provides that the central issue in determining whether the contract was intended to benefit a third party is the relevant intent of the promisee who purchases the promise from the promisor....

In the instant case, the Agreement contains the two requirements noted in *Simpson*: (1) consideration flowing to the promisor, and (2) intent of the promisee to exact a promise directly benefitting the third party. *Simpson*, 677 S.W.2d at 309. Under the Agreement, Ms. Wood promised to distribute the sales proceeds of Berry Hill in payment of a federal tax lien against the assets of Mr. Wood in the amount of $126,471.01 with interest thereon. In consideration for this promise, Mr. Wood conveyed Berry Hill and the three adjacent parcels of land to Ms. Wood, who was to retain the sales proceeds after the payment of the tax lien and mortgages. Moreover, the relevant intent of the promisee, Mr. Wood, is reflected by the terms of the Agreement which provided that "the parties agree that the property shall be sold ... and the net proceeds thereof shall be distributed as received as follows ... a federal tax lien existing against the assets of the husband in the amount of $126,471.01 with interest thereon shall be paid in full." J. App. at 83. Finally, Mr. Wood's intent to exact Ms. Wood's promise for the direct benefit of the Government is evidenced by his prompt notification to IRS of the terms of the property settlement, as well as the uncontradicted affidavit of IRS Revenue Officer, Roy Wyatt, who stated that Mr. Wood "repeatedly assured the Government that the provision in [the Agreement] for payment of the tax lien from Ms. Wood's sale proceeds survived the judicial sale." *Id.* at 33. Given this evidence, we find that the Government was a creditor beneficiary under the Agreement and was entitled to enforce Ms. Wood's promise to pay her husband's tax liability under the Agreement....

The district court held that the Government's right to receive $126,471.01 from the sale of Berry Hill survived an attempt by the Woods to rescind it. Under Kentucky law, when the right to alter, amend or rescind the contract is specifically provided or reserved therein, it may be rescinded without liability to a third party beneficiary. *See Rhodes v. Rhodes*, 266 S.W.2d 790, 792 (Ky.1953). Should an agreement not contain an express reservation, then the parties to the contract cannot rescind the contract without the third party's consent after he has accepted, adopted or relied upon the contract. *Id.* Ms. Wood argues, however, that the district court erred in its application of Kentucky law because, despite *Rhodes*, in the case of a creditor beneficiary, a contract for the benefit of the creditor can be rescinded anytime before the creditor changes his position in reliance on the contract. Finally, Ms.

Wood claims that *Rhodes* does not fully reflect applicable Kentucky law regarding modification of third party beneficiary contracts.

Although the instant Agreement did not reserve a right of rescission, on December 10, 1984 the Woods executed an Addendum to the Agreement. The Addendum provided that Mr. Wood would quitclaim to Ms. Wood his right of redemption arising out of the judicial sale of Berry Hill, and waive any future interest to any proceeds from a subsequent sale of that property. At the district court level, Ms. Wood argued that the Addendum rescinded her obligation to satisfy Mr. Wood's tax liens. Based on the uncontradicted affidavit of IRS officer Roy Wyatt, however, the district court properly held that the Government accepted Mr. Wood's representation regarding his wife's continuing obligations under the Agreement prior to the execution of the Addendum. The district court concluded that since there was no right of rescission reserved in the Agreement, since the Government was never advised of the Addendum, and since the Government accepted Mr. Wood's representation regarding its right as a third party creditor beneficiary before execution of the Addendum, the Government's right to receive payment from the sale of Berry Hill survived the Woods' attempt to rescind it.

Ms. Wood claims that *Rhodes* was not fully applicable in this case because the Addendum was executed before the Government changed its position in reliance upon the Agreement. Consequently, she contends that the Addendum effectively rescinded her obligation to pay Mr. Wood's tax liens for 1980 and 1981. In examining the record, we find that the Government changed its position in reliance upon Mr. Wood's statements regarding Ms. Wood's obligations under the Agreement. Since these statements were made before the Addendum was executed, the Government's reliance occurred prior to the attempted rescission. We base our conclusion on the terms of paragraph 1(a) of the Agreement, and the representations made by Mr. Wood to the IRS concerning payment of the liens by Ms. Wood after the sale of Berry Hill. In addition, even though Kentucky characterizes direct third party beneficiaries as either "donee" or "creditor" beneficiaries, *King v. National Industries, Inc.*, 512 F.2d at 32–33, there is no distinction between donee and creditor beneficiaries for purposes of rescinding a third party benefit. In both instances the power to rescind a contract made for the benefit of a third party terminates upon the third party's acceptance. *Jones v. Higgins*, 80 Ky. 409, 413 (1882) (creditor beneficiary "agreement may be cancelled by the act of the parties making it before acceptance by the party for whose benefit it was made"). . . .

Finally, Ms. Wood argues that *Rhodes* is not fully applicable to this case because there is a split in authority concerning whether a third party beneficiary right becomes vested by merely accepting the contract, or whether the beneficiary must establish some reliance on the contract. *Compare* Restatement (First) of Contracts § 143 (1932) *with* Restatement (Second) of Contracts § 311 (1981). Wood argues that the position of the original Restatement, that the creditor's reliance is necessary to negate the power of the promisee to rescind her promise, will probably be adopted by the Kentucky Supreme Court, and that *Rhodes* is therefore the incorrect rule. We reject this latter argument because the position of the Second Restatement, stating that creditors' rights vest upon their learning of the contract and assenting to it, represents the majority view among the states, *see, e.g., Detroit Bank & Trust v. Chicago Flame Hardening*, 541 F.Supp. 1278, 1283 (N.D.Ind.1982), and because Kentucky law appears to be consistent with this position. *Jones*, 80 Ky. at 413.... For these reasons, we conclude that there was no rescission of the Government's right to receive the benefit promised it under the Agreement....

Questions

1. What are Ms. Wood's defenses to the government's claim as a third party beneficiary to the property settlement agreement?

2. What is the basis for the court's finding that the government changed its position in reliance upon Mr. Wood's statements regarding Ms. Wood's obligations under the agreement? Can you imagine how the government might have relied? Why does it matter?

3. *Problems.*

a. Larry conveyed land to Moe, who assumed and agreed to pay to Bank a debt owed by Larry that was secured by a mortgage on the land. Before Bank learned of the contract, Moe sold it to Curly, who assumed and agreed to pay the debt. At the time of the transaction between Moe and Curly, Larry sent a letter to Moe releasing him from his promise to pay Bank, effective upon Curly's assumption of the duty to pay. Does the Bank have any rights against Moe?

b. Larry conveyed land to Moe, who took the title "subject to" Bank's interest in the land. Before Bank learned of the contract, Moe sold it to Curly, who "assumed" Larry's obligation to pay the mortgage. Does Bank have any rights against Curly? *Compare* Ward v. De Oca, 120 Cal. 102, 52 P. 130 (1898) *with* Schneider v. Ferrigno, 110 Conn. 86, 147 A. 303 (1929).

SECTION 2. ASSIGNMENT AND DELEGATION

In this final section, we introduce two topics involving third parties—assignments of contract rights and delegations of contract duties. These topics will involve one policy in addition to the principles of contract law with which you are now familiar. An assignment is the present transfer of a contract right from one person to another. Unlike a contract, it is an executed rather than an executory transaction. It is therefore more akin to a conveyance of real property or a sale of goods, by contrast with a contract proper. Because the transferability of property (here, intangible property) tends to have considerable economic benefits, a policy of free alienability informs the statutory and case law. However, principles of autonomy and contractual security shape the law here, too.

Free alienability might be related to the general principles of contract law in two ways. Courts could *balance* the policy of free alienability against the principles of autonomy and security. Alternatively, they could *order the priority* of the policy and principles, as by supporting free alienability only when there is no material impairment of the autonomy and security of the contract parties. Consider, as you read the following cases, how free alienability works into the law of contracts. (Note that analysis of the following problems and cases requires especially close attention to the relevant parts of the U.C.C. and the RESTATEMENT (SECOND) OF CONTRACTS.)

————

RESTATEMENT (SECOND) OF CONTRACTS §§ 317, 332

————

Problems

a. Claudette promises Alain that she will give him $100 when David repays $100 to Claudette. Does Alain have a right to $100 from David by assignment from Claudette?

b. Claudette says to Alain "I assign you my car." Does Alain have a right to the car by assignment from Claudette?

c. David promises to give Claudette $100 on her birthday. Claudette owes Alain $100 and says to him, "I assign you the $100 I will get from David on my birthday." Does Alain have a right to $100 from David by assignment from Claudette?

d. Claudette says to Alain: "I assign you the $600 David owes me if you promise to deliver 100 bu. soy beans to me next week." Alain promises. Does Alain have a right to $600 from David by assignment from Claudette?

ADAMS v. MERCED STONE CO.

Supreme Court of California, 1917.
176 Cal. 415, 178 P. 498.

SHAW, JUDGE. The plaintiff appeals from a judgment in favor of the defendant, and from an order denying his motion for a new trial.

The complaint states a cause of action against the defendant, in favor of the decedent, Thomas Prather, upon an indebtedness alleged to be the sum of $112,965.84. The defendant in its answer denied the existence of any indebtedness from it to said Thomas Prather at the time of his death, and on information and belief alleged that prior to his death said Thomas Prather made a gift of said indebtedness, due from the plaintiff to Thomas Prather, to one Samuel D. Prather, and that said Samuel then became and ever since has been the owner of said indebtedness.

The court found that during the last sickness of Thomas Prather, to wit, on April 17, 1913, said Thomas Prather made a gift to his brother Samuel D. Prather, of all of the indebtedness due from the defendant to said Thomas, being the indebtedness sued for by the plaintiff herein. That at that time Samuel was the president, the general manager, and a member of the board of directors of the defendant, said defendant being a corporation, and Thomas Prather knew that Samuel held said offices and by reason thereof of had full and exclusive charge and control of defendant's books of account, including power to make or direct the making of entries and transfers in said books, and knew that by reason thereof Samuel D. Prather had the means of obtaining possession and control of the said indebtedness so given to him. The court further stated that by reason of the fact that Thomas Prather had this knowledge at the time he gave the indebtedness to Samuel, he therefore at that time gave to said Samuel the means of obtaining possession and control of the thing given, that is, of the said indebtedness. This last statement is, of course, a mere conclusion from the facts previously stated. The appellant contends that the transaction as stated in the findings did not constitute a valid gift of the indebtedness in question, and that the finding, so far as it states the ultimate fact of such gift, is contrary to the evidence.

It is conceded that at the time of the asserted gift Thomas Prather knew that Samuel D. Prather held the offices above mentioned, and that it was within his official power by reason thereof to make sufficient changes upon the books of account of the defendant to make them show that the said indebtedness had been transferred by Thomas Prather to Samuel D. Prather, and was owing by the defendant to Samuel D. Prather, instead of Thomas Prather. It is admitted that the asserted gift was made during the last sickness of Thomas Prather, two days before his death, which event occurred on April 19, 1913, and was therefore a gift in view of death. Civ. Code, § 1150. It is also admitted that no change was made upon the books of the defendant regarding said indebtedness, up to the time of the trial of this action, and that when the action was begun the account books of the defendant showed it to be indebted to the said Thomas Prather in the sum claimed in the complaint. The only evidence of the gift asserted in the answer is found in the testimony of Samuel D. Prather, and is as follows:

> "In talking business matters my brother said to me, 'Now, in reference to the account of Thomas Prather in the Merced Stone Company, I want to give you that account, all that is due me from that account. I don't know just how to do this, but I give it to you.' ... A little further in the conversation my brother said to me, 'I give you the keys to my office, the combination of my safe and keys to my desk, and with these I give you all accounts, books, papers, letters, documents, furnishings, pictures, everything that belongs to me in that office. It is yours.' "

This he said occurred on April 17, 1913.

The case depends on the meaning and effect of section 1147 of the Civil Code which reads as follows:

"A verbal gift is not valid, unless the means of obtaining possession and control of the thing are given, nor, if it is capable of delivery, unless there is an actual or symbolical delivery of the thing to the donee."

The contention of the respondent is that this section is complied with in every case of gift of a chose in action where, at the time the donor makes such gift, he knows that the donee has it within his power to secure the possession and control of the thing given, and that in such a case no delivery or transmission from the donor to the donee of the means of obtaining possession and control of the subject of the gift is necessary. We do not think this is the correct construction of the section quoted. It contemplates that the donor shall do something at the time of making the gift which has the effect of placing in the hands of the donee the means of obtaining the control and possession of the thing given. That the fact that the thing was already in possession of the donee at the time of declaring the gift is not enough, is well settled by the authorities. . . .

In order to comply with the section the "means" must be "given." In the connection in which these words occur the effect is that such means must be given by the donor to the donee. This giving of the means is authorized, where the thing given is not capable of delivery, as a substitute for the actual or symbolical delivery of the thing by the donor to the donee required in cases where such thing is capable of delivery. No good reason can be given for supposing that a transmission or delivery by the donor to the donee of the means was not intended to be as essential in the case of intangible property, as the delivery, actual or symbolical, of the thing itself, where it is tangible.

In the case of a chose in action not evidenced by a written instrument, the only means of obtaining control that is recognized by the authorities is an assignment in writing, or some equivalent thereof. . . .

In the present case it is true that Samuel D. Prather was possessed of the physical power and of the official authority, by reason of his relation to the defendant, to make the necessary changes on its books to show that the indebtedness was due to him and not to the decedent. But this power did not emanate from the decedent. Samuel possessed it before the asserted gift as well as after. The decedent did not even authorize him to make such changes, nor suggest that the gift might be effected in that way. It was not shown that such method was in the mind of the donor. The fact that it was a book account, or that a change might be made in the name of the debtor, was not even mentioned in the conversation. The law intends something more than a mere power to make physical entries in the books of the debtor in such a case. The authority to make the change, or cause it to be made, must be vested in the debtor by reason of some act or direction of the creditor. If verbal gifts could be made in such loose manner as this it would open the door to innumerable frauds and perjuries. For this reason the authorities hold that something more than mere physical power is necessary; something more than the previous possession of the property or of the means of obtaining it; something emanating from the donor which operates to give to the donee the means of obtaining such possession and control. . . .

The conclusion of the court below upon the facts found was not in accordance with the law, and its finding of the ultimate fact that Thomas Prather transferred the debt to Samuel D. Prather by way of a verbal gift is not supported by the evidence. Consequently the judgment and order cannot be upheld.

The judgment and order are reversed and the cause is remanded, with directions to the court below to enter judgment upon the findings in favor of the plaintiff for the amount prayed for.

Questions

1. In *Adams*, is it more important that the alleged transaction involved a gift causa mortis or that the thing given was a contract right? Who is the debtor? Who is the creditor-assignor? Who is the assignee? Who sues whom? What is the defense? Why does it fail?

2. Would the result in *Adams* differ under the RESTATEMENT (SECOND) OF CONTRACTS § 332? Why should a gratuitous assignment be revocable unless the conditions in § 332(1) or (3) are satisfied? Should gratuitous assignments be more easily alienable?

3. *Problems*. Apply the RESTATEMENT (SECOND) OF CONTRACTS to the following:

    a. Otherwise on the facts in *Adams*, but, after giving the debt to Sam, Tom assigned the debt to his sister in writing before he died. Can Sam collect from the Merced Stone Co.?

    b. Otherwise on the facts in *Adams*, Tom remained on his deathbed, alive and competent, when Sam demanded payment of the debt by the Merced Stone Co. The company refused. Tom then died. Must the Merced Stone Co. pay Sam if the debt is due and payable to Tom?

    c. The facts are as in problem *b*. but the Merced Stone Co. refused to pay Sam and Sam brought suit. Then Tom died. Must the Stone Co. pay the debt?

    d. The facts are as in problem *b*. but, in addition, the Merced Stone Company paid Sam and then Tom died. Can Tom's estate recover from the Merced Stone Co.?

    e. Otherwise on the facts in *Adams*, assume the debt is for $25,000. Before Tom died, Sam contracted to buy a new car and promised to assign the debt to Seller on delivery of the car. Must the Stone Co. pay the debt to Sam?

UNIFORM COMMERCIAL CODE §§ 9–404, 9–406

ERTEL v. RADIO CORP. OF AMERICA

Supreme Court of Indiana, 1974.
261 Ind. 573, 307 N.E.2d 471.

HUNTER, JUSTICE. This cause originated as an action by a finance company, Economy Finance Corp. (Economy) against its debtor, Delta Engineering Corp. (Delta) for amounts due under a loan and security agreement covering revolving inventory and accounts receivable. Also named as defendants were the guarantors for the payment by Delta, John R. Dugan, President and General Manager of Delta, and John C. Ertel, Secretary–Treasurer of Delta. Delta defaulted on the note, and Dugan's whereabouts are unknown—leaving only Ertel to face the liability.

Ertel, in response to the original complaint, filed a third-party complaint against Radio Corporation of America (RCA) and alleged the following:

RCA was a customer of Delta and, in contracting to purchase machines from Delta, RCA had become Delta's account debtor. To secure its loans from Economy, Delta had assigned its accounts receivable to Economy. RCA was allegedly given notice of this assignment which would in turn require RCA to make all payments to Economy for any machinery purchased from Delta. Contrary to that alleged notice of assignment, RCA made all payments directly to Delta. RCA wrongfully paid these accounts receivable to Delta and allegedly remained liable to Economy. Ertel, as a result of his payment to Economy, claims to be the subrogee of Economy vis-a-vis RCA.

RCA, in its answer, argued that even if it were liable to Economy for the payments made to Delta, it had a right of set-off against Economy. RCA contended that Ertel as subrogee of Delta's assignee (Economy) was, therefore, subject to its right of set-off.

The trial court entered summary judgment against Ertel on Economy's original complaint in the amount of $19,674.10 on May 7, 1971. The Court also entered judgment against Ertel on his third-party complaint on September 14, 1972. The latter judgment was appealed to the Court of Appeals, First District, which reversed the trial court. 297 N.E.2d 446. The Court of Appeals held that Ertel should be subrogated to Economy's rights as assignee of the accounts receivable from RCA and that the assignee-Economy (thus, Ertel as subrogee) would take free of certain set-off rights claimed by the account debtor (RCA) against its account creditor (Delta).

We believe that both the trial court and the Court of Appeals erred and that, therefore, transfer should be granted to rectify the situation.

There are three major issues presented for our consideration:

　　1. Does Economy have a claim against RCA for wrongful payments?

　　2. Is Ertel, as guarantor of the note, subrogated to Economy's rights against RCA?

　　3. Does RCA have rights of set-off against Economy and, therefore, against Ertel?

I. ECONOMY'S CLAIM AGAINST RCA

Section 9–318(3) clearly delineates the legal relationship between the account debtor (RCA) and the assignee (Economy) once the account debtor receives adequate notification of an assignment. The account debtor, upon receipt of said notification, is duty-bound to pay the assignee and not the assignor. Payment to an assignor, after notification of assignment, does not relieve the account debtor of his obligation to pay the assignee unless the assignee consents to such a collection process. (See official Comment #3, § 9–318.) The account debtor's failure to pay the assignee after receiving due notification gives rise to an assignee's claim for wrongful payment.

In order to determine liability for wrongful payment, we must ascertain whether or not RCA received adequate notification as required by § 9–318(3). Notification is nowhere defined in § 9–318(3), but is defined in § 1–201(26)....

The following facts are stipulated in the record:

　　1. On or about May 12, 1969, Economy Finance Corp. mailed written notice of assignment to the RCA Magnetic Products Division, Indianapolis.

　　2. Notice was sent by certified mail.

　　3. A dock employee of RCA Magnetic Products Division receipted for said notice by signature on May 14, 1969.

　　4. The mail was normally delivered by the post office to the receiving dock.

　　5. Dock employees were authorized to sign receipts for certified mail.

　　6. The notice was never received by the accounting department.

The above facts, in our judgment, demonstrate receipt of notification as contemplated by § 1–201(26). The fact that the accounting department never received the notice is of no consequence in this case. The notice was duly delivered and received at the appropriate place by an authorized agent of RCA. The negligence of RCA employees after the initial receipt at the dock should not be charged to Economy Finance, but rather to RCA. To hold otherwise is to circumvent the obvious policy behind § 1–201(26). Therefore, we hold, as the Court of Appeals held, that RCA was notified of the assignment and that, as a consequence, Economy has a claim for wrongful payment.

II. ERTEL'S SUBROGATION CLAIM

The Court of Appeals held that Ertel became subrogated to the rights of Economy upon payment of the debt owing from Delta to Economy. We fully agree with this conclusion.... The general rule, firmly imbedded in Indiana law, is that a surety, upon satisfaction of a debt, is subrogated to all the rights which the creditor had against the principal debtor prior to satisfaction of the debt.... Additionally, the surety is subrogated "to the interests which the creditor has in security for the principal's performance." Restatement of Security, ALI, Ch. 5, § 141. Therefore, it follows that Ertel, as subrogee of Economy, has a right to the accounts pledged by Delta as security for the initial obligation. Of course, this would include the RCA accounts....

III. RCA'S SET-OFF RIGHTS AGAINST ECONOMY (ERTEL)

The assignment agreement between Delta and Economy covered Delta's present and future accounts receivable. The accounts receivable in question were created by contracts for the sale of machinery from Delta to RCA. There were three such sales and each was governed by the same standard contract. RCA now claims that machines transferred in the last sale were substantially incomplete and that RCA had to expend considerable sums of money to make the machines complete and usable. Thus, RCA claims to have a set-off right against Delta for Delta's incomplete performance of the last contract and that, *ergo*, Ertel, as subrogee of Economy, also takes subject to those rights.

Determining against whom RCA can assert its claim is governed by § 9–318(1) of the Commercial Code: ...

The Court of Appeals concluded that RCA had no set-off rights, viewing § 9–318(1)(b) as a bar. Apparently, the Court's decision was based on the fact that the last sales transaction between RCA and Delta (the one out of which RCA's claim arises) occurred after notice of the assignment was given by Economy, and that somehow the third contract was a "separate transaction." We believe that this application of § 9–318(1)(b) to the facts of this case is entirely improper.

It has been held that set-off is the type of claim contemplated by § 9–318(1). Farmers Acceptance Corp. v. DeLozier (1972 Colo.Sup.Ct.), 496 P.2d 1016. The issue here is whether RCA's set-off is the type of claim comprehended by *§ 9–318(1)(a)* or *§ 9–318(1)(b)*. Section § 9–318(1)(a) is clearly the applicable provision in that RCA's claim arose from the contract between itself and Delta.

The Oregon Supreme Court has provided us with the following analysis of § 9–318(1)(a) and (b):

> "The Code distinguishes 'between what might be called the contract-related and the unrelated defenses and claims. *Defenses and claims "arising" from the contract can be asserted against the assignee whether they "arise" before or after notification'* .... Under

the Code, 'any other defense or claim' is available against the assignee only if it 'accrues before ... notification.' "

2 Gilmore, Security Interests in Personal Property, 1090–1091, § 41.4 (1965)....

This interpretation is entirely consistent with UCC § 9–318, Official Comment, No. 1:

> "When the account debtor's defenses on an assigned account, chattel paper or a contract right *arise from the contract between him and the assignor it makes no difference whether the breach giving rise to the defense occurs before or after the account debtor is notified of the assignment.*" (Emphasis added.)

In the case at bar RCA's claim arose from the subsequently assigned contract between itself and Delta. The fact that the claim arose *after* Economy gave notice of the assignment is irrelevant. Therefore, Economy's rights were subject to RCA's herein asserted claim.

Ertel, as subrogee of Economy, succeeds to the rights of Economy vis-a-vis RCA. That is to say, Ertel becomes subrogated to Economy's interest in the RCA accounts. However, the subrogee (Ertel) receives no more or no fewer rights than Economy possessed at the time Ertel satisfied the debt. The Tenth Circuit has characterized the nature of the subrogee's rights in the following manner:

> "One who acquires or succeeds to rights, claims, or securities through subrogation takes them burdened with the limitations and disqualifications to which they were subject in the hands of the person for whom he is substituted. The rights he acquires thereby are not greater nor better than those which the person for whom he is substituted had at the time of the payment which effected the subrogation." (Citing inter alia, In Re Paoli Lithia Springs Hotel Co. (7th Cir.1925), 5 F.2d 902.) Alexander v. Young (1933), 65 F.2d 752, 757.

It follows, therefore, that Ertel has succeeded to the rights of Economy—subject to the RCA claim.

For all the foregoing reasons, transfer is hereby granted and the cause remanded to the trial court to determine liability with respect to the third-party complaint of John C. Ertel.

Transfer granted.

Questions

1. Who is the obligor in *Ertel*? Who is the obligee-assignor? Who is the assignee? What is the contract between Delta and RCA? What is the contract between Delta and Economy? Who is Ertel? How does Ertel come to sue RCA?

2. Are the obligor's contractual interests impaired by the holdings in *Ertel*? Is the policy supporting free alienability upheld at unreasonable cost

to the obligor? Based on the cases you have read, is a question of assignability a matter of balancing the policy of free alienability against the autonomy and security of the contract parties? Or is autonomy to be fully protected, allowing maximum alienability after autonomy is secure?

3. *Problems.*

a. Assignee sues Obligor on The Claim. Obligor defends by claiming that her duty is discharged by full performance rendered to assignor. Who prevails?

b. Assignee sues Obligor on The Claim. Obligor defends by claiming that her duty is discharged by a material breach by the assignor of the contract between Obligor and Assignor. Who prevails? Does it matter whether breach by assignor occurred before or after notice of the assignment to the Obligor?

c. Assignee sues Obligor on The Claim. Obligor defends by claiming a reduction in the amount of the claim as damages for assignor's breach of a related contract. Is the defense sound?

d. Assignee proves that immediately following repudiation by Assignor, Obligor and Assignor entered into a contract governing the same subject matter at the same price with a different payment schedule. Does Assignee acquire rights under the contract as modified?

———

RESTATEMENT (SECOND) OF CONTRACTS § 318

———

UNIFORM COMMERCIAL CODE § 2–210

———

CRANE ICE CREAM CO. v. TERMINAL FREEZING & HEATING CO.

Court of Appeals of Maryland, 1925.
147 Md. 588, 128 A. 280.

Action by the Crane Ice Cream Company against the Terminal Freezing & Heating Company. Demurrer to the declaration was sustained, and from the judgment entered thereon against plaintiff, it appeals. Judgment affirmed.

PARKE, JUDGE. The appellee and one W.C. Frederick entered into a contract for the delivery of ice by the appellee to Frederick, and, before the expiration of the contract, Frederick executed an assignment of the contract to the appellant; and on the refusal of the appellee to deliver ice to the assignee it brought an action on the contract against the appellee to recover damages for the alleged breach....

The contract imposed upon the appellee the liability to sell and deliver to Frederick such quantities of ice as he might use in his business as an ice cream manufacturer to the extent of 250 tons per week, at and for the price of $3.25 a ton of 2,000 pounds on the loading platform of Frederick. The contractual rights of the appellee were (a) to be paid on every Tuesday during the continuation of the contract, for all ice purchased by Frederick during the week ending at midnight upon the next preceding Saturday; (b) to require Frederick not to buy or accept any ice from any other source than the appellee, except in excess of the weekly maximum of 250 tons. . . .

Before the first year of the second term of the contract had expired Frederick, without the consent or knowledge of the appellee, executed and delivered to the appellant, for a valuable consideration, a written assignment dated February 15, 1921, of the modified agreement between him and the appellee. The attempted transfer of the contract was a part of the transaction between Frederick and the appellant whereby the appellant acquired by purchase the plant, equipment, rights, and credits, choses in action, "good will, trade, custom, patronage, rights, contracts," and other assets of Frederick's ice cream business which had been established and conducted by him in Baltimore. The purchaser took full possession and continued the former business carried on by Frederick. It was then and is now a corporation "engaged in the ice cream business upon a large and extensive scale in the city of Philadelphia, as well as in the city of Baltimore, and state of Maryland," and had a large capitalization, ample resources, and credit to meet any of its obligations "and all and singular the terms and provisions" of the contract; and it was prepared to pay cash for all ice deliverable under the contract.

As soon as the appellee learned of this purported assignment and the absorption of the business of Frederick by the appellant, it notified Frederick that the contract was at an end, and declined to deliver any ice to the appellant. Until the day of the assignment the obligations of both original parties had been fully performed and discharged. . . .

The basic facts upon which the question for solution depends must be sought in the effect of the attempted assignment of this executory bilateral contract on both the rights and the liabilities of the contracting parties, as every bilateral contract includes both rights and duties on each side while both sides remain executory. I Williston on Contracts, § 407. If the assignment of rights and the assignment of duties by Frederick are separated, they fall into these two divisions: (1) The rights of the assignor were (a) to take no ice, if the assignor used none in his business, but if he did (b) to require the appellee to deliver, on the loading platform of the assignor, all the ice he might need in his business to the extent of 250 tons a week, and (c) to buy any ice he might need in excess of the weekly 250 tons from any other person; and (2) the liabilities of the assignor were (a) to pay to the appellee on every Tuesday during the continuance of the contract the stipulated price for all ice purchased and weighed by the assignor during the week ending at midnight upon the next preceding Saturday, and (b) not directly or indirectly, during the existence of this agreement, to buy or accept any ice from any other person, firm, or corporation than the said Terminal Freezing & Heating Company, except such amounts as might be in excess of the weekly limit of 250 tons.

Whether the attempted assignment of these rights, or the attempted delegation of these duties must fail because the rights or duties are of too personal a character, is a question of construction to be resolved from the nature of the contract and the express or presumed intention of the parties. Williston on Contracts, § 431.

The contract was made by a corporation with an individual, William C. Frederick, an ice cream manufacturer, with whom the corporation had dealt for 3 years, before it executed a renewal contract for a second like period. The character, credit, and resources of Frederick had been tried and tested by the appellee before it renewed the contract. Not only had his ability to pay as agreed been established, but his fidelity to his obligation not to buy or accept any ice from any other source up to 250 tons a week had been ascertained. In addition, the appellee had not asked in the beginning, nor on entering into the second period of the contract, for Frederick to undertake to buy a specific quantity of ice or even to take any. Frederick simply engaged himself during a definite term to accept and pay for such quantities of ice as he might use in his business to the extent of 250 tons a week. If he used no ice in his business, he was under no obligation to pay for a pound. In any week, the quantity could vary from zero to 250 tons, and its weekly fluctuation, throughout the life of the contract, could irregularly range between these limits. The weekly payment might be nothing or as much as $812.50; and for every week a credit was extended to the eighth day from the beginning of every week's delivery. From the time of the beginning of every weekly delivery of the ice to the date of the payment therefore the title to the ice was in the purchaser, and the seller had no security for its payment except in the integrity and solvency of Frederick. The performances, therefore, were not concurrent, but the performance of the nonassigning party to the contract was to precede the payments by the assignor.

When it is also considered that the ice was to be supplied and paid for, according to its weight on the loading platform of Frederick, at an unvarying price without any reference either to the quantity used, or to the fluctuations in the cost of production or to market changes in the selling price, throughout 3 years, the conclusion is inevitable that the inducement for the appellee to enter into the original contract and into the renewal lay outside the bare terms of the contract, but was implicit in them, and was the appellee's reliance upon its knowledge of an average quantity of ice consumed, and probably to be needed, in the usual course of Frederick's business, at all times throughout the year, and its confidence in the stability of his enterprise, in his competency in commercial affairs, in his probity, personal judgment, and in his continuing financial responsibility. The contract itself emphasized the personal equation by specifying that the ice was to be bought for "use in his business as an ice cream manufacturer," and was to be paid for according to its weight "on the loading platform of the said W.C. Frederick."

When Frederick went out of business as an ice cream manufacturer, and turned over his plant and everything constituting his business to the appellant, it was no longer his business, or his loading platform, or subject to his care, control, or maintenance, but it was the business of a stranger, whose skill, competency, and requirements of ice were altogether different from those of Frederick. The assignor had his simple plant in Baltimore. The assignee, in its purchase, simply added another unit to its ice cream business which it had been, and is now, carrying on "upon a large and extensive scale in the city of Philadelphia and the state of Pennsylvania, as well as in the city of Baltimore and state of Maryland." The appellee knew that Frederick could not carry on his business without ice wherewith to manufacture ice cream at his plant for his trade. It also was familiar with the quantities of ice he would require, from time to time, in his business at his plant in Baltimore, and it consequently could make its other commitments for ice with this knowledge as a basis.

The appellant, on the other hand, might wholly supply its increased trade acquired in the purchase of Frederick's business with its ice cream produced upon a large and extensive scale by its manufactory in Philadelphia, which would result in no ice being bought by the assignee of the appellee, and so the appellee would be deprived of the benefit of its contract by the introduction of a different personal relation or element which was never contemplated by the original contracting parties. Again, should the price of ice be relatively high in Philadelphia in comparison with the stipulated price, the assignee could run its business in Baltimore and furnish its patrons, or a portion of them, in Philadelphia with its product from the weekly maximum consumption of 250 tons of ice throughout the year. There can be no denial that the uniform delivery of the maximum quantity of 250 tons a week would be a consequence not within the normal scope of the contract, and would impose a greater liability on the appellee than was anticipated. 7 Halsbury's Laws of England, § 1015, p. 501....

While a party to a contract may as a general rule assign all his beneficial rights, except where a personal relation is involved, his liability under the contract is not assignable inter vivos, because any one who is bound to any performance whatever or who owes money cannot by any act of his own, or by any act in agreement with any other person than his creditor or the one to whom his performance is due, cast off his own liability and substitute another's liability. If this were not true, obligors could free themselves of their obligations by the simple expedient of assigning them. A further ground for the rule, is that, not only is a party entitled to know to whom he must look for the satisfaction of his rights under the contract, but in the familiar words of Lord Denman in Humble v. Hunter, 12 Q.B. 317, "you have a right to the benefit you contemplate from the character, credit, and substance of the person with whom you contract." For these reasons it has been uniformly held that a man cannot assign his liabilities under a contract, but one who is bound so as to bear an unescapable liability may delegate the performance of his obligation to another, if the liability be of such a nature that its performance by another will be substantially the same thing as performance by the promisor himself. In such circumstances the performance of the third party is the act of the promisor, who remains liable under the contract and answerable in damages if the performance be not in strict fulfillment of the contract. . . .

However, the analysis of the facts on this appeal leaves no room for doubt that the case at bar falls into the category of those assignments where an attempt is made both to transfer the rights and to delegate the duties of the assignor under an executory bilateral contract whose terms and the circumstances make plain that the personal qualification and action of the assignor, with respect to both his benefits and burdens under the contract, were essential inducements in the formation of the contract, and further, that the assignment was a repudiation of any future liability of the assignor. The attempted assignment before us altered the conditions and obligations of the undertaking. The appellee would here be obliged not only to perform the subsequent stipulations of the contract for the benefit of a stranger and in conformity with his will, but also to accept the performance of the stranger in place of that of the assignor with whom it contracted, and upon whose personal integrity, capacity, and management in the course of a particular business he must be assumed to have relied by reason of the very nature of the provisions of the contract and of the circumstances of the contracting parties. . . .

Judgment affirmed.

Questions

1. What does it mean to "assign the contract"? What are Frederick's rights under the assigned contract? What are Frederick's duties? Why was the contract not assignable in the court's view?

2. Would the result differ under U.C.C. § 2–210? Under U.C.C. § 2–306(1)?

3. Assume the result differs under the U.C.C due to §§ 2–306(1), 2–210(5), and that Frederick is available as surety. Would the result then differ if the contract prohibited "assignment of the contract"?

THE BRITISH WAGGON CO. AND THE PARKGATE WAGGON CO. v. LEA & CO.

Court of Queen's Bench, 1880.
5 Q.B.D. 149.

COCKBURN, CHIEF JUSTICE. This was an action brought by the plaintiffs to recover rent for the hire of certain railway waggons, alleged to be payable by the defendants to the plaintiffs, or one of them, under the following circumstances:

By an agreement in writing of February 10th, 1874, the Parkgate Waggon Company let to the defendants, who are coal merchants, fifty railway waggons for a term of seven years, at a yearly rent of £ 600 a year, payable by equal quarterly payments. By a second agreement of June 13th, 1874, the company in like manner let to the defendants fifty other waggons, at a yearly rent of £625, payable quarterly like the former.

Each of these agreements contained the following clause: "The owners, their executors, or administrators, will at all times during the said term, except as herein provided, keep the said waggons in good and substantial repair and working order, and, on receiving notice from the tenant of any want of repairs, and the number or numbers of the waggons requiring to be repaired, and the place or places where it or they then is or are, will, with all reasonable despatch, cause the same to be repaired and put into good working order."

On October 24th, 1874, the Parkgate Company passed a resolution, under the 129th section of the Companies Act, 1862, for the voluntary winding up of the company. Liquidators were appointed, and by an order of the Chancery Division of the High Court of Justice, it was ordered that the winding up of the company should be continued under the supervision of the Court.

By an indenture of April 1st, 1878, the Parkgate Company assigned and transferred, and the liquidators confirmed to the British Company and their assigns, among other things, all sums of money, whether payable by way of rent, hire, interest, penalty, or damage, then due, or thereafter to become due, to the Parkgate Company, by virtue of the two contracts, and all the interest of the Parkgate Company and the said liquidators therein; the British Company, on the other hand covenanting with the Parkgate Company "to observe and perform such of the stipulations, conditions, provisions, and agreements contained in the said contracts as, according to the terms thereof were stipulated to be observed and performed by the Parkgate Company." On the execution of this assignment the British Company took over from the Parkgate Company the repairing stations, which had previously been used by the Parkgate Company for the repair of the waggons let to the defendants, and also the staff of workmen employed by the latter company in executing such repairs. It was expressly found that the British Company have ever since been ready and willing to execute, and have, with all due diligence, executed all necessary repairs to the said waggons. . . .

The main contention on the part of the defendants, however, was that, as the Parkgate Company had, by assigning the contracts, and by making over their repairing stations to the British Company, incapacitated themselves to fulfill their obligation to keep the waggons in repair, that company had no right, as between themselves and the defendants, to substitute a third party to do the work they had engaged to perform, nor were the defendants bound to accept the party so substituted as the one to whom they were to look for performance of the contract; the contract was therefore at an end.

The authority principally relied on in support of this contention was the case of *Robson v. Drummond* (2 B. & Ad. 303), approved by this court in *Humble v. Hunter* (12 Q.B. 310). In *Robson v. Drummond* a carriage having been hired by the defendant of one Sharp, a coachmaker, for five years, at a yearly rent, payable in advance each year, the carriage to be kept in repair and painted once a year by the maker—Robson being then a partner in the business, but unknown to the defendant—on Sharp retiring from the business after three years had expired, and making over all interest in the business and property in the goods to Robson, it was held, that the defendant could not be sued on the contract—by Lord Tenterden on the ground that "the defendant might have been induced to enter into the contract by reason of the personal confidence which he reposed in Sharp, and therefore have agreed to pay money in advance, for which reason the defendant had a right to object to its being performed by any other person;" and by Littledale and Parke, JJ., on the additional ground that the defendant had a right to the personal services of Sharp, and to the benefit of his judgment and taste, to the end of the contract.

In like manner, where goods are ordered of a particular manufacturer, another, who has succeeded to his business, cannot execute the order, so as to bind the customer, who has not been made aware of the transfer of the business, to accept the goods. The latter is entitled to refuse to deal with any other than the manufacturer whose goods he intended to buy. For this *Boulton v. Jones* (2 H. & N. 564), is a sufficient authority. The case of *Robson v. Drummond* comes nearer to the present case, but is, we think, distinguishable from it. We entirely concur in the principle on which the decision in *Robson v. Drummond* rests, namely, that where a person contracts with another to do work or perform service, and it can be inferred that the person employed has been selected with reference to his individual skill, competency, or other personal qualification, the inability or unwillingness of the party so employed to execute the work or perform the service is a sufficient answer to any demand by a stranger to the original contract of the performance of it by the other party, and entitles the latter to treat the contract as at an end, notwithstanding that the person tendered to take the place of the contracting party may be equally well qualified to do the service. Personal performance is in such a case of the essence of the contract, which, consequently, cannot in its absence be enforced against an unwilling party. But this principle appears to us inapplicable in the present instance, inasmuch as we cannot suppose that in stipulating for the repair of these waggons by the company—a rough description of work which ordinary workmen conversant with the business would be perfectly able to execute—the defendants attached any importance to whether the repairs were done by the company, or by any one with whom the company might enter into a subsidiary contract to do the work. All that the hirers, the defendants, cared for in this stipulation was that the waggons should be kept in repair; it was indifferent to them by whom the repairs should be done. Thus if, without going into liquidation, or assigning these contracts, the company had entered into a contract with any competent party to do the repairs, and so had procured them to be done, we cannot think that this would have been a departure from the terms of the contract to keep the waggons in repair. While fully acquiescing in the general principle just referred to, we must take care not to push it beyond reasonable limits. And we cannot but think that, in applying the principle, the Court of Queen's Bench in *Robson v. Drummond* went to the utmost length to which it can be carried, as it is difficult to see how in repairing a carriage when necessary, or painting it once a year, preference would be given to one coachmaker over another. Much work is contracted for, which it is known can only be executed by means of subcontracts; much is contracted for as to which it is indifferent to the party for whom it is to be done, whether it is done by the immediate party to the contract, or by some one on his behalf. In all these cases the maxim Qui facit per alium facit per se applies.

In the view we take of the case, therefore, the repair of the waggons, undertaken and done by the British Company under their contract with the Parkgate Company, is a sufficient performance by the latter of their engagement to repair under their contract with the defendants. Consequently, so long as the Parkgate Company continues to exist, and, through the British Company, continues to fulfill its obligation to keep the waggons in repair, the defendants cannot, in our opinion, be heard to say that the former company is not entitled to the performance of the contract by them, on the ground that the company have incapacitated themselves from performing their obligations under it, or that, by transferring the performance thereof to others, they have absolved the defendants from further performance on their part.

That a debt accruing due under a contract can, since the passing of the Judicature Acts, be assigned at law as well as equity, cannot since the decision in *Brice v. Bannister*, 3 Q.B.D. 569, be disputed.

We are therefore of opinion that our judgment must be for the plaintiffs for the amount claimed.

SALLY BEAUTY CO., INC. v. NEXXUS PRODS. CO., INC.

United States Court of Appeals, Seventh Circuit, 1986.
801 F.2d 1001.

CUDAHY, CIRCUIT JUDGE. Nexxus Products Company ("Nexxus") entered into a contract with Best Barber & Beauty Supply Company, Inc. ("Best"), under which Best would be the exclusive distributor of Nexxus hair care products to barbers and hair stylists throughout most of Texas. When Best was acquired by and merged into Sally Beauty Company, Inc. ("Sally Beauty"), Nexxus cancelled the agreement. Sally Beauty is a wholly-owned subsidiary of Alberto-Culver Company ("Alberto-Culver"), a major manufacturer of hair care products and a competitor of Nexxus'. Sally Beauty claims that Nexxus breached the contract by cancelling;

Nexxus asserts by way of defense that the contract was not assignable or, in the alternative, not assignable to Sally Beauty. The district court granted Nexxus' motion for summary judgment, ruling that the contract was one for personal services and therefore not assignable. We affirm on a different theory—that this contract could not be assigned to the wholly-owned subsidiary of a direct competitor under section 2–210 of the Uniform Commercial Code.

I.

Only the basic facts are undisputed and they are as follows. Prior to its merger with Sally Beauty, Best was a Texas corporation in the business of distributing beauty and hair care products to retail stores, barber shops and beauty salons throughout Texas. Between March and July 1979, Mark Reichek, Best's president, negotiated with Stephen Redding, Nexxus' vice-president, over a possible distribution agreement between Best and Nexxus. Nexxus, founded in 1979, is a California corporation that formulates and markets hair care products. Nexxus does not market its products to retail stores, preferring to sell them to independent distributors for resale to barbers and beauticians. On August 2, 1979, Nexxus executed a distributorship agreement with Best, in the form of a July 24, 1979 letter from Reichek, for Best, to Redding, for Nexxus. . . .

In July 1981, Sally Beauty acquired Best in a stock purchase transaction and Best was merged into Sally Beauty, which succeeded to Best's rights and interests in all of Best's contracts. Sally Beauty, a Delaware corporation with its principal place of business in Texas, is a wholly-owned subsidiary of Alberto–Culver. Sally Beauty, like Best, is a distributor of hair care and beauty products to retail stores and hair styling salons. Alberto–Culver is a major manufacturer of hair care products and, thus, is a direct competitor of Nexxus in the hair care market.

Shortly after the merger, Redding met with Michael Renzulli, president of Sally Beauty, to discuss the Nexxus distribution agreement. After the meeting, Redding wrote Renzulli a letter stating that Nexxus would not allow Sally Beauty, a wholly-owned subsidiary of a direct competitor, to distribute Nexxus products: . . .

In August 1983 Sally Beauty commenced this action by filing a complaint in the Northern District of Illinois, claiming that Nexxus had violated the federal antitrust laws and breached the distribution agreement. In August 1984, Nexxus filed a counterclaim alleging violations of the Lanham Act, the Racketeer Influenced and Corrupt Organizations Act ("RICO") and the unfair competition laws of North Carolina, Tennessee and unidentified "other states." On October 22, 1984, Sally Beauty filed a motion to dismiss the counterclaims arising under RICO and 'other states' law. Nexxus filed a motion for summary judgment on the breach of contract claim the next day.

The district court ruled on these motions in a Memorandum Opinion and Order dated January 31, 1985. It granted Sally's motion to dismiss the two counterclaims and also granted Nexxus' motion for summary judgment. In May 1985, it dismissed the remaining claims and counterclaims (pursuant to stipulation by the parties) and directed the entry of an appealable final judgment on the breach of contract claim.

II.

Sally Beauty's breach of contract claim alleges that by acquiring Best, Sally Beauty succeeded to all of Best's rights and obligations under the distribution agreement. It further alleges that Nexxus breached the agreement by failing to give Sally Beauty 120 days notice prior to terminating the agreement and by terminating it on other than an anniversary date of its formation. Complaint, Count III, Appellant's Appendix at 54–55. Nexxus, in its motion for summary judgment, argued that the distribution agreement it entered into with Best was a contract for personal services, based upon a relationship of personal trust and confidence between Reichek and the Redding family. As such, the contract could not be assigned to Sally without Nexxus' consent.

In opposing this motion Sally Beauty argued that the contract was freely assignable because (1) it was between two corporations, not two individuals and (2) the character of the performance would not be altered by the substitution of Sally Beauty for Best. It also argued that "the Distribution Agreement is nothing more than a simple, non-exclusive contract for the distribution of goods, the successful performance of which is in no way dependent upon any particular personality, individual skill or confidential relationship." Appellant's Appendix at 119.

In ruling on this motion, the district court framed the issue before it as "whether the contract at issue here between Best and Nexxus was of a personal nature such that it was not assignable without Nexxus' consent." ... The district court also rejected the contention that the character of performance would not be altered by a substitution of Sally Beauty for Best: "Unlike Best, Sally Beauty is a subsidiary of one of Nexxus' direct competitors. This is a significant distinction and in the court's view, it raises serious questions regarding Sally Beauty's ability to perform the distribution agreement in the same manner as Best." *Id.* at 7.

We cannot affirm this summary judgment on the grounds relied on by the district court.... We may affirm this summary judgment, however, on a different ground if it finds support in the record. *United States v. Winthrop Towers*, 628 F.2d 1028, 1037 (7th Cir.1980). Sally Beauty contends that the distribution agreement is freely assignable because it is governed by the provisions of the Uniform Commercial Code (the "UCC" or the "Code"), as adopted in Texas. Appellants' Brief at 46–47. We agree with Sally that the provisions of the UCC govern this contract and for that reason hold that the assignment of the contract by Best to

Sally Beauty was barred by the UCC rules on delegation of performance, UCC § 2–210(1), Tex. Bus. & Com. Code Ann. § 2–210(a) (Vernon 1968).

. . .

IV.

The fact that this contract is considered a contract for the sale of goods and not for the provision of a service does not, as Sally Beauty suggests, mean that it is freely assignable in all circumstances. The delegation of performance under a sales contract (whether in conjunction with an assignment of rights, as here, or not) is governed by UCC section 2–210(1), Tex. Bus. & Com. Code § 2–210(a) (Vernon 1968). The UCC recognizes that in many cases an obligor will find it convenient or even necessary to relieve himself of the duty of performance under a contract, *see* Official Comment 1, UCC § 2–210 ("[T]his section recognizes both delegation of performance and assignability as normal and permissible incidents of a contract for the sale of goods."). The Code therefore sanctions delegation except where the delegated performance would be unsatisfactory to the obligee: "A party may perform his duty through a delegate unless otherwise agreed to or unless the other party has a substantial interest in having his original promisor perform or control the acts required by the contract." UCC § 2–210(1), Tex. Bus. & Com. Code Ann. § 2–210(a) (Vernon 1968). Consideration is given to balancing the policies of free alienability of commercial contracts and protecting the obligee from having to accept a bargain he did not contract for....

In the exclusive distribution agreement before us, Nexxus had contracted for Best's "best efforts" in promoting the sale of Nexxus products in Texas. UCC § 2–306(2), Tex. Bus. & Com. Code Ann. § 2–306(b) (Vernon 1968), states that "[a] lawful agreement by either buyer or seller for exclusive dealing in the kind of goods concerned imposes unless otherwise agreed an obligation by the seller to use best efforts to supply the goods and by the buyer to use best efforts to promote their sale." This implied promise on Best's part was the consideration for Nexxus' promise to refrain from supplying any other distributors within Best's exclusive area. *See* Official Comment 5, UCC § 2–306. It was this contractual undertaking which Nexxus refused to see performed by Sally.

In ruling on Nexxus' motion for summary judgment, the district court noted: "Unlike Best, Sally Beauty is a subsidiary of one of Nexxus' direct competitors. This is a significant distinction and in the court's view, it raises serious questions regarding Sally Beauty's ability to perform the distribution agreement in the same manner as Best." Memorandum Opinion and Order at 7. *In Berliner Foods Corp. v. Pillsbury Co.*, 633 F.Supp. 557 (D.Md.1986), the court stated the same reservation more strongly on similar facts. Berliner was an exclusive distributor of Haagen–Dazs ice cream when it was sold to Breyer's, manufacturer of a competing ice cream line. Pillsbury Co., manufacturer of Haagen–Dazs, terminated the distributorship and Berliner sued. The court noted, while weighing the factors for and against a preliminary injunction, that "it defies common sense to require a manufacturer to leave the distribution of its products to a distributor under the control of a competitor or potential competitor." *Id.* at 559–60.[7] We agree with these assessments and hold that Sally Beauty's position as a wholly-owned subsidiary of Alberto–Culver is sufficient to bar the delegation of Best's duties under the agreement.

We do not believe that our holding will work the mischief with our national economy that the appellants predict. We hold merely that the duty of performance under an exclusive distributorship may not be delegated to a competitor in the market place—or the wholly-owned subsidiary of a competitor—without the obligee's consent. We believe that such a rule is consonant with the policies behind section 2–210, which is concerned with preserving the bargain the obligee has struck. Nexxus should not be required to accept the "best efforts" of Sally Beauty when those efforts are subject to the control of Alberto–Culver. It is entirely reasonable that Nexxus should conclude that this performance would be a different thing than what it had bargained for. At oral argument, Sally Beauty argued that the case should go to trial to allow it to demonstrate that it could and would perform the contract as impartially as Best. It stressed that Sally Beauty is a "multi-line" distributor, which means that it distributes many brands and is not just a conduit for Alberto–Culver products. But we do not think that this creates a material question of fact in this case. When performance of personal services is delegated, the trier merely determines that it is a personal services contract. If so, the duty is *per se* nondelegable. There is no inquiry into whether the delegate is as skilled or worthy of trust and confidence as the original obligor: the delegate was not bargained for and the obligee need not consent to the substitution. And so here: it is undisputed that Sally Beauty is wholly owned by Alberto–Culver, which means that Sally Beauty's "impartial" sales policy is at least acquiesced in by Alberto–Culver—but could change whenever Alberto–Culver's needs changed. Sally Beauty may be totally sincere in its belief that it can operate "impartially" as a distributor, but who can guarantee the outcome when there is a clear choice between the demands of the parent-manufacturer, Alberto-Culver, and the competing needs of Nexxus? The risk of an unfavorable outcome is not one which the law can force Nexxus to take. Nexxus has a substantial interest in not seeing this contract performed by Sally Beauty, which is sufficient to bar the delegation under section 2–210, Tex. Bus. Com. code Ann. § 2–210 (Vernon 1968). Because Nexxus should not be forced to accept performance of the distributorship agreement by Sally, we hold that the contract was not assignable without Nexxus' consent.

7. The effort by the dissent to distinguish *Berliner* merely because the court there apparently assumed in passing that distributorship agreements were a species of personal service contracts must fail. The *Berliner* court emphasizes that the sale of a distributorship to a competitor of the supplier is by itself a wholly sufficient reason to terminate the distributorship.

The judgment of the district court is AFFIRMED.

POSNER, CIRCUIT JUDGE, dissenting. My brethren have decided, with no better foundation than judicial intuition about what businessmen consider reasonable, that the Uniform Commercial Code gives a supplier an absolute right to cancel an exclusive-dealing contract if the dealer is acquired, directly or indirectly, by a competitor of the supplier. I interpret the Code differently.

Nexxus makes products for the hair and sells them through distributors to hair salons and barbershops. It gave a contract to Best, cancellable on any anniversary of the contract with 120 days' notice, to be its exclusive distributor in Texas. Two years later Best was acquired by and merged into Sally Beauty, a distributor of beauty supplies and wholly owned subsidiary of Alberto–Culver. Alberto–Culver makes "hair care" products, too, though they mostly are cheaper than Nexxus's, and are sold to the public primarily through grocery stores and drugstores. My brethren conclude that because there is at least a loose competitive relationship between Nexxus and Alberto–Culver, Sally Beauty cannot— as a matter of law, cannot, for there has been no trial on the issue— provide its "best efforts" in the distribution of Nexxus products. Since a commitment to provide best efforts is read into every exclusive-dealing contract by section 2–306(2) of the Uniform Commercial Code, the contract has been broken and Nexxus can repudiate it. Alternatively, Nexxus had "a substantial interest in having his original promisor perform or control the acts required by the contract," and therefore the delegation of the promisor's (Best's) duties to Sally Beauty was improper under section 2–210(1).

My brethren's conclusion that these provisions of the Uniform Commercial Code entitled Nexxus to cancel the contract does not leap out from the language of the provisions or of the contract; so one would expect, but does not find, a canvass of the relevant case law. My brethren cite only one case in support of their conclusion: a district court case from Maryland, *Berliner Foods Corp. v. Pillsbury Co.*, 633 F.Supp. 557 (D.Md.1986), which, since it treated the contract at issue there as one for personal services, *id.* at 559 (a characterization my brethren properly reject for the contract between Nexxus and Best), is not helpful. *Berliner* is the latest in a long line of cases that make the propriety of delegating the performance of a distribution contract depend on whether or not the contract calls for the distributor's personal (unique, irreplaceable, distinctive, and therefore nondelegable) services.... By rejecting that characterization here, my brethren have sawn off the only limb on which they might have sat comfortably....

The fact that Best's president has quit cannot be decisive on the issue whether the merger resulted in a delegation of performance. The contract between Nexxus and Best was not a personal-services contract conditioned on a particular individual's remaining with Best. Compare *Jennings v. Foremost Dairies, Inc.*, [235 N.Y.S.2d 566, at 574]. If Best had not been acquired, but its president had left anyway, as of course he might have done, Nexxus could not have repudiated the contract.

No case adopts the per se rule that my brethren announce. The cases ask whether, as a matter of fact, a change in business form is likely to impair performance of the contract. *Wetherell* asked this. So did *Arnold Productions, Inc. v. Favorite Films Corp.*, 298 F.2d 540, 543–44 (2d Cir.1962), and *Des Moines Blue Ribbon Distributors, Inc. v. Drewrys Ltd.*, 256 Iowa 899, 129 N.W.2d 731, 738–39 (1964). *Green v. Camlin*, 229 S.C. 129, 92 S.E.2d 125, 127 (1956), has some broad language which my brethren might have cited; but since the contract in that case forbade assignment it is not an apt precedent.

My brethren find this a simple case—as simple (it seems) as if a lawyer had undertaken to represent the party opposing his client. But notions of conflict of interest are not the same in law and in business, and judges can go astray by assuming that the legal-services industry is the pattern for the entire economy. The lawyerization of America has not reached that point. Sally Beauty, though a wholly owned subsidiary of Alberto–Culver, distributes "hair care" supplies made by many different companies, which so far as appears compete with Alberto–Culver as vigorously as Nexxus does. Steel companies both make fabricated steel and sell raw steel to competing fabricators. General Motors sells cars manufactured by a competitor, Isuzu. What in law would be considered a fatal conflict of interest is in business a commonplace and legitimate practice. The lawyer is a fiduciary of his client; Best was not a fiduciary of Nexxus.

Selling your competitor's products, or supplying inputs to your competitor, sometimes creates problems under antitrust or regulatory law—but only when the supplier or distributor has monopoly or market power and uses it to restrict a competitor's access to an essential input or to the market for the competitor's output, as in *Otter Tail Power Co. v. United States*, 410 U.S. 366, 93 S.Ct. 1022, 35 L.Ed.2d 359 (1973), or *FTC v. Brown Shoe Co.*, 384 U.S. 316, 86 S.Ct. 1501, 16 L.Ed.2d 587 (1966), or *United Air Lines, Inc. v. CAB*, 766 F.2d 1107, 1114–15 (7th Cir.1985).... There is no suggestion that Alberto–Culver has a monopoly of "hair care" products or Sally Beauty a monopoly of distributing such products, or that Alberto–Culver would ever have ordered Sally Beauty to stop carrying Nexxus products. Far from complaining about being squeezed out of the market by the acquisition, Nexxus is complaining in effect about Sally Beauty's refusal to boycott it!

How likely is it that the acquisition of Best could hurt Nexxus? Not very. Suppose Alberto–Culver had ordered Sally Beauty to go slow in pushing Nexxus products, in the hope that sales of Alberto–Culver "hair care" products would rise. Even if they did, since the market is competitive Alberto-Culver would not reap monopoly profits. Moreover, what guarantee has Alberto-Culver that consumers would be diverted from Nexxus to it, rather than to products closer in price and quality to Nexxus products? In any event, any trivial gain in profits to Alberto–

Culver would be offset by the loss of goodwill to Sally Beauty; and a cost to Sally Beauty is a cost to Alberto-Culver, its parent. Remember that Sally Beauty carries beauty supplies made by other competitors of Alberto–Culver; Best alone carries "hair care" products manufactured by Revlon, Clairol, Bristol–Myers, and L'Oreal, as well as Alberto–Culver. Will these powerful competitors continue to distribute their products through Sally Beauty if Sally Beauty displays favoritism for Alberto–Culver products? Would not such a display be a commercial disaster for Sally Beauty, and hence for its parent, Alberto–Culver? Is it really credible that Alberto–Culver would sacrifice Sally Beauty in a vain effort to monopolize the "hair care" market, in violation of section 2 of the Sherman Act? Is not the ratio of the profits that Alberto–Culver obtains from Sally Beauty to the profits it obtains from the manufacture of "hair care" products at least a relevant consideration?

Another relevant consideration is that the contract between Nexxus and Best was for a short term. Could Alberto–Culver destroy Nexxus by failing to push its products with maximum vigor in Texas for a year? In the unlikely event that it could and did, it would be liable in damages to Nexxus for breach of the implied best-efforts term of the distribution contract. Finally, it is obvious that Sally Beauty does not have a bottleneck position in the distribution of "hair care" products, such that by refusing to promote Nexxus products vigorously it could stifle the distribution of those products in Texas; for Nexxus has found alternative distribution that it prefers—otherwise it wouldn't have repudiated the contract with Best when Best was acquired by Sally Beauty.

Not all businessmen are consistent and successful profit maximizers, so the probability that Alberto–Culver would instruct Sally Beauty to cease to push Nexxus products vigorously in Texas cannot be reckoned at zero. On this record, however, it is slight. And there is no principle of law that if something happens that trivially reduces the probability that a dealer will use his best efforts, the supplier can cancel the contract. Suppose there had been no merger, but the only child of Best's president had gone to work for Alberto–Culver as a chemist. Could Nexxus have canceled the contract, fearing that Best (perhaps unconsciously) would favor Alberto–Culver products over Nexxus products? That would be an absurd ground for cancellation, and so is Nexxus's actual ground. At most, so far as the record shows, Nexxus may have had grounds for "insecurity" regarding the performance by Sally Beauty of its obligation to use its best efforts to promote Nexxus products, but if so its remedy was not to cancel the contract but to demand assurances of due performance. See UCC § 2–609; Official Comment 5 to § 2–306. No such demand was made. An anticipatory repudiation by conduct requires conduct that makes the repudiating party unable to perform. Farnsworth, Contracts 636 (1982). The merger did not do this. At least there is no evidence it did. The judgment should be reversed and the case remanded for a trial on whether the merger so altered the conditions of performance that Nexxus is entitled to declare the contract broken.

Questions

1. In the *British Waggon Co.* case, why does Lea think Parkgate's duties are not delegable? Would the result differ under current law?

2. Does the majority or the dissent present the stronger argument in *Sally Beauty*?

3. How is the legal significance of a delegation of duties different from that of an assignment? Of a third-party beneficiary contract?

3. *Problems.*

    a. Assume the facts are otherwise as in *British Waggon Co.*, except that British Waggon Co. refuses to repair the wagons. Could Lea sue it for breach of contract?

    b. Assume the contract in *British Waggon Co.* required Lea to pay one-half the cost of repairs. The British Waggon Co. repairs the wagons and requests payment. Must Lea pay it? By what legal authority?

    c. Assume the facts are otherwise as in *Sally Beauty*, except that Sally Beauty was only a partially-owned subsidiary of Alberto–Culver. Same result?

    d. Astaire Landscaping Co., an upscale gardening services company, sold its business to Kelly, Inc., including an assignment of all of its contracts with its clients. Astaire wrote to Pangborn that it was going out of business and that Pangborn thereafter must look to Kelly for all performance under their contract for gardening services. Kelly arrived at Pangborn's home and began to cut the lawn. Pangborn immediately called you for advice on this surprising and unwanted switch of gardeners. What are Pangborn's options? What do you advise him?

    e. Winkin and Blinkin concluded a land sale contract under which Winkin promised to pay $135,000 for land owned by Blinkin and Blinkin promised to convey a good title to Winkin. Winkin then changed his plans and, in return for $120,000, assigned "the land sale contract" to Nod. Winkin never paid the price to Blinkin, having left the country. Can Nod get the property? Can Blinkin get the $135,000 from Nod? See RESTATEMENT (SECOND) OF CONTRACTS § 328, *Comment* c.

Index

Reference are to Pages

665

†